1985
The Supreme Court Review

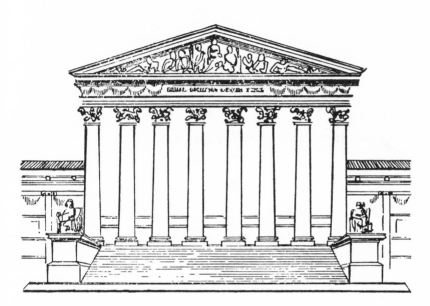

198.
The

"Judges as persons, or courts as institutions, are entitled to
no greater immunity from criticism than other persons
or institutions . . . [J]udges must be kept mindful of their limitations and
of their ultimate public responsibility by a vigorous
stream of criticism expressed with candor however blunt."
–*Felix Frankfurter*

". . . while it is proper that people should find fault when
their judges fail, it is only reasonable that they should recognize the
difficulties. . . . Let them be severely brought to book,
when they go wrong, but by those who will take the trouble
to understand them."
–*Learned Hand*

THE LAW SCHOOL

THE UNIVERSITY OF CHICAGO

Supreme Court Review

EDITED BY

PHILIP B. KURLAND

GERHARD CASPER

AND DENNIS J. HUTCHINSON

 THE UNIVERSITY OF CHICAGO PRESS

CHICAGO AND LONDON

INTERNATIONAL STANDARD BOOK NUMBER: 0-226-46438-5

LIBRARY OF CONGRESS CATALOG CARD NUMBER: 60-14353

THE UNIVERSITY OF CHICAGO PRESS, CHICAGO 60637

THE UNIVERSITY OF CHICAGO PRESS, LTD., LONDON

© 1986 BY THE UNIVERSITY OF CHICAGO. ALL RIGHTS RESERVED. PUBLISHED 1986

PRINTED IN THE UNITED STATES OF AMERICA

TO
JANE SHATTUCK HUTCHINSON

"O may she live
like some green laurel
Rooted in one
dear perpetual place."

CONTENTS

MICHAEL W. McCONNELL

ACCOMMODATION OF RELIGION

It is sometimes forgotten that religious liberty is the central value
and animating purpose of the Religion Clauses of the First Amendment. The separation of church and state—a phrase that does not
appear in the First Amendment or in the debates surrounding its
adoption—is a more problematical, a more contingent, ideal than is
religious liberty. The main components of religious liberty are the
autonomy of religious institutions,[1] individual choice in matters of
religion, and the freedom to put a chosen faith (if any) into practice.
Both free exercise and nonestablishment directly protect religious
liberty: the government may not interfere with a person's chosen
religious belief and practice by prohibiting it or by exerting power
or influence in favor of any faith. The separation of church and
state is a different matter; sometimes separation enhances religious
liberty and sometimes separation diminishes it.

The much-discussed "tension" between the two Religion Clauses
largely arises from the Court's substitution of a misleading formula

Michael W. McConnell is Assistant Professor of Law, The Law School, The University of
Chicago.

AUTHOR'S NOTE: In my former capacity as Assistant to the Solicitor General, I argued
Grand Rapids School District v. Ball as amicus curiae in support of the petitioners and
worked on briefs for the United States in Aguilar v. Felton, Wallace v. Jaffree, Estate of
Thornton v. Caldor, Inc., Alamo Foundation v. Donovan, and Scarsdale Board of Trustees
v. McCreary. The views expressed here are my own. I thank the Sarah Scaife Foundation,
The Morton C. Seeley Fund, and the Sonnenschein Fund for financial support in the
preparation of this article, and Douglas Baird, John Baker, Paul Bator, Mary Becker,
Richard Epstein, Frank Easterbrook, Charles Fried, Geoffrey Miller, Richard Posner, Geoffrey Stone, and Cass Sunnstein for helpful comments on an earlier draft.

[1] The term "church" will be used in this article to denote any religious organization. Its
meaning is not limited to the institution of the Christian church or that of any other faith.

(the three-part *Lemon* test, under which a law or government practice is deemed an establishment of religion if it lacks a "secular"
purpose, if it has the "primary effect" of either "advancing" or
"inhibiting" religion, or if it leads to an "excessive entanglement"
between church and state[2]) and subsidiary, instrumental, values
(especially the separation of church and state) in place of the central
value of religious liberty. This Term's *Aguilar v. Felton*[3] is a ready
example. The Court undoubtedly advanced the separation of
church and state when it prohibited public school professionals
from providing remedial education to needy children on the premises of private religious schools (as they do for similar children in
public and secular private schools). But the most obvious consequence of the ruling was to penalize poor families who decide to
educate their children in religious schools: they forfeit their statutory entitlement to remedial services comparable to those available
to students at public schools.

As *Aguilar* illustrates, the dominant theme of the religion cases in
the 1984 Term was a return to separationist doctrine. This was
quite unexpected. For the two preceding Terms, a majority of the
Court, including the author of *Lemon*, Chief Justice Burger, had
cast doubt on *Lemon*'s continued authority. In cases involving practices far more difficult to justify than those at issue in the 1984
Term, the Court had tempered its commitment to separationism
with the insight that the First Amendment "affirmatively mandates
accommodation, not merely tolerance, of all religions, and forbids
hostility toward any."[4] Looking to historical practice instead of to
Lemon, the Court concluded that practices such as legislative chaplains and Christmas nativity scenes were in keeping with constitutional tradition.[5] Religious pluralism and diversity—not separation
and secularism—were the ascendant values.

While the decisions of the 1982 and 1983 Terms diverged from
the *Lemon* test, the Court did not articulate a new test to take its
place. History was its guide, and if existing doctrine was contradictory the Court would do without doctrine. Expectations (whether

---

[2] Lemon v. Kurtzman, 403 U.S. 602, 612–13 (1971).

[3] 105 S.Ct. 3232 (1985).

[4] Lynch v. Donnelly, 104 S.Ct. 1355, 1359 (1984); see *id.* at 1361.

[5] In the legislative chaplain case, Marsh v. Chambers, 103 S.Ct. 3330 (1983), the Court
did not even purport to apply the *Lemon* test. In Lynch v. Donnelly, the nativity scene case,
the Court applied the test, but in a halfhearted and unconvincing manner.

hopeful or fearful) were therefore high for the 1984 Term. The unprecedented number and diversity of Establishment Clause cases accepted for argument in the 1984 Term appeared to augur doctrinal change that would reflect and explain the Court's new approach. Litigants obliged by offering alternative ways to analyze the issues; briefs and arguments were preoccupied less with the intricacies of *Lemon* analysis and more with effects on religious liberty. But in the end, the Court returned to *Lemon* and applied the test rigidly and emphatically. Justice Powell parted from the majority bloc of the immediately previous Terms. With his fifth vote, a new majority emerged with renewed confidence in the established analytical approach and renewed determination to ferret out religious influences in public life.

What might have been the result if the Court had carried out the promise of reexamining the fundamentals of its approach to the questions of church and state? What interpretation of the First Amendment would be adopted if religious liberty, and not separation or secularism, were the guiding impulse? My intention here is to examine these questions in light of one of the main issues of the 1984 Term: the accommodation of religion.

Accommodation is an increasingly important concept in the Court's thinking about the problem of religion, but one that does not fit comfortably within the current doctrines of free exercise and nonestablishment. It is here that the interests of religious liberty and the rigors of the *Lemon* test are most strikingly at cross-purposes. My thesis is that between the accommodations compelled by the Free Exercise Clause and the benefits to religion prohibited by the Establishment Clause there exists a class of permissible government actions toward religion, which have as their purpose and effect the facilitation of religious liberty. Neither strict neutrality nor separationism can account for the idea of accommodation or define its limits. Only an interpretation of the Religion Clauses based on religious liberty—an interpretation grounded in the political theory underlying the Constitution—satisfactorily distinguishes permissible accommodations from impermissible establishments.

I. THE NATURE OF THE PROBLEM

An accommodation to religion is a practice undertaken specifically for the purpose of facilitating the free exercise of religion, usually by "exempt[ing], where possible, from generally applicable governmental regulation individuals whose religious beliefs and practices would otherwise thereby be infringed, or [by creating] without state involvement an atmosphere in which voluntary religious exercise may flourish."[6] The concept of accommodation, which first appeared in a Supreme Court opinion in 1952,[7] has assumed greater prominence in the Justices' thinking in recent Terms. Every member of the Supreme Court has approved religious accommodations in some circumstances.[8] The concept appears to cut across the usual lines of division on the Court; Justices Brennan and O'Connor, for example, have been among its most forceful expositors.

Despite its prominence in recent Terms, the concept of accommodation has not been precisely defined or located within First Amendment doctrine. It remains a label, not a theory. Is it an exception to the Establishment Clause,[9] an adjunct to the Free Exercise Clause,[10] or simply the result of "play in the joints" between the two Clauses?[11] The Court has not said. But unless informed by a theory grounded in the purposes of the Religion Clauses, the concept might appear to have no limit. "Accommodation" could be invoked as an excuse for rank religious favoritism. Thus, as Justice O'Connor stated in her concurring opinion in the moment-of-silence case, *Wallace v. Jaffree,* "the challenge posed by [the accommodation argument] is how to define the proper Establishment Clause limits on voluntary government efforts to facilitate the free exercise of religion."[12]

---

[6] McDaniel v. Paty, 435 U.S. 618, 639 (1978) (Brennan, J., concurring).

[7] Zorach v. Clauson, 343 U.S. 306, 315 (1952).

[8] Six of the justices have written opinions expressly discussing and endorsing the concept of accommodation. See, *e.g.,* Lynch v. Donnelly, 104 S.Ct. at 1359, 1361 (Chief Justice Burger); Thomas v. Review Board, 450 U.S. 707 (1981) (Chief Justice Burger); *id.* at 727 (Rehnquist, J. dissenting); Marsh v. Chambers, 103 S.Ct. at 3346 (1983) (Brennan, J., dissenting); McDaniel v. Paty, 435 U.S. at 639 (Brennan, J., concurring); Welsh v. United States, 398 U.S. 333, 369–74 (1970) (White, J., dissenting); Trans World Airlines, Inc. v. Hardison, 432 U.S. 63, 90–91 & n.4 (1977) (Marshall, J., dissenting); Gillette v. United States, 401 U.S. 437, 453–54 (1971) (Marshall, J.); Wallace v. Jaffree, 105 S.Ct. at 2502–05 (O'Connor, J., concurring). Each of the others has joined in judgments upholding or requiring accommodations to religious need.

[9] As Justice Brennan treats it in *Marsh,* 103 S.Ct. at 3344, 3346.

[10] As Justice O'Connor treats it in Wallace v. Jaffree, 105 S.Ct. at 2504.

[11] Walz v. Tax Commission, 397 U.S. 664, 669 (1970).

[12] 105 S.Ct. at 2504.

I shall not here attempt a rigorous distinction between accommodations that are a permissible exercise of governmental discretion under the Establishment Clause and those so important that they are compelled under the Free Exercise Clause. Presumably, the distinction requires consideration of such factors as the nature of the religious claim, the openness of the political system to the claims of minority religions, and—most importantly—a general view of the proper relation between elected governments and the courts. From the perspective of judicial power as against the elected branches, constitutionally compelled (*i.e.*, court-ordered) accommodations and discretionary accommodations raise quite different issues. But from the perspective of religious liberty, the nature, justification, and limits of accommodation appear essentially the same when accommodations are instituted by elected officials as when they are ordered by judges. For present purposes it is challenge enough to think about when and why special treatment of religion might be appropriate, leaving to another day the task of determining when it might be constitutionally compelled.

This approach is quite unlike that which the Court has taken. The Court begins by asking whether the case is a "Free Exercise" case or an "Establishment" case and then applies the corresponding test. Thus, if a state denies unemployment compensation to all persons whose refusal to work is due to personal reasons (including religious reasons), the Court—perceiving a "Free Exercise" case—asks first whether the denial of benefits burdens the nonworker's free exercise of religion and, if the answer is "yes," whether the government has a compelling interest in the denial. But if a state voluntarily creates an exception to its unemployment compensation laws, permitting a nonworker to receive benefits when his reasons for not working are grounded in religious conviction (but not other personal reasons), the Court—perceiving an "Establishment" case—will ask whether this exception has a "secular purpose," whether its "primary effect" is to "advance religion," and whether its administration leads to an "excessive entanglement" between church and state. These are quite different sets of questions; they might well lead to different answers.[13]

---

[13] In Thomas v. Review Board, the Court purported to ask both sets of questions. But having concluded that a religious exception was required by the Free Exercise Clause, it gave short shrift to the possibility that the result might violate the *Lemon* test. The Court's explanation why the religious exception satisfied the *Lemon* test was simply that the problem

Indeed, the Court's analysis creates the impression that an accommodation to religion is more likely to be required than permitted. This is for three reasons. First, under free exercise, but not under the *Lemon* test, promoting the liberty of religious exercise is considered a valuable and legitimate objective. Second, under free exercise, once the plaintiff shows that his religious liberty is burdened, the government must grant an accommodation unless the reasons for denying it are "compelling"; that the government's "secular" interests might not be advanced by the accommodation—a dispositive consideration under *Lemon*—is not even relevant. Finally, under the *Lemon* test, but not in free exercise cases, the accommodation must pass the additional hurdle of the "entanglement" test. Accordingly, if taken literally (as lower courts are wont to do), these tests suggest that, when the government views its interest in enforcing a neutral scheme without exceptions to be relatively weak and thus agrees to grant a religious exception, that exception is less likely to be upheld than if the government perceives its interest to be relatively strong, and thus denies it.

A more sensible premise is that the underlying issue in "free exercise" accommodation cases is similar to that in "establishment" accommodation cases. To apply tests that move in opposite directions needlessly creates a "tension" between the Clauses. In short, it is not meaningful to ask whether a government accommodation to religion has a "secular" purpose or whether it "encourages" or "advances" religion; all protections of religious liberty, including the Free Exercise Clause itself, "advance" religion in a sense and are intended to do so. What is needed is an understanding of the role of religion under the Constitution, within a framework that acknowledges the legitimacy of encouraging and facilitating religious liberty.

II. THE SPECIAL STATUS OF RELIGION

Virtually every controversy under the Religion Clauses can be understood as raising the question of the special status of religion. The bulk of the cases arises in four procedural contexts. If the

---

"manifests no more than the tension between the two Religion Clauses" (*id.* at 719) and that carving out a special privilege for religion in this instance "reflects . . . the governmental obligation of neutrality in the face of religious differences" (*id.* at 720). Other decisions are no more enlightening.

government acts neutrally with respect to religion, extending its benefits and burdens among a wide range of persons and institutions without regard to religion, two issues can arise. The first is whether religious practitioners or institutions are entitled to special exemptions or protections; most free exercise cases fall into this category. The leading example is *Sherbert v. Verner*,[14] in which the Court held that the State was constitutionally compelled to grant unemployment benefits when a worker lost her job by refusing to work on her Sabbath day (a Saturday), even though persons who refused to work for nonreligious reasons would receive no benefits. The second issue is whether religious institutions or practitioners must be excluded from government benefits; the leading examples are parochial school cases in which the State seeks to provide educational assistance (textbooks, transportation, remedial instruction) to private school students on the same basis as public school students.[15]

Alternatively, the government might of its own discretion single out religion for special treatment, creating the third and fourth categories of Religion Clauses controversy. The third category consists of challenges to special privileges or exemptions extended to religious individuals or institutions; the Establishment Clause accommodation cases fall into this category. A familiar example is *Gillette v. United States*,[16] in which the Court upheld a statute exempting from the draft persons who objected for religious reasons to fighting in any war. The fourth issue arises when religious organizations or individuals challenge their exclusion from benefits otherwise available to all under the Free Speech, Free Exercise, or Equal Protection Clauses. The leading example is *Widmar v. Vincent*,[17] in which the Court held that a state university may not exclude a student religious group from use of university facilities available to comparable student groups of a secular nature.

The common analytical element in each of these categories of church-state controversy is the special status of religion. When may

---

[14] 374 U.S. 398 (1963).

[15] Everson v. Board of Education, 330 U.S. 1 (1947); Board of Education v. Allen, 392 U.S. 236 (1968); Meek v. Pittenger, 421 U.S. 349 (1975); Aguilar v. Felton, 105 S.Ct. 3232 (1985); School District of Grand Rapids v. Ball, 105 S.Ct. 3216 (1985).

[16] 401 U.S. 437 (1971).

[17] 454 U.S. 263 (1981).

the government treat religion differently and when must it do so? This continuing question—why religion is different—is the issue that gives substance to the debate over the *Lemon* test. I will first consider two prominent, but deficient, approaches to the question and then describe my alternative understanding of the role of religion within the political theory underlying our constitutional system.[18]

A. STRICT NEUTRALITY

An attractively simple answer might be that religion has no special status—that the government may not make any distinction on the basis of the religious or nonreligious character of the activities involved. This view is perhaps most closely associated with Professor Kurland, who has urged that the Religion Clauses of the First Amendment "be read as a single precept that government cannot utilize religion as a standard for action or inaction because these clauses prohibit classification in terms of religion either to confer a benefit or to impose a burden."[19] Applied rigorously, this "strict neutrality" principle would lead to dramatically different results in the religion cases. Not only would benign accommodations to religion (such as that held required as a matter of constitutional law by a vote of eight to one in *Thomas v. Review Board*[20]) be impermissible, but the government could not deny aid to an otherwise eligible organization merely because it is religious.

Despite occasional protestations to the contrary,[21] neither the Court as a whole nor any Justice has ever taken the position that the

---

[18] *Cf.* Smith, The Special Place of Religion in the Constitution, 1983 Supreme Court Review 83 (discussing the reasons offered by members of the Court in opinions since *Everson* for the special treatment of religion).

[19] Kurland, Religion and the Law 18 (1962); Kurland, The Irrelevance of the Constitution: The Religion Clauses of the First Amendment and the Supreme Court, 24 Vill. L. Rev. 3, 24 (1978).

[20] In *Thomas*, the Court required the State to provide unemployment benefits to a person who resigned his job because of religious objections to the work, despite the fact that state law prohibits unemployment compensation for persons who resign for other personal reasons. Only Justice Rehnquist dissented.

[21] In School District of Grand Rapids v. Ball, 105 S.Ct. 3216, 3222 (1985), the Court stated that the "solution" that has been "consistently recognized by this Court" is to "requir[e] the government to maintain a course of neutrality among religions, and between religion and non-religion." Ironically, the Court then proceeded to strike down a state program that did just that.

government must be strictly neutral between religion and nonreligion. Only one Justice—Justice Rehnquist—appears even to believe that the government may maintain such a position of strict neutrality.[22] This reluctance to insist upon strict neutrality should not be too surprising, since the text of the First Amendment itself "singles out" religion for special protections. The Religion Clauses are not framed in terms of neutrality or equal protection. The free exercise of religion is protected in a way that other forms of belief and association are not; similarly, the concept of nonestablishment implies that government's institutional relation to religion is subject to standards different from those applicable to its relation to other forms of belief or association. As Justice White has pointed out, "It cannot be ignored that the First Amendment itself contains a religious classification."[23]

While easy to state, the bare concept of "neutrality" raises serious difficulties in application. How, for example, does one decide between facial neutrality and neutrality of result? If no exception to athletic rules against wearing headgear is made, Orthodox Jewish high school students may not be able to compete in basketball.[24] Is it neutral to apply the no-headgear rule to them, for whom the consequences are so serious, in exactly the way it is applied to others, for whom there is little or no consequence at all? And what course should be taken when no choice available to the government is truly neutral? If teaching creationism in the public schools throws the weight of the government behind a religious belief,[25] does teaching evolution without creationism not throw the weight of the school against it?

Strict neutrality might indeed produce results plainly inconsistent with free exercise. Must restrictions on sex discrimination in employment be applied to the hiring of Roman Catholic priests? Could a Quaker be subpoenaed and required to swear (not merely affirm) that he will tell the truth in court? In such instances exceptions can and should be made. If all religious classifications were forbidden, there would be occasions when the government would

---

[22] See his lone dissent in Thomas v. Review Board.

[23] Welsh v. United States, 398 U.S. at 372 (dissenting opinion).

[24] See Menora v. Illinois High School Athletic Ass'n, 683 F.2d 1030 (7th Cir. 1982).

[25] See Aguillard v. Edwards, 765 F.2d 1251 (5th Cir. 1985).

either forego socially beneficial legislation or be forced to outlaw deep-seated religious practices.

This should not be taken to imply that neutrality between religion and the various forms of nonreligion[26] has no bearing on the proper relation between church and state—merely that strict neutrality cannot be a full explanation for the Religion Clauses. Let us consider the three forms in which the question of neutrality between religion and nonreligion arises: (1) neutrality between religion and unbelief; (2) neutrality between religious and nonreligious moral convictions; and (3) neutrality between religion and various activities or beliefs wholly unrelated to religion or conscience.[27]

Religious liberty demands some degree of neutrality between religion and unbelief. Unbelief is, after all, a system of opinions regarding the existence of God and thus regarding ultimate religious questions of life and value. If "[t]he Religion then of every man must be left to the conviction and conscience of every man,"[28] each person must be as free to disbelieve as he is to believe. Moreover, insofar as unbelief leads the unbeliever to certain actions, not dissimilar to religious practice—for example the calling to preach, proselytize, or attend meetings—these actions are entitled to no less protection from the state than traditional religious actions of a similar nature.[29]

When moving from belief (and communication of belief) to religious observance, however, there is no strict parallel—no coherent requirement of neutrality—between religion and unbelief. It is a commonplace that free exercise protects not just belief but also some action.[30] Beyond a limited number of communicative and associational actions that may, for some unbelievers, be an integral part of their system of unbelief, unbelief entails no obligations and

---

[26] Neutrality between religion and nonreligion must not be confused with neutrality among religions. Neutrality among religions is discussed in the text at notes 143–47, *infra*.

[27] *Cf.* Merel, The Protection of Individual Choice: A Consistent Understanding of Religion Under the First Amendment, 45 U. Chi. L. Rev. 805 (1978) (distinguishing between "irreligion" and "nonreligion").

[28] Madison, Memorial and Remonstrance Against Religious Assessments, ¶ 1, reprinted in an appendix to Everson v. Board of Education, 330 U.S. at 64.

[29] Usually, the Free Speech Clause will be sufficient protection for these actions, which are principally communicative. To the extent, however, that free exercise entails communicative rights for religious spokesmen superior to those demanded by mere free speech (see Murdock v. Pennsylvania, 319 U.S. 105 [1943]), unbelievers are entitled to no less.

[30] Cantwell v. Connecticut, 310 U.S. 296, 303 (1940).

no observances. Unbelief may be coupled with various sorts of moral conviction, which will be considered below. But these convictions must necessarily be derived from some source other than unbelief itself; belief in the nonexistence of God does not in itself generate a moral code. Accordingly, to the extent that religious *actions* are protected under the Religion Clauses, there will be an asymmetry in the treatment of religion and unbelief. The protection of religious opinion will equally benefit religion and unbelief; the protection of religious action will primarily benefit religion.

Neutrality between religiously and nonreligiously motivated moral convictions presents a more difficult question. To some extent, nonreligiously based moral conviction is accorded special respect in our legal system, frequently (if not altogether satisfactorily) under the Free Speech Clause. The right not to proclaim the motto "Live Free or Die" on one's license plate,[31] to opt out of the flag salute in public school,[32] and to refuse financial support for union political activities under a union shop[33] are well known examples.[34] In large part, however, the legal tradition is otherwise: an act of disobedience to the law, however sincerely motivated by moral scruple, is ordinarily thought to be punishable. "The concept of ordered liberty," the Court has said, "precludes allowing every person to make his own standards on matters of conduct in which society as a whole has important interests."[35]

It is when moral conviction most closely resembles religious conviction that it is most likely to be accorded special respect or exemption. This was the basis for the draft exemption cases of the Vietnam War era.[36] There, the Court was faced with principled objectors to participation in war, whose scruples were indistinguishable from those of religious objectors but for the fact that the ultimate source of value they recognized was not a Supreme Being or any other recognizable religious concept. It may have seemed to the

---

[31] Wooley v. Maynard, 430 U.S. 705 (1977).

[32] West Virginia Department of Education v. Barnette, 319 U.S. 624 (1943).

[33] Abood v. Detroit Board of Education, 431 U.S. 209 (1977).

[34] The objections in *Wooley* and *Barnette* were religiously based, but the Court treated them as matters of moral opinion.

[35] Wisconsin v. Yoder, 406 U.S. 205, 215–16 (1972); see, *e.g.*, United States v. O'Brien, 391 U.S. 367 (1968).

[36] *E.g.*, Welsh v. United States, 398 U.S. 333 (1970); United States v. Seeger, 380 U.S. 163 (1965).

Court that to condition exemption for so weighty a moral principle upon belief in a theistic faith would, in effect, interfere with the freedom to determine one's own religious beliefs. The underlying theory here seems to be that religious scruple is the strongest and most firmly grounded basis for exemption from morally repugnant requirements but that other scruples may in particular circumstances be entitled to similar treatment, on an analogy to religious scruple—much as other "suspect classes" have been accorded special protection under the Equal Protection Clause on an analogy to race.

The Court has consistently treated religiously grounded moral objections as worthy of greater consideration.[37] "Under the Free Exercise Clause," Justice Brennan has stated, "religiously motivated claims of conscience may give rise to constitutional rights that other strongly-held beliefs do not."[38] In *Wisconsin v. Yoder*, the Court stated that "[a] way of life, however virtuous and admirable, may not be interposed as a barrier to reasonable state regulation . . . if it is based on purely secular considerations; to have the protection of the Religion Clauses, the claims must be rooted in religious belief."[39] The Court has not articulated any rationale for this difference in treatment; but it seems plausible in light of the fact that there is no explicit textual basis, parallel to the Free Exercise Clause, for requiring governmental toleration of secular moral systems. Why such a textual difference might be justifiable under the political theory underlying the Constitution will be considered later.[40] For present purposes, it suffices to note that absolute neutrality between religious and nonreligious moral convictions cannot be squared with the constitutional text.

Neutrality between religion and activities wholly unrelated to religion or conscience—tennis, for example, or the study of history—is a much clearer matter. Government may regulate, sup-

---

[37] *E.g.*, Thomas v. Review Board, 450 U.S. 707 (1981) (religious objection to nature of work); Wisconsin v. Yoder, 406 U.S. 205 (1972) (religious objection to compulsory schooling); Gillette v. United States, 401 U.S. 437 (1971) (religious objection to military service); Sherbert v. Verner, 374 U.S. 398 (1963) (religious objection to work schedule); Zorach v. Clauson, 343 U.S. at 313 (religious conflicts with school schedules). As *Gillette* and *Zorach* indicate, the Court's special solicitude for religious conflicts extends beyond free exercise cases.

[38] Marsh v. Chambers, 103 S.Ct. at 3346 (dissenting opinion).

[39] 406 U.S. at 215–16.

[40] See text at notes 47–85 *infra*.

port, or require such activities without constraint under the Religion Clauses. They are not like religion in any significant respect and need not be treated as if they were. The government can exempt churches from taxation without exempting tennis clubs. Conversely, government schools are prohibited from teaching the tenets of a religion as fact, but they can teach the tenets of history as fact. Most importantly for present purposes, government may show respect for religious conviction and facilitate the practice of an individual's freely chosen religion, without being forced to accord the same respect to the myriad nonreligious preferences of the people. There is, in short, no requirement of neutrality between religion and nonreligion in this sense. Any constitutional constraint must arise because the special treatment of religion would have a deleterious effect on religious liberty—not because other activities or systems of thought are of equal constitutional dignity.

B. STRICT SEPARATION

A second common view of the constitutional status of religion is that of strict separation between church and state. Under this view, the government may not aid religion in any way, direct or indirect, large or small. Since the government's assistance generally arises from its coercion of others (through taxation or otherwise), any government aid to religion forces some persons to support a religious exercise against their will. Accordingly, it has been said that the government is "stripped of all power to tax, to support, or otherwise to assist any or all religions."[41]

This "no-aid" view, too, while it had considerable support on the Court at one time,[42] has now been rejected by even the most separationist Justices.[43] The principal support for this view was a mistaken reading of the history of the Religion Clauses by the Court and, more conspicuously, by the dissent in *Everson v. Board of Education*.[44] In light of the purposes of the Religion Clauses, it has

---

[41] Everson v. Board of Education, 330 U.S. at 11.

[42] See, *e.g.*, *Everson*, 330 U.S. at 28–63 (Rutledge, J., dissenting).

[43] McDaniel v. Paty, 435 U.S. at 638–43 (Brennan, J., concurring); see Mueller v. Allen, 463 U.S. 388, 393 (1983).

[44] The flaws in the Court's historical analysis are discussed in Cord, Separation of Church and State: Historical Fact and Current Fiction (1982); see also Wallace v. Jaffree, 105 S.Ct. 2379, 2509–17 (1985) (Rehnquist, J., dissenting).

little to commend it.[45] Excluding religious institutions and individuals from government benefits to which they would be entitled under neutral and secular criteria, merely because they are religious, advances secularism, not liberty. In the extreme case—denial of access to basic public services such as sewage hookup or fire and police protection—denial of "aid" would be tantamount to prohibition. Thus the Court recognized, even in *Everson*, that "we must be careful, in protecting . . . against state-established churches, to be sure that we do not inadvertently prohibit [the state] from extending its general state law benefits to all its citizens without regard to their religious belief."[46]

C. RELIGIOUS PLURALISM

An alternative view is that religion is a welcome element in the mix of beliefs and associations present in the community. Under this view, the emphasis is placed on freedom of choice and diversity among religious opinion. The nation is understood not as secular but as pluralistic. Religion is under no special disability in public life; indeed, it is at least as protected and encouraged as any other form of belief and association—in some ways more so. The idea of accommodation of religion, which is foreign to interpretations of the Religion Clauses based on strict neutrality or separation, follows naturally from the pluralist understanding. I believe that this view is more consistent than its competitors with the liberal political theory which underlies the Constitution.[47]

Religion poses a special problem for a liberal republic. The experience of religious strife and persecution associated with the various establishments of religion in Europe has demonstrated the dangers

---

[45] The arguments in favor of the no-aid view are each reviewed, and rejected, in Schwartz, No Imposition of Religion: The Establishment Clause Value, 77 Yale L.J. 692, 708–20 (1968).

[46] 330 U.S. at 16.

[47] This discussion of liberal political theory is not intended to be comprehensive but merely to indicate the place of church-state relations within the dominant strain of that theory. For more extended discussions of liberal thought at the time of the Founding, see Bailyn, The Ideological Origins of the American Revolution (1967); Berns, The First Amendment and the Future of American Democracy 1–32 (1976); Robbins, The Eighteenth-Century Commonwealthmen: Studies in the Transmission, Development, and Circumstances of English Liberal Thought from the Restoration of Charles II until the War with the Thirteen Colonies (1959); Smith, The Convention and the Constitution: The Political Ideas of the Founding Fathers (1965); Storing, What the Anti-Federalists Were For (1981).

of an overbearing church.[48] If a single church obtained political supremacy, the result would be tyranny. The dominant church might be expected to use the power of the state to enforce conformity, even to the point of persecution, among adherents to other forms of belief. And if even the prospect of political supremacy existed, the various sects would contend with one another for preferment. "It was impossible," Justice Story stated in his famous commentaries on the Constitution, "that there should not arise perpetual strife and perpetual jealousy on the subject of ecclesiastical ascendancy, if the national government were left free to create a religious establishment."[49]

But, while unable to establish a national religion, the liberal state also cannot reject in principle the possibility that a religion may be true; and if true, religious claims are of a higher order than anything in statecraft. The individual and the state may disagree on a point of secular ethics, but the claims of right arising from such a disagreement, even if assumed to be valid, do not give a priority to one or the other. The individual must do what he thinks right; the state (that is, the citizens collectively) must do what it thinks right. Though natural law may be viewed as higher authority than positive law, controversies arising from natural law claims will take the form of disputes over what the natural law is. Neither the individual's nor the government's interpretative power is presumptively superior.[50] By contrast, religious claims—if true—are prior to and of greater dignity than the claims of the state. If there is a God, His authority necessarily transcends the authority of nations; that, in part, is what we mean by "God." For the state to maintain that its authority is in all matters supreme would be to deny the possibility that a transcendant authority could exist. Religious claims thus differ from secular moral claims both because the state is constitutionally disabled from disputing the truth of the religious claim and because it cannot categorically deny the authority on which such a claim rests.

---

[48] See, *e.g.*, 3 Story, Commentaries on the Constitution of the United States 728–31 (1833).

[49] *Id.* at 731.

[50] To be sure, radical individualists and collectivists each may differ with this proposition, the one granting priority to individual and the other to collective judgments. The liberal republicanism of the American Constitution, however, departs from both of these extremes: it recognizes and attempts to differentiate individual and collective spheres of action.

These considerations lead to both pragmatic and principled reasons for government deference to religious scruple. The state might defer on issues of less than compelling importance in order to preserve harmony. Since some persons, otherwise good and law abiding citizens, will view religious claims as higher authority than civil law, it may be preferable to accommodate them than to provoke confrontation and disobedience. The state might also defer—again on issues of less than compelling importance—simply because liberalism recognizes, in principle, the possibility of higher claims than those of government.[51]

Finally, the liberal state itself cannot ultimately be the source (though it can be the reflection) of the people's values. Liberalism is foremost a regime of fair procedures. It leaves to the citizens the right and responsibility for determining their own interests and values. Other than by education—which at the time of the Founding was predominately private and certainly not secular—and by the example of its laws, the liberal state has no direct means of shaping the nation's moral thinking. In a liberal regime, the recesses of mind and conscience are exempt from governmental regulation; the state "is not an examiner of consciences."[52]

Nonetheless, any form of civil society must depend, in part, on the citizens' commitment to order and morality. Coercion is an insufficient basis for civil order, except perhaps in the more ruthless despotisms. And any democratic form of society must inevitably reflect the values of its people. The need for internalized constraints and natural sentiments of justice is thus particularly acute for citizens of a republic, in which rule by force is replaced by self-rule. As the Founders understood it, the republic was peculiarly dependent on public virtue to maintain the mutual respect and harmony on which republican liberty rests.[53] If the people are corrupt, how

---

[51] See Gillette v. United States, 401 U.S. at 452–53 (religious draft exemption supported by "considerations of a pragmatic nature, such as the hopelessness of converting a sincere conscientious objector into an effective fighting man," as well as by "the view that 'in the forum of conscience, duty to a moral power higher than the State has always been maintained' "), quoting United States v. Macintosh, 283 U.S. 605, 633 (1931) (Hughes, C. J., dissenting).

[52] Poe v. Ullman, 367 U.S. 497, 546, 547 (1961) (Harlan, J., dissenting). This is not to say that the state may not "concern[ ] itself with the moral soundness of its people," but only that "it must operate in the realm of behavior, of overt actions." Ibid.

[53] See, e.g., The Federalist Papers, No. 55 (Madison), at 346 (1787) (New American Library ed. 1961) ("[T]here are other qualities in human nature which justify a certain

can a republican government—in which sovereignty resides in the people—be just?

If the state is not itself responsible for morality and self-restraint, how is the deficiency to be supplied? A partial answer may be found in indirect democracy, whereby the views of the people are expected to be "refine[d]" and "enlarge[d]"—not merely reflected—through the process of representation and deliberation.[54] By the constitutional scheme, the Founders hoped to remedy the defects in human nature.[55] But no less important an element in republican theory was its reliance on the "genius" of the American people and their social institutions for the formation of national character. Madison himself defended the proposed Constitution on the ground that "the people will have virtue and intelligence to select men of virtue and wisdom" and acknowledged that if there is "no virtue among us . . . , we are in a wretched situation. No theoretical checks, no form of government, can render us secure."[56]

A source of public virtue outside of government was therefore necessary to the ultimate success of the republican experiment. Private associations—families, civic groups, colleges and universities, above all, churches—supply the need. They are the principal means by which the citizens in a liberal polity learn to transcend their individual interests and opinions and to develop civic responsibility. These associations bear the brunt of the responsibility for articulating and inculcating values of morality and justice in the liberal republic. Frequently denominated "mediating" structures or institutions,[57] these associations "have played a critical role in the culture and traditions of the Nation by cultivating and transmitting

---

portion of esteem and confidence. Republican government presupposes the existence of these qualities in a higher degree than any other form"). The need for "public virtue" and "republican virtue," by which were understood the willingness to restrain private interests and passions for the common good, was a frequent theme of speeches, articles, and sermons throughout the period of the Revolution and the 1780s. Many of these sources are collected and quoted in Wood, Creation of the American Republic, 1776–1787 65–70, 413–29 (1969). In this, as in other matters, the Founders followed the lead of de Montesquieu. See Montesquieu, The Spirit of Laws, bk. 4, ch. 5, at 34 (1748) (Hafner Press ed. 1949).

[54] The Federalist Papers No. 10 (Madison), at 82.

[55] *Id.*, No. 51 (Madison), at 322.

[56] 3 Elliot, The Debates of the State Conventions on the Adoption of the Federal Constitution 536–37 (2d ed. 1854). See also The Federalist Papers, No. 55, at 346.

[57] See, *e.g.*, Berger & Neuhaus, To Empower People: The Role of Mediating Structures in Public Policy (1977); Kerrine & Neuhaus, Mediating Structures: A Paradigm for Democratic Pluralism, 446 Annals 10 (1970).

shared ideals and beliefs."[58] It is in the context of these communal associations that individual citizens commonly derive their system of values, even their sense of personal identity and integrity.[59] If the liberal community ultimately has worth in the classical sense of promoting the good for its citizens—that is, the virtuous life[60]— that end is met not by the government but by the free associations of the people.

In differing degrees and largely without explicit textual foundation, the Court has recognized the protected status of key mediating institutions. This is especially true of the family[61] but can also be seen in other areas—witness the Court's recognition of the constitutional autonomy of political and civic associations[62] and social clubs[63] and of academic freedom.[64] Historically and to the present day, however, no such institutions are as important to the process of developing, transmitting, communicating, and enforcing concepts of morality and justice as are the churches. It is in this sense that Tocqueville described religion as "the first of [America's] political institutions."[65] The role of the churches has been especially notable in connection with public morality and justice, as recent public controversies over matters such as racial discrimination, nuclear disarmament, abortion, and immigration illustrate. The special status of religion under the Constitution—both the individual's choice of faith and the institution's autonomy—derives in large part from these considerations.[66]

---

[58] Roberts v. United States Jaycees, 104 S.Ct. 3244, 3250 (1984).

[59] Id. at 3250.

[60] See Aristotle, Nicomachean Ethics, bk. 1, sec. 2 (Bobbs-Merrill ed. 1962); Aristotle, Politics, bk 1, sec. A, ch. 1 (Clarendon Press ed. 1946).

[61] Roberts v. United States Jaycees, 104 S.Ct. at 3250; see Zablocki v. Redhail, 434 U.S. 374, 383–86 (1978); Moore v. City of East Cleveland, 431 U.S. 494, 503–04 (1977); Pierce v. Society of Sisters, 268 U.S. 510, 534–35 (1925); Sexton v. Wheaton (8 Wheat.) 227, 239–40 (1823); but see, e.g., Bellotti v. Baird, 443 U.S. 622 (1979).

[62] See, e.g., Democratic Party of the United States v. Wisconsin ex rel. La Follette, 450 U.S. 107 (1981); NAACP v. Alabama, 357 U.S. 449 (1958). See generally Roberts v. United States Jaycees, 104 S.Ct. at 3250–52.

[63] Moose Lodge No. 107 v. Irvis, 407 U.S. 163, 179–80 (1972) (Douglas, J., dissenting); see Gilmore v. City of Montgomery, 417 U.S. 556, 575 (1974).

[64] Keyishian v. Board of Regents, 385 U.S. 589, 603 (1967); Sweezy v. New Hampshire, 354 U.S. 234, 250 (1957); see also Epperson v. Arkansas, 393 U.S. 97, 104 (1968).

[65] Tocqueville, Democracy in America 292 (Anchor Books ed. 1969).

[66] This is not to disparage the spiritual value of the church for believers, which undoubtedly has influenced thinking about religious liberty as well.

The "political" effects of religion must be distinguished, in this sense, from individual morality. Unlike individual moral thought, religion is communal and institutional.[67] It is poised between the individual and the state; it is social but not universal. Religious thought is not the product solely of individual reason but is rooted in history and tradition. It commands veneration and not mere assent. It carries with it a system of internalized discipline (most pronounced in traditional theistic religions with their belief in divine punishments and rewards) far stronger than mere opinion of right and wrong. It was accordingly widely thought by the Founders that republican self-government could not succeed unless religion continued to foster a moral sense in the people.[68]

The problem for liberal theory was how to realize the benefits of religion in public life without suffering the dangers. The typically Madisonian solution was to rely on the number and diversity of religious views to foster strong and vigorous religion and at the same time guarantee against religious tyranny. Madison wrote in *Federalist* 51:[69]

> In a free government the security for civil rights must be the same as that for religious rights. It consists in the one case in the multiplicity of interests, and in the other in the multiplicity of sects. The degree of security in both cases will depend on the number of interests and sects; and this may be presumed to depend on the extent of country and number of people comprehended under the same government.

Liberal political theory thus favored religion, but it did not favor any one religion. It guaranteed religious freedom in the hope and expectation that religious observance would flourish, and with it

---

[67] Intensely private and noninstitutional religion may be more similar to secular morality than to religion in the traditional sense.

[68] Each of the early Presidents spoke on the theme. John Adams, for example, stated that "[w]e have no government armed with power capable of contending with human passions unbridled by morality and religion. Our constitution was made only for a moral and a religious people. It is wholly inadequate for the government of any other." Hauerwas, A Community of Character 79 (1981). See also Washington, Farewell Address, in 1 Messages and Papers of the Presidents 212 (1897); Jefferson, Notes on the State of Virginia 163 (1787). Early commentators on constitutional law agreed. See 3 Story, note 48 *supra*, at 722–23; Cooley, Constitutional Limitations 470 (4th ed. 1878). See also Tocqueville, note 65 *supra*, at 294 ("Despotism may be able to do without faith, but freedom cannot. Religion is much more needed in the republic . . . than in the monarchy . . . , and in democratic republics most of all").

[69] The Federalist Papers, No. 51, at 324.

morality and self-restraint among the people. But it feared monopoly in religion, especially at the national level. This is the theory that best explains the Religion Clauses of the First Amendment. James Madison, foremost expositor of the pluralist theory of the Constitution itself, appeared in Congress as the foremost expositor of the proposed Religion Clauses as well.[70] Whatever may have been Madison's view of church-state relations in the smaller, more homogeneous jurisdiction of Virginia,[71] the position he took in Congress in propounding an Establishment Clause was based firmly on the theory of religious pluralism, parallel to that espoused in *The Federalist Papers*.

Madison's principal explanations of the committee draft of what are now the Religion Clauses of the First Amendment ("no religion shall be established by law, nor shall the equal rights of conscience be infringed"[72]) were as follows. Each was preceded by remarks to the effect that the nonestablishment provision might injure the cause of religion.[73] "Mr. Madison said, he apprehended the meaning of the words to be, that Congress should not establish a religion, and enforce the legal observation of it by law, nor compel men to worship God in any manner contrary to their conscience."[74]

Prevention of religious coercion, then, was the first principal concern. Multiplicity of sects was the second:[75]

---

[70] Madison did not think a Bill of Rights necessary, since he believed that the powers of Congress under Article I did not extend so far as to endanger individual liberties. 1 Annals of Congress 449, 757 (J. Gales ed. 1834). Nonetheless, he viewed the amendments as consistent with the principles of the original Constitution and of some value in making liberties more secure. *Id.* at 449.

[71] Given Madison's general views on the relationship between the size of the republic and the dangers of factions (including religious sects), it is highly dubious to rely on his views on disestablishment in Virginia as an indication of his intention as framer of the First Amendment, as the Court has done. See, *e.g.*, Everson v. Board of Education, 330 U.S. at 13.

[72] 1 Annals, *supra*, at 757.

[73] A full discussion of the debates is contained in Malbin, Religion and Politics 3–17 (1978); Cord, note 44 *supra* at 7–15; and, in somewhat less complete form, Justice Rehnquist's dissent in Wallace v. Jaffree, 105 S.Ct. at 2510–12. Although I differ with these sources (as they do with each other) in matters of emphasis and specific interpretation of individual statements, they support the general interpretation offered here. Until Justice Rehnquist's dissent, no opinion of the Supreme Court—majority, concurring, or dissenting—ever comprehensively analyzed the congressional debates on the drafting of the Establishment Clause.

[74] 1 Annals, *supra*, at 758.

[75] *Id.* at 758–59.

He believed that the people feared one sect might obtain a pre-eminence, or two combine together, and establish a religion to which they would compel others to conform. He thought if the word national was introduced, it would point the amendment directly to the object it was intended to prevent.

In other words, the "object it [the Establishment Clause] was intended to prevent" was the same as that intended to be prevented by the basic structure of the Union, according to the *Federalist Papers:* avoidance of the tyranny of faction, here religious faction.

This pluralist understanding of the First Amendment was dominant in early interpretation, as statements by the Supreme Court of that era,[76] exegeses by early constitutional scholars,[77] and actions by Congress demonstrated. Beginning in the very session that framed the Bill of Rights, Congress openly signaled its approval and endorsement of religion in general through such diverse actions as calling on the President to recommend to the people a day of prayer,[78] appointing House and Senate chaplains,[79] and making land grants for schools in the territories on the theory that "[r]eligion, morality, and knowledge [are] necessary to good government."[80] This evidence has recently been rehearsed in other places and need not be elaborated here.[81] In brief, the principal objects of the Religion Clauses were consistent with the liberal political theory summarized above. They were to prevent coercion

---

[76] See Terrett v. Taylor, 9 Cranch 43, 48–49 (1815) (interpreting the Virginia disestablishment laws) ("Consistent with the constitution of Virginia, the legislature could not create or continue a religious establishment which should have exclusive rights and prerogatives, or compel the citizen to worship under a stipulated form or discipline, or to pay taxes to those whose creed they could not conscientiously believe. But the free exercise of religion cannot be justly deemed to be restrained, by aiding with equal attention the votaries of every sect to perform their own religious duties").

[77] See 3 Story, note 48 *supra* at 726–28; Cooley, note 68 *supra* at 470–71 (both quoted in Wallace v. Jaffree, 105 S.Ct. at 2515–16 [Rehnquist, J., dissenting]). The Senate Judiciary Committee in 1853 defined "establishment" as "the connexion with the state of a particular religious society, by its endowment, at public expense, in exclusion of, or in preference to, any other, by giving to its members exclusive political rights, and by compelling the attendance of those who rejected its communion upon its worship or religious observances." S. Rep. No. 376, 32d Cong., 2d Sess. 1 (1853).

[78] 1 Annals, *supra*, at 949–50.

[79] See Marsh v. Chambers, 103 S.Ct. 3330, 3333–34 (1983).

[80] 1 Stat. 50, 52n.(a).

[81] See Wallace v. Jaffree, 105 S.Ct. at 2509–16 (Rehnquist, J., dissenting); Cord, note 44 *supra;* Malbin, note 73 *supra;* see also Antieau, Downey, & Roberts, Freedom From Federal Establishment (1964).

(and lesser forms of governmental pressure) in matters of religion and to encourage a multiplicity of religious sects. Government respect for, and encouragement of, religion in general—in ways that do not compel religious exercise or invade the religious liberty of others—was considered appropriate and even necessary.[82]

An incident during debate over what is now the Second Amendment casts light on the specific issue of accommodation. The committee draft of the Amendment included a clause that "no person religiously scrupulous shall be compelled to bear arms."[83] Interestingly, no House member opposed the clause on the ground that it favored religion. Even Representative Jackson, who thought it was "unjust" to require "one part [of the country] to defend the other in case of invasion" was willing to permit the religious exemption "upon paying an equivalent, to be established by law."[84] Nonetheless, Representative Benson moved to strike the clause, stating,[85]

> No man can claim this indulgence of right. It may be a religious persuasion, but it is no natural right, and therefore ought to be left to the discretion of the Government. . . . I have no reason to believe but the Legislature will always possess humanity enough to indulge this class of citizens in a matter they are so desirous of; but they ought to be left to their discretion.

Benson's motion was defeated by a vote of 24–22. The Senate, however, rejected inclusion of the military religious exemption clause and it was deleted in conference.

This incident, while of course not dispositive in itself of the meaning of the Religion Clauses, establishes a link between the understanding of religious liberty reflected in the First Amendment and the idea of accommodation of religion. Two important points that remain central to the argument for accommodation today emerge from the debate: that preferential treatment for religion in some matters is desirable (and perhaps sometimes mandatory), and

---

[82] This does not mean, as Justice Rehnquist appears to have concluded (Wallace v. Jaffree, 105 S.Ct. at 2516), that the Religion Clauses will permit any form of "non-discriminatory aid to religion." Certain benefits, if extended to religion alone and not to competing activities or institutions, would endanger religious liberty by inducing citizens to engage in religious practices. This point is treated in the text at notes 135–38 *infra*.

[83] 1 Annals, *supra*, at 778.

[84] *Id.* at 779.

[85] *Id.* at 780.

that the government is not limited in making religious accommodations to those required under the Constitution. While the state
must retain authority to protect the vital collective interests of the
people, it will "possess humanity enough" to recognize the higher
claims of religion when it can.

My premise is that this understanding of the Religion Clauses
remains sound today. Religious liberty—both in the sense of individual choice in matters of religion and in the sense of autonomous
churches operating without governmental intrusion—is the appropriate central value for the regulation of church-state relations. Yet
I offer two caveats. First, to view the Religion Clauses solely as
protectors of religious liberty is incomplete as a matter of history.
Considerations of state-federal power were as important—if not
more important—to the drafting of the First Amendment. As originally enacted, the Amendment did not apply to the States; indeed,
its language was crafted not only to prevent Congress from establishing a national church but also to prevent it from taking any steps
that would weaken the various state establishments. I have not
discussed this aspect of the Religion Clauses because the Court's
application of the First Amendment to the States, through the
medium of the Fourteenth Amendment, has made it of little continuing importance. Second, this analysis of the values underlying
the Religion Clauses should not be taken to imply that every practice supported by early Congresses or Presidents is necessarily in
conformity to the Constitution. I do not suggest that specific cases
must be decided as the Founders did but that a modern theory of
the Religion Clauses should be guided by a similar assessment of the
role of religion in public life.

In another sense, change in historical circumstance has
strengthened my argument. The Religion Clauses were adopted in
1789 as limitations on an already-limited government. The sphere
of federal governmental action was narrow; conflicts between religion and the federal government, as originally envisioned, would
be few. The growth of the modern welfare-regulatory state has
vastly increased the occasions for conflict between government and
religion. The government has entered areas formerly private and
often religious, such as education and charity ("welfare"), and has
enacted regulations affecting religious institutions, such as labor
and antidiscrimination laws. To maintain the vitality and independence of religious life as it was in 1789 requires, even more clearly

than it did at that time, a recognition of the special character and needs of religion.

III. THE NATURE, PURPOSE, AND LIMITS OF ACCOMMODATION

A. EXAMPLES OF ACCOMMODATION

The Supreme Court has had occasion to discuss specific accommodations to religion in a surprisingly large number of cases. In each of the following instances, the religious accommodation was upheld, required, or discussed approvingly by the Supreme Court during Terms prior to 1984.

The largest and most important category of accommodation is that targeted specifically to religion, whether to religious believers or to religious institutions. Examples of accommodations to individual believers include providing unemployment benefits to persons who resign their jobs for religious reasons;[86] exempting self-employed persons from the Social Security system if they are religiously opposed to participation and belong to a religious organization that provides for its dependent members;[87] exempting jurors with a religious objection from jury duty;[88] releasing children from public schools to receive religious education in their own churches;[89] expending trust funds in the discretion of the Secretary of the Interior for sectarian education;[90] exempting members of the Old Order Amish sect from compulsory education laws;[91] providing chaplains in prisons and in the military;[92] exempting adherents to "well-recognized" faiths opposed to participation in war from military conscription;[93] exempting distributors of religious materi-

---

[86] Thomas v. Review Board, 450 U.S. 707 (1981); Sherbert v. Verner.

[87] United States v. Lee, 455 U.S. 252, 260 & n.11 (1982) (discussing and apparently approving 26 U.S.C. § 1402[g] [1982]).

[88] In Re Jenison, 375 U.S. 14 (1963), vacating and remanding 265 Minn. 96 (1963), 120 N.W.2d 515. See In Re Jenison Contempt Proceedings, 267 Minn. 136 (1963), 125 N.W.2d 588 (on remand).

[89] Zorach v. Clauson.

[90] Quick Bear v. Leupp, 210 U.S. 50 (1908).

[91] Wisconsin v. Yoder, 406 U.S. 205 (1972).

[92] Cruz v. Beto, 405 U.S. 319, 322 n.2 (1972); Marsh v. Chambers, 103 S.Ct. at 3346 (Brennan, J., dissenting).

[93] Selective Draft Law Cases, 245 U.S. 366 (1918).

als from municipal tax on door-to-door vending;[94] exempting non-Sunday Sabbatarians from Sunday Closing Laws;[95] and requiring employers to make "reasonable accommodations" to the religious practices of their workers.[96] Examples of accommodations to religious institutions include exempting churches and church-operated schools from certain payroll taxes[97] and exempting pervasively religious private elementary and secondary schools from labor laws.[98] (The category of accommodations to religious institutions is actually much larger, especially in the fields of taxation and regulation, but has received comparatively little attention in the Court's opinions.)

Some accommodations are broader in scope; while instituted partly or even principally for the protection of religion, they extend their benefits to comparable nonreligious, as well as religious, circumstances. Examples of these broader accommodations include exemptions from the requirement of saluting the flag in public school, instituted at the behest of religious objectors but extended to dissenters on the ground of religion, politics, nationalism, or any other "matters of opinion;"[99] zoning protections for churches and schools;[100] and property tax exemptions for churches and other nonprofit organizations.[101]

Finally, some accommodations are specifically targeted to religion, but the concept of "religion" is broadened beyond systems of belief ordinarily considered "religious" to encompass moral convictions in many ways comparable to religion. The clearest example of this in the Court's decisions is the draft exemption cases of the Vietnam War era, already discussed.[102] There, the Court inter-

---

[94] Follett v. McCormick, 321 U.S. 573 (1944); Murdock v. Pennsylvania, 319 U.S. 105 (1942).

[95] Arlan's Department Store, Inc. v. Kentucky, 371 U.S. 218 (1962) (dismissing challenge to the accommodation for want of a substantial federal question); see also Braunfeld v. Brown, 366 U.S. 599, 608 (1961).

[96] Trans World Airlines, Inc. v. Hardison, 432 U.S. 63 (1977) (accommodation claim rejected on statutory grounds).

[97] St. Martin Evangelical Lutheran Church v. South Dakota, 451 U.S. 772 (1981).

[98] NLRB v. Catholic Bishop of Chicago, 440 U.S. 490 (1979).

[99] West Virginia Board of Education v. Barnette, 319 U.S. 624, 642 (1943).

[100] Larkin v. Grendel's Den, Inc., 459 U.S. 116, 123–24 (1982).

[101] Walz v. Tax Commission, 397 U.S. 664 (1970).

[102] See text at note 16 *supra*.

preted a statutory exemption for persons who "by reason of religious training and belief" were opposed to participation in war to include persons who hold "moral, ethical, or religious beliefs" against war "with the strength of more traditional religious convictions."[103]

B. THE PURPOSES OF ACCOMMODATION

The special status of religion under the Constitution, discussed above, provides a framework for understanding both the purposes and the limits of accommodation. Accommodation comes in two forms: accommodation to the individual believer and accommodation to the religious institution. While similar, they have somewhat different purposes.

1. *Individual accommodation*. The need for accommodation to the individual believer arises, in the clearest case, from conflicts between religious duties and obligations and the demands of society. The believer perceives these obligations as having an objective validity, a source outside himself. They are not mere preferences, nor are they mere opinions about right conduct. The Virginia Declaration of Rights refers to "religion" as "the duty which we owe to our creator."[104] Since religious obligations are not perfectly congruent with civil or social obligations, a believer can be faced with a conflict between authorities. Mrs. Sherbert could obey her employer by working on a Saturday or obey her God by observing the Sabbath and keeping it holy. A religious objector to war can obey his government and fight; or obey his God and refrain from fighting. The purpose of a religious accommodation is to relieve the believer—where it is possible to do so without sacrificing significant civic or social interests—from the conflicting claims of religion and society. When rendering to God and rendering to Caesar are in irreconcilable conflict, it does not offend a proper notion of separation of church and state for Caesar to recede when he can conveniently do so.

---

[103] Welsh v. United States, 398 U.S. at 343, 344.

[104] 1 Virginia Collection of Acts, ch. 1, sec. XVI, at 2 (1803) (enacted May 6, 1776) (emphasis added). Professor Howe has called attention to a revealing formulation proposed for the bill of rights in the Maine Constitution: "All men have a natural and inalienable right to exercise the duty of worshipping Almighty God." Howe, The Garden and the Wilderness 25 (1965), quoting The Debates and Journal of the Constitutional Convention of the State of Maine, 1819–1820, at 99 (1894).

Yet accommodation is not confined to duties or obligations in the strictest sense. Religions recognize degrees of righteousness in various forms of conduct. Not all actions are necessarily required (duties) or forbidden (sins); religion addresses what is "better" as well as what is "good." To take a simple example, to teach Sunday school at church may be viewed as praiseworthy; not to teach Sunday school is not commonly viewed as sinful. It may be difficult, however, for an outsider to distinguish religious duties from other religious practices. The distinction turns to a great extent on the particular religious tradition or language involved. Some religions promulgate complex and detailed sets of behavioral codes, creating many "duties" even in the strictest sense, while others emphasize the motives and individual situation of the believer. A person in one religious tradition may feel a religious motivation—not a "duty"—to engage in a particular action; a person in another tradition might understand the same motivation as a divine calling, the neglect of which would be unfaithful.

These differences, when they can be discerned, are not irrelevant to the strength of a claim for accommodation. The assault on a person's religious identity is far greater if he is prevented from performing what he understands to be a duty than what he understands to be a religiously praiseworthy practice. Accommodations compelled under the Free Exercise Clause thus tend to involve religious duties, strictly understood.[105] But discretionary accommodations to religiously motivated conduct do not lose their legitimacy merely because they do not involve a duty in this strict sense. The distinction is of importance principally within the religious community. Legislators and administrators are not well equipped to draw the distinction; nor, for the most part, would it be useful for them to attempt to do so. The purpose of accommodation is furthered when the broadest scope of religiously motivated actions is permitted, within the constraints of countervailing governmental interests.

2. *Institutional accommodation.* The pertinent need of religious institutions is autonomy. Government interference will tend to undermine both vitality and diversity among the churches. For example, application of the labor laws to sectarian elementary and secondary schools would put the government into the position of

---

[105] See text at note 132 *infra.*

arbiter in disputes between clergy-administrators and teachers over matters that may well involve religious doctrine. Part of the freedom of a church to operate a school is its ability to deal with its agents in accordance with church doctrine; otherwise the church's strength and distinctiveness as a religious educator would be threatened. Accordingly, the Court has held (in an act of creative statutory interpretation) that the National Labor Relations Act does not cover teachers in parochial schools.[106]

Church autonomy is a shared value of accommodationists and separationists alike. One of the principal purposes of the First Amendment has thus been to "keep the state from interfering in the essential autonomy of religious life."[107] This emphasis explains, for example, both the special rules about religious property disputes under the Free Exercise Clause[108] and the prohibition on "comprehensive, discriminating and continuing state surveillance" of religious institutions and actors by public officials under the "entanglement" aspect of the *Lemon* test.[109] The purpose of an accommodation, in this context, is to protect religious institutions from unnecessary interference by the government.[110]

Although relatively rare, there are also instances in which an accommodation to religious institutions may be justified to protect the institutions from needless interference from private parties. For example, a special need to protect religious institutions from the hostile or incompatible actions of other persons might well justify imposing penalties for acts of religious vandalism[111] or banning liquor sales in the vicinity of churches.[112]

---

[106] NLRB v. Catholic Bishop.

[107] Marsh v. Chambers, 103 S.Ct. at 3342 (1983) (Brennan, J., dissenting).

[108] See, *e.g.*, Jones v. Wolf, 443 U.S. 595 (1979); Presbyterian Church v. Mary Elizabeth Blue Hull Memorial Presbyterian Church, 393 U.S. 440 (1969).

[109] Lemon v. Kurtzman, 403 U.S. at 619.

[110] For elaboration on legal protections of church autonomy, see Esbeck, Establishment Clause Limits On Governmental Interference With Religious Organizations, 41 Wash. & Lee L. Rev. 347 (1984); Laycock, Towards a General Theory of the Religion Clauses: The Case of Church Labor Relations and the Right to Church Autonomy, 81 Colum. L. Rev. 1373 (1981).

[111] See Note, Protecting Religious Exercise: The First Amendment and Legislative Responses to Religious Vandalism, 97 Harv. L. Rev. 547 (1983).

[112] See Larkin v. Grendel's Den, Inc., 459 U.S. at 123–24.

C. THE LEGITIMACY OF ACCOMMODATION BEYOND THAT REQUIRED UNDER THE FREE EXERCISE CLAUSE

It might be argued that the government's right to accommodate religious practice extends no further than is required under the Free Exercise Clause itself. Indeed, this is one interpretation of the holding in the recent moment of silence case, *Wallace v. Jaffree*.[113] Under this view, the dangers of religious favoritism are so great that the legislature cannot be trusted to make specific provisions safeguarding the liberty of religious exercise without using the power of the state to induce conformity to majoritarian religious conceptions.

Such a holding would be difficult to square with many of the Court's decisions. The very term "accommodation" was first used in the religious context in an often cited decision by the Supreme Court, *Zorach v. Clauson*,[114] in which the accommodation—an off-premises release time program of religious instruction for public school students—was clearly *not* required by the Free Exercise Clause. In *Walz v. Tax Commission*,[115] the Court stated, "The limits of permissible state accommodation to religion are by no means co-extensive with the noninterference mandated by the Free Exercise Clause. To equate the two would be to deny a national heritage with roots in the Revolution itself." And in *NLRB v. Catholic Bishop*,[116] the Court interpreted a statute to create a specific religious exemption, precisely to avoid having to reach the constitutional question whether such exemption was required under the Religion Clauses. If the limits of permissible accommodation were identical (or even very close) to the limits of mandatory accommodation under the Free Exercise Clause, the *Catholic Bishop* decision would have been nonsense.[117]

---

[113] See text at note 155 *infra*.

[114] 343 U.S. 306 (1952).

[115] 397 U.S. at 673.

[116] 440 U.S. 490 (1979).

[117] Interestingly, the present Court's most separationist member, Justice Brennan, has three times in recent years acknowledged the legitimacy of governmental accommodations to religion "even when the government is not compelled to do so by the Free Exercise Clause." Marsh v. Chambers, 103 S.Ct. at 3346 (dissenting opinion); McDaniel v. Paty, 435 U.S. 618, 638–39 (1978) (concurring opinion); Lynch v. Donnelly, 104 S.Ct. at 1378 (dissenting opinion).

Most importantly, the argument for limiting religious accommodations to those mandated by the Free Exercise Clause is not persuasive. While courts might be presumed to be more responsive than elected officials to the needs of minority religions and, thus, perhaps more willing to grant accommodations to them, this is merely an argument for allowing the courts to require accommodations under the Free Exercise Clause. It is not an argument for denying elected officials the discretion to do so as well.[118] And considering the tremendous diversity of religious persuasion in the country (including staunchly secularist interests), there is no serious reason to expect that the evils of an official ecclesiastical ascendancy are likely to appear.

Moreover, the elements of a free exercise claim are not apposite to an accommodation freely adopted by the government. There are two elements to a free exercise claim. First, the religious observer must demonstrate that his freedom to practice his faith is substantially infringed by a governmental practice. This is the prima facie case. Then, the burden shifts to the government to show that its practice is justified by a compelling governmental interest.[119]

The Court has not often found that neutral government policies violate the Free Exercise Clause—only three times in the last 25 years.[120] The restrictive character of its approach to free exercise is evidently a product of judicial restraint. Given the numerous opportunities for conflict between faith and government, the Free Exercise Clause would become a serious infringement on the government's ability to perform its functions were the Clause not confined to the most serious burdens on religious exercise and did it not take into account the government's legitimate interests in denying religious exemptions and exceptions.[121] The concerns about judicial restraint do not apply where the elected government chooses to accommodate religion; they cut the other way. The same presumption of constitutionality of legislation that protects against

---

[118] For a parallel problem in the context of political association, see Stone & Marshall, Brown v. Socialist Workers: Inequality as a Command of the First Amendment, 1983 Supreme Court Review 583.

[119] United States v. Lee, 455 U.S. at 256–57 (1982).

[120] Thomas v. Review Board; Wisconsin v. Yoder; Sherbert v. Verner.

[121] Free exercise might be viewed as an "underenforced constitutional norm," and the accommodation of religion justified, in part, on that basis. See Sager, Fair Measure: The Status of Underenforced Constitutional Norms, 91 Harv. L. Rev. 1212 (1978).

free exercise claims also supports the legality of government actions accommodating religion.

The most important reason not to confine accommodation to instances compelled by the Free Exercise Clause is that the government is in a better position than the courts to evaluate the strength of its own interest in governing without religious exceptions. Where the government determines that it can make an exception without unacceptable damage to its policies, there is no reason for a court to second-guess that conclusion, unless the constitutional rights of other persons are adversely affected. Such a determination advances the pluralistic goals of the First Amendment. The "compelling state interest" element of the free exercise test is for the protection of the government defendant; it is in the nature of an affirmative defense. If the government does not choose to invoke it, no other party has cause to complain. Accordingly, unless there are other problems of a constitutional nature, a governmental decision to accommodate religion should be upheld at least in instances where the individual believer or religious institution could make out a prima facie case under the Free Exercise Clause. The relative strength of the governmental interest counter to the accommodation is purely a matter for legislative concern and ought not affect the constitutional analysis.

Considering the other side of the free exercise balance, the plaintiff's burden, there are two respects in which the requirement ought to be relaxed under a concept of permissive accommodation. First, an accommodation ought not be confined to conflicts between an individual's faith and the government; conflicts with other forms of societal authority may provide appropriate occasion for accommodations as well. Justice O'Connor stated in *Jaffree*:[122]

> The text of the Free Exercise Clause speaks of laws that prohibit the free exercise of religion. On its face, the Clause is directed at government interference with free exercise. Given that concern, one can plausibly assert that government pursues free exercise clause values when it lifts a government-imposed burden on the free exercise of religion.

She would therefore not recognize the validity of an accommodation where the interference with religious exercise arises from pri-

---

[122] 105 S.Ct. at 2504.

vate sources.[123] This seems an unnecessary and undesirable limitation.

Some "rights" are constitutional rights insofar as they may be infringed by the government; but are rights under statute or common law as against private persons. Guarantees of life and property are an example. And some constitutional rights without parallel in traditional private law have been "extended" to the private sector through modern legislation. Racial nondiscrimination and religious liberty are both of this sort. Just as the government pursues "equal protection values" when it enacts laws prohibiting racial discrimination in private markets, so also it pursues "free exercise values" when it facilitates religious liberty in society at large. The "state action" limitation on constitutional rights does not logically imply any limit on government's power to extend statutory rights under its power to regulate commerce. As Justice Marshall has commented, "[i]f the State does not establish religion over nonreligion by excusing religious practitioners from obligations owed the State, . . . the State can [not] be said to establish religion by requiring employers to do the same with respect to obligations owed the employer."[124] To be sure, most occasions for religious accommodation will involve state action, but there is no reason in the logic of accommodation or of the Establishment Clause to limit the principle in this way.

Accommodation in the private sector might, admittedly, be criticized from the perspective of the minimalist state. If the government is foreclosed from interfering with private contractual relationships in pursuit of social objectives, then its authority to require religious accommodations in the private sector is correspondingly limited. If it is conceded, however, that the government may regulate the marketplace (and thereby impose uncompensated costs) in the interest of health, safety, esthetics, racial equality, freedom of sexual proclivity, or the like, there can be no constitutional objection to doing so to promote religious liberty, which is a social value of constitutional dimension.

Justice O'Connor's suggested limitation generates unnecessary complications. For example, the lower courts have generally upheld the provisions of Title VII of the Civil Rights Act of 1964 that

---

[123] She relied on this point in Estate of Thornton v. Caldor, Inc., 105 S.Ct. at 2919.

[124] Trans World Airlines, Inc. v. Hardison, 432 U.S. at 90 (dissenting opinion).

require employers to make "reasonable accommodations," short of "undue hardship," to the "religious observances and practices" of their employees and prospective employees.[125] Under Justice O'Connor's view of accommodation, Title VII is not a permissible accommodation. In order to explain in *Estate of Thornton v. Caldor, Inc.*[126] why Title VII is nonetheless consistent with the Establishment Clause, Justice O'Connor had to find a "secular purpose" for the statute. The difficulty is that the religious accommodation provisions of Title VII were explicitly inspired by the plight of Saturday Sabbatarians whose religious liberty was infringed by neutral employment practices requiring Saturday work.[127] The sponsor of the amendment, Senator Randolph, was himself a Seventh Day Baptist, and he expressed concern that because of employer pressure for Saturday work there had been a "dwindling of the membership."[128] Although Title VII is applicable to private employers, the Senators who supported the legislation were of the view that it would "promote[] the constitutional demand" of free exercise of religion,[129] and that it would protect "religious liberty."[130] Surely it is "disingenuous to look for a purely secular purpose when the manifest objective of a statute is to facilitate the free exercise of religion"—as Justice O'Connor herself has said[131]—whether it is by "lifting a government-imposed burden" or by lifting one imposed by private citizens or society at large.

Second, discretionary accommodations ought to be possible even where the religious interest is not substantial enough to rise to a free exercise violation. In furtherance of judicial restraint, the Court has confined its protections for religious practice under the Free Exercise Clause to those instances in which the religious infringement is

---

[125] Sections 701(j) and 703(a)(1), 42 U.S.C. § 2000e(j) and 2000e(a)(1); see McDaniel v. Essex International, Inc., 696 F.2d 34, 37 (6th Cir. 1982); Tooley v. Martin-Marietta Corp., 648 F.2d 1239 (9th Cir. 1981); Nottelson v. Smith Steel Workers, 643 F.2d 445, 454–55 (7th Cir. 1981); but see Isaac v. Butler's Shoe Corp., 511 F. Supp. 108, 112 (N.D. Ga. 1980). The Supreme Court impliedly confirmed the lower court consensus that Title VII is constitutional in Thornton. See text at notes 195–97 *infra*.

[126] 105 S.Ct. 2914 (1985).

[127] 118 Cong. Rec. 705–06 (Jan. 21, 1972) (comments of Sen. Randolph).

[128] *Id.* at 705.

[129] *Id.* at 706 (comments of Sen. Williams).

[130] *Id.* at 730 (comments of Sen. Randolph).

[131] Wallace v. Jaffree, 105 S.Ct. at 2504.

extremely serious. In *Wisconsin v. Yoder*,[132] the Court described the religious practices as "central," "fundamental," "important," and "essential" to the Amish faith. This is understandable, because, if the practice in question is not central and important, the Court has little warrant for interfering with decisions of elected officials. But if government is willing to make the accommodation and other constitutional constraints are respected, why should less extreme religious conflicts not be accommodated as well?

Indeed, it may be awkward for the government to confine an accommodation to persons who can demonstrate that they seriously need it. As discussed above,[133] the distinction between a religious "duty" and other forms of religiously motivated conduct may be difficult for the government to draw. The government must operate according to general rules—unlike the courts' case-by-case adjudication—and may not be able conveniently to make individual judgments. For example, some government employees may view attendance at religious services on a holy day a sacred duty; they could make out a plausible free exercise case if the government refused them leave. Others may view attendance at services as no more than a spiritually wholesome activity; their free exercise claim would be much weaker. It is not unreasonable for the government to disregard these distinctions—to implement a general policy permitting leave for employees on the holy days of their faith.[134] There seems little reason to confine the government to the exacting standards appropriate to courts when they exercise their function of judicial review. Religious liberty is not enhanced by a rule confining government accommodations to the minimum compelled under the Constitution.

D. LIMITS ON PERMISSIBLE ACCOMMODATION

The limits on the power of government to accommodate the religious practices of individuals follow naturally from the analysis of the special status of religion and of the need for accommodation. The essential distinction is between permissible accommodations, which facilitate religious liberty, and unwarranted benefits, which

---

[132] 406 U.S. at 210–19.

[133] See text at notes 104–05 *supra*.

[134] See 5 U.S.C. § 5550a (1982).

channel and constrain religious choice. The three principles which follow assist in making this distinction. While there may be other useful ways of approaching the matter, these principles focus attention on the main points that have been developed thus far: What is the effect of the challenged action on the religious liberty of the targeted beneficiaries—does it accommodate the exercise of a religion independently adopted or does it induce religious practices acceptable to the state? What is its effect on the religious liberty of others? Does it interfere with religious liberty by preferring one sect or form of belief over another?

1. *An accommodation must facilitate the exercise of beliefs and practices independently adopted rather than inducing or coercing beliefs or practices acceptable to the government.* The purpose of an accommodation is to enable a person to practice his faith, usually by removing social or governmental obstacles. It is not to cause or induce a person to adopt a religious practice he would not freely choose. This is an essential principle if accommodations are to advance the cause of religious liberty—and not the cause of government-favored religion.[135] Two potential responses by the intended beneficiary are of concern. First, an individual might be persuaded or induced to adopt a religion or religious practice because of the influence of the government's support. Second, the person might decide to feign a religious belief or practice in order to qualify for the accommodation. The former problem is the more serious problem for religious liberty, but the latter is almost certainly more likely.

The possibility that a religion may be influenced or feigned as a result of an accommodation can never be entirely dismissed. On the margin, the accommodation will affect the costs and benefits—the attractions and the drawbacks—of adopting the faith or the practice. A close analysis of the specifics of the case, however, including record evidence, will enable a court to draw reasonable distinctions. The extremes are relatively clear. For example, an exemption permitting high school basketball players to wear a skullcap with their uniforms during games will facilitate religious observance by Orthodox Jews without any appreciable risk that others would be induced to adopt or feign the religion. At the opposite extreme, for the government to offer a cash reward for regular church atten-

---

[135] Professor Alan Schwartz has argued that this principle—which he calls the "no-imposition standard"—is the sole Establishment Clause value. Schwartz, note 45 *supra*.

dance would be an unwarranted inducement. The former decreases the obstacles to a religious practice, while the latter increases its desirability. The former removes disincentives, while the latter creates positive incentives to practice religion.

Other cases—draft exemptions for example—are more difficult. On the one hand, to allow sincere religious pacifists to avoid conscription without going to jail removes a powerful legal obstacle to following religious conscience. On the other hand, since not being obliged to fight in war is a privilege desired by many, the availability of religious exemptions might well be an inducement to conversion, if exemption were confined along strict statutory lines.

Where the benefit is so desirable that a religious accommodation would likely induce—and not merely facilitate—religious practice, the preferred solution may be to widen the benefit rather than to deny the accommodation. That, presumably, was one of the factors that led the Court to adopt a broader definition in the draft cases; it decreased the likelihood that the government's exemption policy would pressure secular conscientious objectors into accepting a theistic faith, while retaining the accommodation for religious objectors. For another example, if one agreed with the dissenters in *Zorach v. Clauson*[136] that a release time program for religious instruction, during which all other students must remain in study hall, has the effect of inducing students to undertake religious training, the solution would be to offer other attractive alternatives during the release time period, to neutralize this effect. There is no reason to forbid the accommodation.[137]

Although it is relatively easy to posit hypothetical accommodations so alluring that they would distort rather than facilitate religious choices, most actual accommodations adopted by governments and tested in the courts have not been troublesome. Some accommodations contain internal guarantees against fraud or undue inducement. Exemption from social security for self-employed persons is limited to those whose church maintains an alternative system for retirement support; exemption from the payment of union

---

[136] 343 U.S. 306 (1952).

[137] Compare the Sunday Closing laws, which made church attendance easier and more likely. The "alternatives open to non-laboring persons" were so diverse that the laws would not likely induce a person to attend church who did not otherwise wish to do so. McGowan v. Maryland, 366 U.S. at 451.

dues is accompanied, where possible, by the requirement of an equal contribution to charity; the advantage of receiving unemployment compensation because of religious objection to Saturday work is balanced by the more serious and long-term disadvantage of increased difficulty in locating a new job; to take one's child out of high school in Wisconsin requires immersion into the unworldly life of the Amish.

Where the problem is insincere attempts to gain the benefits of an accommodation rather than inducement to adopt a religious practice, the government can adopt screening devices designed to separate faith from fraud. Here, as the Court has consistently recognized,[138] there is less threat to religious liberty so long as the government confines its inquiry to the sincerity—as distinguished from the truth—of the individual's professed beliefs.

2. *An accommodation must not interfere with the religious liberty of others by forcing them to participate in religious observance.* The reasons for this limitation are straightforward; the facilitation of one person's liberty cannot be at the expense of another's. Religious liberty means the freedom to choose whether to engage in religious practice and which (if any) to adopt, without government coercion or interference. The principles of religious pluralism demand that the government respect the dignity of all religious beliefs, including the right to disbelieve and to refrain from religious practices. This is one reason why vocal public school prayers might not be considered an appropriate accommodation to the needs of some children to engage in prayer at the beginning of the school day. To conduct state-selected or state-composed prayers in public school classrooms may violate the rights of other children not to participate and may channel religious practice into state-prescribed forms.

It must be acknowledged, however, that religious accommodations often, perhaps always, impose some costs on others. Sometimes these costs are not inconsiderable. A young man's chances of being drafted, and perhaps killed, are increased if some of his coevals are exempted by virtue of their beliefs. A merchant's economic position may be seriously injured if some of his competitors are exempted from the Sunday Closing Laws because they observe

---

[138] Thomas v. Review Board; United States v. Seeger, 380 U.S. 163 (1965); United States v. Ballard, 322 U.S. 78 (1944); see Braunfeld v. Brown, 366 U.S. at 615 (Brennan, J., dissenting).

the Sabbath on Saturday.[139] The question, however, as recognized by the Court in *Sherbert v. Verner*, is whether recognition of the believer's right to accommodation "serve[s] to abridge any other person's religious liberties."[140] The economic and other interests of other persons are properly weighed by the legislature and need not automatically yield to religious needs;[141] but neither is the legislature required to treat religious conviction as if it had no greater weight or dignity under the Constitution than economics or similar interests.[142]

It may be objected that some purely economic costs were viewed by the Framers of the First Amendment as infringements on religious liberty. The religious assessment against which Madison wrote his *Memorial and Remonstrance* was, after all, a purely "economic" injury. There is a crucial distinction, however, between a compulsory church contribution, like that Madison opposed, and an indirect economic injury caused by the exercise by others of religious rights. In cultural and religious terms, the problem with the religious assessment was that it extended a specifically religious obligation—the giving of tithes and offerings—to nonbelievers. The injury, as Madison noted, was not the money—"three pence" would have been just as objectionable—but the obligation to render obedience and sustenance to a church. In contrast, the person drafted in place of a religious objector, to take one example, is obliged only to render obedience to his country.

A mandatory church contribution scheme can also be distinguished from indirect economic injury in a more analytical sense. The economic cost and the religious benefit of a direct tax and subsidy are one and the same; the taxpayer pays the tax and the

---

[139] See Braunfeld v. Brown, 366 U.S. at 608.

[140] 374 U.S. at 398. The same point is made by Dean Choper (though he disagrees with its application in Sherbert). Choper, The Religion Clauses of the First Amendment: Reconciling the Conflict, 41 U. Pitt. L. Rev. 673, 690–92 (1980). His analysis differs from mine principally in that he would not permit government programs that "intensify or meaningfully encourage even independently chosen beliefs." *Id.* at 696.

[141] United States v. Lee, 455 U.S. 252 (1982) (upholding Congress' failure to exempt Amish employers from payment of Social Security tax).

[142] As Justice Douglas said for the Court in *Murdock*, "[a] license tax certainly does not acquire constitutional validity because it classifies the privileges protected by the First Amendment along with the wares and merchandise of hucksters and peddlers and treats them all alike. Freedom of press, freedom of speech, freedom of religion are in a preferred position." 319 U.S. at 115.

church receives it. In contrast, the religious benefit in other instances is obtained without regard to whether any injury is suffered
by other parties. The injury is incidental to the benefit. Exempting
Orthodox Jewish merchants from Sunday Closing laws may cause
economic injury to their competitors, but the religious benefit does
not depend on the injury. Even if there is no injury, the Orthodox
merchants will be enabled to practice their faith without economic
penalty. Other examples of accommodations which entail incidental costs are draft exemptions, workplace accommodations, and
release time programs. Where the injury is incidental, it cannot be
said that a person is forced to engage in or support a religious
practice against his will.

3. *An accommodation must not favor one form of religious belief over
another.* Since the objective of religious accommodations is to enhance the freedom of choice, it is important that they be extended
on an evenhanded basis. Religious pluralism demands that, where
possible, the government's actions must not be permitted to affect
the previously existing religious mix. One church, or an alliance of
churches, must not be permitted to wrest advantages from the state
that are not available to other sects. Along with the prohibition of
religious coercion, the "clearest command of the Establishment
Clause is that one religious denomination cannot be officially preferred over another."[143]

Accordingly, if a privilege or immunity is extended to one faith,
it should be extended to all, to the extent that the nature of the
subject matter permits. Accommodations must not be "religious
gerrymanders."[144] If a state allows a Sunday Sabbatarian to receive
unemployment compensation when a conflict between work schedules and religious conviction results in resignation or discharge but
does not extend the same privilege to Saturday or Friday Sabbatarians, it violates the Establishment Clause.[145] If a state exempts the
Amish from compulsory education, it must exempt members of
other faiths with similar scruples and similar systems of alternative
education.[146]

---

[143] Larson v. Valente, 456 U.S. 228, 244 (1982); see text at note 75 *supra.*

[144] Walz v. Tax Commission, 397 U.S. at 696 (Harlan, J., concurring).

[145] This is one reason why Sherbert v. Verner may have been correctly decided even if
Thomas v. Review Board was not. See 374 U.S. at 406.

[146] *Yoder* does not make this point explicitly, but I assume it is implicit.

This does not mean, however, that an accommodation must be of equal value to members of all sects. Practitioners of religions which do not faithfully observe a Sabbath will have little use for the accommodation required in *Sherbert*, and persons who do not object to war (or object only to some wars) will be no better off—indeed, worse off—as a result of the accommodation upheld in *Gillette*. This is in the nature of things. Since conflicts between faith and society are of varying types and intensities, accommodations to those conflicts will inevitably be of little interest to some faiths even while of great value to others. And an accommodation cannot reasonably be thought to discriminate against nonbelievers merely because it relieves believers of a burden or conflict that nonbelievers do not share.

Indeed, most religious accommodations are of principal interest to members of minority faiths, since it is far more likely that their beliefs will come into conflict with society than it is for members of the larger denominations. But as society becomes more secularized (assuming that is its direction), believers of every stripe may have greater need for accommodation. An accommodation should not be deemed inappropriate merely because it benefits members of few faiths. Only if an accommodation is not neutral on its face, or if the terms of a facially neutral accommodation are so specifically targeted as to suggest religious favoritism, is there likely to be a constitutional problem.

Moreover, the obligation of neutrality among sects does not mean that the government may not address specific religious needs without also addressing others. Religious accommodations tend to be enacted piecemeal, as part of the laws pertaining to the particular subject matter. It is not a sign of religious favoritism that a state, in the course of considering one area of the law, should make accommodation to a religious practice directly pertinent to that area without surveying other areas of law for appropriate accommodations to other practices or forms of belief. On the other hand, if the legislature has singled out one specific religious conflict for accommodation, leaving others in the same subject area untouched, or if it has systematically accommodated some faiths but not others, there is reason to question the evenhandedness of the legislature.

Nor is the government disabled from making distinctions among religious beliefs where those distinctions are relevant to legitimate civic or social interests. Merely because the government is willing to exempt from the draft those who object to all war does not mean that it must exempt the much larger and more indeterminate category of those who object to a particular war.[147] If distinctions cannot be explained, however, they may reasonably be attributed to religious favoritism—especially if the accommodations in question have been made to politically powerful groups.

These three principles of limitation should enable the courts to distinguish between permissible accommodations to individual believers and unwarranted benefits to religion. The underlying theme is that individual choice in religion is a public value; the state itself is religiously pluralistic—not secular.

The limits on accommodations to religious institutions derive from the same source and are in many respects the same. The primary difference is in the effect on the targeted beneficiary of the accommodation. Rather than being a protector of individual religious conscience, the accommodation in the institutional context is a protector of church autonomy. The basis for this form of accommodation has already been discussed.[148] As in the case of individual accommodations, this purpose defines the limit of permissible accommodation. To assist religion is not a sufficient basis for an accommodation. A church might be exempted from a form of regulation—the labor laws, for example—in order to avoid governmental interference with internal church discipline in matters touching on doctrine. It is not a sufficient reason simply to spare the church the expense of compliance. The other limiting principles applicable to individual accommodations are equally applicable to institutional accommodations.

IV. APPLICATION TO THE CASES

This statement of the basis and limits of the accommodation principle should be tested against the facts of the two major accommodation cases of the 1984 Term, *Wallace v. Jaffree*,[149] and *Estate of Thornton v. Caldor, Inc.*[150]

---

[147] Gillette v. United States, 401 U.S. at 448–60.

[148] See text at notes 106–10, *supra*.

[149] 105 S.Ct. 2479 (1985).

[150] 105 S.Ct. 2914 (1985).

A. WALLACE V. JAFFREE

Jaffree involved the constitutionality of an Alabama statute authorizing public school teachers at the beginning of the first class of each day to announce a "period of silence" for "meditation or voluntary prayer." The moment-of-silence statute—along with other statutes and practices involving vocal prayer—was challenged by Ishmael Jaffree, parent of children in kindergarten and second grade. The State argued that the statute was "a permissible accommodation of religion." What would have been the reasoning if the Court had followed the accommodation analysis set forth above?

1. *Does the moment of silence accommodate or facilitate a preexisting religious practice?* The principal effect of the moment of silence is to allow students who wish to do so to pray. Many persons feel a need to incorporate prayer into all of life's significant activities and understand this need to include school. Since the practice of vocal prayer was eliminated from the public schools, these individuals have felt a void. It is no answer to such people that they may pray freely at home or at church, for they do not believe their faith can be so confined. Children are compelled by compulsory schooling laws to attend school but are denied an appropriate occasion in which to dedicate the school day to God. To be sure, they might snatch a moment during the day for a brief prayer, but there is no time during which noise, distractions, classroom activity, and other school responsibilities cease; and to take a moment off by oneself for prayer is likely, in this secular age, to bring down upon the child's head the scorn of his peers. The moment of silence is a response to this need. Some twenty-five states have determined that a moment of silence is an appropriate way to accommodate the religious needs of the children without infringing on the rights of other children.

2. *Does the moment of silence induce or coerce belief? Does it interfere with the religious liberty of those who feel no need to pray?* Examining the face of the statute, the answer to these questions must be no. The teacher simply announces that a there will be a moment of silence "for meditation or voluntary prayer." Students can pray if they choose, but there is no pressure to do so. They can also meditate on secular matters, daydream, or doze. No one will know how they use the time; nor can they know what goes on in the minds of the others. As Justice O'Connor commented, "[d]uring a moment of

silence, a student who objects to prayer is left to his or her own thoughts, and is not compelled to listen to the prayers or thoughts of others."[151] Only if the statute is insensitively or abusively administered—as by a teacher conspicuously assuming a posture of prayer or urging children specifically to pray—is the voluntary character of the opportunity threatened.

The cost imposed on other students is minimal—a moment of time during which ordinary classroom activities do not take place. Indeed, this may not be a cost at all, even to the nonreligious student, since he may appreciate the chance to gather his thoughts. The problem with vocal prayer—that nonparticipating students might be made to feel "different"—is minimized or eliminated, since no one will know what the others are thinking or whether, in fact, he is "different."

3. *Is the moment of silence neutral among religions?* In all the major theistic religions, a brief silent prayer is one of the ways to communicate with God.[152] But for religions that do not recognize brief, individual, silent prayer, and for nonreligion, the moment of silence is at worst an idle moment and may well be valued as an opportunity for reflection. The statutory language itself emphasizes neutrality: students may use the moment for meditation *or* voluntary prayer. The moment of silence thus appears to be, as the State contended, a legitimate accommodation to the religious needs of many students.

The Supreme Court disagreed. In a majority opinion by Justice Stevens, the Court held the moment-of-silence law unconstitutional under the *Lemon* test. In fact, the Court found it unnecessary to run through all three parts of the *Lemon* test, because in its view the moment-of-silence law so "unambiguous[ly]" violated the first part—whether the statute has a "secular purpose."[153]

The Court could answer the "purpose" question so easily because the sponsor of the legislation and the State's trial attorneys made the work easy. Although there was no legislative history in the usual sense, the sponsor, Senator Holmes, inserted a statement in the legislative record after enactment explaining that the purpose

---

[151] 105 S.Ct. at 2499.

[152] Whittier, Silent Prayer and Meditation in World Religions (Congressional Research Service May 27, 1982).

[153] 105 S.Ct. at 2490.

was to "return voluntary prayer to the public schools." Then, in district court, Senator Holmes (in testimony) and the lawyers (in interrogatories) stated that that was the *only* purpose for the law. There was, moreover, the unfortunate circumstance (for the defendants) that the moment-of-silence law, though separately enacted, was considered in court as part of a "package" of laws designed to provoke reconsideration of the *School Prayer* cases by authorizing vocal prayer in the Alabama public schools. This history, and this context, convinced the Court that there was no secular purpose for the law. Given the nature of the *Lemon* test, no further analysis was needed.

But does it make any sense to apply the "purpose" prong of the *Lemon* test to religious accommodations? Justice O'Connor would seem to be correct that "[i]t is disingenuous to look for a purely secular purpose when the manifest objective of a statute is to facilitate the free exercise of religion."[154] Indeed, under the *Lemon* test, taken literally, no accommodation to religion could ever be upheld. The "purpose" of an accommodation is plainly to facilitate religion, and that will be its "effect" as well. Perhaps recognizing that its "no secular purpose" conclusion is less than dispositive in the accommodation context, the Court expressly considered the State's accommodation argument and supplied two somewhat inconsistent answers.

The Court's first answer, in footnote 45, appears to be based on the view that the government may not make any accommodation not required by Free Exercise Clause. Relying on a statement in the Solicitor General's brief that "it is unlikely that in most contexts a strong Free Exercise claim could be made that time for personal prayer must be set aside during the school day," the Court stated:[155]

> it is undisputed that at the time of the enactment of [the moment of silence law] there was no governmental practice impeding students from silently praying for one minute at the beginning of the school day; thus, there was no need to "accommodate" or to exempt individuals from any general governmental requirement because of the dictates of our cases interpreting the Free Exercise Clause.

---

[154] *Id.* at 2504.

[155] *Ibid.*

For reasons already discussed, this view contradicts substantial Supreme Court precedent and is inconsistent with a sound understanding of the relation between the two Religion Clauses.[156]

The Court's second response to the State consisted of a detailed examination into whether the State's claim that it was merely accommodating religion was plausible in light of the existence of an earlier statute, not challenged by the plaintiff, which also provided for a moment of silence. The earlier statute (called by the Court the "1978 statute") applies only to the elementary grades and requires a moment of silence for purposes of "meditation." The 1981 statute, at issue in *Jaffree*, applies to "all grades" and states that the moment of silence is for "meditation or voluntary prayer."

The Court seemingly affirmed the constitutionality of the 1978 moment-of-silence law, stating that "[t]he legislative intent to return prayer to the public schools is, of course, quite different from merely protecting every student's right to engage in voluntary prayer during an appropriate moment of silence during the school day. The 1978 statute already protected that right."[157] Apparently, the purpose of "protecting every student's right to engage in voluntary prayer" is deemed to be a "secular purpose" under *Lemon*.

One might have thought that, if the 1978 law is constitutional, the 1981 law must be constitutional as well: the extension of the moment of silence to the upper grades is surely unobjectionable, and the addition of the words "or voluntary prayer" merely makes its meaning explicit.[158] The Court concluded, however, that the statutory changes had *no* legitimate justification—that is, the 1981 law either was intended to convey the State's endorsement of prayer or it was "meaningless" or "irrational."[159] The Court dismissed the extension of the moment of silence to the upper grades as "of no relevance" because it did not affect the plaintiff's children, who are in kindergarten and second grade.[160] This reasoning is obviously faulty. That Mr. Jaffree's children were not among those

---

[156] See text at notes 113–34 *supra*.

[157] 105 S.Ct. at 2491.

[158] This was the construction placed by a three-judge federal district court on the Massachusetts legislature's similar amendment of an almost identical moment of silence law by addition of the words "or prayer." Gaines v. Anderson, 421 F. Supp. 337, 343 (D. Mass. 1976).

[159] 105 S.Ct. at 2492.

[160] *Id.* at 2491.

affected does not make the legislature's action meaningless or irrational; there are other children in Alabama.

The issue, therefore, should not have been viewed as whether the Alabama legislature had *any* legitimate purpose in enacting the 1981 moment-of-silence law, but whether the legislature's inclusion of the words "or voluntary prayer" in the statute tainted the legislature's otherwise legitimate extension of the moment of silence to the secondary grades. The Court stated that "[t]he addition of 'or voluntary prayer' indicates that the State intended to characterize prayer as a favored practice."[161] Perhaps the State so intended. But it is difficult to see how the Court divined that intent from the language of the statute. The addition of the words "or voluntary prayer" does no more than indicate that prayer is one of the permissible uses of the time.[162] Given the common misperception that the Supreme Court has forbidden children to pray in the schools, the legislators might have thought a clarification useful.[163]

The decisive factor in the Court's decision was Senator Holmes' express statement that the purpose of the 1981 law was "to return voluntary prayer to the public schools." A moment-of-silence law enacted with a different legislative history would in all likelihood withstand challenge. What principle can be deduced from this result? The distinction would seem to be between the genuine desire to accommodate religious needs and the desire to use the resources and prestige of government to encourage or inculcate religion among the unwilling or the indifferent. In Justice O'Connor's words, the line must be drawn between "creating a quiet moment during which those so inclined may pray, and affirmatively endorsing the particular religious practice of prayer."[164]

If the focus were on the students, this line would be precisely on point. I have argued that an accommodation, to be legitimate, must facilitate an independent religious choice and not coerce or pressure

---

[161] *Ibid.*

[162] Perhaps the term "meditation" itself might be understood as having a religious connotation; in that event, both the 1978 and the 1981 laws are vulnerable. The solution, however, would be to require the State to supplement its explanation to the students by language to the effect that they can use the moment of silence for any thoughts of their choice, including, but not limited to, prayer or meditation.

[163] Portions of Senator Holmes' testimony not quoted by the majority (see 105 S.Ct. at 2506 (Burger, C. J., dissenting)) support this surmise.

[164] *Id.* at 2505.

that choice. The Court's distinction between creating an opportunity for "those so inclined" to pray and "affirmatively endorsing" prayer reflects essentially the same principle.

Neither the Court nor Justice O'Connor, however, focused on the students themselves. The Court looks to the subjective motivations of the legislators, and Justice O'Connor looks also to the reactions of a hypothetical "objective observer." Neither alternative is likely to be fruitful. The distinction between protecting the right to pray and encouraging the use of that right is far less clear (and far less important) from the perspective of legislative motivation than it is from the perspective of effects on the individuals involved. Ordinarily, one protects a right when he believes that the exercise of that right is in some way valuable or important. Legislative history in an accommodation case is quite likely to reveal that the legislators who cared enough to sponsor the legislation were those who approved of the religious practice in question. If the line is drawn so as to invalidate accommodations in such cases, many legitimate and commendable attempts to facilitate religious liberty will be struck down.

Undoubtedly, Senator Holmes hoped that Alabama schoolchildren would use the moment of silence for prayer; he said as much. But if the result of Senator Holmes's efforts was to open up an opportunity for children to pray or not, as they choose, and if the government exercises neither force nor suasion to influence them in their choice, what difference do Senator Holmes's motives make? Would extension of subsidized bus service to weekends be invalid if it could be shown that its proponents hoped thereby to increase church and synagogue attendance? Without unconstitutional effects, legislative motivation is an empty concept. Indeed, if there are no unconstitutional consequences, it is hard to see why anyone has standing to sue.

The Court's treatment of legislative motivation under the Establishment Clause is a constitutional oddity. In equal protection cases, there is no inquiry into "intent" unless there are disparate results; the function of legislative motivation is to determine whether discriminatory effects are unconstitutional.[165] In free

---

[165] Compare Personnel Administrator of Massachusetts v. Feeney, 442 U.S. 256 (1979), and Washington v. Davis, 426 U.S. 229 (1976), with Palmer v. Thompson, 403 U.S. 217 (1971).

speech cases, there is no inquiry into "intent" unless some speakers are treated differently from others.[166] In free exercise cases, there is no inquiry into the government's motivations (its "compelling interest") unless the plaintiff first has demonstrated a burden on religious liberty stemming from the government's conduct. The Establishment Clause would seem to be the sole doctrinal field in which intent, divorced from results, can lead to a finding of unconstitutionality.

Nor is Justice O'Connor's notion of the "objective observer" likely to prove illuminating. Whether an observer would "perceive" an accommodation as "endorsement of a particular religious belief"[167] depends entirely on the observer's view of the proper relation between church and state. Justice O'Connor, for example, assumes that her " 'objective observer' . . . is acquainted with the Free Exercise Clause and the values it promotes."[168] An objective observer holding separationist views of the First Amendment might be quick to perceive government's contact with religion as endorsement; one following the approach of this article might have a different reaction. Looking to an "objective observer" cannot substitute for a constitutional standard. Such a formulation serves merely to avoid stating what considerations inform the judgment that a statute is constitutional or unconstitutional. If Justice O'Connor's "objective observer" standard were adopted by the courts, we would know nothing more than that judges will decide cases the way they think they should be decided.

If the core value of the Religion Clauses is religious liberty, the test under those Clauses should be the actual consequences for religious liberty. The motivations of legislators may be evidence of how the accommodation will function in practice. But the ultimate inquiry should be directed not at legislative motivation—which may or may not predict results—but on effects. And no unconstitutional effects have been persuasively shown to flow from a moment of silence.[169]

---

[166] See Cornelius v. NAACP Legal Defense & Education Fund, 105 S.Ct. 3439, 3455 (1985) (where exclusions from federal employee charity drive are not "precisely tailored," the excluded groups must be permitted to raise claim that the exclusions were based on the government's "bias against their viewpoints").

[167] *Thornton*, 105 S.Ct. at 2919 (O'Connor, J., concurring).

[168] 105 S.Ct. at 2504.

[169] As Justice Powell, a member of the majority in *Jaffree*, conceded. 105 S.Ct. at 2495 n.9 (concurring opinion).

A final word should be said in defense of the decision in *Jaffree*. It seems clear that the Court's objections to the Alabama moment-of-silence law were based on the peculiarities of the postenactment legislative history and the connection to Alabama's vocal prayer law. While this approach seems unsound in its details and invites ad hoc decision making by the lower courts, it is preferable to a holding that, in principle, a State may not take account of the religious needs of schoolchildren by allowing a moment of silence for prayer or other forms of reflection. This had been the basis for the lower court decisions striking down moment-of-silence statutes in other states.[170]

Such a holding could not be justified on the basis of a concern for voluntarism or neutrality; it would establish secularism in place of pluralism and liberty. The underlying question in *Jaffree*, as it was in the earlier city creche and legislative chaplaincy cases,[171] was whether all manifestations of religion must be removed from the public sphere.[172] The answer in those earlier cases was that certain religious observances have become "part of the fabric of our society."[173] In truth, religious observances antedated our society and are in no small part responsible for the path it has taken. It would be a dangerous experiment, as the Founders understood,[174] to cordon off from public life those motivating influences which, in the view of many of our citizens, supply the foundation for public justice and individual restraint. It is a large step to take from the proposition that "the Religion . . . of every man must be left to the conviction and conscience of every man"[175] to the notion that citizens must leave behind their religious convictions and practices when they enter the (ever-expanding) realm of the state.

Court watchers may disagree about whether the specifically Christian symbol of the Nativity or the specifically Presbyterian prayers of the Nebraska chaplain run counter to the ideal of reli-

---

[170] May v. Cooperman, 572 F. Supp. 1561 (D. N.J. 1983); Duffy v. Las Cruces Public Schools, 557 F. Supp. 1013 (D. N.M. 1983); Beck v. McElrath, 548 F. Supp. 1161 (M.D. Tenn. 1982). See also Note, The Unconstitutionality of State Statutes Authorizing Moments of Silence in the Public Schools, 96 Harv. L. Rev. 1874 (1983); Note, Daily Moments of Silence in Public Schools: A Constitutional Analysis, 58 N.Y.U. L. Rev. 364 (1983).

[171] Lynch v. Donnelly; Marsh v. Chambers.

[172] See Neuhaus, The Naked Public Square (1984).

[173] *Marsh*, 103 S.Ct. at 3336.

[174] See text and notes at notes 65–68 *supra*.

[175] Madison, Memorial and Remonstrance, 330 U.S. at 64.

gious pluralism. A moment of silence should have presented an easier case. In principle, and divorced from its peculiar "legislative history," the moment of silence is entirely nonsectarian. Its offense is that it allows a religious practice in the most sacredly secular precinct of the state, the public school—and it does not merely suffer the practice to occur but openly acknowledges it as one of the appropriate parts of the school day for those who wish it. The moment of silence offends the modern vision of a strictly secular society where religion must be kept out of sight, at least out of the sight of impressionable youngsters. That the Court did not adopt the sweeping prohibition espoused by the lower courts may be difficult to square with *Lemon*'s insistence on a "secular" purpose for all governmental practices, but it accords, more importantly, with a proper recognition of the place of religion in our society.

B. ESTATE OF THORNTON V. CALDOR, INC.

In 1976, the Connecticut House of Representatives voted to repeal the State's 300-year-old practice of requiring most businesses to be closed on Sunday. But before doing so, it considered the objections of legislators that the repeal might force workers who observe Sunday as their Sabbath to work in violation of religious conviction. In response, the House amended the bill to guarantee the right of any employee who "states that a particular day of the week is observed as his Sabbath" not to work on that day.[176] The effect of the House bill, as amended, was to permit non-Sabbath observers for the first time to do business on any day they chose, to permit non-Sunday Sabbath observers for the first time to refrain from working on their Sabbath, and to preserve the right of Sunday Sabbath observers not to work on their Sabbath.

The State Senate did not agree with the House proposal to repeal the Sunday Closing laws altogether but voted to exempt certain businesses from the law. The Senate accepted the House proposal for Sabbath protection. Senator Hudson, for example, stated that the House bill "gives people the right not to work on the Sabbath if they choose to and I think that that is a responsible action on the part of the government to guarantee those who wish to observe

---

[176] Conn. Gen. Stat. Sec. 53-303e(b) (1982). At the same time, the House adopted a provision for a maximum six-day week. *Id.*, Sec. 53-303e(a).

their Sabbath, whatever day it is, not to have to work."[177] Later, the Connecticut Supreme Court invalidated the Sunday Closing law but left the Sabbath protection provisions intact.

The protections of the law were invoked by Donald Thornton, a managerial employee of Caldor, Inc., a large department store chain, and challenged in state court by Caldor under the Establishment Clause of the First Amendment, as applied to Connecticut through the Fourteenth Amendment. Under the accommodation principles set out above, the Connecticut statute would appear to be permissible.

1. *Does the Sabbath provision facilitate or accommodate a preexisting religious practice? Or does it induce workers to adopt a religious practice favored by the government?* Much more than for the moment-of-silence law, the answers to these questions are difficult here. The difficulty is not unlike that already discussed in connection with religious draft exemptions.[178] On the one hand, from the perspective of a sincere Sabbath observer, the law merely accommodates the religious practice. It does not make a Sabbath any more attractive; it removes obstacles to its observance. On the other hand, the ability to designate a particular weekend day as one's day off is desirable to many workers. The law might therefore create an incentive in some to adopt or, more likely, to feign Sabbath belief. It is useful to consider these two aspects separately.

a). The need for accommodation is clear; Mr. Thornton was caught in a conflict between the demands of his employer that he work on Sunday and the tenets of his faith that he not. To be sure, as the Court pointed out,[179] "[o]ther employees . . . have strong and legitimate, but non-religious reasons for wanting a weekend day off." Workers may have moral obligations—the duty to take care of a family member, for example—that are more than mere preferences and that conflict with work obligations but that are not accommodated by the Connecticut law. The Supreme Court has not had any difficulty in distinguishing between such reasons—however strong and legitimate—and the specifically religious clash of authority confronted by Sabbath observers. There were vigor-

---

[177] 19 Conn. S. Proc. (Pt. 5), at 2039–40 (Apr. 28, 1976).

[178] See text at notes 135–36 *supra*.

[179] 105 S.Ct. at 2918 n.9.

ous dissents in *Sherbert v. Verner*[180] and *Braunfeld v. Brown*,[181] on the issue whether special provision for Sabbath observers must be made under the Free Exercise Clause. But no Justice in those cases expressed any reservation regarding whether it would be appropriate or legitimate for special provision to be made to Sabbath observers—even where no provision is made for alleviating other conflicts.

This reflects the Court's longstanding view that religious scruple is entitled to special protection. Nonreligious moral scruple may be entitled to respect similar in some ways to religious scruple, but there is no explicit textual basis in the Constitution for it, and the significance of religion within liberal political theory, already discussed,[182] justifies the textual distinction. Moreover, as a practical matter, it is difficult for legislation of this sort to extend beyond Sabbath protection. Conflicts between work schedules and moral obligations are likely to occur at erratic intervals; the need to care for a family member or attend a funeral may occur at any time. It is not unlikely that informal arrangements or contractual leave policies will accommodate most such conflicts, but to draft a statute that would adequately define a generalized right of accommodation for moral conflicts with work schedules might well be impossible. The Sabbath, being a concrete, well-defined concept, is more susceptible to accommodation. Whatever may be the reasons, it is clear that the Court treats as legitimate, and at times mandatory, the drawing of lines between religious scruple and other forms of moral obligation.[183]

Nothing in the majority opinion suggests a change. But Justice O'Connor's concurring opinion strikes a somewhat different note. She commented that "[a]ll employees, regardless of their religious orientation, would value the benefit which the statute bestows on Sabbath observers—the right to select the day of the week in which to refrain from labor,"[184] as if a Sabbath observer, like Mr. Thornton, "selects" the Sabbath day. In Mr. Thornton's belief, Sunday is a holy day, ordained by God as a day of rest. The Court has

---

[180] 374 U.S. 398 (1963).

[181] 366 U.S. 599 (1961).

[182] See text at notes 47–70 *supra*.

[183] See text at notes 31–40 *supra*.

[184] 105 S.Ct. at 2919.

recognized (in earlier cases) that when the Sabbath observer is denied the Sabbath day off, he is "put to a choice of fidelity to religious belief or cessation of work."[185] The statute thus did not reward Mr. Thornton for "adher[ing] to a particular religious belief" by conferring on him a "valued and desired benefit," as Justice O'Connor implied.[186] It eliminated a burden his co-workers did not face, the burden of choosing between disobeying his religion and losing his job.

b). Since employees tend to prefer to take their day off on a weekend for a variety of reasons, however, the possibility that some might adopt a Sabbath-observing religion because of the statute must be considered. More realistically, the fear is less that the statute might induce someone actually to adopt a faith that recognizes a Sabbath than that some might feign such a religion in order to be guaranteed a particular weekend day off. While the possibility cannot be dismissed (and it would be helpful to know more about experience under the statute in order to assess the case), this does not appear to be a sufficient concern to outweigh the strong interests already discussed in favor of the accommodation.

Several factors support this conclusion. As construed by the state courts, the statute guards against the possibility of feigned Sabbath observance by allowing the arbitrators to inquire into the employee's "sincerity."[187] Sincere Sabbath observance has its own restrictions; most workers would probably be unwilling to be so constrained in their activities during their day off. Moreover, the statute has been invoked only six times during its existence; this suggests that the level of abuse is not high in actual practice. The judgment of private employers like Caldor, Inc. (other than in litigation) appears to be that this is not a problem. By contract, Caldor grants its rank-and-file employees the right not to work on their Sabbath. (Only because Mr. Thornton was a manager did this contractual right not apply.) If such a right were a significant inducement to feign a religion, a private employer would not be likely voluntarily to confer it.

2. *Does the accommodation infringe the religious liberty of others?* The

---

[185] Thomas v. Review Board, 450 U.S. at 717.

[186] 105 S.Ct. at 2919.

[187] The Board of Arbitration specifically concluded that Mr. Thornton's religious views on the Sabbath were sincerely held.

other persons affected by the Connecticut statute were the fellow employees and the employer. The fellow employees might not be adversely affected at all. The most likely means of complying with the Sabbath protection requirement is for the employer to offer premium pay for weekend work, at levels sufficient to attract enough workers. Under such a scheme, the employees are as well or better off as a result of the statute. On the other hand, if the employer were able to require additional weekend work without additional compensation, the fellow employees would bear the cost of accommodating the Sabbath observer. So long as the increase in weekend work does not affect their own religious practices, however, this cost is a purely secular one—not unlike the cost to other employees entailed by a liberal sick leave or maternity leave.

There will likely be a cost to the employer of complying with the statute. But this, too, is purely an incidental economic cost—not the sort of injury prevented by the Religion Clauses. As noted above,[188] virtually every form of accommodation to religion entails some cost—sometimes very substantial—on others. There is no reason to accord the economic interests of employers extraordinary judicial protections from the majoritarian processes; their problems, if serious, will not fall on deaf ears in the legislature.

The employer's religious freedom is not infringed by the statute. Caldor was not "taxed" for the support of Mr. Thornton's religion; its injury (if any) was wholly incidental to the benefit to the employee. Mr. Thornton's ability to observe his Sabbath would not be diminished if it turned out that Caldor could accommodate him without cost (if, for example, other employees agreed to work on Mr. Thornton's Sabbath without additional financial inducement). The injury to Caldor is analogous to the injury to competitive merchants if Orthodox Jews are permitted to operate on Sundays despite Sunday Closing laws, to other men of draft age if exemptions to compulsory military service are made, or to other taxpayers if church property is exempt from tax. Such injuries, while appropriate matters for legislative consideration, fall outside the protection of the Religion Clauses.[189] The decisive question under the Religion Clauses is whether the "cost" is an infringement on religious liberty. Other costs must look elsewhere for their protection.

---

[188] See text at note 139 *supra*.

[189] See text at notes 140–43 *supra*.

It is interesting that Caldor itself did not view exempting Sabbath observers from Sabbath work as an infringement on its liberty. It was happy to include such a provision in the contract for rank-and-file workers. The reason it did not extend the courtesy to managerial employees is that the cost and inconvenience of doing so was significantly greater.

3. *Is the accommodation neutral among religions?* A Sabbath is common to all the major religions of the country—Christianity, Judaism, Islam. The Connecticut statute makes no distinction; it confers its protection equally to all. Even the Connecticut Supreme Court, which held the statute unconstitutional, acknowledged that the statute "does not favor one religion over another."[190] Indeed, the statute was enacted as a substitute for the prior Sunday Closing law, under which the usual Christian Sabbath was legally protected and members of other faiths forced to comply. The new statute was more neutral in every respect. Under it, each individual was free to observe the Sabbath commanded by his faith, or none at all.

To be sure, most people—including many Christians, Jews, and Moslems—no longer view Sabbath observance as a duty. They, along with adherents to non-Sabbath observing religions (and perforce adherents to no religion at all), will not benefit from the statute. But they were not caught in the conflict to begin with. The accomodation is narrow but, within its scope, available to all. It shows no religious favoritism. That most people have no need for the accommodation does not undermine its neutrality; most accommodations are of value only to members of minority religions.

Justice O'Connor's suggestion in this context, that the "message conveyed is one of endorsement of a particular religious belief, to the detriment of those who do not share it,"[191] is difficult to understand, unless every specific accommodation to a particular religious practice is suspect. Admittedly, the Connecticut law "singles out Sabbath observers for special . . . protection without according similar accommodation to ethical and religious beliefs and practices of other private employees."[192] This is equally true of the moment of silence (which singles out the practices of prayer and medita-

---

[190] 191 Conn. at 350 (1983).

[191] 105 S.Ct. at 2919 (concurring opinion).

[192] *Ibid.*

tion), the draft exemption (which singles out opposition to war), the release time program of *Zorach* (which singles out religious education), or any other specific accommodation. The reason why the legislature "singled out" Sabbath observance is plain from the legislative context: Sabbath observance was the sole religious practice adversely affected by repeal of the Sunday Closing laws. When the legislature turns its attention to laws regulating the days of the week during which workers may be required to work, there is no reason to demand that it simultaneously examine unrelated "ethical and religious beliefs" that might require accommodation.

According to this analysis, the law should have been sustained. The Court disagreed, by a lopsided vote of eight to one. The majority opinion, however, is essentially bare of analysis or precedent. The Court stated that "the statute goes beyond having an incidental or remote effect of advancing religion" because the right it gives Sabbath observers is "absolute and unqualified."[193] The one precedent relied upon—a 1953 Second Circuit decision—is not on point.[194] The ground relied upon—the "absolute" character of the statute—is undoubtedly important to its wisdom as a matter of labor policy but of dubious relevance under the Establishment Clause.

Significantly, the Court did not hold that it violates the First Amendment for the government to require a private party to accommodate the religious needs of another, even when nonreligious needs receive no such accommodation. Such a holding would have invalidated the religious accommodation provisions of Title VII of the Civil Rights Act of 1964[195] as well as the Connecticut statute.

---

[193] 105 S.Ct. at 2918. The Court may have leaped too quickly to the conclusion that the Connecticut Sabbath protection law is absolute. The Connecticut Supreme Court's decision did not expressly state, nor do the facts of the case compel the inference, that the employee's right to refrain from work on the Sabbath is unqualified. The State itself informed that Court that the statute was subject to a "reasonableness" limitation.

[194] The decision, Otten v. Baltimore & Ohio R. Co., 205 F.2d 58 (2d Cir. 1953), rejected the claim that the Free Exercise Clause compels a private employer to make an exception to a union shop agreement for a worker whose religious faith would not permit his joining the Union. That the Constitution does not, of its own force, protect a right is not dispositive of the question whether the government may do so through its power to regulate the terms and conditions of employment. *Cf.* Nottelson v. Smith Steel Workers, 643 F.2d 445 (7th Cir. 1981) (Title VII requires an employer to make an exception to a union shop agreement for a worker whose religious faith would not permit his making contributions to a union).

[195] Sections 701(j) and 703(a)(1) of Title VII of the Civil Rights Act of 1964, 42 U.S.C. §§ 2000e(j) and 2000e–2(a)(1). Under these provisions, an employer is prohibited from taking

Nor did the Court cast any doubt on the legitimacy of the Connecticut legislature's purpose in passing the statute, even though it was
not "secular" in any recognizable sense of the term. That would
have invalidated not just Title VII, which has a similar legislative
history, but most other accommodations as well. The *Thornton*
decision appears to be rooted in just one factor: the "absolute"
nature of the accommodation.

This emphasis is consistent with the Court's analysis in an earlier
brush with the Title VII accommodation requirements. In *Trans
World Airlines, Inc. v. Hardison*,[196] the Court construed the Title
VII requirements narrowly—far more narrowly than the language
and legislative history would suggest. This may have been to avoid
deciding the constitutional question that, the dissenters noted,[197]
would "be posed by interpreting the law to compel employers (or
fellow employees) to incur substantial costs to aid the religious
observer." If the imposition of "absolute" costs were constitutionally permissible, then the restrictive reading of Title VII in *Hardison* would have been unnecessary.

The *Thornton* decision makes eminent sense from a practical
viewpoint, without weakening in any way the general argument for
religious accommodations. An unqualified right of any employee to
refrain from work on his Sabbath would cause severe problems for
some employers. The Court cited several apt examples: the Friday
Sabbath observer employed in an occupation (such as teaching) that
operates Monday through Friday; the employer with a high percentage of workers adhering to the same Sabbath day; the employer
who would have to impose significant burdens on other employees
in order to accommodate the Sabbath observer.[198] The absence of
any exceptions for such cases makes the statute appear ill-advised.

But are these considerations properly understood as arising
under the Establishment Clause? Under the analysis here, the answer is no. The relevant issue is the nature, not the magnitude, of

---

adverse employment actions against applicants or employees on the basis of their religious
observances and practices, including their observance of a Sabbath, "unless an employer
demonstrates that he is unable to reasonably accommodate to an employee's or prospective
employee's religious observance or practice without undue hardship on the conduct of the
employer's business." See text at notes 125–31 *supra*.

[196] 432 U.S. 63 (1977).

[197] *Id.* at 90.

[198] 105 S.Ct. at 2918.

the cost imposed on other parties. Protecting businesses from excessive and unreasonable regulation went out with substantive due process. The question should have been whether the religious liberty of the employer or the other employees was infringed by the statute, not whether the costs associated with complying were reasonable.

The Court's emphasis on the "absolute" character of the Connecticut law, which strongly implies the validity of the "reasonable accommodation" provision of Title VII as interpreted in *Hardison*, thus suggests a commonsensical, rather than a doctrinal, limitation on the accommodation of religion. The message seems to be that religion may be singled out for special protection, but not if excessive costs are thereby imposed on other specific, identifiable, private actors. As a matter of policy, this is not a bad solution—especially since Title VII will accomplish most of the good that the Connecticut statute attempted, with less economic disruption. A better solution as a matter of constitutional law, however, would have been to sustain the statute and to leave to the legislature the task of protecting economic interests.

V. Conclusion

One striking fact about both the *Jaffree* and the *Thornton* decisions is the irrelevance of the *Lemon* test. It is useless to look to *Lemon* for an explanation of the distinctions drawn by the Court between some moment-of-silence statutes and the Alabama statute and between "absolute" protections for the Sabbath and reasonable accommodations. While the Court cannot be said to have followed the analysis outlined here—for its conclusions were to the contrary—the Justices evidently have concluded that in accommodation cases a new analysis is required. Contrary to expectation, *Jaffree* and *Thornton* may actually have impeded the development of new doctrine—*Jaffree* because the legislative background seemed to call out for Supreme Court repudiation and *Thornton* because the practical consequences of the statute were so unreasonable. These, apparently, were not the cases in which to break new ground. On the other hand, the Court's generally favorable view of accommodation—manifested here in its implied approval of most moment-of-silence laws (but not Alabama's) and for non-"absolute" accommodations in the workplace (but not Connecticut's)—speaks more loudly than its explicit, but irrelevant, reaffirmation of *Lemon*.

It is therefore likely that these questions will return to the Court in the near future. The opinions in *Jaffree* and *Thornton*, despite their surface appearance, present no obstacles to the development of a principled doctrine of the accommodation of religion, under which the purposes of the Free Exercise and Establishment Clauses are harmonized. In this article I have attempted to show why the accommodation of religion is consistent with the political theory underlying the Constitution and how an emphasis on the central value of religious liberty can generate principles for distinguishing between legitimate accommodations and unwarranted benefits to religion. Under this view, pluralism and liberty—not secularism or separation—define the relation between church and state under the Constitution.

JOHN GARVEY

ANOTHER WAY OF LOOKING
AT SCHOOL AID

In the 1983 and 1984 Terms the Supreme Court decided several controversial cases about government aid to schools. In 1984 it held in *Grove City College v. Bell*[1] that scholarship aid to college students counted as assistance to the school for purposes of Title IX[2] but that only the school's financial aid program had to comply with that law. Last Term the Court held that remedial and other aid for parochial school students counted as assistance to their schools and that the aid programs were altogether invalid under the Establishment Clause. Though both events caused quite a stir,[3] no one seems to have noticed that the problems were virtually identical. The solutions were not, though I think they should have been.

Grove City involved a small private school that refused as a matter of principle to accept federal or state aid. It did, however, admit students who paid their tuition with congressionally authorized Pell grants.[4] The Court held that that money was indirect aid to the school and that the school was therefore required to abide by the

John H. Garvey is Visiting Professor of Law, University of Michigan Law School.

AUTHOR'S NOTE: I would like to thank Alex Aleinikoff, Paul Bator, and Fred Schauer for reading an earlier version of this paper. While on leave in the Office of the Solicitor General, I participated in briefs in *Grove City* and in *Mueller* v. *Allen;* the views expressed here are my own.

[1] 104 S.Ct. 1211 (1984).

[2] Education Amendments of 1972, 20 U.S.C. § 1681 *et seq.* (1982).

[3] Congress is considering several bills designed to overturn *Grove City.* H.R. 700, 99th Cong., 1st Sess. (1985); S. 272, 99th Cong., 1st Sess. (1985); S. 431, 99th Cong., 1st Sess. (1985).

[4] 20 U.S.C. § 1070(a) (1982).

prohibition against sex discrimination in Title IX. But Title IX only applies to the "education program or activity receiving Federal financial assistance,"[5] not to the recipient institution as a whole. The Court found that in the case of Pell grants the only program covered by the antidiscrimination principle was the school's financial aid program.

Last Term's cases were *Grand Rapids School District v. Ball*[6] and *Aguilar v. Felton*.[7] In *Grand Rapids* the school district offered two programs in the parochial schools. One (Shared Time) provided remedial and "enrichment" math and reading, art, music, and physical education. These were taught during regular class periods by full-time public school employees, in rooms "leased" (at $6.00 per room per week) from the parochial schools, with materials supplied by the public school system. The other (Community Education) offered such courses as arts and crafts and chess in voluntary classes at the end of the school day. These were taught in large part by instructors already teaching at the schools where the courses were offered. No attempt was made to monitor either program for religious content.[8]

The Court held both programs unconstitutional under the *Lemon* antiestablishment test[9] because they had the effect of advancing religion. This effect, the Court said, might occur in three ways. First, the teachers might "become involved in intentionally or inadvertently inculcating particular religious tenets or beliefs."[10] There was no evidence that this had happened, but the Court found evidence unnecessary since the classes weren't monitored and no one had any incentive to report violations. Second, the programs might subsidize the schools' religious function by providing "direct aid to [their] educational function."[11] Third, "the programs may provide a crucial symbolic link between government and religion[.]"[12]

---

[5] 20 U.S.C. § 1681(a) (1982).

[6] 105 S.Ct. 3216 (1985).

[7] 105 S.Ct. 3232 (1985).

[8] 105 S.Ct. at 3218–20.

[9] See Lemon v. Kurtzman, 403 U.S. 602, 612–13 (1971).

[10] 105 S.Ct. at 3223.

[11] *Id.* at 3229.

[12] *Id.* at 3223. The Chief Justice and Justice O'Connor each concurred in the judgment as to the Community Education program but dissented as to the Shared Time program. *Id.* at 3231. Justices White (*id.* at 3249) and Rehnquist (*id.* at 3231) would have upheld the constitutionality of both programs.

In *Aguilar* the Court struck down New York City's program for using Title I money[13] to provide remedial reading and math, English as a second language, and guidance services to parochial school students at their own schools. The offerings were staffed by regular public school employees and monitored by field personnel and program coordinators.

New York City's program was thus similar to the Shared Time program in *Grand Rapids*, but the issue was different because New York had monitored its classes for religious content and found no improper effects. Catch-22. New York's monitoring violated the entanglement part of the *Lemon* test. Having government agents work with parochial school personnel on matters like schedules and students' needs posed a danger for nonadherents of the school's denomination.[14] Having them "guard against the infiltration of religious thought"[15] threatened the religious liberty of those at the school.

I. ANTIESTABLISHMENT AND ANTIDISCRIMINATION

A. THE ANTIESTABLISHMENT PRINCIPLE

I begin by pointing out the similarity in structure and function of the antiestablishment principle applied in *Grand Rapids* and *Aguilar* and the antidiscrimination principle applied in *Grove City*. The antiestablishment principle in parochial school aid cases is really a "state action" rule written in substantive First Amendment terms. In the typical state action case a private institution (a school,[16] a hospital,[17] a nursing home,[18] a restaurant[19]) has done something

---

[13] Title I of the Elementary and Secondary Education Act of 1965, as amended, Pub. L. No. 96-561, 92 Stat. 2153 (1978), authorized the Secretary of Education to distribute money to local educational agencies to meet the needs of educationally deprived children from low-income families. (It has been superseded by Chapter I of the Education Consolidation and Improvement Act of 1981, 20 U.S.C. § 3801 *et seq.* (1982), but the relevant provisions are virtually identical.) The statute gives local educational agencies some freedom to design programs (§ 3805(a)), but they must include services for deprived children in private schools (§ 3806(a)).

[14] 105 S.Ct. at 3237.

[15] *Id.* at 3239.

[16] Rendell-Baker v. Kohn, 457 U.S. 830 (1982).

[17] Simkins v. Moses H. Cone Memorial Hospital, 323 F.2d 959 (4th Cir. 1963), cert. denied, 376 U.S. 938 (1964).

[18] Blum v. Yaretsky, 457 U.S. 991 (1982).

[19] Burton v. Wilmington Parking Authority, 365 U.S. 715 (1961).

(discriminated, interfered with speech, denied a hearing) that the Constitution forbids government to do. The plaintiff will claim that the institution's behavior should be considered "state action" because the government has given the institution a lot of money or otherwise significantly involved itself in the institution's affairs.

In cases where the plaintiff is successful it doesn't really matter whether the government intended that the institution should misbehave.[20] But the plaintiff does have to show that the government is "responsible"[21] in the sense that there is some causal nexus between what it has done and the specific institutional activity complained of.

In parochial school aid cases private institutions are engaged in behavior (religious activity) that the Constitution forbids to government. There is nothing wrong with such activity if it remains private—indeed it is then protected by the Free Exercise Clause. But *Lemon v. Kurtzman* says that the government may not purposefully promote such activity nor take action whose principal or primary *effect* is to do so. *Lemon* also says (though this is really just another kind of effect) that the government "must not foster 'an excessive government entanglement with religion.' "[22]

B. THE ANTIDISCRIMINATION PRINCIPLE

The antidiscrimination principle in Title IX is also a "state action" rule, though one that is broader than the Constitution alone would require. Title IX says that[23]

> No person in the United States shall, on the basis of sex, be excluded from participation in, be denied the benefits of, or be subjected to discrimination under any education program or activity receiving Federal financial assistance[.]

If discrimination occurs, the granting agency must see that it is eradicated. If it is not, the agency is authorized to cut off assistance

---

[20] When the plaintiff accuses the government itself of discrimination, he or she usually has to show such an improper intent. Personnel Administrator of Mass. v. Feeney, 442 U.S. 256, 279 (1979); Washington v. Davis, 426 U.S. 229, 239–44 (1976). The Court hasn't altogether squared this comparatively recent rule with more ancient state action principles. See Choper, Thoughts on State Action: The "Government Function" and "Power Theory" Approaches, 1979 Wash. U.L.Q. 757, 765–69.

[21] Blum v. Yaretsky, note 18 *supra*, 457 U.S. at 1011.

[22] 403 U.S. at 612–13 (emphasis added).

[23] 20 U.S.C. § 1681(a) (1982).

"to the particular program, or part thereof, in which" discrimination is occurring.[24]

As the cutoff sanction shows, Title IX's objective is not to forbid discrimination by private or other nonfederal institutions outright but to assure that the federal government does not support it either on *purpose* or in *effect*. The statute deems the government responsible, regardless of its intent, for any discrimination that occurs in an "education program or activity receiving Federal financial assistance." To say that the government is deemed to support discrimination is really to say that it is thought to "cause" discriminatory "effects" under these circumstances. Other statutes apply the same principle to discrimination based on race (Title VI of the 1964 Civil Rights Act),[25] physical handicap (§ 504 of the Rehabilitation Act),[26] and age (the Age Discrimination Act).[27]

It should not be surprising that the antiestablishment and antidiscrimination principles look so similar. Both are designed to assure that the government does not get involved in constitutionally forbidden activity when it gives aid to private educational institutions. Both began as principles of constitutional law ("state action"), though the constitutional antidiscrimination rules have been largely displaced by statute, beginning with the 1964 Civil Rights Act. It is only because the statutory rules are the effective ones (and because they are so well developed through regulations and case law) that I am not comparing what are really companion constitutional doctrines.

II. Causes and Effects

Here I propose to consider the Court's concern with "effects" in school aid cases.[28] In Title IX law the presumption that government has caused improper effects is limited in three ways: (1) it only applies if there is "Federal financial assistance"; (2) it only applies to the actions of "recipients" (*i.e.* those who are "receiving"

---

[24] 20 U.S.C. § 1682 (1982).

[25] 42 U.S.C. § 2000(d) *et seq.* (1982).

[26] 29 U.S.C. § 794 (1982).

[27] 42 U.S.C. § 6101 *et seq.* (1982).

[28] For reasons I will relate below, the "purpose" prong of the *Lemon* and antidiscrimination rules has been irrelevant in these cases. See pages 73–74 *infra*.

assistance); and (3) in the case of any recipient, it only applies if the discrimination occurs in the particular "program or activity" to which federal aid is going. The development of these Title IX rules offers a sense of organization and direction that has been missing in First Amendment cases. Yet the very same rules are being applied, when government "causes" religious "effects" by giving aid to educational institutions.[29] The only difference concerns factor (3) (the "program or activity" rule). In applying that rule the Court has been much more willing to find institution-wide effects in Establishment Clause cases. The statutory rules thus provide a useful standard for judging where parochial school aid cases have taken a wrong turn.

A. PRELUDE

Before I take up the effects rules, it may be useful to provide a list of things they permit (col. A) and forbid (col. B) government to provide to parochial schools (see table 1). Then I can try to explain how this division came about.

Though there are family resemblances within each column, there are distressing conflicts when they are laid side-by-side. A review of comparable problems under the antidiscrimination principle may make the results seem at least coherent, if not correct.

B. WHAT IS "FINANCIAL ASSISTANCE"?

As the term "financial assistance" suggests, the nondiscrimination principle only applies where the government gives educational institutions something of value for nothing. The same is true in Establishment Clause cases. Such assistance may cause forbidden effects in a number of ways: it may provide new opportunities for the institution to work "harm" (discrimination or indoctrination); it may also suggest government approval of the harmful enterprise. I will take up later the precise ways in which these effects are thought to be caused. They do not always occur when financial

---

[29] Coverage is the only question that occurs in parochial school aid cases. There is no question but that the schools are engaged in religious activity. In antidiscrimination cases, by contrast, there are difficult questions about whether the institutional conduct that the government may be assisting counts as "discrimination" for statutory purposes. See, *e.g.*, Guardians Assn. v. Civil Service Comm'n, N.Y.C., 463 U.S. 582 (1983); Alexander v. Choate, 105 S.Ct. 712, 716–20 (1985).

TABLE 1

A	B
Property tax exemptions[30]	. . .
Tax deductions for parents[31]	Tax credits for parents[44]
Scholarships (college)[32]	Tuition grants (lower schools)[45]
Lunches[33]	. . .
Books[34]	Other materials[46]
State-prepared tests[35]	Teacher-prepared tests[47]
Reimbursement for state-prepared tests and record keeping[36]	. . .
Diagnostic services[37]	. . .
Bus rides to school[38]	Bus rides on field trips[48]
Therapeutic services off premises[39]	Therapeutic services on premises[49]
Counseling off premises;[40] remedial instruction off premises[41]	Counseling on premises;[50] remedial, accelerated, or supplemental instruction on premises[51]
Construction grants (college)[42]	Maintenance and repair grants (lower schools)[52]
Noncategorical grants (college)[43]	Teachers' salaries[53]

[30] See Walz v. Tax Commission, 397 U.S. 664 (1970).

[31] Mueller v. Allen, 463 U.S. 388 (1983).

[32] Americans United for Separation of Church and State v. Blanton, 433 F. Supp. 97 (M.D. Tenn.), aff'd, 434 U.S. 803 (1977); Smith v. Bd. of Governors of University of N.C., 429 F. Supp. 871 (W.D.N.C.), aff'd, 434 U.S. 803 (1977). *Cf.* Witters v. Wash. Dept. of Services for the Blind, 54 USLW 4135 (Jan. 27, 1986).

[33] See *Lemon*, note 9 *supra*, 403 U.S. at 616.

[34] Board of Education v. Allen, 392 U.S. 236 (1968).

[35] Wolman v. Walter, 433 U.S. 229 (1977).

[36] Committee for Public Education v. Regan, 444 U.S. 646 (1980).

[37] *Wolman*, note 35 *supra*.

[38] Everson v. Board of Education, 330 U.S. 1 (1947).

[39] Wolman, note 35 *supra*.

[40] *Ibid.*

[41] *Ibid.*

[42] Tilton v. Richardson, 403 U.S. 672 (1971); *cf.* Hunt v. McNair, 413 U.S. 734 (1973).

[43] Roemer v. Maryland Public Works Bd., 426 U.S. 736 (1976).

[44] Committee for Public Education v. Nyquist, 413 U.S. 756 (1973).

[45] *Nyquist*, note 44 *supra*; Sloan v. Lemon, 413 U.S. 825 (1973).

[46] Wolman, note 35 *supra*; Meek v. Pittenger, 421 U.S. 349 (1975) (given to school).

[47] Levitt v. Committee for Public Education, 413 U.S. 472 (1973).

[48] *Wolman*, note 35 *supra*.

[49] *Meek*, note 46 *supra*.

[50] *Ibid.*

[51] *Grand Rapids*, note 6 *supra*; *Aguilar*, note 7 *supra*; *Meek*, note 46 *supra*. *Cf.* Public Funds for Public Schools of N.J. v. Marburger, 358 F. Supp. 29 (D.N.J. 1973), aff'd, 417 U.S. 961 (1974) (grants ot nonpublic schools to be used for hiring public school personnel for remedial services).

[52] *Nyquist*, note 44 *supra*.

assistance is given to an institution;[54] but that is a necessary condition, if not a sufficient one.

1. *Grants.* The paradigm of "financial assistance" under both principles is the outright grant or loan of money to a school.[55] And there is no real difference between a grant of cash and a gift of property[56] or, as in *Grand Rapids* and *Aguilar*, services.[57] All are cases where the institution gets something for nothing. All may provide new opportunities for discrimination or indoctrination.[58] All may involve a suggestion of government approval. "Why else," one may ask, "would the government bestow favors on the institution?"

2. *Procurement.* Dealing with the "leases" of classrooms in *Grand Rapids* is a trickier matter, and perhaps for that reason the Court ignored the issue. The arrangement is like the Pennsylvania law held invalid in *Lemon*, which authorized the state Superintendent of Public Instruction "to 'purchase' specified 'secular educational services' from nonpublic schools."[59] What's going on in both cases is an attempt to build on the intuition—made explicit in antidiscrimination cases—that government procurement contracts do not count as "financial assistance." The reason is that the purchase[60] or

---

[53] *Lemon*, note 9 *supra*.

[54] A state may give cash to a religious college without violating the Establishment Clause. See col. A at notes 42 and 43.

[55] Compare 34 C.F.R. § 106.2(g)(1) (1984) (Department of Education Title IX regulation) with *Nyquist*, 413 U.S. at 762 (maintenance and repair grants to nonpublic elementary and secondary schools). Whether the grant violates the antidiscrimination or antiestablishment rule is a different question. All three coverage questions—including the "program or activity" rule—must be satisfied before one can reach that conclusion.

[56] See 34 C.F.R. § 106.2(g)(2) (1984) ("A grant of Federal real or personal property . . . , including surplus property"). Plaintiffs challenging federal assistance of this type will have difficulty in Establishment Clause cases after Valley Forge College v. Americans United, 454 U.S. 464 (1982), which denied standing because the donation of surplus property was not an exercise of the spending power. That problem will ordinarily not afflict those challenging state aid.

[57] *Cf.* 34 C.F.R. § 106.2(g)(3) (1984).

[58] As *Grand Rapids* and *Aguilar* show, it may be harder to pervert services provided in kind to religious or discriminatory ends.

[59] 403 U.S. at 609. See also the schemes for "reimbursing" schools for giving and grading tests that the Court dealt with in *Levitt* and *Regan*, notes 36, 47 *supra*. The Court in *Lemon* never actually decided whether this form of aid had the effect of promoting religion. Instead, it said that the effort to find out would entail impermissible entanglement. 403 U.S. at 611–25.

[60] Randolph v. Alabama Inst. for Deaf and Blind, 27 Fair Empl. Prac. Cas. (BNA) 1718 (N.D. Ala. 1982) (§ 504).

rental[61] of services or goods at fair market value for the government's own account does not cause forbidden effects because it does not subsidize or suggest approval of the contractor's behavior.

There are a few flaws in the analogy. If the services provided in *Lemon* were not, say, 1,000 hours of secular education but 900 hours mixed with 100 of religious indoctrination, then the government would get no value for part of its dollar and would to that extent be giving the school something for nothing.[62] More important, the government is not really buying for its own account in these cases. Paying for the rooms (*Grand Rapids*) and providing "secular educational services" (*Lemon*) are things the parochial schools would do for their students anyway. So the government really is giving them something for nothing—no change of behavior on their part.[63]

3. *Tax benefits.* A third type of "financial assistance" problem is the treatment of tax benefits. It now seems undisputed that tax exemptions do not subject institutions to the requirements of Title IX and its cognate statutes.[64] The statutory language is fairly clear.[65] Anyway, treating exemptions as subsidies assumes that some ideal share of everyone's property and earnings already belongs to the government, which can hand out money by either (i) releasing its claim or (ii) collecting on its claim and then giving the money back.[66] In deciding what should count as getting some-

---

[61] Cook v. Budget Rent-A-Car Corp., 502 F. Supp. 494 (S.D.N.Y. 1980) (§ 504); 28 C.F.R. § 41.3(e) (1984) ("any grant, loan, contract (other than a procurement contract . . .)") (Department of Justice § 504 regulation).

[62] *Cf.* Bernard B. v. Blue Cross and Blue Shield, 528 F. Supp. 125, 132 (S.D.N.Y. 1981), aff'd, 679 F.2d 7 (2d Cir. 1982).

[63] See New York v. Cathedral Academy, 434 U.S. 125, 134 (1977). A better Establishment Clause analogy might be an Army base buying bread or brandy from local Benedictine monks. Or maybe even Bradfield v. Roberts, 175 U.S. 291, 294 (1899).

[64] Paralyzed Veterans of America v. CAB, 752 F.2d 694, 709–710 (D.C. Cir. 1985), cert. granted, No. 85-289 (Oct. 21, 1985); Bachman v. American Society of Clinical Pathologists, 577 F. Supp. 1257, 1263–65 (D.N.J. 1983). McGlotten v. Connally, 338 F. Supp. 448, 460–62 (D.D.C. 1972), held that some tax exemptions were tantamount to "Federal financial assistance" for purposes of Title VI. The case was roundly criticized in Bittker & Kaufman, Taxes and Civil Rights: "Constitutionalizing" the Internal Revenue Code, 82 Yale L.J. 51 (1972), and has not been followed since.

[65] 20 U.S.C. § 1682 (1982) equates "Federal financial assistance" with "grant, loan, or contract other than a contract of insurance or guaranty." See also 42 U.S.C. § 2000d-1 (1982).

[66] Why stop there? One might with equal justification object that repeal of the income tax would violate the Fifth Amendment since that—like an exemption—would release to dis-

thing for nothing in this context, Congress and the courts seem to agree that keeping "your own" money rather than paying it in taxes does not count as "something."

The Court has reached a similar result in Establishment Clause cases for similar reasons. As it said in *Walz v. Tax Commissioner*: "The grant of a tax exemption is not sponsorship since the government does not transfer part of its revenue to churches but simply abstains from demanding that the church support the state."[67]

C. WHO IS A "RECIPIENT"?

A persistent tactic of those who want to give aid to parochial schools has been to structure the transaction so that the aid is formally given to the child or to the parents. This approach has had some, but not uniform, success. It was an argument the Court rejected in *Grand Rapids*:[68]

> Petitioners claim that the aid here, like the textbooks in *Allen*, flows primarily to the students, not to the religious schools. . . . Where, as here, no meaningful distinction can be made between aid to the student and aid to the school, "the concept of a loan to individuals is a transparent fiction."

Identical questions have arisen under the antidiscrimination statutes, and the results have been parallel. In both areas the difficulty has been making a "meaningful distinction . . . between aid to the student and aid to the school."

1. *General purpose assistance for individuals.* That there is a difference is not open to doubt. One who receives welfare[69] or Social Security[70] payments may spend them at a sexist institution without subjecting himself or the institution to the requirements of Title IX. And the same money can be given to a church or a parochial school without creating any Establishment Clause questions.[71] The

---

criminating institutions money that belongs to the government. The argument would be vulnerable to the objection that the government had no discriminatory intent, though that claim might not be successful if the plaintiff chose his defendant carefully. See note 20 *supra*.

[67] 397 U.S. 664, 675 (1970).

[68] 105 S.Ct. at 3229.

[69] See *Grove City*, 104 S.Ct. at 1218 n.13.

[70] See Soberal-Perez v. Heckler, 717 F.2d 36 (2d Cir. 1983) (Title VI). See also 45 C.F.R. Pt. 84, App. A, p. 302 (1984) (HHS § 504 regulation) (Medicare); 110 Cong. Rec. 10076 (1964) (letter of Atty. Gen. Kennedy regarding agricultural support payments) (Title VI).

[71] See Choper, The Establishment Clause and Aid to Parochial Schools, 56 Calif. L. Rev. 260, 316–17 (1968).

government is not seen as the cause of forbidden effects in such cases. The reason is that the law here, as elsewhere, is unwilling to follow a chain of causation back beyond a voluntary and unforeseen human act in order to explain or attribute responsibility.[72] In making such grants the government has no way of knowing how they will be spent and no practical means of controlling expenditures. The individual beneficiary chooses what to do with the money, uninfluenced by anything the government has done. The case is otherwise when the government gives aid directly to an institution that propagates religion (or promotes discrimination). Then the government should foresee, and can control, the effects of its action. In fact, to take an intermediate case, the result is also different when the government gives aid to individuals in a form that can only be used at such an institution.[73]

2. *Tax benefits for individuals.* Let me first mention a problem one step short of the intermediate case—tax breaks for individuals who contribute money to religious or discriminating institutions. The Court has never suggested that the charitable deduction for contributions to churches is suspect under the First Amendment.[74] And in *Mueller v. Allen* it held that a deduction for tuition paid to parochial (or other) schools was not forbidden aid to the schools.[75] The outcome seems to be the same when deductions are taken for contributions to institutions that discriminate.[76]

One approach to justifying the practice has been to emphasize

---

[72] "If a guest sits down with a table laid with knife and fork and plunges the knife into his hostess's breast, her death is not in any context thought of as caused by, or the effect or result of the waiter's action in laying the table[.]" Hart & Honoré, Causation in the Law 66 (1959). This is the paradigm adopted by the Court in *Witters*, note 32 *supra*, which approved the expenditure of state vocational rehabilitation assistance money at a Bible college. 54 USLW at 4136.

[73] "If the murder occurred in a prison dining hall, . . . where knives are never set on tables and diners may be expected to get violent, then the laying of the table would be the abnormal event of great explanatory power, and the provision of opportunity 'the cause.' The pertinent principle here is that *the more expectable human behavior is, whether voluntary or not, the less likely it is to 'negative causal connection*[.]" Feinberg, Doing and Deserving 166 (1970) (emphasis in original).

[74] See *Nyquist*, 413 U.S. at 790 n.49.

[75] 463 U.S. 388 (1983).

[76] McGlotten v. Connally, note 64 *supra*, which held that exemptions for fraternal organizations counted as "financial assistance," also held that deductions for contributors subjected such organizations to Title VI. 338 F. Supp. at 462. This conclusion, like the first, has never been followed. The question can no longer arise under Title VI after Bob Jones University v. United States, 461 U.S. 574 (1983), though it may under Title IX, § 504, and the ADA.

that (as with Social Security) the benefit to an institution is "ulti-mately controlled by the private choices of individual parents."[77] That will not work. The government knows exactly what parents will take the deduction *for* (tuition); the only question is *whether* they will take it. The real explanation for these cases is not that the school is not a "recipient" but that tax deductions for con-tributors—like tax exemptions for the schools—do not count as "financial assistance."

3. *Tuition.* That explanation of the tax benefits rule is confirmed by the intermediate case: tuition grants. *Grove City* held that a college whose students paid for their education with Pell grants "receive[d] Federal financial assistance" within the meaning of Title IX.[78] And *Committee for Public Education v. Nyquist* held that a New York tuition reimbursement program for students at private grade and high schools was really "assistance to private schools."[79] Such grants are different from Social Security because the government foresees, indeed intends, that they will be spent at educational (parochial) institutions.[80] On the other hand, such grants differ from tax deductions because their effects are, as the Court put it in *Grand Rapids*, "unmediated by the tax code."[81]

---

[77] Mueller v. Allen, 463 U.S. at 400. Hence the emphasis, in all these "child benefit" cases, on whether the aid is available to public as well as to private school children. *Id.* at 398; *Nyquist*, 413 U.S. at 782–83 n.38. If it is, one can argue that the state doesn't really know what use a parent will make of the aid (whether he will use it in public school, in a private secular school, or in a parochial school), just as it does not know how Social Security benefits will be spent. And so, the argument concludes, the state can't be considered the cause of any unforeseen religious effects. See Witters, note 32 *supra*, at 4136–37.

[78] 104 S.Ct. at 1216–20.

[79] 413 U.S. at 783. The Court's summary affirmances in Americans United for Separation of Church and State v. Blanton and in Smith v. University of North Carolina, note 32 *supra*, might suggest that the Establishment Clause treats college scholarships differently. Both cases at least hold that scholarships that college students may use at any public or private school do not necessarily have an unconstitutional effect of promoting religion when they are used at religious colleges. That, however, is entirely consistent with my point, which is simply that a school is a "recipient" of aid when students spend scholarships there. As I shall suggest later, to prove an Establishment Clause violation one must also show that the aid goes to a "program or activity," within the "recipient" institution, where religious practices occur.

[80] "[G]eneral assistance programs, unlike student aid programs, [are] not designed to assist colleges and universities. . . . [I]ndividuals' eligibility for general assistance is not tied to attendance at an educational institution." *Grove City*, 104 S.Ct. at 1218 n.13. "[I]t is precisely the function of New York's law to provide assistance to private schools, the great majority of which are sectarian." *Nyquist*, 413 U.S. at 783.

[81] 105 S.Ct. at 3229 n.13. I should here say something about the tax credit to parents that was condemned in *Nyquist*. 413 U.S. at 789–794. Mueller v. Allen admitted that "the economic consequences of [that] program [were] difficult to distinguish" from the deduction that the Court upheld. 463 U.S. at 397 n.6. I agree. What made it impossible to sustain the

4. *Materials and services for individuals.* These crucial features of tuition grants are shared by books, bus rides, and other materials and services (diagnosis, therapy, counseling, remedial help). All those kinds of aid can be structured as assistance to child or parent, but such an arrangement should not in itself exonerate the government from responsibility for religious indoctrination. As may be seen from column A and column B in table 1, however, the Court has approved some such arrangements and not others. The reason is that, under the Establishment Clause and under Title IX, there is still a further question: whether the aid goes to any "program or activity" where forbidden conduct is occurring.

D. WHAT "PROGRAM OR ACTIVITY" IS ASSISTED?

Like the "financial assistance" and "recipient" rules, the "program or activity" rule is concerned with the effects of government aid. The "financial assistance" rule eliminates certain government actions (procurement, tax exemptions) as not causally relevant. The "recipient" rule deals with aid delivered to institutions through intermediaries, who may sometimes sever the causal nexus. The "program or activity" rule assumes that there are discontinuities within institutions—that aid to one aspect of a school's affairs does not necessarily produce effects everywhere else in the school. Seven theories have been used to explain what intrainstitutional effects are forbidden.

1. *Purpose.* The most obvious reason for holding government responsible for private discrimination, or private religious activity, is that it has intended its assistance to cause such effects. One would expect the law to be rather unforgiving in blaming government for effects when it has such a purpose, much as it is in blaming a defendant for remote damages caused by intentional torts or in finding complicity in someone else's criminal conduct.[82] The

---

credit in *Nyquist* was that it was integrated with the system of tuition grants to produce a carefully graduated benefit scale. 413 U.S. at 764–67. To have held only the grants invalid would have eliminated benefits for the poor (those with incomes of less than $5,000) while approving them for the rich. That was something the Court just couldn't bring itself to do.

[82] See, *e.g.*, A.L.I. Restatement (Second) of Torts § 435B, comment a (1965) ("responsibility for harmful consequences should be carried further in the case of one who does an intentionally wrongful act than in the case of one who is merely negligent or is not at fault"); A.L.I. Model Penal Code and Commentaries (Official Draft and Revised Comments) § 2.06, comment 6(b) (1985) ("One who solicits an end, or aids or agrees to aid in its achievement, is an accomplice in whatever means may be employed, insofar as they constitute or commit an offense fairly envisaged in the purpose of the association.").

issue is pretty much hypothetical, though. The courts rarely find evil intentions in government assistance programs.[83]

2. *Opportunity.* As a practical matter, when we say that the government has caused improper "effects" we do not mean that its conscious objective is to achieve such results. We do not even mean that the government has unwittingly made something happen. There are voluntary actions by people in the institution that intervene between the government's act and its "effects,"[84] and it would be strange to say that the government "made" those people engage in religious or discriminatory activity. What we really mean, most often, is that the government has provided an opportunity for the institution to misbehave. It is as though the government has left the keys in a parked car, which a thief drives away. Or better, it is like the opportunity for harm that a Dram Shop Act seeks to prevent.[85]

Suppose that a bartender gives his customer a free drink (to make the dram shop case look like "financial assistance" rather than procurement). The most obvious cause-and-effect relation envisioned by a Dram Shop Act is that the customer will get drunk and injure himself or someone else. If he does, the bartender is held responsible. Other consequences are possible too. The customer may linger over his drink, when he should be at work, and get fired. Or he may spend the money he saves on his free drink with a bookmaker. But we would not say that the bartender was the cause of the customer's unemployment or gambling. Those harms do not exploit the dangerous aspects of the opportunity that he provided.

The Opportunity Theory envisions something like the first type of harm in this example. Title IX worries in large part that customers (recipients) will put the sustenance they are given (federal dol-

---

[83] The purpose prong of the *Lemon* test has been invoked only in cases where the government itself has engaged in religious activity. See, *e.g.*, Wallace v. Jaffree, 105 S.Ct. 2479 (1985); Stone v. Graham, 449 U.S. 39 (1980). At the time Title VI was passed there were several federal aid programs that authorized recipients to spend assistance under a "separate but equal" formula, 7 U.S.C. § 323 (1958) (Second Morrill Act); 20 U.S.C. §636(b)(1)(F) (1958) (impact aid); 42 U.S.C. § 291e(f) (1958) (Hill-Burton Act), and much was made of these in the debates. 110 Cong. Rec. 1527–1528 (Rep. Celler), 6544 (Sen. Humphrey), 7054, 7057, 7062 (Sen. Pastore) (1964). We have problems nowadays, but not of this kind.

[84] In the "recipient" problems discussed above there are actually two intervening voluntary actions: one by the individual who first gets the assistance and one by the institution to which it is remitted.

[85] But with this difference: in the parochial school case we take away the bartender's license (declare the aid statute unconstitutional); in the discrimination case we only take away the customer's drink (revoke the aid).

lars) to harmful use (discrimination).[86] To avoid that harm it suffices to trace the federal dollars and insist that they be spent for proper purposes.

If this were the only harm Title IX was concerned with, the term "program or activity" would refer to the federal grant program (*e.g.*, Pell grants) rather than to some program conducted by the recipient (a college financial aid program) that includes both federal and school money. It would not matter if the recipient caused harm with its own time or money; what would count is what it did with the drink. Many of the early Title VI cases emphasized this point,[87] though the Supreme Court took a broader view in *Grove City*.

The Court has also flirted with the Opportunity Theory for aid to religious colleges. *Roemer v. Maryland Public Works Board* held that a state could give noncategorical grants to private (including religious) colleges, provided the schools segregated the funds in separate accounts, agreed not to spend the money for sectarian purposes, and accounted for the funds at the end of the year.[88] The important thing was the assurance that the government's money would not itself be misused: "if secular activities can be separated out, they . . . may be funded."[89]

---

[86] "That principle is [that] taxpayers' money, which is collected without discrimination, shall be spent without discrimination." 110 Cong. Rec. 7064 (1964) (Sen. Ribicoff) (Title VI). "Here we have this scholarship money—much of it federal—going to students. Which students receive this scholarship money is decided upon by the individual colleges and universities—where there are often quota restrictions on women recipients." Discrimination Against Women: Hearings on Section 805 of H.R. 16098 Before the Special Subcomm. on Education of the House Comm. on Education and Labor, 91st Cong., 2d Sess., Pt. 1, at 235 (1970) (Rep. May) (Title IX).

[87] See, *e.g.*, Board of Public Instruction of Taylor County, Fla. v. Finch, 414 F.2d 1068, 1077 (5th Cir. 1969) ("the school lunch program, * * * the agricultural extension program for home economics teachers, * * * the farm-to-market road program"). This is also the most natural reading of some of the statutory language. Title IX speaks, for example, of "termination of . . . assistance *under* such program or activity to any recipient" and says that termination reports have to be filed "with the committees on the House and Senate having legislative jurisdiction over the program or activity involved[.]" 20 U.S.C. § 1682 (1982) (emphasis added).

[88] 426 U.S. 736 (1976). *Regan* upheld cash payments to lower schools on the same theory. The payments there were reimbursement for the costs of recordkeeping and of administering and grading state-prepared tests. 444 U.S. at 657–59.

[89] *Id.* at 755 (opinion of Blackmun, J.) (emphasis omitted). *Roemer* was a challenge to Maryland's statute on its face, so the Court had no occasion to say how much space had to be left around secular activities when they were "separated out"—*e.g.*, whether the entire French department (the recipient's "program") had to be free of religious taint before money could be spent there. If it did, the relevant effects would include not just opportunities but also symbolism. See pages 83–85 *infra*.

The government can often avoid the consequences of this theory by providing assistance in kind rather than in cash. That technique has succeeded for books, tests, and diagnostic services delivered to parochial schools on their premises (see col. A, table 1). Such aid is thought to be self-policing: it does not create any opportunity for abuse and so cannot be said to cause any forbidden effects. It is as though the bartender in the dram shop gave his customer a glass of water rather than something more potent. But *Grand Rapids*, like *Grove City*, takes a view of forbidden effects that is broader than the Opportunity Theory allows for. The Court does not look only at the government grant program.

3. *Infection*. One justification for reaching out beyond the grant program to other parts of the institution might be called the Infection Theory. The idea is that misbehavior elsewhere in the school (upstream, as it were, from the grant program) can infect the use of government funds and should therefore be covered as well. The Infection Theory thus adds one link to the chain described in the previous section.

An example under Title IX is admissions. In *Cannon v. University of Chicago* the Court allowed a female applicant to challenge a medical school's admissions practices without any showing that federal money was spent on admissions.[90] The reason may have been that federal aid *was* extended to other parts of the medical school, and the school would give it all to men if women could not get in the front door.[91] A more difficult infection question would be presented if the medical school got federal money to teach anatomy and discriminated against women by barring them from a school honor society.[92]

In deciding whether Title IX covers such outside activities, these cases have not insisted on a showing that federal money was misspent. They have instead relied on regulations—delineating the

---

[90] 441 U.S. 677, 680–81 (1979).

[91] Rice v. President and Fellows of Harvard College, 663 F.2d 336, 339 n.2 (1st Cir. 1981), cert. denied, 456 U.S. 928 (1982); Othen v. Ann Arbor School Board, 507 F. Supp. 1376, 1388 (E.D. Mich. 1981), aff'd, 699 F.2d 309 (6th Cir. 1983). Norwood v. Harrison, 413 U.S. 455, 469 (1973), applied this same theory as a matter of constitutional (rather than statutory) law to racially segregated schools.

[92] See Iron Arrow Honor Soc. v. Heckler, 702 F.2d 549 (5th Cir. Unit B), vacated and remanded, 104 S.Ct. 373 (1983).

path that infection can be expected to follow[93]—that permit them
to assume that the ultimate forbidden effect (abuse of the federal
grant funds) occurs once discrimination is shown outside the grant
program.

Grand Rapids relied on the Infection Theory for its first effects
argument. The Court found that "the presence of the [parochial
school] environment" might cause even public school teachers to
"conform their instruction to the environment."[94] There is a kind of
fox-guarding-the-chickens plausibility to this with regard to the
Community Education program, which was taught in large part by
parochial school teachers hired *pro hac vice* by the school district. It
is downright implausible as to the Shared Time program, which
was taught almost entirely by full-time public employees who
had no connection whatever with the schools to which they were
assigned.[95]

The presumption that infection would occur is not just implausible; it is contradicted by the evidence of nineteen years' experience
with the Title I program in *Aguilar*.[96] And there are no agency
regulations on which the Court can rely, as it does in discrimination
cases, for support of its unproved empirical assumptions. One may
ask why, in that event, the Court adhered to this dubious causal
inference. The answer is the entanglement theory, which, as I will
show, disqualified the Court from looking at the evidence. The
situation is a bit like the flat-earth problem in the thirteenth century. The Court has adopted a view of the world that is immune
from refutation because the very nature of the Court's view makes
it unwilling to gather evidence.

4. *Benefits*. This theory is something like the Infection Theory
run in reverse. The Infection Theory holds that discrimination (or
religion) upstream from the grant program can flow into and corrupt it. The Benefits Theory holds that an innocent grant program

---

[93] See *Iron Arrow*, 702 F.2d at 554; 34 C.F.R. § 106.31(b)(7) (1984) (school support of
student social organizations); 34 C.F.R. § 106.15(c) (1984) (ED Title IX admissions regulation); 45 C.F.R. § 84.42(a) (1984) (HHS § 504 admissions regulation).

[94] 105 S.Ct. at 3225, quoting *Wolman*, 433 U.S. at 247. The Court reached the same
conclusion in *Meek*, 421 U.S. at 370–72, and *Lemon*, 403 U.S. at 617.

[95] See 105 S.Ct. at 3231 (O'Connor, J., concurring in part and dissenting in part).

[96] 105 S.Ct. at 3245 (O'Connor, J., dissenting).

can sometimes provide a benefit to discrimination (or religion) that occurs downstream. This theory has had mixed success in discrimination law, but more in religion cases.

One example of the Benefits Theory is tuition grants, which can be passed on from one program to another. *Grove City* rejected the argument that Title IX should cover every classroom and activity at the college because Pell grants went from the financial aid office into the general operating budget and out again in every direction.[97] *Committee for Public Education v. Nyquist* reached the opposite conclusion about tuition grants to parochial school students.[98]

A different kind of example concerns government aid that is used up in program x with side effects on program y. Suppose that the government gives money for teaching math classes and that students who take the classes do better in physics as a result. The Title IX regulations suggest that both physics and math are covered.[99] It is not clear whether they survive *Grove City*. *Grand Rapids* may also have had something like this in mind when it said that "state programs providing [instructional materials and services] advance[] the 'primary, religion-oriented educational function of the sectarian school.' "[100] The Court may have meant that remedial reading classes make the school's own reading classes a more effective way of putting religion across.

The Benefits Theory of causation depends (as the Infection Theory does) on the more basic idea of providing an opportunity that the institution can exploit for purposes of discrimination or religion. The fear about tuition grants is that the school will misspend the government's money after moving it from one pocket to another. Insofar as it lends itself to that abuse, tuition looks like noncategorical aid that can benefit almost any part of the institu-

---

[97] "[We] have found no persuasive evidence suggesting that Congress intended that the Department's regulatory authority follow federally aided students from classroom to classroom, building to building, or activity to activity." 104 S.Ct. at 1222.

[98] "The tuition grants here are subject to no . . . restrictions. There has been no endeavor 'to guarantee the separation between secular and religious educational functions and to ensure that State financial aid supports only the former.' " 413 U.S. at 783.

[99] 34 C.F.R. § 106.11 (1984): "This Part . . . applies to every recipient and to each education program or activity operated by such recipient which receives *or benefits* from Federal financial assistance."

[100] 105 S.Ct. at 3229, quoting *Meek*, 421 U.S. at 364.

tion, and there is some sense in following it into every classroom as *Nyquist* does.[101]

The problem of side effects is more difficult. Suppose that the physics building at Grove City College is inaccessible to the handicapped. We might hold the government responsible for that if it paid for the physics building. But if it has only given money for teaching math, the opportunity that the school abuses is not the government assistance itself. It is a side effect (benefit) of that assistance that the school prevents the handicapped from utilizing. So too with remedial reading and religion: the parochial school does not touch the remedial reading classes but puts one of their benefits (increased literacy) to use in other classes where it teaches religion.[102]

These arguments stretch the idea of causation quite far. There is a sense in which Grand Rapids has contributed to the propagation of religious faith. But it has in the same sense contributed to the spread of pornography, the belief in creationism, and the growth of the Republican party since those are all things that increased literacy will lead one to read about.

5. *Freed-up funds.* In holding that the Grand Rapids programs were an "indirect subsidy" to parochial schools[103] the Court may have had in mind not the Benefits Theory but a different kind of

---

[101] The contrary outcome in *Grove City* was based on indications of congressional intent (104 S.Ct. at 1221–22) that do not apply to Establishment Clause questions. The result is also different under the Establishment Clause where tuition assistance is given to students at religious colleges. See col. A. Since the cases approving such aid were only summary affirmances, see note 32 *supra*, one can only speculate about the reasons. One possible explanation is that in such cases, unlike primary and secondary school cases, the schools are not "pervasively sectarian." See *Aguilar*, 105 S.Ct. at 3237. It is thus far less certain that tuition funds, even after having been moved around from one program to another, will end up benefiting religious activity. This matters because we are less willing to attribute responsibility to the government for effects it cannot foresee when it acts—particularly if they are produced by another institution's intervening voluntary choice. See text at notes 107–10 *infra*. The district court in *Smith* emphasized that the tuition aid there could not be spent at a seminary or bible college—institutions that, like lower parochial schools, would be pervasively sectarian. 429 F. Supp. at 872. But *cf.* Witters v. Washington Department of Services for the Blind, note 32 *supra*.

[102] Another possible side effect in the religion cases, more remote still, is that the remedial reading program paid for by the government will make it more likely that children will attend parochial school and receive the religious instruction offered in other classes there. That is a consequence the Court has not found sufficient in other cases. *Nyquist*, 413 U.S. at 775; *Allen*, 392 U.S. at 244; *Everson*, 330 U.S. at 17.

[103] 105 S.Ct. at 3229 n.12.

ripple effect. The Freed-up Funds Theory says that, even if the government aid is not itself abused, and even if it has no benefits that spill over into other programs, the institution may work new harm with the money that government aid displaces in its budget. If the federal government gives a college $500,000 to spend on teaching physics, the college may then take $500,000 of its own money out of the physics budget to spend on men's athletics. The Freed-up Funds Theory is one that several courts found persuasive in antidiscrimination cases[104] before the Supreme Court rejected it in *Grove City*. The movement in religion cases has been in the opposite direction: the Court consistently rejected the theory before *Grand Rapids*,[105] which might be understood to have resurrected it.

Like the Benefits Theory, this theory holds that the government causes all the ripple effects that flow from its assistance. *Grove City* picks out two obvious weaknesses with this idea. First, the government aid may not really cause any diversion of funds.[106] If someone gives me an automatic garage door opener, I won't have more money to spend on other things, if I should never have purchased a garage door opener for myself. Second, if money is freed up, it may be very hard to tell where it goes, and it may not go toward forbidden acts.[107] This matters because we are less willing to attribute responsibility for effects one cannot foresee when he acts— particularly if they are produced by another person's intervening voluntary choice. (Remember the problem of Social Security.) We would not say that the bartender was the cause of the customer's gambling, even though the customer may have had no funds to gamble with had the bartender not given him a free drink.

If we assume that parochial schools are "pervasively sectar-

---

[104] See, *e.g.*, Grove City College v. Bell, 687 F.2d 684, 696 (3d Circ. 1982), rev'd, 104 S.Ct. 1211 (1984) (Title IX); Haffer v. Temple University, 688 F.2d 14 (3d Cir. 1982) (Title IX); Wright v. Columbia University, 520 F. Supp. 789, 792 (E.D. Pa. 1981) (§ 504); Poole v. South Plainfield Bd. of Ed., 490 F. Supp. 948, 951 (D.N.J. 1980) (§ 504); Bob Jones University v. Johnson, 396 F. Supp. 597, 602 (D.S.C. 1974), aff'd, 529 F.2d 514 (4th Cir. 1975) (Title VI).

[105] See, *e.g.*, *Regan*, 444 U.S. at 658; *Roemer*, 426 U.S. at 747 (plurality opinion); *Hunt*, 413 U.S. at 743; *Nyquist*, 413 U.S. at 775; *Tilton*, 403 U.S. at 679 (plurality opinion); *Lemon*, 403 U.S. at 664 (opinion of White, J.). *Cf. Cathedral Academy*, 434 U.S. at 134.

[106] 104 S.Ct. at 1221.

[107] *Ibid.*

ian,"[108] this second point loses force. In that case the government might foresee that almost anything for which the freed-up funds will be spent will be religious. But there are still several problems with saying that the government has caused religious effects. In other religion cases,[109] as in *Grove City*, the Court has not been willing to assume that government aid for nonessentials actually frees up funds. And the evidence in *Grand Rapids* showed that the parochial schools had not previously offered the challenged courses. The Court's response was that there was no way of knowing that they would not have done so in the future[110]—a kind of counterfactual conditional not subject to rebuttal.

A third kind of problem with the Freed-up Funds Theory is that it applies to a surprising variety of causes. One may say that remedial reading services free up money for teaching religion, but one could with equal justice point to city sewer services as a cause of the same effect. If the city did not provide sewer service, the parochial schools would have to install septic tanks, and you can buy a lot of catechisms for what you'd spend on a septic tank.[111]

It is true that reading is part of the curriculum (a point emphasized in *Grand Rapids*) and sewers are not.[112] But that actually counts against this theory. When school money earmarked for septic tanks is freed up and spent on religion, there is a net gain in funded religious activity. School money budgeted for the curriculum, however, is already going for religious activity,[113] so moving it somewhere else may cause no new harm. If the Shared Time program has actually erased religion from "10 percent of the school day,"[114] it is queer to say that the program has caused religious effects simply because the school looks for a way to make up the time.

---

[108] *Grand Rapids*, 105 S.Ct. at 3223.

[109] See, *e.g.*, *Allen*, 392 U.S. at 244 n.6.

[110] 105 S.Ct. at 3230.

[111] This argument impressed the Court in *Regan*, 444 U.S. at 658 & n.6, and *Roemer*, 426 U.S. at 747 (opinion of Blackmun, J.).

[112] 105 S.Ct. at 3230.

[113] That is the basic assumption behind saying that the government cannot aid the school's "educational function" (105 S.Ct. at 3229)—the curriculum is "pervasively sectarian" (*id.* at 3223).

[114] 105 S.Ct. at 3230.

6. *Proof problems.* The paradigm cause-and-effect relation in all the theories I have discussed so far is one where the government provides an opportunity for harm that the institution exploits. For all of these theories the relevant "program or activity" is the government grant program, though activities elsewhere in the institution may also be covered if they infect, or benefit from, or are funded by money freed up by, the government's program. But suppose that the government contributes half the cost of building a school library and that the school contributes the other half. It would be arbitrary, given the way libraries are built and paid for, to say that the government's money built one part of the library and the school's another or that the government's money paid for the first twenty years of its useful life and the school's for the remainder. Even if the effect we worry about is misuse of the government's money, the impossibility of tracing it requires us to say that the "program or activity" here is the recipient's program, not the grant program. This is what the antidiscrimination regulations and the Establishment Clause cases say about construction grants.[115]

Grand Rapids and *Aguilar* may accept a variation on this theory. One way of expressing their conclusion is to say that the relevant "program or activity" is the school's entire educational program,[116] not the government assistance program. But one cannot rely on the Proof Problems Theory for that conclusion. There was no ambiguity in either case, as there is with construction grants, about where the government's money went. Nor was there any ambiguity in the other cases (see col. B, table 1) where states supplied materials or services, rather than cash, for use on the parochial school premises. The question in all these cases was not where the assistance went but whether harm occurred (whether religion was sponsored by the government's contribution).

The Court said in *Grand Rapids* that it can be hard to prove the fact of harm, just as it is hard to trace government funds. We cannot require taxpayer plaintiffs to show harm in schools they do not attend, the argument went, when no one at the school has an

---

[115] As to paying for part of a building, compare *Nyquist*, 413 U.S. at 774–79, with 45 C.F.R. § 80.5(e) (HHS Title VI regulation). As to paying for part of a building's useful life, compare *Tilton*, 403 U.S. at 674–75, 681–84, with 34 C.F.R. § 106.4(b)(1) (ED Title IX regulation).

[116] 105 S.Ct. at 3229 ("educational function").

incentive to report abuses.[117] But the government itself can monitor for harm, as it did in *Aguilar*.[118] The real reason the Court presumed harm was not proof problems but the discovery process. *Aguilar* makes this clear:[119]

> When the state [monitors for harm] the freedom of religious belief of those who are not adherents of that denomination suffers, even when the governmental purpose underlying the involvement is largely secular. In addition, the freedom of even the adherents of the denomination is limited by the governmental intrusion into sacred matters.

The solution to the discovery problem is the same as the solution to the proof problem: define "program or activity" more broadly than the government assistance program. The outer limits are fixed by the area in which discovery is likely to cause problems. In lower school cases the program is the education program on the school premises. In the case of colleges, which are not "pervasively sectarian," discovery presents no problem and this theory does not apply.

Whether this variation on the Proof Problems Theory is a convincing reason for expanding the notion of "program or activity" depends on the assumption that discovery really does cause problems. I will argue later that it does not.

7. *Symbolism.* The other effect on which *Grand Rapids* relied, unlike all of those up to this point, has nothing to do with the recipient abusing opportunities. The Court said that the government would also improperly aid religion if it "convey[ed] a message of . . . endorsement or disapproval of religion." In *Grand Rapids* the message was sent via symbols: "the symbolic union of church and state" in one joint enterprise.[120] It's as though the school paid for religious activity with its own money, but its partner the government said, "We are in this together."

In this instance, as in the last (Proof Problems), the relevant "program or activity" is not the government grant program but something broader—the joint venture in which government and school

---

[117] 105 S.Ct. at 3225–26.

[118] "[T]he supervision in this case would assist in preventing the Title I program from being used, intentionally or unwittingly, to inculcate the religious beliefs of the surrounding parochial school." 105 S.Ct. at 3236–37.

[119] *Id.* at 3237.

[120] 105 S.Ct. at 3226.

are engaged. This might explain why *Grove City* held the college's financial aid program, not just the Pell grant program, subject to Title IX.[121] To hold otherwise could suggest that the government approved of sex discrimination carried on by the school with its own scholarship funds.

The obvious problem with the implementation of this theory is defining the scope of the joint venture. In *Grove City* it did not encompass any classes the school gave, even though the government was paying tuition for all of them. In *Grand Rapids* it seemed to include all classes, even though the government was only offering a few. The Court said that the scope of the joint venture there was determined by the public's (and especially the parochial school student's) perception:[122]

> [The question] is whether the symbolic union . . . is sufficiently likely to be perceived by adherents of the controlling denominations as an endorsement, and by the nonadherents as a disapproval, of their individual religious choices. . . . The symbolism . . . is most likely to influence children of tender years.

I am not sure that a Gallup poll would measure this effect any better than the Court's intuitive method does, but my own intuition is different. The private religious activities of the government's joint venturers are, unlike discrimination, something the Constitution protects and deems valuable. That is why *Norwood v. Harrison* said that government can give free books to religious schools but not to segregated schools.[123] So, if English classes are not covered in *Grove City*, a fortiori they should not be covered in *Grand Rapids*. It is harder to see endorsement when the government's partner does things the government has no control over than when it does things the government could forbid but does not.

There is another difficulty with the Court's conclusion about symbolic effects. Remember that we are speculating about people's impressions of how the government views its joint venturer's reli-

---

[121] The Court did not say why it chose the recipient's program, rather than the grant program, as the relevant unit for purposes of coverage. It simply said that "students who participate in the College's federally assisted financial aid program but who do not themselves receive federal funds [are] protected against discrimination on the basis of sex." 104 S.Ct. at 1221 n.21. Some of the statutory language supports this conclusion. Section 901(a) speaks, for example, of an "education program or activity receiving Federal financial assistance." 20 U.S.C. § 1681(a) (1982). But see note 87 *supra*.

[122] 105 S.Ct. at 3226.

[123] Note 91 *supra*.

gious activity. It seems as though the government could neutralize any symbolic effects by making perfectly clear that it did not approve of what its partner was doing. New York succeeded fairly well at that in *Aguilar:* "[T]he religious school . . . must endure the ongoing presence of state personnel whose primary purpose is to monitor teachers and students in an attempt to guard against the infiltration of religious thought."[124] No one would suppose that the government in that case applauded the schools' religious activities. But this most obvious means of neutralizing symbolic effects is forbidden by the entanglement rules.

E. REPRISE

The antiestablishment and antidiscrimination principles are sufficiently similar that one could restate the *Lemon* test in the terms used by Title IX without causing any real change in the results of the cases.[125] The rephrased test would read:

> No person in the United States shall . . . be [given religious instruction] in . . . any education program or activity receiving Federal [or State] financial assistance.

With but one exception the terms "financial assistance," "receiving," and "program or activity" have the same meaning and scope as they do under Title IX. The exception is that, in cases involving aid to parochial grade and high schools, the term "education program or activity" means the entire on-premises educational function of the school.[126] Any government contribution to on-premises education must be cut off because students are receiving religious instruction in that program.

This reading of "program or activity" is broader than what *Grove City* says Title IX would require. Under the antidiscrimination

---

[124] 105 S.Ct. at 3239.

[125] This is slightly overstated. See note 126 *infra.*

[126] Education assistance (therapeutic, counseling, remedial, accelerated, and supplemental services) can be given to parochial school students off campus. See col. A. Bus rides for field trips do not fall within this category, perhaps because the teacher goes along. See col. B and *Wolman,* 433 U.S. at 253. Aid that does not contribute to the educational process (lunch, diagnostic services) can be provided on campus. See col. A. Given this expansive definition of "education program or activity," I cannot account for allowing books or tests (nor reimbursement for tests). See col. A. But the Court has as much as said that it cannot either, *Wolman,* 433 U.S. at 252 n.18, so I shall not apologize for this shortcoming. See also note 81 *supra* (on the problem of tax credits).

principle it would be appropriate to distinguish between a high school's industrial arts program, or its athletics program, and its program for use of Title I funds.[127] As the Court said in *Grove City*, "[W]e have found no persuasive evidence suggesting that Congress intended that the Department's regulatory authority follow federally aided students from classroom to classroom . . . or activity to activity."[128]

This difference between parochial school and Title IX cases results from the Court's greater willingness to find intrainstitutional religious effects under nearly all of the "program or activity" theories I discussed. In *Grand Rapids* the Court assumed that the parochial school atmosphere would infect Shared Time, notwithstanding a lack of evidence on that point (Infection Theory). It said that both Shared Time and Community Education would have ripple effects (Benefits or Freed-up Funds) that promoted religion. But there was no evidence that funds were actually freed up or that, if they were, their expenditure resulted in a net increase in religious activity.[129] In fact the Court dispensed altogether with proof of harm because it believed that the process of discovering harm would itself be detrimental to religion (Proof Problems). Finally, the Court worried about symbolic effects in *Grand Rapids* (Symbolism), though neither evidence nor intuition supported its concerns. And it forbade in *Aguilar* the very means for countering any symbolic effects that might occur.

To put it more briefly, the chief difference between parochial school and Title IX cases is that the former make strained assumptions about cause and effect that the entanglement rule precludes people from disproving. The decision in parochial school aid cases must depend entirely, as it did in *Grand Rapids*, on "risks" rather than on "effects," on what "might" happen rather than on what did.[130]

---

[127] See, *e.g.*, Dougherty County School System v. Bell, 694 F.2d 78, 81 (5th Cir. 1982); *Finch*, note 87 *supra*, 414 F.2d at 1078; *Othen*, note 91 *supra*, 507 F. Supp. at 1380.

[128] 104 S.Ct. at 1222.

[129] And the benefits—things like literacy—have such a variety of applications that it seems arbitrary to pick out religious belief as the effect they primarily advance.

[130] See, *e.g.*, 105 S.Ct. at 3223–24 ("*may* impermissibly advance religion"; "teachers . . . *may* become involved"; "programs *may* provide a crucial symbolic link"; "programs *may* . . . provid[e] a subsidy"). As to the problem of infection, see *id.* at 3224–26 ("an unacceptable *risk*"; "[t]he *potential* for impermissible fostering of religion"; "too great a *risk*"; "a substantial

III. ENTANGLEMENT

Aguilar said that the entanglement rule rested on two concerns that prevented the collection of evidence about improper effects. Both rely on unsupported speculation that *other* kinds of forbidden effects will occur if the government tries to monitor the services it provides. One concern is that the government, in administering assistance, will show too much favor for the recipient and thereby threaten nonmembers of the sect. The other is that "the freedom of even the adherents of the [school's] denomination is limited by governmental intrusion into sacred matters."[131]

A. CAPTURE

The first entanglement problem mentioned in *Aguilar* concerned the effect that administration of the aid program might have on people outside the school:[132]

> When the state becomes enmeshed with a given denomination in matters of religious significance, the freedom of religious belief of those who are not adherents of that denomination suffers, even when the governmental purpose underlying the involvement is largely secular.

The phrase "enmeshed . . . in matters of religious significance" here refers to the issues that may arise when program administrators monitor teachers and classrooms to make sure that religion does not creep in.

The Court did not explain how this harm would come about, though one proposal has been that it is like the "capture" of administrative agencies by those they are supposed to regulate.[133] Or to put the same idea in the terms I have been using, it's the Infection

---

risk"; "the pressures of the environment *might* alter his behavior"; "[t]eachers . . . *may* well subtly . . . conform their instruction"; "the *absence of proof* of specific incidents *is not dispositive*.") As to the problem of symbolism, see *id.* at 3226–27 ("sufficiently *likely*"; "students would be *unlikely* to discern the . . . difference"). As to the problem of subsidy, see *id.* at 3230 ("there is *no way of knowing* whether the religious schools would have offered some or all of these courses"; the schools "*could* surely discontinue existing courses"; approval here would "let the genie out of the bottle").

[131] 105 S.Ct. at 3237.

[132] *Ibid.*

[133] Nowak, The Supreme Court, the Religion Clauses and the Nationalization of Education, 70 Nw. L. Rev. 883, 904 (1976).

Theory at one remove. The Infection Theory says that public school teachers working in the Title I program in parochial schools may be swept up in the sectarian spirit of the enterprise and modify their instruction along religious lines. This variation says that administrators who go into the parochial schools to make sure that does not happen will catch the same bug and ignore or approve abuses they see in the program.

We have heard this kind of thing in school aid cases for so long now that I think we are inured to how really extraordinary it is. Suppose, just to make it sound fresh, that we transpose the same idea to Title IX. The modified Infection Theory in that context would say that a school subject to Title IX could for that very reason not receive federal aid because, in the process of looking for sex discrimination, Department of Education officials might be captured by chauvinists. I do not mean to deny that the problem of "capture" is sometimes a real one. But the mere possibility that it will occur cannot be a sufficient reason for refusing to give government aid because any program for giving assistance to institutions will require government supervision to assure that the aid is not abused. The only sensible solution[134] is to deal with the problem if and when it happens by cutting off aid to the captors.

There is one possible difference between the two cases. *Aguilar* stressed that parochial schools are "pervasively sectarian,"[135] and Title IX recipients are by and large not pervasively discriminatory. Perhaps capture is so much more likely in the former kind of case that it is not worth running the risk. The Court's treatment of religious colleges is consistent with this idea. They, unlike lower schools, are not "pervasively sectarian," and so the Court does not worry much about entanglement.[136]

The problem with this hypothesis is that it does nothing to explain why capture is more likely in a case like *Aguilar*. The people at risk there—Title I administrators—were supervising public school teachers, and it is hard to see a threat of entanglement in the government supervising its own employees. It does that in the public schools. The only contacts Title I administrators had with

---

[134] "Deregulation" is not an option.

[135] 105 S.Ct. at 3237.

[136] See 105 S.Ct. at 3237–38. See also *Roemer*, 426 U.S. at 758–59; *Tilton*, 403 U.S. at 684–89; and *Hunt*, 413 U.S. at 745–49.

parochial school personnel (the only time they risked capture or infection) concerned the time and place for classes, the choice of students, and reporting about performance.[137] The latter two are things that would happen even if parochial school students went outside the building for Title I instruction. And none of those contacts can remotely be considered a "matter of religious significance."

The "capture" argument is so implausible that it is hard to believe that this first entanglement concern should make any difference. And in fairness to the Court, I must say that the opinion in *Aguilar* did not dwell on it. It was more interested in a second variety.

B. INSTITUTIONAL AUTONOMY

In addition to its statutory arguments against Title IX coverage, Grove City College claimed "that conditioning federal assistance on compliance with Title IX infringe[d] First Amendment rights of the College and its students[.]"[138] The school did not contend that it had a right to discriminate against women. On the contrary, it said that "to engage in discrimination . . . would be repugnant to [its] moral principles[.]"[139] Instead it argued that pervasive regulation by the Department of Education to enforce Title IX "would impermissibly interfere with the College's autonomy and the values which it seeks to promote among its students."[140] Those values derived in large measure from religious principles (Grove City is affiliated with the United Presbyterian Church),[141] but the First Amendment freedom the school feared for was academic and associational rather than religious.[142]

---

[137] 105 S.Ct. at 3239.

[138] 104 S.Ct. at 1223.

[139] Pet. Br. 48, Grove City College v. Bell, 104 S.Ct. 1211 (1984). The case arose out of the college's refusal to execute an Assurance of Compliance with Title IX. The Department of Education then began administrative proceedings to terminate financial assistance (Pell grants) to the college and its students. Departmental regulations and the statute authorize termination for failure to execute an Assurance. 20 U.S.C. § 1682 (1982); 34 C.F.R. § 106.4 (1984); 104 S.Ct. at 1222–23. There was thus no claim that the college had actually discriminated.

[140] Grove City College v. Bell, 687 F.2d at 701.

[141] *Id.* at 688, 701 n.29.

[142] *Id.* at 701.

The Court gave a short but sufficient answer to this claim:[143]

> Congress is free to attach reasonable and unambiguous conditions to federal financial assistance that educational institutions are not obligated to accept. Grove City may terminate its participation in the [Pell grant] program and thus avoid the requirements of [Title IX]. Students affected by the Department's action may either take their [Pell grants] elsewhere or attend Grove City without federal financial assistance.

Since the college had no obligation to accept federal assistance in the first place, it could easily avoid the restrictions that it found so bothersome. In any event, Title IX's restrictions were quite "reasonable," given the Court's holding that the statute only covered Grove City's financial aid program. If the college accepted federal money, it could "segregate its activities according to the source of its funding"[144] and would remain free to do as it wished outside the boundaries of the federally assisted program.

Grove City's argument has a familiar ring to it. It is the second entanglement argument the Court made in *Aguilar:* that "[a] comprehensive, discriminating, and continuing state surveillance"[145] is "pregnant with dangers of excessive government direction of church schools."[146] The peculiar thing about the argument in religion cases is that it is never made by the schools, as it was in *Grove City.* It is instead made by plaintiffs challenging school aid, and accepted by the Court, in order to protect "the freedom of religious belief of . . . the denomination[s]" running the schools.[147] That peculiarity seems to make the argument even weaker. If the government can attach restrictions to aid over the recipient's objection without violating the First Amendment, it should certainly be able to do so with the recipient's consent.

There are several differences between the two cases that might make the analogy inapt. One is that the conditions on grants to parochial schools might not be as "reasonable" as they are in Title IX cases because the "program or activity" under surveillance is

---

[143] 104 S.Ct. at 1223 (citation omitted).

[144] FCC v. League of Women Voters of California, 104 S.Ct. 3106, 3128 (1984). See Regan v. Taxation with Representation of Wash., 461 U.S. 540 (1983).

[145] 105 S.Ct. at 3237, quoting *Lemon*, 403 U.S. at 619.

[146] *Lemon*, 403 U.S. at 620.

[147] *Aguilar*, 105 S.Ct. at 3237.

broader. That is only true, however, because the Court is uniquely willing in religion cases to assume that improper effects will occur outside the boundaries of the grant program. A more realistic view of effects would resolve at one stroke the entanglement problem as well.[148]

A second difficulty with the analogy is that the First Amendment right relied on by Grove City College was academic freedom, while the threat to parochial schools concerns their "freedom of religious belief."[149] It is possible that the Court is more concerned about the latter right than about the former and is therefore willing to go to great lengths to protect schools (even against their own wishes) from "the bewitching power of governmental largesse."[150] The fear, I suppose, is that parochial schools will have to so change their practices in order to qualify for aid that they will lose much of their religious character—and will come to regret this in the end.

That the Court is more solicitous of religious freedom than of other First Amendment freedoms is a proposition that has some support. The odd thing is that the cases substantiating it show a greater willingness to give government money to free exercise

---

[148] That solution to the problem is strongly supported by *League of Women Voters*, note 145 *supra*. The Court there held invalid § 399 of the Public Broadcasting Act, 47 U.S.C. § 399 (1982), which forbids broadcasting stations that receive grants from the Corporation for Public Broadcasting to engage in editorializing. Congress enacted that section because it feared that recipients would "promulgate [their] own private views on the air at taxpayer expense" (104 S.Ct. at 3130 (Rehnquist, J., dissenting)), just as the Court has adopted institution-wide effects rules because it fears that recipients will promote religion at taxpayer expense. *League of Women Voters* held, however, that an institution-wide prohibition violated First Amendment freedoms of speech and press:

[A] noncommercial educational station that receives only 1% of its overall income from CPB grants is barred absolutely from all editorializing. . . . [Such] a station is not able to segregate its activities according to the source of its funding. The station has no way of limiting the use of its Federal funds to all noneditorializing activities, and, more importantly, it is barred from using even wholly private funds to finance its editorial activity.

Of course, if Congress were to adopt a revised version of § 399 that permitted noncommercial educational broadcasting stations to [segregate their activities and] use the station's facilities to editorialize with non-federal funds, such a statutory mechanism would plainly be valid.

Id. at 3128. In short, the Constitution actually requires a narrower ("program-specific") view of the effects of government grants where the recipient institution wants to exercise some kinds of First Amendment freedoms with its own money. Why that view should be limited to freedoms of speech and press, and not extend to religion, is not clear.

[149] 105 S.Ct. at 3237.

[150] *League of Women Voters*, 104 S.Ct. at 3122.

claimants (and to dispense with restrictions) than to those asserting other freedoms.[151] Moreover, this difficulty, like the last one, varies with the scope of the restrictions that attend government grants. If the recipient school is required to do no more than refrain from putting the government's money to religious ends, it is hard to see how the government has worked any change in the extent of religious exercise that private initiative would produce in the absence of government intervention.

IV. CONCLUSION

I have shown that the antiestablishment and antidiscrimination principles in school aid cases are both ultimately concerned with preventing the government from causing improper effects by giving financial assistance to private institutions. The agencies and courts implementing Title IX have developed elaborate and fairly consistent rules for determining how and when such effects occur. Perhaps it should not be surprising that those effects rules work in nearly the same way when applied to the problem of parochial school aid. But it is reassuring, in a way, that the Supreme Court— acting in an ad hoc fashion over a period of nearly 40 years—has worked out an architecture for the Establishment Clause that matches up so well, point for point, with a statutory and regulatory system designed as a coherent whole.

The only anomaly in the two systems is the Court's willingness to stretch the "program or activity" rule to cover entire institutions (or at least their educational functions) in primary and secondary religious school cases. In doing so, the Court credits theories of causation that it rejects under Title IX, and it does so without any evidence that they are more plausible in the Establishment Clause context. Its reasons for adopting those theories is the entanglement rule—itself a collection of hypotheses about causation that is even less supportable than the "program or activity" theories. Abandoning those hypotheses would bring the effects rules into line with Title IX law and would straighten out the major kink in Establishment Clause law.

---

[151] See, *e.g.*, Thomas v. Review Bd., 450 U.S. 707 (1981); Sherbert v. Verner, 374 U.S. 398 (1963); Garvey, Freedom and Equality in the Religion Clauses, 1981 Supreme Court Review 193.

ALFRED C. AMAN, JR.

SEC v. LOWE: PROFESSIONAL REGULATION AND THE FIRST AMENDMENT

> O body swayed to music, O brightening glance,
> How can we know the dancer from the dance?*

I. INTRODUCTION

What is a professional? Is there anything, in particular, about professionals that might justify special treatment under the law? Do professionals differ significantly from those who produce or sell more tangible commodities than, for example, legal services or medical assistance? Are professional services analogous to commodities?

Questions such as these often have arisen, directly or indirectly, in cases challenging professional regulations that are self-serving and anticompetitive in nature.[1] While purporting to protect the public from incompetent or unethical individuals, such regulations

Alfred C. Aman, Jr., is Professor of Law, Cornell Law School.

AUTHOR'S NOTE: I would like to thank Professors Carol Greenhouse, James Henderson, Shiela Jasanoff, Peter Martin, E. F. Roberts, Gary Simson, and Charles Wolfram for their very helpful comments. I also wish to thank Carol Grumbach, '86, for her valuable critical and research assistance and Kathleen Hernandez for her superb secretarial support.

* William Butler Yeats, Among School Children, in The Collected Poems of W. B. Yeats 212, 214 (1956).

[1] See generally Regulating the Professions (Blair & Rubin eds. 1980); Gellhorn, The Abuse of Occupational Licensing, 44 U. Chi. L. Rev. 6, 11 (1976).

can also keep important information from consumers[2] and erect unnecessary barriers to entry[3] into an ever-growing number of professions.[4] Courts have responded by invalidating regulations unduly restricting the flow of information to the consuming public, in the form of advertising the services of a lawyer[5] or the price of prescription drugs.[6] They also have struck down minimum fee schedules[7] and so-called ethical rules against competitive price bidding.[8] In such contexts, courts have given legal defenses grounded on professionalism increasingly short shrift.[9]

On one level, the decisions striking down the cartel-like aspects of professional regulation increasingly contribute to a view of the services a professional renders as commodities.[10] While some of these cases recognize that there may be a public service aspect to the services provided,[11] their sale is, in the final analysis, tantamount to the sale of any other commodity: legal counsel, medical help, investment assistance, or used cars. Is there really a difference?

One difference is that a significant component of the ultimate product or commodity produced and sold by many professions is in the form of words—spoken or written. This difference can raise important First Amendment issues, particularly when less self-serving forms of professional regulation are involved such as the imposition of justifiable disciplinary sanctions. When a professional misbehaves, the ultimate administrative sanction that can be imposed is the revocation of that person's license to practice the pro-

---

[2] See, *e.g.*, Virginia Board of Pharmacy v. Virginia Citizens Consumer Council, 425 U.S. 748 (1976).

[3] See, *e.g.*, Gellhorn, note 1 *supra*, at 13–19.

[4] See *id.* at 10–13.

[5] Bates v. State Bar of Arizona, 433 U.S. 350 (1977).

[6] Virginia Board of Pharmacy v. Virginia Citizens Consumer Council, 425 U.S. 748 (1976).

[7] Goldfarb v. Virginia Bar, 421 U.S. 773 (1975).

[8] National Society of Professional Engineers v. United States, 435 U.S. 679 (1978).

[9] Kissam, Antitrust Law, the First Amendment, and Professional Self-Regulation of Technical Quality, in Regulating the Professions, note 1 *supra*, at 150.

[10] Compare Dorsen & Gora, Free Speech, Property, and the Burger Court: Old Values, New Balances, 1982 Supreme Court Review 195.

[11] See, *e.g.*, Goldfarb v. Virginia State Bar, 421 U.S. 773, 778 n.17 (1975); National Society of Professional Engineers v. United States, 435 U.S. 679, 686 (1978).

fession. When this occurs, the right of that individual to associate and to speak to others in a professional context is severely curtailed. A disbarred lawyer, for example, can no longer provide clients his services or, in effect, speak or write to them in these particular ways.

The impact that professional sanctions have on speech usually has been upheld as an acceptable form of regulation.[12] Because lawyers and doctors, for example, may be entrusted with the fortune, health, life, or livelihood of clients, ethics and competence have long been important and uncontroversial regulatory concerns. When a license revocation is due to gross misconduct or incompetency, the impact of the regulation on speech has usually been treated by reviewing courts as incidental to the primary purpose of the regulation.[13]

Like lawyers or doctors, investment advisers are also entrusted with great personal responsibility for the welfare of the clients they serve. The clients' trust often involves investment advice and custody of substantial amounts of money that the investment advisers are responsible for investing profitably or at least prudently. The ultimate disciplinary administrative sanction for an investment adviser found to be unethical in his dealings with clients also has been license revocation and, in effect, a prohibition from selling financial advice to clients and associating with other investment advisers.[14]

This was the sanction the Securities and Exchange Commission (SEC) applied to Christopher S. Lowe after it found that Lowe had engaged in serious criminal misconduct in areas relating directly to his work as an investment adviser.[15] But both Lowe and the SEC went a step further. Despite the fact that Lowe and his corporations' licenses to engage in investment advising had been revoked, Lowe continued to publish financial advice in the form of various

---

[12] See, *e.g.*, Schutrum v. Grievance Comm., 70 A.D.2d 143, 420 N.Y.S.2d 429 (1979); Florida Bar v. Nagel, 440 So. 2d 1287 (Fla. 1983); Mitchell v. Association of Bar of City of N.Y., 40 N.Y.2d 153, 386 N.Y.S.2d 95 (1976); People v. Hilgers, 612 P.2d 1134 (Colo. 1980); Florida Bar v. Page, 419 So. 2d 332 (Fla. 1982). For cases involving the curtailment of speech in a nondisciplinary context, see, *e.g.*, Giboney v. Empire Storage & Ice Co., 336 U.S. 490 (1499); National Labor Relations Board v. Retail Store Employees Union, Local 1001, 447 U.S. 607 (1980); National Society of Professional Engineers v. United States, 435 U.S. 679 (1978).

[13] See sources cited in note 12 *supra*.

[14] SEC v. Lowe, 105 S.Ct. 2557, 2560 (1985).

[15] *Ibid.*

newsletters to hundreds of paid subscribers.[16] The Commission treated these publications as simply another way of practicing the profession he no longer was licensed to pursue and therefore sought to enjoin his publications as a violation of the 1940 Investment Advisers Act.[17] The Supreme Court ultimately granted *certiorari* in *SEC v. Lowe*[18] to decide "the important constitutional question whether an injunction against the publication and distribution of [Lowe's] newsletters is prohibited by the First Amendment."[19]

The majority opinion, written by Justice Stevens, nonetheless, sidestepped the very issue the Court granted certiorari to resolve. In so doing, Justice Stevens engaged in a kind of statutory rehabilitation that went far beyond the traditional bounds of statutory construction. It would be wrong, however, to assume that *Lowe* was just a statutory case. Indeed, the statutory gymnastics that the majority as well as some lower court judges were willing to go through seemed to be directly related to their view of the outcome of the case on constitutional grounds. As Justice White pointed out in his dissent, the peculiar kind of constitutional avoidance used by the majority resulted in it "deciding constitutional questions without explaining [its] reasoning."[20]

As a result, *SEC v. Lowe* does more to confuse the meaning of the 1940 Investment Advisers Act than it does to deepen our understanding of what constitutes a profession and, more important, what the constitutional limits of professional disciplinary regulation should be. At what point should the perspective of the administrative state give way to the individual rights perspective of the First Amendment? Put another way, at what point, in the analysis of a regulation that affects the right of a professional to speak, does one shift from a regulatory perspective that presumes the reasonableness of the government's rules to a First Amendment perspective that presumes just the opposite? In short, when are we dealing with regulatory attempts to control unethical behavior, and when are we dealing with protected speech? The opinions in this case do little to address, let alone answer, these questions in any meaningful way.

---

[16] *Ibid.*

[17] *Ibid.*

[18] See *id.* at 2557.

[19] *Id.* at 2562.

[20] *Id.* at 2582.

II. FACTS

Christopher L. Lowe was the president, principal share-
holder, research chairman, and editor of Lowe Management Corporation.[21] From March 1974 until May 1981, Lowe Management
was registered with the SEC as an investment adviser pursuant to
Section 203(c) of the Investment Advisers Act of 1940.[22] It published investment advice and had custody of and managed client
funds on a discretionary basis.[23] During this period, Lowe was
charged with and convicted of serious misconduct relating directly
to his investment advisory activities.[24] In 1977, he pleaded guilty to
a charge of failing to register in New York State as an investment
adviser.[25] He also pleaded guilty to a charge of appropriating the
funds of an investment client. He had apparently told his client not
only that he had invested $2,200 for the client's benefit but also that
the investment was earning a most encouraging 27 percent return.
In fact, Lowe had misappropriated the funds for his own use.[26]

In 1978, he was convicted of two felonies. He pleaded guilty to
tampering with physical evidence by altering a copy of a ten dollar
money order to have it appear to be one for $10,000. He also
pleaded guilty to third-degree larceny for fraudulently drawing
checks on a bogus account.[27] He was sentenced to prison and ordered to make restitution.[28]

The SEC began administrative proceedings in 1979 under Section 203 of the Investment Advisers Act against Lowe personally
and the Lowe Management Corporation. After a full hearing on the
record, the Commission revoked the registration of the Lowe Corporation as an investment adviser and prohibited Lowe personally
from associating with any investment adviser.[29] The Commission's

---

[21] SEC v. Lowe, 556 F. Supp. 1359, 1361 (E.D.N.Y. 1983).

[22] SEC v. Lowe, 725 F.2d 892, 894 (2d Cir. 1984).

[23] *Ibid.*

[24] In re Lowe Management Corp., Investment Advisers Act of 1940, Release No. 759,
1091 (May 11, 1981).

[25] *Ibid.*

[26] *Ibid.*

[27] *Ibid.*

[28] See note 22 *supra* at 894.

[29] See note 24 *supra* at 1097.

order affirmed the Administrative Law Judge's findings that Lowe Management Corporation, "aided and abetted by Lowe, violated antifraud and reporting provisions, and that Lowe had been convicted of various crimes, including the misappropriation of funds."[30] In addition, the Commission agreed with the law judge's finding that "respondents failed to comply with reporting requirements" set forth in Section 204 of the Act.[31]

Lowe's attorneys argued that sanctions for this past misconduct were no longer necessary. Restitution had been made to those whose funds had been taken, and, more important, Lowe and his corporation no longer handled clients' funds or securities. They argued that Lowe was now engaged "solely in the business of publishing two advisory newsletters on a subscription basis, and that the publications enjoy an excellent reputation in the investment community."[32] They contended that the past charges against Lowe and his corporations were unrelated to those publications. The license revocations proposed by the Administrative Law Judge would thus constitute an unwarranted "second round of punishment."[33] Moreover, they would amount to an unconstitutional prior restraint of their right to publish.[34]

The Commission rejected these arguments and emphasized that it did not intend to punish Lowe for his past actions but rather to protect the public from potential future harm. In the Commission's view, Lowe's distribution of investment advice by selling newsletters to paid subscribers was simply another means of practicing his profession and, as such, was fully subject to the Commission's remedial powers. The Commission thus saw its decision to prohibit Lowe's publications as a reasonable prophylactic measure necessary to ensure that the kinds of unethical and illegal dealings Lowe had engaged in in the past would not occur in the future. As the Commission's final order of May 11, 1981, stated:[35]

---

[30] *Id.* at 1094.

[31] *Id.* at 1095.

[32] *Id.* at 1096.

[33] *Id.* at 1095.

[34] *Ibid.*

[35] *Ibid.*

> Although we recognize the serious effect of the sanctions . . . we
> are convinced that lesser remedies will not suffice. . . .
> [R]espondents are still free to engage in all aspects of the advi-
> sory business. And, as the Administrative Law Judge noted,
> even their present activities afford numerous "opportunities for
> dishonesty and self-dealing."

Lowe did not appeal the Commission's order, nor did he render
the Commission's concerns as to the possibility of future misconduct unfounded. In 1982, he pleaded guilty to two charges under
New Jersey law of fradulently misrepresenting that checks drawn
on his personal account and one of the Lowe Publishing accounts
were good and negotiable. He was sentenced to a three-year prison
term and probation and ordered to make restitution of $27,000 to
the defrauded banks.[36] Despite these incidents and the Commission's order revoking his SEC registration, he continued to publish
and distribute two investment and advisory services, the *Lowe Investment and Financial Letter* and the *Lowe Stock Advisory*, and to
solicit subscriptions for a third, the *Lowe Stock Chart Service*.

The *Lowe Investment and Financial Letter* had a list of subscribers
that ranged from 3,000 to 19,000.[37] The legend on the masthead of
the publication read: "Market Timing and Stock Selection for Maximum Profits."[38] A typical issue "contained general commentary
about the securities and bullion markets, reviews of market indicators and investment strategies, and specific recommendations for
buying, selling or holding stocks and bullion."[39] It also advertised a
"telephone hot line" that would provide subscribers of the service
up-to-date information.[40] Though advertised as a semimonthly
publication, only eight issues were published in the 15 months
between the Commission's 1981 revocation order and the beginning
of the Commission's suit in federal court.[41] The *Lowe Stock Advisory*
published only four issues and had only 278 paid subscribers. "It

---

[36] See note 22 *supra* at 895.

[37] *Ibid.*

[38] See Brief for the Securities and Exchange Commission, 5.

[39] See note 14 *supra* at 2560.

[40] *Ibid.*

[41] *Ibid.*

too analyzed and commented on the securities and bullion markets, but specialized in lower priced stocks. Subscribers were advised that they receive periodic letters with updated recommendations about specific securities and also could make use of the telephone hot line."[42] Its masthead legend read "Sensible Speculations in Low Priced Stocks."[43] The *Lowe Chart Service* was intended to be a weekly publication that would contain charts for all securities listed on the New York and American Stock Exchanges but would offer no specific investment advice. Though approximately forty subscribers paid for this service, no issues were published at the time this litigation began.[44]

Approximately one year after issuing its administrative order, the SEC filed suit in the Federal District Court for the Eastern District of New York. The complaint alleged that, in publishing two newsletters and soliciting subscriptions for a third, Lowe and his corporations were "engaged in the business of advising others . . . 'as to the advisability of investing in, purchasing, or selling securities . . . and as a part of a regular business . . . issuing reports concerning securities.' "[45] Lowe and his corporations were no longer registered under Section 203 of the Act, nor were they legally exempt from such registration. The use of the mails in connection with this advisory business specifically violated various provisions of the Act.[46] Moreover, Lowe's actions also violated the terms of the Commission's 1981 order, which was judicially enforceable pursuant to Section 209 of the Act.[47] The Commission thus sought permanent injunctive relief prohibiting further publication of the newsletters, enforcing the Commission's 1981 order, and directing the defendants to disgorge all subscription monies received from their publications since the issuance of that Commission order.[48]

---

[42] See *id.* at 2560 n.7.

[43] See Brief for the Securities and Exchange Commission, 6.

[44] *Ibid.*

[45] *Id.* at 2560.

[46] *Ibid.*

[47] See note 21 *supra* at 1362.

[48] *Ibid.*

III. THREE PERSPECTIVES

There are three broad perspectives on which the various opinions in this case are either explicitly or implicitly based: a regulatory perspective, a pure First Amendment perspective, and the arguably somewhat lesser First Amendment perspective provided by the commercial speech or, perhaps more precisely, the commercial advertising doctrine. The adoption of either the regulatory or the pure First Amendment perspective is virtually determinative of the outcome of this case, while the commercial speech perspective triggers a kind of judicial balancing approach that renders the ultimate outcome of the case relatively unpredictable. Since the fundamental issue in this case requires a resolution of what Justice White calls a "collision between the power of government to license and regulate those who would pursue a profession or vocation and the rights of freedom of speech and of the press guaranteed by the First Amendment,"[49] it is useful to set forth these basic perspectives before analyzing the opinions in the case and attempting to determine not only which perspective applies but also how one goes about choosing among them.

A. THE REGULATORY PERSPECTIVE

When courts review governmental action from a regulatory perspective, they usually engage in at least a two-step analysis. First, the court will implicitly or explicitly decide whether the governmental action taken or anticipated is within the scope of the agency's authority and, thus, not *ultra vires*.[50] It is only after a court concludes that an agency's action was legally authorized that it reaches the second question, the reasonableness of the agency's action. Generally, the wisdom of the action taken by the agency is presumed.[51] The burden of proving otherwise is on the challenging

---

[49] See note 14 *supra* at 2582.

[50] See, *e.g.*, National Labor Relations Board v. Hearst Publications, Inc., 322 U.S. 111 (1944). See also Stark v. Willard, 321 U.S. 288 (1944); Chrysler Corp. v. Brown, 441 U.S. 281 (1979); Meade Township v. Andrus, 695 F.2d 1006 (6th Cir. 1982).

[51] See, *e.g.*, Chemical Mfrs. Ass'n v. Natural Resources Defense Council, 105 S.Ct. 1102 (1985); Chevron U.S.A., Inc. v. Natural Resources Defense Council, Inc., 104 S.Ct. 2778 (1984); Woodward & Levin, In Defense of Deference: Judicial Review of Agency Action, 31 Ad. L. Rev. 329 (1979).

party.[52] While courts might engage in so-called "thorough, probing in-depth review"[53] to determine if the agency action is, in fact, *ultra vires*, they usually use some version of a rational basis test to assess the validity of challenges to the reasonableness of an agency action, as opposed to its legality.[54] The likelihood of the government prevailing in cases involving challenges only to the reasonableness of a government's action is very high.[55]

Along with the statutory standards and scopes[56] of judicial review that usually govern judicial review of agency action, as well as notions of agency expertise that underlie them,[57] there are certain assumptions inherent in the regulatory perspective itself that militate in favor of a deferential judicial posture when the agency's judgment is questioned. The essential purpose of most regulation is to prevent future harm. It is thus prospective in orientation and as such deals with probabilities, not certainties. Environmental Protection Agency regulations dealing, for example, with lead in the environment are not likely to prevent all significant health hazards, but regulators usually assume that they are at least likely to decrease the frequency with which these harms occur.[58] The reasonableness of regulation turns on the reasonableness of predictions often made on the basis of limited data.[59]

In making regulatory judgments about the future, the past usually is considered as prologue. Regulators reason from data amassed in the past about harms they wish to prevent in the future. They make predictions by playing the odds.[60] There may not necessarily be, in fact, a high correlation between the harm to be prevented and

---

[52] See, *e.g.*, Woodward & Levin, note 51 *supra*, at 332.

[53] Citizens to Preserve Overton Park, Inc. v. Volpe, 401 U.S. 402, 415 (1971).

[54] *Ibid.* Cases involving the so-called hard look doctrine, however, often result in greater judicial scrutiny than what some variant of a reasonableness test would seem to warrant. See, *e.g.*, Motor Vehicle Mfrs. Ass'n v. State Farm Auto. Ins. Co., 436 U.S. 29 (1983).

[55] See Breyer & Stewart, Administrative Law and Regulatory Policy 336 (2d. ed. 1983).

[56] See, *e.g.*, The Administrative Procedure Act, 5 U.S.C. § 706.

[57] See generally Beth Israel Hosp. v. NLRB, 437 U.S. 483 (1978); NLRB v. Universal Camera Corp., 340 U.S. 474 (1951); Orvis v. Higgins, 180 F.2d 537, 540 n.7 (2d Cir. 1950), cert. denied, 340 U.S. 810 (1950).

[58] See, *e.g.*, Ethyl Corp. v. EPA (II), 541 F.2d 1 (D.C. Cir. 1976); see generally, Ashford, Regan, & Caldart, Law and Science Policy in Federal Regulation of Formaldehyde, 222 Science 894 (November 1983).

[59] *Ibid.*

[60] *Ibid.*

the regulation proposed, but if it is reasonable to assume that there may be, a regulatory judgment to move ahead usually will be upheld.[61] In many areas, the magnitude of the harm that the agency seeks to prevent often gives it even more leeway when courts assess the reasonableness of their predictions.[62] Huge amounts of certain substances injected into mice may create cancer at a high and certain rate. But does it follow that much lower amounts generally found in the atmosphere will have a similar effect on human beings? The gravity of the danger posed by cancer, however, often means that all doubts are resolved in favor of avoiding risks, even when regulators are not entirely sure of the connection between the harm that is feared and the regulation that is proposed.[63] Because regulation deals in probabilities, with the future, and often with serious potential harm, the regulatory perspective has great tolerance for imprecision. The regulatory discourse is about reasonable guesses, not certainties.

The regulatory perspective usually also involves groups, not individuals. Regulatory judgments are based on averages, general trends, likelihoods, and the possibilities of groups, broadly defined, engaging in a certain kind of activity. Regulation seldom is or can be tailored to fit the peculiar circumstances of an individual in the regulated class.[64] If anything, the regulatory perspective often takes a least-common-denominator approach. When it imagines a hypothetical firm that may be producing a harmful chemical or endangering the lives of workers, it imagines the prototype of the worst in the industry and designs its regulations to ensure that the "bad apples" are clearly covered. This usually raises the regulatory costs of the majority in the industry who, on balance, may pose less risk of harm on a daily basis. Nevertheless, once an agency decides that such an approach is necessary, the sloppy fit that regulations have when they actually are applied to a particular entity usually is tolerated because of the reasonableness of the broad policy goals

---

[61] *Ibid.* See also Amoco Oil Co. v. EPA, 501 F.2d 722 (D.C. Cir. 1975).

[62] *Ibid.* See generally Brickman, Jasanoff, & Iegen, Controlling Chemicals: The Politics of Regulation in Europe and the United States, ch. 5, at 119–22 (1985).

[63] See note 58 *supra.*

[64] See generally Aman, Administrative Equity: An Analysis of Exceptions to Rules, 1982 Duke L. Rev. 277, 278–86; Shuck, When the Exception Becomes the Rule: Regulatory Equity and the Formulation of Energy Policy through an Exceptions Process, 1984 Duke L. Rev. 163.

involved.[65] The peculiarities of individuals are seldom recognized. Like legislation at the Congressional level, the perspective is societywide.

Applying these elements of the regulatory perspective to the facts in *Lowe* makes the remedial action of the SEC appear eminently reasonable. The basis of the Commission's decision to enjoin Lowe from publishing his newsletters was essentially regulatory in nature: "We do not seek to punish respondents but, in light of their egregious misconduct, we must protect the public from future harm at their hands."[66] This prediction was based on Lowe's checkered past. If the agency had used a bad-apple approach to determine the composite characteristics of the general type of individual they would regard as a very high risk and a most likely candidate for the kind of prophylactic regulation they sought to apply in this case, they could not do better than Lowe. It was thus eminently reasonable, from a regulatory point of view, to suspect that he might, at some point in the future, misuse the trust accorded him by virtue of his position as an investment adviser.

Two aspects of the SEC's remedial approach, however, suggest that *Lowe* might not be a regulatory as opposed to a constitutional case. First, the regulatory means chosen by the SEC resulted in a complete prohibition of Lowe's publishing activities that constituted investment advising. Second, the basis of this ban on publishing was the possibility of future harm to the public. The ban was not viewed as a punishment for past actions and, in effect, as a simple common-law case based on a record consisting of primarily retrospective facts. Banning publications based on future possible harm takes on a different perspective when viewed through the constitutional lens of the First Amendment. Under these circumstances, Lowe's attempt to continue to practice his profession solely by using the press arguably converts reasonable regulatory attempts to control potential future harm into prior restraints on free speech.

B. THE FIRST AMENDMENT PERSPECTIVE

The First Amendment perspective is, in many ways, the antithesis of the regulatory perspective. When an individual's right to free

---

[65] See Aman, note 64 *supra*, at 311–13.

[66] See note 24 *supra* at 1096.

speech or a free press is materially infringed by government action, the government bears a heavy burden of proof. Far more than a showing of reasonableness is needed to sustain its action.[67] There is, if anything, a presumption in favor of the individual's rights and against the government's interest.[68] Particularly in a First Amendment context involving what might be construed as a prior restraint on speech, the government's regulatory attempts must survive a level of scrutiny that seldom results in upholding the government's actions.[69] To decide to adopt this perspective in a case is, in many instances, also to decide its outcome.

Basic to this perspective and the heavy presumption it accords against the validity of regulatory attempts is a deep respect for individual differences. Attempts to justify regulation in terms of averages, general trends or probabilities, and noble but uncertain regulatory goals are not part of the First Amendment discourse.[70] For regulation impinging on protected speech to survive judicial review, it must be tailored to the situation. The least restrictive means possible must be used.[71] For the government to carry its burden, it usually must talk in terms of certainties, not predictions, and the application of its rules is judged on how well it fits the individual, not groups. Moreover, an individual's past usually is considered irrelevant in assessing whether that person has a present right to speak. Thus, Lowe's past record of misconduct, if it is separated from the publications he seeks to sell, cannot be used against him. Even a scoundrel has the freedom to speak and publish. The First Amendment is not intended to protect the public from those it may not want to hear. Nor is it intended to protect the public from what it might not want to hear. Unlike regulatory

---

[67] See, *e.g.*, Organization for a Better Austin v. Keefe, 402 U.S. 415, 419 (1971) ("Any prior restraint on expression comes to this Court with a 'heavy presumption' against its constitutional validity [citations]. Respondent thus carries a heavy burden of showing justification for the imposition of such a restraint.") See also New York Times v. United States, 403 U.S. 713 (1971); Nebraska Press Ass'n v. Stuart, 427 U.S. 539, 559 (1976); Near v. Minnesota, 283 U.S. 697 (1931).

[68] *Ibid.* Organization for a Better Austin v. Keefe, 402 U.S. at 419; Near v. Minnesota, 283 U.S. at 713–21.

[69] *Ibid.* See, *e.g.*, Nebraska Press Ass'n v. Stuart, 427 U.S. 539, 559 (1976) ("[P]rior restraints [are] the most serious and least tolerable infringement on First Amendment rights"); New York Times Co. v. United States, 403 U.S. 713 (1971).

[70] See, *e.g.*, NAACP v. Alabama, 357 U.S. 449 (1958).

[71] See, *e.g.*, O'Brien v. United States, 391 U.S. 367, 377 (1968); Note, Less Drastic Means and the First Amendment, 78 Yale L. J. 464 (1969).

schemes based on probabilities that resolve all doubts in favor of regulation, in a constitutional framework all such doubts are resolved in favor of the exercise of that individual's constitutional rights.

Viewed from this perspective, Lowe's case is also an easy one, but the result is very different from that when the regulatory perspective is employed: if Lowe's newsletters are protected by the First Amendment as a kind of speech indistinguishable from the expression of religious or political views, for example, attempting to enjoin these future publications on the grounds that they might be deceptive is tantamount to a prior restraint. Though the government has a strong interest in avoiding unethical conduct in the securities profession in general and has every reason to believe that Lowe might abuse his position in the future, such concerns are not likely to justify preventing Lowe from publishing in advance of any such misbehavior. As Chief Justice Hughes stated in *Near v. Minnesota*, "the fact that the liberty of the press may be abused by miscreant purveyors of scandal does not make any the less necessary the immunity of the press from previous restraint in dealing with offical misconduct. Subsequent punishment for such abuses as may exist is the appropriate remedy."[72]

C. THE COMMERCIAL SPEECH PERSPECTIVE

These two perspectives are based on such different assumptions and approaches to government regulation that attempting to reconcile them is like mixing oil and water. Most courts that have dealt with regulatory problems having First Amendment overtones tend to opt for either one perspective or the other. Prior to the development of the commercial speech doctrine, courts' opinions in professional regulation cases involving license revocations usually have not identified significant First Amendment issues. Courts have tended to view the impact of such disciplinary action on speech as, at best, incidental to the disciplinary action, not as a regulation of speech itself.[73] This conclusion was consistent with the way courts traditionally treated speech in the context of commercial relationships. In *Valentine v. Christensen*,[74] the Supreme Court upheld a

---

[72] 283 U.S. 697, 720 (1931).

[73] See cases cited in note 12 *supra*.

[74] 316 U.S. 52 (1942).

New York statute that prohibited the distribution of any "handbill, circular . . . or other advertising matters whatsoever in or upon any street."[75] The court noted that, though the First Amendment would forbid the banning of all communication by handbilling in the public thoroughfares, it imposed no such restraint on the government with respect to purely commercial speech.[76] Government regulation involving such transactions evoked the regulatory perspective, thus minimal judicial interference with the government's regulatory efforts. Regulation of commercial transactions that happen to involve speech as well was routinely upheld. With the development of the commercial speech doctrine, however, an area of speech previously viewed as unprotected became subject to the First Amendment.[77]

In *Virginia State Board of Pharmacy v. Virginia Citizens Consumers Council*,[78] the Court squarely held that speech that does "no more than propose a commercial transaction"[79] is nonetheless entitled to First Amendment protection. Yet this protection is apparently something less than that in a "pure" First Amendment case.[80] As the Court noted in *Virginia Board*, the commercial speech or advertising doctrine is thus very much tied to the "consumer's interest in the free flow of commercial information."[81] Relying on this narrower basis for First Amendment protection and the "common-sense differences between speech that does 'no more than propose a commercial transaction' . . . and other varieties,"[82] the Court appears to be considerably more indulgent of regulation of this kind of speech than of speech "integrally related to the exposition of thought—thought that may shape our concepts of the whole universe of man."[83] As a consequence, cases to which this doctrine applies often evince a greater degree of tolerance on the part of the court for regulatory justifications that would not be likely to withstand full First Amendment scrutiny.

---

[75] *Id.* at 53 n. 1.

[76] *Id.* at 54.

[77] See Bigelow v. Virginia, 421 U.S. 809 (1975), and note 6 *supra*.

[78] 425 U.S. 748 (1976).

[79] *Id.* at 760, 762.

[80] See, *e.g.*, Zauderer v. Supreme Court of Ohio, 105 S.Ct. 2265 (1985); Bolger v. Youngs Drug Prod. Corp., 463 U.S. 65 (1982).

[81] 425 U.S. at 763.

[82] *Id.* at 779.

[83] *Id.* at 771 n.24.

The adoption of the commercial speech perspective itself, thus, is seldom determinative of the outcome of the case. Assessing the reasonableness of regulation that effects commercial speech usually triggers a judicial balancing approach that partially blends the regulatory and pure First Amendment perspectives sketched above. Prospective regulatory goals often are balanced against the narrower First Amendment consumer or market values that seemingly underlie the commercial speech doctrine. Prophylactic rules and the uncertainty they imply vis-à-vis the exercise of First Amendment rights are not automatically rejected. Thus, for example, the Supreme Court, in *Ohralik v. Ohio State Bar Association*,[84] upheld the Ohio State Bar Association rules governing personal solicitation by lawyers, noting that:[85]

> The Rules prohibiting solicitation are prophylatic measures whose objective is the prevention of harm before it occurs. The Rules were applied in this case to discipline a lawyer for soliciting employment for pecuniary gain under circumstances likely to result in the adverse consequences the State seeks to avert. In such a situation, which is inherently conducive to overreaching and other forms of misconduct, the State has a strong interest in adopting and enforcing rules of conduct designed to protect the public from harmful solicitation by lawyers whom it has licensed.

More recently, in *Zauderer v. Supreme Court of Ohio*,[86] however, the Court struck down certain bar association rules prohibiting printed advertising that contained advice and information regarding specific legal problems. As long as the printed advertisement was nondeceptive and truthful, it could be distinguished from the person-to-person solicitation in *Ohralik*.[87]

One result of the commercial speech doctrine is that it provides an alternative mode of analysis to what are often almost predetermined judicial outcomes when either the regulatory or the pure First Amendment approaches are applied. Because it is not, as yet, clear whether this doctrine applies only to commercial advertising or whether it applies to commercial transactions in general, the doctrine plus this definitional ambiguity has several effects. One

---

[84] 436 U.S. 447 (1978).

[85] *Id.* at 464.

[86] 105 S.Ct. 2265 (1985).

[87] *Id.* at 2277.

possibility is that the doctrine might be extended to cases arguably now subject to full First Amendment protections, thus diluting these protections with an approach willing to tolerate a wider range of governmental regulatory interests. More relevant to the *Lowe* case, however, is the possibility that the doctrine will be extended to various commercial transactions that were once routinely subject to the judicial application of the regulatory perspective described above. This would have the ultimate effect of substantially increasing the degree of judicial scrutiny previously applied in such cases. Moreover, the question may be raised whether a commmercial transaction that does not fit within the commercial speech doctrine now demands, at least presumptively, that the pure constitutional perspective of the First Amendment apply unless it can be shown by the government that the regulatory perspective is, in fact, appropriate.

The opinions in the *Lowe* case do little to explain either the contours of this doctrine or its applicability to the facts of the case. To the extent the doctrine is applied in *Lowe*, it has little integrity of its own. The ambiguity of the commercial speech or advertising doctrine lends itself ultimately to the control of either the regulatory or the pure First Amendment perspective. Judges who see *Lowe* as a case on the regulatory end of the spectrum reason that, even if Lowe's newsletter might qualify as commercial speech, the regulation involved was appropriate.[88] Judges who see this as a case closer to the pure First Amendment end of the spectrum reason that, even if this is commercial speech, the remedy sought by the Commission was nonetheless too extreme to uphold.[89]

Which perspective should apply to the facts in *Lowe* and how one determines the answer to this issue are important questions scarcely addressed in any explicit way by any of the opinions in the case. The resolution of these questions, however, clearly is implicit in the judicial approaches evident in the opinions that I shall now examine.

IV. THE LOWER COURT OPINION

For Judge Weinstein, the District Court Judge, this was not a simple case requiring the judicial assessment of the reasonableness

---

[88] See note 21 *supra* at 1367.

[89] See, *e.g.*, Justice White's dissent in *Lowe*.

of an agency's choice of remedy. The contents of Lowe's newsletters were essentially indistinguishable from speech traditionally protected by the First Amendment and therefore were entitled to full First Amendment protection:[90]

> The State of the nation's economy and finances is often an issue uppermost in the minds of voters, and politicians regularly point to the performance of the stock market as an index of public confidence in their office. There exists . . . no sharp demarcation in the range of economic observation that runs from comment on economic policy to prediction of the performance and recommendation of specific securities. Financial news and analysis is persistently flavored with projected consequences of political events and both may form the predicate for particular investment advice.

Under such circumstances no court could indulge in a presumption of validity in favor of the government's attempt to enjoin this speech, nor could it simply defer to the SEC's interpretation of its own statute. The government would have to justify what amounted to a prior restraint.[91]

In the district court's view, this heavy burden of proof could not properly be lightened by characterizing the speech involved as a form of commercial speech. The category of cases in which the speech involved might justifiably be called commercial was limited strictly to the advertising of a product or service. Investment advisory publications "are not the words of a seller peddling his own wares or services, but those of an apparently detached observer commenting on the value of shares offered or held by others."[92] While recognizing that "the investment publisher has a financial motivation to disseminate his analyses and recommendations,"[93] the lower court emphasized that "so may the literary publisher or pamphleter."[94] For Judge Weinstein, there was a basic difference between advertising and selling a printed product, and that difference "reflects in part basic distinctions 'between commercial price and product advertising, on the one hand, and ideological com-

---

[90] See note 21 *supra* at 1367.

[91] *Id.* at 1366.

[92] *Ibid.*

[93] *Ibid.*

[94] *Ibid.*

munication on the other.' "[95] But even if the Lowe publications were to qualify as commercial speech, a matter that the lower court seriously doubted, the constitutional result would still be the same. The SEC's remedy failed to meet the least restrictive alternative requirement of the Supreme Court's four-part test in *Central Hudson Gas & Electric Corp. v. PSC*, a case in which the New York Public Service Commission attempted to ban utility advertising designed to promote the use of electricity: "Given the disclosure mechanisms available to the SEC to put subscribers on their guard against interested investment advice, the censorship that the SEC would impose on Lowe is more extreme than necessary to effectuate the congressional goal of a confident and informed investing public."[96] In short, if, in fact, the SEC had the statutory power to prohibit publication of the Lowe newsletters, the Court had to face "unanswered questions concerning the conditions, if any, under which an absolute restraint may constitutionally be imposed upon them."[97]

Given the constitutional perspective adopted by the district court, however, it had every reason to hope that Congress was aware of this problem when it drafted the Investment Advisers Act in 1940. It was thus against a constitutional backdrop that viewed the SEC's attempt to regulate the Lowe newsletters as a prior restraint that the lower court formulated what it considered to be the fundamental statutory issues in this case: (1) "whether the SEC is authorized to withhold registrant status of anyone seeking to sell impersonal investment advice through subscription newsletters and by this denial to cut off publication"[98] and (2) "whether under the statute and the rules and regulations of the Commission, defendants had a duty to disclose to their subscribers Lowe's convictions and the 1981 order of the Commission, so that their failure to do so constituted a fraud in violation of section 206 of the Act."[99]

In resolving these issues, Judge Weinstein combined the regulatory perspective and approach taken in *ultra vires* cases with the breadth and scope of judicial review used when constitutional issues are, in fact, being decided. The end result is an approach to

---

[95] *Ibid.*

[96] 447 U.S. 557, 566 (1980).

[97] See note 21 *supra* at 1367.

[98] See note 21 *supra* at 1366.

[99] *Ibid.*

statutory construction that improperly attempts to justify what amounts to judicial amendment of the legislation involved. To understand this opinion, however, it is helpful, first, to set forth the basic outlines of the 1940 Investment Advisers Act, Judge Weinstein's interpretation of that Act, and, finally, his approach to judicial interpretation or, as it turns out, judicial amendment of otherwise constitutionally infirm statutes.

A. THE STATUTE

The Investment Advisers Act in 1940 was, like most New Deal legislation, a direct product of the Great Depression. It was the last of a series of Acts designed to eliminate abuses in the securities industry "found to have contributed to the stock market crash of 1929 and the depression of the 1930's."[100] Along with other similarly inspired legislative enactments, it endeavored "to substitute a philosophy of full disclosure for the philosophy of *caveat emptor*" and thus sought "to achieve a high standard of business ethics in the securities industry."[101] In accord with this approach, Section 203(a) of the Investment Advisers Act requires that all persons subject to the Act register with the SEC and disclose crucial facts concerning the nature and scope of their business.[102] In addition, they must disclose "whether they or any person associated with them are subject to disqualification under Section 203(e)."[103] The SEC may deny applications for registration on the basis of any of the reasons for disqualification set forth in that section,[104] and Section 203(e) also authorizes the Commission "to censure, place limitations on the activities, or operation of, suspend or revoke the registration of any investment adviser" if similar kinds of disqualifying factors come to light after a license has been granted.[105] Similarly, Section 203(f) empowers the Commission "to censure, place limitation on, suspend, or bar the association of any person with an investment adviser."[106]

---

[100] SEC v. Capital Gains Bureau, 375 U.S. 180, 186 (1963).

[101] *Ibid.* See generally Lovitch, The Investment Advisers Act of 1940—Who Is an "Investment Adviser"? 24 Kan. L. Rev. 67 (1975).

[102] 15 U.S.C. § 80b-3(c)(1)(A)–(H) (1982).

[103] *Id.* at § 80b-3(c)(1)(G).

[104] *Id.* at § 80b-3(c)(2)(B).

[105] *Id.* at § 80b-3(e).

[106] *Id.* at § 80b-3(f).

These provisions and the sanctions with which the Commission is empowered to enforce them apply to all persons who fall within the statutory definition of "investment adviser" and are not subject to any statutory or discretionary exemptions. Section 202(a)(11) broadly defines "investment adviser" to include[107]

> [a]ny person who, for compensation, engages in the business of advising others, either directly or through publication or writings, as to the value of securities or as to the advisability of investing in, purchasing, or selling securities, or who, for compensation and as part of a regular business, issues or promulgates analyses or reports concerning securities.

The statute provides for three mandatory exemptions from the requirement that investment advisers must register with the SEC[108] and also gives the Commission the discretion to grant additional exemptions to "any class . . . of persons . . . to the extent that such exemption is necessary or appropriate in the public interest."[109] The only possibly relevant mandatory exemption for the purposes of this case is that set forth in Section 202(D), which exempts "the publisher of any bona fide newspaper, news magazine or business or financial publication of general and regular circulation."[110] The district court, however, did not find that this exemption applied to the Lowe newsletters. In its view, Section 202(D) pertained to "publications providing general business and financial information" because such publications "pose less danger to the public than specialized advisory publications designed particularly for potential investors."[111] Since this was precisely what the Lowe newsletters were intended to be, a statutory solution to this case required a more creative approach.

B. JUDGE WEINSTEIN'S INTERPRETATION OF THE ACT

Judge Weinstein focused his attention on the disclosure requirements and remedial provisions laid down in Section 203. He read

---

[107] *Id.* at § 80b-2(a)(11).

[108] *Id.* at § 80b-3(b). See generally, Lovitch, note 101 *supra*, at 70–72.

[109] 15 U.S.C. § 80b-6a. It is at least arguable that the Commission could have granted newsletter writers a discretionary exemption under this provision if it could show that this would be in the public interest. The Commission, of course, did not do this, and it is unclear what the statutory basis of such an exemption would have been if it did. See text at note 126 *infra*.

[110] *Id.* at § 80b-2(a)(11)(D).

[111] See note 22 *supra* at 1362.

the broad definition of investment adviser set forth in Section 202 to include investment advisers engaged in personal, one-on-one relationships with individual clients as well as advisers rendering more impersonal advice through publications such as the Lowe newsletter. He nevertheless concluded that the disclosure and remedial provisions of Section 203 of the Act did not apply when the advice given was, as in this case, impersonal investment advice published for all those in the general public willing to purchase it.[112]

> These provisions were of limited applicability to advisers and their associates as publishers of impersonal investment advice for general or subscription distribution in section 203(c)(2)(13) . . . insofar as it speaks of denial of registration; the last sentence of section 203(c)(2) . . . ; section 203(e) . . . insofar as it speaks of suspension or revocation of registration; and section 203(f) . . . insofar as it speaks of suspension or bar from association with an investment adviser.

Judge Weinstein recognized that "there is no suggestion on the face of the statute"[113] that supported his reading of a distinction between personal and impersonal investment advice into Section 203; however, not to do so would force one to conclude that Congress had, in effect, authorized the SEC to request "a prior restraint on would-be publishers of impersonal market information."[114] Judge Weinstein argued that his interpretation was thus "suggested by constitutional considerations."[115] Moreover, there was a compelling logic behind it:[116]

> The newsletter publisher . . . plays a role different from that of the broker, dealer or personal adviser, so that observations and procedures directed toward securities practitioners generally are not necessarily applicable to him. For example, in enacting the anti-fraud provisions of the Advisers Act, Congress observed that the "occupations [of broker-dealer and advisers] involve similar delegations of trust and responsibility." The analogy is apt for the personal adviser, but not for the editor of a market publication who has no direct person to person contact with his readers and to whom there is no delegation of authority.

---

[112] *Id.* at 1369.

[113] *Id.* at 1365.

[114] *Ibid.*

[115] *Ibid.*

[116] *Ibid.*

Based on this logic as well as on the demands of "constitutional considerations," Judge Weinstein argued that his interpretation is what Congress "may have assumed" or "might have concluded" when it included in its broad definition of "investment adviser" both personal and impersonal advisers:[117]

> In the Advisers Act the common grouping of personal and impersonal advisers need not imply that Congress intended that they be treated identically under all provisions or for all purposes. In particular, Congress may have assumed that disclosure of past misdeeds alone would be inadequate protection against an adviser who, through personal contact, could improperly dilute the force of such disclosure. The only effective protection would be a bar to the adviser's practice. But Congress might have concluded that disclosure was adequate in the case of an impersonal client who could more calmly weigh the gravity of the publisher's misdeeds against his advisory qualifications and in an unpressured atmosphere decide to accept or reject the publisher's services or recommendations.

In other words, for Judge Weinstein, regulation of the personal activities of an investment adviser may, from a remedial perspective, be the only and thus the least restrictive means available of protecting the public in such circumstances. The First Amendment arguably imposes greater limits on Congress if it attempts to substitute regulation for the doctrine of *caveat emptor* when only print is involved.

Having read this distinction between personal and impersonal investment advisers into portions of the Act, Judge Weinstein denied the SEC's request for an injunction against Lowe's newsletters on *ultra vires* grounds. His decision nonetheless left much of the statute intact. Though the SEC could not enjoin the newsletters in advance, Lowe was not necessarily exempt from the more general disclosure requirements of the Act:[118]

> The defendants, whose registration has been revoked by the SEC for all purposes on May 11, 1981, cannot be cited for or enjoined from a violation of the registration provisions of the Advisers Act insofar as their activities are limited to publishing. So long as the defendants stand ready to submit to registration and provide all information that is now or may in the future be

---

[117] *Ibid.*

[118] *Id.* at 1369.

properly required by the SEC pursuant to sections 203(c)(1) and 204 of the Advisers Act, but are denied registration by the Commission, they may continue to publish their market newsletters and news services.

In the publisher's context, registration constitutes no more than a feature of the disclosure mechanism.

As to the SEC's charge that Lowe illegally failed to divulge his past convictions to his subscribers, Judge Weinstein seemed to imply that disclosure of the sort demanded by the Commission might very well have been an appropriate or less restrictive means of achieving the overall regulatory purpose of the Act. Lowe could continue to publish his newsletters, but only by disclosing at least the fact that the SEC had revoked his registration for past misconduct. But as Judge Weinstein noted:[119]

> [B]ecause there is no rule presently in force that would require a subscription market letter publisher to disclose to its readers the past misconduct or criminality of its owners, employees or associates, the defendants cannot be found to have violated any reporting requirements. It would be patently unfair to hold defendants accountable under the anti-fraud provisions of section 206 for failure to disclose when the reporting rules are silent on any such requirement and may even imply the absence of such a requirement.

The district court did, however, enjoin Lowe's continued use of a recorded hot-line service, presumably on the somewhat strained grounds that this mode of communication provided the kind of personal advice that the SEC clearly had the power to regulate under the Act.

Judge Weinstein felt constitutionally compelled to read the statute as he did but not to invalidate it. In his view, and, as we shall see, in the opinion of a majority of the Supreme Court as well, finding a statutory distinction between rendering personal as opposed to impersonal investment advice would salvage an otherwise unconstitutionally overbroad statute. Presumably, such a saving construction would exclude from coverage of the Act a clear category of conduct privileged by the First Amendment, that is, the right to publish without prior restraint.[120] But to read this distinction into the Act with no basis other than what Congress might

---

[119] *Id.* at 1370.

[120] See generally Tribe, American Constitutional Law § 12-27 at 717.

have intended in light of the constitutional gloss the lower court now places on a statute drafted over forty years ago is to cross even a deliberately vaguely drawn line between the judicial act of statutory interpretation and the legislative act of statutory amendment.

C. STATUTORY CONSTRUCTION, STATUTORY REHABILITATION, AND STATUTORY AMENDMENT

Deciding constitutional questions only when necessary has been considered a basic tenet of judicial restraint. Separation of powers principles require that courts recognize that there is or should be a difference between statutory interpretation and statutory amendment.[121] Lawmaking power lies with Congress, and courts should not interfere with legislative schemes unless it is necessary to do so. It is usually assumed that avoiding a constitutional question in favor of a statutory solution results in less judicial interference with the legislature's powers, not more.[122] But that is not the case with Judge Weinstein's approach.

Judge Weinstein's reasons for avoiding the constitutional issues in this case are based more on an assessment of the policy implications of the various solutions to the legal problems presented than on a careful determination of who has the power to implement these solutions. For Judge Weinstein, the policy implications of his declaring the Investment Advisers Act unconstitutional are enough to encourage, if not require, a search for an alternative judicial approach. To declare the Act unconstitutional "would seriously impede the regulation of securities markets. Its effect on investors as well as those in the securities business might be highly damaging. It seems doubtful that Congress or the SEC would welcome such a result."[123] Building on the theme of what Congress would welcome today, and presumably assuming that that is, therefore, what they may, in fact, have intended in 1940, he turned to a provision in the statute that presumably authorizes this kind of judicial creativity. He noted that the Act allows the Commission to "exempt . . . any class . . . of persons . . . from any provision [of the Act] . . . to the extent that such exemption is necessary or appropri-

---

[121] *Ibid.*

[122] *Ibid.*

[123] See note 21 *supra* at 1367.

ate in the public interest."[124] It is at best unclear whether the SEC itself could have, pursuant to this provision, exempted newsletter writers from any of the requirements of the Act.[125] But even if it could, it does not follow that such agency discretion in any way authorizes the judicial creation of a permanent exemption. Nevertheless, based on this provision, Judge Weinstein argues that since "Congress has apparently encouraged a flexible approach in the interpretation and execution of the Advisers Act so as to advance the public good . . . [a] similar liberality is called for in the construction of the Advisers Act to preserve its constitutionality and basic design."[126]

This is, at least, a candid attempt to empower a court to rehabilitate a statute about to be applied in an arguably unconstitutional manner. Just as we have a living constitution, so too, arguably, did Congress seek to provide for a living statute. Such an approach, however, improperly equates Congressional authorization of agency interpretation within the boundaries of the statute involved with a judicial interpretative approach that ultimately results in the alteration of those very boundaries. In authorizing the SEC to grant exemptions on a discretionary basis, Congress, in effect, provided the agency with the power to dispense administrative equity.[127] Exemptions could be granted to certain classes of persons, but only if those exemptions were in the public interest, as defined by purposes and goals of the statute itself.[128] Granting exemptions gives the agency an opportunity to fine tune its own statute but not to alter its basic scope and structure.[129] The fact that Congress expressly granted the agency this kind of discretionary power has nothing to do with the scope of a court's interpretative powers. When reviewing the statute on an *ultra vires* basis, a court, like the agency itself, is limited by the statutory assumptions and goals set forth by Congress. Even the best of constitutional purposes cannot add what Congress did not create.

---

[124] *Id.* at 1368.

[125] Public interest exemptions require a rationale based on the general purposes of the statute. Given Congress's apparent intent, at least from the SEC's point of view, of regulating certain investment activities carried on in print, it is difficult to say just what this rationale could have been.

[126] *Ibid.*

[127] See Aman, note 64 *supra*, at 317.

[128] See note 126 *supra*.

[129] Aman, note 64 *supra*, at 280–86.

To do otherwise improperly blends a regulatory *ultra vires* statutory approach with that used by courts when interpreting open-ended, arguably vague constitutional provisions. It would, in effect, equate the flexibility of an agency's enabling act—its regulatory constitution, if you will—with the perceived demands of the Constitution. But agency flexibility to alter the coverage of its own enabling act requires that it take that Act as a given. If a portion of it is, in fact, unconstitutional, this does not give either the agency or the court the authority to excise it by reading a provision into it that does not exist. At times an agency's regulatory constitution must be asked to square with the U.S. Constitution. If it does not measure up, the Court is not empowered to rewrite the statute but to interpret it in light of a higher authority. In such a case, the appropriate judicial result is not to rewrite the statute but to "remand" the law to Congress.

Avoiding constitutional issues through this kind of judicial rehabilitation is a far cry from judicial restraint. Judicial restraint is based, fundamentally, on an overriding respect for the separation of powers principle that courts ought not to interfere with legislative enactments unless they have no other choice. Judge Weinstein's approach, however, stands for the opposite: courts can amend a statute when they believe that Congress encouraged flexibility in its interpretation and would probably amend it in a similar way, if it took the time and expended the political capital necessary to do so. This may have been, in the district court's view, the only straightforward way of saving an otherwise unconstitutional statute, but if the court believed that this statute as applied to Lowe was unconstitutional, it should have so held.

V. THE COURT OF APPEALS

The Court of Appeals, in a decision written by Judge Oakes and specially concurred in by Judge Van Graafeiland, rejected both the lower court's approach to statutory interpretation and the constitutional perspective underlying it. The majority "did not believe that the Investment Advisers Act may be rewritten as the district court would rewrite it. The Act does not distinguish between 'personal' and 'impersonal' advice, but rather between publications or writing 'as to the value of securities or as to the advisability of investing in, purchasing, or selling securities,' on the one hand, and 'bona fide newspaper[s], news magazine[s], or business or financial publication[s] of general and regular circulation;' on the other."[130] The court also rejected the pure First Amendment constitutional perspective that drove Judge Weinstein to such creative interpretive lengths, noting that it was "preferable to analyze this case as one involving the permissible 'regulation of economic activity.' "[131] From a regulatory point of view, the SEC's proposed actions were both fully within its statutory powers and represented a reasonable exercise of those powers. Lowe was continuing to practice his profession, albeit solely in print, and he was no longer licensed to do so. For the majority, it was hornbook law that "[t]he denial of a professional license for criminal conduct has been a traditional, and perhaps necessary, aspect of this type of regulation. . . . Thus, we believe that the SEC may bar Lowe from the profession of investment adviser because of his past criminal conduct."[132]

To the extent that First Amendment considerations entered the majority's analysis, it did not treat the speech involved in the case as entitled to full First Amendment protection. The First Amendment interests had to be examined in the light of the regulatory context in which they arose. As such, the nature of the speech involved in this case was characterized as "potentially deceptive commercial speech."[133] As such, it was not the kind of speech entitled to the "identical constitutional protection provided for certain forms of social, political or religious expression."[134]

In taking this approach the majority relied heavily on *SEC v. Wall Street Transcript*,[135] in which the Second Circuit reversed and remanded a federal district court decision that refused to enforce a subpoena duces tecum issued by the SEC under the Investment Advisers Act.[136] At issue was whether the Wall Street Transcript Corporation was, in fact, an investment adviser. The purpose of the SEC's subpoena was to obtain information that would help resolve this question. The Commission sought disclosure of all

[130] See note 22 *supra* at 896–97.

[131] *Id.* at 901.

[132] *Ibid.*

[133] *Ibid.*

[134] *Id.* at 899.

[135] SEC v. Wall Street Transcript Corp., 442 F.2d 1371 (2d Cir. 1970), cert. denied, 398 U.S. 958 (1970).

[136] *Ibid.*

documents, arguments, or other writings pertaining to the sale of the *Transcript*, correspondence with its subscribers or prospective subscribers, and all writings relating or containing reference to obtaining materials printed in the publication.[137] The president refused to comply, and the district court upheld his refusal on the ground that the *Wall Street Transcript* was "a bona fide newspaper and thus exempt from the Act." The Second Circuit reversed, holding that the district court's determination that the *Transcript* was a "bona fide newspaper" was premature and inappropriate.[138] Even if this ultimately were to be proven true, the court reasoned, an initial investigation of the sort planned by the Commission would not so circumscribe freedom of expression during this interim period as necessarily to violate the First Amendment.[139] In so doing, the Court treated commercial investment advice as a kind of speech not "entitled to the identical constitutional protection provided for certain forms of social, political or religious expression."[140] It bolstered this conclusion with Justice Harlan's comments in *Curtis Publishing Co. v. Butts:*[141]

> A business "is not immune from regulation because it is an agency of the press. The publisher of a newspaper has no special immunity from the application of general laws. . . ." Federal securities regulation, mail fraud statutes, and common-law actions for deceit and misrepresentation are only some examples of our understanding that the right to communicate information of public interest is not "unconditional."

Wall Street Transcript and *Curtis Publishing*, however, were decided before the Supreme Court's landmark decision in *Virginia State Board of Pharmacy v. Virginia Citizens Consumer*[142] establishing the principle that commercial speech was entitled to at least some First Amendment protection. Lowe's attorneys claimed that, because of *Virginia Board* and its aftermath, *Wall Street Transcript* was no longer good law. Courts could no longer adopt the regulatory perspective when commercial speech was involved. Appellees ar-

---

[137] *Id.* at 1374.

[138] *Id.* at 1379.

[139] *Id.* at 1380.

[140] *Id.* at 1379.

[141] *Ibid.* Curtis Publishing Co. v. Butts, 388 U.S. 130 (1967).

[142] See note 6 *supra*.

gued that, since the speech in this case did more than just propose a commercial transaction, it was entitled to full First Amendment protection, but at the very least, the Lowe newsletters were protected commercial speech. Even if some regulation might be appropriate, only the least restrictive means possible could be used.[143] Prohibition, particularly in the form of a prior restraint on publication, was, in fact, far more restrictive than necessary.

In Judge Oakes's view, however, the commercial speech cases did not in any way undermine the Second Circuit's fundamental approach to the Investment Advisers Act set forth in *Wall Street Transcript* but rather fully supported the constitutionality of the statutory provisions applied to Lowe in this case: "[C]onsidered in light of *Virginia Pharmacy* and its progeny, . . . the provisions of the Investment Advisers Act at issue here are precisely the kind of commercial activity permissible under the First Amendment."[144] The government did not "lose its power to regulate *commercial activity* deemed harmful to the public whenever speech is a component of the activity."[145] Given Lowe's track record, the regulatory goals of the Act, and the consequently strong government interest in avoiding future harm to the public, Judge Oakes easily concluded that Lowe was simply continuing to practice his profession in print and that the SEC had every right to stop him:[146]

> [T]he regulation of the professions is intended to prevent harm to the public before it occurs, not after it is done. Saying that appellees may not sell their views as to the purchase, sale, or holding of certain securities is no different from saying that a disbarred lawyer may not sell legal advice. Thus, we hold that the authority to revoke Lowe's registration as an investment adviser, and as a result to bar him from publishing his newsletter, does not violate the First Amendment.

In the alternative, Judge Oakes rejected the lower court's narrow view that commercial speech was confined solely to advertising, concluding that "commercial speech is linked inextricably to commercial activity" and as such was clearly broad enough to encom-

---

[143] See note 24 *supra*.

[144] See note 22 *supra* at 900–901.

[145] *Id.* at 900.

[146] *Id.* at 899.

pass Lowe's publications.[147] But viewing the Lowe newsletters as a form of commercial speech did not change the result for Judge Oakes.

Having rejected both the need for and the statutory basis of a distinction based on the rendering of personal or impersonal advice, Judge Oakes nonetheless used another distinction to determine when, in fact, a serious First Amendment issue might be involved in a case such as *Lowe*. In emphasizing what his opinion did *not* do, he noted that what Lowe "is prohibited from doing is selling to clients advice and counsel, analysis and reports as to the value of specific securities or as to the advisability of investing in, purchasing or selling or holding specific securities."[148] In a footnote Judge Oakes left "to another day the question whether a publication dealing only with market indicators generally or making recommendations only as to groups of securities . . . could be barred on facts such as those of this case."[149] Presumably, there is a point at which the speech being published becomes general enough to be protected by the First Amendment. But at what point does that occur?

This problem of where this line is to be drawn was the focus of the dissenting judge's opinion. A district court judge sitting by designation, he was very sensitive to the difficulty trial judges might have in drafting such injunctions. In his view, without a bright line to guide the district court, it would be virtually impossible to frame a constitutional injunction:[150]

> No logical basis is presented for the court on remand to allow the recommendation of groups of securities but not individual stocks. Faced with the necessity of framing an injunction which

---

[147] *Id.* at 902. This approach was similar to that taken by the Seventh Circuit in Savage v. CFTC, 548 F.2d 192 (7th Cir. 1977). In a situation closely analogous to *Lowe*, the Court rejected a First Amendment challenge to the Commodity Futures Trading Commission's denial of registration of a publisher of a weekly commodities newsletter. Registration was denied on the basis of the applicant's prior violations of federal securities laws. The Commission argued that the violations were evidence of the applicant's unfitness to act as an adviser. The publisher, on the other hand, argued that the denial was an unconstitutional prior restraint. The Court rejected the publisher's argument. For the proposition that *Savage* is inapposite to *Lowe*, see Case Comment, SEC v. Lowe: The Constitutionality of Prohibiting Publication of Investment Newsletters under the Investment Advisers Act, 69 Minn. L. Rev. 937 (1985).

[148] Note 22 *supra* at 902.

[149] *Id.* at 902 n.7.

[150] *Id.* at 909.

> preserves Lowe's conceded right to express his views as to the
> effect of current events on market conditions, and yet prevents
> any "recommendation" of specific securities, the district judge
> will be presented with extreme difficulty. The injunction decree
> of a court of equity must be intelligible and practical; it must
> draw a bright line, and should produce benefits at least equal to
> its social burdens.

The concurring judge was more optimistic: "Judge Brieant's concern about the terms of the injunction to be issued by the district
court is, I suggest, premature and fails to take into account the skill
and ingenuity of Judge Brieant's colleagues in the district court. . . .
I have no doubt that, upon remand, the district court can frame an
injunction so that Mr. Lowe 'will know what the court intends to
forbid.' "[151]

This exchange highlights the real issues in this case. (1) At what
point should the regulatory perspective give way to a constitutional
perspective? Implicit in this question is another. (2) At what point
does the practice of investment advising give way to a more journalistic enterprise that is more clearly protected by the First Amendment? For the majority, the answers to these questions were relatively easy because, in its view, the *Lowe* case easily fit on the
regulatory end of the judicial review spectrum, but its recognition
of these questions nicely raised the very issues the Supreme Court
granted certiorari to decide. The Supreme Court majority, however, avoided these issues. It construed the statute in a way that
paid only lip service to the line between judicial and legislative
power, and it approached the legislative record in a way that calls to
mind Namier's statement about history: "We imagine the past so
that we may remember the future."[152]

VI. THE SUPREME COURT OPINIONS

Like Judge Weinstein, Justice Stevens, writing for the majority, looks at the statute through a pure First Amendment lens. In
interpreting the statute, he too attempts to reconstruct what Congress intended when it passed the Advisers Act in the light of
constitutional demands, both past and present. Unlike Judge

---

[151] *Id.* at 903.

[152] Namier, Conflicts 70 (1942).

Weinstein, however, Justice Stevens does not purport to speculate on what Congress might have intended or may have assumed when it came to the passage of the Investment Advisers Act. Rather, he sets out to prove what, in fact, Congress did intend. The end result of his opinion is a judicial invasion of the legislature's domain that cuts much deeper than Judge Weinstein's attempt to save the statute. In the process of deciding the case, the opinion evinces so casual a regard for statutory language and Congressional history as to render sadly ironic the judicial restraint rhetoric used to justify the statutory approach the Court claims to be so compelled to follow.

A. THE MAJORITY'S OPINION

The majority opinion concludes that Congress did not give the SEC the power to regulate publications such as the Lowe newsletter, implying that for it to interpret the statute and legislative history in any other way would suggest that Congress did not know its constitutional law. "Congress was undoubtedly aware of two major first amendment cases that this Court decided before the enactment of the Act," *Near v. Minnesota* and *Lovell v. City of Griffin*.[153] To support a statutory determination that Lowe was not engaged in the business of investment advising within the meaning of the Act, Justice Stevens also reads into the Act a distinction between person-to-person or personal investment advice and impersonal advice given in printed publications, a distinction that he claims is firmly grounded in the Act's legislative history. According to the opinion, Congress fully intended to submit only personal investment advice to the kind of regulation the SEC sought to apply in this case. He acknowledges that this distinction is not explicit in the statute,[154] but in arguing that it is implicit he blurs the differences between investment counsel and investment adviser by selectively relying on congressional testimony and certain provisions of the statute that usually refer to the personalized functions carried on by investment counsel and omitting all reference to the nonpersonalized advisory functions of the more broadly defined class of investment advisers.

---

[153] See note 14 *supra* at 2570.

[154] *Id.* at 2569 n.45.

The face of the Act distinguishes between investment counsel and investment advisers.[155] Certain investment advisers are also characterized as investment counsel if a substantial part of their business consists of rendering investment supervisory services.[156] The Act defines supervisory services as "the giving of continuous advice as to the investment of funds on the basis of the individual needs of each client."[157] There is, therefore, a personal nexus with clients if one is an investment counsel. But the Act also contains a broad definition of "adviser" that encompasses advice that is both "direct or through publications or writings."[158] Nowhere in the Act, however, is this distinction between investment adviser and investment counsel relevant for purposes of determining the Act's coverage. On the face of the statute, the SEC's licensing and disciplinary powers over both types of advisers are identical.[159]

At one point in the opinion, Justice Stevens argues that the terms "investment counsel," "investment counselor," and "investment adviser" were understood by Congress to share a common definition.[160] Though this flies in the face of the broad definition of "investment adviser" in Section 202, he nonetheless maintains that "it does not follow, as Justice White seems to assume, that the term 'investment adviser' includes persons who have no personal relationship at all with their customers."[161] His evidence that it does follow, however, is based largely on the merging of the categories of investment counsel and investment advisers.

For example, Justice Stevens begins his opinion with a discussion of the SEC Report to Congress that preceded the passage of the Act. That report dealt almost exclusively with "investment counsel organizations," and Justice Stevens implies that this focus was carried through in the Act as well.[162] Similarly, he quotes, at length,

---

[155] Compare 15 U.S.C. §§ 80b-2(a)(11)–80b-8(c).

[156] Id. at § 80b-8(c).

[157] Id. at § 80b-2(a)(13).

[158] Id. at § 80b-2(a)(11).

[159] Id. at § 80b-2(a)–(h).

[160] See note 14 supra at 2569 n.45.

[161] Ibid.

[162] Id. at 2563–65. See Investment Trusts and Investment Companies, Report of the Securities and Exchange Commission, Pursuant to Section 30 of the Public Utility Holding Company Act of 1935, Investment Counsel, Investment Management, Investment Supervisory, and Investment Advisory Services, H.R. Doc. No. 477, 76th Cong., 2d Sess. (1939).

"one witness distinguishing the investment-counsel profession from investment firms and businesses"[163] to illustrate the personal nexus between adviser and client that he claims underlies the definition of investment adviser. But this again was testimony that dealt with investment counsel, not broadly defined investment advisers.

Justice Stevens is similarly selective when he argues that certain provisions of the Act support the personal/impersonal distinction. He argues, for example, that "the repeated use of the term client in the statute contradicts the suggestion that a person who is merely a publisher of non-fraudulent information in a regularly scheduled periodical of general circulation has the kind of fiduciary relationship the Act was designed to regulate."[164] He then refers to eight provisions of the Act that contain the word "client," but nowhere is that term used in a context that supports this position. For example, in Section 201(1),[165] the term "client" is used in reference only to specific functions that an investment adviser may perform. It does not characterize or in any way limit the scope of an adviser's functions. On the contrary, the provision broadly defines the role of investment adviser to support the proposition that investment advisers are of national concern. In so doing, it includes functions that can be rendered impersonally, such as "their advice, counsel, publications, writings, analyses, and reports,"[166] as well as functions most likely rendered on a personal basis such as the negotiation and performance of "their contracts, subscription agreements and other arrangements with clients."[167] The term "client" is used in relation to certain personalized aspects of the adviser's role, but the definition of "adviser" is clearly composed of personalized and nonpersonalized functions.[168]

---

[163] Note 14 *supra* at 2565–66. See Hearings on S. 3580 before the Subcommittee on Securities and Exchange of the Senate Committee on Banking and Currency, 76th Cong., 3d Sess. 713–16 (1940) (statement of Charles M. O'Hearn, Vice President and Director of Clarke, Sinsabaugh & Co., Investment Counsel) (hereinafter cited as Hearings).

[164] Note 14 *supra* at 2569 n.45.

[165] 15 U.S.C. § 80b-1(1).

[166] *Ibid.*

[167] *Ibid.*

[168] Three additional provisions noted by Justice Stevens, [15 U.S.C. §§ 80b-3(b)(1)–(b)(3), pertain to exemptions from registration. Section 80b-3(b)(1) exempts those advisers whose clients are residents of the state within which the adviser maintains his [sic] principal office and principal place of business. The provision also exempts those advisers, though, who do not furnish advice or issue analyses or reports with respect to certain types of securities.

In addition to merging congressional history and statutory provisions that deal with investment counsel with investment advisers, Justice Stevens fails to take into account the motivation of those whose testimony emphasized the personalized aspects of their business. Justice Stevens uses this testimony to bolster his argument that Congress intended to regulate only personalized investment advice. But those who testified were not arguing for regulation that falls only on the personalized aspects of their business. They were, quite the contrary, arguing that, because of the personalized aspect of their business, they should not be regulated at all.[169] Not surprisingly, Justice Stevens can find ample testimony from investment counsel who stress the "personalized nature" theme, and he dwells on this theme and the testimony that supports it:[170]

> It is a personal-service profession and depends for its success upon a close personal and confidential relationship between the investment-counsel firm and its client. It requires frequent and personal contact of a professional nature between us and our client. . . . We are quite clearly not "hit and run" tipsters, nor do

---

Sections 80b-3(b)(2) and (b)(3) exempt, respectively, those investment advisers whose clients are solely insurance companies and those investment advisers with a minimum number of clients. These provisions do not restrict the scope of the adviser definition. They simply exempt from coverage those advisers who give personalized advice to specific individuals, on certain designated securities or in a limited capacity. Thus the registration of a category of personal advisers is exempted in the same manner in which a category of publishers is exempted from registration.

In § 80b-3(c)(1)(E), referred to by Justice Stevens, the term "client" pertains to the requirement that the registration form must contain information with respect to the adviser's authority over a client's funds and accounts. The term "client" is used because this provision concerns the fiduciary discretion of advisers. However, in a preceding subsection, § 80b(3)(c)(1)(C), not cited by Justice Stevens, the statute specifies that the registration form must also contain a description of the adviser's business, "including the manner of giving advice and rendering analysis or reports."

Finally, Justice Stevens cites the use of the term "client" in 15 U.S.C. §§ 80b-6(1)–6(3). But these subsections refer to certain prohibited transactions by investment advisers. Section 80b(6) refers not only to prohibited acts vis-à-vis clients but to any act, practice, or course of business that is fraudulent, deceptive, or manipulative. Thus, again, "client" pertains to one particular manner of rendering advice, not to the entirety of the adviser's functions. Because the statute defines the "investment adviser" in terms of individuals who give advice both directly and through publications, specific provisions will sound more or less oriented toward personal advice, depending on which investment service is being referred to. The repeated reference to "publications, writings, analysis and reports" in conjunction with concerns addressed to clients indicates that the definition of "investment adviser" includes individuals who have no personal or direct relation with their customers as well as those who do. Justice Stevens, however, cites only the client provisions and excludes the publications provisions to buttress his argument that the latter were not of concern to Congress.

[169] See Hearings, note 163 *supra*, at 717–18.

[170] See note 14 *supra* at 2566; Hearings, note 163 *supra*, at 713–16.

we deal with our clients at arms' length through the advertising columns of the newspapers or the mails; in fact, we regard it as a major defeat if we are unable to have frequent personal contact with a client and with his associates and dependents. We do not publish for general distribution a statistical service or compendium of general economic observations or financial recommendations. To use a hackneyed phrase, our business is "tailor made."

Justice Stevens, however, omits that part of the testimony that makes clear the actual motivation behind testimony such as this:[171]

Whatever may be the merits of a plan to regulate the activities of the tipsters and others on the fringe, it seems to us that what they do is so different from what we do, in principle, in purpose, and in method, that they constitute a separate category in which we should not be involved merely because we also give financial advice. The whole effort of our business life has been to offer a service which, because it avoided the superficialities and instability characteristic of the tipster service and related enterprises, could establish for itself an enduring professional reputation.

However, we would not have the committee believe that we think we should be immune from regulation merely because we conduct a business which is different from that of others who are or perhaps should be regulated. Our case for believing that the business we conduct does not need to be regulated in the manner provided by the proposed legislation, rests on other grounds. We and our profession have a good record for honest dealing with the public and with our clients. We have gone to great lengths to protect our clients from a wider range of abuses than could possibly be covered by law. We do not claim unique virtues for the profession. We do not claim exemption from the supervision which "ordinary mortals" must endure. The outstanding fact of the investment counsel profession is that unless it can demonstrate that it possesses these virtues, it will pass out of existence in the long run for the most cogent of all reasons—it will be worthless.

Investment counsel thus stressed the "personalized nature" of their profession simply to distinguish themselves from the "tipsters and touts" who they felt should be the focus of regulation. Justice Stevens's reliance on this testimony to support his assertion that "the dangers of fraud, deception, or overreaching that motivated the enactment of the statute are present in personalized communications but are not replicated in publications that are advertised and

---

[171] Hearings, note 163 *supra*, at 717–18.

sold in the open market" is thus clearly suspect.[172] The threat and practice of fraud in the publications setting was of foremost concern to Congress; it is precisely these publishers who may constitute the "tipsters and touts" repeatedly referred to in Congressional testimony and specifically designated for the Act's coverage, and it is these very individuals that the Act sought to deal with. According to David Schenker, Chief Counsel, Securities and Exchange Commission Investment Trust Study, the title of the statute relating to investment advisers "encompasses that broad category ranging from people who are engaged in the profession of furnishing disinterested, impartial advice to a certain economic stratum of our population to the other extreme, individuals engaged in running tipster organizations, or sending through the mails stock market letters."[173] He put stock market letters in the same category as tipster organizations.[174] There seems to be little doubt that Congress intended to regulate individuals who published nonpersonalized investment advice. According to one witness, who was asked to define the procedure or operation of an investment adviser:[175]

> This is a fairly broad statement because the term includes people who send out bulletins from time to time on the advisability of buying or selling stocks, or even giving tips on cheap stocks, and goes all of the way from that to individuals and firms who undertake to give constant supervision to the entire investments of their clients on a personal basis and who even advise them on other matters and other financial matters which essentially are not a question of choice of investments.

Having thus concluded that Congress intended to distinguish between personal and impersonal investment advising functions, Justice Stevens did not read this distinction into the relevant enforcement provisions of Section 203 as did Judge Weinstein. He used the distinction as a basis for his conclusion that the Lowe

---

[172] See note 14 *supra* at 2573.

[173] Hearings on S. 3580 before Subcommittee of the Committee on Banking and Currency, 76th Cong., 3d Sess. 47 (1940).

[174] *Ibid.*

[175] Hearings on H.R. 10065 before the Subcommittee of the House Committee on Interstate and Foreign Commerce, 76th Cong., 3d Sess. 86–91 (1940).

Newsletters actually fell within Section 202(D)[176] and were, in effect, exempt as a "bona fide newspaper."[177]

In construing the "bona fide" and "general and regular" requirements of Section 202(D), Justice Stevens tries to distinguish what he calls "hit and run tipsters" and "touts" from "genuine" publishers. He states:[178]

> Presumably a "bona fide" publication would be genuine in the sense that it would contain disinterested commentary and analyses as opposed to promotional material disseminated by a "tout." Moreover, publications with a "general and regular" circulation would not include "people who send out bulletins from time to time on the advisability of buying and selling stocks," or "hit and run tipsters." On this basis, petitioners newsletters are within the exclusion because the publications are disinterested and offered to the general public on a regular schedule.

If we take as a given the personal/impersonal distinction Justice Stevens worked so hard to create, however, it is difficult to understand how the exemption could include even tipsters and touts. If the Act merely extends to those persons who "provide personalized advice attuned to a client's concerns," it would seem that the Act cannot extend to disingenuous publishers unless they also render personal advice. The publishers' motive would not seem to be an issue. Furthermore, frequency of publication would be irrelevant. The Act could no more apply to publishers who furnish information from "time to time" than to those individuals who publish on a regular schedule. Similarily, Justice Stevens's interpretation of what constitutes a regular schedule appears, particularly on the facts of this case, to be based on mere intentions rather than reality. As Justice White points out:[179]

> [I]f a "tout" or "tipster" promised to publish his recommendations at more or less regular intervals, he, like petitioner, would meet the regularity requirement. Moreover, a truly "hit and run" practitioner . . . would not fall within the definition of an investment adviser because he would not deem to "engage in the business of advising others."

---

[176] See note 14 *supra* at 2573–74.

[177] *Id.* at 2573.

[178] *Id.* at 2571.

[179] See *id.* at 2576 n.3.

Justice Stevens's statutorily based decision is likely to have a greater deregulatory impact than a decision declaring the Investment Advisers Act unconstitutional as applied to Lowe. Because a truly hit-and-run tipster would not be considered an investment adviser, the Act presumably could not apply to a person who "purchases shares for his own account shortly before recommending that security for long-term investment and then immediately sell[ing] the shares at a profit upon the rise in the market place following the recommendation."[180] Justice Stevens attempts to deal with this situation by claiming that "bona fide" means genuine in the sense that it refers to a publication produced by one who is disinterested. Yet as Justice White points out, nowhere in the Act or its history "is there any suggestion that whether a person is an investment adviser depends on whether his advice is disinterested."[181] Moreover, as White added, such an approach would be not only a content-based test but one that the SEC would not have the power to apply.[182]

There is little to recommend the strained, indeed tortured, statutory approach taken by Justice Stevens and the majority in this case. Though it was inspired by a constitutional perspective that viewed the SEC's attempt to prohibit publication of the Lowe newsletters as tantamount to a prior restraint, the statutory basis of the decision was, in many ways, much more intrusive vis-à-vis the legislature than the constitutionally based decision proposed by the dissent.

In arguing that the portion of the Act that applies to publishers like Lowe was unconstitutional, Justice White's approach would not have interfered with the overall scope of the SEC's jurisdiction.

---

[180] Id. at 2580, citing SEC v. Capital Gains Research Bureau, 375 U.S. 180, 181 (1963).

[181] Note 14 supra at 2576 n.3.

[182] Ibid. The SEC is currently arguing that it is not precluded, on the basis of Lowe, from enjoining the publication of a particular investment advisory newsletter because the publisher is a "tout" within the meaning of lowe. Wall Street Publishing Institute, Inc. v. SEC, No. 84-5485 (D.C. Cir. filed July 24, 1985). This case involves a motion for summary reversal in which the Appellant is arguing that Lowe is new law that renders invalid the district court's injunctions requiring it, among other things, to comply with the antifraud provisions of Sec. 206 of the Investment Advisers Act and to cease publishing its investment advisory magazine until it applies for registration as an investment adviser under Sec. 203 of the Act. The SEC is taking the position that this premise is erroneous because, first, Lowe did not decide the constitutional issue of whether the Commission could, consistent with the First Amendment, enjoin publication of an investment advisory newsletter and, second, the publisher here, unlike Lowe, is not entitled to the exclusion because he is allegedly a tout.

Under his analysis, publishers of investment advice would remain investment advisers within the meaning of the Act.[183] They would continue to register with the SEC, thereby providing the SEC with the kind of information it needs to play its role as a regulatory watchdog.[184] Without this information, the Commission would have great difficulty discovering scalping practices and prosecuting such individuals either through extra administrative mechanisms such as the mail fraud statute or through administrative sanctions pursuant to Section 10(b)(5) of the Securities Act.[185] Moreover, the dissent was the only opinion that explicitly reached the constitutional issues in this case, and it is this aspect of the opinion that I shall now examine.

B. THE DISSENTING OPINION

For Justice White the constitutional issue was squarely put: does the First Amendment permit the Federal Government to prohibit the publication of investment advice in this case? In deciding this issue, White makes clear that "the power of government to regulate the professions is not lost whenever the practice of a profession entails speech." He is sympathetic to the government's concern that "bad investment advice may be a cover for stockmarket manipulations designed to bilk the client for the benefit of the adviser; worse, it may lead to ruinous losses for the client."[186] Thus it is reasonable for the government to insist that "investment advisers, like lawyers, evince the qualities of truth speaking, honor, discretion, and fiduciary responsibility."[187] Yet Justice White notes that there also are limits: "*At some point*, a measure is no longer a regulation of a profession but a regulation of speech or of the press; beyond that point, the statute must survive the level of scrutiny demanded by the First Amendment."[188]

For Justice White, just where that point is is primarily a question for courts to decide. Deference to either Congress's or an agency's

---

[183] Note 14 *supra* at 2586.

[184] *Id.* at 2586–87.

[185] *Id.* at 2581 n.9.

[186] *Id.* at 2583.

[187] *Ibid.*

[188] *Ibid.* (emphasis added).

views on this matter is not appropriate: "It is for us, then, to find some principle by which to answer the question whether the Investment Advisers Act as applied to petitioner operates as a regulation of speech or of professional conduct."[189] To determine just where those limits are and at what point a constitutional perspective replaces the regulatory perspective, Justice White starts with an approach first outlined by Justice Jackson, who concluded that "the distinguishing factor was whether the speech in any particular case was 'associated . . . with some other factor which the state may regulate so as to bring the whole within its official control.' "[190] In cases where "the association or characterization is a proven and valid one, the regulation may stand."[191] Justice White builds on this approach by attempting to locate the point at which speech is no longer associated "with some other factor which the state may regulate"[192] by relying on a personal/impersonal distinction similar to that used both by Judge Weinstein and the Supreme Court majority:[193]

> One who takes the affairs of a client personally in hand and purports to exercise judgment on behalf of the client in the light of the client's individual needs and circumstances is properly viewed as engaging in the practice of a profession. . . . Where the personal nexus between professional and client does not exist, and a speaker does not purport to be exercising judgment on behalf of any particular individual with whose circumstances he is directly acquainted, government regulation ceases to function as legitimate regulation of professional practice with only incidental impact on speech; it becomes regulation of speaking or publishing as such, subject to the First Amendment.

Justice White thus concludes that, while regulation of "investment advice tailored to the individual needs of each client . . . is not subject to scrutiny as a regulation of speech,"[194] the application of the Act's enforcement provisions to prevent unregistered persons from engaging in the business of publishing investment advice for

---

[189] *Id.* at 2584.

[190] *Ibid.*, citing Thomas v. Collins, 323 U.S. 516, 547 (1944).

[191] Note 14 *supra*.

[192] *Id.* at 2584.

[193] *Id.* at 2584–85.

[194] *Id.* at 2585.

the benefit of any who would purchase their publications, however, is a direct restraint on freedom of speech and of the press subject to the searching scrutiny called for by the First Amendment.[195]

The dissent goes on to consider briefly whether the commercial speech doctrine might apply in this case. Since, however, it finds that the result would not be different if it did, it does not find it "necessary to the resolution of this case to determine whether petitioner's newsletters contain fully protected speech or commercial speech."[196]

VI. PROFESSIONALS AND THE FIRST AMENDMENT

With the exception of the majority of the court of appeals, every judge that reviewed this case either decided or sidestepped the constitutional issues involved by relying on a personal/impersonal distinction. By pointing out the deficiencies of this distinction, we may not necessarily substitute a better or more accurate litmus test for determining when we are regulating professional conduct as opposed to speech, but we may, at least, begin to suggest a kind of discourse that will enable courts to think about this issue within a broader, more realistic framework.

A. THE PERSONAL/IMPERSONAL DISTINCTION
FROM A REGULATORY PERSPECTIVE

The personal/impersonal distinction makes little sense from a regulatory perspective. It is difficult to apply to cases such as *Lowe*, and, in any event, it grossly understates the potential harm to the public that can occur through the so-called impersonal provision of investment advice.

In *Lowe*, it is difficult to say the service in question was not, in fact, a personal one. Unlike advertising, Lowe's newsletters did not arrive in an individual's home unannounced or uninvited. They were personally subscribed to by individuals who found his advice useful and relevant to their own circumstances. While Lowe may not have dealt personally with each of his subscribers, his views certainly were capable of being treated and relied on as personal

---

[195] *Ibid.*
[196] *Id.* at 2586.

advice by his subscribers. They knew of Lowe, and, presumably, they knew what kind of advice they wanted. That is why they were willing to pay the subscription price in the first place. To say this is not personal advice is to view this only from Lowe's perspective. The advice was very personal indeed to those who used it.

Moreover, it is difficult to say with certainty that Lowe himself did not know these individuals in some sense. He knew his market. There is evidence in the record to suggest that at least one of his newsletters was aimed at small and arguably lower- or average-income investors.[197] Having a basic composite profile of a certain class of subscribers in mind and then seeking to provide the kind of advice these individuals would find useful is impersonal in only a technical and irrelevant sense. Lowe's service to such a class of subscribers is not unlike legal services rendered in the context of a large class action. The lawyer representing the class may know the named plaintiffs, but he or she also represents hundreds or perhaps even thousands of others with similar interests and claims. What is relevant from a professional point of view are the personal characteristics that make someone an interested member of the class, not his or her direct relationship with the lawyer involved.[198]

In this sense, Lowe provides specific investment advice presumably tailored enough to a certain class of individuals to make it worth their while to purchase it. Moreover, given the regularized nature of the publication and the natural desire to retain and expand one's subscription list, it is reasonable to assume that the newsletter would begin to respond to requests from subscribers for particular kinds of advice or information about matters of interest to them. The more successful the newsletter, the more likely it is to speak directly to the perceived interests of its subscribers. To call it impersonal because Lowe does not speak to each subscriber personally or because he does not know for a fact that the advice given is tailored to the needs of the particular individual willing to pay for it is as erroneous as is concluding that a recorded hot-line service is, on the other hand, personal and capable of regulation.[199] The fact is

---

[197] See note 21 *supra* at 1361. One of Lowe's bulletins, the Lowe Stock Advisory, specialized in low-priced stocks costing under twenty dollars listed in the New York and American Stock Exchanges and traded in the over-the-counter market. Lowe Stock Advisory subscriptions cost thirty-nine dollars for one year and seventy-nine dollars for three years.

[198] See generally Rule 23 FRCP.

[199] Note 14 *supra* at 2562 n.23.

that both the hot line and the newsletter are personal statements to those who find the advice offered relevant to their own financial situation.

The personal/impersonal distinction is even more problematic when one considers the rapid changes in technology taking place in many professions and the emergence of computerized professional services.[200] As in other phases of modern life, standardized services are and will continue to become more available. While the wealthy may still be able to afford—or prefer—person-to-person, individualized professional help, the poor or low- to average-income consumer of professional services increasingly will be buying them off the computerized rack. One can easily imagine computer programs that provide a variety of services for individuals without any direct personal contact with the professional who made the video- or audiotape or devised the computer program.[201]

In short, the distinction between personal and impersonal advice is relatively useless from a regulatory perspective. The greater distance between the professional and the client, the increased reliance on computers, and the prevalence of providing advice to classes of consumers, standardized on the basis of composites of their essential characteristics, render a distinction between face-to-face service and service in print almost quaint. From a purely regulatory point of view, if there are dangers to be feared in the rendering of professional services face to face, those dangers are not necessarily decreased when the advice is put in print; indeed, they may be increased. More important, there is no way to distinguish a competent or ethical professional from an incompetent or unethical one simply on the basis of the mode of speech employed. To argue that this distinction is constitutionally compelled is also suspect.

B. THE PERSONAL/IMPERSONAL DISTINCTION
FROM A CONSTITUTIONAL PERSPECTIVE

The regulatory reasons that might justify the regulation of printed investment advice provided to voluntary subscribers at a

---

[200] Similarly, consumers frequently turn to "how to do it kits" published by lawyers and nonlawyers. For a discussion of the case law involving such kits, see generally, Wolfram, Modern Legal Ethics 840-1 (1985).

[201] The securities industries are not, of course, immune from a whole range of technological changes that raise, as a serious question, whether an entirely new approach to regulation is, in fact, now required. See generally, Langevoort, Information Technology and the Structure of Securities Regulation, 98 Harv. L. Rev. 747 (1985).

price undercut the usefulness of a distinction between personal and impersonal advice. These reasons are based, in large part, on a consumer's perspective and the need to protect the public from future harm. One would expect the constitutional justifications for maintaining this distinction as a means of determining when free speech has been violated to be of a different order of magnitude. But Justice White tells us very little as to why he uses this distinction for constitutional purposes or what underlies his decision to draw this particular line between the regulatory and the constitutional perspectives.

Justice White's approach, in effect, marks the point at which the regulation of a profession becomes the regulation of speech by defining what a profession is, for constitutional purposes. He states that "one who takes the affairs of a client personally in hand and purports to exercise judgment on behalf of the client in the light of the client's individual needs and circumstances is properly viewed as engaging in the practice of a profession."[202] Given this personal nexus, "the professional's speech is incidental to the conduct of the profession."[203] But where this personal nexus does not exist "and a speaker does not purport to be exercising judgment on behalf of any particular individual with whose circumstances he is directly acquainted, government regulation ceases to function as legitimate regulation of professional practice with only incidental impact on speech."[204] This approach not only results in a narrow definition of what a profession is; it has little to do explicitly, at least, with First Amendment values and concerns. On an individual level it would seem that the regulation of personal relationships and the ability to associate with clients and other professionals would be even more intrusive from a First Amendment point of view than the regulation of less personal professional services. Indeed, from the point of view of what, in fact, might inhibit an individual's free expression more, it would seem logical to allow regulation of the impersonal aspects of professional services and be more protective of the personal aspect. Justice White seems to be suggesting, however, that personal speech is so intertwined with the provision of professional services that it would be impossible to separate the two. From a

---

[202] See note 14 *supra* at 2584.

[203] *Ibid.*

[204] *Id.* at 2585.

remedial point of view, the regulation involved constitutes the least restrictive means available because it is the only effective way of regulating this kind of professional conduct.

The same, however, can be said of professional advice rendered in print or in a so-called impersonal manner. The printed word can be even more authoritative than the spoken word. The argument that information conveyed in print is "more conducive to reflection and the exercise of choice on the part of the consumer"[205] must be balanced against the consumer's inability to raise questions and engage in a dialogue with a professional who is selling information in print rather than in person. Moreover, there may be a tendency, perhaps particularly on the part of judges and others whose daily work consists of analyzing texts and the relationships among words, to overestimate the ability of people to be appropriately skeptical of the printed word. To those whose livelihood does not daily depend on this kind of analysis and reflection, investment advice printed in a slick newsletter and published with the apparent blessing of a federal governmental agency can be even more persuasive than a face-to-face encounter with the newsletter's author.

It is against this backdrop that one should assess the argument that a disclaimer in the newsletter itself would represent a less restrictive means of regulation and thus be more appropriate from a First Amendment remedial point of view. A disclaimer certainly would be less restrictive, but is it realistic to assume it would be at all effective? The answer depends, in large part, on what the disclaimer says, and it is by no means clear what that may be. A disclaimer setting forth Lowe's past criminal convictions and making clear their relationship to his present business of selling an investment newsletter would likely be subject to the same objections raised in this case. If it were allowed, its effect would most likely be similar to a ban on publication. On the other hand, a disclaimer that simply said that Lowe no longer was a licensed broker would undercut all regulation of professions that could be carried on in print: anyone could practice a profession in print as long as he or she admitted to not being licensed to do so. Such an approach accords with Justice White's position that what can be considered the practice of a profession ends when the advice rendered is impersonal rather than personal in nature. Such an ap-

---

[205] 105 S.Ct. 2265, 2277 (1985).

proach, however, does not accord with the realities of an increasingly standardized modern world. But even if it were possible to devise an appropriate and effective disclaimer to give consumers the information they need without resorting to a complete ban of this means of practicing one's profession, the ability to do so would turn on the peculiar facts of particular cases. Fact-specific remedial choices are hardly the bases for drawing general lines between the constitutional protection accorded the provision of impersonal as opposed to personal advice.

There is, however, another assumption implicit in this distinction that also has First Amendment significance. Since advice provided by a newsletter is likely to reach a larger audience than advice given in one-on-one encounters, the sheer numbers involved may imply that this kind of speech is of more general interest and thus worthy of greater First Amendment protection. Whether one communicates his professional advice in a personal or impersonal manner and whether that advice reaches, in this way, 100 or 1,000 individuals would seem to have little to do with whether what is being communicated transcends the practice of one's profession and is the kind of speech the First Amendment was intended to protect. In this regard, Judge Oakes's suggested approach to when we shift from a regulatory to a constitutional perspective is superior. His proposed distinction between general speech involving a substantial portion of religious, political, or ideological opinions and the kind of speech necessary to carry out the functions of an investment adviser—namely, speech that gives advice regarding specific securities—would at least generate a discourse that directly involved fundamental First Amendment values. Moreover, it results in a more realistic determination of when one is, in fact, practicing a profession and when, in fact, one is engaging in a more journalistic enterprise.

This is not to say that the general/specific line suggested by Judge Oakes's opinion is an easy one to draw or that, on balance, the difficulty of dealing with such cases may not militate in favor of a decision or line that errs in favor of the practice of individual constitutional rights. If there are First Amendment values at stake, particularly in cases less clear cut than *Lowe*, and the court concludes that there is no way really to distinguish between general and specific speech, the application of Justice Holmes's aphorism from another context would have provided a more direct way of washing one's judicial hands of the problem than the mechanical application of a personal/impersonal distinction: it is better to let a rascal slip through the net of the law than the law play an ignoble role.[206]

An examination of the commercial speech cases, however, suggests that such a judicial hands-off approach is not necessary. To date, these cases constitute what might be called the commercial advertising doctrine and, as such, would not be applicable directly to *Lowe*. Their inapplicability would not, however, mean that Lowe's newsletters were entitled to full First Amendment protection. Rather an examination of the personal/impersonal distinction as it arises in the commercial advertising context suggests that the regulation in *Lowe* belongs at the regulatory rather than the constitutional end of the analytic spectrum.

C. THE PERSONAL/IMPERSONAL DISTINCTION
IN THE COMMERCIAL SPEECH CASES

From the beginning, the commercial advertising cases have made clear that they did not intend to interfere with legitimate professional regulation. Indeed, to extend First Amendment protection to speech incidental to otherwise valid economic regulation risks, as Professors Jackson and Jeffries have noted, "the revivication of economic due process in the guise of commercial speech."[207] Thus there is good reason to give substantial weight to the court's comment in *Virginia Board* that "high professional standards, to a substantial extent, are guaranteed by the close regulation to which pharmacists in Virginia are subject. And this case concerns the retail sale by the pharmacist more than it does his professional standards. Surely, any pharmacist guilty of professional dereliction that actually endangers his customers will promptly lose his license."[208] Moreover, these cases suggest that "high professional standards" and license revocations for those "guilty of professional dereliction" are not necessarily inconsistent when impersonal as opposed to personal services are involved, particularly if one exam-

---

[206] *Cf.* Olmstead v. United States, 277 U.S. 438, 470 (1927).

[207] Jackson & Jeffries, Commercial Speech: Economic Due Process and the First Amendment, 65 Va. L. Rev. 1 (1979).

[208] 425 U.S. at 768–69.

ines the reasons that underlie this distinction and not simply the distinction itself.

In *Ohralik v. Ohio State Bar Ass'n*,[209] the court considered the validity of regulations that prohibited in-person solicitation by an ambulance-chasing lawyer. The lawyer involved sought to obtain the business of two young individuals hurt in an automobile accident. He visited one of them in the hospital and the other shortly after she was released. He had a hidden tape recorder with him to "prove" that they authorized him to take their case on a contingency basis. When his high-pressure tactics were reported, he challenged the rules involved as a violation of his First Amendment rights, arguing strenuously that he engaged in no wrongdoing in his solicitation efforts. The Court framed the question narrowly: "whether the Bar, acting with state authorization, may discipline a lawyer for soliciting clients in person, for pecuniary gain, under circumstances likely to pose dangers that the state has a right to prevent."[210] The court found that the in-person solicitation involved in this case was subject to protection under the commercial speech doctrine but noted that "[i]n-person solicitation by a lawyer of renumerative employment is a business transaction in which speech is an essential but subordinate component. While this does not remove the speech from the protection of the First Amendment, as was held in *Bates* and *Virginia Pharmacy*, it lowers the level of appropriate judicial scrutiny."[211] Thus the court concluded that a lawyer's procurement of remunerative employment "is a subject only marginally affected with First Amendment concerns. It falls within the state's proper sphere of economic and professional regulation. While entitled to some constitutional protection, appellant's conduct is subject to regulation in furtherance of important state interests."[212]

The Court further noted that the State interests implicated in this case were particularly strong. Not only did the State have an interest in protecting consumers and regulating commercial activities, but the State "bears a special responsibility for maintaining

---

[209] 436 U.S. 447 (1978).

[210] *Id.* at 449.

[211] *Id.* at 457.

[212] *Id.* at 459.

standards among members of the licensed professions."[213] The
Court thus rejected appellant's assertion that the State must show
actual harm to the solicited individual before it is entitled to impose
disciplinary sanctions. The Court approved the prophylactic aspect
of the rules involved, noting that their "objective is the prevention
of harm before it occurs"[214] and that they were appropriately applied in a context "likely to result in the adverse consequences the
State seeks to avert."[215]

The rationale that underlies the regulation in this case can be
applied to *Lowe*, arguably without any First Amendment overtones. The State has a similarly strong interest to engage in prophylactic rule making in cases like *Lowe* to prevent potentially harmful
future conduct. The conduct is not publishing, but it is practicing
one's profession after so abusing one's trust as to justify a fear that,
however one goes about one's business, the same thing may happen
again. The in-person solicitation aspect of the case in *Ohralik* was
relevant because it increased the likelihood that fraud could occur.
The use of this distinction did not define the outer bounds of what
constitutes the practice of a profession but was a circumstance that
made the very dangers the state wished to prevent more likely to
occur. In *Lowe*, the fact that his advice is rendered in print rather
than in person does not at all lessen the possibility of Congress's
fears coming to pass, especially since those fears had to do explicitly
with activities such as scalping or touting a stock that were likely to
occur in print. The Supreme Court's recent decision in *Zauderer v.
Office of Disciplinary Counsel of the Supreme Court of Ohio*[216] suggests
that, when print as opposed to in-person solicitation is involved, a
higher standard is applied to regulation of the former. The underlying reasons for drawing a distinction between in-print and in-
person advertising, however, are not applicable to a case like *Lowe*.

In *Zauderer*, the Court considered two unresolved questions regarding the regulation of commercial speech by attorneys: whether a
state may discipline an attorney for soliciting business by running
newspaper advertisements containing nondeceptive illustrations
and legal advice and whether a state may seek to prevent potential

---

[213] *Id.* at 460.

[214] *Id.* at 464.

[215] *Ibid.*

[216] 105 S.Ct. 2265 (1985).

deception of the public by requiring attorneys to disclose in their advertising certain information regarding fee arrangements. In resolving these issues, Justice White's opinion for the Court perhaps sheds some light on his use of the personal/impersonal distinction in his dissent in *Lowe*. As to the first issue, he rejected the State's argument that it could apply a prophylactic rule to the appellant in this case, notwithstanding the fact that the particular advertisement in issue was neither deceptive nor misleading. In so doing, Justice White distinguished print advertising from in-person solicitation. Citing *Ohralik*, he noted:[217]

> In-person solicitation by a lawyer, . . . was a practice rife with possibilities of overreaching, invasion of privacy, the exercise of undue influence, and outright fraud. . . . In addition, . . . in-person solicitation presents unique regulatory difficulties because it is "not visible or otherwise open to public scrutiny." These unique features of in-person solicitation by lawyers we held, justified a prophylactic rule prohibiting lawyers from engaging in such solicitation for pecuniary gain, but we were careful to point out that "in-person solicitation of professional employment by a lawyer does not stand on a par with truthful advertising about the availability and terms of routine legal services."
>
> It is apparent that the concerns that moved the Court in *Ohralik* are not present here. . . . [A]ppellant's advertisement— *and print advertising generally*—poses much less risk of overreaching or undue influence. Print advertising may convey information and ideas more or less effectively, but in most cases, it will lack the coercive force of the personal presence of a trained advocate. In addition, a printed advertisement, unlike a personal encounter initiated by an attorney, is not likely to involve pressure on the potential client for an immediate yes-or-no answer to the offer of representation. Thus, a printed advertisement is a means of conveying information about legal services that is more conducive to reflection and the exercise of choice on the part of the consumer than is personal solicitation by an attorney. Accordingly, the solicitation upheld in *Ohralik* cannot justify the discipline imposed on appellant for the content of his advertisement.

It is important to emphasize the context in which this distinction between print and in-person solicitation was made. *Zauderer* is a case in which the print medium was employed solely in an advertis-

---

[217] *Id.* at 2277.

ing context by a person who has not knowingly abused this opportunity in the past. No commercial or trust relationship, as yet, actually exists between the advertising attorney and the potential clients who may read the advertisement. Lowe's newsletter, however, is not a mere advertisement but a professional document, voluntarily used by consumers who have paid for the opportunity to rely on Lowe's advice. Having accepted his clients' money, Lowe is in a different relationship to these individuals than if he simply published his views in a newspaper or professional journal. Expectations are created in this context that simply do not exist when only advertising is involved. Clients are more predisposed to trust and believe his advice having decided to seek investment advice and having made a judgment that his product was worth purchasing. Even if the difference between advertising a product and the actual product itself does not remove this case from the purview of the commercial speech doctrine, the government's interest in regulating the actual practice of one's profession in print is certainly stronger than the need to regulate what one claims to do in his advertisement. When one is engaged in the practice of his profession, we are one step closer to the actual harm that false advertising claims may or may not cause. In this context and at this stage of the relationship between the professional and the client, it is equally difficult to prevent the kind of harm the regulations in *Lowe* were conceived to prevent whether the advice rendered is in print or in person.

Furthermore, to extend protection accorded by the commercial speech doctrine to newsletters such as Lowe's proves too much. It suggests that the constitution now requires that certain markets must go unregulated because the consumer in the marketplace of goods is like the consumer in the marketplace of ideas. Similarly it also suggests that all sellers are functionally identical because they all "speak." On the basis of this extended metaphor, a wide range of regulation, involving, for example, tipee trading under the Securities Act or the supervision of union elections under the National Labor Relations Act, could be placed in constitutional jeopardy. It would be no less than remarkable if the First Amendment were to rekindle the fires of substantive due process that the Court has repeatedly assured us have long since died out.[218]

---

[218] See, generally, Jackson and Jeffries, note 207 *supra*.

Finally, and more important, since *Lowe* involves the actual practice of one's profession, albeit in print, the government's interest is not just the future well-being of consumers but the integrity of the profession itself. Quite apart from the deterrent effect on other brokers of the government's decision to revoke Lowe's license in this case and the protection that decision may provide to future clients of Lowe's, his past track record is relevant to the broader governmental interest of maintaining the integrity of the profession. The license revocation in this case can be based simply on the retrospective fact that Lowe has abused his trust so badly, so many times, that he no longer deserves to practice his profession. This rationale for regulation suggests a punitive, retrospective perspective that has nothing to do with the mode of expression one chooses to practice a profession. It also implies a very different definition of what a professional is than that which seems to underlie both the personal/impersonal distinction and the opinions that rely on it.

D. WHAT IS A PROFESSIONAL?

The personal/impersonal distinction overemphasizes the future relationships of a professional with the consumers of his services and underemphasizes the significance of the character of the person rendering that service and the relationship of that character to the product produced. Such an approach is particularly inappropriate in a disciplinary case. There is, and should be, a punitive aspect to such a case that applies quite apart from what the future may bring. After reasonable opportunity to prove oneself, there comes a point at which the abuse of a public trust in a professional context disqualifies a person from continuing to pursue a particular career, not simply because this kind of abuse may or may not happen again but because of the extent to which it occurred in the first place. Such a basis for regulation would seem crucial to the overall integrity of a profession, and it suggests a definition of a professional that does not separate the service rendered from the person who provides it. As Judge Tuttle has written:[219]

> The professional man is in essence one who provides service. But the service he renders is something more than that of a laborer, even the skilled laborer. It is a service that wells up from

---

[219] Tuttle, Heroism in War and Peace, 13 Emory Q. 129 (1957).

the entire complex of his personality. True, some specialized and highly developed techniques may be included, but their mode of expression is given its deepest meaning by the personality of the practitioner. In a very real sense his professional service cannot be separate from his personal being. He has no goods to sell, no land to till. His only asset is himself. . . . If he does not contain the quality of integrety, he is worthless. If he does, he is priceless. The value is either nothing or it is infinite.

A profession should have the right to police its own members and bar from practice those who have proven themselves in the past as unworthy of the public's trust. That is what the SEC sought to do and what, under any straightforward reading of the statute involved, Congress authorized. This kind of case invokes not only a regulatory perspective but an adjudicatory, common-law view of the facts as well. In the final analysis, this was, in fact, a simple case in the common-law meaning of that term, but deciding cases as opposed to broad policy issues seems, unfortunately, very much out of fashion.

VII. Conclusion

SEC v. Lowe is a case filled with irony. Apparently for the sake of avoiding a constitutionally based decision, the district court rewrote the statute, and the majority of the Supreme Court rewrote both the statute and its legislative history. While relying on a doctrine normally associated with judicial restraint, both courts engaged in a kind of judicial activism that renders illusory any serious notion that courts should not interfere with legislative judgments. Under the guise of a narrow statutory decision, the Supreme Court majority opinion had a much greater impact on Congress's overall regulatory scheme than if they had simply and directly declared a portion of the statute unconstitutional.

Moreover, it is a decision that suggests a romanticized view of a face-to-face society, at least when it comes to professional relationships. Yet the decision the Court reached will make it easier for fraud to occur in the provision of professional services for mass markets. It turns these services and those that provide the services into commodities by suggesting that, at least when they are in print, they can somehow be detached from their maker.

But perhaps the greatest irony of this case is that it results in further deregulation of professional rules of conduct that are not at all the self-servicing, cartel-like rules found in many of the professional regulation cases. At a time when ethical concern is increasing in the professions, when the codes by which professionals live or used to live seem to be crumbling, and when the almighty dollar dominates the structure and primary goal of many professions today, we have a decision that puts legitimate disciplinary actions out of regulatory reach because they do not conform to an image of small-town personal relationships that may have typified another America.

R. GEORGE WRIGHT

A RATIONALE FROM J. S. MILL
FOR THE FREE SPEECH CLAUSE

I. INTRODUCTION

My purpose here is to defend a simple if unpopular thesis. I assume that the Free Speech Clause of the First Amendment has an appropriate range of applicability. The scope of the First Amendment should be determined by the broadest range of purposes or values that can coherently be thought to underlie the Free Speech Clause. Where free speech values are not significantly implicated by any given expression or conduct, the expression is not entitled to protection under the Free Speech Clause. The distinction between expression that is not protected and expression to be accorded limited free speech protection is often not difficult to recognize. When properly drawn, this distinction should expedite the sound resolution of many otherwise problematic free speech cases.

The unpopularity of this argument flows from its incompatibility with two schools of thought. The first would substitute "expression" for "speech," and considers tolerance, pluralism, and diversity to be ultimate goods. It therefore detects speech, and free speech issues, in the most curious of contexts. This school flirts with constitutionalizing libertarianism in an outer sphere of general social conduct in order, it is alleged, more securely to protect the

---

R. George Wright is Bigelow Fellow and Instructor in Law, The Law School, The University of Chicago.

inner sphere of genuine speech. The second, opposing school, of less current practical influence but with unquestioned intellectual credentials, would limit the protection of the Free Speech Clause to a few selected free speech values. Both schools impose unnecessary costs in establishing free speech values.

"Speech" for free speech purposes is not an unproblematic concept in all contexts. It is simultaneously broader and narrower than speech in its literal sense of the spoken word. Free speech values may conflict in a given case, tugging a given instance of expression simultaneously toward or away from recognition as "speech." The approach offered here, however, aims at increased analytical simplicity while preserving the possibility of vigorous application of the Free Speech Clause within its proper and legitimate sphere.

II. FREE SPEECH VALUES

Were we able to ask the drafters of the First Amendment, "Now, when you refer to freedom of speech, do you mean to include, say, commercial nude dancing as a form of speech?" the answer, one suspects, would square poorly with current judicial decisions. But the possibility remains that the drafters chose the open-textured term "speech" just so that we, of a later generation, could include such activities within its purview.

It seems evident that "[w]e know very little of the precise intentions of the framers and ratifiers of the speech and press clauses of the first amendment."[1] Under these circumstances, one approach that might set constitutional theory on a sound jurisprudential basis would be to turn to the classic texts in defense of First Amendment activities for guidance in delimiting the concept of speech; Socrates, John Milton, Locke, Hume, and John Stuart Mill would be obvious sources. We should be disturbed if the classic philosophical exponents of freedom of thought and discussion cannot be fairly enlisted in support of our contemporary free speech case law.

This course, however, is rarely taken directly or explicitly, both because there is ample free speech case law precedent, and because it can hardly be claimed that someone like Mill, however titanic his stature, influenced the drafters of the First Amendment. Moreover, the classic texts are themselves not without difficulties of interpre-

---

[1] Ollman v. Evans, 750 F.2d 970, 996 (D.C. Cir. 1984) (en banc) (Bork, J., concurring).

tation. The reader may therefore wish to interpret "Millian" values as referring simply to all coherently defensible values particularly underlying the Free Speech Clause.

There is at least a fair consensus as to the major contemporary and historical candidates for free speech values or underlying purposes. One broad formulation refers to: "1. The development of the faculties of the individual; 2. The happiness to be derived from engaging in the activity; 3. The provision of a safety valve for society; and, 4. The discovery and spread of political truth."[2] Another frequently cited broad formulation holds:[3]

> Maintenance of a system of free expression is necessary (1) as a method of assuring individual self-fulfillment, (2) as a means of attaining the truth, (3) as a method of securing participation by the members of the society in social, including political, decision-making, and (4) as a means of maintaining the balance between stability and change in the society.

Other relatively inclusive formulations of First Amendment or, more specifically, free speech values include those of Professor Stone, who cites the "search for truth," meaningful participation in self-government, and individual "self-fulfillment,"[4] and perhaps Chaffee, who refers to both an "individual interest" in "the need of many men to express their opinions on matters vital to them if life is to be worth living, and a social interest in the attainment of truth, so that the country may not only adopt the wisest course of action but carry it out in the wisest way."[5]

Before such broader formulations can be adopted, they must survive the critique of those who have taken any of a variety of narrower views of free speech, and they must have their own internal ambiguities resolved. What will be left in the end is a set of considerations with some surprising implications that I shall refer

---

[2] Bork, Neutral Principles and Some First Amendment Problems, 47 Ind. L.J. 1, 24–25 (1971)(reformulating for purposes of critique the doctrine of Justice Brandeis expressed in Whitney v. California, 274 U.S. 357, 375 (1927)).

[3] Emerson, Toward a General Theory of the First Amendment 3 (1966). See also Bloustein, The Origin, Validity, and Interrelationships of the Political Values Served by Freedom of Expression, 33 Rutgers L. Rev. 372, 373 (1981); Baker, Scope of the First Amendment Freedom of Speech, 25 UCLA L. Rev. 964, 990–91 (1978).

[4] Stone, Content Regulation and the First Amendment, 25 Wm. & Mary L. Rev. 189, 193 (1983).

[5] Chaffee, Free Speech in the United States 33 (1967).

to as Millian values.[6] To fail to implicate Millian values in some respect is, in that respect, not to be speech at all for free speech purposes.

Three of the most eminent contemporary American scholars who have sought to limit the scope of coverage of the free speech clause have been Alexander Meiklejohn,[7] Alexander Bickel,[8] and Robert Bork.[9] Professor Meiklejohn's distinction between speech implicating the public welfare and speech implicating merely private goods[10] is perhaps elastic enough to encompass most of what would be considered protected speech under the broader free speech value conceptions.[11] But to the extent that for Meiklejohn the touchstone of free speech coverage is speech bearing on "issues with which voters have to deal,"[12] Meiklejohn's theory is either unduly narrow or misleadingly phrased.

An exclusive concern with issues that we must or may address as voters, expansive as such a category may be, does not seem a felicitous way of capturing what we recognize intuitively as at least one among other free speech values: "[o]ur personal growth. . .intellectual, emotional, aesthetic, professional, vocational, civic, and

---

[6] The term "Millian values" is used for convenience, but the concept draws its strength as well from the writings of the consensually acknowledged classic champions of liberty of inquiry, thought, and discussion, dating from Socrates' Apologia.

[7] See, *e.g.*, A. Meiklejohn, Political Freedom 26–27, 79–80 (1965).

[8] See Bickel, The Morality of Consent 61–75 (1975).

[9] See Bork, note 2 *supra*, at 23–25. Ronald Dworkin's approach is difficult to classify. He suggests that the "strongest arguments" ordinarily marshaled in free speech cases—a right to listen to argument or to an equal voice in the political process—are not implicated in most pornography cases. Dworkin, A Matter of Principle 335 (1985). He finds "the literature celebrating freedom of speech and press" to be unpromising in justifying a reluctance to censor in the context of pornography. *Id.* at 336. Dworkin goes on to support a "rights-based," as opposed to a "goals-based," approach to pornography. Dworkin's argument is that, even if pornography in its various forms imposes long-term net costs on the community, censorship is wrong where it violates an egalitarian "right of moral independence." He ultimately concludes "that the right to moral independence, if it is a genuine right, requires a permissive legal attitude toward the consumption of pornography in private." *Id.* at 358. Dworkin's argument is not addressed to a particularly American or constitutional context, so it is unclear whether he wants to protect most private consumption of pornography by expanding the Free Speech and Press Clauses or by calling into play substantive due process "privacy" rights or even the Equal Protection Clause.

[10] See A. Meiklejohn, Free Speech and Its Relation to Self-Government 94 (1948).

[11] See Meiklejohn, The First Amendment Is an Absolute, in 1961 Supreme Court Review 245, 262–63.

[12] Meiklejohn, note 10 *supra*, at 93–94.

moral."[13] While it is far from true that everything implicating our emotional growth, for example, or every expression of emotionality implicates free speech values, certainly the category of personal development[14] is useful in accounting for why a given expression counts as speech or as protected speech.[15]

Alexander Bickel may also be taken to have restricted the broad free speech value formulations when, in modifying Chaffee's formulation,[16] he confines the scope of the "social" interest to "the interest in the successful operation of the political process."[17] The political can obviously be defined in narrower or broader terms, and conceptions of what is required successfully to operate a constitutional government vary in breadth.[18] Paradoxically, what is required to operate the political process successfully probably itself depends on the scope of constitutional protection accorded to speech, so Bickel's formulation may be of limited value. If the political process is thought of narrowly, Bickel's formulation is arbitrarily underinclusive, in that civic-minded persons would, as civic-minded persons, tend to care about and wish to express publicly their opinions on "nonpolitical" matters as much as on "political" concerns.[19]

---

[13] Bloustein, note 3 *supra*, at 373.

[14] This formulation raises the unsolved problem of whether a system of free speech, or meaningful free speech, requires the affirmative availability, perhaps by government provision, of open opportunities for education, travel, employment, social class interaction, and such.

[15] It should be said in partial defense of Meiklejohn's "voter-issue" formulation that it properly includes a portion of what Professor Baker refers to as "solitary" uses of speech, *e.g.*, recording, cataloging, outlining, and writing notes to oneself. See Baker, note 3 *supra*, at 993. Recording and organizing privately one's thoughts on political issues would be protected by both Meiklejohn and Baker, even if the recorded and organized thoughts are not intended for any direct subsequent communication. But certainly not all private acts of expression, or self-definition qualify as speech, with or without the presence of an audience. One can certainly help define the kind of person one is by riding horses and chopping wood by hand at one's ranch or by consuming particular products, but such acts are not ordinary speech. Contra *id.* at 994.

[16] See note 5 *supra* and accompanying text.

[17] Bickel, note 8 *supra*, at 62.

[18] See Wellington, On Freedom of Expression, 88 Yale L.J. 1105, 1112 (1979).

[19] The Supreme Court has properly observed that "[e]ven though political speech is entitled to the fullest possible measure of constitutional protection, there are a host of other communications that command the same respect. An assertion that 'Jesus Saves,' that 'Abortion is Murder,' that every woman has the 'Right to Choose,' or that 'Alcohol Kills,' may have a claim to a constitutional exemption . . . that is just as strong as 'Robert Vincent—City Council.' " Members of the City Council v. Taxpayers for Vincent, 104 S.Ct. 2118, 2135 (1984).

In focusing attention on "explicitly and predominantly political speech,"[20] Bork notes:[21]

> The First Amendment indicates that there is something special about speech. We would know that much even without a first amendment, for the entire structure of the Constitution creates a representative democracy, a form of government that would be meaningless without freedom to discuss government and its policies. Freedom for political speech could and should be inferred even if there were no first amendment.

The problem with proceeding thus to confine the scope of the Free Speech Clause is, of course, that this interpretation assumes the Clause's redundancy. While it is certainly possible to argue that the drafters inserted this express protection of political speech merely for reasons of expediency, and not genuinely to amend the Constitution, it is at least equally plausible to suggest that the Free Speech Clause was intended to add something meaningful and that the drafters could well have inserted the qualifier "political" had they meant to so confine the Clause.

Narrow formulations of the scope of and values underlying the Free Speech Clause tend, therefore, to be unduly arbitrary. But this does not mean that the broader formulations of free speech values are unproblematic. Writers such as Martin Redish[22] have explicitly recognized that what is variously referred to as the value of self-realization, or development, of "self-fulfillment," or autonomy, conceals an ambiguity.[23] For convenience, this ambiguity will be referred to in terms of autonomy$_1$ and autonomy$_2$. Autonomy$_1$, which can safely be regarded as a Millian value and is at least arguably defensible as a coherent element of distinctive free speech

---

[20] Bork, note 2 *supra*, at 26.

[21] *Id.* at 23.

[22] See Redish, The Value of Free Speech, 130 U. Pa. L. Rev. 591, 593 (1982).

[23] *Cf.* Schauer, Free Speech: A Philosophical Inquiry 56–58 (1982) (not acknowledging a broader and narrower sense of autonomy but rejecting autonomy as a value underlying a distinctive free speech principle). It should be noted that, while Schauer does not recognize even autonomy$_1$ or self-realization in the narrow sense as an element of a distinctive free speech principle, this will make no significant difference to the argument that follows. One may conclude that Schauer either underplays the direct and substantial connection between autonomy$_1$ and free speech or else that he is precisely on target. Whichever, the analysis of the case law areas below should be unaffected. See *id.* at 56. The ambiguity at issue is illustrated by Emerson's use of the phrase "the affirmation of self." Emerson, note 3 *supra*, at 5, and by Scanlon's use of "autonomy" in Scanlon, A Theory of Freedom of Expression, 1 Phil. & Pub. Affairs 204 (1972).

values, is connected with self-realization in the sense utilized by Mill and draws on the developmental dynamic that is described by writers as diverse as Aristotle and Hegel. This sense of autonomy or self-realization is associated with what Isaiah Berlin has referred to as "positive liberty."[24]

Autonomy$_2$, or autonomy in the broader sense, has no essential reference to progress, growth, development, or cultivation of one's "higher powers" and is associated more with simply doing as one likes, generally, or with an absence of socially imposed restraint on one's actions and choices. Autonomy$_2$, or Berlin's "negative liberty," however valuable it may be, is simply too broadly conceived to support a free speech principle above and beyond a general libertarianism.[25] Then, too, it will be a rare case indeed in which suppression of the freedom of speech of one group does not simultaneously advance the broad "negative liberty" or autonomy$_2$ of another, perhaps larger, group. Autonomy$_2$ may therefore be at most of limited usefulness in deciding free speech cases or in deciding what is to count as speech.

Of course, even the theorists subscribing to a broader conception of free speech values have occasionally been subject to criticism for excessively restrictive categorization. Professor Tribe has warned that[26]

> [h]owever tempting it may be to resist governmental claims for restricting speech by retreating to an artificially narrowed zone and then defending it without limit, any such course is likely in

---

[24] See Berlin, Two Concepts of Liberty, in Four Essays on Liberty 118, 122–31 (1969). But *cf*. MacCallum, Negative and Positive Freedom, 76 Phil. Rev. 321 (1967) (critically placing Berlin's negative versus positive freedom distinction in proper perspective). See also Bay, The Structure of Freedom (1958); F. Oppenheim, Dimensions of Freedom (1961).

[25] While Mill could, with some qualifications, be classified in at least certain respects as a conduct libertarian, his defense of freedom of "thought and discussion" has much more to do with "flourishing" than with any value associated more broadly with "doing as one likes." In any event, Schauer's dismissal of autonomy as a distinctive First Amendment value is at least as cogent when confined to autonomy$_2$. Schauer was on this score anticipated by Robert Bork, who argued that "the development of individual faculties and the achievement of pleasure . . . do not distinguish speech from any other activity. An individual may develop his faculties or derive pleasure from trading on the stock market." Bork, note 2 *supra*, at 25. Again, the case law argument below does not depend on whether one perceives a special relationship between autonomy$_1$ and free speech, or at least a closer relationship than between autonomy$_2$ and free speech. For a critique of Bork's approach, see Wellington, note 18 *supra*, at 1120–21. But see Yudof, In Search of a Free Speech Principle, 78 Nw. U.L. Rev. 1139, 1348–49 (1983).

[26] See Tribe, American Constitutional Law 579 & *id*. n.25 (1978).

the end to sacrifice too much to strategic maneuver: the claims
for suppression will persist, and the defense will be no stronger
for having withdrawn to arbitrarily constricted territory.

The trick, of course, is to tell artificial from principled constriction,
and it will be argued here that the "Millian values" help us to do so.

In the meantime, it should be recognized that artificially expanding the zone of protected speech beyond that justified by the principles and purposes underlying freedom of speech may disserve those
values and impose costs in other ways. Strategically, it is not true
that the free speech "army" cannot overextend its position.[27] It is
certainly plausible to argue, as against Tribe, that a refusal to trivialize or debase the Free Speech Clause by extending its application
beyond the bounds of its coherent, identifiable purposes helps to
enhance and dignify the invocation of the Clause within the full
extent of its legitimate scope. If we wish to honor its intrinsic
importance, we do so by supporting free speech principles inten-
sively, on every appropriate occasion.

III. Millian Values and the Requirement
of a Social Idea

The recognizable, distinctive values or purposes underlying
a free speech principle, tied together as Millian values, impose
certain requirements on what is to count as speech. In terms of
Millian values, for something to be speech it must embody or convey a more or less discernible idea, doctrine, conception, or argument of a social nature, where "social" is understood to include
broadly political, religious, ethical, and cultural concerns. For language or gesture or conduct to be speech, it must carry implications
beyond the speaker's individual and immediate circumstances.
Speech must communicate; it must be, at least potentially, socially
"fertile," and not socially sterile or exclusively ego-referential.

Speech, certainly, can be almost purely factual and empirical or
normative and evaluative, or informal, or false, or internally inconsistent, or pernicious, or irresponsible; it can go unheard or even be
intended for an audience of only the speaker. What it cannot be is

---

[27] *Cf.* Schauer, note 23 *supra*, at 134–35 ("[t]he broader the scope of the right, the more
likely it is to be weaker, largely because widening the scope increases the likelihood of
conflict with other interests, some of which may be equally or more important").

patently sterile, without implication for our collective arrangements and institutions, broadly understood. Self-servingness is not
definitive, though; self-serving speech in a marketplace may well
not be protected speech, but self-serving speech about the marketplace probably is.

Generalizations about putative speech in particular contexts,
such as commercial speech or, as discussed below, in the context of
nude dancing or other entertainment, or disorderly conduct arrests,
should only be drawn inductively by examining a run of individual
cases, judicially decided on a case-by-case basis. The stakes involved—the risks of either trivializing the guarantee or of suppressing legitimate speech—are so high that conclusively
presuming putative speech in any particular social context to be
or not to be First Amendment speech seems ill advised.

While speech can be vague, or equivocal, or metaphorical, or
guarded, or aesopic, this does not mean that the presence of speech
depends on the efforts, or successful efforts, of an intended audience, bystanders, or third parties. A verbalization may causally
provoke or incite action or inspire thought, speech, or action in
others without being speech. A glimpse of a starving child may
inspire an ethical debate or change a foreign policy without the
child's presence being speech, just as a flower placed in a crannied
wall may inspire the poet without speaking or amounting to speech.
If one has no significant social message to impart, however confused or apparently foolish or inarticulate or ill formed, the creativity of the listener cannot constitute one's words as speech in this
sense. If one has sent a social message, however, even if none was
received, or if an entirely different message was received, one has
engaged in speech, even if imperfectly.

If talk or conduct does not rise to the level of speech, symbolic or
otherwise, this does not mean that such talk or conduct is without
practical, statutory, or even constitutional protection. If talk is
genuinely or even widely perceived as sterile, there may be little
incentive for a government to expend resources in suppressing it.

Even where such incentives exist, other constitutional safeguards
apart from the Free Speech Clause may come into play. These may
include, beyond due process,[28] the Free Exercise of Religion
Clause, the Equal Protection Clause, the right to vote, the right to

---

[28] See Meiklejohn, note 7 *supra*, at 79.

travel, free assembly and the right to petition, as well as freedoms of association and privacy.[29] Whatever the constitutional concept, there may be some comfort to be secured from the strong historical tendency of dictatorial regimes to suppress on the ground of alleged harmfulness, or falsity, or unorthodoxy, or as blasphemous, or reactionary, none of which denies the presence of a social idea. Selective enforcement problems are minimized because potential oppressors cannot resist the temptation to label opposing ideas as bad social ideas, thereby admitting that they are some sort of social ideas, and thereby giving the game away.

The reasons for placing these restrictions on the concept of speech reflect the nature of Millian values. Mill's defense of the regime of free speech or, more particularly, of liberty of thought and discussion, was informed not by an undifferentiated libertarianism but by a vision of the progressive enlightened development of a society. Victorian progressives such as Mill were perhaps not so sanguine as to believe that humanity's "prospects of creating a rational and enlightened civilization [were] virtually unlimited,"[30] but it is clear that Mill's thinking is not adequately reflected by focusing on a condition of "negative liberty" or on a mere absence of restraint. The end is social progress through individual character development. Without suggesting, of course, that good character should generally be legally enforced, Mill believed that character could be better or worse, higher or lower, and his approach to free speech is inseparable from this assumption.

Mill indeed presupposes a "prior ideal of excellence for human beings further realized by allowing liberty of action and thought."[31] This is reflected in Mill's estimation not of mere idiosyncrasy of speech and behavior[32] but of "individual growth"[33] and the "due study and preparation"[34] typically required therefor.

---

[29] The freedom of the press may be added, if it is thought that this protection of the printed word rests on a different base than freedom of speech.

[30] Emerson, note 3 *supra*, at 14.

[31] Ladenson, A Philosophy of Free Expression and Its Constitutional Implications 152 (1983).

[32] *Id.* at 150 ("it is . . . a *non sequitur* to hold that someone who opposes conforming to custom merely as custom must also believe that people should be encouraged to be idiosyncratic simply for the sake of being idiosyncratic").

[33] See Scanlon, Freedom of Expression and Categories of Expression, 40 U. Pitt L. Rev. 473, 483 (1974) (Mill's focus on "true belief and individual growth"; concern for "fostering the development of better (more independent and inquiring) individuals").

[34] Mill, On Liberty 33 (D. Spitz ed. 1975).

Mill recognizes that not all forms and instances of speech in the literal sense significantly implicate the values and aims underlying freedom of speech. For example, "[t]he scope of Mill's defense of freedom of expression does not cover the dissemination of information, whether true or false, about a person's private life which has no bearing on the scientific, moral, political, religious, and social issues with which he is concerned."[35]

Outside the context of his narrow discussion of free speech, but with implications for current free speech issues, Mill observed unhesitatingly that[36]

> there are many acts which, being directly injurious only to the agents themselves, ought not to be legally interdicted, but which, if done publicly, are a violation of good manners, and coming thus within the category of offenses against others, may rightly be prohibited. Of this kind are offenses against decency; on which it is unnecessary to dwell.

This is plainly some distance from the late twentieth century free speech jurisprudence that fashionably, if ultimately incoherently, rejects ethical skepticism while settling for an ethical relativism in which one man's indecency is another man's lyric. It also reinforces the necessity for some sort of social idea for protected speech to be present. For Mill, the indecent is, at least sometimes, not only recognizable and is not simply to be shunned as a matter of unconstrained moral preference, but it is also subject to authoritative legal prohibition.

Even where the issue is not susceptibility to prohibition, Mill is not reluctant to distinguish greater and lesser value on grounds other than mere subjective preference. He unselfconsciously asserts that "[i]t may be better to be a John Knox than an Alicibiades,[37] but it is better to be a Pericles than either; nor would a Pericles, if we

---

[35] Ten, Mill on Liberty 136 (1980).

[36] Mill, note 34 *supra*, at 91. See also Ten, note 35 *supra*, at 106–07; Honderich, 'On Liberty' and Morality-Dependent Harms, 30 Pol. Studies 504–11 (1983). A computer research session suggests that this interesting passage has been quoted only once in recent reported American jurisprudence, and that, appropriately, in dissent. See In re Excelsior Pictures Corp. v. Regents of the University of the States, 3 N.Y.2d 237, 256, (1957) (Burke, J., dissenting). But *cf.* Solzhenitsyn, A World Split Apart, in East and West 50–51 (1980) (reference to "destructive and irresponsible freedom" being granted "boundless scope").

[37] For evidence of Alcibiades' less than sterling character, see Thucydides, The Peloponnesian War 456, 565, 570, 585–86 (R. Warner trans. 1954).

had one in these days, be without anything good which belonged to John Knox."[38]

This, again, is to suggest not that Mill advocated the legal proscription of all that he considered decadent or depraved but merely that there can be no Millian reasons for barring any legal action against that which does not implicate Millian values. Within the sphere of liberty of thought and discussion, Mill is concerned essentially with that which rises to the level of "doctrine," as when he asserts at his most radical that "there ought to exist the fullest liberty of professing and discussion, as a matter of ethical conviction, any doctrine, however immoral it may be considered."[39]

For speech in a literal sense to be speech in a protectable, First Amendment sense, though, it must rise to the level of recognizable "doctrine" or of factual assertion or evaluative "opinion" that may in at least some sense be either true or false. This much is clear even from Mill's famous recapitulation of his arguments for liberty of thought and discussion, where he iterates his arguments on infallibility, on the likelihood of partial truth, and on the necessity of vigorous contest to promote vital, as opposed to thoughtless, merely prejudiced belief.[40] If the putative speech cannot be envisioned as some sort of direct, if minor, contribution to a social or intellectual debate continuing over time, in which there is perhaps a consensus or an array of contesting schools of thought that now approach, now recede from the truth, Millian values are not significantly implicated.

We resist this clear understanding of Mill largely on the assumption that Mill, like many of us, must have subscribed to a sort of nonjudgmental, nonhierarchical general libertarianism.[41] But this is

---

[38] Mill, note 34 *supra*, at 59. See also Mill, Utilitarianism 12–13 (Sher ed. 1977) ("no intelligent human being would consent to be a fool . . . even though they should be persuaded that the fool is better satisfied with his lot than they are with theirs").

[39] Mill, note 34 *supra*, at 17 n.2.

[40] *Id.* at 50.

[41] It should be clear at this point that any claim that a broad conduct libertarianism underlies and informs the Free Speech Clause is illogical on its own terms, obviously historically anachronistic, contrary to Millian logic, language, and assumptions, and currently inconsistent with a vast panoply of widely accepted paternalistic statutes and judicial decisions, none of which is commonly thought by libertarian opponents to be in logical tension with the Free Speech Clause. Certainly, a broadly libertarian society, however conceived, would by definition proscribe at least certain kinds of restraints on speech, but it remains unclear why liberty of speech must be more central to a libertarian society, or receive greater

inconsistent not only with Mill's arguments and their underlying premises but also with the unmistakable tone or flavor of Mill's language throughout *On Liberty*. Mill insists on the capacity for "being improved" as a prerequisite to the regime of free speech.[42] He appeals "to the permanent interests of man as a progressive being."[43] His emphasis is on not merely thinking for oneself but also thinking for oneself "with due study and preparation."[44] He approves Humboldt's exaltation of "the highest and most harmonious development of [humanity's] powers to a complete and consistent whole"[45] as the dictate of reason. Choosing one's "plan of life" calls for "observation to see, reasoning and judgment to foresee, activity to gather materials for decision, discrimination to decide, and . . . firmness and self-control to hold to [one's] deliberate decision."[46]

Mill refers without embarrassment to "human excellence"[47] and goes on to specify that "individuality is the same thing with development."[48] He is careful to link eccentricity with "strength of character"[49] and to observe that "the amount of eccentricity in a society has generally been proportional to the amount of genius, mental vigor, and moral courage it contained."[50] The ultimate aim remains "cultivation of higher nature."[51]

This is not to suggest that only that which is universally recog-

---

protection, than liberty in plainly nonspeech commercial market transactions, or in child raising and family relations, or in education, or physical movement. In a word, just as the Due Process Clause does not enact Mr. Spencer's Social Statics, the Free Speech Clause does not enact Mr. Nozick's Anarchy, State and Utopia. *Cf.* Commonwealth v. Kautz, 491 A.2d 864, 865 (Pa. 1985) (citing Mill's principle of "liberty of tastes and pursuits" and declining to adhere to it in the context of mandatory motorcycle helmets). But *cf.* Linmark Associates, Inc. v. Township of Willingboro, 431 U.S. 85, 96 (1977) (rejecting paternalistic elements of ordinance restricting the flow of housing market information).

[42] Mill, note 34 *supra*, at 11.

[43] *Id.* at 12.

[44] *Id.* at 33.

[45] *Id.* at 54.

[46] *Id.* at 56. None of this is to suggest, of course, that Mill would seek to suppress the speech of those who disagree with the worthiness of Millian values or with any particular conception of their realization.

[47] *Id.* at 59.

[48] *Id.* at 60.

[49] *Id.* at 63.

[50] *Ibid.*

[51] *Id.* at 64.

nized as decent and uplifting can be entitled to special protection.[52] The point is merely to elaborate on Millian values, in the absence of which there is no point in according special constitutional protection to a given instance of expression.

It is only the prestige and convenience of Mill's elaborate theory that suggests focusing on Mill and "Millian values." One could, as well, imaginatively resurrect Socrates in the role of constitutional arbiter, to the same end.

It is occasionally suggested that a linkage between the Free Speech Clause and Millian or other values is illegitimate and not textually warranted. William Van Alstyne has said:[53]

> The first amendment does not link the protection it provides with any particular objective and may, accordingly, be deemed to operate without regard to anyone's view of how well the speech it protects may or may not serve such an objective. The second amendment expressly links the protection it provides with a stated objective . . . and might, therefore, be deemed to operate only insofar as the right it protects . . . can be shown to be connected with that objective.

The problem is that, if we try to remain agnostic about the aims, purposes, or values underlying the Free Speech Clause, there is no reliable, nonarbitrary guide for inclusion or exclusion as "speech." Literalism fails us, since a Morse Code message or sign language may plainly implicate First Amendment values without being speech in a literal sense.[54] Can something be "symbolic" speech?[55]

---

[52] See, e.g., Pring v. Penthouse Int'l, Ltd., 695 F.2d 438, 443 (8th Cir. 1982), cert. denied, 462 U.S. 1132 (1983). See also Fraser v. Bethel School Dist. No. 403, 755 F.2d 1356 (9th Cir.) cert. granted, 106 S.Ct. 56 (1985), in which the court confessed that: "[w]e fear that if school officials had the unbridled discretion to apply a standard as subjective and elusive as 'indecency' in controlling the speech of high school students, it would increase the risk of cementing white, middle-class standards for determining what is acceptable and proper speech and behavior in our public schools. Language that may be considered 'indecent' in one segment of our heterogeneous society may be common, household usage in another." Id. at 1363. What the public schools may have overlooked in their rush toward standardlessness along with the Ninth Circuit, aside from the utility of the Equal Protection Clause, is that one defends the decency or propriety of one's language not by claiming that it is common in one's own ethnic or other group to speak or act as one did but by claiming that one's language gave no gratuitous, unnecessary offense to significant numbers of likely hearers from other ethnic or class groups.

[53] Van Alstyne, A Graphic Review of the Free Speech Clause, 70 Cal. L. Rev. 107, 112 n.13 (1982).

[54] See Hart, The Concept of Law 124, 126 (1961) on the logic and practical necessity of recourse to underlying purposes. This need could not be dispensed with merely by the framers' omission of a prefatory statement of purposes in the text of the Amendment itself.

[55] See, e.g., Clark v. Community for Creative Non-Violence, 104 S.Ct. 3065 (1984)

Recourse to the purposes of the Free Speech Clause, as recognized by one or more drafters or by other persons, is necessary in order to decide.

Bearing the Millian values in mind not only permits the principled resolution of free speech cases but also permits, in many instances, their more expeditious and less logically tortuous resolution as well. The complexity of the Supreme Court's treatment, in various contexts, of "low value" speech, meriting some, but only limited, free speech protection, has been described by Professor Stone.[56] At least some "low value" speech is, in the absence of any significant implication of Millian values, actually "zero value" or, more simply, nonspeech, meriting no Free Speech Clause protection at all.[57]

(prohibition of demonstrators from sleeping in Lafayette Park); Spence v. Washington, 418 U.S. 405 (1974) (attachment of peace symbol to flag); Tinker v. Des Moines School Dist., 393 U.S. 503 (1969) (wearing black armband in school); United States v. O'Brien, 391 U.S. 367 (1968) (draft card–burning case). In the recent case of Monroe v. State Court, 739 F.2d 568 (11th Cir. 1984), a flag-burning case, the court held that, if there is an "intent to convey a particularized message . . . and in the surrounding circumstances the likelihood was great that the message would be understood by those who viewed it . . . , the activity falls within the scope of the first and fourteenth amendments.' " Id. at 570 (quoting Spence, 418 U.S. at 410–11). While it is disheartening to learn that to speak unclearly or over the heads of one's audience is to forfeit free speech protection, and while it is not clear that just any kind of "particularized message" will do, the main point is that this requirement is certainly not drawn from the text of the First Amendment, even by fair inference.

[56] See Stone, note 4 supra, at 194–96. See also Stone, Restrictions of Speech because of Its Content: The Peculiar Case of Subject-Matter Restrictions, 46 U. Chi. L. Rev. 81 (1978).

[57] This is not to suggest, of course, that no close case will appear, or that interesting problems cannot be devised in Millian analysis. Consider the actual, if perhaps unlitigated, case of a sticker reading, in full, "the invasion of Nicaragua." By itself, the sticker conveys no social idea nor otherwise implicates Millian values. It is therefore not "speech" at all. But consider that the sticker is red, and assume that it is designed to be not easily removed once applied. Apparently, the only use for the sticker is an illegal one: to be affixed just below the word "Stop" on a traffic sign. The aim of an ordinance flatly prohibiting the manufacture of such a sticker would be to narrowly effectuate reasonable time, place, and manner restrictions. But the effect of prohibition may be just that. It is certainly not obvious precisely what tests to impose on putative speech that does not rise to the level of a social idea absent illegality.

Some instances of speech may more deeply implicate Millian values than others, independent of any assessment of the speech's falsity or perniciousness. It may be, for instance, that certain forms or modes of speech, apart from subject matter, tend to more deeply implicate Millian values than others.

Mill suggests that "[a]n opinion that corn-dealers are starvers of the poor, or that private property is robbery, ought to be unmolested when simply circulated through the press, but may justly incur punishment when delivered orally to an excited mob assembled before the house of a corn-dealer, or when handed about among the same mob in the form of a placard." Mill, note 34 supra, at 53. While Mill's emphasis here is on a clear and present danger rule, there is also the suggestion that speech in the form of articles may implicate Millian values more deeply than mass oratory or placards, as a general rule. The general hierarchy seems clear: books, articles, and leaflets may tend to be more precise, richer, more articulate, or

It is possible that the speech-nonspeech distinction may turn out, eventually, to bear a family resemblance to the doctrine of public issue or public matter speech versus private interest speech as developed by the Supreme Court in several contexts.[58] Of course, the Court has thus far continued to accord concededly private or personal interest speech some limited measure of Free Speech Clause protection.[59] The public-private interest speech distinction must be further clarified if it is to be consistently applied in a convincing way.[60]

IV. ENTERTAINMENT AND MILLIAN VALUES

Entertainment is not necessarily beyond the compass of the Free Speech Clause. Some instances of entertainment, such as protest songs or satiric comedy, clearly tend to implicate Millian values. But many forms of entertainment do not. It is unmistakably the law that even, or especially, in a commercial context, "nude dancing is not without its First Amendment protections from official regulation."[61] While this result has not been univer-

---

self-incriminating intellectually than placards, slogans, banners, and bumper stickers. The world may be better off to the extent that there is a reasonably social class–neutral legal incentive to publish, rather than to sloganeer. Articulateness is not the sole Millian value, or even the dominant or controlling Millian value, but it is a Millian value.

Frederick Schauer has denied the wisdom of drawing this general qualitative distinction in constitutional terms. His argument is that we are bombarded with so much speech nowadays that, in order to be heard, we must each perhaps speak more offensively, or literally or figuratively raise our voice above the din of other speech to acquire or maintain an audience. See Schauer, Note 23 *supra*, at 201–02. The general futility of this advice seems clear; one might as well counsel all spectators at a football game to stand up in order to see better.

[58] See *e.g.*, Dun & Bradstreet, Inc. v. Greenmoss Builders, Inc., 105 S.Ct. 2939 (1985) (commercial defamation case); Connick v. Myers, 461 U.S. 138 (1983) (public employment discharge case). See also Chaffee, note 5 *supra*, at 6, 11, 18, 19 (focus on "matters of public interest").

[59] See, *e.g.*, *Connick*, 461 U.S. at 147 ("We do not suggest . . . that Myers' speech, even if not touching upon a matter of public concern, is totally beyond the protection of the First Amendment"). But see Jones v. Memorial Hosp. System, 677 S.W.2d 221, 224 (Tex. Civ. App. 1985) ("The federal courts have declined to require protection of speech on matters solely of personal interest. To be entitled to first amendment protection, speech must relate to matters of 'political, social, or other concern to the community.' ") (quoting *Connick*, 461 U.S. at 146); Meiklejohn, note 7 *supra* at 79 ("Private speech, or private interest in speech . . . has no claim whatever to the protection of the First Amendment").

[60] Part of the lack of clarity of this distinction, resulting in a very dubious analysis in Greenmoss, is attributable to the near emptiness of the Court's "content, form, and context" test, Connick, 461 U.S. at 147–48, and part to the conceptual ambiguity of "interest." See generally Held, The Public Interest and Individual Interests (1970).

[61] Schad v. Borough of Mount Ephraim, 452 U.S. 61, 66 (1981).

sally acclaimed,[62] it seems solidly entrenched. The problem is that not all nonobscene commercial nude dancing, for example, purports to convey a social idea in the relevant sense, nor need Millian values otherwise be significantly implicated. As a result, the courts feel "bound to treat topless dancing as a form of expression which is protected at least to some extent by the first amendment," while recognizing that " 'few of us would march our sons and daughters off to war' to protect that form of expression."[63]

It has been suggested in a broader context, though, that sexually related "speech" "will almost invariably carry an implicit, if not explicit, message in favor of more relaxed sexual mores. . . . In our society, the very presence of sexual explicitness in speech seems ideologically significant, without regard to whatever other messages might be intended."[64]

It would seem, however, that advocacy of relaxed sexual mores is something imputed to commercial nude dancing or something invested by the third parties in the concept, rather than a message in any sense sent and received. One clue is that "sexual mores" is obviously broader than the activities encompassed by commercial nude dancing. One might even suspect that the hidden agenda of commercial nude dancing may be not the relaxation of sexual mores but keeping them the way they are so that the customers will be motivated to return and pay to watch again. Then again, there may be no intent, explicit or implicit, in operation other than merely to profit or merely to entertain—diversion for its own sake, rather than to make a point.[65]

---

[62] See, *e.g.*, Judge Richard Posner's reiterated misgivings in Douglass v. Hustler Magazine, Inc., 769 F.2d 1128, 1141 (7th Cir. 1985) ("Art . . . even of the artless sort represented by 'topless' dancing—today enjoys extensive protection in the name of the First Amendment") (contrasting an alternative of protecting only "political" speech); Piarowski v. Illinois Community College Dist. 515, 759 F.2d 625, 628 (7th Cir. 1985) (citing Doran v. Salem Inn, Inc., 422 U.S. 922, 932–34 (1975)); Reed v. Village of Shorewood, 704 F.2d 943, 949–50 (7th Cir. 1983) (contrasting "political" and "cultural" expression) (relying on Chaffee, note 5 *supra*, at 7–33). See also Bork, note 2 *supra*, at 27. But see Wellington, note 18 *supra*, at 1115–16. Attempting to distinguish between the political and the cultural, at least in broad senses of the terms, appears to be profoundly difficult. Nor does Mill give us any reason to do so.

[63] Krueger v. City of Pensacola, 759 F.2d 851, 854 (11th Cir. 1985) (quoting Young v. American Mini Theaters, 427 U.S. 50, 70 (1976)).

[64] Stone, note 56 *supra*, at 111–12. But *cf.* the sexually explicit, but ideologically pointless, language of the "cop abuse" cases discussed *infra* at notes 99–111 and accompanying text.

[65] See, *e.g.*, State v. House, 676 P.2d 892, 896 (1984) (en banc) (Rossman, J., dissenting), aff'd 299 Or. 78, 698 P.2d 951 (1985). It is certainly possible, of course, that requiring merely the conveyance of some social idea, as a necessary and sufficient condition to acquir-

If the "message" of commercial nude dancing is so shadowy and equivocal, however, it is too attenuated and insubstantial significantly to implicate Millian values.[66] Further, and more controversially, there is no reason necessarily to assume that the Millian pointlessness of commercial nude dancing must depend on a finding of bad taste, lewdness, indecency, obscenity, or widespread offensiveness. A claim of free speech protection for a given activity may "trivialize"[67] the Free Speech Clause because of the Millian pointlessness of the activity, and not because the activity is judged immoral, or harmful, or lewd, or misleading.[68]

In a slightly different context, the Eleventh Circuit recently has detected no advocacy or expression of ideas in connection with nude sunbathing, despite plaintiffs' claim that nude sunbathing "is the practice by which they advocate and communicate their philosophy that the human body is wholesome and that nudity is not indecent."[69] The plaintiffs sought to analogize their situation to that involved in the protected commercial nude dancing cases, but the Eleventh Circuit rejected the argument on the grounds that the nude dancing cases, unlike nude sunbathing, involved "nudity in combination with a protection form of expression."[70] A problem lies in the fact that non-sexually oriented social or recreational

---

ing at least some free speech protection, would in some contexts generate close questions by setting up incentives for nonspeakers to clothe themselves with some free speech protection by adorning themselves with some minimal speech. If the social idea is not expressed by or integrated into the nude dance routine but is merely "worn about the neck" to ward off constitutional attack, then only the readily severable social idea communication itself should be protected by the Free Speech Clause. There is generally no need to inquire whether the invokers of the Free Speech Clause "really" believe in, or even vaguely understand, their own protected and protective social idea.

[66] The assumption that commercial nude dancing is ordinarily sought to be suppressed because of its "content," in the same sense in which a regime might seek to suppress Das Kapital or Mein Kampf because of dislike of or unpopularity of its content, seems doubtful. See Krueger, 759 F.2d at 854.

[67] Highway Tavern Corp. v. McLaughlin, 105 A.D.2d 122, 139, 483 N.Y.S.2d 323, 338 (1984).

[68] Of course, the state is understandably required to show more than mere triviality before obtaining a criminal conviction. See, e.g., State v. Jacobson, 459 So. 2d 1285, 1290 (La. Ct. App. 1984) (obscenity conviction); Erhardt v. State, 468 N.E.2d 224, 225 (Ind. 1984) (vacating 463 N.E.2d 1121 (Ind. Ct. App. 1984)) (public indecency conviction).

[69] South Florida Free Beaches, Inc. v. City of Miami, 734 F.2d 608, 609–10 (11th Cir. 1984). In contrast, a Florida court has recognized a free speech right to beg alms for oneself, despite the presumably limited message content involved. See C.C.B. v. State, 458 So. 2d 47, 48 (Fla. Ct. App. 1984).

[70] 734 F.2d at 610.

dancing is generally not accorded any free speech protection at all, despite the ability of articulate persons to generate plausible "messages," such as antipuritanicalism, that might be imputed to recreational or social dancing.[71]

Sorting these cases out, it appears that the courts attach crucial First Amendment significance to a strict separation of performer and audience. Persons in a group of social dancers are not viewed as performing for themselves or for each other as an audience. Performance dancing, nude or, presumably, otherwise, with an audience, is protected, unlike social dancing, and it does not lose its "expressive," protected quality when associated with nudity. Sunbathing clad, however, is not an otherwise free speech protected activity, and nudity adds or subtracts nothing in the way of free speech protection to the sunbathing.[72]

The cases can probably thus be reconciled. What should not be overlooked, however, is that there is no Millian value-based rationale available to defend the results obtained if it is recognized that the courts often protect putative speech that does not even purport to convey any social idea.

If one turns to the video game free speech cases, one finds that the possible analogy of video game screens to movies is generally downplayed and that video games, at least at the present state of technology, are typically said to fall afoul of the requirement that, to enjoy free speech protection, the entertainment be intended to convey some idea or information.[73] This is an eminently sensible result from a Millian standpoint and, despite contentions that some video games vaguely inculcate distinctively martial values, should stand until the video screen conveys, in a manner inextricable with

---

[71] See, *e.g.*, Jarman v. Williams, 753 F.2d 76, 78 (8th Cir. 1985) (assuming that the "message" intended is merely that dancing is not wrong); Kent's Lounge, Inc. v. City of New York, 104 A.D.2d 397, 398, 478 N.Y.S.2d 928, 929 (1984) ("recreational dancing is not a form of speech protected by the First Amendment") (further noting the absence of free speech protection for rollerskating).

[72] Break dancers are therefore advised to gather a discrete, separate audience—an audience of one's fellow break dancers may not suffice; one must argue for their "receptivity" while not taking their turn—and, secondarily, to try to think of some articulable message above and beyond approval of break dancing.

[73] See, *e.g.*, Marshfield Family Skateland, Inc. v. Town of Marshfield, 389 Mass. 436, 450 N.E.2d 605, 609, cert. dismissed, 104 S.Ct. 475 (1983); Caswell v. Licensing Comm'n, 387 Mass. 864, 868, 444 N.E.2d 922, 926–27 (1983); People v. Walker, 135 Mich. App. 267, 275, 354 N.W.2d 312, 316–17 (1984), appeal dismissed sub. nom. Walker v. Warren, 106 S.Ct. 32 (1985).

what is sought to be prohibited, some sort of recognizable social idea.

The idea or information requirement tends to go out the window, however, in other entertainment contexts, such as musical performances. The First Amendment, it has been held, protects the right to produce jazz concerts.[74] Similarly, the bands marching in Philadelphia's Mummers Parade, complete with "thematic arrangement," are engaged in "a form of expressive entertainment" protected by the First Amendment.[75] The problem in focusing on the "expressiveness" or performance aspect of the entertainment is, of course, the determination to ignore the absence of any social idea. Expressive entertainment in the form of juggling, plate balancing, and the swallowing of swords or goldfish cannot be distinguished in principle from the above sorts of performances. If anything is clear about the First Amendment, it is that such activities, however captivating, are simply not speech.[76]

Again, though, these generalizations are subject to some exceptions. One could theoretically employ plate balancing as a medium of social criticism. Since there are substantial risks, potentially, in erroneously deciding free speech cases for or against the speaker, which may be summed as the risks of decadence or loss of purpose versus the risk of suppression, a case-by-case determination process without the aid of specific presumptions seems called for here, even if most cases of plate balancing do or do not turn out to involve speech.

The logic of the entertainment cases is ultimately derived from the now rather quaint "crime magazine" case of *Winters v. New York*.[77]

---

[74] See Fact Concerts, Inc. v. City of Newport, 626 F.2d 1060, 1063 (1st Cir. 1980), rev'd on other grounds, 453 U.S. 247 (1981).

[75] See Tacynec v. City of Philadelphia, 687 F.2d 793, 796 (3d Cir. 1982), cert. denied, 459 U.S. 1172 (1983).

[76] A somewhat more complex case is presented by Cinevision Corp. v. City of Burbank, 745 F.2d 560 (9th Cir. 1984), cert. denied, 105 S.Ct. 2115 (1985). The court, in a case involving the concert promotion of several rock groups of arguably varying "hardness," indicated that "constitutional safeguards are not applicable only to musical expression that implicates some sort of ideological content." *Id.* at 569. From a Millian value standpoint, one would at least want to inquire into such matters as life-style endorsements or the contents of song lyrics for the Free Speech Clause to be implicated. Actually, there was some evidence of genuine, easily judicially detected content-based broadly political discrimination in *Cinevision*. See *id.* at 573.

[77] 333 U.S. 507 (1948).

The court indicated, in a free press clause context:[78]

> We do not accede to appellee's suggestion that the constitutional protection for a free press applies only to the exposition of ideas. The line between the informing and the entertaining is too elusive for the protection of that basic right. Everyone is familiar with instances of propaganda through fiction. What is one man's amusement, teaches another's doctrine.

The Court in *Winters* was otherwise confident, of course, of its ability reliably to detect the lewd, the indecent, and the absence of social value in a publication.[79] Its otherwise consistent judicial modesty, however, is appropriate only with respect to recognizable borderline cases. Obviously, propaganda in the guise of fiction is ordinarily protectable speech on any theory. But it is unreasonable to suggest that since there are undeniably borderline cases, it is either impossible or pointless to recognize the substantial numbers of instances in which the absence of any intent to convey a social idea can be fairly and reliably detected.

V. Profanity and the Abuse of Cops, Meter Maids, and Civilians: The Conjunction of Chaplinsky and Cohen

It may be that the very triviality of much pure entertainment perversely inspires First Amendment protection: If it is socially inconsequential, why permit its suppression? This brings into isue the judicial refusal to defer to the legislative balancing of the benefits and costs associated with the literally pointless prohibited activity. There are a wide variety of cases of allegedly socially pointless "speech" in which the alleged associated harms range from public "pollutant" effects, such as a general coarsening in the tenor of public discourse, to the taking of justified personal offense, to the threat of physical violence.[80]

It must be conceded at the outset that, while the well-known

---

[78] *Id.* at 510.

[79] *Ibid.*

[80] See, *e.g.*, Archibald Cox's argument that the expression at issue in *Cohen* imposed social costs in the form of a lowering of the standard of public debate, in Cox, The Role of the Supreme Court in American Government 47–48 (1976).

Cohen case[81] should not be defended in unduly romantic terms, *Cohen* was probably correctly decided in Millian value terms. In *Cohen*, a jacket bearing the inscription[82] "Fuck the Draft" inspired a divided Court to observe that it is "often true that one man's vulgarity is another's lyric"[83] and to decline to "indulge the facile assumption that one can forbid particular words without also running a substantial risk of suppressing ideas in the process."[84] Whether or not an attempt generally to forbid any particular words was ever at issue, the Court in effect constitutionalized protection of the emotive, as opposed to cognitive, force of language.[85]

But the *Cohen* result is defensible as a recognition of a particular phrase, in historical context, that barely made it into the category of "speech" by expressing a remarkably vague social idea about a reasonably clearly specified social phenomenon, the draft. Whether or not "Fuck" would have been speech by itself or not, "Fuck the Draft," in context, probably was. More enthusiastic defenses seem questionable.

It is suggested, for example, that "Resist the Draft" and "Fuck the Draft" do not convey the same meaning,[86] or that "Fuck the Draft" says it twice as well,[87] or that the manner of expression in *Cohen* is "more powerful,"[88] or that, more generally, "[t]he use of profanity . . . is often an effective means for individuals to convey

---

[81] Cohen v. California, 403 U.S. 15 (1971).

[82] Evidently, Cohen was not the author of the inscription, and the jacket in question was covered with writing, among which the words "Fuck the Draft" did not particularly stand out. See Farber, Civilizing Public Discourse: An Essay on Professor Bickel, Justice Harlan, and the Enduring Significance of Cohen v. California, 1980 Duke L.J. 283, 286 & 286 n.21. These details accord rather poorly with the image of a protester so overwrought with intensity of indignation that he, unlike, say, Henry David Thoreau in Civil Disobedience, could not reasonably be expected to convey this depth of feeling through mere nonprofane speech.

[83] 403 U.S. at 25. Despite its judicial modesty in this respect, the Court remains fully inclined to review judgments that distinguish protected material that "provokes only normal, healthy sexual desires" from material that arouses "morbid" and presumably unhealthy responses. See Brockett v. Spokane Arcades, 105 S.Ct. 2794, 2799 (1985).

[84] 403 U.S. at 26.

[85] *Ibid.*

[86] See, *e.g.*, Rutzick, Offensive Language and the Evolution of First Amendment Protection, 9 Harv. C.R.-C.L. L. Rev. 1, 19 n.98 (1974) (quoting Maiman, Speech v. Privacy: Is There a Right Not to Be Spoken To? 67 Nw. U. L. Rev. 153, 189 (1972)).

[87] See Van Alstyne, note 53 *supra*, at 142.

[88] See Redish, The Content Distinction in First Amendment Analysis, 34 Stan. L. Rev. 113, 141 (1981).

dramatically otherwise inexpressable emotions."[89] It is pointed out that "[n]ot everyone can be a Daniel Webster."[90]

None of these arguments is without point. Yet each can easily be oversold. Despite its non-McCluhanesque tenor, there is some sense in the observation that "[a] requirement that indecent language be avoided will have its primary effect on the form, rather than the content, of serious communication. There are few, if any thoughts that cannot be expressed by the use of less offensive language."[91] If a surgically neat form-content distinction is impossible, it remains true that the slope connecting the proscribing of Cohen's language in that particular context and banning or regulating Thoreau is not terribly slippery.

The more central problem is that, without projecting our own sentiments into *Cohen*, we simply cannot tell what "Fuck the Draft" means well enough to pass informed judgments as to its power, aptness, or effectiveness. We can, admittedly, dispute at the margins what Thoreau meant in a literal sense. But "Fuck the Draft," while it conveys enough meaning of a social character to cross the line into speech, is not far from a blank sheet of paper. Does it mean, roughly, as C. L. Stevenson might suggest, "I strongly disapprove of the draft," do so as well? Perhaps it means, in alienated fashion, "I strongly disapprove of the draft, but/and I don't care what you think": an entirely different message and one to which we know Thoreau would not have subscribed.

The grounds of the objection are not hinted at. The draft may be abhorrent for a variety of moral reasons or out of practical self-interest. Obviously, a slogan can say only so much, and it is unreasonable to expect a speaker to pack an expository essay into a slogan, but this only bespeaks the limited communicative value of slogans and the riskiness at best of assuming that a slogan, profane or otherwise, is likely to be particularly apt in expressing deep frustrations.[92] If we can't tell what Cohen meant at some level of

---

[89] Stone, note 4 *supra*, at 244.

[90] People v. Callahan, 168 Cal. App. 3d 631, 214 Cal. Rptr. 294, 296 (1985), op. withdrawn, cert. denied, 54 USLW 3484 (Jan. 21, 1986).

[91] FCC v. Pacifica Foundation, 438 U.S. 726, 743 n.18 (1978) (opinion of Stevens, J., joined by Burger, C. J., and Rehnquist, J.). Note that of these three, only Chief Justice Burger was available to joint the dissenters in *Cohen*.

[92] It is interesting to note that Cohen's expression scans well only with moderate-level alleged evil as a target. "Fuck Nazism," or "Fuck Genocide," or "Fuck Slavery," or "Fuck Terrorism" are uninspiring partly because of the abstractness of the institution denounced

detail, how can we know how well his slogan expressed his feelings?

An interesting assumption at work in the defense of *Cohen* is that a person's willingness consciously to violate basic norms of social propriety, etiquette, or concern for the sensibilities of others, including those of some of one's allies, implies that the person must feel more strongly, deeply, or intensely than the rest of us, or than Thoreau did, or than the person himself does on many other subjects.

This is a fallacy, though. Some of us simply have a low threshold of resort to predictably socially offensive behavior, quite apart from the intensity of our "feelings."[93] The feelings of others may simply not be thought to matter much. So even if we are to accord free speech protection to emotions, as opposed to ideas, we must not assume the emotion from the willingness to offend.

Occasionally, the more enthusiastic defenders of *Cohen* discuss social trends and touch on the incentives set up by *Cohen*.[94] One court has observed that "[w]hat is vulgar to one may be lyric to another. . . . Some people spew four-letter words as their common speech such as to devalue its currency; Billingsgate thus becomes commonplace."[95] This sort of argumentation, along with the observation that many words are less shocking now than they used to be,[96] is curiously reversible in its import. It would seem, all else equal, that the degeneration of language or of the quality of discussion is to be avoided. Any process of having to outbid one's competitors for linguistic shock effect, worked out as a kind of Gresham's

---

but also because they are immediately recognizable as adolescent-minded trivialization of the evils involved. We would not view them as "effective" or "powerful" statements.

[93] Consider the facial expression of the next person who violates the rules and breaches decorum by playing his radio aloud on the bus. Does he seem to have an unusually intense devotion to music that has resulted in the dictates of social propriety being outweighed? Or does he merely look as bored as the rest of us? We must not simply read fervor and commitment into Cohen-type situations.

[94] 403 U.S. at 25. See also Rutzick, note 86 *supra*, at 20; Bollinger, Free Speech and Intellectual Values, 92 Yale L.J. 438, 470 (1983). If one does not believe that there are long-term, subtle, but significant consequences flowing from this judicial relativism, one need not fear being soon confronted by clear, vigorous, empirical proof to the contrary. We tend to be skeptical that societies decay culturally, but we do recognize this phenomenon writ small, as in the obviously decaying morale of a baseball team as it slides toward the cellar.

[95] Callahan, note 90 *supra*.

[96] *Ibid.*

Law among the tokens of language, would similarly seem a bad thing.

Lost amid the relativism of *Cohen* is the obvious point that even if we cannot reliably tell vulgarity from lyric, we can reasonably well predict that what we view as lyric will or will not be found gratuitously offensive by substantial numbers of reasonably tolerant people. Protected speech may be rude or offensive, particularly where the rudeness or offensiveness is inseparable from the message. But elevating or at least maintaining the level or quality of the debate is a Millian value. While not all of us can rise to the level of a Daniel Webster or a Thoreau, this is not what the detractors of *Cohen* would require. The question is whether it would be constitutionally permissible, under the Free Speech Clause, to require an even slightly closer approach to the level of a Daniel Webster than *Cohen* manifests if we are to address the public. The aim is not to ban any usage per se or to disenfranchise the inarticulate but to require of all speakers a certain minimum, easily attained level of respect for the feelings of many among the audience. It has been suggested that[97]

> offensiveness is often an important part of a speaker's message. Use of offensive language reveals the existence of something offensive and ugly, whether in the situation described by the speaker or in the speaker's mind itself. In either event, the language reveals an important though unpleasant truth about the world. Suppressing this language violates a cardinal principle of a free society, that truths are better confronted than repressed. . . . We cannot expect to have, nor should we require, true civility in discourse until we achieve civility in society.

Of course, an assassination attempt on a popular political figure also may reveal an important truth, but the issue is whether the price is worth paying. By the time of Cohen's speech, the "truth" about the draft—that it was profoundly immoral, let us say—had already been "said" and was already generally "known." From contrary speech, we also already generally "knew" the "truth" that the draft was a fine thing. What we actually learned from Cohen's speech was mostly about Cohen, and, as we have seen, Cohen's speech told us very little about him or the state of his mind at all.

---

[97] Farber, note 82 *supra*, at 302.

What we learned probably qualifies as neither particularly unpleasant nor important.

At the time of Cohen's speech, no one doubted the controversiality of the draft or the willingness of many persons to speak indecorously. Nor is there, ultimately, any clear reason to hold a minimal civility in public discourse hostage until such a time as we have achieved civility in society. The former has not been shown to be an impediment to achieving the latter, and it may perhaps be its prerequisite. If the two forms of civility are causally independent, why not enjoy the former while we await the arrival of the latter? At a minimum, it is unclear why we are bound by the Free Speech Clause never to accord the effect of a given speech on the level of discussion any weight at all, even where the effect on the level of debate is undisputed.

Perhaps on the theory, though, that grievances are better aired than compulsorily bowdlerized, a recent Louisiana Court of Appeals case has, on the strength of *Cohen*, given free speech protection to the display on a pickup truck bumper of a sticker reading "Fuck Charles Foti, Jr."[98] Mr. Foti was a local sheriff. The court displayed no great interest in attempting to distinguish *Cohen*, perhaps on the grounds that, while a jacket may be discreetly taken off and folded up, there may be a felt necessity to park a truck in a given space regardless of the presence of, say, a school yard or playground in the vicinity.

Actually, it may be that the only way of distinguishing the case is to take the direct route. Except under rare circumstances not discussed in the *Foti* opinion itself, "Fuck Charles Foti, Jr." does not convey even a rudimentary social idea, even if Mr. Foti is relatively well known locally. Whether such an expression is printed on a bumper sticker, inscribed on a jacket, or chiseled in marble on the author's front lawn, it is, in most circumstances, simply too diffuse and "open" to significantly implicate Millian values, even granting that it rises in significance above mere random lettering. Unlike "Fuck the Draft," it does not even psychologically tie in with or trigger thoughts on any particular social issue.[99] Attempts at selec-

---

[98] See State v. Meyers, 462 So. 2d 227, 227 (La. Ct. App. 1984).

[99] Apparently, though, there are limits to Cohen's power to sanctify the emotive. In a recent case, the Seventh Circuit announced that it was unable to locate "any authority for the proposition that the first amendment . . . protects [a person's] right to kick and rock a video

tive enforcement should be obvious where the political context suggests that a particular idea, far from being so diffuse and open as to be unrecognizable, is actually being suppressed as unpopular or disfavored by the judge.

A much more common instance of Millian nonspeech involving the police, though often adjudicated as protected "low" speech, is that of directing streams of epithets, sometimes for remarkably prolonged periods of time, at an arresting or investigating police officer. Typically, the speaker is indignant, for reasons that are only rarely ascertainable from the judicial opinion, at the prior arrest of himself or a friend or relative.[100] One suspects that, in some of the cases, the motivation is simply the inconvenience associated with being arrested. Often, the purported speech is associated with a physical disturbance or resistance to arrest. Sometimes a crowd gathers. In a noteworthy proportion of the cases, the speaker appears to have been drinking immoderately. Despite perhaps even an intent to offend, and the absence of any social idea being communicated,[101] the purported speech is often judicially protected as free speech,[102] the disorderly conduct or breach of

---

game to retrieve fifty cents." Friedman v. Village of Skokie, 763 F.2d 236, 239 (7th Cir. 1985). In this case, the coin return had been welded inoperable and a no-refund policy instituted. *Cohen* was not mentioned, despite the obvious possibility of arguing for a largely emotive, and perhaps efficacious, "expressive" protest over a legitimate or imagined "grievance." Apparently, no property was damaged or threatened, and mere words would not have sufficed, under the circumstances. See *id.* at 237. If it turned out that Mr. Friedman did not literally speak in the course of having "attracted the attention of 20 to 30 people who looked on," *ibid.*, it must be pointed out that constitutionally protected nude dancers need not keep up a monologue.

[100] It is difficult to envision the typical defendant as exercising autonomy in the literal form of Kantian legislation. See Kant, The Fundamental Principles of the Metaphysic of Ethics 38, 47, 52 (Manthey-Zorn ed. 1966).

[101] Occasionally, a brief, unelaborated reference to the race of one or more of the officers is made. See, *e.g.*, State in re W. B., 461 So. 2d 366, 368 (La. Ct. App. 1984). A coherent focus on the unjustness of "the system" would also help the defendant in Millian terms.

[102] When such results are reached, the most typical rationale is that the police are or should be inured to abusive language, that they did not in fact react to the verbal provocation, and that they are paid to not be provoked and are under a legal duty in that regard. The case is therefore held not to fall within the scope of the "fighting words" exception laid down in Chaplinsky v. New Hampshire, 315 U.S. 568 (1942). Sometimes the strand of the Chaplinsky test focusing on the tendency of the language to inflict injury drops out of the analysis entirely. See, *e.g.*, Harbin v. State, 358 So. 2d 856 (Fla. Ct. App. 1978); Rutzick, note 86 *supra*, at 22–27. Police restraint or indifference, however, does not add social content to the prior "speech." Occasionally, the invective is defended on a theory of the beneficial effects of catharsis. See, *e.g.*, Redish, note 22 *supra*, at 626. While theories of catharsis or of "blowing off steam" in various contexts have a long and distinguished intellectual pedigree, the experimental support for such theories is limited at best. See J. Goldstein, Aggression and Crimes

peace charge dismissed, and any "reasonably necessary" force used physically to resist the "illegal" arrest immunized.

An example, selected for the moderation, and not the extremity, of its facts, would be the case of *State v. Montgomery*.[103] The appellant in *Montgomery* initiated the incident by loudly shouting a series of profanities, for example, "fucking pigs, fucking pig ass hole,"[104] at 10:50 P.M. on a cold February night in downtown Seattle as the two targeted police officers were passing by on patrol in their car. When the police stopped to investigate, the appellant, who was eventually charged with possession of marijuana, continued in a similar linguistic vein. Eventually, it was determined that a recent drinking citation had left the fifteen-year-old appellant irate.

Despite repeated attempts to settle the appellant down, he continued to express himself loudly. Eventually a crowd gathered, which, though sizable enough to block the sidewalk, was not itself threatening or hostile. The appellant did not physically threaten the officers and was not carrying a weapon. Largely because of the sidewalk blocking, the appellant was, after a total of about five to ten minutes, arrested and charged with disorderly conduct and possession of a controlled substance.

On appeal, the convictions for disorderly conduct and for possession of marijuana were reversed on free speech grounds,[105] with the court citing *Chaplinsky* and *Cohen* and determining that the appellant's conduct deserved moral, but not legal, "censure and rebuke."[106] The majority, unmoved by a dissenter's observation that "I fail to see that the 'freedom of speech' contemplated by the First Amendment has anything whatsoever to do with this case,"[107] in-

---

of Violence 36, 48, 50, 53, 55, 164 (1975). It is certainly equally plausible to suppose that tolerating, if not actually rewarding, prolonged screaming at police officers legitimizes or encourages such behavior. In any event, this kind of theorizing would not seem to fall within the special competence of the judiciary.

[103] 31 Wash. App. 745, 644 P.2d 747 (1982).

[104] *Id.* at 747–48, 644 P.2d at 748–49.

[105] *Id.* at 760, 644 P.2d at 756.

[106] *Ibid.* Courts that reverse misdemeanor convictions on this kind of analysis often seek, at least rhetorically, to have it both ways. In one case, the conviction was reversed, but the defendant was solemnly informed that the special restraint required of the police "does not give the public a right to abuse a police officer." People v. Justus, 57 Ill. App. 3d 164, 167, 372 N.E.2d 1115, 1118 (1978). Presumably, a constitutional right is indeed some sort of a right.

[107] 31 Wash. App. at 761, 644 P.2d at 757.

stead noted the "commonplace" nature of the language employed.[108]

The logical centerpiece of the majority's own independent analysis of the issues noted that[109]

> were the use of the invectives and vulgarisms used by the defendant to be held to be grounds for arrest, a number of professional tennis players and other public figures in sports and entertainment would be subject to arrest for their language, oft repeated.

Shrinking from this disturbing prospect, the court in effect constitutionalized its own weighting of the competing interests involved. Because there are some sound, practical reasons for not arresting tennis players, free speech must be involved.[110]

But it is not a mere verbal quibble to distinguish, for Millian value or free speech purposes, between the proposition that fifteen-year-olds, including the speaker, should be permitted publicly to drink or to smoke marijuana, and the almost purely emotive expressions of a negative attitude, of some sort, toward one's own arrest. If no particular grounds for concluding that the original arrest was unfair or discriminatory or arbitrary or illegitimate are given, we are left merely with a negative attitude toward one's own arrest, in particular, principle aside. Verbalizing merely this attitude does not rise to the level of a recognizable attempt to convey or express a social idea in the relevant sense.[111] If a social idea is not present, the fact that the target of verbal abuse did not or, if reasonable, would

---

[108] *Id.* at 756 n.2, 644 P.2d at 754 n.2. Courts rarely pause to inquire whether there may be any connection between the increasing frequency of "reprehensible and disgraceful" language and their own increasing inclination to protect it on free speech grounds. See *id.* at 760, 644 P.2d at 756.

[109] *Ibid.*

[110] Perhaps part of the problem is that affirming a disorderly conduct or breach of peace conviction involves at least some modest cost to the particular, identifiable individual defendant, whereas on the other side of the ledger, a presumably desensitized police officer aside, there are only abstract, longer term principles and broader policy considerations, the validity of many of which cannot be rigorously demonstrated.

[111] The role in the analysis of the defendant's use of profanity becomes equivocal, particularly in light of the inclination of some courts to focus exclusively on a threat of breach of peace issue, rather than the injurious offensiveness of the language, in *Chaplinsky*-type cases. See Gooding v. Wilson, 405 U.S. 518 (1972); see also note 102 *supra*. There is sometimes the sentiment that the disorderly conduct conviction should be upheld even if, under the circumstances, the defendant had loudly and prolongedly recited nursery rhymes. See, *e.g.*, Morris v. State, 335 So. 2d 1, 2 (Fla. 1976); Mesarosh v. State, 459 N.E.2d 426, 430 (Ind. Ct. App. 1984) (Young, J., concurring).

Yet it is difficult to believe that courts would not take into consideration the saltiness of the language if a loud, extended, socially pointless tirade were directed by a nonthreatening

not be expected to breach the peace in response is not relevant to the adjudication of the free speech constitutional claim.[112]

VI. Conclusion

Obviously, the notion of "Millian" values has a broader range of operation than its application to the cases here considered. Perhaps they are more readily invoked in the cases noted than in more controversial areas of application, such as the realm of defamation and dissemination of commercial information or misinformation. I meant here only to start a debate, not to conclude it. Understandably, we should be leery about not crediting a free speech claim. But it should be clear that not every principled attempt to limit the expansion of the scope of coverage of the Free Speech Clause reflects a desire to impose orthodoxy or to root out error. While the scope of the Clause should not be artificially circumscribed, as by narrowing its coverage to plainly political issues, neither should it be assumed that the Free Speech Clause has a scope unrelated to its recognizable purposes.[113]

---

defendant, say, at a nun. We may assume that the nun would not be expected to breach the peace by reacting violently. At least she would be under a recognizable duty not to do so. This scenario is what currently passes for a fiendishly difficult free speech case. While no nun abuse case appears to have been recently decided on appeal, there is the interesting meter maid abuse case of Commonwealth v. Mastrangelo, 489 Pa. 254, 414 A.2d 54, appeal dismissed, 449 U.S. 894 (1980). In *Mastrangelo*, the disorderly conduct conviction was upheld despite the lack of evidence of any immediate breach of the peace. The court may have been moved by the fact that the absence of any breach of the peace may have been attributable to the meter maid's having been too frightened to patrol in the area of the defendant's car for a week. The court may also have believed that the injuring, desensitizing process is confined to regular police officers, as opposed to meter maids. *Cf.* People v. John V., 167 Cal. App. 3d 761, 213 Cal. Rptr. 503 (1985) (sixteen-year-old civilian female target of repeated profane abuse; previous reaction by target included swinging baseball bat at offender and hitting boyfriend instead; speaker's conviction upheld under free speech challenge).

[112] The sociological richness of the "fighting words" cases is only hinted at by the examples cited above. See also Wilson v. Attaway, 757 F.2d 1227 (11th Cir. 1985); Bovey v. City of Lafayette, 586 F. Supp. 1460 (N.D. Ind. 1984); aff'd mem., 774 F.2d 1166 (7th Cir. 1985); State v. Beckenbach, 1 Conn. App. 669, 476 A.2d 591 (Conn. 1984); State v. Nelson, 38 Conn. Super. 349, 448 A.2d 214 (1982); Cavazos v. State, 455 N.E.2d 618 (Ind. Ct. App. 1983); State v. Beck, 9 Kan. App. 2d 459, 682 P.2d 137 (1984); State in re W. B., 461 So. 2d 366 (La. Ct. App. 1984); State v. John W., 418 A.2d 1097 (Me. 1980); State v. Groves, 219 Neb. 382, 363 N.W.2d 507 (1985); People v. DuPont, 107 A.D.2d 247, 486 N.Y.S.2d 169 (1985); City of Seattle v. Camby, 38 Wash. App. 462, 685 P.2d 665 (1984), rev'd, 104 Wash. 2d 49, 701 P.2d 499 (1985) (en banc); State v. Yoakum, 30 Wash. App. 874, 638 P.2d 1264 (1982).

[113] Confining the application of the Free Speech Clause to its defensible and proper scope might well vaguely and minimally advantage some persons and disadvantage others in certain contexts, but these effects cannot in principle extend to conflicts between recognizable interest groups, parties, or political forces and causes. Social cause speech remains within the scope of speech and cannot be legitimately exiled as nonspeech.

GEOFFREY P. MILLER

INTERSTATE BANKING
IN THE COURT

Banking has undergone a revolution in the past decade. One can no longer recognize a bank just by looking at its housing. Many enterprises offering banklike services turn out not to be banks at all. And banks or bank holding companies are doing very "unbanklike" things—brokering stocks, operating mutual funds, performing commercial messenger services, even distributing ordinary merchandise through mail order catalogues. Bankers, for their part, have become aggressive marketers and creative competitors in a rapidly evolving financial marketplace. In banking today, there is much that is being done for the first time.

The causes of this revolution are manifold. Changes in technology have enabled bankers to offer diverse packages of financial services and to communicate instantaneously in a world financial market. Inflation and high nominal interest rates have destroyed the comfortable world of government-imposed price controls for bank products. New, unregulated competitors have appeared on the scene. And the old guard bankers have ceded the field to a new generation who knew not the Great Depression and its trauma.

Geoffrey P. Miller is Assistant Professor of Law, The Law School, The University of Chicago.

AUTHOR'S NOTE: Financial support for this article was provided by the John M. Olin and the Sarah Scaife Foundations. I would like to thank Douglas G. Baird, Daniel R. Fischel, Roberta Karmel, and Cass R. Sunstein for helpful comments and Jeremy Hobbs for valuable research assistance.

Among the principal causes of these changes, one is conspicuously absent. It is sobering, if edifying, to realize that banking, the world's most regulated industry, is evolving in almost blithe disregard of regulatory constraints. The industry has changed through the use of previously dormant statutory powers, through the aggressive manipulation of loopholes, or (sometimes) in apparent disregard of well-established legal principles. But legislators and the regulators have not forced the action. They have been relegated to cleaning up after the party—closing loopholes, ratifying changes that have occurred extralegally, or removing regulatory constraints in order to allow banks and thrift institutions to survive competition from their unregulated rivals. "Deregulation" has indeed taken place, but it has not been the result of deliberate policy initiatives on the part of the legislative or executive branches.

The courts, for their part, have faced something of a dilemma. Because of pervasive anticompetitive regulation, the financial services industry is fractured into many different groups and subgroups, each jealously guarding the economic rents that it has appropriated while enviously eyeing the rents appropriated by others. Poaching by any party instantly triggers a lawsuit. How should the court decide? The governing statutes are hopelessly dated, both with regard to the structure of the industry and to the theory of competition and regulation on which they depend. Strictly following the rules would often be awkward, to say the least, and might sometimes be nonsensical. But bending the rules to account for changes in mores—or markets—would be untrue to the charge one is trying to fulfill.

This judicial dilemma was acutely illustrated last Term in the so-called "Regional Banking Compact Case," *Northeast Bancorp, Inc. v. Board of Governors.*[1] At issue was the legality of state laws that allowed bank holding companies from certain states, but not others, to establish or acquire subsidiary banks within the regulating state. In upholding these laws against statutory and constitutional challenge, the Supreme Court paved the way for the regionalization of the nation's banking industry.

---

[1] 105 S.Ct. 2545 (1985).

I. Legal and Economic Background of the Decision

A. LEGAL REGULATION OF INTERSTATE BANKING

The banking system in this country has long been contained by geographic barriers. Although the First and Second Banks of the United States branched nationwide,[2] state banks were typically unit banks (limited to a single office) and had no authority to branch interstate. The state pattern of unit banking was carried over into the system of national banks established in 1864 by the National Banking Act.[3]

When the states began to permit branching by state banks within the state of origin, the national banks were placed at a competitive disadvantage because they could not offer their customers the convenience of a branch network. Congress partially rectified the disparity in 1927 with the McFadden Act,[4] which permitted national banks to branch within the borders of their home city if state banks were permitted to do so. National banks were still at a disadvantage, however, because they could not branch outside their home city even when state chartered banks could do so. Accordingly, Congress amended the McFadden Act in 1933 to permit national banks to branch within a state on the same terms and conditions as state banks.[5]

While both state and national banks can now branch intrastate as permitted by state law, there has never been a corresponding authority to branch into other states. The McFadden Act prohibits

---

[2] Huertas, The Regulation of Financial Institutions: A Historical Perspective on Current Issues, in Financial Services—The Changing Institutions and Government Policy 6, 8 (Benston ed. 1983). The Second Bank of the United States operated branches in twenty different states and the District of Columbia. Remini, Andrew Jackson and the Bank War 26 n.18 (1967).

[3] Huertas, note 2 supra, at 13.

[4] Act of Feb. 25, 1927, ch. 191, § 7, 44 Stat. 1224, 1228–29 (current version at 12 U.S.C. § 36(c) (1982)). The Comptroller of the Currency had earlier permitted national banks to establish nonbank "teller's windows" that could take deposits but could not make loans. See Huertas, note 2 supra. It appeared for a time as if national banks would eventually obtain full branching privileges without the need for new legislation. The Supreme Court destroyed these hopes in 1924 when it ruled that national banks had no authority to establish full service branches. First National Bank in St. Louis v. State of Missouri ex rel. Barrett, 263 U.S. 640 (1924).

[5] Banking Act of 1933, ch. 89, § 23, 48 Stat. 162, 189–90.

interstate branching by national banks and state banks that belong to the Federal Reserve System.[6] State nonmember banks are not expressly prohibited by federal law from branching into other states. Most state banking statutes, however, prohibit out-of-state banks from branching into the state.[7]

These branching limitations restricted the activities of state and national banks to areas smaller than their natural markets. In the 1950s the banking community discovered that these limits could be circumvented through holding companies. A bank would turn itself into a subsidiary of a holding company, which could then establish or acquire new subsidiary banks located outside the original bank's branching area. The holding company allowed banking organizations to expand not only within a state but also to other states. Moreover, nonbank subsidiaries of the holding company could engage in all sorts of activities prohibited to the bank itself. The holding company loophole undermined the entire system of legal restrictions on bank expansion.

Congress rescued the system—temporarily—with the Bank Holding Company Act of 1956 (BHCA).[8] The BHCA limited bank holding companies[9] to activities that resembled the activities already permissible for banks.[10] And it generally prohibited bank holding companies from acquiring or establishing subsidiary banks in more than one state.[11]

Congress did not, however, completely prohibit interstate ex-

---

[6] See 12 U.S.C. § 36(c) (1982) (national banks); *id.* § 321 (1982) (member banks).

[7] Ginsburg, Interstate Banking, 9 Hofstra L. Rev. 1133, 1166 (1981). For a suggestion that state chartered banks might be used as a means of penetrating into regional banking regions from outside, see Miller, A Different Approach to Interstate Banking, American Banker, August 8, 1985, at 4; Miller, Interstate Branching and the Constitution, 41 Business Lawyer 337 (1986).

[8] Bank Holding Company Act of 1956, 70 Stat. 133 (codified at 12 U.S.C. §§ 1841–50 (1982)).

[9] The BHCA originally applied only to multibank holding companies—organizations controlling two or more banks. It was amended in 1970 to cover single bank holding companies as well. 84 Stat. 1760 (current version at 12 U.S.C. § 1841 [1982]).

[10] See § 4(c)(8) of the BHCA, 12 U.S.C. § 1843(c)(8) (1982); 12 C.F.R. § 225.4 (1985) (Regulation Y).

[11] 12 U.S.C. § 1842(d)(1) (1982). Existing interstate bank holding company networks were grandfathered. The largest such organization, First Interstate Bancorporation, has 626 interstate offices in 11 states. Whitehead, Interstate Banking: Probability or Reality? Economic Review of the Federal Reserve Bank of Atlanta 6 (March 1985). These networks, however, are not major factors in the current marketplace evolution toward interstate banking.

pansion by bank holding companies. The "Douglas Amendment"[12] gave the states the option to allow entry by bank holding companies from other states. The Douglas Amendment provides that interstate acquisitions by bank holding companies are permitted if they are "specifically authorized by the statute laws of the state in which [the acquired] bank is located, by language to that effect and not merely by implication."

These, then, are the legal restraints on interstate bank expansion: state banks are generally forbidden to branch interstate by provisions of state law; national banks are forbidden to branch interstate by the McFadden Act; and bank holding companies are forbidden to establish or acquire subsidiary banks in other states unless the state legislature has expressly allowed the expansion. The law seems firmly established that banks are to do their business within the borders of the state in which they are chartered or have their principal place of business.

B. THE MARKETPLACE REALITIES

In banking law, however, as in other areas of economic regulation, the market often mocks the laws. Geographic limitations on banking operations have proved porous in the extreme.[13] Banks found any number of ways to do business interstate. Grandfathered interstate holding companies continued their operations.[14] Banking chains—groups of banks linked by common ownership but not held in holding company form—expanded across state lines.[15] Commercial loan officers trekked the country soliciting business for big money center banks in California, Illinois, and New York. Bank holding companies established nonbank subsidiaries to perform all sorts of banklike services free of geographic

---

[12] 12 U.S.C. § 1842(d)(1) (1982). The amendment is named after its sponsor, Senator Paul H. Douglas of Illinois.

[13] See generally U.S. Dept. of the Treasury, Geographic Restrictions on Commercial Banking in the United States—The Report of the President (1981) (hereafter cited as "Treasury Report") (discussing de facto system of interstate banking); Horvitz, Alternative Avenues to Interstate Banking, Economic Review of the Federal Reserve Bank of Atlanta 32 (May 1983).

[14] See note 11 *supra*.

[15] See Interstate Chain Banking, Majority Staff Report to the Subcommittee on Financial Institutions Supervision, Regulation, and Insurance of the House Committee on Banking, Finance and Urban Affairs, 99th Cong., 1st Sess. (May 20, 1985) (128 interstate bank chains).

limitations.[16] Banks established brick and mortar loan production offices in other states which solicited business subject to "approval" in the home office;[17] provided international banking services through interstate "Edge Act" subsidiaries;[18] supplied a substantial portion of the nation's consumer credit through nationwide credit card operations; offered deposit, cash dispensing, and other consumer banking services across state lines through automated teller machine networks;[19] acquired failing thrift institutions located in other states;[20] solicited deposits from other states through the mails[21] or by retaining the services of professional deposit brokers;[22]

---

[16] Many of the services on the Federal Reserve Board's "laundry list" of activities permissible for nonbank subsidiaries of bank holding companies are also permissible for subsidiary banks. See Ginsburg, Interstate Banking, 9 Hofstra L. Rev. 1133, 1162–63 (1981). As of early 1985 there were over 5,500 interstate offices serving 328 nonbank subsidiaries of 139 bank holding companies. Whitehead, note 11 supra, at 9.

[17] See 12 C.F.R. § 7.7380 (1985). As of early 1985 there were 202 interstate loan production offices, operated by forty-four different banking organizations in thirty-four states. Whitehead, note 11 supra, at 8.

[18] See 12 U.S.C. §§ 611–632 (1982) (Edge Act). As of early 1985 there were 143 interstate Edge Act offices, operated by forty-nine domestic banking organizations. Whitehead, note 11 supra, at 9.

[19] An automated teller machine (ATM) owned or rented by a national bank is considered a "branch" for purposes of the McFadden Act and therefore cannot be established across state lines. Independent Bankers Ass'n v. Smith, 534 F.2d 921 (D.C. Cir.), cert. denied sub. nom. Bloom v. Independent Bankers Ass'n, 429 U.S. 862 (1976). However, an ATM is most likely not a branch for McFadden Act purposes if the bank merely participates in a shared ATM network on a fee-for-service basis. See Independent Bankers Ass'n of New York State v. Marine Midland Bank, 757 F.2d 453 (2d Cir. 1985), pet. for cert. filed, June 27, 1985; 12 C.F.R. § 5.31(b) (1985). As of 1984 there were roughly 200 ATM networks operating on an interstate basis, serving over 7,500 commercial banks with more than 16,000 ATMs. Statement of Michael A. Mancusi, Senior Deputy Comptroller of the Currency, in Status of ATM's under State Branching Laws, Hearings on S. 2898 before the Senate Comm. on Banking, Housing and Urban Affairs, 98th Cong., 2d Sess. (1984).

[20] See, e.g., Citicorp, 70 Fed. Res. Bull. 149 (1984) (approving Citicorp's acquisition of First Federal Savings and Loan Association of Chicago, a failing Illinois thrift with $4 billion in assets and sixty-two offices); Citicorp, 70 Fed. Res. Bull. 157 (1984) (approving Citicorp's acquisition of New Biscayne Federal Savings and Loan Association, a failing Florida thrift with $1.9 billion in assets and thirty-five offices).

[21] See Weinstein, "Check's in the Mail" is Music to Some, American Banker, August 12, 1985, at 1 (reporting on bank programs to gather deposits from consumers around the country by persuading them to mail their funds to addresses in New York, Delaware, and South Dakota).

[22] The activities of deposit brokers have become so pervasive as to stimulate attempts by the Federal Deposit Insurance Corporation and the Federal Savings and Loan Insurance Corporation to deny federal deposit insurance to certain forms of deposit brokerage thought to be detrimental to the safety and soundness of banking institutions. See Proposed Restrictions on Money Brokers, Hearing before a Subcommittee of the House Committee on Government Operations, 98th Cong., 2d Sess. (1984). These regulations, however, have been overturned in court. FAIC Securities, Inc. v. United States, 768 F.2d 352 (D.C. Cir. 1985).

and established "stakeout" positions in out-of-state banking firms in order to have a head start on the competition if and when a full acquisition were legally permissible.[23] The list could be extended.

All these devices permit substantial interstate activity by banks. But none compares with that wonderful oxymoronic creature, the nonbank bank. In most respects the nonbank bank is just like any other bank. It is chartered by the state or federal authorities; it is entitled to federal deposit insurance; it has access to the Federal Reserve Board's discount window; it has the power to do almost anything ordinary banks can do. But the nonbank bank is not a "bank" for purposes of the BHCA. That statute defines a bank as an institution that *both* accepts demand deposits *and* engages in the business of making commercial loans.[24] The definition implies that an institution can accept demand deposits and make personal loans without being classified as a bank under the Act, so long as it doesn't make commercial loans. This is the so-called "consumer bank." Or an institution can make both commercial and personal loans and offer various deposit accounts with transaction features, so long as the customer doesn't have a legal right to withdraw the funds on demand. The institution could even offer NOW accounts, which are technically savings deposits even though in practice they are nothing more than interest-bearing checking accounts.[25] Other permutations are possible.

It requires but little imagination to see the stunning power of the nonbank bank. Because it is not a "bank" for purposes of the BHCA, it is not subject to that statute's limitations on interstate banking. A bank holding company could establish national nonbank banks in all fifty states regardless of whether the state legislatures have authorized such expansion. The nonbank bank's potential to destroy the putative limits on interstate banking was first demonstrated by the Dimension Financial Corporation, a Colorado-based financial company which sought national bank charters for nonbank banks in twenty-five different states.[26] It was

---

[23] See Huston v. Board of Governors, 758 F.2d 275 (8th Cir. 1985).

[24] 12 U.S.C. § 1841(c)(1982) (" 'bank' means any institution . . . which (1) accepts deposits that the depositor has a legal right to withdraw on demand, and (2) engages in the business of making commercial loans").

[25] See First Bancorporation v. Board of Governors, 728 F.2d 434 (10th Cir. 1984); Oklahoma Bankers Ass'n v. Federal Reserve Board, 766 F.2d 1446 (10th Cir. 1985).

[26] King, Nonbank Banks: What Next? Economic Review of the Federal Reserve Bank of Atlanta 40, 41 (May 1985).

obvious that if Dimension's application succeeded, then all bets were off so far as interstate banking was concerned.

The subsequent history of the nonbank bank epitomizes the complex politics of banking in this country. The Comptroller of the Currency, carrying out free-market policies of the Reagan Administration, endorsed the concept of interstate expansion through federally chartered nonbank banks but bowed to political pressure and declared a moratorium on the granting of such charters in order to give Congress time to act.[27] In Congress, there was widespread consensus that the nonbank bank loophole should be closed, and bills to close it were introduced in both houses.[28] But the movement foundered on a disagreement between the House and Senate on whether banks should be allowed to engage in expanded product lines. The Comptroller thereupon announced an end to his moratorium.[29] The Federal Reserve Board, for its part, broke with the Comptroller and attempted to plug the nonbank bank loophole by expanding the definition of "commercial loan" to include various money market instruments that banks commonly include in their portfolios of liquid assets and by broadening the definition of demand deposits to include NOW accounts and other arrangements that are functionally similar to checks.[30] The Court of Appeals for the Tenth Circuit, however, overturned both parts of the Board's regulation.[31] The Supreme Court recently upheld the Tenth Circuit's decision.[32]

In the meantime, the Federal Reserve Board reluctantly abandoned its opposition and began to approve applications by bank holding companies for interstate nonbank banks.[33] Word of the Fed's surrender precipitated an avalanche of applications for non-

---

[27] See letter from Comptroller C. T. Conover to Rep. Fernand St. Germain, April 5, 1983, reprinted in CCH Fed. Banking L. Rep. ¶ 99,528 (1982–1983 Transfer Binder).

[28] S. 2851, 98th Cong., 2d Sess. (1984); H.R. 5916, 98th Cong., 2d Sess. (1984).

[29] Statement by C. T. Conover, Comptroller of the Currency, October 15, 1984, reprinted in CCH Fed. Banking L. Rep. ¶ 86,083 (Current Binder).

[30] 12 C.F.R. § 225.2(a)(1)(ii)(A) (1985).

[31] First Bancorporation v. Board of Governors, 728 F.2d 434 (10th Cir. 1984); Dimension Financial Corporation v. Board of Governors, 744 F.2d 1402 (10th Cir. 1984), cert. granted, 105 S.Ct. 2137 (1985). See also Oklahoma Bankers Ass'n v. Federal Reserve Board, 766 F.2d 1446 (10th Cir., July 9, 1985).

[32] Board of Governors v. Dimension Financial Corp., 106 S.Ct. 681 (1986).

[33] See U.S. Trust Corporation, 70 Fed. Res. Bull. 371 (1984).

bank banks from all parts of the country. Enter the Court of Appeals for the Eleventh Circuit, which, in a broadly worded opinion, declared interstate nonbank banks contrary to the congressional purpose of giving states the option whether to allow entry by out-of-state bank holding companies.[34] Meanwhile, a district court enjoined the Comptroller of the Currency from issuing any more interstate nonbank bank charters on the ground that such institutions are not authorized by the chartering provisions of the National Bank Act.[35] Several states enacted legislation barring nonbank banks.[36] And the House Banking Committee has reported legislation that would close the nonbank bank loophole.[37] At present writing, the nonbank bank, remains a serious threat to the continued vitality of rules against interstate banking.

C. THE REGIONAL BANKING MOVEMENT

Interstate banking can also be accomplished pursuant to state statutes that lift the Douglas Amendment ban on interstate bank holding company expansion. Such statutes can take a number of forms. The first states to lift the ban allowed out-of-state bank holding companies to charter only limited-purpose banks in the state.[38] The evident object of these statutes was to bring jobs into the state without subjecting the state's own banks to increased competition. Other states opened their borders to any and all out-of-state bank holding companies; these tended to be geographically remote states, such as Maine and Alaska, that wished to attract capital to their borders and that did not have an entrenched local

---

[34] Florida Dept. of Banking and Finance v. Board of Governors, 760 F.2d 1135 (11th Cir. 1985). The Supreme Court has vacated and remanded this decision in light of *Dimension Financial. U.S. Trust Corp.* v. *Board of Governors*, 54 USLW 3493 (Jan. 27, 1986).

[35] Independent Bankers Association v. Conover, No. 84-1403 (N.D. Fla., December 14, 1984).

[36] See Easton, States Attempt Fill Banking Enforcement Gap, Legal Times of Washington, January 28, 1985, at 17. These laws may be constitutionally suspect. See Hinkle & Rushdoony, States May Lack Authority to Bar Nonbank Banks, Legal Times of Washington, April 1, 1985, at 17.

[37] H.R. 20, 99th Cong., 1st Sess. (1985). The house bill would redefine a "bank" as an entity that is insured by the FDIC or that is a state or federally chartered institution that makes commercial loans and also accepts demand deposits or other accounts withdrawable for payment to third parties. See H.R. Rep. No. 174, 99th Cong., 1st Sess. (1985).

[38] See, *e.g.*, S.D. Codified Laws Ann. §§ 51-16-40, 41 (1984); 5 Del. Code Ann. §§ 801 *et seq.* (Supp. 1984).

banking lobby.[39] Still other states permitted entry on a reciprocal basis—that is, an out-of-state bank holding company was allowed to enter a state if the home state of the entering bank holding company permitted similar entry by bank holding companies head-quartered in the forum state.[40]

The regional banking movement, the subject of the *Northeast Bancorp* suit, is the latest of these variants on Douglas Amendment legislation. Born in New England, the cradle of recent banking innovations,[41] a regional bank statute is simply a state law that permits entry only by bank holding companies located in a defined region of the country. Massachusetts, which passed the first such law in the waning days of 1982,[42] limited its statute to bank holding companies with their principal places of business in Connecticut, Maine, Vermont, New Hampshire, or Rhode Island. Conspicuously absent from this list was New York. It was well understood by all concerned that the omission was intentional. The giant New York bank holding companies—Citicorp, Chase Manhattan Corporation, Manufacturers Hanover Corporation and their ilk—were not welcome to the Boston party. This pattern of excluding banks from money center states has been repeated in other existing or proposed regional banking areas.

II. THE NORTHEAST BANCORP CASE

The New England compact, the original regional banking arrangement, was the first to face judicial challenge. At issue were three interstate acquisitions. The Bank of New England Corporation, a Massachusetts bank holding company, sought to acquire CBT Corporation, a Connecticut bank holding company; Hartford National Corporation, a Connecticut bank holding company,

---

[39] See, *e.g.*, Alaska Stat. § 06.05.235 (Supp. 1984); Me. Rev. Stat. tit. 9-B, § 1013 (Supp. 1984).

[40] See, *e.g.*, New York Banking Law § 141, 142-b (McKinney Supp. 1984).

[41] The NOW account, currently available nationwide, was developed in Massachusets and New Hampshire and was first congressionally authorized on an experimental basis only for banking organizations in the New England region. See S. Rep. No. 368, 96th Cong., 2d Sess., at 7–8 (1980). The development of the NOW account is entertainingly recounted in Mayer, The Bankers 176–79 (1974).

[42] Mass. Gen. Laws Ann. ch. 167A, § 2 (West 1971 & Supp. 1984).

sought to acquire Altru Bancorporation, a Massachusetts bank
holding company; and Bank of Boston Corporation, a Massachusetts bank holding company, sought to acquire Colonial Bancorp,
Inc., a Connecticut bank holding company.[43] Each of these acquisitions was submitted to the Federal Reserve Board for approval as
required under the BHCA.[44] The applications were opposed by
Citicorp, the huge New York bank holding company, which complained that Connecticut and Massachusetts had acted illegally in
excluding New York from their enabling statutes. The eponymous
Northeast Bancorp, Inc., a Connecticut bank holding company,
joined in opposing one of the applications. Northeast had agreed to
be acquired by the Bank of New York Corporation, a New York
bank holding company, if and when such an acquisition was legally
permissible.[45]

The Board approved all three acquisitions.[46] The Second Circuit
upheld the Board's order.[47] On writ of certiorari, the Supreme
Court affirmed in an opinion by Justice Rehnquist.[48]

A. THE OPINION

The most significant question in *Northeast Bancorp* was the meaning of the Douglas Amendment. If the Douglas Amendment barred
regional banking compacts, then the Connecticut and Massachusetts statutes would be illegal on statutory grounds and the Court
would have no occasion to address the constitutional issues. If, on
the other hand, the Douglas Amendment authorized these statutes,
then the constitutional analysis would be considerably simplified
since Congress would have approved the state action under attack.
Accordingly, it was to this issue of statutory interpretation that
Justice Rehnquist turned first.

---

[43] See Northeast Bancorp, Inc. v. Board of Governors, 740 F.2d 203, 204 (2d Cir. 1984),
aff'd, 105 S.Ct. 2545 (1985).

[44] Section 3(a) of the BHCA, 12 U.S.C. § 1842(a) (1982).

[45] Brief of Petitioners Northeast Bancorp, Inc. and Union Trust Co., at 3.

[46] 70 Fed. Res. Bul. 353; *id.* at 376; *id.* at 524.

[47] Northeast Bancorp, Inc. v. Board of Governors, 740 F.2d 203 (2d Cir. 1984), aff'd, 105
S.Ct. 2545 (1985).

[48] 105 S.Ct. 2545 (1985). Justice O'Connor filed a concurring opinion and Justice Powell
did not participate.

In accordance with axiomatic interpretative principles,[49] Justice Rehnquist looked first to the language of the Douglas Amendment. The language, however, did not resolve the legality of regional banking compacts; while such compacts were not excluded, neither were they specifically authorized by the amendment.[50] In the absence of dispositive language, Justice Rehnquist turned to the legislative history.[51] And in the legislative history he found a "sufficient indication of Congress' intent"[52] to permit regional banking compacts.

This legislative history consisted of two statements by Senator Douglas during floor debate. The Senator announced that his proposed amendment would allow bank holding companies to acquire banks in other states "to the degree" that state laws expressly permit them to do so[53] and stated further that his proposal carried the provisions of the McFadden Act over to the holding company form.[54] Justice Rehnquist interpreted these remarks to mean that state power to permit out-of-state entry was a matter of degree; states were not limited to the binary choices of nationwide entry or nothing. Congress, in the McFadden Act, had decided to subject national banks to the same branching limits as applied to state banks in the state. But states were not limited to an all-or-nothing choice about branching; they could adopt statewide branching, limit branching to specified regions within a state, or prohibit branching altogether. By analogy, the Douglas Amendment gives states the power to allow nationwide bank holding company entry or to limit entry to particular regions of the country. Ergo, regional compacts were authorized by the Douglas Amendment.

Justice Rehnquist then turned to the only substantial constitu-

---

[49] For example, BankAmerica Corp. v. United States, 462 U.S. 122, 128 (1983); North Dakota v. United States, 460 U.S. 300, 312 (1983); Watt v. Alaska, 451 U.S. 259, 266–67 (1981); American Textile Manufacturers Institute v. Donovan, 452 U.S. 490, 545–47 (1981) (Rehnquist, J., dissenting); Blue Chip Stamps v. Manor Drug Stores, 421 U.S. 723, 756 (Powell, J., concurring).

[50] 105 S.Ct. at 2551.

[51] Ibid.

[52] Ibid.

[53] 105 S.Ct. at 2552, quoting 102 Cong. Rec. 6858 (1956).

[54] 105 S.Ct. at 2552, quoting 102 Cong. Rec. 6869 (1956) ("our amendment will permit out-of-state holding companies to acquire banks in other States only to the degree that State laws expressly permit them; and that is the provision of the McFadden Act").

tional issue in the case:[55] Did Connecticut and Massachusetts deny New York banking organizations the equal protection of the laws by excluding them from the New England compact.[56] Justice Rehnquist rejected the argument that invalid purposes infected the regional banking statutes. With respect to the business of banking, "we do not write on a clean slate."[57] The "historical fact" is that "our country traditionally has favored widely dispersed control of banking."[58] In this respect, Justice Rehnquist observed, the pattern of banking in the United States differs from that observed elsewhere: "While many other western nations are dominated by a handful of centralized banks, we have some 15,000 commercial banks attached to a greater or lesser degree to the communities in which they are located."[59] The history of local control of banks informed the purposes underlying the challenged statutes. The Connecticut legislature wanted to "preserve a close relationship between those in the community who need credit and those who provide credit"[60] and worried that "immediate acquisition of Connecticut banks by bank holding companies headquartered outside the New England region [could] threaten the independence of local banking institutions."[61] "No doubt similar concerns motivated the Massachusetts legislature."[62] Because these were legitimate state concerns, the challenged statutes had a rational basis sufficient to withstand equal protection scrutiny.

---

[55] The Court's construction of the Douglas Amendment destroyed petitioners' arguments under the Commerce and Compact Clauses. Because Congress authorized the Massachusetts and Connecticut statutes, they were not invalid as discriminations against interstate commerce under the dormant Commerce Clause. Nor did they implicate the concerns underlying the Compact Clause, since they did not enhance state power at the expense of the federal government. See 105 S.Ct. at 2553–55.

[56] Petitioners raised this argument by supplemental briefing in the wake of the Court's decision in Metropolitan Life Insurance Co. v. Ward, 105 S.Ct. 1676 (1985). See 105 S.Ct. at 2555–56. *Ward* invalidated, under the Equal Protection Clause, a state tax that treated domestic insurance companies more generously than out-of-state insurance companies. The Court held in *Ward* that encouraging the formation of new domestic insurance companies and encouraging capital investment in the state's assets and government securities were not, standing alone, legitimate state purposes which could permissibly be furthered by discriminating against out-of-state corporations.

[57] 105 S.Ct. at 2555.

[58] *Ibid.*

[59] *Ibid.*

[60] *Ibid.*

[61] *Ibid.*

[62] *Ibid.*

B. ANALYSIS OF THE OPINION

Northeast Bancorp is likely to be remembered less for what it said than for what it omitted to say. The opinion breaks no doctrinal ground. Nevertheless, it is instructive to examine Justice Rehnquist's reasoning as an object lesson in how the Court, in the guise of "interpretation," attempts to conform an outmoded statute to demands of a changing environment.

The Court's interpretation of the Douglas Amendment is largely fictional. Senator Douglas' remarks, on which the Court rested its analysis, hardly convey an intent to endorse regional banking. Little, if anything, can be inferred from the Senator's statement that holding companies could enter "to the degree" a state permitted; and his reference to the McFadden Act seems rather clearly to be a standard debating move of associating a controversial proposal with a measure that is already on the books. The context in which the words were uttered gives even less support to the Court's interpretation. The very idea of interstate regional banking was unknown in 1956. The most farsighted lawmaker could not be expected to predict the revolutionary marketplace changes that would bring about regional compacts in 1985. Even if Senator Douglas had known of regional banking, it is unlikely that he would have approved the idea. His home state of Illinois, because of its own political dynamics, long resisted efforts to allow banks to expand geographically even within the state.[63] And the giant Chicago banks were likely to be excluded from any regional compacts that might develop—a prospect not calculated to gladden the heart of a Senator from Illinois. Douglas, in his autobiography, expresses disapproval for all forms of geographic bank expansion, whether through branching, holding companies, or merger.[64] His motivation in proposing the Douglas Amendment was probably not to encourage regional banking but to fashion a political compromise

---

[63] See Ill. Ann. Stat., ch. 17, §§ 311, 313 (Smith-Hurd 1981 & Supp. 1984).

[64] See Douglas, In The Fullness of Time 360 (1971): "I decided that I did not favor branch banking, or chain banking, where one group controlled a chain of separate banks through a given corporation or by any form of holding company. I also opposed bank mergers where these would significantly reduce competition. The one exception was where one bank was losing heavily and its failure would throw a great burden on its depositors and the community or upon the Federal Deposit Insurance Corporation."

that could ward off the specter of federally authorized nationwide banking.[65]

Moreover, it is disingenuous to rely, in statutory interpretation, on the remarks of a single legislator in floor debate, even when that legislator happens to have sponsored the measure in question. The intent of Congress should account for all those whose votes were neccessary to passage. There is no reason to suppose that an intent to permit regional compacts was shared by the other Senators who voted for the measure, by members of the House of Representatives, or by the President. Indeed, if the Douglas Amendment had been understood to endorse regional banking, it is entirely likely that legislators from money center states would have objected, as indeed they did when a proposal to permit regional banking was introduced in the 1984 Congress.[66]

Similar difficulties mar the Court's treatment of the equal protection issue. Justice Rehnquist's conclusion that Massachusetts and Connecticut acted out of legitimate and nondiscriminatory motives is charitable but not realistic. The reason Massachusetts and Connecticut excluded New York from their compact is obvious to anyone familiar with politics of banking regulation. The larger banking organizations in those states wanted the ability to acquire banks in the region without fear of competition from the big New York banks. The motive behind the regional legislation was economic protectionism in favor of one interest group which happened to be represented in the states—larger domestic banks—and against another group with no local legislative muscle—the New York banks.

Even if the Court was justified in accepting the states' self-serving rationalizations for their actions, the legislation would still be highly questionable. The states' desire to ensure that local credit needs are met is but a thinly disguised wish to channel credit to local communities at the expense of distant ones, surely a dubious motivation even under the relaxed standards of rational basis equal protection scrutiny. The other stated justification—maintaining

---

[65] At the time Senator Douglas offered his amendment there was considerable support in Congress for a proposal to allow full-scale interstate banking through bank holding companies. See 105 S.Ct. at 2551.

[66] See 42 Cong. Q. 2183 (1984) (reporting on filibuster led by Senator Moynihan of New York against a bill that would have given congressional approval to regional banking).

the "independence" of local banking institutions—is similarly suspect, translating rather directly into a preference for one set of institutions (banks and bank holding companies within the region) over others (similar institutions outside the region).

Finally, even if the states' justifications were bona fide and legitimate, there are serious questions about the fit between legislative means and ends. The statutes in question distinguish between out-of-state institutions within the New England compact region, on the one hand, and out-of-state institutions outside of the region, on the other. But there is no reason to suppose that the former would serve local credit needs better than the latter. And the "independence" of local banks is necessarily undermined by the very legislation at issue in the case, since the Massachusetts and Connecticut statutes allow takeovers of local institutions by bank holding companies from other states within the New England region.

The essentially fictional nature of the opinion in *Northeast Bancorp* raises the inference that the Court was influenced by unstated factors. What those factors were is a matter of speculation. It is likely, however, that the Justices were aware, at least in a general sense, of the marketplace developments mentioned earlier: the growth of de facto interstate banking; the revolution in technology; the upsurge of competition from nonbanking institutions; the breakdown of government-enforced price controls; and so on. All of these factors point toward the virtual inevitability of full-scale interstate banking. If marketplace forces are not allowed to expand directly, through the Douglas Amendment, they will find less desirable means of doing so indirectly. The New England regional compact, while it does not go the whole way toward interstate banking, is at least a first step, and perhaps a necessary step, in the orderly marketplace evolution. Or so the Justices might have believed. Indeed, Justice Rehnquist hinted as much when he praised a Connecticut legislative commission for viewing regional banking as an "experiment" which "would afford the legislature an opportunity to make its own calculus of the benefits and detriments that might result from a broader program of interstate banking."[67]

The *Northeast Bancorp* decision can be viewed as an attempt by the Court to conform an outmoded statute to the needs of a radi-

---

[67] 105 S.Ct. at 2553, quoting Report to the General Assembly of the State of Connecticut (January 5, 1983), at 1230, 1240–41.

cally changed environment.[68] The Congress that passed the Douglas Amendment had not the slightest inkling that thirty years later regional banking would suddenly sweep across the nation. If they had thought about the matter, it is far from clear that they would have approved the idea. At least the legislative coalition that passed the Douglas Amendment would have been unlikely to coalesce around an amendment that expressly approved regional banking. Nevertheless, because the language of the amendment did not expressly forbid regional banking, the Court had the flexibility to update the statute, in the guise of interpretation, in order to meet current needs. Congress, of course, has the power to overrule the Court's interpretation; in this sense the Court may be said to have shifted the "burden of inertia"[69] to those who wish to retain the old system of state-limited banking. That Congress is unlikely to reverse the ruling may say something about the wisdom of the Court's decision.

The same general factors may explain the Court's treatment of the equal protection issue. In this area, to be sure, the Court operated under the constraints of the rule that distinctions based purely on economic grounds are subjected to highly deferential scrutiny.[70] But the Court had plentiful doctrinal support to strike down the statutes if it wished to do so. Indeed, just a few months earlier it had struck down a statute on grounds that could not easily be distinguished from the case at bar.[71] That it chose to uphold the statutes probably indicates the Court's view that regional arrangements are a positive first step on the road to true nationwide banking.

III. Implications of the Decision

Northeast Bancorp sets forth a fundamental charter for geographic expansion in the banking industry. Henceforth, bank holding companies within interstate banking regions may offer

---

[68] See Calabresi, A Common Law for the Age of Statutes (1982).

[69] *Id.* at 104.

[70] See generally Note, Legislative Purpose, Rationality, and Equal Protection, 82 Yale L.J. 123 (1972).

[71] See 105 S.Ct. at 2556–57 (O'Connor, J., concurring). The earlier case, Metropolitan Life Ins. Co. v. Ward, 105 S.Ct. 1676 (1985), is discussed in note 56 *supra*.

full-service banking throughout the region. But a bank holding company outside a banking region may not offer full-service banking where it has not been admitted. In particular, bank holding companies in the money center states—New York, Illinois, California, and Texas—are likely to be barred, at least in the short term, from expanding into any of the regional compact areas.

The Supreme Court's endorsement of regional banking launches the industry on a new and uncharted course. Powerful marketplace forces will now be redirected along regional lines. Those forces, expressed at the level of politics, will cause realignments of traditional coalitions. Interest groups may find themselves supporting measures they once opposed; and new and unusual alliances may develop as old ones crumble.

A. MARKETPLACE ADAPTATIONS

1. *Growth of interstate institutions.* Initially, it seems reasonable to ask, skeptically, Is *Northeast Bancorp* anything to get excited about? If only a few bank holding companies take advantage of their new powers to establish interstate bank subsidiaries, then the case will signify little. But if bank holding companies move vigorously into interstate markets, then the decision will have very great importance.

The odds are high that regional banking will indeed have significant and long-lasting effect on the structure of the banking industry. The available evidence indicates that over time a class of institutions will emerge as truly interstate bank holding companies. Some of these institutions may come to rival the biggest money center banks for power and influence in the national and international financial arenas.

The support for this prediction lies in the virtually universal experience that banks grow ever larger unless they are stymied by regulatory constraints. This tropism, as it were, for bank expansion has manifested itself in states that have liberalized their restrictions on branch banking. In such states a relatively small number of banking institutions typically grow to immense size. These giants dominate their markets even though they constitute only a small proportion of the banks chartered in the state.[72] In 1983, for ex-

---

[72] See Shull, Multiple Office Banking and Competition: A Review of the Literature, reprinted in Subcommittee on Financial Institutions of the Senate Committee on Banking,

ample, there were over 400 banks in California, a state that has long allowed statewide branching.[73] Of these, the five largest banks controlled more than three quarters of the deposits statewide; and one bank alone, Bank of America, controlled roughly 40 percent.[74] Big California banks exercised a comparable dominance in terms of bank assets.[75] New York, which liberalized its branching laws more recently, shows much the same pattern.[76] These figures are instructive even after discounting the fact that New York and California attract more than their share of deposits from other states and foreign countries.

The picture becomes even starker when we turn our attention to other Western nations, none of which has followed the United States' model of restricting bank expansion. In Canada, for example, where banks enjoyed branching privileges from the start,[77] there are only seventy-two chartered banks, of which the largest five account for 80 percent of the total assets.[78] In France, the three biggest deposit banks maintain more than 5,500 branches through-

---

Housing and Urban Affairs, Compendium of Issues Relating to Branching by Financial Institutions 113, 126 (94th Cong., 2d Sess., 1976)(5-firm concentration ratios in 1973 were 75.4 for statewide branching states, 41.1 for limited branching states, and 34.3 for unit banking states). Similar concentration figures are reported in more recent studies. See Rhoades, Concentration in Local and National Markets, Economic Review of the Federal Reserve Bank of Atlanta 28 (March 1985).

[73] See State of California Banking Department, Statistical Tables (December 31, 1983) at 1, 29 (on file with the author).

[74] Ibid.

[75] See Interstate Banking, Hearings before the Subcommittee on Financial Institutions Supervision, Regulation and Insurance of the House Comm. on Banking, Finance and Urban Affairs, 99th Cong., 1st Sess. 36 (1985) (hereafter cited as Interstate Banking Hearings) (six largest California banks controlled 73.96 percent of total state banking assets as of year end 1984).

[76] See Interstate Banking Hearings at 39 (thirteen largest New York banks controlled 89.46 percent of total state banking assets as of year-end 1984).

[77] O'Brian & Lermer, Canadian Money and Banking 25 (1969).

[78] Canadian Department of Finance, The Regulation of Financial Institutions: Proposals For Discussion 58, 27 (1985). Some of the concentration in Canadian banking is due to restrictions on entry. Prior to 1980 a chartered bank could be created only by special legislation passed by Parliament. Id. at 22. The 1980 Bank Act revisions allowed chartered banks to be created by letters patent, a process which requires approval by the Federal Cabinet but not special legislation. The 1980 legislation also allowed foreign bank subsidiaries to gain bank status. The result has been an increase in the number of banks from eleven in 1977 to seventy-two today. Compare Revell, Costs and Margins in Banking: An International Study 101 (1980). At present there are only 12 domestic chartered banks in Canada. Martin, Troubles at Canadian Banks, New York Times, October 4, 1985, at 29. Two domestic banks recently failed in Canada, the first bank failures in that country in sixty-two years. Ibid.

out the country and account for more than 60 percent of the total deposit banking assets.[79] The pattern is similar, although somewhat less pronounced, in West Germany and Japan.[80] These comparisons must be evaluated with a critical eye because of different government policies toward banking, especially in the areas of antitrust and the connection permitted between banks and commercial enterprises.[81] Nevertheless, the overwhelming testimony of countries most similar to our own is this: where branching is free, banks grow large.

Why banks have this powerful growth instinct is not clear. Indeed, the puzzle of bank expansion is one of the major theoretical problems in banking studies today. Over the past twenty years economists have performed numerous studies of economies of scale in banking. Although the early studies showed slight economies of scale, the more recent work has been virtually unanimous that there are no measured economies of scale in commercial banking beyond the very smallest banks.[82] And the marketplace evidence shows that smaller banks are not, in fact, always driven out by competition from the giants. In some local markets they have been able to hold their own or better,[83] and in California, despite the size dominance of the banking giants, a substantial number of new bank charters are granted each year, indicating that incentives for new bank formation have not been extinguished.[84]

Whatever the causes of bank expansion, it is clear that in an unregulated environment some banks grow to huge proportions. Now that regional banking is permitted, a substantial number of banking organizations will attempt to grow by acquiring subsidiary

---

[79] Baer & Mote, The Effects of Nationwide Banking on Concentration: Evidence from Abroad, Economic Perspectives of the Federal Reserve Bank of Chicago 3, 12 (January/February 1985).

[80] *Id.* at 8–10. As of year-end 1984, only three of the top twenty-five banks in the world were American. Thirteen were Japanese, four were French, three were English, one was German and one was Canadian. Top 25 Banks in the World, American Banker, July 6, 1985, at 16.

[81] See Baer & Mote, note 79 *supra*.

[82] See Benston, Hanweck & Humphrey, Scale Economies in Banking: A Restructuring and Reassessment, 14 J. Money, Credit & Banking 435 (1982).

[83] See King, Upstate New York: Tough Market for City Banks, Economic Review of the Federal Reserve Bank of Atlanta 30 (June/July 1985).

[84] See Interstate Banking Hearings, note 75 *supra*, at 37 (61 new bank charters granted in California in 1983, accounting for 16.9 percent of the total new charters nationwide).

banks in other states. Accordingly, the marketplace response to the *Northeast Bancorp* decision is likely to be significant and sustained.[85]

2. *Stages of marketplace expansion.* The market is likely to respond to *Northeast Bancorp* in four broad stages: a stage of mergers between major regional institutions; a stage of market expansion through acquisition or de novo chartering of smaller banks; a stage of contested expansion through unfriendly takeovers and intramarket competition for market share; and, finally, a stage of equilibrium as the market settles down into a relatively steady state. These stages are, of course, schematic in that the actual course of bank expansion will be far more complex than described here. All forms of bank expansion will no doubt occur simultaneously to some extent. Nevertheless, a four-stage expansion path catches some important features of the evolution of the market in an environment of regional compacts.

The first stage is characterized by interstate mergers between larger institutions. Such mergers are likely to dominate the early days of regional banking for several reasons. First, larger banks are sophisticated in their contingency planning. Many of them discussed mergers with regional partners well before *Northeast Bancorp* was decided. Second, mergers between larger institutions achieve substantial interstate expansion at a relatively low cost in terms of planning and negotiation. If there are scale economies or marketing advantages to be had from interstate expansion, then we would expect banking institutions to seek the greatest amount of these benefits at the lowest cost to themselves. The most beneficial mergers are likely to be the earliest ones consummated. Third, mergers between big regional institutions will result in a dramatic increase in the size of the merged entity. This rapid growth could recommend itself to the merging partners for defensive reasons. If the industry eventually moves beyond regional banking to full scale interstate banking—as many believe is inevitable[86]—the largest regional institutions will be much better positioned than smaller organizations to resist unfriendly takeovers by the big money center banks.[87]

---

[85] Market professionals appear to have made a similar judgment. See Forde, A Regional-Bank Mutual Fund, American Banker, August 2, 1985, at 2.

[86] See text at notes 113–14 *infra*.

[87] See Bennett, Interstate Banking's Difficult Birth, New York Times, Sunday, June 2, 1985, 1st Business Page (reporting on merger agreement between Georgia and Florida bank

This first stage of regional banking is already underway. Banks have been quick to use their new powers to expand interstate. Within weeks after the Supreme Court's decision, two giant interstate mergers were announced in the Southeast region.[88] Rumors of mergers involving big Ohio banks circulated in the financial community even before that state's interstate banking legislation took effect.[89] Other big interstate mergers have been announced.[90]

This stage should exhaust itself within a few years, both because there are a limited number of suitable partners and because the advantages to this type of merger are greater the sooner the merger is consummated. Accordingly, we are likely to see the banking market move to a second stage—that of interstate expansion through de novo chartering and purchase of smaller banks. This stage should come somewhat more slowly than the stage of big regional mergers because of the significantly higher costs per dollar of interstate banking business which these forms of expansion entail. There will ordinarily be economies of scale associated with negotiating a large merger as compared with a small one. And de novo chartering will require substantial investigation and start-up costs. These forms of expansion, moreover, do not offer the protections against unfriendly takeovers that are afforded by mergers between large firms. Accordingly, expansion-minded organizations are likely to exhaust the merger opportunities with larger partners before looking to acquire or charter smaller interstate banks.

The third stage of regional bank expansion involves acquisition of market share by subsidiary interstate banks and unfriendly acquisitions of existing institutions. Obviously, competition for market share cannot occur until the initial acquisition of an interstate

---

holding companies in which the two organizations, although formally held in a joint holding company, would continue to operate as if each were still independent. The combination would produce an entity with $15 billion in assets and total equity of almost $1 billion, making it much more costly to acquire than either of the two institutions separately).

[88] Marshall, Handshakes in the Southeast, American Banker, June 25, 1985, at 9. The mergers—one between Wachovia Corp. (North Carolina) and First Atlanta Corp. (Georgia) and the other between First Union Corp. (North Carolina) and Atlantic Bancorp (Florida)— established the merged entities as two of the four largest bank holding companies in the region. *Ibid.*

[89] Solomon, Banks May Arrange Interstate Mergers Long Before New Ohio Bill Takes Effect, Wall Street Journal, July 12, 1985, at 4.

[90] Fraust, Big Deals: Another North Carolina Banking Firm Leads Interstate Charge, American Banker, August 13, 1985, at 16; Fraust, Once-Rare Interstate Combinations Proliferate in August, American Banker, September 12, 1985, at 1.

bank has been completed; and even after an organization has begun to compete in another state, the market share figures will not change overnight. Accordingly, changes in market share are likely to become significant at a later stage in the evolution of regional banking. Similar reasoning holds for unfriendly acquisitions. These are extremely costly because entrenched management can muster a battery of defensive tactics against the suitor, driving up the purchase price and requiring substantial expenditures for lawyers, investment bankers, proxy solicitation firms, and the like. Further, there is no guarantee of success, so that a potential acquiror needs to consider the possibility of spending large amounts of money for no return. Unfriendly acquisitions are therefore likely to be attempted only when reasonable avenues for noncontested bank expansion have been exhausted.

This stage of market share expansion and unfriendly acquisitions is likely to be controversial. If the out-of-state entrant is successful in gaining market share, the success will inevitably be at the expense of an existing bank. Local institutions that are suffering from out-of-state competition are likely to use the specter of bank failure to seek renewed legislative protections against interstate banking. Similarly, unfriendly takeovers will be at least as controversial in the banking area as they have been in other sectors of the economy. Incumbent management will seek the protections of the courts and the legislatures in order to maintain the powers and perquisites of their offices. Bank takeovers, particularly large-scale acquisitions, will raise special concerns because of the potential conflict between banks as suppliers of credit to the economy and banks as users of credit in their acquisition efforts. In addition, bank holding companies engaged in unfriendly takeover battles will have an incentive to raise capital through low-grade debt offerings or other financing devices that increase the firm's riskiness. The Federal Reserve Board's Capital Adequacy Guidelines[91] provide some protection against excessively risky financing, but bank holding companies are likely to find ways to increase their effective leverage to very high levels while remaining in technical compliance with the guidelines.

Finally, the market is likely to settle into a state of relative equilibrium. The equilibrium condition for regional banking—and also

---

[91] See 1 Fed. Res. Reg. Serv. § 3-1506 (1983); Fed. Res. Reg. Serv. Transmittal No. 52 (June 1985).

for national banking, if that is the stopping place in the political evolution of interstate banking[92]—is likely to show the following characteristics. First, there will be many fewer banks than exist today. A large number of smaller banks and some larger banks and bank holding companies will have lost their identity through merger or failure. Second, there will be a small group of banking giants which carry on the business of banking on a nationwide as well as international basis. Included in this group will be the current industry leaders from the money center states. In addition, new banking giants are likely to arise from among the regional banks which are currently expanding by means of interstate mergers. Finally, a substantial number of small and medium sized banks will remain on the scene as independent organizations. The experience of New York and California strongly indicates that smaller banking institutions are able to hold their own against larger competitors if they are well managed.[93] In this respect the effects of geographical restrictions on bank expansion are likely to live on as a relatively permanent part of our heritage even after the legal restraints have disappeared. The smaller banks that do survive are likely to find a competitive niche by maintaining good business relations in smaller communities or by providing specialized "boutique" financial services to limited ("upscale") segments of the consuming public.

B. POLITICAL AND REGULATORY RESPONSES

These marketplace developments should have a profound influence on the regulatory structure for interstate banking as it develops over the next few years. The current situation is highly fluid. State legislatures all over the country are considering proposals to allow interstate banking in one form or another. Laws already passed are being amended in response to rapidly shifting political pressures. There will probably be three discernible phases in the political evolution of interstate banking: a stage of consolidation, a stage of destabilization, and a stage of national banking.

1. *Consolidation.* The first stage—that of consolidation—refers to a period during which the interstate banking regions are estab-

---

[92] See text at notes 113–14 *infra.*

[93] See text at note 135 *infra.*

lished. This stage is already well under way. The growth of regional banking in the past three years has been phenomenal. At least five regional banking areas are now forming: Pacific Northwest; North Central and Plains; New England, Mid-Atlantic; and Southeast. Regional banking legislation of one type or another has been passed or proposed in at least twenty-one states.[94] The national banking system, like a supercooled liquid, is crystallizing with incredible speed into different regional banking markets.

This is not to say that the regionalization of the nation's banking market has yet followed any set pattern. While some states have adopted pure regional legislation, others have declined to lift the Douglas Amendment bar at all, have lifted it on a nationwide rather than a regional basis, or have otherwise enacted nonconforming legislation. Of the New England states, for example, only Connecticut and Massachusetts have adopted true regional statutes. Maine permits entry by bank holding companies from anywhere in the nation; Rhode Island has a regional statute that permits nationwide interstate acquisitions in 1987; and Vermont and New Hampshire have not adopted any legislation.[95] Regional patterns are evident, but they are as yet undefined.

As this stage of consolidation progresses, the nation's banking market is likely to display three different geographic models of banking simultaneously. First, some states will not open themselves up to interstate banking at all. States like Arkansas and New Hampshire, for example, have rejected legislative proposals to lift the Douglas Amendment barrier.[96] Political forces in these and other states may defeat any attempt to permit interstate banking, at least in the next few years. Accordingly, the traditional model of banking limited to the borders of a state will remain with us for some time to come in at least a few states.

The second model of banking is the regional market. The events described above indicate that the forces for regional consolidation are far from spent. A substantial number of new states can be expected to join regional banking compacts. In addition, state legis-

---

[94] See American Bankers Association, State Legislation on Interstate Acquisitions by Bank Holding Companies, reprinted in Interstate Banking Hearings, note 75 *supra*, at 242.

[95] See Northeast Bancorporation v. Board of Governors, 105 S.Ct. at 2549; 4 Banking Expansion Reporter 6–7 (September 2, 1985).

[96] American Bankers Association, note 94 *supra*, at 257.

lation will probably evolve toward greater interstate conformity. At present, the boundaries of interstate regions are not always uniform from state to state. For example, Florida's regional banking statute includes Maryland, Arkansas, and West Virginia, but not Kentucky;[97] Georgia's includes Kentucky, but not West Virginia, Arkansas, or Maryland;[98] and South Carolina's includes Arkansas, Maryland, and West Virginia.[99] Many states are likely to enact amendatory legislation to admit states which other states in the region have included in their interstate banking statutes.[100] The overall trend should be toward greater conformity of legislation within regional areas, with the impetus being to expand the scope of a region when the laws of different states are inconsistent.

The third model of banking, which is likely to coexist with the other two, is full-scale national banking limited to certain states scattered throughout the country. The states most likely to adopt this strategy are geographically remote states with weak banking lobbies and strong interests in attracting capital to their borders. In these states bank holding companies from anywhere in the country can acquire existing banks or establish banks de novo. This group of states will form a laboratory in which the effects of unrestricted nationwide banking can be assessed.

2. *Destabilization.* The stage of consolidation should result in a banking market characterized by a few relatively well defined regional banking areas. But even as the consolidation progresses, forces will begin to undermine the stability of these banking regions.

The regional system could break down in either of two ways. The first potential cause of breakdown is federal legislation. Congress is even now debating whether to authorize nationwide interstate expansion by bank holding companies at some "trigger" date in the future. The House Banking Committee has approved legislation setting a nationwide banking trigger for 1990.[101] The nation-

---

[97] Fla. Stat. Ann. § 658.295 (West 1984).

[98] Ga. Code Ann. §§ 7-1-620–7-1-625 (Supp. 1985).

[99] S.C. Code Ann. §§ 34-24-10–34-24-100 (Law Co-op. 1984 Supp.).

[100] But see American Bankers Association, note 94 *supra*, at 257 (Georgia defeated legislation to include Arkansas in the interstate banking region, even though most other Southern states included Arkansas).

[101] See H.R. 2707 (99th Cong., 1st Sess.); H.R. Rep. No. 174 (99th Cong., 1st Sess.).

wide trigger has also been endorsed by Paul Volcker, the influential Chairman of the Federal Reserve Board.[102] However, the American Bankers Association, which at first approved the trigger idea, has recently withdrawn its support,[103] and the measure faces an uncertain future in the Senate.[104]

If past history is a guide, Congress will either act soon on a nationwide trigger—within a year or so—or will take no action for some time to come. Congress's normal condition on banking issues is one of paralysis. It can act only in situations of dire peril, as in the emergency legislation of 1980 and 1982 responding to the economic and regulatory shocks of record high interest rates[105] or when no potent political coalition has mobilized to oppose the action, as in the 1978 legislation imposing limits on the activities of foreign banks in this country.[106] Until quite recently regional banking was such a new phenomenon that the usual paralyzing forces were not fully effective. No organized interest group had a sufficient stake in maintaining regional banking to justify the expenditure of large amounts of political capital to oppose a nationwide trigger. However, the moment for action, if ever there was one, may already have passed. As long as the outcome of the *Northeast* decision was in doubt, all forces working toward interstate banking could find some merit in a nationwide trigger. But the Supreme Court's decision has changed the political calculus by giving the larger banks within regional areas an incentive to oppose any further loosening of the

---

[102] Volcker, Statement Before the Subcomm. on Financial Institutions Supervision, Regulation, and Insurance of the House Comm. on Banking, Finance and Urban Affairs (April 24, 1985), reprinted in 71 Fed. Res. Bull. 430 (1985).

[103] The American Bankers Association originally endorsed the concept of nationwide banking, with certain reservations. See Interstate Banking Hearings, note 75 *supra*, at 216 (statement of James G. Cairns, Jr., President, American Bankers Association) (qualified endorsement). However, the ABA subsequently abandoned its support for the concept, apparently in response to pressure from small banks in its membership. See Rosenstein, ABA Leaders Drop Backing for Interstate Bill, American Banker, September 13, 1985, at 1.

[104] Rosenstein & Naylor, Key Senators Scorn House Banking Bill, American Banker, June 14, 1985, at 1; Rosenstein, Interstate Banking Won't Concentrate Industry, Says Garn, American Banker, June 20, 1985, at 1.

[105] Depository Institutions Deregulation and Monetary Control Act of 1980, Pub. L. 96-221, 94 Stat. 189; Garn–St. Germain Depository Institutions Act of 1982, Pub. L. No. 97-320, 96 Stat. 1469.

[106] International Banking Act of 1978, Pub. L. No. 95-369, 92 Stat. 607 (1978).

limits on bank expansion that would open them to competition from banks in the money center states.[107]

Another factor that may influence the course of federal legislation is the nonbank bank. As noted above,[108] the nonbank bank holds the potential for undermining most of the remaining geographical barriers on bank expansion. The nonbank bank is currently in a state of some uncertainty as a result of judicial decisions.[109] However, the Supreme Court's decision in *Dimension Financial* has gone far toward establishing the legality of nonbank banks.[110] If the nonbank bank manages to survive judicial and congressional review, it could play a wildcard role in the politics of interstate banking. While it is likely that Congress will close the nonbank bank loophole if judicial decisions do not, the price of congressional action might well be agreement to mandate nationwide banking at some future date.

In the absence of federal legislation the regional banking system can be dismantled only through changes in state legislation. Accordingly, the issue is one of political economy at the state level. There is good reason to suppose that, over time, the political coalitions supporting the state regional banking laws will begin to undergo severe strains.

It appears that state regional banking statutes are favored by two primary interest groups. First are the larger banks that wish to expand interstate and are willing to tolerate competition from other states in the region so long as money center institutions are excluded. Second are the smaller banks that wish to enhance their market value by increasing the number of potential bidders and are willing to tolerate some increased operating competition in order to achieve this goal.

As the marketplace evolves, these groups may begin to disintegrate. Some larger banks may expand to the point where they no longer fear competition or acquisition by money center banks.

---

[107] Naylor & Fraust, Trigger Bill's Prospects Dim, American Banker, June 12, 1985, at 1.

[108] See text at notes 24–37 *supra*.

[109] See *ibid*.

[110] The Supreme Court's decision in the *Dimension Financial* case, see note 32 *supra*, does not definitively resolve the question of the legality of interstate nonbank banks. See notes 35–37 *supra*.

These larger banks might then become proponents of nationwide banking, which would give them the opportunity to expand into other states. Smaller banks, for their part, might come to favor full interstate banking on the theory that the increased competition they would face would be marginal, while the market value of their stock could be significantly increased by the addition of a large group of potential acquirors. Although many of these smaller banks might yearn for the world of state-limited banking,[111] it is doubtful that they could muster the political clout necessary to effect a return to the old system.

Other forces could arise to undermine the system of regional banking. Once the consolidation phase is completed, consumers within banking regions will be able to travel to many other states and obtain banking services not significantly different from those they enjoy at home. The convenience of this system will not be lost on the public. And once regional banking has destroyed the mystique of the state as the sole legitimate banking arena, the public is unlikely to accept the sanctity of the multistate banking region. Accordingly, consumer advocates may come to favor full-scale national banking.

The regional banking system is also likely to be undermined by its own success. The horror stories sometimes told about interstate banking probably will not come to pass. While there may be temporary disruptions, the system as a whole is likely to withstand the strains well.[112] Particularly important, in this respect, will be the experience of states that allow unrestricted entry by bank holding companies from anywhere in the country. These states will be viewed as models for what interstate banking would look like if extended to the nation as a whole. If their experience is positive, many of the arguments against full-scale interstate banking will lose much of their force.

3. *Nationwide Banking.* Eventually, more and more states can be expected to adopt laws that permit entry from anywhere in the country. Most such statutes are likely to require reciprocity by the entering organization's home state, but some may follow the example of Maine and Alaska and allow unrestricted entry. States

---

[111] See text at note 91 *supra*.

[112] See text at notes 92–93 *supra*, 121–36 *infra*.

may also adopt "trigger" mechanisms similar to that currently under consideration at the federal level.[113]

The forces blocking federal nationwide banking legislation will lose much of their potency as states increasingly permit nationwide banking. If the number of holdout states becomes sufficiently small, it may be possible for Congress to clean up the situation by enacting a nationwide banking bill, perhaps with a trigger to give the holdouts time to adjust to the expected changes in their banking markets. If Congress does not act, the system might evolve into a regime of predominantly nationwide banking, with a few backwater states permitting only regional or even state-limited banking.

Accordingly, regional banking is unlikely to be the stopping point in the evolutionary process. Over time, the market will move toward full-scale nationwide banking. In this respect the American banking system will eventually come into conformity with the systems elsewhere in the industrialized world which in general have long permitted free nationwide bank expansion.[114]

IV. POLICY IMPLICATIONS

Finally, a word is in order about the policy implications of the Supreme Court's opinion. Given the likely response of the banking marketplace and the regulatory environment in which it operates, what can be said about a decision endorsing the legality of regional banking compacts? I am not here concerned with the correctness of the Court's decision as a matter of statutory or constitutional interpretation but rather with its wisdom from a legislative or policy standpoint.[115]

The short of it is that there are no intellectually credible justifications for pure geographic restrictions on bank expansion. These restrictions are nothing but special-interest measures that protect

---

[113] See text at notes 101–04 *supra*. Several existing or proposed state statutes already contain triggers for nationwide banking. See, *e.g.*, R.I. Gen. Laws §§ 19-30-1–19-30-2 (1984 Supp.).

[114] See text at notes 77–80 *supra*.

[115] As noted above, there are good reasons to suspect that the Court's decision was in fact heavily influenced by policy considerations even though it was couched in the language of interpretation. See text at notes 68–71 *supra*.

entrenched local banks from outside competition.[116] Loosening geographic restrictions is bound to increase competition and therefore to enhance consumer satisfaction and overall economic welfare. While nationwide banking, under this analysis, is the optimal structure for the industry, regional banking arrangements are obviously preferable to the old system of state-by-state restrictions. And if it is correct, as argued above, that regional banking compacts will eventually give way to nationwide banking, the Court's opinion will tend toward the economically optimal outcome. To the extent that loosening geographic restrictions causes difficulties—for example, in the areas of bank safety and soundness or concentration and competition in particular markets—those difficulties should be addressed by regulation directly aimed at rectifying them, rather than through the old system of inefficient and overbroad geographic restrictions.

A. SERVING LOCAL NEEDS

The fear that faraway banks will inadequately serve local needs is an old saw in the bank expansion debate. It is often alleged by those seeking to maintain geographic barriers that distant institutions will drain credit out of the community by taking local deposits and then making loans elsewhere. Commonly associated with this argument is the image of the local banker, the pillar of the community and supporter of local charities, who, it is suggested, is an indispensible part of our American heritage. Geographic restrictions are said to be necessary in order to maintain the "independence" of this local banker and of his bank. The Supreme Court accepted this argument from folklore as a sufficient justification for the overt discrimination against money center institutions contained in the New England regional banking compact.[117]

This argument is hardly credible as a matter of economics. The

---

[116] Geographic restrictions and other entry barriers in banking have received powerful criticism in the economics literature. See, *e.g.*, Black, Miller & Posner, An Approach to the Regulation of Bank Holding Companies, 51 J. Bus. 379 (1978); Pelzman, Entry into Commercial Banking, 8 J. Law & Econ. 11 (1965); Benston, Federal Regulation of Banking: Analysis and Policy Recommendations, 14 J. Bank Research 8 (1981); Ginsburg, Interstate Banking, 9 Hofstra L. Rev. 1133 (1981).

[117] See text at notes 57–62 *supra*.

purpose of a market system is to direct resources to those sectors of the economy and those parts of the country where they can be put to the most constructive use.[118] Banks are profit-maximizing private institutions. They will make loans where they can obtain an optimal combination of risk and return for their investment. If, therefore, banks choose to direct funds away from the area where they are deposited to some other part of the country, or to some foreign land, then this is presumably because the funds are more efficiently used outside the local community. The argument for serving local credit needs is a thinly disguised suggestion that banks should act contrary to their self-interest and to the interest of the public as a whole in order to provide a special favor for one set of customers.

It might be said that economic efficiency should not be the sole criterion, that there are other important public values served by a dispersed system of local banks serving local needs. It is difficult to rebut this contention, except to observe that "public values," more often than not, are nothing but masks for private interests. Many charming pieces of Americana immortalized by Norman Rockwell are far more desirable as nostalgia than as current realities. The corner grocery store has disappeared because the public prefers the convenience and low prices of the supermarket. The banker devoted to the local community, as epitomized by James Stewart's portrayal of a struggling savings and loan president in the movie "It's A Wonderful Life," does not, in principle, present a different case. If the public truly values local banking, then the local banker need not fear competition from the business school MBAs with their computers and big-city values. But if the public prefers the services offered by the bigger bank, then it is hard to see the point of maintaining an outmoded system for delivering financial services, however attractive the incidents of that system might be. One suspects that the proponents of "local control" are often manipulating the image of the local banker in the service of their own self-interest.

Even accepting the local control argument, however, there is little to be said for excluding out-of-state banking institutions. Banks owned by out-of-state holding companies are likely to serve local credit needs just as effectively as local banks. Local banks are

---

[118] See generally Stigler, The Theory of Price (revised ed. 1952); Hirshleifer, Price Theory and Applications (2d ed. 1980).

no less profit-oriented, in general, than out-of-state banks. They will not provide credit to local businesses unless doing so is in their economic self-interest. They are fully capable of investing their funds in other states or abroad, through loan participations, sales of federal funds to other banks, eurodollar transactions, and the like. While local banks might find it slightly more costly to invest funds interstate as compared with affiliates of interstate bank holding companies, the effect is likely to be marginal. Conversely, there is no reason to suppose that out-of-state organizations would inadequately serve local credit needs.[119] An out-of-state institution is likely to be highly motivated to extend loans to local businesses and consumers in order to build up goodwill in the community. And subsidiaries of out-of-state institutions, no less than local banks, are subject to the local service requirements of the Community Reinvestment Act.[120]

B. SAFETY AND SOUNDNESS

A second possible justification for geographic restrictions on bank expansion is the concern for bank safety and soundness. This is a legitimate and important governmental concern. Banks occupy a unique role in the implementation of the nation's monetary policy and in the effective functioning of the payments system. Widespread bank failure could devastate the nation's economy. At the same time banks are uniquely vulnerable to failure. Because of the fractional reserve nature of banking, no bank has sufficient funds on hand at any given time to repay more than a small percentage of its depositors. A public loss of confidence in a bank can trigger a run, in which depositors, for quite rational reasons, rush to withdraw their funds before the bank closes. And weakness or failure in one bank can quickly spread to others because of the intricately interconnected nature of our financial system.

The bank failure rate during the past few years has been higher

---

[119] Unfortunately, there is very little empirical evidence as to the actual effect of geographic bank expansion on credit services to local communities. Treasury Report, note 13 *supra*, at 138.

[120] 12 U.S.C. §§ 2901–2905 (1982). The purpose of the Community Reinvestment Act is "to require each appropriate Federal financial supervisory agency to use its authority when examining financial institutions, to encourage such institutions to help meet the credit needs of the local communities in which they are chartered consistent with the safe and sound operation of such institutions." 12 U.S.C. § 2901(b) (1982).

than at any time since the Depression.[121] The vulnerability of our financial system was vividly illustrated in the recent, highly publicized Penn Square imbroglio, where the failure of a small bank in an Oklahoma shopping mall sent ripples of instability throughout the banking system. Losses related to the Penn Square failure, coupled with other factors, eventually precipitated a huge run on Continental Bank, one of the nation's largest commercial banks. The imminent failure of Continental, in the estimation of the federal regulators, threatened the safety and soundness of the banking system as a whole and required the largest federal rescue of a private institution in history.[122]

Much of the federal regulatory policy toward banks is designed to prevent this kind of disruption in the banking system. The federal deposit insurance funds for banks, savings and loans, and credit unions now provide depositors in federally insured institutions with nearly absolute security that their deposits (up to $100,000) will be repaid even if their institution fails. Although not without its problems, federal deposit insurance is the centerpiece of federal policy toward the safety and soundness of the financial system. Even Milton Friedman, a scholar not ordinarily known for his advocacy of regulatory intrusion into private markets, has strongly endorsed the concept of deposit insurance.[123] Complementing the deposit insurance program is the Federal Reserve Board's discount window, which provides emergency assistance to banks suffering temporary liquidity problems. And the whole safety and soundness scheme is backed up by a comprehensive and intricate system of supervision and inspection by various federal and state banking authorities.

---

[121] See Short, O'Driscoll, & Berger, Recent Bank Failures: Determinants and Consequences (Federal Reserve Bank of Dallas, May 1985) (on file with the author) (average failure rate for entire post–WWII period was .07 percent; failure rate for the past three years was .36 percent).

[122] For background on the Continental fiasco, see Inquiry into Continental Illinois Corp. and Continental Illinois National Bank, Hearings Before the Subcomm. on Financial Institutions Supervision, Regulation and Insurance of the House Committee on Banking, Finance and Urban Affairs, 98th Cong., 2d Sess. (1984). The failure of Penn Square Bank is recounted in Singer, Funny Money (1985), and Zweig, Belly-up: The Collapse of Penn Square Bank (1985). For a muckraker's perspective see Lernoux, In Banks We Trust 4–19 (1984).

[123] See Friedman & Schwartz, A Monetary History of the United States 1867–1960 11 (1963).

Regional banking raises concerns about bank safety and soundness for two primary reasons. First, as noted above,[124] the opportunities for expansion offered by regional banking are likely to create a new class of giant financial institutions. These huge banks may, on balance, prove to be somewhat more risky than their smaller predecessors. It is true that the larger a bank, the greater its ability to diversify its asset portfolio and its deposit base. In theory, at least, this increased diversification on both sides of the balance sheet should reduce a bank's vulnerability to adverse economic shocks in discrete sectors of the economy or geographic regions.[125] This principle of diversification does appear to apply in some instances. For example, the nation's largest banks have not generally been severely damaged by the recent farm depression that has wreaked havoc with many rural banks. On the other hand, a large bank's greater opportunity to diversify is anything but a guaranty of safety. Large banks have proved highly vulnerable to shocks in discrete economic sectors. A disastrous downturn in the energy industry was the underlying cause of the loan losses that brought down the Continental Bank. Bank of America recently suffered huge losses from downturns in agriculture, shipping, commercial real estate, and loans to foreign countries.[126] Other big banks have experienced problems similar in kind, although less serious in degree. Moreover, as banks increase in size new types of risky investments become attractive. The nation's largest banks routinely speculate on interest rates in the short-term money market[127] and engage in risky foreign currency transactions. The short of it is that banks enjoy an exquisite ability to fine-tune the risk and return in their investment portfolio. No big bank is going to operate below its optimal level of risk and return merely because it can diversify its portfolio; it will simply make up for the reduction in risk due to diversification by increasing the riskiness (and therefore the ex-

---

[124] See text at note 92 *supra*.

[125] See Baltensperger, Economies of Scale, Firm Size, & Concentration in Banking, 4 J. Money, Credit and Banking 467 (1972). There is some empirical support for this thesis. See Larch & Murphy, A Test for the Impact of Branching on Deposit Variability, 5 J. Fin. & Quantitative Analysis 323 (1970).

[126] See Carroll, BankAmerica's Bombshell $338 Million Loss in Second Quarter Jolts Financial Community, American Banker, July 18, 1985, at 1.

[127] See Stigum, The Money Market: Myth, Reality, and Practice (1978).

pected return) of the individual investments within the diversified portfolio.[128]

The available evidence shows that big banks operate at somewhat higher levels of risk than do small banks. They have a larger percentage of nonperforming loans and a worse liquidity position than their smaller rivals.[129] In addition, they have tended historically to operate at a significantly lower level of capitalization, thus (in theory) subjecting themselves to greater bankruptcy risk.[130] This phenomenon is not fully understood. Partial explanations may be found in the lower levels of personal risk that big bank executives may experience in connection with their bank's fortunes; in the big bank's need to operate at risk levels similar to those which its foreign competitors are willing to incur; and in the realistic perception that deposits in the nation's largest banks are de facto 100 percent guaranteed, while deposits in smaller banks are effectively insured only up to the $100,000 federal deposit insurance ceiling.[131]

Whatever the explanation for the heightened riskiness of big banks, the equation for regional banking is obvious. Regional banking facilitates the growth of larger banks; larger banks incur greater risk; and greater risk imposes additional strains on the system of safety and soundness regulation. But while this equation may be correct, it does not follow that regional banking is undesirable. Regional banking may have benefits in the form of consumer convenience and enhanced competition that outweigh its increased risks.

---

[128] See Wall & Eisenbeis, Risk Considerations in Deregulating Bank Activities, Economic Review of the Federal Reserve Bank of Atlanta 6 (May 1984) (banking firms can take as much risk as they like by exercising traditional banking powers).

[129] See Rose, A New Scoring System, American Banker, July 23, 1985, at 1 (study showing that banks with over $40 billion in assets had adequate return on assets but "deplorable" risk scores as compared with smaller institutions).

[130] See Eisenbeis, Interstate Banking's Impact on Financial System Risk, Economic Review of the Federal Reserve Bank of Atlanta 31 (March 1985).

[131] See Statement by Comptroller General of the United States to the Subcomm. on Financial Institutions Supervision, Regulation and Insurance of the House Comm. on Banking, Finance and Urban Affairs (December 14, 1984) (explaining agency's concern that failure to rescue Continental Bank might cause a broader financial crisis of uncertain dimensions and duration); Working Group of the Cabinet Council on Economic Affairs, Recommendations for Change in the Federal Deposit Insurance System 45 (January 1985) ("a serious problem facing the current deposit insurance systems is how to deal with the insolvency of one of the largest banks or thrifts. Some have become so large that the regulatory authorities appear unwilling to accept the direct and indirect costs of letting them fail in the conventional sense. Currently, no workable methods have been developed to handle a very large institution's failure or near-failure. The current system therefore encourages large depositors and creditors to use those institutions that are perceived to be 'too large to fail' ").

More importantly, to the extent that big banks are riskier, the solution is not to prevent banks from getting bigger but to control the risk directly. Indeed, the federal banking regulators have done just that by increasing minimum capital requirements for larger financial institutions.[132] In addition, the supervisory process could be stepped up for large banks if it looks as if they are likely to operate in an excessively risky manner. And some form of risk-based deposit insurance could be developed to correct for the moral hazard inherent in the present fixed-premium system that rewards risk-taking by banks.[133] As compared with the option of retaining state-by-state limits on bank expansion, these regulatory approaches would be much more effective at controlling excessive risk-taking by big banks.

Regional banking also raises safety and soundness issues for smaller banks. Interstate banking will inevitably increase competition in many of the nation's local banking markets. Increased competition necessarily means increased risk of failure for the market participants. Accordingly, regional banking can be expected to drive a substantial number of small banks out of business.

This does not mean that all or even most small banks will suffer losses as a result of regional banking. A well-run small bank should be capable of holding its own or even increasing its market share in competition with its larger rivals.[134] But of the roughly 14,000 or so small banks in this country, a substantial number are certainly inefficiently operated.[135] Badly managed small banks will no doubt

---

[132] See 1 Fed. Res. Reg. Serv. § 3-1506 (1983); Fed. Res. Reg. Serv. Transmittal No. 52 (June 1985). But see O'Hara, A Dynamic Theory of the Banking Firm, 38 J. Fin. 127 (1983); Koehn & Santomerro, Regulation of Bank Capital and Portfolio Risk, 35 J. Fin. 1235 (1980) (banking firms might increase the riskiness of their assets if forced to increase capital). Chairman Volcker has indicated that the Federal Reserve Board intends to take risk explicitly into account in its capital adequacy program. See Naylor, Volcker to Propose Risk-Based Capital Role, American Banker, September 12, 1985, at 1.

[133] See Comptroller General of the United States, An Economic Overview of Bank Solvency Regulation 24–29 (1981).

[134] See King, Upstate New York: Tough Market for City Banks, Economic Review of the Federal Reserve Bank of Atlanta 30 (June/July 1985) (small upstate banks are able to compete effectively with major New York City firms).

[135] Incompetent management is frequently identified as one of the prime causes of bank failure. See, e.g., Comprehensive Reform in the Financial Services Industry, Hearings Before the Senate Committee on Banking, Housing and Urban Affairs 175 (99th Cong., 1st Sess. 1985) (letter from Chairman of the FDIC indicating that "management deficiencies" were the major causes of failure in all but one of the 25 banks that failed between October 19, 1984, and February 8, 1985).

feel the lash of competition from interstate rivals; many will not survive. This expected increased failure rate in small banks will naturally put pressure on the system of safety and soundness regulation. Disbursements from the federal deposit insurance funds will be required more frequently; and the drain on the administrative capacities of the safety and soundness regulators—the Federal Deposit Insurance Corporation, the Federal Home Loan Bank Board, the Federal Credit Union Administration, and various state agencies—will be substantial. In addition, overall public confidence in the banking system may be undermined by a pronounced and sustained trend of increasing bank failures.

The expected winnowing among the nation's small banks creates some cause for concern. But this is an inevitable consequence of a system that for so many years has protected inefficient or lazy bank managers from the natural consequences of their misbehavior. That the introduction of competition into a market should result in failure is in itself no cause for concern. Indeed, if some failure did not occur, one would suspect that the competition was more ephemeral than real. Competition-induced bank failure, like the failure of any business enterprise, is unfortunate for the owners and employees of a particular firm but is a necessary consequence of a market structure that is desirable for the public as a whole.[136]

Again, as in the case of risky large banks, the optimal regulatory solution for small banks is not to return to the era of protected markets and government-supported inefficiencies. The marketplace itself provides substantial safeguards against the threat of excessive bank failures. The owners of small banks have every incentive to sell before their equity is dissipated through competition. In a regime of interstate banking the number of potential acquirors will be considerably larger than in a state-by-state system, increasing the probability that a merger can be arranged before a bank fails. Thus the bank's assets can be placed in more capable hands before failure occurs. And an unfriendly takeover is possible if a bank's managers abuse their office by resisting bona fide acquisition efforts. The market for corporate control, of course, is not perfect, and in any event some banks are doomed to fail in a highly competitive market regardless of the skills of their management. But even if a bank fails, a supervisory merger may be possible under which the de-

---

[136] See Tussig, The Case for Bank Failure, 10 J. Law & Econ. 129 (1967).

mands on the federal deposit insurance system are minimized. Bank failures that do require disbursements from the insurance funds—as long as they stay below some maximum level—represent a cost which the nation long ago determined to be reasonable in light of the benefits afforded by a system of federal deposit insurance. And the regulatory correctives of increased supervision and marketplace discipline are just as available for small banks as for large ones.

Accordingly, while regional banking can be expected to increase the overall riskiness of banks, maintaining the rigid system of state-limited banking is not an appropriate solution to the problem. The Court's decision in *Northeast Bancorp* was reasonable as far as the safety and soundness of the banking system is concerned.

C. CONCENTRATION AND COMPETITION

A third concern of banking regulation is that of concentration and competition. If banking markets become overconcentrated, the danger of collusion arises, with the attendant concern for monopolistic pricing, consumer inconvenience, and economic inefficiency. If regional banking increases levels of concentration in particular markets, it might be objectionable on competitive grounds.

Analysis of the competitive effects of regional banking starts with a model of the banking market. Banking is not a unitary function with a single well defined geographic market. It is an intricate complex of financial services, each with a different geographic configuration. Take the extension of credit. The relevant geographic market for loans is impossible to identify in the abstract. Small business and consumer loans are usually (but not always) made by nearby banks; larger business loans and loan participations can be made to borrowers in other states or even foreign countries. Similar factors apply to the liability side of the balance sheet. Smaller deposits tend to come from nearby consumers of bank services; but larger deposits can come from anywhere in the country, through the mediation of corporate treasurers or deposit brokers, and may even be obtained abroad. Variability in geographic scope also characterizes the services which banks render to one another and to businesses and individual consumers.

It is a useful analytic device—if an obvious oversimplification—to divide the bank product market into institutional and consumer banking. I am using these words in a somewhat unusual sense. By "institutional" banking I do not refer specifically to services bankers provide to other bankers. Instead, I am using the phrase in a more general sense, as denoting all forms of banking services as to which effective competition is possible outside a local geographic market. The paradigm case of institutional banking is the multimillion dollar business loan. Consumer banking, as I use the phrase, consists of the complex of services as to which effective competition is possible only within a local geographic market such as a Standard Metropolitan Statistical Area. These services usually involve lower dollar amounts per transaction and higher costs per dollar of transaction. The paradigm case of consumer banking is a bank's relationship with an individual customer who maintains a checking account at a nearby bank and borrows from the bank for expenditures such as an automobile purchase or a child's college tuition.

Although institutional and consumer banking are distinguishable both in the types of products offered and in the geographic area within which the business is conducted, it is apparent from the structure of the industry that there is an intimate economic connection between the two. Almost all banks engage in both types of banking simultaneously. Only the very smallest banks engage solely in consumer banking; and none of the larger public banks—with the possible exception of Morgan Guarantee Trust Company—engage solely in institutional banking. The nature of the connection between institutional and consumer banking has received almost no attention in the economic literature, although the issue is intriguing. The testimony of the marketplace, however, is that there are strong synergies of operation between the two activities.

Partly as a consequence of these synergies, geographic restrictions on banking have had widely different impacts on the concentration levels in institutional and consumer banking. At the consumer level, geographic restrictions have tended to increase concentration. The most egregious case is that of unit banking, in which banks are prohibited from branching at all. Unit banking, in its pure form, is a system of isolated local banks subject to retail competition only by other banks chartered in the same locality. Although pure unit banking is a thing of the past, restrictions on branching of various degrees of severity still subsist in many states. These states tend to be characterized by relatively high levels of concentration in local banking markets. High concentration levels, according to the structure-performance hypothesis,[137] translate into lower levels of service or higher prices for consumers. Morever, concentration alone does not tell the whole story; the severe barriers to entry imposed by unit banking—and to a lesser extent by restricted branching—drastically reduce the amount of potential competition in local markets and therefore eliminate much of the spur to efficient operations that the fear of new entry can provide.[138] Even in states with statewide branching, the prohibitions on entry by banking organizations located in other states has the effect of deterring some actual and potential competition in retail banking markets.

Geographic barriers to entry have quite a different effect at the institutional level. Institutional banking is highly unconcentrated. A manufacturing company seeking a loan for the purchase of new equipment has hundreds or thousands of potential sources of capital. Some of these providers are nonbank financial intermediaries such as life insurance companies or pension funds. Or the company might seek to obtain the funds without intermediation by selling commercial paper. But the primary suppliers of large business credits are still commercial banks; and for a loan of a sufficient size there are large numbers of banks willing to provide the capital.

Geographic restrictions may well have contributed to the atomization of the institutional banking market. This hypothesis depends on the observed connection between consumer and institutional banking. It appears that a bank's ability to engage profitably in institutional banking is limited by the amount of consumer banking

---

[137] The structure-performance hypothesis posits that the level of industry concentration is a reliable index of an industry's market power. The empirical implication is that a relatively high level of concentration facilitates collusion or dominant-firm pricing, with associated industrywide monopoly rents. See generally Scherer, Industrial Market Structure and Economic Performance (1970); Weiss, The Concentration-Profits Relationship and Antitrust, in Industrial Concentration: The New Learning (Goldschmid, Mann, & Weston ed. 1974); Bain, Industrial Organization (1959). The empirical literature identifies a weak positive relationship between structure and performance in banking. See, e.g., White, Price Regulation and Quality Rivalry in a Profit-Maximizing Model, 8 J. Money, Credit & Banking 97 (1976) (more competitive market structure correlated with higher levels of bank services); Higgestad & Mingo, Prices, Nonprices, and Competition in Commercial Banking, 8 J. Money, Credit & Banking 107 (1976) (weak positive relationship between monopoly power and bank prices). But see Smirlock, Evidence on the (Non)relationship Between Concentration and Profitability in Banking, 17 J. Money, Credit & Banking 69 (1985) (observed correlation between concentration and profitability may be spurious).

[138] See Baumol, Panzar, & Willig, Contestable Markets and the Theory of Industrial Structure (1981).

it conducts. Thus, geographic restrictions, by limiting the amount of consumer banking a bank can conduct, apparently restrict a bank's institutional operations as well. But while at the consumer level the effect of these restrictions is to increase concentration by limiting the number of banks that can compete in a given market, at the institutional level the effect is to reduce concentration by limiting the amount of institutional business which a bank can transact and therefore providing the opportunity for many different institutions to compete in the market.

The breakdown of geographic restrictions through regional banking should reverse the polarities at both the institutional and consumer levels. At the consumer level, interstate banking will increase the number of actual or potential entrants. Here we may draw on the model of market evolution proposed in Part III of this article. When a state enters a regional compact, the number of potential entrants into its consumer banking markets is increased to include all the likely entrants from other states in the region. The immediate effect of a state's entering a regional compact is therefore a sharp increase in the amount of potential competition and, by hypothesis, an improvement in the expected performance of the state's existing banks.

In the first stage of marketplace development after a state has joined a banking region, as discussed above, the primary means of interstate banking will likely be mergers between larger banks in the region. These mergers will not, in themselves, increase competition in local markets. Indeed, they should slightly reduce competition because they remove a potential de novo entrant from the market. Such mergers might be challenged under the antitrust laws as violations of the actual potential entrant doctrine.[139] Although courts have endorsed the theoretical viability of the doctrine in the banking context,[140] it is unlikely that a potential competition claim could succeed in the context of market expansion mergers pursuant

---

[139] The actual potential entrant doctrine views as anticompetitive the acquisition by an outside firm of a leading firm within a concentrated market. The premise is that if the outsider is barred from acquiring a larger firm in the market it will enter de novo or through a toehold acquisition and will then compete vigorously for market share, eventually leading to deconcentration of the market. See generally Areeda & Turner, Antitrust Law 69–161 (1980).

[140] Mercantile Texas Corp. v. Board of Governors, 638 F.2d 1255 (5th Cir. 1981); Republic of Texas Corp. v. Board of Governors, 649 F.2d 1026 (5th Cir. 1981).

to a regional banking agreement. The existence of numerous other potential entrants would ordinarily be sufficient to sustain a merger between larger banking organizations in different states. Accordingly, the first phase of marketplace evolution is not likely to affect the concentration of local banking markets but may have an inhibiting effect on competition as potential entrants are eliminated by merger with existing institutions. The reduction in competition, however, is likely to be slight and would rarely be so serious as to run afoul of the antitrust laws.

The second phase of marketplace expansion involves the acquisition of smaller existing institutions and the establishment of de novo interstate banks. Acquisition of existing institutions may raise concern because of the elimination of a potential entrant, but the reduction in competition here is likely to be even less serious than in the first phase. This is so because smaller banks may be acquired by institutions that would not be in a position to make a toehold acquisition or charter a de novo bank in the market. Such acquisitions would not result in the elimination of any potential competition. Establishment of a de novo bank, the other activity typifying the second stage of marketplace evolution, necessarily involves increased competition in local markets because the de novo bank begins with zero market share and seeks to wrest business away from existing banks in the area. Accordingly, this second phase, as a whole, should be one of increasing competition in local markets.

The third phase of marketplace evolution involves competition for market share by subsidiaries of interstate banks and unfriendly takeovers of banks. Competition for market share is procompetitive by definition. The only danger here is that larger banking institutions will use their financial resources to engage in predatory practices that drive smaller independent banks from the market. If the subsidiary of the interstate bank gains too much market share as a result of such practices, then the market could again become concentrated. But the antitrust laws will be available to police against overt predation.[141] There is little or no evidence that big banks have engaged in predatory practices when they enter markets dominated by smaller independent banks. A big bank would have little to gain from predation because of the ease of de novo entry into the market

---

[141] *E.g.*, Utah Pie Co. v. Continental Baking, 386 U.S. 685 (1966); F.T.C. v. Anheuser-Busch, Inc., 363 U.S. 536 (1959).

by other large institutions, a factor which would place a cap on any monopoly profits expected from successful predation. It is likely, however, that small banks will charge their bigger rivals with predatory practices, even if the charges are unjustified, as they begin to feel the pinch of competition.

Unfriendly takeovers are the other distinguishing characteristic of this third phase of marketplace evolution. Such acquisitions do not in themselves reduce concentration in a market because they entail the acquisition of an existing institution. Unfriendly takeovers are most likely to occur when the target bank is poorly managed. The acquiring institution believes that its managers can use the bank's resources more profitably than can the incumbent officers. A large body of empirical evidence supports the view that takeovers usually enhance the value of the acquired firm.[142] Thus, the threat of an unfriendly takeover should act as a spur to incumbent management to operate their banks in an efficient—and therefore competitive—manner. If the officers fail to improve their performance, they can be replaced by better ones through the takeover mechanism. In either case the market for corporate control should operate to enhance competition in local banking markets, at least so long as incumbent managers do not prevail on the legislators or the courts to place roadblocks in the way of unfriendly bank takeovers.

Accordingly, the consumer marketplace is likely to evolve toward decreasing concentration and increasing competition as a result of regional banking. If this prediction holds, then the final stage of consumer market reaction to regional banking—the equilibrium stage—will be characterized by increased customer convenience and enhanced overall economic efficiency.

At the institutional level, however, concentration levels are likely to increase. As hypothesized above, state-limited banking has inhibited the growth of concentration in institutional banking. Interstate banking is likely to remove those limits. Interstate banking should result in a substantial reduction in the number of banks nationwide, as smaller banks are acquired by bigger ones or fail due

---

[142] *E.g.*, Dodd & Ruback, Tender Offers and Stockholder Returns: An Empirical Analysis, 5 J. Fin. Econ. 351 (1977); Kimmer & Hoffmeister, Valuation Consequences of Cash Tender Offers, 33 J. Fin. 505 (1978); Bradley, Interfirm Tender Offers and the Market for Corporate Control, 53 J. Bus. 345 (1980); Jarrell & Bradley, The Economic Effects of Federal and State Regulations on Cash Tender Offers, 23 J. L. & Econ. 371 (1980); Jensen & Ruback, The Market for Corporate Control—The Scientific Evidence, 11 J. Fin. Econ. 5 (1983).

to increased competition. Thus the number of banks offering large commercial loans or other institutional services will be reduced as the marketplace evolves. Concentration in institutional banking will increase.

The antitrust laws are unlikely to provide any sort of a brake to this increase in concentration. First, the geographic banking market, as identified by the Supreme Court, is essentially an extended local market. The Court has been unwilling to treat banking as a set of distinct activities each with its own product markets. But in viewing banking as a unitary activity, the Court has had to adopt a geographic market definition that does not account for concentration at the regional or national levels. In the *Philadelphia National Bank* case,[143] the Court observed that "[i]n banking, as in most service industries, convenience of location is essential to effective competition. Individuals and corporations typically confer the bulk of their patronage on banks in their local community; they find it impractical to conduct their banking business at a distance."[144] By thus establishing the extended local market as the relevant geographic market for banking, the Court effectively excluded from the ambit of the antitrust laws the effect of a bank merger on the wholesale market.

Philadelphia National Bank has long been outmoded.[145] The Court may well be inclined to rethink its position if it ever faces another significant bank merger case. In the meantime, however, *Philadelphia National Bank* places limits on the power of antitrust doctrine to police against excessive concentration at the wholesale level. But as a practical matter this limitation is unlikely to be problematic, at least in the foreseeable future. The wholesale banking market is so highly unconcentrated and so rife with competition from nonbank financial institutions that even a very substantial consolidation in the banking industry would not create serious concern about collusive or anticompetitive practices.

Accordingly, *Northeast Bancorp*, although it paves the way for increased concentration in the institutional market, does not thereby raise undue problems of anticompetitive behavior. The growth of

---

[143] United States v. Philadelphia National Bank, 374 U.S. 321 (1963).

[144] *Id.* at 358.

[145] *Cf.* Note, The Line of Commerce for Commercial Bank Mergers, 96 Harv. L. Rev. 907 (1983) (criticizing outmoded approach to product market definition and suggesting alternative analysis).

huge banking institutions facilitated by the decision does, however, raise policy issues of another sort.

D. SIZE OF FINANCIAL INSTITUTIONS

A final criterion for evaluating *Northeast Bancorp* is the concern for limiting the size of financial institutions. This is not an economic matter, strictly speaking, but a political one. Since the early days of the Republic citizens have worried about vast amounts of financial power being consolidated in the hands of a few private citizens. President Jackson gave early and eloquent voice to these concerns in his message vetoing the bill to recharter the Second Bank of the United States. Jackson warned that the bank's immense economic power might fall into the hands of a "few designing men" who could then perpetuate themselves in office during the entire period of the bank's charter.[146] "It is easy to conceive," he said, "that great evils to our country and its institutions might flow from such a concentration of power in the hands of a few men irresponsible to the people."[147] Jackson's theme has struck a responsive chord throughout our history. Worry about excessive size of financial institutions was probably the principal justification for the extension of the BHCA to one-bank holding companies in 1970.[148] More recently, the theme has found expression in both the Carter[149] and Reagan[150] administrations and in Congress.[151]

---

[146] Message by President Andrew Jackson Returning the Bank Bill, With His Objections, H.R. Doc. No. 300, 22d Cong., 1st Sess. (1832).

[147] *Ibid.*

[148] See Bank Holding Company Act Amendments—Hearings on H.R. 6778 Before the House Comm. on Banking and Currency, 91st Cong., 1st Sess. 9, 21 (1969); One-Bank Holding Company Legislation of 1970, Hearings on S. 1052, S. 1211, S. 1664, S. 3823 and H.R. 6778 Before the Senate Comm. on Banking and Currency, 91st Cong., 2d Sess. 13 (1970). See also Statement by the President Endorsing Proposed Legislation for Further Regulation, 5 Weekly Comp. of Pres. Doc. 461 (March 24, 1969).

[149] See Treasury Report, note 13 *supra*, at 1 ("This Administration is committed to the avoidance of an undue concentration of economic resources and supports the continuation of a viable dual banking system").

[150] See Interstate Banking Hearings, note 75 *supra*, at 6 (testimony of Federal Reserve Board Chairman Volcker) (noting that "[h]istorically, a counter-argument to interstate banking has been a strong antipathy to concentration of economic power, particularly in the banking system").

[151] See H.R. Rep. No. 174 (99th Cong., 1st Sess.) (House Banking Committee is "deeply concerned that without appropriate safeguards, interstate banking could lead to an undue concentration of financial resources in the hands of a few giant banking companies").

If we accept this political judgment, is there cause for concern in the *Northeast Bancorp* decision? In one sense there is. As demonstrated above, the regional compact movement is likely to facilitate the growth of a small class of very large banking institutions. So long as the money center states are excluded from the banking regions, the new banking giants are unlikely to grow even as large as the big money center banks. But we have also seen that regional banking is likely to prove unstable, giving way eventually to full-scale national banking. In an unfettered interstate system, the biggest banking firms are likely to grow almost beyond measure unless checked by regulation. National banking poses the danger of giantism, which the politics of this country have always abhorred.

If the political judgment is that banks should not grow too large, the solution is not to prevent interstate banking but to place some reasonable ceiling on the size which a bank can attain. Such ceilings have already been proposed. Chairman Volcker, for example, has endorsed an approach that would prohibit the nation's largest bank holding companies from merging with each other or from otherwise obtaining through acquisition of smaller banks more than some maximum share of the total nationwide banking assets.[152] Such a direct approach to the problem of size would be an effective solution that would still allow most if not all the benefits of interstate banking in terms of enhanced competition and consumer convenience. Even if size is a legitimate concern, *Northeast Bancorp* is not objectionable merely because it facilitates the growth of banking organizations.

Accordingly, the opinion in *Northeast Bancorp*, whatever its merits from the standpoint of judicial craftsmanship, is reasonable in terms of its likely effects on the complex and rapidly changing political and economic institutions that together constitute the world of banking in the United States today.

---

[152] Interstate Banking Hearings, note 75 *supra*, at 7.

MAURICE KELMAN

THE FORKED PATH OF DISSENT

Anglo-American appellate courts are neither perfectly collegial nor purely individualized tribunals. Courts of last resort in some European countries, particularly those influenced by French practice, proceed in all instances collectively, corporately. Their opinions are, as we say, per curiam. Public dissent is unknown. No matter how dissimilar the judges may be in temperament and outlook, they are united on the need to foster the myth of the law's impersonality and inexorability.[1] So much importance is attached to solidarity that it is valued even above consistency of decision from case to case—one of the reasons, perhaps, why the doctrine of precedent enjoys little if any official stature.[2]

To place our rather different judicial customs in a clearer perspective, suppose we inverted the continental system totally. Imagine a court of last resort whose members decided every question according to nothing save their individual notions of law, never bending to the views of colleagues, making no effort to compose

Maurice Kelman is Professor of Law, Wayne State University.

AUTHOR'S NOTE: I am grateful to my colleagues Robert Glennon, Joseph Grano, Robert Sedler, Stephen Schulman, and Edward Wise for their comments on an earlier draft of this paper.

[1] See Nadelmann, The Judicial Dissent: Publication v. Secrecy, 8 Am. J. Comp. L. 415, 422–29 (1959). See also Schlesinger, Comparative Law 416–20 (4th ed. 1980). An exception to the English custom of open dissent is found in opinions of the Privy Council before 1966. See Patterson, The Law Lords 102 n. 64 (1982).

[2] For comparisons of English and French attitudes toward judicial precedent, see Allen, Law in the Making 178–87 (7th ed. 1964); Lawson, A Common Lawyer Looks at the Civil Law 84 (1955); Goodhart, Precedent in English and Continental Law, 50 Law. Q. Rev. 40, 42 (1934).

differences, and unconcerned with the way in which a majority of the judges has decided similar controversies in the past. Let it be noted that we are not postulating judges who operate in the undisciplined style of Justice Frankfurter's proverbial kadi issuing judgments under a tree.[3] We are imagining a system in which the performance of an appellate judge is measured not only by the persuasiveness of his opinions but by personal consistency from case to case and term to term. The integrity of individual positions would be all-important, and achieving collective coherence a matter of profound indifference to such egocentric judges. In that system the "Court's" decision would amount to nothing more than the result decreed by a majority of votes, each of which might be cast for separate reasons. Beyond terminating the litigants' dispute, a decision would be without public importance except as a showcase of the autonomous minds of the justices. Advocacy in later cases would not be built on Court precedents but would necessitate multiple arguments—why not separate briefs?—tailored to the specific jurisprudence of each of the justices.

Judicial individuality of course is liberally indulged in the courts of America and Great Britain. Dissent and separate opinions are venerable institutions, as is the practice of publicly attributing the authorship of the Court's pronouncements. Yet the extreme individualism of our imaginary model is as alien to our judicial traditions as the European lockstep.[4] Our real-world appellate courts combine both qualities of collegialism and individuality; they perform in many ways as an ensemble and in other respects as an assortment of soloists. There are no distinct lines of demarcation.[5] In none of the highest courts, so far as I know, have the obligations

---

[3] Terminiello v. Chicago, 337 U.S. 1, 11 (1949) (Frankfurter, J., dissenting).

[4] In a recent article, Professor (now Judge) Easterbrook comes close to celebrating that model of judging. See Ways of Criticizing the Court, 95 Harv. L. Rev. 802 (1982).

[5] Depending on the point to be made, the stress can be placed on either theme. Justice Frankfurter thus speaks with nostalgia of "the early healthy practice whereby the Justices gave expression to individual opinions," Graves v. New York ex rel. O'Keefe, 306 U.S. 466, 487 (1939) (concurring opinion), and praises multiple opinions as "mak[ing] for the clarity of candor," McGowan v. Maryland, 366 U.S. 420, 459 (1961) (concurring opinion), but elsewhere chooses to emphasize the group aspect of Supreme Court decision making, asserting that "the judgments of this Court are collective judgments. They are neither solo performances nor debates between two sides, each of which has its mind quickly made up and then closed," Kinsella v. Krueger, 351 U.S. 470, 485 (1956) (separate opinion "reserv[ing] for a later date an expression of my views").

of collegiality or the limits of individuality ever been precisely defined. Certainly there is no formal court rule or training manual for new justices to indicate the extent to which it is permissible for a judge to reject the holdings of the Court's majority. Nor, if one looks at the Supreme Court over the last half century, can it be said that group decision making is the rule and broken ranks the exception.[6] Justice Jackson observed in the 1950s that the Court "functions less as one deliberative body than as nine,"[7] and that was never more the case than today.

Nevertheless there are forces, whose strength should not be underestimated, that work against much greater fragmentation of opinion and prevent multimember courts from becoming the antithesis model we posited earlier. First and foremost, there is the pressure felt by all the judges to achieve as often as possible an "opinion of the Court" reflecting the agreement of a majority of the members on a single rationale.[8] It is generally considered a failure in performance of the Court's creative mission of making and clarifying law when cases chosen for review from the mass of petitions are not decided on doctrinally significant grounds but disposed of by the anticlimax of a headcount. A second force that reduces individuality of judgment is stare decisis, the requirement of fitting the current decision into the body of past decisions in a rationally satisfying way in order to promote private legal planning, assure equal treatment of like litigants, and inspire respect for the courts.

---

[6] See Nelson, Book Review, 131 U. Pa. L. Rev. 480, 514 (1982). An analysis of the 1982 Term reveals that the Court was unanimous in only one of every five cases decided by full opinion and that dissenting opinions were written in nearly two-thirds of the cases. The Supreme Court, 1982 Term, 97 Harv. L. Rev. 295 (table I[A]), 297 (table I[C]) (1983). For the 1983 Term the unanimity rate was one in four cases and the incidence of dissenting opinions was 60 percent. The Supreme Court, 1983 Term, 98 Harv. L. Rev. 309 (table I [C]) (1984).

[7] Jackson, The Supreme Court in the American System of Government 16 (1955).

[8] My colleague Edward Wise refers to "the practice of having a single opinion of the court, which American lawyers seem to prefer but which builds a risk of unreliability because judges who concur in the opinion are not necessarily committed to everything said in it." Wise, The Doctrine of Stare Decisis, 21 Wayne L. Rev. 1043, 1051 (1975). Partial disagreement with the Court's opinion may (*a*) go unspoken, (*b*) find expression in a separate concurring opinion by a signatory to the majority opinion, or (*c*) provoke a justice to limit his concurrence to the Court's judgment. The choice seems to be fitfully ad hoc. Compare Justice Powell's preference for course *b* in some cases where his vote was needed to produce a five-justice majority opinion—e.g., Gannett Co. v. De Pasquale, 443 U.S. 368 (1979); Zurcher v. Stanford Daily, 436 U.S. 547 (1978); Branzburg v. Hayes, 408 U.S. 665 (1972)—with his recourse to *c* on other occasions, as in Mills v. Habluetzel, 456 U.S. 91 (1982). *Cf.* University of California Regents v. Bakke, 438 U.S. 265 (1978).

Yet these conformist pressures prevent internal divisions only to a limited extent. When one considers the close and difficult questions that the highest courts undertake to decide, wide scope for disagreement remains a normal—an inevitable—state of affairs. (Indeed, unanimity of opinion in the Supreme Court arouses the suspicion that some of the justices must not have been paying close attention.) Accepting dissent as a legitimate and basically wholesome facet of the judicial enterprise, this essay seeks to examine the significance of dissent for the dissenter himself as new cases present the Court with questions spawned by the original holding. Is the dissenter's position in successor cases to be governed by the views put forward in his initial dissent, or will the dissenter now accept the majority's decision as his point of departure?

In fact the dissenter's road forks in three directions. One course of action is to abandon past dissent under the pressure of stare decisis.[9] If the erstwhile dissenter sees the issue as one that should be put to rest, then the Court's first answer will suffice simply because it is an answer. It follows that reiteration of past disagreement on the merits is pointless, or worse, mischievous. The former dissenter's duty in these circumstances is to rejoin his colleagues, approaching new cases as if he had concurred (albeit reluctantly) in the first place.

The second major option is for the dissenter to cling to his own doctrinal position. This course calls for a renewal of the first dissent whether by perfunctory notation or with fresh vigor and elaboration. In purest form this choice also includes a refusal to take part in the business of refining the foundation decision—working out its implications, its applications, its limits—even when the current litigation is framed around just those questions.

The third course does not to my knowledge have a recognized name nor is it much discussed in the literature, although the practice is commonplace in appellate courts. It does not call for the permanent sacrifice of the dissenter's own theories, as does stare decisis, but asks him to put his views into temporary cold storage and meanwhile to accept the original decision as the predicate for

---

[9] Dershowitz, The Best Defense 307 (1982): "I am reminded of my colleague Alan Stone's observation that there are no Nobel prizes in law because law is the only profession where you lose points for originality and gain points for demonstrating that somebody else thought of your idea first."

his judicial reasoning in the next cases. Exactly how long must the dissenter table his own position? Until the Court is sufficiently disillusioned with the original decision to consider an overruling—a day which may arrive sooner or later or perhaps never or at least not during the dissenter's remaining time on the Court. Judge Traynor is one of the few writers to have commented on this option (which for want of a settled vocabulary is variously termed in this essay "temporary suppression of dissent," "temporary acquiescence," or "self-subordination"). Traynor writes:[10]

> Once [the dissenter has issued his dissent] he has had his day. He should yield to the obligation that is upon him to live with the law as it has been stated. He may thereafter properly note that he is concurring under compulsion, *abiding the time when he may win over the majority*, but he should regard dearly enough the stability of the law that governs all the courts in the state not to renew the rataplan of his dissent.

I. Abandoned Dissent: The Stare Decision Option

In a system of precedent the benefits of consistency and stability of judgment will generally override the evils of perpetuated error. According to Brandeis' familiar apothegm, "it is usually more important that a rule of law be settled than that it be settled right."[11] One could quarrel with the terms "generally" and "usually" when the capacity for toleration of error varies so widely from court to court, judge to judge, and era to era and when so much depends on the subject matter of the precedents (courts refusing to refashion property rules or statutory interpretations as freely as they revise doctrines of tort liability or constitutional rights). But however loosely one cares to formulate the principle of stare decisis, however generous the allowance for reconsideration and correction, still it must be true that some mistaken decisions will resist judicial reversal. To deny the inertial force of all past errors is to repudiate the concept of precedent itself. If courts only accepted those decisions that are thoroughly agreeable in reasoning and result, all questions in the end would be addressed de novo.[12]

---

[10] Traynor, Some Open Questions on the Work of State Appellate Courts, 24 U. Chi. L. Rev. 211, 219 (1957) (emphasis added).

[11] Di Santo v. Pennsylvania, 273 U.S. 34, 42 (1927) (dissenting opinion).

[12] See Radin, Case Law and Stare Decisis, 33 Colum. L. Rev. 199, 201 (1933).

To be sure, it is the later court that chooses for itself whether to follow or deviate from the precedents. Internal stare decisis is a policy, not a cast iron imperative of appellate courts. It is not our theory that the first pronouncement exhausts the court's power of decision over a point, as the British thought until only a few years ago.[13] But the choice depends on more than simple disagreement with previous cases. Justice Stevens correctly observes that while demonstrated error is a necessary—or at any rate a usual— condition for overruling, it is not a sufficient condition:[14]

> [T]he question whether a case should be overruled is not simply answered by demonstrating that the case was erroneously decided and that the Court has the power to correct its past mistakes. The doctrine of *stare decisis* requires a separate examination. Among the questions to be considered are the possible significance of intervening events, the possible impact on settled expectations, and the risk of undermining public confidence in the stability of our basic rules of law.

Not even in American constitutional law, where the idea of a "living Constitution" invites judicial innovation and reinterpretation, can stare decisis be dismissed as an insignificant restraining force—a neglected truth that Professor Monaghan has been at pains to remind us of.[15] Any list of dubious constitutional propositions that realistically are irreversible, because they are too deeply entrenched and not so insufferable, would include these: corporations count as "persons" for purposes of Fourteenth Amendment due

---

[13] With its Practice Statement on Precedent [1966] All E.R. 77, the House of Lords freed itself from the rigid, no-exceptions version of stare decisis that had captured judicial thinking in the latter part of the nineteenth century. For a study of the Law Lords' post-1966 use of their overruling power, see Patterson, note 1 *supra* at 154–69.

[14] Stevens, The Life Span of a Judge-Made Rule, 58 N.Y.U. L. Rev. 1, 9 (1983). Justice Stevens' philosophy of stare decisis as applied to older precedents is expressed in Thomas v. Washington Gas Light Co., 448 U.S. 261, 272 (1980) (plurality opinion), and Rose v. Mitchell, 443 U.S. 545, 593 (1979) (dissenting in part). His view of recent decisions as precedents is found in the cases cited in note 30 *infra*.

[15] Monaghan, Taking Supreme Court Opinions Seriously, 39 Md. L. Rev. 1 (1979). See also Reed, Stare Decisis and Constitutional Law, 35 Pa. B.A.Q. 131, 137 (1938) (citing cases where justices voted solely on the strength of stare decisis). For a compilation of express overrulings in constitutional cases, see Burnet v. Coronado Oil & Gas Co., 285 U.S. 393, 407–11 (1932) (Brandeis, J., dissenting). This was updated by Blaustein and Field, "Overruling" Decisions in the Supreme Court, 57 Mich. L. Rev. 151, 184–94 (1958), and again by Maltz, Some Thoughts on the Death of Stare Decisis in Constitutional Law, 1980 Wis. L. Rev. 467, 494–96 (appendix).

process and equal protection;[16] all manner of classifications besides those drawn on racial lines are subject to the requirement of "equal protection of the laws";[17] the "privileges and immunities" of national citizenship are few in number and of limited importance compared to the companion safeguards of due process and equal protection;[18] First Amendment freedom of speech limits the authority of states to the same degree that it limits the federal government's power;[19] the establishment of religion prohibition reaches the states as well as the federal government.[20] These propositions were settled before any of the present justices came on the scene. And that fits with the conventional thinking about stare decisis, which views the controlling case law as the work of past judges, either dead or pensioned off, and which sees the decision to follow or reject precedent as a choice to be made by another set of judges who bear no authorial responsibility for the challenged decision. Hart and Sacks thus speak of "the propriety of according respect to the conclusions of *predecessor* judges."[21] And Justice Douglas, writing about policies of stare decisis in constitutional cases, sets up the same model: "A judge . . . remembers above all else that it is the Constitution which he is sworn to support and defend, not the gloss which his *predecessors* may have put on it."[22]

A decision need not be hoary to be precedential. Last year's decision, or this morning's dewy pronouncement, also has stare decisis

---

[16] Santa Clara County v. Southern Pac. R.R., 118 U.S. 394 (1886). Objection to this proposition has been voiced from time to time, either with a call for overruling, Connecticut Gen'l Ins. Co. v. Johnson, 303 U.S. 77, 83 (1938) (Black, J., dissenting), or without, First Nat'l Bank of Boston v. Bellotti, 435 U.S. 765, 822 (1978) (Rehnquist, J., dissenting).

[17] Gulf, Colo. Ry. v. Ellis, 165 U.S. 150 (1897), is perhaps the earliest use of the Equal Protection Clause to invalidate an economic regulation. See Justice Rehnquist's rueful observation about nonracial equal protection in Weber v. Aetna Cas. & Sur. Co., 406 U.S. 164, 178 (1972) (dissenting opinion).

[18] Slaughterhouse Cases, 83 U.S. (16 Wall.) 36 (1873).

[19] This proposition derives from the decision to "incorporate" the First Amendment speech guarantee into the Fourteenth Amendment, Gitlow v. New York, 268 U.S. 652 (1925).

[20] Everson v. Board of Educ., 330 U.S. 1 (1947). Justice Rehnquist condemns another facet of *Everson*—its "wall of separation" principle—as "a metaphor based on bad history," which "should be frankly and explicitly abandoned." Wallace v. Jaffree, 105 S.Ct. 2479, 2517 (1985) (dissenting opinion). But at the same time Justice Rehnquist accepts as a "given" the applicability of the Establishment Clause to the states. *Id.* at 2520.

[21] Hart & Sacks, The Legal Process 588 (tent. ed. 1958) (emphasis added).

[22] Douglas, Stare Decisis 9 (1949) (emphasis added).

potency. There are new and rapidly evolving fields of law, indeed, where all the germane precedents are contemporary cases—the opinions, sometimes closely divided, of the current justices. The usual stare decisis considerations that urge acceptance of the errors of one's judicial predecessors can also enjoin a judge to accept his coeval's mistaken judgments in the larger interests of repose and predictability. "My dissent from the holding," says Justice Stevens of a recent decision, "does not qualify my duty to respect it as a part of our law."[23]

The freshness of a precedent is nonetheless a factor that can be assigned either a plus or a minus value in determining the role of stare decisis. There is a sense in which the newly minted precedent deserves a special immunity from overruling. Among the standard grounds for overruling are the sobering lessons of long experience with the case and its progeny or the loss of vitality caused by shifting circumstances or by antithetical developments elsewhere in the law.[24] These justifications ordinarily are lacking in the case of new decisions.[25] That is why some dissenters are willing to take a wait-and-see attitude toward the majority decision—respecting it as, one might say, a probationary precedent that deserves a chance to demonstrate its merits and to dispel the doubts raised by the dissent.[26] In effect the initial dissenter reserves his future options: he may in the end embrace the case as the conclusive precedent or

---

[23] H.L. v. Matheson, 450 U.S. 398, 421 (1981) (concurring opinion).

[24] *E.g.*, Hughes v. Oklahoma, 441 U.S. 322, 326 (1979), overruling an eighty-three-year-old precedent, Geer v. Connecticut, 161 U.S. 519 (1896), with the comment that "time has revealed the error of the early resolution reached in that case." In a 1985 overruling of an 1887 decision, the Court noted that the precedent "has simply not survived" later cases. United States v. Miller, 105 S. Ct. 1811, 1819 (1985), expressly overruling Ex parte Bain, 121 U.S. 1 (1887).

[25] See Oregon v. Corvallis Sand & Gravel Co., 429 U.S. 363, 395 (1977) (Marshall J., dissenting): "[T]he majority has advanced neither experience nor changed circumstances to justify its interment of a 7–1 decision of this Court issued barely three years ago." But see Swift & Co. v. Wickham, 382 U. S. 111, 116 (1965), overruling a three-year-old decision, Kesler v. Dept. of Pub. Safety, 369 U.S. 153 (1962), because it "proved to be unworkable in practice."

[26] Justice Black disagreed with Trupiano v. United States, 334 U.S. 699 (1948), but objected to its overruling only two years later, thinking "it would be wiser judicial policy to adhere to the *Trupiano* rule of evidence, at least long enough to see how it works." United States v. Rabinowitz, 339 U.S. 56, 66 (1950) (dissenting opinion). Conversely, majority justices may become disenchanted with their handiwork after a short time. See United States v. Scott, 437 U.S. 82 (1978), overruling United States v. Jenkins, 420 U.S. 358 (1975).

he may remount a challenge to it, depending on its near-term consequences. A former dissenter may also be sensitive to what can only be called the public relations difficulty associated with frequent or rapid overrulings. Among the "very weighty considerations" behind the doctrine of precedent the Court is frank to include "the necessity of maintaining public faith in the judiciary as a source of impersonal and reasoned judgments."[27] When the Court alters course too abruptly, especially on questions of intense national debate, it severely taxes that "public faith." The clumsy flip-flop in the Legal Tender Cases[28] a century ago is still remembered as one of the Supreme Court's most grievous "self-inflicted wounds."[29] Traumatic memories of this sort do much to explain why even one of the Court's most independent justices can say, "I am firmly convinced that we have a profound obligation to give recently decided cases the strongest presumption of validity."[30]

Conversely, there are arguments by which recent decisions can be disparaged as serious precedents. The newer the decision the less the opportunity for accretion of reliance interests, and it is after

[27] Moragne v. States Marine Line, 398 U.S. 375, 403 (1970).

[28] Knox v. Lee (Legal Tender Cases), 79 U.S. (12 Wall.) 457 (1871), overruling Hepburn v. Griswold, 75 U.S. (8 Wall.) 603 (1870).

[29] See Hughes, The Supreme Court of the United States 50–53 (1928). Hughes' two other "notable instances" of self-inflicted wounds are the *Dred Scott* case, Scott v. Sandford, 60 U.S. (19 How.) 393 (1857), and the income tax case, Pollock v. Farmers' Loan & Trust Co., 158 U.S. 601 (1895).

[30] Florida Dept. of Health v. Florida Nursing Home Ass'n, 450 U.S. 147, 151 (1981) (concurring opinion). To similar effect, see Solem v. Stumes, 104 S. Ct. 1338, 1354 (1984) (Stevens, J., dissenting); General Bldg. Contractors Ass'n v. Pennsylvania, 458 U.S. 375, 405 (1982) (Stevens, J., concurring); California v. Sierra Club, 451 U.S. 287, 298 (1981) (Stevens, J., concurring); Dougherty Bd. of Educ. v. White, 439 U.S. 32, 47 (1978) (Stevens, J., concurring); Planned Parenthood of Missouri v. Danforth, 428 U.S. 52, 101 (1976) (Stevens, J., concurring in part and dissenting in part); Runyon v. McCrary, 427 U.S. 160, 189 (1976) (Stevens, J., concurring). The "strongest presumption of validity" falls short of a conclusive presumption. See Justice Stevens' advocacy of overruling of National League of Cities v. Usery, 426 U.S. 833 (1976), by separate concurrence in EEOC v. Wyoming, 103 S.Ct. 1054, 1067 (1983) ("[I] think it so plain that National League of Cities not only was incorrectly decided, but also is inconsistent with the central purpose of the Constitution itself, that it is not entitled to the deference that the doctrine of stare decisis ordinarily commands for this Court's precedents"). Notice also Justice Stevens' shift from initial acceptance of the Court's recent sovereign immunity decisions to a posture of out-and-out opposition. Compare Florida Dept. of Health, *supra* (concurring opinion yielding to the precedential authority of Edelman v. Jordan, 415 U.S 651 (1974)), with Atascadero State Hosp. v. Scanlon, 105 S.Ct. 3142, 3180 (1985) (dissenting opinion urging "a fresh examination of the Court's Eleventh Amendment jurisprudence").

all the reliance element that is one of the chief inhibitors of judicial overruling.[31] It is less painful to correct a single decision than to uproot a line of cases or for that matter a whole sector of jurisprudence.[32] Moreover, recent decisions have differing densities that are not visible to the outsider but are known to the participating justices.[33] Some decisions are the product of haste or fragile compromise or inattention on the part of some of the majority subscribers and so are more susceptible to early reexamination than decisions which embody firmly held views. As Justice Jackson reminds us,[34]

> The first essential of a lasting precedent is that the court or the majority that promulgates it be fully committed to its principle. That means such individual study of its background and antecedents, its draftsmanship and effects that at least when it is announced it represents not a mere acquiescence but a conviction of those who support it. When the thoroughness and conviction are lacking, a new case, presenting a different aspect or throwing new light, results in overruling or in some other escape from it that is equally unsettling to the law.

As for the Court's public image, a quick self-correction poses nothing like a Legal Tender threat where the repudiated recent decision is not of "landmark" stature but involves only technical or other low-profile matters.[35]

---

[31] Brandeis, calling for the overruling of several decisions within the previous seven years, says, "The decisions are recent ones. They have not been acquiesced in. They have not created a rule of property around which vested interests have clustered." Washington v. Dawson & Co., 264 U.S. 219, 228 (1924) (dissenting opinion).

[32] Walker v. Armco Steel, 446 U.S. 740, 749 (1980). On the other hand, Justice Frankfurter denigrates a case decided only a year earlier: "A single decision by a closely divided Court, unsupported by the confirmation of time, cannot check the living process of striking a wise balance between liberty and order as new cases come here for adjudication." Kovacs v. Cooper, 336 U.S. 77, 89 (1949) (concurring opinion) (speaking of Saia v. New York, 334 U.S. 558 (1948)).

[33] For example, although Justice Stewart joined the eight to zero opinion in Red Lion Broadcasting Co. v. FCC, 395 U.S. 367 (1969), he later acknowledged that it was "with considerable doubt." See Columbia Broadcasting System v. Democratic Nat'l Comm., 412 U.S. 94, 138 (1973) (concurring opinion). Likewise Justice Harlan in Welsh v. United States, 398 U.S. 333, 344 (1970) (concurring in result), recanted his earlier vote with the majority in United States v. Seeger, 380 U.S. 163 (1965). And Justice Douglas disparaged as "casual, almost off hand" a unanimous ruling in which he had joined seventeen years earlier. See Cammarano v. United States, 358 U.S. 498, 514 (1959) (concurring opinion) (referring to Valentine v. Chrestensen, 316 U.S. 52 (1942)).

[34] Jackson, Decisional Law and Stare Decisis, 30 A.B.A. J. 334, 335 (1944). See the similar observations by Illinois's Justice Schaefer, Precedent and Policy, 34 U. Chi. L. Rev. 3, 7 (1966).

[35] When the Court reverses itself in the same case by a rehearing, the situation is closer to abortion than infanticide.

A. CESSATION OF DISSENT

One place where a cessation of dissent occurs with some regularity is in cases of statutory interpretation. As Dean Ely has observed, "[d]issenting views . . . are seldom maintained beyond the original case in which they are announced (for the obvious reason that Congress can correct a construction it did not intend or does not presently approve, a move ordinarily not open to it in the constitutional context)."[36] A confirming illustration was recently provided by two justices who are not usually identified with stare decisis self-denial. Justices Marshall and Brennan were among the dissenters in the five to four decision, *Buffalo Forge Co. v. Steelworkers*,[37] which read the Norris-LaGuardia Act as prohibiting federal injunctions of sympathy strikes by unions not directly party to a labor dispute. Some years later, in *Jacksonville Bulk Terminals v. International Longshoremen's Ass'n*,[38] the question was whether federal judges could intervene injunctively against the politically inspired refusal by longshoremen to handle cargo bound for the Soviet Union. The four *Buffalo Forge* dissenters were still on the Court and evidently still in disagreement with the decision (they were Justice Powell and Justice Stevens as well as Justices Marshall and Brennan). In addition one member of the *Buffalo Forge* majority, the Chief Justice, was prepared to disavow his vote in that case. Another member of the earlier majority was Justice Stewart, who had retired and been succeeded by a jurist of unknown views on the scope of Norris-LaGuardia, Justice O'Connor. Finally, Jacksonville Terminals' specific request for a reconsideration of *Buffalo Forge* created a procedurally congenial setting for an overruling. Yet that did not happen. For reasons essentially of stare decisis Justices Marshall and Brennan discarded their original dissenting views and contributed the decisive votes for adherence to the construction put on the statute by *Buffalo Forge*, with Justice Marshall performing the further service of delivering the Court's opinion.[39]

---

[36] Ely, The Supreme Court, 1977 Term—Foreword: On Discovering Fundamental Values, 92 Harv. L. Rev. 5, 10 n.33 (1978).

[37] 428 U.S. 397 (1976).

[38] 457 U.S. 702 (1982).

[39] See also Dougherty Bd. of Educ. v. White, 439 U.S. 32, 47 (1978) (concurring opinion), where Justice Stevens cast the fifth vote for a liberal application of the Voting Rights Act contrary to his own prior dissent. But *cf.* Oklahoma City v. Tuttle, 105 S.Ct. 2427, 2441 (1985) (dissenting opinion) (Justice Stevens argues for imposing respondeat superior liability

Given the lesser force of stare decisis in constitutional litigation, we do not encounter as much surrender of dissent as in statutory cases—and much of what appears superficially to be stare decisis-induced resignation is in fact "temporary acquiescence." Still, some capitulation by recent dissenters does occur. An interesting specimen was provided by Justices White and Stewart in connection with Congressional reapportionment. When the Court first considered the constitutionality of minor population disparities in the 1969 cases of *Kirkpatrick v. Preisler*[40] and *Wells v. Rockefeller*,[41] those two justices objected to the Court's mathematical rigidification of the new "one man, one vote" principle. But in the next case on the subject four years later, Justice White, joined by Justice Stewart, delivered the Court's opinion in *White v. Weiser*,[42] standing by the *Kirkpatrick* and *Wells* rulings in the face of a direct plea for overruling and notwithstanding the appearance of an embryonic majority for overruling formed by the addition of three new justices who were plainly unpersuaded by the earlier decisions.

As an exercise in constitutional law there is something to be said for giving precedential finality to the decisions insisting on digit perfection equality in a state's congressional districts. Even if the Court did mishandle the issue, it did not inflict an injustice or threaten any vital state concerns. The margin of disagreement between the majority and dissenters was narrow (shall the districts be perfectly equal or substantially equal in population?). Whatever the majority lacked in doctrinal felicity was offset by the bright-line clarity of the instructions given to Congressional map makers. This too can be said for Justices White and Stewart: when a judge grants controlling effect to a decision from which he had dissented only a short while before, he has the minor consolation of knowing that, as Judge Traynor puts it, "he has had his day," that is, a personal opportunity to influence the Court's choice when the matter was res nova, something he cannot say about more ancient precedents which claim his allegiance without his input. Moreover, acceptance of precedent is not a wholly unselfish action. Insofar as the justices

---

on cities in suits under 42 U.S.C. § 1983, although that is contrary to Monell v. Dep't of Social Services, 436 U.S. 658 (1978)).

[40] 394 U.S. 256 (1969).

[41] 394 U.S. 542 (1969).

[42] 412 U.S. 783 (1973).

have comparably respectful attitudes toward past decisions, the "losing" justice's embrace of the majority's decision is reciprocated in situations in which the precedential shoe is on the other foot.[43]

And yet there is more than a trace of gall and wormwood here, for not only is the dissenter required to desist after once registering his objections, but he must avoid the temptation of striking an alliance with new justices who may well be amenable to an overruling (*vide White v. Weiser, vide Jacksonville Bulk Terminals*). And if his devotion to stare decisis is stronger than his colleagues', he may find himself once more in dissent, vainly protesting the renunciation or impairment of a decision whose wisdom he never personally accepted. For stare decisis, properly understood, means that the past decision should be upheld not merely because there are not enough votes for overruling but despite the conviction of a majority of—or all—the current judges that the decision was incorrect. The precedent is to be followed not for lack of critics but for paramount reasons of stability in the law.

But what, we may ask, is the point of dissenting in the first place if the dissenter does not intend and hope that his views will prevail in time? Charles Curtis tells us in his charming book, *Lions Under the Throne*:[44]

> Dissents serve a larger purpose than either to cover scruples of conscience or to save your judicial reputation as a good lawyer. Dissents are competing opinions in their own right. They are what the dissenter would have said if he had persuaded enough of his colleagues to agree with him. * * * The majority exercise all the powers of the Court, but the minority have a curious concurrent jurisdiction over the future. For a dissent is a formal appeal for a rehearing by the Court sometime in the future, if not on the next occasion.

This, of course, echoes Chief Justice Hughes' famous description of dissent as "an appeal to the intelligence of a future day, when a later decision may possibly correct the error into which the dissenting judge believes the court to have been betrayed."[45] If a dissent is *not*

---

[43] And the converse: those who wield the sword of overruling expose themselves to the swords of Jacobite restorers. See Garcia v. San Antonio Metro. Transit Auth., 105 S.Ct. 1005 (1985), overruling National League of Cities v. Usery, 426 U.S. 833 (1976), which had overruled Maryland v. Wirtz, 392 U.S. 183 (1968).

[44] Curtis, Lions Under the Throne 74–75 (1947).

[45] Hughes, note 29 *supra*, at 68.

"an appeal to the intelligence of a future day," is it then bereft of a function? Chief Justice Taft certainly thought so. His well known aversion to displays of dissent on the Court in fact was a corollary of his firm attachment to stare decisis. "I don't approve of dissents generally," he is quoted as remarking to a colleague, "for I think in many cases where I differ from the majority, it is more important to stand by the Court and give its judgment weight than merely to record my individual dissent where it is better to have the law certain than to have it settled either way."[46] In this statement Taft conflates the Brandeis formulation of stare decisis and the practice of selective dissent. He says in effect that to warrant public exposure, a judge's disagreement with his colleagues must be a prayer for overruling; if it does not amount to that, the dissent ought to remain *in pectore*.[47]

In cases of statutory interpretation, given the greater locking-in effect of stare decisis, a nonrenewable dissent might serve as an

---

[46] Mason, William Howard Taft: Chief Justice 223–24 (1965). For Taft this was not only a matter of statecraft; it was a question of judicial ethics. In 1924 he engineered the inclusion of Canon 19 in the American Bar Association's Canons of Judicial Ethics: "It is of high importance that judges constituting a court of last resort should use effort and self-restraint to promote solidarity of conclusions and the consequent influence of judicial decision. A judge should not yield to pride of opinion or value more highly his individual reputation than that of the court to which he should be loyal. Except in case of conscientious difference of opinion on fundamental principle, dissenting opinions should be discouraged in courts of last resort." Wisely, this canon was deleted from the reformulated Code of Judicial Conduct in 1972.

Although in Taft's eyes Justice Brandeis was a libertine of dissent (as were Holmes and Stone), we know of many cases where Brandeis scrapped his draft dissents though he still thought the majority opinion was wrong. In one such case Brandeis "suppressed my dissent, because, after all, it's merely a question of statutory interpretation." Bickel, The Unpublished Opinions of Brandeis 210 (1957). By the standards of today's Court, Brandeis, Holmes, and Stone are models of collegiality. See Nelson, note 6 *supra*. A common criticism of the Burger Court is voiced by Archibald Cox, who says: "The most striking aspect of the work of the Burger Court has been the insistence of the Justices upon presenting individual views, and their persistence in advancing those views even after a majority has disagreed. This is not a new development, but the trend has been more pronounced." Cox, Freedom of Expression in the Burger court, 94 Harv. L. Rev. 1, 72 (1980).

[47] But when it is the majority that is doing the overruling, an aggrieved defender of precedent will not hesitate to dissent despite a general Taftlike reluctance to do so. Often the strongest formulations of the doctrine of stare decisis appear in such dissenting opinions. See, *e.g.*, Pollock v. Farmers Loan & Trust Co., 157 U.S. 429, 652 (1985) (White, J., dissenting). It has been calculated that in his 27-year career on the Court, Justice (later Chief Justice) White dissented in only 33 cases. Lambeth, The Lawyers in Statuary Hall, 66 A.B.A. J. 1254 (1982). Even the formidable John Marshall, who abhorred dissent on his court, published a minority opinion when one of his decisions was overruled by his colleagues. Hudson v. Guestler, 10 U.S. (6 Cranch) 281 (1810), overruling Rose v. Himely, 8 U.S. (4 Cranch) 241 (1808). Cf. Bank of U.S. v. Dandridge, 25 U.S. (12 Wheat.) 64, 90 (1827) (Marshall, C. J., dissenting despite "my custom, when I have the misfortune to differ from this court, [of] acquiesc[ing] silently in its opinion").

appeal to the legislative branch for corrective amendment rather than as advocacy of judicial overruling—although that is surely not every dissenter's specific intention.[48] In any event, the concept of dissent as a call for rectification by nonjudicial hands does not explain once-only dissent in constitutional cases, such as Justice White's in the first of the Congressional redistricting cases, for to describe his original dissent as a petition to the nation for a formal constitutional amendment to legalize mildly nonuniform Congressional districts would be, in a word, silly.

The plain fact is that dissents are not always written as pleas for future correction, by the court or anyone else. Some dissents are academic exercises having, *pace* Charles Curtis, "no larger purpose than either to cover scruples of conscience or to save [the judge's] reputation as a good lawyer." However, I would not be quick to dismiss those motives as sheer self-indulgence. Even if stare decisis factors overcome "scruples of conscience" in successor cases, why must conscience be denied expression the first time? Lord Denning speaks for most judges, I think, when he says in his memoirs: "I was reluctant to dissent. But in the last resort I did so. It was for my own peace of mind. So long as I did what I thought was just, I was content. I could sleep at night. But if I did what was unjust, I stayed awake worrying."[49] Beyond assuring a judge the sleep of the just, the dissent that does not "appeal to the intelligence of a future day" has a valuable informing function. Despite the efforts of John Marshall or William Howard Taft to forge a tradition of corporate opinions,[50] our system of appellate justice still lodges responsibility

---

[48] The dissent may also furnish forensic material for later interpretation of the revisory legislation. The dissenting opinions in General Electric Co. v. Gilbert, 429 U.S. 125 (1976), thus were an influential component of the Court's first interpretation of the anti-Gilbert Pregnancy Discrimination Act of 1978. See Newport Shipbuilding Co. v. EEOC, 103 S.Ct. 2622 (1983) (majority opinion by Justice Stevens, a *Gilbert* dissenter).

[49] Denning, The Family Story 183 (1981).

[50] See Baker, John Marshall: A Life in Law 414–16 (1974) (discussing Marshall's introduction of collective opinions); Mason, note 46 *supra*, at 198 (discussing Taft's aversion to open dissent). Other Chief Justices have voted against their own beliefs in the interest of showing solidarity (if not for the purpose of controlling the opinion assignment). See Mason, The Supreme Court From Taft to Warren 155–56 (1958) (commenting on Chief Justice Hughes' propensity for vote switching). Not only do Chief Justices dissent more sparingly than most associate justices, but they are less persistent in their dissenting positions. Chief Justice Burger discernibly fits this pattern. In nine of fifteen Terms (1969–70 through 1983–84), he issued fewer dissenting opinions than any of his colleagues. By comparison to his average of seven dissenting opinions per Term, Justice Powell averages over nine and Justice Rehnquist almost fourteen (through the 1983–84 Term). Representative examples of the Chief Justice's

for decisions in the individual judges who compose the tribunal rather than in the court as a bloodless abstraction. Certainly, where appellate judges are subject to periodic reelection or reappointment, the data for appraising an incumbent's worth come from his recorded votes and opinions. As for judges who hold lifetime tenure, the publication of dissents and separate opinions is a safeguard against arbitrary or slipshod decision making by fellow judges. When anonymity of pronouncement is combined with security in office, it is all too easy for the politically insulated officials to lapse into arrogant *ipse dixits*. Taft's conviction that most dissent is incompatible with stare decisis duties therefore crosses the grain of our legal traditions. We remember that the dissenting opinion is a fixture of British judicial practice and that individual dissent flourished during that long era in which all the English judges, dissenters included, were in thrall to a rigid stare decisis that had no room whatever for "appeals to the intelligence of a future day."[51] This surely attests to the institutional legitimacy of dissent even when it is less than a clarion call for future overruling.

B. THE CREDIBILITY FACTOR

One does not have to be an enthusiast in order to form a reasonable opinion about the meaning of previous cases, and there is nothing disabling ethically or intellectually about earlier dissent. Yet when the original dissenter takes a narrower view of the precedent than that taken by charter members of the majority, can he avoid giving the impression of still resisting the Court's ruling? Here one needs to be more precise about the requirements of stare decisis. The foremost obligation is for a judge to integrate the current case into the body of past decisions. If he claims to respect a

---

readiness to discontinue his dissent even when fellow dissenters do not are Branti v. Finkel, 445 U.S. 507 (1980) (joining majority opinion based on Elrod v. Burns, 427 U.S. 347 [1976]), and Arizona v. Rumsey, 104 S.Ct. 2305 (1984) (joining majority opinion adhering to Bullington v. Missouri, 451 U.S. 430 [1981]). In addition, compare the Chief Justice's separate concurrence in Dun & Bradstreet v. Greenmoss Builders, 105 S.Ct. 2939, 2948 (1985) (temporarily accepting but distinguishing Gertz v. Welch, 418 U.S. 323 [1974], with *id.* at 2953 (White, J., concurring in judgment) (Justice White, another *Gertz* dissenter, is totally "unreconciled to the Gertz holding").

[51] For an instance of surrendered dissent in the House of Lords even after the 1966 relaxation of stare decisis, see Lord Reid's concurring speech in Knuller v. Director of Public Prosecutions, [1973] A.C. 435, 455. For other functions of nonrenewed dissent, see Patterson, note 1 *supra*, at 100.

precedent, the judge should either follow it, explaining how it compels or what it contributes to his conclusion, or he should distinguish it, pointing out why the present outcome does not contradict the earlier decision. Perhaps because of their greater inhibitions about outright overruling, the English courts tend to look at cases in terms of their narrow facts and to distinguish them in ways that, to American eyes, look like hair splitting.[52] Though American judges differ from their British cousins in giving more consideration to the rationale of the precedent, they are still left with considerable leeway when it comes to interpreting the past decisions, often finding it possible to draw relatively narrow or relatively broad propositions from the case law. Since it is in the nature of courts of last resort (unlike intermediate reviewing courts) to deal in the novel and the debatable, fidelity to Case A does not automatically solve the problem of Case B. As Brandeis put it, "The process of inclusion and exclusion, so often applied in developing a rule, cannot end with its first enunciation."[53] So while the dissenter may regard himself as precedentially bound by the original decision, that does not mean he is forced to any *a priori* understanding of the meaning of the case, and a conservative reading of the precedent is not necessarily disingenuous.[54] What does cause an acute credibility problem is the dissenter's current attempt to put forward a limiting interpretation of the first decision after having originally, in the overstated fashion of many dissenters, projected all the gloomy ramifications of the majority's action. One sometimes sees justices earnestly, and awkwardly, drawing distinctions that previ-

---

[52] See generally Cross, Precedent in English Law 38–102 (3d ed. 1977).

[53] Washington v. Dawson & Co., 264 U.S. 219, 236 (1924) (dissenting opinion).

[54] Indeed, even if every justice is equally dedicated to stare decisis, succeeding cases can be decided by shifting majorities, with the result that there is no justice on the Court who endorses each and every interpretation and application of the original ruling; and yet all are obliged, as are the lower courts, to make sense, if possible, out of the entire body of decisions. Or a pattern of decisions may conform in toto to the views of just one justice, who thereby commands special authority. See, *e.g.*, the unique role played by Justice Powell in cases involving claims of unconstitutional discrimination against illegitimate children. In nine such decisions since 1972, seven found a denial of equal protection and two found no constitutional violation. Justice Powell was the "swing" voter in two of the cases, decided five to four, making him the only justice to support the Court's result in all nine cases: Weber v. Aetna Cas. & Sur. Co., 406 U.S. 164 (1972); Gomez v. Perez, 409 U.S. 535 (1973); N.J. Welfare Rights Org. v. Cahill, 411 U.S. 619 (1973); Jiminez v. Weinberger, 417 U.S. 628 (1974); Mathews v. Lucas, 427 U.S. 495 (1976); Trimble v. Gordon, 430 U.S. 762 (1977); Lalli v. Lalli, 439 U.S. 259 (1978); Mills v. Habluetzel, 456 U.S. 91 (1982); Pickett v. Brown, 103 S.Ct. 2199 (1983).

ously they dismissed and even ridiculed.[55] Dissenting chickens of that sort have a way of coming home to roost.[56]

But contrast the position of the former dissenter who now extends generous effect to the majority decision as a blueprint for future cases, broader scope than even the original authors of the precedent case are prepared to grant it. There is a series of decisions involving the constitutionality of health inspections of private premises without a search warrant in which Justice Stewart provides a fascinating model of an erstwhile dissenter who, in the grasp of stare decisis, becomes more Catholic than the Pope.[57] Stewart's own views about such administrative inspections are reflected in *Frank v. Maryland*,[58] where he joined the majority in a five to four decision allowing warrantless entry. Understandably enough he dissented from the six to three overruling of *Frank* by *Camara v. Municipal Court*.[59] But then, in *Marshall v. Barlow's, Inc.*,[60] his vote created a five to three majority for a *Camara*-premised decision finding the Fourth Amendment violated by the OSHA inspection procedure. Finally in a fourth case on the subject, *Donovan v. Dewey*,[61] Justice Stewart

---

[55] As a dissenter in Lloyd Corp. v. Tanner, 407 U.S. 551, 570 (1972), Justice Marshall complained that the Court was sub silentio overruling Amalgamated Food Employees Union v. Logan Valley Plaza, Inc., 391 U.S. 308 (1968), even though the majority professed to find the cases distinguishable. Then when the Court in Hudgens v. NLRB, 424 U.S. 507 (1976), declared that *Lloyd Corp.* had indeed overruled *Logan Valley*, Justice Marshall, again dissenting, said: "upon reflection I am of the view that the two cases are reconcilable." *Id.* at 535. For a contrastingly canny analysis by an initial dissenter, see Justice Stevens' opinion in Caban v. Mohammed, 441 U.S. 380, 415 (1979) (appreciating "the risk that the arguments one advances in dissent may give rise to a broader reading of the Court's opinion than is appropriate," the dissenters chose instead to emphasize "why [they] regard [the majority's] holding in this case as quite narrow"). See also the minimizing dissents by Justice Brennan in Marsh v. Chambers, 103 S.Ct. 3330, 3337 (1983), and Lynch v. Donnelly, 104 S.Ct. 1355, 1370 (1984).

[56] The awkwardness is mitigated somewhat when the former dissenter is now the spokesman for the Court, since the views he expresses in that capacity are not, or may not be, as purely individual as views expressed by separate opinion. See Weinberger v. Salfi, 422 U.S. 749 (1975) (Justice Rehnquist's majority opinion distinguishes United States Dept. of Agriculture v. Murry, 413 U.S. 508 (1973), on a ground which he had sought to discredit as a *Murry* dissenter).

[57] In addition to the series of cases discussed in the text, see NLRB v. Pipefitters Local, 429 U.S. 507, 543 (1977) (Stewart, J., dissenting) (protesting the Court's rough handling of a statutory interpretation precedent, Nat'l Woodwork Mfrs' Ass'n v. NLRB, 386 U.S. 612 [1967], from which Justice Stewart himself had dissented).

[58] 359 U.S. 360 (1959).

[59] 387 U.S. 523 (1967).

[60] 436 U.S. 307 (1978).

[61] 452 U.S. 594 (1981).

filed a dissenting opinion, charging the Court with backsliding from *Camara* and *Barlow* by its decision to allow warrantless mine safety inspection. The full extent of Justice Stewart's self-subordination can be seen in the following passages:[62]

> In *Frank v. Maryland* . . . , the Court concluded that warrantless administrative inspections are not subject to the restrictions that the Fourth and Fourteenth Amendments place upon conventional searches. The *Frank* decision was overruled eight years later in *Camara v. Municipal Court* . . . , over the dissent of three Members of the Court, of whom I was one. I believed then that the *Frank* Case had been correctly decided, and that warrantless health and safety inspections do not "require . . . the safeguards necessary for a search of evidence of criminal acts." . . . I must, nonetheless, accept the law as it is and the law is now established that administrative inspections are searches within the meaning of the Fourth Amendment. . . . Because the Court today departs from this principle, I respectfully dissent.

One wonders: suppose Justice Stewart had continued on the Court for another, post-*Donovan* case of administrative inspection without warrant. Would he then have embraced and defended the *Donovan* apostacy with the same generosity with which he yielded to the *Camara* majority in *Barlow*? The trouble is that, for a justice who sees it as his obligation to uphold the last relevant precedent, a meandering course of decisions leaves him a step behind his colleagues, treading unhappily in their footprints without the satisfaction of voting his own views on the merits or the consolation that he is bringing uniformity to the law.[63]

We cannot take leave of Justice Stewart without giving him credit for perhaps the most breathtaking abandonment of individual views in the annals of constitutional law. I am referring to his remarkable concurring opinion in the abortion case, *Roe v. Wade*.[64] The precursor to *Roe* was *Griswold v. Connecticut*,[65] striking down a

---

[62] *Id.* at 609–10.

[63] I have suggested elsewhere that persistent zigzagging by an appellate court should release lower courts from stare decisis obligations. Kelman, The Force of Precedent in the Lower Courts, 14 Wayne L. Rev. 3, 28 (1968). The freedom is available, a fortiori, to individual members of the higher Court, including those who place utmost stress on the doctrine of precedent. See Wolman v. Walter, 433 U.S. 229, 265 n.2 (1977) (Stevens, J., concurring in part and dissenting) ("the doctrine of stare decisis cannot foreclose an eventual choice between two inconsistent precedents").

[64] 410 U.S. 113 (1973).

[65] 381 U.S. 479 (1965).

law against contraception. There Justice Stewart dissented, seeing the majority's strained attempt to tie the decision to the Bill of Rights by means of emanations and penumbras radiating from specific guarantees of privacy as nothing less than a revival of the doctrine of open-ended substantive due process, a concept thought to have been thoroughly and permanently discredited by the modern Court. Next came *Roe*, decided by an opinion that dropped the pretense of direct derivation from the Bill of Rights. For his part Justice Stewart accepted the decision. His concurring opinion reads in part:[66]

> [I]t was clear to me then, and it is equally clear to me now, that the Griswold decision can be rationally understood only as a holding that the Connecticut statute substantively invaded the "liberty" that is protected by the Due Process Clause of the Fourteenth Amendment. As so understood Griswold stands as one in a long line of pre-Skrupa cases decided under the doctrine of substantive due process, and I now accept it as such.

Justice Stewart's position amounts to this: I myself reject the theory that due process is a substantive limitation on state law, as did the full Court in the long post-*Lochner* period and as I made clear in my dissent in *Griswold*. But the implication, although not the avowed basis, of the *Griswold* majority decision is that due process is a substantive check after all, and giving *Griswold* the respect due it as the latest precedent, I will apply the Fourteenth Amendment substantively now and hereafter.[67] And, as the record shows, that is

---

[66] 410 U.S. at 167–68.

[67] Dean Ely asserts that "Justice Stewart rather clearly intends his *Roe* opinion as a repudiation of his *Griswold* dissent, and not simply as an acquiescence in what the Court did in the earlier case." Ely, The Wages of Crying Wolf: A Comment on Roe v. Wade, 82 Yale L.J. 920, 940–41 n.109 (1973). I agree that Justice Stewart "repudiates" his *Griswold* dissent, but only out of respect for stare decisis and not because he suddenly became a road-to-Damascus convert to substantive due process. Further reflection apparently satisfied Justice Stewart that the Court had given recognition to unenumerated liberties of a noneconomic character not only in the "long line of pre-Skrupa cases decided under the doctrine of substantive due process" but in several other contemporary decisions besides *Griswold*. Among those he mentions are the racial intermarriage case, Loving v. Virginia, 388 U.S. 1 (1967), and the right-to-travel decisions, Shapiro v. Thompson, 394 U.S. 618 (1969) (domestic travel) and Aptheker v. Sec'y of State, 378 U.S. 500 (1964) (foreign travel). Thus Justice Stewart concludes that the idea of substantive due process had not been rejected as definitely as he had thought when he dissented in *Griswold*. On this reanalysis of the case law, he is making a clinical observation rather than voicing a personal preference when he says that "[c]learly the Court today is correct in holding that the right [of abortion] is embraced within the personal liberty protected by the Due Process Clause of the Fourteenth Amendment." 410 U.S. at 170.

precisely what Justice Stewart did in cases after *Roe*. He conscientiously attempted to decide whether the claimed nontextual right was or was not "implicit in the concept of ordered liberty," accepting some such substantive due process claims[68] and rejecting others on their merits.[69] He also insisted that substantive due process questions should be recognized in those terms and not decided, as his colleagues sometimes did, under other rubrics (notably equal protection of laws).[70]

Justice Stewart's course after *Griswold*, let it be noted, is not a simple matter of a dissenter imputing a broader rather than a narrower holding to the precedent decision and then following the broader holding in new cases. *Roe v. Wade* raised questions about the significance of written constitutions and about the proper role of the judiciary in a democratic society, matters of first principle really—which is why *Roe* set off a tidal wave of books and articles about the evils or virtues of "noninterpretive" decision making by the Supreme Court. Did the doctrine of precedent, even granting it a nonnegligible role in constitutional cases, force Justice Stewart to show the white flag when he was outvoted once (or even twice) on such profound questions?[71] Should a modern generation of Court decisions, supported in turn by a stream of classic Holmes and Brandeis dissents, have been cast aside so quickly? If the answer is "no"—as I think it is—then it follows that *Roe* is not a sacrosanct precedent. It can be overruled with an easy conscience by a reconstituted Supreme Court, even if the new justices are institutional conservatives with relatively strong stare decisis instincts.[72]

---

[68] Carey v. Population Services Int'l, 431 U.S. 678 (1977) (Justice Stewart joins the Court's opinion upsetting restrictions on distribution of contraceptives to minors, on *Griswold-Roe* grounds); Zablocki v. Redhail, 434 U.S. 374, 391 (1978) (Justice Stewart concurs separately, recognizing a due process right to remarry).

[69] Moore v. East Cleveland, 431 U.S. 494, 531 (1977) (Justice Stewart, in dissent, rejects a claimed fundamental right of an "extended family" to live together in violation of zoning restrictions).

[70] Zablocki v. Redhail, 434 U.S. 374, 391 (1978) (majority applies the strict scrutiny form of equal protection analysis; Justice Stewart concurs separately to insist that the proper basis for decision is pure substantive due process).

[71] In contrast to his quick capitulation to revived substantive due process, Justice Stewart remained stalwart in opposition to the *Miranda* doctrine concerning police interrogation of suspects. See Orozco v. Texas, 394 U.S. 324, 331 (1969) (Stewart, J., dissenting).

[72] I differ with Professor Monaghan, who says of *Roe*, "While I think the case incorrectly decided, I would be reluctant now to disturb its authority." Monaghan, note 15 *supra*, at 8.

II. Sustained Dissent: The Never-Say-Die Option

Assume that the dissenter still nurtures hope that eventually the Court will recognize and correct its error and so is unwilling to grant a final settling effect to the majority's decision. The choice for such a justice then reduces to this: either he can "renew the rataplan of his dissent" (as Judge Traynor puts it) or he can turn to the practice I have termed temporary subordination until the Court agrees to reconsider the question.[73]

Stubborn dissent is a characteristic of many constitutional cases not only because the doctrine of precedent weighs less heavily but also because justices form such strong and matured convictions about organic law that they find it exceedingly hard to make even the limited shift from dissent to temporary accommodation.[74] If there was less persistence in dissent on the nineteenth-century Supreme Court than we see today, I think it is because constitutional cases represented a smaller part of the Court's work in that era and major rulings did not regularly drive lawyers back to court for doctrinal fine-tuning.

The justice regarded as the Court's "First Dissenter," the Jeffersonian Republican William Johnson, was hardly a promiscuous writer of minority opinions by modern standards. In his twenty-nine years as a justice, Johnson issued thirty-four dissenting opinions.[75] None was strictly a repetitious dissent. Indeed, a biographer calls attention to a period in his mid-career on the Court when Justice Johnson "lapse[d] into silent acquiescence" suggestive of "a limited acceptance on Johnson's part of Marshall's presuppositions."[76]

---

[73] Of course, there are instances in which the transformation from dissenter to overruler occurs in a single triumphant leap, sparing the justice from having to choose between further dissent and temporary acquiescence in the interim. Thus Justice Stone was a dissenter in Di Santo v. Pennsylvania, 273 U.S. 34, 37 (1927), and author of the overruling opinion in California v. Thompson, 313 U.S. 109 (1944). Justice Stewart was the lone dissenter in Bonnelli Cattle Co. v. Arizona, 414 U.S. 313, 332 (1973), and member of the overruling majority in Oregon v. Corvallis Sand & Gravel Co., 429 U.S. 363 (1977).

[74] Justice Rehnquist has said that "it may well be that the nature of constitutional adjudication invites, if it does not require, more separate opinions than does adjudication in other areas." The Supreme Court: Past and Present, 59 A.B.A. J. 361, 363 (1973). Professor Maltz, note 15 supra, at 476 n.46, relates the multiplication of individual opinions to the lesser role of stare decisis.

[75] Morgan, Justice William Johnson: The First Dissenter 189 (table 2) (1954).

[76] Id. at 290.

On the other hand, a protomodern dissenter in frequency and tenacity was Justice Peter Daniel (1841–60). Daniel subscribed to the philosophy, held by more than a few twentieth-century justices, that the oath of office obliges each justice to follow his own version of constitutional truth no matter how singular it is. As he declared in the *License Cases*,[77]

> [I]n matters involving the meaning and integrity of the Constitution, I can never consent that the text of that instrument shall be overlaid and smothered by the glosses of essay-writers, lecturers, and commentators. Nor will I abide the decisions of judges, believed by me to be invasions of the great *lex legum*. I, too, have been sworn to observe and maintain the Constitution. I possess no sovereign prerogative by which I can put my conscience into commission. I must interpret exclusively as that conscience shall dictate.

Justice Daniel had such deep antipathy to federal authority, including the judicial branch's, that a successor observed that "he seemed to consider himself not so much a member of the Supreme Court as a delegate sent from the States to break down the growing power of the national judiciary."[78] Among many propositions to which he took running exception was that a business corporation is a citizen of the chartering state for purposes of the federal courts' diversity jurisdiction. This was laid down in a unanimous 1844 decision.[79] Daniel exploded in disagreement eight years later, with this excuse for his belated dissent:[80]

> Against this position it may be urged, that this matter is no longer open for question. In answer to such an argument, I would reply, that this is a matter involving a construction of the Constitution, and that wherever the construction or the integrity of that sacred instrument is involved, I can hold myself trammelled by no precedent or number of precedents. That instrument is above all precedents.

Within two years Daniel delivered another dissent on the same point[81] and by the time his Court service ended, he had reiterated

---

[77] 46 U.S. (5 How.) 504, 612 (1847) (concurring opinion).

[78] Brown, The Dissenting Opinions of Mr. Justice Daniel, 21 Am. L. Rev. 869, 886 (1887).

[79] Louisville & Cincinnati R.R. Co. v. Letson, 43 U.S. (2 How.) 497 (1844). It is not known why Justice Daniel let this ruling go without a protest.

[80] Rundle v. The Delaware & Raritan Canal Co., 55 U.S. (14 How.) 80, 95 (1852).

[81] Northern Indiana R.R. v. Mich. Cent. R.R., 56 U.S. (15 How.) 233, 251 (1854).

his dissent in sixteen cases involving corporate litigants in diversity suits.[82]

Still later in the nineteenth century several of the justices proved unyielding in their opposition to the Legal Tender Act, which the Court in rapid sequence struck down and then upheld.[83] Chief Justice Chase and Justices Clifford and Field continued in succeeding cases to haul out the argument that paper money impaired contracts ("We have considered with great deliberation the views of the majority who differ from us and we are unable to yield our assent to them").[84] And even after the death of his dissenting comrades left Justice Field the Court's only exponent of the antilegal tender position, he still pressed his point of view resolutely and with passion.[85]

Finally, the first Justice Harlan merits attention. He ranks with Johnson and Daniel as one of the three great dissenters of the nineteenth-century Court. Harlan was not as chronically out of harmony with his colleagues as was Justice Daniel, but he was no stranger to repeated dissent.[86] After delivering a dissenting argument in *Hurtado v. California*[87] for treating grand jury presentment as a Fourteenth Amendment requirement in state criminal cases, Justice Harlan thereafter took what we can term "dissenter's notice" of the absence of indictment in capital cases reaching the Court on entirely different claims of error.[88] Paradoxically, Harlan never displayed equivalent tenacity in opposing racial segregation after his eloquent dissent in *Plessy v. Ferguson*.[89]

---

[82] Brown, note 78 *supra*, at 888.

[83] See note 28 *supra*.

[84] Doley v. Smith, 80 U.S. (13 Wall.) 604 (1872) (dissenting opinion). Further dissents were registered in The Telegraph v. Gordon, 81 U.S. (14 Wall.) 258, 269 (1872); Norwich & Worcester R.R. Co. v. Johnson, 82 U.S. (15 Wall.) 195, 196 (1873); Maryland v. R.R. Co., 89 U.S. (22 Wall.) 105 (1874) (dissent without opinion).

[85] Julliard v. Greenman, 110 U.S. 421, 451 (1884).

[86] For a comparison of Daniel and Harlan as dissenters, see Brown, The Dissenting Opinions of Mr. Justice Harlan, 46 Am. L. Rev. 321 (1912).

[87] 110 U.S. 516, 538 (1884).

[88] Baldwin v. Kansas, 129 U.S. 52, 57 (1889) (dissenting opinion).

[89] 163 U.S. 537, 552 (1896). Harlan fell silent on the constitutional propriety of racial segregation of school children in a case in which the appellant raised the issue for the first time at oral argument. Indeed, he wrote the Court's opinion rejecting the appeal, an action that was generally understood as a countenancing of school segregation and, even worse, of grossly inferior facilities for black pupils. Cummings v. Board of Educ., 175 U.S. 528 (1899).

When we come to the twentieth-century Court, there is no short-age of repeated dissenters, but the foremost justice in this category is Hugo Black. For the most part he declined to judge constitutional cases by any principles but his own.[90] He did not retreat from his pet notions no matter how often or forcefully his views were dis-missed by the Court—not even in cases where the official jurispru-dence could be made to yield the same results as his own ideas. To a greater degree than other justices, Black defined himself as a textualist and also an originalist, relying on the words of the Con-stitution[91] and the understanding of the Framers[92] as the touch-stones of decision. One who claims to discern clear answers in the text or history, as Black so often did, will not be diverted by a false or casuistic gloss placed on the document by others. In a sense Black's indifference to case law is a corollary to his belief that the best constitutionalist is semanticist-cum-historian rather than law-yer.[93]

The intransigence of Black's views is well known in freedom of speech cases. His reading of the First Amendment led him to dis-tinguish pure forms of speech, which he held to be absolutely immune from government interference (hence Black's renown as an "absolutist"), from physically expressive actions, which he did not consider "speech" in the constitutional sense and which he ex-cluded from the First Amendment's protective mantle.[94] Presented

---

[90] In contrast to his irreverence toward precedent in constitutional law, Justice Black argued for the strictest sort of stare decisis in matters of statutory interpretation. See Boys Markets, Inc. v. Retail Clerks Union, 393 U.S. 235, 255 (1970) (dissenting opinion).

[91] See, e.g., Katz v. United States, 389 U.S. 347, 373 (1967) (dissenting opinion); Gris-wold v. Connecticut, 381 U.S. 479, 510 (1965) (dissenting opinion).

[92] See McGautha v. California, 402 U.S. 183, 226 (1971) (concurring opinion); Adamson v. California, 332 U.S. 46, 74 (1947) (dissenting opinion), criticized by Fairman, Does the Fourteenth Amendment Incorporate the Bill of Rights? The Original Understanding, 2 Stan. L. Rev. 5 (1949), and answered by Justice Black in Duncan v. Louisiana, 391 U.S. 145, 162 (1968) (concurring opinion).

[93] See Bobbitt, Constitutional Fate 33 (1982). Other justices have also spoken of the primacy of the text. See, e.g., Graves v. New York ex rel. O'Keefe, 306 U.S. 446, 491–92 (1939) (Frankfurter, J., concurring); Coleman v. Alabama, 399 U.S. 1, 22–23 (1970) (Burger, C. J., dissenting).

[94] Compare New York Times Co. v. Sullivan, 376 U.S. 254, 293 (1964) (concurring opinion); Konigsberg v. State Bar of California, 366 U.S. 36, 56 (1961) (dissenting opinion); Beauharnais v. Illinois, 343 U.S. 250, 267 (1952) (dissenting opinion), with Street v. New York, 394 U.S. 576, 609 (1969) (dissenting opinion); Cox v. Louisiana (Cox II), 379 U.S. 559, 575 (1965) (dissenting opinion); Giboney v. Empire Storage & Ice Co., 336 U.S. 490 (1949) (opinion for the Court). For a critical analysis, see Kalven, Upon Rereading Mr. Justice Black on the First Amendment, 14 UCLA L. Rev. 428 (1967).

with a case in the first category, Black's response was automatic: no regulation, no punishment is constitutional allowable. That his fellow justices might rule in favor of the speaker through different principles and analyses—for example, by evaluating the importance of the government interest at stake, the restrictiveness of the regulation, and the availability of less burdensome alternatives— simply meant that Black's separate opinion was a concurrence in the judgment rather than a dissent. One wonders, without disparaging his theory of free speech, whether there was any point to his attending the arguments in a "pure speech" case. What he heard from either side was almost certain to be foreign to his own thought processes.[95]

Another of Justice Black's go-it-alone positions was his thesis of total incorporation of the Bill of Rights through the Fourteenth Amendment.[96] In case after case he addressed the due process claim from that perspective, undaunted by the majority's repeated rejection of wholesale incorporation. What emerged instead as the Court's ruling doctrine was the philosophy of "selective incorporation" of those parts of the Bill of Rights that are "fundamental." In the long run that approach produced nearly as much restriction of local police practices as Black's theory, a point he was not bashful about making. But while Justice Black allied himself with the piecemeal incorporators in specific cases, he did not merge his views with theirs; he wrote separately, and his position remained distinctively his own.[97] However, no justice is a purist in all things,

---

[95] While Black did not go to the length of ducking out of the oral arguments, he did make a point of absenting himself from the Court's private screening of assertedly obscene motion pictures—a necessary part of the decisional process for other justices but for him an irrelevance and in itself an unconstitutional ritual of censorship. Dunne, Hugo Black and the Judicial Revolution 356–57 (1977). In speaking of Justice Black's closed mind on free-speech matters, I do not mean to intimate that he was somehow unfit to participate in such cases. Judicial impartiality does not require a judge to be persuadable to any point of view in every case. Justice Douglas addressed this in a public speech, saying: "[I]t would have been a gross erosion of judicial independence to have undertaken to drive Hugo Black out of a case involving First Amendment rights because he felt passionately that the First Amendment was the heart of our constitutional system." Douglas, The Court Years 371 (1980) (quoting his own public remarks in 1975).

[96] Adamson v. California, 332 U.S. 46, 68 (1947) (dissenting opinion). The earliest exponent of this thesis was Justice Harlan, dissenting in Twining v. New Jersey, 211 U.S. 78, 114 (1908).

[97] See Duncan v. Louisiana, 391 U.S. 145, 162 (1968) (concurring opinion). In contrast to Justice Black's self-adherence is the nonchalance with which the dissenters in Gannett Co. v. De Pasquale, 443 U.S. 368 (1979), who had argued unsuccessfully for recognition of a Sixth

and certainly not in the things that this essay treats. Hugo Black, the premier straight-line dissenter, occasionally confounds us with appeals to stare decisis in constitutional cases[98] and with uncharacteristic acts of temporary accommodation.[99]

Repeated dissent appears on the current Court in many important aspects of constitutional law. Justices Brennan and Marshall habitually assert that the death penalty is per se cruel and unusual punishment, despite decisive rulings to the contrary.[100] The same two justices, joined by Justice Stewart, continually voted to reverse criminal obscenity convictions on the basis of their dissenting views in *Miller v. California*.[101] Justice Brennan also persists in the uncanonical opinion that the double-jeopardy clause is violated when a defendant is subjected to separate trials for offenses stemming from a single criminal transaction.[102] And Justice White maintains a running disagreement with the three-part constitutional analysis laid down in *Lemon v. Kurtzman*[103] for aid to religion cases[104] and ad-

---

Amendment right of public access to criminal proceedings, switched over to an alternative theory of First Amendment access in the next case, Richmond Newspapers, Inc. v. Virginia, 448 U.S. 555 (1980) (see especially the concurring opinions by Justices White, *id.* at 581, and Blackmun, *id.* at 601).

[98] See United States v. Rabinowitz, 339 U.S. 56, 66 (1950) (Black, J., dissenting) (opposing the overruling of a recent 5–4 decision in which he had been on the dissenting side, Trupiano v. United States, 334 U.S. 699 (1948)). Years later Justice Black in turn objected to the overruling of *Rabinowitz* by Chimel v. California, 395 U.S. 752 (1969).

[99] See Boulden v. Holman, 394 U.S. 478, 482 (1969) (concurring notation) ("Mr. Justice Black, while still adhering to his dissent in Witherspoon v. Illinois, 391 U.S. 510 [1968], acquiesces in the Court's judgment and opinion" remanding to the lower court an unconsidered *Witherspoon* issue).

[100] See, *e.g.*, Pulley v. Harris, 104 S.Ct. 871, 884 n.1 (1984) (dissent).

[101] 413 U.S. 15, 47 (1973). Justices Brennan, Stewart, and Marshall reiterated their *Miller*-dissenting views in Millican v. United States, 418 U.S. 974 (1974) (dissent from denial of cert.); Jenkins v. Georgia, 418 U.S. 153, 162 (1974) (concurring in result); Marks v. United States, 430 U.S. 188, 196 (1977) (concurring in part and dissenting in part); Smith v. United States, 431 U.S. 291, 310 (1977) (dissenting opinion); Pinkus v. United States, 436 U.S. 293, 305 (1978) (concurring in result); Ballew v. Georgia, 435 U.S. 223, 246 (1978) (separate concurrence); New York v. Ferber, 458 U.S. 747, 775 (1982) (Brennan and Marshall, JJ., concurring in judgment); Maryland v. Macon, 105 S.Ct. 2778, 2783 (1985) (Brennan and Marshall, JJ., dissenting); Brockett v. Spokane Arcades, 105 S.Ct. 2794, 2805 (1985) (Brennan and Marshall, JJ., dissenting).

[102] Typical is Brooks v. Oklahoma, 456 U.S. 999 (1982) (Brennan, J., dissenting from denial of cert.).

[103] 403 U.S. 602 (1971).

[104] See Justice White's dissenting opinions in Wallace v. Jaffree, 105 S.Ct. 2479, 2508 (1985); Grand Rapids School Dist. v. Ball, 105 S.Ct. 3216, 3249 (1985); Aguilar v. Felton, 105 S.Ct. 3232, 3249 (1985); Committee for Pub. Educ. v. Nyquist, 413 U.S. 756, 820 (1973); Roemer v. Maryland Bd. of Pub. Works, 426 U.S. 736, 768 (1976); New York v.

heres to his dissenting position in *Buckley v. Valeo*[105] that campaign spending ceilings do not violate the First Amendment.[106]

In favor of the course of unremitting dissent as against the alternative of temporary subordination of minority views is its quality of directness. The dissenter speaks in his own unmistakable voice, says what he thinks the law ought to be, and wields his vote in conformity to that vision. There is no over-subtlety, no distortion by any other concerns than the intrinsic merits of the case. But all this guilelessness is not without a tactical dimension. By acting on the basis of his own counterdoctrine, the dissident may imagine that he is preventing the official position from settling into a marmoreal hardness that will defy future displacement. He may suppose that the continuing exhibition of his opposition shows the world that the issue remains in dispute, that while battles are lost the war goes on, and in this way he encourages litigants to mount fresh assaults on the official position, creating new opportunities for reconsideration and hastening the "intelligence of a future day."

The idea of keeping the issue alive is perfectly legitimate. Whatever its actual effectiveness, it is not an act of institutional treachery on the part of the dissenter. There is no ethical imperative that confines a dissenter to a single, not-to-be-repeated statement of disagreement. Contrary to Chief Justice Taft's belief, rejection of the Court's decisions by a minority of justices does not "leave the dissenters to be the only constitutional lawbreakers in the country."[107] They are in a unique position, to be sure. For lower court judges to disregard Supreme Court decisions is to forget their place

---

Cathedral Academy, 434 U.S. 125, 134–35 (1977). But note Justice White's nominal acceptance of the *Lemon* formula as author of the Court's opinion in Committee for Pub. Educ. v. Regan, 444 U.S. 646 (1980) (an opinion assignment whose wisdom I would question, for reasons developed in the text *infra* at note 268), and his joining without cavil a majority opinion applying the *Lemon* tests to a law guaranteeing workers their Sabbath day off, Estate of Thornton v. Caldor, Inc., 105 S.Ct. 2914 (1985).

[105] 424 U.S. 1, 257 (1976) (concurring in part and dissenting in part).

[106] First Nat'l Bank of Boston v. Bellotti, 435 U.S. 765, 802 (1978) (dissenting opinion); Citizens Against Rent Control v. Berkeley, 454 U.S. 290, 303 (1981) (dissenting opinion); FEC v. National Conservative Political Action Comm., 105 S.Ct. 1459, 1471 (1985).

[107] Mason, note 46 *supra*, at 223. As a majority opinion writer recently observed about a chronic dissenter: "Justice Brennan has long maintained that the settled view of Hans v. Louisiana, as established in the holdings and reasoning of the above cited cases, is wrong. [There follows a string citation of Justice Brennan's dissents.] It is a view, of course, that he is entitled to hold." Atascadero State Hosp. v. Scanlon, 105 S.Ct. 3142, 3148 n.3 (1985).

in the judicial hierarchy.[108] But members of the highest Court stand apart. By tradition, not by logical necessity, they are allowed the privilege of rejecting the majority's decisions. A dissenting justice who exercises that prerogative can be accused of stubbornness, lack of collegiality, or undue pride of opinion,[109] but none of that makes him a "constitutional lawbreaker." Although this is an elementary point, Justice Frankfurter thought it worthwhile to remind the judiciary[110] that as a Supreme Court dissenter he was not inviting or in any sense sanctioning lower court disregard of the controlling precedents.[111]

It is a nice question whether dissent, be it singular or sustained, actually does contribute to later doctrinal change in a causal sense. When a new generation of judges engages in overruling, the historical dissent may provide nothing more than some quotable support for a decision that would have been the same in any event. The dissent, in other words, may be a correct prophesy yet not a source of the change. One writer asks whether we are not falling into the *post hoc ergo propter hoc* fallacy when we give "credit" to early dissenters in these situations:[112]

> Would the Fourteenth Amendment have come a day later had not Mr. Justice Curtis dissented in the Dred Scott case? Was the Supreme Court of 1954 dependent upon, or even substantially influenced by, the wisdom of Mr. Justice Harlan when it discovered that "separate but equal" had become a constitutional non-sequitur? To so frame the questions is to require answers that I believe to be obviously in the negative.

And even if past dissent were one in a set of factors producing turnaround by a later Court, there is nothing in the cases to suggest that sustained dissent is more potent than dissent uttered once and then suspended. If any Supreme Court dissenter can be said to have influenced the thinking of his successors, it was Justice

---

[108] See, *e.g.*, Hutto v. Davis, 454 U.S. 370, 375 (1982). See generally Kelman, note 63 *supra*.

[109] See Toll v. Moreno, 458 U.S. 1, 19 (1982) (Blackmun, J., concurring) (criticizing Justice Rehnquist).

[110] Schwartz v. Texas, 344 U.S. 199, 204–05 (1952) (concurring in result).

[111] Accord, Oregon v. Hass, 420 U.S. 714 (1975).

[112] ZoBell, Division of Opinion in the Supreme Court: A History of Judicial Disintegration, 44 Cornell L.Q. 186, 211 n.129 (1959).

Holmes. Yet as Brandeis remarked, Holmes had a "reluctance to dissent again after he had once had his say on a subject."[113] Typical of that reluctance was Holmes' role in successive cases concerning the constitutionality of minimum wage laws. Charles Curtis describes the sequence:[114]

> Among the great dissents were those of Taft, Sanford, and Holmes in the Atkins case, where a minimum wage was held unconstitutional. A few years later, in 1925, the same question came up and the same majority again held a minimum wage void. And all three dissenters acquiesced. "Mr. Justice Holmes," the report says, "requests that it be stated that his concurrence is solely upon the ground that he regards himself bound by the decision in *Adkins v. Children's Hospital.*"

Did Holmes blunt the impact of his initial dissent on a future Court? Not at all. As Curtis says, "it was their dissent which persisted, not their acquiescence, and was the base on which the *Adkins* case was later overruled."[115]

But doesn't continuation of dissent stimulate challenges to the foundation precedents that might have been inhibited by a Holmesian suspension of dissent? Again there is reason to be skeptical. For one thing, every repetition of a minority view advertises the dissenter's inability to win over his colleagues. Why should a mere attorney think he will succeed in attacking established doctrine after a talented Supreme Court justice has repeatedly failed at intramural persuasion? What seems in practice to inspire direct challenges to case law is not the tenacity of the original dissenters but shifting winds within the Court, brought about by such developments as change in the Court's composition or indications of misgiving on the part of justices who helped to fashion the ruling cases or by the doctrine's visible deterioration over the course of time. Thus it was not surprising in the Pentagon Papers Case[116] that, despite the repeated dissents of Justice Black and Douglas on behalf of an absolutist interpretation of the First Amendment, the lawyers

---

[113] Bickel, note 46 *supra*, at 18.

[114] Curtis, note 44 *supra*, at 75 (Holmes was speaking in Arizona v. Sardell, 269 U.S. 530 (1925), about Adkins v. Children's Hosp., 261 U.S. 525 (1923)).

[115] *Ibid.* For another reference to Holmes' cessation of dissent, see Evans, The Dissenting Opinion—Its Use and Abuse, 3 Mo. L. Rev. 120, 132 (1938). But for a counterexample of repeated dissent by Holmes, see Stevens, note 14 *supra*, at 7.

[116] New York Times Co. v. United States, 403 U.S. 713 (1971).

for the *New York Times* and *Washington Post* put pragmatism before vain posturing and chose not to advocate First Amendment absolutism but to concede the remote possibility of a constitutionally sustainable injunction against certain press reports revealing military secrets. Their moderation no doubt irritated Justices Black and Douglas, but their votes in favor of freedom to publish could be taken for granted anyway. The key to victory was in wooing the Court's First Amendment "balancers," for whom the Black-Douglas position was too doctrinnaire and too coarse to cope with the factual subtleties of specific cases.[117]

INDEFINITE VERSUS SHORT-TERM DISSENT

Two very different factors seem to account for the maintenance of dissenting views on an issue. One is the factor of deep conviction—Charles Curtis's "scruples of conscience"—the justice's belief not only in the soundness of his position but in its righteousness. Deep conviction is the fuel that drives dissent past the limits of hope, beyond appeal to the intelligence of a future day, and into the realm of the quixotic. It is why a justice champions a lost cause. But the other factor behind continued dissent is distinctly the child of hope. It is the dissenter's assessment that the decisions which he opposes will prove to be short-lived. Perhaps the cases were so closely divided or so disfigured by compromise or superficiality that corrective action seems to him almost inevitable.[118] Here further dissent is a serious form of counterattack, a response to perceived instability. But should the majority decisions turn out to be more durable and more fertile than anticipated, the dissenter needs to reassess his own position. At that point dissent can give way to subordination or even all-out stare decisis acceptance.

In connection with short-term dissent, one is reminded of Felix Frankfurter's less than worshipful attitude toward recent deci-

---

[117] See Godofsky, Protection of the Press From Prior Restraints and Harassment Under Libel Laws, 29 U. Miami L. Rev. 462, 471–72 (1975). A similar piece of advocacy is recounted in Lewis, Gideon's Trumpet 174 (1964).

[118] Justice Walter Schaefer says: "The instrinsic quality of the precedent relied upon is significant in determining its fate. . . . [A]n opinion which does not within its own confines exhibit an awareness of relevant considerations, whose premises are concealed, or whose logic is faulty is not likely to enjoy either a long life or the capacity to generate offspring." Schaefer, note 34 *supra*, at 10, 11.

sions[119] and especially of his role in the cases considering the application of antitrust laws to professional athletics. After the Court reaffirmed baseball's antitrust immunity in 1953,[120] it proceeded to hold professional boxing subject to the Sherman Act in 1955, over Frankfurter's dissent.[121] He dissented again two years later when the Court added football to the list of sporting enterprises governed by antitrust laws.[122] "Respect for the doctrine of stare decisis," Frankfurter wrote, "does not yet require me to disrespect the view I expressed [as a dissenter] in the Boxing case."[123] "Yet" implies a time limitation on his disagreement with the Court.[124] One can only wonder if *Flood v. Kuhn*[125] would have been the point at which Frankfurter's inclination to further dissent was exhausted. In any event, we can look on short-term dissent as the antithesis of temporary acquiescence. The temporary acquiescer goes along for now but in hope of ultimate reversal; the short-term dissenter disagrees for the present but is prepared to yield when hope for change runs out.

III. SUSPENDED DISSENT: THE OPTION OF TEMPORARY ACQUIESCENCE

We come to the postdissenting alternative which I choose to call temporary acquiescence—granting governing effect to the majority's decision until a countermajority can be marshalled for cor-

---

[119] See Helvering v. Hallock, 309 U.S. 106, 119 (1940). See also Frankfurter's continued dissent, begun in United States v. Kahriger, 345 U.S. 22, 37 (1953), and reiterated in Lewis v. United States, 348 U.S. 419, 425 (1955). Several years after Frankfurter's departure from the Court, *Kahriger* and *Lewis* were overruled, although not for the reasons that provoked Frankfurter to dissent but rather for the reasons stated by dissenters Black and Douglas in those cases. See Marchetti v. United States, 390 U.S. 39 (1968).

[120] Toolson v. New York Yankees, Inc., 346 U.S. 356 (1953).

[121] United States v. International Boxing Club, 348 U.S. 236, 248 (1955).

[122] Radovich v. National Football League, 352 U.S. 445, 455 (1957).

[123] *Id.* at 456.

[124] Indeed, Justice Frankfurter said in his *Radovich* dissent, *id.* at 455: "It would disregard the principle [of stare decisis] for a judge stubbornly to persist in his views on a particular issue after the contrary had become part of the tissue of the law. Until then, full respect for stare decisis does not require a judge to forego his own convictions promptly after his brethren have rejected them."

[125] 407 U.S. 258, 284 (1972) ("we adhere once again to Toolson . . . to International Boxing and Radovich").

rective action.[126] This choice differs from true acceptance of stare decisis in that the original dissenter, counting on time and tide to bring about a reconsideration of the precedent, reserves the right to join, indeed to rally, his colleagues to an express reversal when the moment is opportune.

A. DAMAGE CONTROL

What commends temporary acquiescence as against sustained dissent? One might start with the simple observation that a justice who is willing to participate on an equal footing, doctrinally speaking, may be in a position to limit or ameliorate the Alpha principle, whereas a justice's adherence to outvoted views estranges him from the precise questions posed by succeeding cases and wastes his potential influence on the evolutionary direction of the case law. We are speaking, in short, about a strategy of damage control, of a judicial Fabianism looking toward the gradual reshaping of a bad decision into good, or at least less noxious, law.

But that is an incomplete explanation for temporary acquiescence. In the first place, the damage containment concern becomes operative only when there are four other votes on the Court for limiting the foundation decision and when an original dissenter can furnish the pivotal fifth vote. If a majority exists without him for a restriction of Case Alpha, it makes little difference whether the original dissenter adds a surplus signature to an already precedential opinion of the Court or keeps up a running opposition to the Case Alpha principle.[127] And, on the other hand, if there is a

---

[126] A cynic might say that "indefinite submission" or "acquiescence in perpetuity" are more descriptive terms than temporary acquiescence, considering the infrequency of express overrulings by the Court, particularly overrulings that take place within the career span of the original dissenters. For lists of express overrulings, see note 15 *supra*. However, it is not my argument that suspension of dissenting views is more conducive to early reversal than is sustained dissent. Either course faces formidable odds, and most dissent, whether repeated or not, proves in the fullness of time to have been futile. The point is simply that a justice's alternative vision of the law, expressed either as sustained dissent or as provisional concurrence, may promote the chances of future reconsideration at least marginally, and if it does nothing else it spares the minority justice from estopping himself by a premature surrender should the reconsideration come to pass while he is still on the Court.

[127] In these circumstances the original dissenter, while joining the Court's opinion distinguishing the prior case, may wish to record his standing objection to the earlier decision as a precedent. See, *e.g.*, Hills v. Gautreau, 425 U.S. 284, 306–07 (1976) (Marshall, J., concurring) ("In this case the Court distinguishes Milliken [v. Bradley, 418 U.S. 717 (1974)]. I join the Court's opinion except insofar as it appears to reaffirm the decision in Milliken").

current majority for an Alpha-extending decision, placing our justice again on the minority side, what is the advantage of arguing for a narrower reading of Alpha rather than repeating the justice's basic objections to Alpha itself?

Secondly, the attractiveness of the damage control tactic is qualified by the factor of intellectual self-respect. It is not always possible for a fairminded judge to blunt the impact of a precedent decision, and even the most tendentiously nimble cannot sidestep precedent in every situation. Temporary acquiescence forces a justice, when push comes to shove, to vote in accordance with the Court's ruling decisions.[128] For this reason we need to distinguish temporary acquiescence from a look-alike behavior that I will term spurious acceptance of the precedents. Spurious or one-sided acceptance is a method used by an unreconciled dissenter to reach via the Court's own decisions the same end result that his own theories call for. If the justice does not reproclaim his dissent as an alternative ground, his opinion may appear to be operating within the majority's current terms of reference. But this reliance on the prior cases is unfailingly result oriented. The precedents are quoted or explained away only to support a conclusion that sorts with the justice's dissident views. When all the allowable techniques for manipulation of precedent fail,[129] the one-sided judge does not hesitate to resurface his original opposition.[130]

---

[128] Intellectual high-mindedness may also be combined with a desire to let the ramifications of the foundation case be felt in full, the more effectively to discredit the precedent. An example is Justice Jackson's swing vote in Magnolia Petroleum Co. v. Hunt, 320 U.S. 430 (1943), for a position he and four other justices claimed to derive from Williams v. North Carolina, 317 U.S. 287 (1942), decided a year earlier over Jackson's strong dissent. See 320 U.S. at 446–47 (concurring opinion). However, Justice Jackson discarded the hairshirt when he joined in a unanimous decision four years later, holding that *Magnolia Petroleum* "does not control this case," Wisconsin Indus. Comm'n v. McCartin, 330 U.S. 622, 630 (1947)—a conclusion that a later generation of justices regarded as quite unfounded. See Thomas v. Washington Gas & Light Co., 448 U.S. 261 (1980).

[129] Llewellyn lists sixty-four "precedent techniques," including some for "avoidance of 'the decided,'" Llewellyn, The Common Law Tradition: Deciding Appeals 77–91 (1960), and especially at 84–86. Avoidance techniques subdivide into the legitimate and the illicit. In the latter category are such malpractices as deliberately ignoring the adverse precedent ("flatly illegitimate," says Llewellyn) or drawing a meaningless distinction (something Llewellyn characterizes as "dubiously legitimate, except in a system which will not face up to overruling").

[130] A justice may revert to his basic dissent even when one-sided acceptance is still a feasible alternative. Thus Justice Stevens, a dissenter in National League of Cities v. Usery, 426 U.S. 833 (1976), joined in a series of subsequent decisions in all of which a majority, and sometimes a unanimous Court, was able to distinguish and limit *National League of Cities*:

Reversion to original opposition in some instances never becomes necessary. Certain precedents are undermined by a course of limiting decisions before they are finally swept away. An original dissenter's one-sided acceptance provides a basis for ad hoc alliances with other justices whose support for the precedent is waning but who are not yet prepared for outright disavowal. If the Court is steady in its retreat from the foundation case during that transitional period, it may be impossible to discern from the actions and statements of the original dissenter whether we are witnessing temporary subordination or merely feigned submission. Indeed, the former dissenter has no need in these circumstances to resolve his true position in his own mind. That is why I hesitate to offer the renowned overruling in *Erie Railroad Co. v. Tompkins*[131] as a rare specimen of temporary acquiescence with a happy ending, that is, as a case where a dissenter's self-subordination was rewarded during his time on the Court with an express overruling. It is true that Justices Brandeis and Stone joined the Holmes dissent in 1928, which described *Swift v. Tyson* jurisprudence as "an unconstitutional assumption of powers by the Courts of the United States which no lapse of time or respectable array of opinion should make us hesitate to correct."[132] But in three cases after Holmes left the Court, Brandeis and Stone quietly joined unanimous opinions strengthening the role of state law in diversity of citizenship cases without directly criticizing the *Swift* doctrine of federal common law.[133] Thus we are hard put to say whether Brandeis and Stone, before staging the famous *coup de main* in *Erie*, were resorting to a jaundiced reading of *Swift* or were truly engaged in temporary acquiescence.[134]

Hodel v. Virginia Surface Mining Ass'n, 452 U.S. 264 (1981); United Transportation Union v. Long Island R.R., 455 U.S. 678 (1982); FERC v. Mississippi, 456 U.S. 742 (1982). But in EEOC v. Wyoming, 103 S.Ct. 1054 (1983), while others continued to confine the foundation precedent, Justice Stevens wrote separately to call for "a prompt rejection of National League of Cities' modern embodiment of the spirit of the Articles of Confederation." *Id.* at 1067 (concurring opinion). The call was answered in Garcia v. San Antonio Metro Transit Auth., 105 S.Ct. 1005 (1985).

[131] 304 U.S. 64 (1938).

[132] Black & White Taxicab Co. v. Brown & Yellow Taxicab Co., 276 U.S. 518, 533 (1928) (dissenting opinion).

[133] Hawks v. Hamill, 288 U.S. 52 (1933) (*per* Cardozo, J.); Burns Mortgage Co. v. Fried, 292 U.S. 487 (1934) (*per* Roberts, J.); Mutual Life Ins. Co. v. Johnson, 293 U.S. 335 (1934) (*per* Cardozo, J.).

[134] Similar ambiguity attends Chief Justice Hughes' actions concerning laws against yel-

One-sided acceptance has slight appeal to a dissenter who wants only to display the sapience of his own doctrines. Such a justice would not try to tame the objectionable precedents or put them to work for his own ends; when he was not denouncing the majority's decisions he would ignore them altogether. This kind of sustained boycott on the part of dissenters is rare, as Dean Acheson learned during his clerkship with Brandeis. In his memoirs Acheson comments on the justice's willingness to cite cases he reviled:[135]

> For a long time apparent inconsistencies in his use of certain cases led to my being constantly overruled in attempts to produce uniformity. These were such cases as *Lochner v. New York*, *Coppage v. Kansas*, and *Adair v. United States*, in which, over Holmes' dissent, the Court had declared unconstitutional statutes, today accepted everywhere, affecting labor relations. While the Justice declined to be bound by them, I argued that as a matter of principle he should never make use of them to make a point in dissenting opinions. He answered only that the Court had gotten into these errors and must not be permitted to escape the consequences.
>
> At first this attitude seemed to me an Old Testament one like Lincoln's conception in the Second Inaugural that it might be God's will that the war continue "until all the wealth piled by the bond-man's two hundred and fifty years of unrequited toil shall be sunk, and until every drop of blood drawn with the lash, shall be paid by another drawn with the sword. . . . " But I came to see that this was not so. He wanted some of the brethren to see both that they could escape from the bondage of language in these cases and that their doctrine might be very costly if developed.

It must be emphasized that a dissenter is not transformed into a temporary acquiescer according to my definition simply by saying "I still disagree with *Flotsam v. Jetsam* but my decision in this case

---

low-dog contracts. He dissented from a decision striking down such laws, Coppage v. Kansas, 236 U.S. 1 (1915). When he returned to the Court as Chief Justice, he had occasion to minimize *Coppage* and its predecessor, Adair v. United States, 208 U.S. 161 (1908). See Texas & N.O.R. Co. v. Ry. Clerks, 281 U.S. 548, 571 (1930), although his purported distinction of those cases has been termed "casual and unconvincing." See Taylor, The Unconstitutionality of Current Legislative Proposals, 65 Judicature 199, 206 (1981). *Coppage* and *Adair* were expressly overruled while Hughes was still on the Court, Phelps Dodge Corp. v. NLRB, 313 U.S. 177, 187 (1941), but somewhat anticlimactically Hughes dissented on an unrelated issue in the case.

[135] Acheson, Morning and Noon 95 (1965).

would be the same even were I to apply *Flotsam*."[136] The hallmark of a self-subordinator is that he actually accepts the interim authority of the decision in which he was outvoted. If he can steer a reasonable course around that decision to the result favored by his own dissenting principles, well and good. But an acquiescing justice is one who is ready to follow the majority holding even when it leads him to an outcome in conflict with his individual views. A soloist, on the other hand, always votes for the judgment dictated by his own theories. He may volunteer the comment that "I would join the Court's opinion and judgment today if I could accept *Flotsam v. Jetsam*," but the operative statement is this: "Adhering as I do to the views stated in my dissent in *Flotsam*, I come to a contrary conclusion in this case and accordingly I dissent from today's judgment."[137]

For an illustration of one-sided acceptance on the modern Court we can turn to Hugo Black. In tracing opinion patterns for this essay I assumed that a vivid display of Black's tenacious attachment to his own dissenting views would be found in the cases concerning the right of indigent criminal defendants to be provided with appointed counsel. In *Betts v. Brady*[138] Justice Black proposed an entitlement to counsel in every felony case, but the majority rejected such a right except in cases presenting "special circumstances" of need. After a score of years in which the special circumstances doctrine held sway, Justice Black was able to write his dissenting

---

[136] See, *e.g.*, Brown v. Glines, 444 U.S. 348, 361 (1980) (Brennan, J., dissenting) (Greer v. Spock, 424 U.S. 828 (1976)); Great Am. Fed. Savings & Loan Ass'n v. Novotny, 442 U.S. 366, 381 (1979) (Stevens, J., concurring) (Brown v. General Services Adm'n, 425 U.S. 820 (1976)); Abood v. Detroit Bd. of Educ., 431 U.S. 209, 242 (1977) (Rehnquist, J., concurring) (Elrod v. Burns, 427 U.S. 347 (1976)).

[137] This describes Justice Black's posture in cases involving the scope of the "preclearance" section of the federal Voting Rights Act, requiring certain states and localities in the South to secure Justice Department approval for changes in their electoral practices. See Allen v. State Bd. of Elections, 393 U.S. 544, 595 (1969) (Black, J., dissenting); Perkins v. Matthews, 400 U.S. 379, 401 (1971) (Black, J., dissenting). Justice Black retained his constitutional objection to the preclearance procedure, as forcefully stated in his dissenting opinion in South Carolina v. Katzenbach, 383 U.S. 310, 355 (1966). He also agreed with the Court's expansive interpretation of the preclearance provision of the statute in *Allen* and *Perkins*. Instead of formulating his position as a concurrence in the Court's judgment in those cases, he placed himself in dissent again, saying that as he still considered the statute null and void he was constrained to side with the state officials who were seeking to escape federal preclearance. *Cf.* American Textile Mfrs. Inst. v. Donovan, 452 U.S. 490, 543 (1981) (Rehnquist, J., dissenting) (refusing to take part in interpreting a statute which, in an earlier dissent, he deemed unconstitutional).

[138] 316 U.S. 455, 475 (1942) (dissenting opinion).

position into law in *Gideon v. Wainwright*,[139] expressly overruling *Betts*. Surely, I thought, in the many cases leading up to *Gideon*, Justice Black must Catolike have renewed his demand for an unrestricted right of counsel for indigent defendants. No. What Black actually did was to oscillate between his own anti-*Betts* views and an application (obviously a generous application) of the *Betts* exception. Sometimes he wrote separately to renew his call for an absolute right to an attorney;[140] at other times he joined majority opinions that scraped together enough "special circumstances" to require the appointment of counsel[141] (Justice Black even authored some of those opinions for the Court).[142] Only rarely did Black write conjunctively, siding with the defendant on the basis of his own minority view as well as the *Betts* exception.[143] There even is a case virtually on the eve of *Gideon* in which Justice Black elected to join the opinion of six other justices predicated on special circumstances rather than a separate concurring opinion by Justice Douglas, joined by Justice Brennan, directly attacking *Betts*.[144]

The one constant in Black's actions was that he never failed to support the claim for appointment of counsel. His occasional resort to *Betts* analysis never was at the expense of upholding the conviction of an unrepresented indigent. If a given case eluded the reach

---

[139] 372 U.S. 335 (1963).

[140] Bute v. Illinois, 333 U.S. 640, 677 (1948) (joining Justice Douglas' dissenting opinion); Carnley v. Cochran, 369 U.S. 506, 518–19 (1962) (concurring opinion).

[141] DeMeerleer v. Michigan, 329 U.S. 663 (1947); Wade v. Mayo, 334 U.S. 672 (1948); Moore v. Michigan, 355 U.S. 155 (1957); Cash v. Culver, 358 U.S. 633 (1959); Hudson v. North Carolina, 363 U.S. 697 (1960); Chewning v. Cunnigham, 368 U.S. 443 (1962).

[142] Pennsylvania ex rel. Herman v. Claudy, 350 U.S. 116 (1956); Palmer v. Ashe, 342 U.S. 134 (1951). Notice, however, that Justice Black managed to cite only post-*Betts* cases, not the detested *Betts* itself. Compare this disclaimer by Justice Black in Terry v. Ohio, 392 U.S. 1, 31 (1968): "Mr. Justice Black concurs in the judgment and opinion except where the opinion quotes from and relies upon this Court's opinion in Katz v. United States, 389 U.S. 347 (1967) [in which Black dissented vigorously], and the concurring opinion in Warden v. Hayden, 387 U.S. 294 (1967) [a case in which Black concurred only in result]."

[143] See Gibbs v. Burke, 337 U.S. 773, 782 (1949), where Justices Black and Douglas concurred with this notation: "They think that Betts v. Brady should be overruled. If that case is to be followed, however, they agree with the Court's opinion insofar as it holds that petitioner is entitled to relief under the Betts v. Brady doctrine." *Cf.* Uveges v. Pennsylvania, 335 U.S. 437 (1948) (Black signs Justice Reed's six to three opinion, which simply recites the two views within the Court respecting the right to counsel and finds in defendant's favor under either position).

[144] McNeal v. Culver, 365 U.S. 109 (1961). But the next year Justice Black renewed his call for overruling of *Betts*. See Carnley v. Cochran, 369 U.S. 506, 518–19 (1962) (concurring opinion).

of the special circumstances rule, even in its most generous possible form, no one could doubt how Justice Black would respond to the defendant's appeal.[145]

One-sided acceptance is not hard to spot on the current Court. Conspicuous examples are Justice Brennan's and Marshall's opinions in capital punishment cases. They vote consistently to grant review and to set aside death sentences. In some cases the only reason given is their continuing total opposition to capital punishment.[146] More often they also speak to the majority's issues, and when they do they can be counted on to find a procedural flaw or other error warranting reversal of the death penalty in the case.[147]

B. AVOIDING NONMAJORITY DECISIONS

There is, apart from any strategy of damage control, a neutral reason for the temporary sacrifice of dissent: to ensure that the case at hand produces a clear-cut opinion "of the Court." It is trite but

---

[145] See Bute v. Illinois, 333 U.S. 640, 677 (1948) (Justice Black joins in a four-justice dissent challenging "the ill-starred decision in Betts v. Brady").

[146] They have a stock statement: "adhering to our views that the death penalty is in all circumstances cruel and unusual punishment prohibited by the Eighth and Fourteenth Amendments." See their recent notation of dissent from denial of certiorari in Celestine v. Blackburn, 105 S.Ct. 3490 (1985). Cases in which their basic dissenting position was the only stated reason for their votes include Lockett v. Ohio, 438 U.S. 586, 619 (1978) (Marshall, J., concurring in judgment); Coker v. Georgia, 433 U.S. 584, 600 (1977) (Brennan and Marshall, JJ., each and separately concurring in judgment); Gregg v. Georgia, 428 U.S. 153, 227, 231 (1976) (Brennan and Marshall, JJ., separately dissenting); Woodson v. North Carolina, 428 U.S. 280, 305, 306 (1976) (Brennan and Marshall, JJ., each and separately concurring in judgment); Roberts v. Louisiana, 428 U.S. 325, 336 (1976) (Brennan and Marshall, JJ., each and separately concurring in judgment).

[147] See Baldwin v. Alabama, 105 S.Ct. 2727, 2739 (1985) (joining Justice Stevens' dissent); Spaziano v. Florida, 104 S.Ct. 3154, 3167 (1984) (joining Justice Stevens' dissent); Arizona v. Rumsey, 104 S.Ct. 2305 (1984) (joining Court's opinion based on double-jeopardy grounds); Pulley v. Harris, 104 S.Ct. 871, 884 (1984) (dissent); Zant v. Stephens, 103 S.Ct. 2733, 2757 (1983) (dissent); Endmund v. Florida, 458 U.S. 782, 801 (1982), and Eddings v. Oklahoma, 455 U.S. 104, 117 (1982) (Justice Marshall joins majority opinion without separate comment; Justice Brennan appends a concurrence repeating his basic opposition to death penalties); Bullington v. Missouri, 451 U.S. 430 (1981) (joining five to four opinion on double-jeopardy grounds); Godfrey v. Georgia, 446 U.S. 420 (1980) (concurring in result); Presnell v. Georgia, 439 U.S. 14, 17 (1978) (both justices join majority opinion but also file short reiteration of their anti-capital punishment views); Lockett v. Ohio, 438 U.S. 586, 619 (1978) (Marshall, J., concurring in result); Roberts v. Louisiana, 431 U.S. 633, 638 n.7 (1977) (both justices join five to four per curiam opinion but add a footnote repetition of their anti-capital punishment position); Gardner v. Florida, 430 U.S. 349, 364, 365 (1977) (separate opinions). Justice Marshall even turns up in the 1984–85 Term as the author of a majority opinion setting aside a death sentence. Caldwell v. Mississippi, 105 S.Ct. 2633 (1985). In that uncommon role he refrains from voicing his categorical objection to all capital punishment. The wisdom of the opinion assignment is discussed in note 268 *infra*.

nevertheless true to say that the Supreme Court's *raison d'etre* is not to dispense justice in the relative handful of cases it is possible to hear but to settle the troublesome questions presented by those cases, questions that, if the Court has managed its jurisdiction wisely, are of considerable public (at any rate professional) significance. When a single member of the Court refrains from addressing the issues specifically tendered by an appeal, the chances of securing a majority opinion are proportionally diminished. If the original dissenter agrees that the present occasion demands a clear majority pronouncement—not as a permanent solution but as an interim settlement to guide the lower courts until the Supreme Court is receptive to a full scale reexamination of the basic doctrine—and if the justice's vote is needed to create a majority opinion, then the public-spirited choice is temporary acquiescence. (This course can, but it need not, also serve the cause of damage containment.)

Justice Powell has written, "We have an institutional responsibility not only to stare decisis but also to make every reasonable effort to harmonize our views on constitutional questions of broad practical application."[148] Justice Stewart seconded the thought in a post-retirement interview:[149]

> It's always seemed to me that one of the duties of this Court, one of the reasons for its existence, is to produce a Court opinion in every case, for the guidance of lawyers and, ultimately, the people of the United States. While it's tempting to write a separate, original essay on a subject, I think it's important that there be a Court opinion when one can be achieved, through accommodation and compromise.

Of course we do not know how often justices suppress their own views in cases of initial impression, since the act is a silent one, but the reports give public view to case sequences in which the first decision produces an array of nonmajority positions and a later decision reflects the open surrender of individual views by one or

---

[148] Robbins v. California, 453 U.S. 420, 436 n.4 (1981) (concurring in judgment). Faithful to that conception of judicial duty is Justice Powell's fifth vote concurrence in Scott v. Illinois, 440 U.S. 367, 374–75 (1979). Compare Justice Powell's fifth vote concurrence in Reed v. Ross, 104 S.Ct. 2901, 2912 (1984), putting to one side his dissident views expressed in Hankerson v. North Carolina, 432 U.S. 233, 246 (1977) (concurring in result), because that issue had not been raised by the parties in *Reed*; by addressing the somewhat different question before the Court, Justice Powell made a majority pronouncement possible.

[149] "Justice Stewart (Retired)," New Yorker, Oct. 19, 1981, p. 36.

more of the justices in the interest of putting the law to rest until a different majority position is achievable. Among the more notable compromises of individual views in order to settle festering disputes on the Court, one recalls Taney's yielding to the notion that the dormant commerce power precludes state legislation in some cases[150] and more recently Justice Brennan's shift in gender classification cases from his favored policy of "strict scrutiny"[151] to a milder but still exacting intermediate standard, "substantially related to achievement" of "important governmental objectives."[152]

Justice Blackmun has yielded his own position in several cases in order that an opinion of the Court could be achieved. In *Gertz v. Welch*[153] he retreated from his own broader definition of "public figures" in libel litigation, as previously expressed in the plurality opinion in *Rosenbloom v. Metromedia, Inc.*,[154] in this way:[155]

> The Court was sadly fractionated in Rosenbloom. A result of that kind inevitably leads to uncertainty. I feel that it is of profound importance for the Court to come to rest in the defamation area and to have a clearly defined majority position that eliminates the unsureness engendered by Rosenbloom's diversity. If my vote were not needed to create a majority, I would adhere to my prior view. A definitive ruling, however, is paramount.

To dispel some of the confusion about warrantless searches of automobiles and their contents, Justice Blackmun provided a self-sacrificing fifth vote for the Court's opinion in *United States v. Ross*,[156] saying:[157]

> It is important . . . not only for the Court as an institution but also for law enforcement officials and defendants, that the appli-

---

[150] Cooley v. Board of Wardens of the Port of Philadelphia, 53 U.S. (12 How.) 299 (1851), giving up the position that state power is fully concurrent with the federal commerce power, his position in The License Cases, 46 U.S. (5 How.) 504, 573 (1847) (separate opinion), and The Passenger Cases, 48 U.S. (7 How.) 283, 464 (1849) (dissenting opinion). See Frankfurter, The Commerce Clause under Marshall, Taney and Waite 56–57 (1937); Lewis, Without Fear or Favor 300 (1965).

[151] Frontiero v. Richardson, 411 U.S. 677 (1973) (plurality opinion).

[152] Craig v. Boren, 429 U.S. 190, 197 (1976) (opinion for the Court).

[153] 418 U.S. 323 (1974).

[154] 403 U.S. 29 (1971) (three-justice plurality opinion by Brennan, J.).

[155] 418 U.S. at 354 (concurring opinion).

[156] 456 U.S. 798 (1982).

[157] *Id.* at 825 (concurring opinion).

cable legal rules be clearly established. Justice Stevens' opinion
for the Court now accomplishes much in this respect, and it
should clarify a good bit of the confusion that has existed. In
order to have an authoritative ruling, I join the Court's opinion
and judgment.

The point of fifth vote acquiescence is called into some question
by a theory of case reading that the Court seems to have endorsed,
according to which a holding of precedential value for the lower
courts (although not for the Supreme Court itself) can be extracted
from a fragmented decision. Suppose that two justices support the
Court's disposition of the case on the strength of legal analysis, X,
and three others under a broader analysis, Y, with four justices
dissenting (on anti-X and/or anti-Y grounds or for reasons unrelated to X or Y).[158] Any future case which comes within the scope
of analysis X should produce the same outcome in the Supreme
Court, assuming no personnel changes on the Court and no shifting
of original positions. For predictive purposes, then, the narrower
line of reasoning in support of the judgment (X) can be deemed the
effective ratio decidendi of the case—despite the fact that it was
adopted only by a minority of the justices or, as in our example, by
the numerically smaller of the two factions combining in the judgment.[159] Even a single "swing" justice can provide the effective
holding of the case if his view happens to be the narrowest rationale
for the Court's judgment.[160] And this seems to be true not only as

[158] Although nonmajority decisions are usually cases of close voting division (six to three,
five to four), with the majority being subdivided as to the rationale, there are also situations
in which the Court is fully unanimous as to the outcome and still unable to produce an
"opinion of the Court." E.g., Ballew v. Georgia, 435 U.S. 223 (1978).

[159] Greg v. Georgia, 428 U.S. 153, 169 n.15 (1976): "Since five justices wrote separately in
support of the judgment in Furman, the holding of the Court may be viewed as that position
taken by those members who concurred in the judgments on the narrowest grounds."
Accord, Marks v. United States, 430 U.S. 188, 193 (1977): "When a fragmented Court
decides a case and no single rationale explaining the result enjoys the assent of five Justices,
'the holding of the Court may be viewed as that position taken by those Members who
concurred on the narrowest grounds.'" See Note, The Precedential Value of Supreme
Court Plurality Decisions, 80 Colum. L. Rev. 756 (1980).

[160] It is this theory that finds precedential elements in Justice Powell's swing opinion in the
Bakke case, University of California Regents v. Bakke, 438 U.S. 265 (1978). See Blasi, Bakke
as Precedent: Does Mr. Justice Powell Have a Theory? 67 Calif. L. Rev. 756 (1980).
Similarly influential on lower courts is Justice Powell's concurring opinion on the subject of
journalists' source privileges, Branzburg v. Hayes, 408 U.S. 665, 709 (1972). See, e.g.,
United States v. Liddy, 478 F.2d 586, 587 (D.C. Cir. 1972). There are, nevertheless, cases in
which the combined effect of separate lines of reasoning produces a precedent that, while
significant in itself, plainly is an anomaly. Justice Powell's singular position in Apodaca v.

to pivotal minority positions that are ignored by the other justices in favor of alternative reasons (Y rather than X, or Z rather than X or Y) but of positions that are explicitly rejected by all the other justices, concurrers and dissenters alike.[161] Given this concept of precedent, one can wonder whether Justice Powell's belief in the importance of "harmoniz[ing] our views on constitutional questions of broad practical application" really ought to persuade a soloist to join in forming an artificial majority. Indeed, by helping to create a five-vote opinion, doesn't the justice cause an internal stare decisis obstacle to the Supreme Court's future reconsideration, an impediment that does not arise from a fragmented decision?[162]

C. DISCONTINUATION OF DISSENT AS AN "INSTITUTIONAL DUTY"

Some opinions by former dissenters declare that they and their companions in earlier dissent have a "judicial responsibility"[163] or an "institutional duty"[164] to respect the majority decision until it is

---

Oregon, 406 U.S. 404 (1972), in the context of the even division of his colleagues, created just such a precedent.

[161] National Mut. Ins. Co. v. Tidewater Transfer Co., 337 U.S. 582, 644 (1949) (Frankfurter, J., dissenting) ("And so, conflicting minorities in combination bring to pass a result—paradoxical as it may appear—which differing majorities of the Court find unsupportable").

[162] While the "utterly without redeeming social value" test of obscenity, as formulated by the three-justice plurality in Memoirs v. Massachusetts, 383 U.S. 413 (1966), was deemed by Marks v. United States, 430 U.S. 188 (1977), to be the operative holding of the case for the lower courts, it was easily—breezily—dismissed by the Supreme Court itself in Miller v. California, 413 U.S. 15, 24–25 (1973), with the comment that it "has never commanded the adherence of more than three Justices at one time." There is a considerably different reason impelling a justice to vote out of line with his own doctrinal stance, and that is to assure a majority disposition of the case at bar, rather than to produce a majority rationale. See Justice Rutledge's strictly limited concurrence "in the result" in Screws v. United States, 325 U.S. 91, 113, 134 (1945). Contrast the position of Justices Black and Douglas in Time, Inc. v. Hill, 385 U.S. 374, 402 (1967) ("[We] have joined the Court's opinion in order to make possible an adjudication that controls this litigation"). Query whether that could not have been accomplished by a Rutledge-style concurrence in result only, without helping to create a precedential opinion of the Court on doctrinal lines that Justices Black and Douglas manifestly do not support, even as temporary acquiescers. See the more limited concurrence by those justices in Associated Press v. Walker, 388 U.S. 130, 170 (1967) (for dispositional purposes only), and Justice Black's concurrence in the judgment in Rosenbloom v. Metromedia, 403 U.S. 29, 57 (1971). But see Justice Stevens' fifth vote concurrence in Pinkus v. United States, 436 U.S. 293, 305 (1978) ("The opinion that the Chief Justice has written is faithful to the cases on which it relies. For that reason, and because a fifth vote is necessary to dispose of this case, I join his opinion").

[163] Burns v. Richardson, 384 U.S. 73, 98 (1966) (Harlan, J., concurring in result).

[164] Hudgens v. NLRB, 424 U.S. 507, 518 (1976) (per Stewart, J.). See Justice Stewart's similar assertion in Burns v. Richardson, 384 U.S. 73, 99 (1966) (concurring in judgment).

reversed. Is this rhetorical excess? Is the posture of temporary accommodation in any sense compulsory rather than a matter of variable temperament and tactics?

There are, to be sure, some appellate courts which specifically require dissenters to submit to the majority's decision in dealing with succeeding cases. The practice, well known in the federal courts of appeal, avoids the issuance of contradictory pronouncements by different three-member panels of the court.[165] For that reason the decision by the first panel to address a question automatically becomes "circuit authority," binding on all the Court of Appeals judges, dissenter and nonpanelist alike, just as it binds all the district judges of the circuit. In my taxonomy the deference mandated by the practice amounts to temporary acquiescence, not stare decisis acceptance, because the dissenter's duty to put aside his opposition is *ad interim*—until the Court of Appeals agrees to give the matter en banc consideration, at which time all the judges are freed to act according to their favored positions on the merits.[166]

In a tribunal like the Supreme Court, which decides all cases "en banc," there is no corresponding need to enforce internal conformity of views. It is interesting to observe that on those few occa-

---

Justice Rehnquist, although himself a repeated dissenter in many cases, says, "I . . . agree with the statements as to institutional responsibility contained in the separate opinions in Burns v. Richardson," Lockett v. Ohio, 438 U.S. 586, 628 (1978) (concurring in part and dissenting in part). And Chief Justice Burger, while continuing to hope that Gertz v. Welch, 418 U.S. 323 (1974), will be overruled, declares in the meantime that it is "the law of the land, and until it is overruled, it must, under the principle of stare decisis, be applied by this Court." Dun & Bradstreet v. Greenmoss Builders, 105 S.Ct. 2939, 2948 (1985) (concurring in judgment). (The "principle" is not stare decisis but temporary acquiescence as here defined).

[165] See Schaefer, Reducing Circuit Conflicts, 69 A.B.A. J. 452, 455 (1983). When the Eleventh Circuit was carved out from the old Fifth Circuit, the new court took the occasion of its first case to announce its intention to follow the parent circuit's rule of intracircuit stare decisis. Bonner v. City of Prichard, 661 F.2d 1206, 1209 (11th Cir. 1981) (en banc). Because the same practice has long been observed in the Second Circuit, the often-dissident Jerome Frank wrote many separate opinions that in form were concurrences but in substance were dissents inviting Supreme Court intervention and reversal. See, *e.g.*, In re Luma Camera Service, Inc., 157 F.2d 951, 952 (2d Cir. 1946) (concurring opinion), rev'd sub nom. Maggio v. Zeitz, 33 U.S. 56 (1948). The English House of Lords resembles the federal circuits more than the Supreme Court in that it decides cases by "appellate committees" of five or seven judges rather than by the full membership, and for this reason some of the law lords are hesitant to reject recent decisions by other "committees." See Jones v. Sec'y of State for Social Services [1972] A.C. 944, 1024 (*per* Lord Simon).

[166] A variation is the practice whereby a second panel rejects the precedent panel decision after notifying all the active judges of the circuit without eliciting any requests for en banc rehearing. See Heirins v. Mizell, 729 F.2d 449 (7th Cir. 1984).

sions when a single justice acts as surrogate for the whole Court—
as in deciding as Circuit Justice whether to stay a lower court order
pending action on a cert petition—all the justices acknowledge that
a chambers decision must be based on an appraisal of the merits as
defined by the Court's precedents (to be distinguished from the
justice's own past dissents) and on a clear-eyed estimate of the
chances that four votes will be cast to grant review.[167]

The only other sense in which temporary acquiescence is, arguably, a justice's obligation rather than an option has to do with the
nature of the advocacy in the case. Our adversary system assumes a
connection between arguments made to the Court and the ultimate
judicial reasoning. Judges normally do not stray far from the issues
and arguments presented by the litigants, thinking that to do so is
to act without the informing (or cautionary) value of adversary
debate and to leave the defeated party with a sense of ill treatment.[168] Article III courts in particular, confined as they are to
actual "cases or controversies," insist on "that concrete adverseness
which sharpens the presentation of issues upon which the Court so
largely depends for illumination of difficult constitutional questions."[169] If no litigant draws into question the vitality of any of the
key precedents, a sua sponte overruling by the Court verges on a
breach of faith.[170] Should the justices wish to reconsider past deci-

---

[167] For example, Justice Rehnquist observes in Los Angeles Bd. of Educ. v. Superior
Court, 448 U.S. 1343 (1980) (chambers opinion), that the petitioner's arguments comport
with his own published dissents but he cannot "in good conscience . . . say that four
Justices of the Court would vote to grant certiorari in this Case" to reexamine the past
rulings. See generally Stern & Gressman, Supreme Court Practice 871–75 (5th ed. 1978).

[168] Indeed, a justice who misses the oral argument does not participate in the decision. See
Red Lion Broadcasting Co. v. FCC, 395 U.S. 367, 401 (1969) ("Not having heard oral
argument in these cases, Mr. Justice Douglas took no part in the Court's decision").

[169] Baker v. Carr, 369 U.S. 186, 204 (1962).

[170] That did not deter the Brandeis-led Court from acting independently of the parties in
Erie R.R. Co. v. Tompkins, 304 U.S. 64 (1938), in deciding to scrap Swift v. Tyson, 41
U.S. (16 Pet.) 1 (1842). Not surprisingly, the dissenters objected to the Court's eagerness to
overrule. See 304 U.S. at 88 (dissent). See also Michelin Tire Corp. v. Wages, 423 U.S. 276,
302 (1976) (White, J., concurring), where the concurring justice criticized the majority for
overruling Low v. Austin, 80 U.S. (13 Wall.) 29 (1872), when "[n]one of the parties has
challenged that case here, and the issue of its overruling has not been briefed or argued." Cf.
Mapp v. Ohio, 367 U.S. 643 (1961), in which the only frontal challenge to Wolf v. Colorado,
338 U.S. 25 (1949), came in a perfunctory paragraph at the end of the ACLU's amicus brief.
See Stewart, The Road to Mapp v. Ohio and Beyond: The Origins, Development and
Future of the Exclusionary Rule in Search-and-Seizure Cases, 83 Colum. L. Rev. 1365,
1367–68 (1983).
Despite these instances of unbidden overrulings, the reversal of precedent is generally seen

sions in the face of conservative advocacy based on the precedential status quo, it is always possible to invite or direct further briefing and argument addressed to that issue, as well as amicus involvement by interested groups.[171]

When we place judicial decisions against the template of the advocacy, much of what passes for precedential adherence lacks the personal commitment that I consider a defining feature of true stare decisis. There is a difference, and an important difference, between reasoning from foundation cases which none of the parties attempts to impugn and consciously upholding precedent against a direct challenge. Adherence of the first kind is not the outcome of a careful weighing of competing values that would lead a court to validate a wrong decision as the definitive settlement of the point; it is simply the result of narrowly focused advocacy and hence of inertial forces. This is not to say that a past decision is never authoritative until it has survived a plea for overruling, and certainly a long history of unchallenged application is itself an important argument against judicial self-reversal. But where today's

---

as an issue of last resort, much like a question of constitutional interpretation—to be reached only if the case cannot be decided on less sensitive grounds. *E.g.*, Brewer v. Williams, 430 U.S. 387 (1977). From a procedural standpoint it is incumbent on a party who wishes to attack a precedent to say so explicitly. Supreme Ct. Rule 21.1(a) provides that "[o]nly the questions set forth in the petition or fairly comprised therein will be considered by the Court." It is not at all certain that a question formulated in terms of the scope or applicability of a precedent decision "fairly comprise[s]" arguments for overruling. *Cf.* Burch v. Louisiana, 441 U.S. 130, 139 (1979) (Stevens, J., concurring). However, amici curiae often are bolder than the parties in interest, and they may inject arguments for overruling into a conservatively constructed appeal. Sometimes this is good enough for the Court and sometimes it is not. Compare Oregon v. Corvalis Sand & Gravel Co., 429 U.S. 363, 368 n.3 (1977), and Mapp v. Ohio, *supra*, with Monsanto Co. v. Spray-Rite Service Corp., 104 S.Ct. 1464, 1469 n.7 (1984). In any event the Court is not as constrained by the rules as is counsel. Under Rule 34.1(a) the Court reserves to itself the authority "[a]t its option . . . [to] consider a plain error not among the questions presented but evident from the record and otherwise within its jurisdiction to decide." Perhaps it could be said that the "record" exhibits "a plain error" whenever the lower court's decision is bottomed on a precedent the Supreme Court wishes, without prompting by the parties, to overrule (although the Court has not quite said so).

[171] For an early use of this technique, see United States v. Coolidge, 14 U.S. (1 Wheat.) 415 (1816) (in the end, the parties rebuffed the Court's request for reconsideration of United States v. Hudson & Goodwin, 11 U.S. [7 Cranch] 32 [1812]). More modern instances include United States v. Ross, 456 U.S. 798 (1982); Blonder-Tongue Laboratories, Inc. v. Univ. of Illinois Foundation, 402 U.S. 313 (1971); Moragne v. State Marine Lines, Inc., 398 U.S. 375 (1970). *Cf.* Illinois v. Gates, 103 S.Ct. 2317, 2321 (1983) (Court avoids decision on invited issue of overruling "with apologies to all"). The procedure of ordering reargument is still subject to the criticism that it usurps the issue-framing initiative of the attorneys. See New Jersey v. T.L.O., 104 S.Ct. 3583, 3585 (1984) (Stevens, J., dissenting).

judges are not the authors of the precedent decisions, they do not as individuals become stare decisis acceptors (rather than temporary acquiescers) unless they are actually asked to certify the inherited cases as irreversible.

In the case of contemporary precedents, the unreconciled dissenter is, of course, always ready to talk about overruling, with or without specific prompting from a litigant. In this respect individual justices tend to be more freewheeling about the questions presented by an appeal than the Court as a collective body.[172] An irritated majority sometimes points that out by way of criticism.[173]

But when an original dissenter accepts for himself the same procedural discipline that confines the rest of the Court to the issues framed by counsel, he can be said to be fulfilling an "institutional duty."[174] This, then, is the duty-based version of temporary acquiescence—the former dissenter's sense of the inappropriateness of continued debate over the wisdom of Case A when the only issues raised by the parties in Case B, considered by the lower courts, and brought within the Court's grant of review are issues based on or allied to Case A.[175] An instance of this variety of self-subordination was Justice Robert's misunderstood vote with the majority in *Morehead v. New York ex rel. Tipaldo*,[176] to invalidate a minimum

---

[172] Another feature distinguishing separate opinions from Court opinions is the tone of the prose. See Cardozo, Law and Literature 34 (1931). Because a dissenting opinion by definition lacks authority, one might not expect dissenters to avoid "obiter" or shun "unnecessary" issues. Thus in Defunis v. Odegaard, 416 U.S. 312 (1974), the Court dismissed the appeal on mootness grounds, but dissenting Justice Douglas was not content to register his disagreement with the mootness analysis; he went on to the merits and offered an individual opinion on the sensitive constitutional issue of benign racial preferences. Yet dissenters sometimes do refrain from speaking to constitutional questions which are relevant to their own view of the case but not to the majority's. See Kolender v. Lawson, 103 S.Ct. 1855, 1865 (1983) (White, J., dissenting); NLRB v. Catholic Bishop of Chicago, 440 U.S. 490, 508 (1979) (Brennan J., dissenting).

[173] See Branti v. Finkel, 445 U.S. 507, 512 n.6 (1980) ("Unlike Mr. Justice Powell in dissent . . . , petitioners do not ask us to reconsider the holding in Elrod").

[174] This was a major consideration in Justice Harlan's career as a temporary acquiescer. See Coleman v. Alabama, 399 U.S. 1, 19 (1970) (concurring in part and dissenting in part) ("The continued viability of the cases . . . is not directly before us for decision, and if and when such an occasion arises I would face it in terms of considerations that I have expressed elsewhere").

[175] Suppose the alternative of overruling is raised by the appellant but only in a feeble way. Should a pro-overruling justice hold his fire if the majority are unwilling to reexamine the precedent? Compare Justice Murphy's dissent with Justice Rutledge's special concurrence in Cleveland v. United States, 329 U.S. 14 (1946), on the question of overruling Caminetti v. United States, 242 U.S. 470 (1917).

[176] 298 U.S. 587 (1936).

wage law on the authority of the *Lochner*-era relic, *Adkins v. Children's Hospital.*[177] Within a year, Roberts cast the decisive vote in *West Coast Hotel Co. v. Parrish*[178] to overrule *Adkins.* His action was sarcastically dubbed "the switch in time that saved the Nine" from Franklin Roosevelt's Court packing plan. But the "switch" was satisfactorily explained on the procedural distinction pointed out in *West Coast Hotel,* that is, that the overruling of *Adkins* was specifically requested in that case in contrast to *Morehead,* where "the only question before [the Court] was whether the Adkins case was distinguishable."[179] That Justice Roberts' "switch" was so widely interpreted as personal inconsistency under President Roosevelt's pressure is some indication that acquiescence-in-authority-absent-an-argument-for-overruling is not a universally recognized "institutional obligation," though it is a practice of many of the justices much of the time.

IV. JUSTICE HARLAN

If Hugo Black is the diehard dissenter, the second Justice Harlan is the modern Court's leading accommodationist. A constitutional conservative on an increasingly activist Court, Justice Harlan opposed many of his colleagues' expansive interpretations of due process and equal protection. He then had to determine what his role would be after voicing his dissent.[180] To some of the decisions he extended full precedential respect and to most others his interim allegiance. While inclined to use the nomenclature of stare decisis in both settings, his opinions in the latter category

---

[177] 261 U.S. 525 (1923).

[178] 300 U.S. 379 (1937).

[179] *Id.* at 389. See Frankfurter, Mr. Justice Roberts, 104 U. Pa. L. Rev. 311 (1955). In fact the majority in *Morehead,* 298 U.S. at 604–05, was equally explicit about what it was and wasn't deciding: "The petition for the writ sought review upon the ground that this case is distinguishable from that one [*Adkins*]. No application has been made for reconsideration of the constitutional question there decided. The validity of the principles upon which that decision rests are [sic] not challenged. This Court confines itself to the ground upon which the writ was asked or granted."

[180] Dorsen, Mr. Justice Black and Mr. Justice Harlan, 46 N.Y.U. L. Rev. 649, 652 (1971); Lumbard, John Harlan: In Public Service 1925–1971, 85 Harv. L. Rev. 372, 376 (1971); Warren, Mr. Justice Harlan As Seen by a Colleague, 85 Harv. L. Rev. 369, 370 (1971) (all commenting on Harlan's role as the Court's leading dissenter after the disappearance of the "Frankfurtian majority").

clearly project the hope that Harlan's own position would someday win majority favor. Indeed, one of the things that sets Harlan apart from other subordinators is that the provisional character of his acquiescence was always spelled out in a separate opinion. He wrote either a concurrence saying that he accepted the Court's reasoning from *Flotsam v. Jetsam* in the present case although still convinced that the decision was unsound and deserving of overruling, or a dissenting opinion which took off from *Flotsam* but protested against its undue extension or its misapplication in the present case. Unlike more slothful acquiescers, Justice Harlan was not content to join an opinion for the Court by a *Flotsam* majority justice writing on the uncriticized foundation of *Flotsam*.[181]

His subordination of views is nowhere more evident than in cases involving the constitutionality of state criminal procedures. What drove Harlan to initial dissent was his rejection of the doctrine of Fourteenth Amendment "incorporation," which transfers to the states all restrictions expressed in the first eight amendments that the Court deems "necessary to an Anglo-American regime of ordered liberty,"[182] and which, moreover, makes those incorporated sections of the Bill of Rights applicable to the states "root and branch," "jot for jot," "bag and baggage," "hide and tail,"—that is, with the same degree of stringency as in their primary application to federal authorities.[183] Harlan belonged to the once dominant school of thought[184] that understands Fourteenth Amendment due process to prohibit only governmental conduct that "shocks the conscience."[185] This approach, usually described as the fundamental fairness principle, denies any direct linkage between the due process guarantee of the Fourteenth Amendment and the particulars of the Bill of Rights; a challenged state practice may satisfy due process even if the same practice by the federal government runs afoul of some stricture in the Bill of Rights, and a state practice can

---

[181] Nesson, Mr. Justice Harlan, 85 Harv. L. Rev. 390 (1971); Lewin, Justice Harlan: "The Full Measure of the Man," 58 A.B.A. J. 579, 583 (1972).

[182] Duncan v. Louisiana, 391 U.S. 145, 150 n.14 (1968).

[183] See Nowak, Rotunda, & Young, Constitutional Law 455–57 (2d ed. 1983).

[184] See Adamson v. California, 332 U.S. 46 (1947); Palko v. Connecticut, 320 U.S. 319 (1937); Twining v. New Jersey, 211 U.S. 78 (1908).

[185] Rochin v. California, 342 U.S. 165, 171 (1952).

deny due processes in the Fourteenth Amendment sense without offending any prohibition found in the first eight amendments.[186]

The Harlan version of due process was overtaken in the 1960s by the incorporationist philosophy. Incorporation produced sequences of cases in which the first typically exhibited a Bill of Rights violation by the state but not necessarily a conscience-jolting injustice, and the question for the Court was whether Fourteenth Amendment due process was thereby denied.[187] For the majority of justices such a case afforded a vehicle for "selective incorporation" of the constitutional safeguard in question. And, as it transpired, most of the justices treated nearly everything in the Bill of Rights as worthy of Fourteenth Amendment incorporation. Justice Harlan of course rejected the incorporationist methodology and predictably dissented, often with force and eloquence, from what he considered a woeful misconstruction of the text and an injury to the constitutional system of federalism.

Once having settled a matter of incorporation, the Court turned next to cases presenting questions of interpretation of the incorporated provision of the Bill of Rights. These second generation cases illuminate Justice Harlan's accommodation to the majority. Unlike a Justice Black or Douglas, who habitually maintained their original dissenting positions in succeeding cases, Harlan generally accepted as *fait accompli* the Court's decision to extend the federal right in question to state criminal practice.[188] His acceptance fell short of all-out stare decisis surrender, however. As doubtful as it may seem to us that any future Court will overturn the incorporating actions of the Warren Court (something the Burger Court has so

---

[186] Griswold v. Connecticut, 381 U.S. 479, 499 (1965) (Harlan, J., concurring in judgment).

[187] *Cf.* Benton v. Maryland, 395 U.S. 784 (1969).

[188] However, for the duration of the Term in which he issued his basic dissent, Justice Harlan voted on any similar cases on the Court's calendar in accordance with his own views. Acquiescence did not replace dissent until the next Term. But see North Carolina v. Pearce, 395 U.S. 711, 745 (1969) (concurring in part and dissenting in part) (a departure from "my usual practice"). Some justices seem to think that proper etiquette is for dissenters to join with the majority in docket-clearing remands for further consideration "in light of" the newly released decision. Klein v. Doe, 434 U.S. 915 (1977) (separate notation by Blackmun, J.). But *cf.* Boston Police Patrolmen's Ass'n v. Castro, 104 S.Ct. 3576 (1984) (Blackmun, J., dissenting from remand "for further consideration in light of" a case decided three weeks earlier).

far refrained from doing), Justice Harlan still salted his acquiescence with reminders that the majority's course was exceedingly bad constitutional law that ought to be set right someday.[189]

A special motive for joining with the other justices in addressing postincorporation issues was Harlan's fear that the Court might dilute the protections of the Bill of Rights once it became necessary to hold all the states to the exacting requirements of federal criminal justice. When he saw this happening, Harlan dissented even if that put him in the paradoxical position of opposing the disposition of the appeal that his own nonincorporationist conception of due process called for (in favor of the state, against the criminal defendant).[190] He also stood ready to revise older case law that did not give federal defendants their constitutional due, knowing he was also tightening the straitjacket in which incorporation had bound state law enforcement.[191] He was prepared, too, to furnish the pivotal fifth vote for a generous construction of an incorporated part of the Bill of Rights when, by reasserting his narrower view of due process, he could have produced a five to four judgment the other way.[192] On the other hand, if Justice Harlan detected no infringe-

---

[189] See Griffin v. California, 380 U.S. 609, 617 (1965) (concurring opinion): "Although compelled to concur in this decision [by Malloy v. Hogan, 378 U.S. 1 (1964), applying the Fifth Amendment privilege against self-incrimination to state proceedings, over Harlan's dissent], I am free to express the hope that the Court will eventually return to constitutional paths which, until recently, it has followed throughout its history." To the same effect is Justice Harlan's concurring opinion in Coolidge v. New Hampshire, 403 U.S. 443, 490 (1971) (proceeding from Mapp v. Ohio, 367 U.S. 653 [1961], and Ker v. California, 374 U.S. 23 [1963], while still urging their overruling).

[190] See, e.g., Chambers v. Maroney, 399 U.S. 42, 55 (1970) (concurring in part and dissenting in part).

[191] See Chimel v. California, 395 U.S. 752 (1969), overruling Harris v. United States, 331 U.S. 145 (1947), and United States v. Rabinowitz, 339 U.S. 56 (1950). Justice Harlan, concurring, said: "[The] federal-state factor has not been an easy one for me to resolve, but in the last analysis I cannot in good conscience vote to perpetuate bad Fourth Amendment law." 395 U.S. at 769.

[192] See Coolidge v. New Hampshire, 403 U.S. 443, 490 (1971) (Harlan, J., concurring) (addressing the case along with the other justices in Fourth Amendment terms, Justice Harlan contributed the critical fifth vote for a finding that the search was impermissible). For the "insider" account of the struggle for Harlan's vote in Coolidge, see Woodward & Armstrong, The Brethren 116–19 (1979). Contrast Justice Black's soloist action in United States v. White, 401 U.S. 745, 754 (1971) (concurring in judgment). Black stood by his dissent in the progenitor case, Katz v. United States, 389 U.S. 347 (1967), while his colleagues were splitting four to four on the application of Katz to the instant case.

ment of the Bill of Rights in a state case, he pitched his decision on that ground rather than coming to the same outcome by way of fundamental fairness analysis (a choice that of course is not explicable by concerns about "dilution" of federal standards).[193]

In the manner of a true self-subordinator, Justice Harlan was prepared to adapt to successive defeats. If the Court extended the foundation precedent in a way he thought unwarranted, he said so in another dissent but thereafter he accepted the majority's second decision as no less binding on him than the parent decision.[194] But while acceding to the majority's specific holding in a case, Justice Harlan never considered himself bound by the constitutional philosophy or interpretive technique that led to the mistaken holding. In his view, therefore, the Court's decision to read the Fifth Amendment[195] self-incrimination privilege into the Fourteenth Amendment guided his own approach to future cases involving self-incrimination claims[196] but did not foreclose his objections to additional efforts at selective incorporation. When the Court later came to consider a defendant's constitutional right to jury trial in a state criminal case, Harlan felt free to address the matter as a dissenting nonincorporationist;[197] and likewise he dissented once more when the Court's "march toward 'incorporation' " swept up the double-jeopardy clause.[198]

In a similar fashion, having become disenchanted with the Court's frequent resort to prospective limitation as a way of mitigating the unsettling effect of newfound constitutional rights for defendants, Justice Harlan did not consider himself locked into

---

[193] See California v. Byers, 402 U.S. 424, 434 (1971) (concurring in judgment) (self-incrimination); Terry v. Ohio, 392 U.S. 1, 31 (1968) (concurring opinion) (search and seizure); cf. Ashe v. Swenson, 397 U.S. 436, 448 (1970) (concurring opinion) (agreeing with the majority that double jeopardy was inflicted on the defendant but writing to challenge a more extravagant interpretation of the Fifth Amendment safeguard put forward separately by Justice Brennan).

[194] Thus Justice Harlan dissented from Miranda v. Arizona, 384 U.S. 436, 504 (1966), and from *Miranda*'s extension in Mathis v. United States, 391 U.S. 1, 5 (1968) (joining Justice White's dissent). Thereafter, he deferred to *Mathis* as well as to *Miranda*. See Orozco v. Texas, 394 U.S. 324, 327 (1969) (concurring opinion).

[195] Malloy v. Hogan, 378 U.S. 1 (1964).

[196] Griffin v. California, 380 U.S. 609, 615 (1965) (concurring opinion).

[197] See Duncan v. Louisiana, 391 U.S. 145, 181 n.18 (1968) (dissenting opinion).

[198] Benton v. Maryland, 395 U.S. 784, 808–09 (1969) (dissenting opinion).

continued use of the technique.[199] Deference to narrow holdings, yes; deference to the majority's methodology of decision, no.

Nor did Justice Harlan's collegiality stop him from taking a microscopic view of the "holding" by which he felt bound. For him, *Mapp v. Ohio*[200] settled no more than that the exclusionary rule applies to the use of illegally acquired evidence in state trials as it does in federal cases. In the Court's first post-*Mapp* encounter with local search and seizure, *Ker v. California*,[201] eight justices understood *Mapp* as subjecting state and federal searches to the same Fourteenth Amendment standard of reasonableness. Harland disagreed: "*Mapp v. Ohio* . . . did not purport to change the standards by which state searches and seizures were to judged; rather it held that the 'exclusionary' rule of Weeks v. United States . . . was applicable to the States."[202] This narrow reading freed Harlan to address *Ker* on nonincorporationist premises: "In judging state searches and seizure I would continue to adhere to the established [sic] Fourteenth Amendment concepts of fundamental fairness."[203] Of course, *Ker* in the end settles, if *Mapp* itself did not, that state searches are held to uniform Fourth Amendment standards, and Justice Harlan must have realized even as he wrote his *Ker* dissent that he would acquiesce to that proposition in all cases after *Ker*.[204]

In order to place Harlan's practice of self-subordination in full perspective, one needs to account for the situations in which he pointedly refused to budge from a dissenting position. One such

---

[199] See Justice Harlan's successive dissents in Desist v. United States, 394 U.S. 244, 256 (1969), and Williams v. United States, 401 U.S. U.S. 667, 675 (1971). See also his reiterated objection to the use of the Equal Protection Clause to remedy the disadvantages that indigency imposes on a criminal appellant. Griffin v. Illinois, 351 U.S. 12, 29 (1956) (dissenting opinion); Douglas v. California, 372 U.S. 353, 360 (1963) (dissenting opinion). His insistence that such cases should be addressed as due process matters seems to have been vindicated. See Ake v. Oklahoma, 105 S.Ct. 1087 (1985); Evitts v. Lucey, 105 S.Ct. 830 (1985).

[200] 367 U.S. 653 (1961).

[201] 374 U.S. 23 (1963).

[202] *Id.* at 45 n.1 (dissenting opinion).

[203] *Id.* at 46.

[204] Aguilar v. Texas, 378 U.S. 108 (1964); Coolidge v. New Hampshire, 403 U.S. 443, 491 (1971) (concurring in judgment) ("Because of Mapp and Ker . . . this case must be judged in terms of federal standards, and on that basis I concur . . . in the judgment of the Court"). Notice that Justice Harlan's tie-breaking vote for the defendant in *Coolidge* prevented a "diluted" interpretation of the Fourth Amendment, as discussed in the text *supra* at note 190. But he seemed unconcerned about possible relaxation of the federal standard in *Ker*, where his refusal to speak to the Fourth Amendment validity of the search left the Court divided four to four on that issue.

instance, a clear exception to his usual pattern in incorporated Bill of Rights cases, was his attitude toward jury rights in state prosecutions. Not only did Justice Harlan dissent, as was his custom, in the maiden decision in *Duncan v. Louisiana*,[205] incorporating the Sixth Amendment right into the due process clause, but he refused to accept *Duncan* as controlling in subsequent cases. Hence in *Baldwin v. New York*,[206] concerning the right to jury trial on misdemeanor charges carrying a maximum punishment of one year's imprisonment, Harlan could agree that the Sixth Amendment "right to jury trial attaches where an offense is punishable by as much as six months' imprisonment,"[207] but nevertheless he cast his vote to affirm the defendant's nonjury conviction as compatible with fundamental fairness. Decided with *Baldwin* was *Williams v. Florida*,[208] in which one of the issues was the constitutionality of six member juries in criminal cases. The majority, lending substance to Harlan's often voiced fear of dilution resulting from the incorporation approach, held that the tradition of twelve jurors was not a constitutional requisite of trial by jury. Harlan strongly disagreed with that interpretation of the Sixth Amendment but concurred in the result of the appeal on the basis of his own principle of fundamental fairness. In a separate opinion applicable both to *Baldwin* and *Williams*, he declared his continuing rejection of *Duncan* ruling and urged his colleagues to "reconsider the 'incorporation' doctrine before its leveling tendencies further retard development in the field of criminal procedure by stifling flexibility in the States and by discarding the possibility of federal leadership by example."[209] Why this break from his habit of temporary acquiescence? Why on this occasion did Harlan reject the *Duncan* premise? His only attempt at explanation is this sentence: "In taking that course in *Baldwin*, I cannot, in a matter that goes to the very pulse of sound constitutional adjudication, consider myself constricted by *stare decisis*."[210]

---

[205] 391 U.S. 145 (1968).

[206] 399 U.S. 66 (1970).

[207] *Id.* at 120.

[208] 399 U.S. 78 (1970).

[209] *Id.* at 138.

[210] *Id.* at 118. Manifestly, Justice Harlan uses "stare decisis" here to mean, in my terminology, temporary acquiescence.

This is not say that Harlan's tolerance of incorporationist due process had finally expired, for while defying *Duncan's* extension of Sixth Amendment jury requirements to the states, Justice Harlan dealt with a separate issue of self-incrimination in the six-member jury case on the premise that due process incorporates the Fifth Amendment privilege, as held in *Malloy v. Hogan.*[211] "Given *Malloy v. Hogan*," wrote Justice Harlan in *Williams v. Florida*, "I join that part of the Court's opinion."[212] And during the *Baldwin-Williams* term of the Court, Harlan maintained his practice of temporary accommodation on questions of double jeopardy arising in state proceedings.[213] In short, there was something especially disturbing about *Duncan v. Louisiana*, something more meretricious than the other cases of selective incorporation, that made even temporary acquiescence an impossible choice for Justice Harlan ("a matter that goes to the very pulse of sound constitutional adjudication").

One also sees the reemergence of Harlan's dissenting views in Fourteenth Amendment voting rights cases, and for the same reasons of deep conviction. His position was that the Equal Protection Clause had no application either to the problem of legislative malapportionment or to restrictive voting qualifications. He expressed himself fully by dissent in *Reynolds v. Sims*[214] on the subject of reapportionment and in a shorter dissent in *Carrington v. Rash*[215] on the matter of suffrage restrictions. But whereas he approached all further questions of reapportionment on a *Reynolds v. Sims* foundation[216]—a deference that continued to his last year on the Court[217]—he lost his stomach for subordination of dissenting views in the eligibility-to-vote cases. After a few years of uneasy acquies-

---

[211] 378 U.S. 1 (1964).

[212] 399 U.S. at 119 (concurring in result).

[213] Ashe v. Swenson, 397 U.S. 436, 448 (1970) (concurring in a Fifth Amendment based ruling, as required by Benton v. Maryland, 395 U.S. 784 [1969]).

[214] 377 U.S. 533, 589 (1964) (dissenting opinion).

[215] 380 U.S. 89, 97 (1965). Justice Harlan also explained why he did not consider *Reynolds* controlling in *Carrington*. *Id.* at 97–98.

[216] Hadley v. Junior College Dist., 397 U.S. 50, 60 (1970) (dissenting opinion) ("I deem myself bound by Reynolds"); Kirkpatrick v. Preisler, 394 U.S. 526, 552 (1969) (dissenting opinion) ("a case whose constitutional reasoning I still find it impossible to swallow, but by whose dictate I consider myself bound," referring to Wesberry v. Sanders, 376 U.S. 1 [1964]).

[217] See Whitcomb v. Chavis, 403 U.S. 124, 165 (1971) (Harlan J., concurring).

cence,[218] Justice Harlan reverted in *Oregon v. Mitchell*[219] to his original position that the Fourteenth Amendment was not meant to affect state voting qualifications. He took this course because he was "deeply convinced" it was what "the Constitution demands."[220]

I think we obtain an apt description of Harlan's outlook by making a slight emendation in Chief Justice Taft's guidelines for ethical dissent. Former Canon 19 discourages dissenting opinions "except in cases of conscientious difference on fundamental principle." While Taft did not differentiate first dissent from repeated dissent on the same point, Harlan's actions depend on that distinction. Never one to censor his initial disagreement with his colleagues, Justice Harlan did subscribe to the Taft philosophy when it came to the continuation of dissent. That was an admissible course, his record in the later years of the Warren Court seems to say, only in "cases of conscientious difference of opinion on fundamental principle."

In sum, Justice Harlan traveled all three postdissent roads. He fully relinquished his opposition and gave authoritative effect to a

---

[218] When the constitutionality of state poll taxes came to the Court a year after *Carrington* (which involved state definitions of voter residency), Justice Harlan wrote: "I do not propose to retread ground covered in my dissents in Reynolds v. Sims . . . and Carrington v. Rash . . . , and will proceed on the premise that the Equal Protection Clause of the Fourteenth Amendment now reaches both state apportionment (*Reynolds*) and voter qualifications (*Carrington*) cases." Harper v. Virginia Bd. of Elections, 383 U.S. 663, 681 (1966) (dissenting opinion). Harlan participated in several other voting rights cases on the same *Carrington* premise, although he only went so far as to apply the rational basis standard of equal protection. See Kramer v. Union Free School Dist., 395 U.S. 621 (1969); Cipriano v. City of Houma, 395 U.S. 701 (1969); Phoenix v. Kolodziejski, 399 U.S. 204 (1970).

[219] 400 U.S. 112, 152 (1970) (concurring in part and dissenting in part).

[220] Professor Monaghan, note 15 *supra*, finds this choice an unacceptably selfish act on Harlan's part. He says: "I do not think an individual appointed to the Court could responsibly base his vote, in relevant cases, on the theory that . . . the Fourteenth Amendment was never intended to reach suffrage qualifications." *Id.* at 7. That is so not because the Harlan position lacks merit—indeed, there is much to be said in its favor from the standpoint of original understanding—but because in Monaghan's opinion its assertion today or in 1970 amounts to a major breach of stare decisis. Professor Monaghan particularly disapproves of Harlan's resort to a dissident interpretation when, as in Oregon v. Mitchell, it tips the outcome of a closely balanced case. *Id.* at 7–8 n.25. But what about Justice Black, who single-handedly controlled the outcome in *Mitchell* by voting, as his biographer says, "on opposite sides of two propositions that every one of his colleagues saw as organically inseparable"? Dunne, note 95 *supra*, at 427–38. Both these soloist actions by Justices Black and Harlan are, in my judgment, defensible and should not be equated to the situation described by Judge Traynor, note 10 *supra* at 291, in which a multiple-issue appeal tempts a single judge "to achieve a reversal or affirmance that would not otherwise have materialized" by adding "his vote on the basis solely of his ancient dissent" to "a nucleus of dissenters on other issues." This is the antithesis of principled action.

majority decision settling a question that needs a final answer more than it requires a right answer. When he was not prepared to concede the majority the last word on the subject, Harlan's instinct was to subordinate himself to the decision until the Court, disillusioned or altered in membership, agreed to reconsideration. When convinced, however, that the prevailing doctrine was exceptionally bad constitutional law, Harlan kept to his own competing position. He thus introduces another element into the choice between dogged dissent and temporary acceptance, and that is the wretchedness of the majority's decisions. Either choice presupposes the justice's desire for eventual reconsideration by the Court— which is to say that he sees the recent cases as both unsound and harmful. But Justice Harlan appears to subdivide such decisions into (1) the temporarily endurable and (2) the wholly insufferable— a classification that corresponds roughly to the academic grades of D (less than satisfactory but still earning course credit) and E (out and out flunk, no credit). The infrequency of his sustained dissent shows that Harlan was one of the Court's most generous graders.

V. NEWCOMER JUSTICES

A. SIGNIFICANCE TO PAST DISSENTERS

For a justice who has become a full-fledged stare decisis acceptor, changes in the Court's membership should be an utter irrelevance. The stare decisis principle, as discussed above, asks more of a dissenter than that he retreat only while the original majority remains intact; it calls for acceptance of that majority's decisions as the permanent institutional settlement. By the stare decisis choice the dissenter is recast as a loyal follower of the misbegotten precedent, its defender if need be. Turnover of justices, nonetheless, is a mind-concentrating event. The appointment of new members to the Court quite naturally induces a clarification if not a reassessment of positions by previous dissenters. One who fancied himself a stare decisis acceptor may realize that he is not prepared to surrender to precedent when actually given a chance to reverse the Court's ruling. What he discovers is that he had been granting his colleagues all along a merely transitory and revocable assent, that is, he was a temporary acquiescer in the guise of a stare decisis acceptor.

On the other hand, a justice who in the past made a point of qualifying his deference with words of temporary acquiescence may come to realize at the moment of truth that he is not yet ready to join newcomers in an overruling. Sometimes even a continuous dissenter develops a case of cold feet just when new appointments to the bench open a genuine prospect of overturning decisions of the recent past. Far from being active proselytizers, the justices I am here describing prefer to invest their hope for change in the actions of a future Court rather than in alliances with a new set of sympathetic colleagues. Contributing to such an attitude—perhaps the chief reason for it—is fear that the Court's reputation will suffer if the doctrinal shift is perceived to be the result of nothing except altered membership, "bringing adjudication of this tribunal," as Justice Roberts lamented, "into the same class as a restricted train ticket, good for this day and this train only."[221]

Still, whatever the institutional cost of a prompt overruling, it is only one factor in a larger equation—a cost to be weighed with other costs against the importance of judicial self-correction. When the balance of considerations tilts in favor of overruling, there is no virtue in delay and temporizing.[222] Before the dissenting veteran

---

[221] Smith v. Allwright, 321 U.S. 649, 669 (1944) (dissenting opinion). For an extreme application (or misapplication) of this concern by state appellate judges, see People v. Lewis, 88 Ill. 2d 129, 430 N.E.2d 1346 (1981), cert. denied, 456 U.S. 1011 (1982). The Illinois Supreme Court had upheld the state's death penalty law two years earlier by a four to three division. After one of the majority justices retired, the question was revisited in *Lewis*. Justice Simon, the new member of the court, urged the three original dissenters to collaborate with him in an overruling. All three declined, invoking stare decisis and asserting (too categorically, I think) that "the circumstances which warrant changes in the law do not include changes in personnel." 88 Ill. 2d at 169, 430 N.E.2d at 1365 (Clark, J., concurring).

[222] Professor Brest poses this question in his excellent casebook, Brest, Processes of Constitutional Decisionmaking 1128 (1st ed. 1975): "Suppose a justice dissents from a holding one year, and the next year a case arises involving the application of the holding to a different fact situation. Might the justice properly feel more freedom to reiterate his dissent to the original holding if he is still in the minority than to join or make a majority to overrule the holding?" From the context in which the question is put, it is clear that Professor Brest assumes there has been an intervening change of personnel on the Court and therefore is thinking of the trauma of reversal that is nakedly attributable to a turnover of justices. But to answer Brest's question in the affirmative is to put forward the curious idea that opposing a recent decision is acceptable behavior for a justice only when the opposition is ineffectual. If original dissent is issued as an appeal to the intelligence of a future day, should the dissenter falter because that day arrives sooner than anyone expected? And suppose the original dissenter were to switch sides in order to prevent too sudden an overruling. How then is he supposed to behave in succeeding cases? Is he to lapse back to the original dissent once it is again a certifiably harmless eccentricity? Or does his precedent-rescuing vote establish him as an all-out stare decisis acceptor/defender for the rest of his time on the Court?

reaches that conclusion, however, he may suffer a temporary am-
bivalence of the kind so well described by Jimmy Durante: "Did ya
ever get the feeling that you wanna go, and then you wanna stay?"
That seems to have been Justice Stewart's difficulty in the case of
National League of Cities v. Usery,[223] if we can credit Woodward and
Armstrong's account of the matter.[224] In 1968 Justice Stewart was a
dissenter in *Maryland v. Wirtz*,[225] a six to three decision upholding
Congress' authority to prescribe minimum wages for state government workers. Eight years and several new justices later, *National
League of Cities* offered a chance to overturn *Wirtz*.[226] As the tale is
told, the conference voting placed Justice Stewart in the position of
tie-breaker. The four Nixon-appointed justices favored a repudiation of *Wirtz*. Stewart, though, "felt it was important that he
should not be the fifth vote, particularly by joining the four Nixon
justices, to overrule Warren Court decisions."[227] He was challenged
on this by, of all people, a *Wirtz* supporter, Justice White, who
objected to "keep[ing] the jurisprudence of the Court tied up for
reasons that are not on the public record."[228] Seeing the merit of
White's point, Stewart agreed that he should not pull his punches,
whereupon he furnished the fatal fifth vote against *Wirtz*.

Had Stewart refrained from overruling in *National League of Cities*
an opportunity as propitious might not have come his way again.
Justice White could attest to that on the strength of his own experience in cases involving Congressional redistricting. In an earlier
section of this essay the 1973 case of *White v. Weiser*[229] was offered
as a clear illustration of full stare decisis acceptance by ex-dissenters
on a point of constitutional law (in that instance by Justices White

---

[223] 426 U.S. 833 (1976).

[224] Woodward & Armstrong, note 192 *supra*, at 406–10.

[225] 392 U.S. 183 (1968).

[226] A year before *National League of Cities*, Justice Stewart joined in a *Wirtz*-premised
decision, Fry v. United States, 421 U.S. 542 (1975). Because he did not write separately, it is
unclear whether his vote was an act of stare decisis acceptance or nothing more than temporary acquiescence. It is also conceivable that Justice Stewart saw *Fry* as legitimately distinguishable from *Wirtz*. That possibility, as well as the failure of any party to challenge *Wirtz*
directly, made *Fry* an awkward vehicle for a fundamental reconsideration (although the sole
dissenter, Justice Rehnquist, urged it anyway).

[227] Woodward & Armstrong, note 192 *supra*, at 406.

[228] *Id.* at 407.

[229] 412 U.S. 783 (1973).

and Stewart).[230] There the Court, with significantly reconstituted membership, gave governing effect to a Warren Court precedent, *Kirkpatrick v. Preisler*,[231] which required all Congressional districts in a state to have numerically equal populations. Three new justices, writing separately in *White v. Weiser*, associated themselves with the *Kirkpatrick* dissents, which were prepared to uphold minor population disparities. Nevertheless, the newcomers—Justice Powell, Justice Rehnquist, and the Chief Justice—were resigned at least for the time being to the rigid one-man, one-vote formula of *Kirkpatrick*. It was the White-Stewart surrender to stare decisis that fostered temporary acquiescence in place of rebellion on the part of the three recent arrivals. Justice Powell wrote: "unless and until the Court decides to reconsider [*Kirkpatrick*], I will follow it"[232] (translation: I will happily overturn the precedent any time the Court cares to reexamine it). And the allusion to "the Court" takes in, with a hint of reproof, the former dissenters, Justices White and Stewart.

A decade later Justice White had reason to regret his status quo posture in *White v. Weiser*. Another decennial census triggered a new round of Congressional redistricting and brought *Karcher v. Daggett*[233] to the Court, testing once again the strictness of the one-man, one-vote standard, this time not in a case of modest population variances but one of truly de minimis disparities. To five justices *Kirkpatrick* and *White* left no room for anything less than exact numerical equality, and stare decisis, among other reasons, required a rejection of the ever-so-slightly unequal districts in the latest case. The majority included the Court's two newest members, Justice Stevens (who said in a concurring opinion that "the doctrine of stare decisis requires that result")[234] and Justice O'Connor (who joined the majority opinion without separate explanation). Justice White this time was provoked into dissent, complaining that the majority had carried *Kirkpatrick* and *White* to arbitrary lengths "and if the Court is convinced that our cases demand the result reached today, the time has arrived to reconsider these prece-

---

[230] See text at notes 40–42 *supra*.

[231] 394 U.S. 526 (1969).

[232] 412 U.S. at 798 (concurring opinion).

[233] 103 S.Ct. 2653 (1983).

[234] *Id*. at 2667.

dents."[235] In this he was joined by the same three justices—Powell, Rehnquist, and the Chief Justice—whose opposition to *Kirkpatrick* he (as well as Justice Stewart) had elected not to exploit in the *White* case. The trouble was that once Justice White was in an overruling mood, he was a vote short of his objective. The chances for repudiating the *Kirkpatrick* standard of "slide-rule precision"[236] in Congressional reapportionment were better, hindsight tells us, in 1973 than in 1983. If there is a moral here it is: embrace potential allies while you may (or, it is never too soon to get rid of a precedent that deserves overruling).

B. POSTURE OF NEWCOMERS VIS-A-VIS RECENT DECISIONS

Should a new justice be any more or any less respectful of recent decisions than the justices who participated in those cases? When the veteran justices divide into two camps—those who think the decisions should stand because they are right and those who think the decisions are bad and ought to be reversed (an attitude common to sustained dissenters and temporary acquiescers)—the advent of a stare decisis acceptor changes the climate but not the voting outcome.[237] If the authors of the case law are somewhat disappointed by the newcomer's lack of enthusiasm for their handiwork, by the condescension inherent in the stare decisis ground, the dissidents are much more frustrated by what to them is the defeatist attitude of their new associate. Here, for example, is Justice Black chiding Chief Justice Burger and Justice Blackmun for taking too much docile a position toward recent decisions:[238]

---

[235] *Id.* at 2678.

[236] The phrase is Justice Powell's. White v. Weiser, 412 U.S. 783, 798 (1973) (concurring opinion).

[237] If the newcomer succeeds a dissenter or is now joined by one or more of the original dissenters in granting precedential respect to the first decision, the arithmetic in support of the precedent shows an improvement. Thus a five to four decision, Bullington v. Missouri, 451 U.S. 430 (1981), was reaffirmed by a seven to two vote in Arizona v. Rumsey, 104 S.Ct. 2305 (1984), thanks to (*a*) newcomer Justice O'Connor's obeisance to precedent and (*b*) the stare decisis surrender of two of the *Bullington* dissenters (including the author of the original dissenting opinion, Justice Powell).

[238] Perkins v. Matthews, 400 U.S. 379, 409 n.8 (1971) (dissenting opinion). But see Rogers v. Bellei, 401 U.S. 815 (1971), where Justice Blackmun authored and Chief Justice Burger joined the majority decision, which Justice Black, in dissent, accused of overruling in all but name his own earlier decision for a five to four Court, Afroyim v. Rusk, 387 U.S. 253 (1967). Black's criticism included a rebuke of the new justices for failing to show proper respect for

My brothers, the Chief Justice and Mr. Justice Blackmun have stated that "given the decision in Allen [a two year old case] [they] join in the judgment" of the Court in this case. I have to admit that I do not precisely understand what they mean by "given Allen." Neither the Chief Justice nor Mr. Justice Blackmun was a member of the Court when Allen was decided. They are certainly not bound by the Court's past mistakes if they think, as I do, that Allen was a mistake. Yet I do not understand that "given Allen" necessarily means that they now agree to what was decided in that case. I believe that Allen was wrongly decided and would overrule it now.

Conversely, a newcomer's zeal for overruling may be too much for a senior dissenter. So in a 1980 case[239] Justice Rehnquist issued a call for full re-examination of *Massiah v. United States*,[240] a 1964 decision, while Justice White, a *Massiah* dissenter, countered that there was "no need to abandon *Massiah* . . . as Mr. Justice Rehnquist does,"[241] and contented himself with pointing out the distinguishing features of the present case. On another occasion[242] Justice Rehnquist flatly rejected a 1969 decision. *O'Callahan v. Parker*,[243] at the same time that Justice Stewart, an original *O'Callahan* dissenter, yielded temporary acquiescence.[244]

When a new justice replaces a dissenter, the voting balance on the Court is, of course, effectively unchanged. If the new justice subscribes to his predecessor's views, things remain in status quo, and if he shares or otherwise bows to the majority position the status quo not only continues but gains an extra vote. Does it follow that when the newcomer does not hold a pivotal fifth vote for reaffirming or reversing the Court's position, he should not help to

---

precedent: "This precious Fourteenth Amendment American citizenship should not be blown around by every passing political·wind that changes the composition of this Court." 401 U.S. at 837. Nor was this the first time that Justice Black called attention to the effect of changes in the Court's membership. See Boys Markets, Inc. v. Retail Clerks Local, 398 U.S. 235, 255 (1970) (dissenting opinion); Rutkin v. United States, 343 U.S. 130, 139 (1952) (dissenting opinion).

[239] United States v. Henry, 447 U.S. 264 (1980).

[240] 377 U.S. 201 (1964).

[241] 447 U.S. at 277 n.1 (Justice White joining in Justice Blackmun's dissenting opinion).

[242] Gosa v. Mayden, 413 U.S. 665 (1973).

[243] 395 U.S. 258 (1969).

[244] 413 U.S. at 693 (concurring opinion). See also United States v. Biswell, 406 U.S. 311 (1972) (original dissenters are now content to distinguish Colonnade Catering Corp. v. United States, 397 U.S. 72 [1970], while newly arrived Justice Blackmun declares himself in *Biswell* to be a *Colonnade* opponent).

bring the issue back to the Court on a grant of certiorari? That indeed was Justice Stevens' position. His predecessor, Justice Douglas, was one of the four dissenters in the important 1973 decision, *Miller v. California*,[245] providing strengthened constitutional support for criminal laws against obscenity. A chance to reconsider *Miller* presented itself shortly after Justice Stevens' accession to the Court. The three remaining *Miller* dissenters voted to grant certiorari; the still-intact *Miller* majority opposed review. Under the "Rule of Four," the decision was in the hands of Justice Stevens. He chose not to force the issue back to the Court, reasoning that "regardless of how I might vote on the merits after full argument, it would be pointless to grant certiorari in case after case of this character only to have *Miller* reaffirmed time after time."[246]

There have been rare occasions when a death or resignation has left the surviving justices deadlocked on a question and both wings of the Court openly have invited the replacement justice to arbitrate the matter.[247] Normally, however, a new justice's independent consideration of a recently decided matter lacks the blessing of the remaining members of the original majority[248] and may fail even to draw support from previous dissenters. We have seen, for instance, how Justice Powell was alone in *Apodaca v. Oregon*[249] on the issue of jury unanimity because, unlike all his colleagues, he rejected the recent holdings that federal and state jury requirements in criminal cases are coextensive under the Sixth and Fourteenth amendments.

---

[245] 413 U.S. 15 (1973).

[246] Liles v. Oregon, 425 U.S. 963 (1976) (separate statement). Although Justice Stevens did not have it in his power to overturn *Miller*, a reconsideration by the full Court would have spread his views on the record and perhaps encouraged (or depending on where he stood, discouraged) additional challenges to *Miller*. In the event, Justice Stevens did not have long to wait for other opportunities to speak his mind on the constitutionality of obscenity law. See, *e.g.*, Marks v. United States, 430 U.S. 188, 198 (1977) (concurring in part and dissenting in part); Smith v. United States, 431 U.S. 291, 311 (1977) (dissenting opinion). *Cf.* Young v. American Mini Theatres, 427 U.S. 50 (1976).

[247] The Court set Jones v. Opelika, 316 U.S. 584 (1942), a five to four decision, for reargument on the same day Justice Rutledge was sworn in as successor to Justice Byrnes (a member of the *Jones* majority). The result of rehearing was a five to four *volte face*. Murdock v. Pennsylvania and Jones v. Opelika, 319 U.S. 103 (1943). See Harper, Justice Rutledge and the Bright Constellation 49–67 (1965).

[248] See, *e.g.*, Reid v. Covert, 351 U.S. 487 (1956), in which rehearing was granted at the next Term over the objections of the depleted majority bloc, 352 U.S. 901, followed by a reversal by the reconstituted Court, 354 U.S. 1 (1957). And, of course, the second Legal Tender Case, Knox v. Lee, 79 U.S. (12 Wall.) 457 (1871), certainly was not welcomed by any of the majority participants in the first case.

[249] See note 160 *supra*.

His position created a contrapuntal effect, injecting a fugue of new dissent while an earlier dissenter was sounding a note of resignation.[250]

VI. IMPLICATIONS FOR OPINION WRITING ASSIGNMENTS

A traditional prerogative of the Chief Justice, when he is part of the majority, is to designate the Court's opinion writer.[251] Although the reasons for particular assignments "normally remain with the breast of the Chief Justice,"[252] a major consideration surely must be good public relations. I use the term unpejoratively to refer to the legitimate interest in making a controversial decision more palatable, or at least slightly less disturbing, to predictably hostile segments of the public. Justice Douglas observes in his memoirs that "[e]very Chief Justice, when assigning opinions, has an eye to public relations and to history—and naturally so. A so-called liberal Justice will be certain to get the opinion holding a so-called liberal law unconstitutional."[253]

The operative idea is that there is something disarming about an opinion that is out of character for its author, one that must have

---

[250] The earlier dissenter was Justice Stewart, who joined with Justice Harlan in dissent in Duncan v. Louisiana, 391 U.S. 145, 171 (1968), the decision "incorporating" Sixth Amendment jury rights into the Fourteenth Amendment, and in two post-*Duncan* cases, Baldwin v. New York, 399 U.S. 66 (1970), and Williams v. Florida, 399 U.S. 78, 117 (1970). By the time of *Apodaca* in 1972, Justice Stewart was willing to proceed from a *Duncan* premise, as did all the other justices except Justice Powell. (Stewart's earlier dissenting compatriot, Justice Harlan, was no longer on the Court). What Justice Stewart did not explain was why he resigned himself to *Duncan* in 1972 when he was still resistant in 1970. One scholar, comparing Justices Stewart and Powell and drawing a distinction between institutional conservatism and doctrinal conservatism, points out that Stewart generally felt himself bound by Warren Court decisions while Powell did not. Tushnet, untitled article, National Law Journal, Feb. 18, 1980, p. 27, col. 2 (a profile of Justice Stewart). But when we update Justice Powell's voting record in cases after *Apodaca*, we discern a pattern not unlike Stewart's. After repeating his anti-*Duncan* position in Ludwig v. Massachusetts, 427 U.S. 618, 632 (1976) (concurring opinion), and Ballew v. Georgia, 435 U.S. 223, 245 (1978) (concurring in judgment), Justice Powell seems finally to have conceded the *Duncan* premise. See Burch v. Louisiana, 441 U.S. 130 (1979), where he joined without separate explanation a decision barring state court conviction by a nonunanimous six-member jury, as a Sixth-cum-Fourteenth Amendment matter. Moreover, there are other instances in which Justice Powell, at first encounter, bowed to Warren Court authority while registering his personal disagreement. See Carter v. Kentucky, 450 U.S. 288, 307 (1981) (concurring opinion) ("I . . . would have joined Justices Stewart and White in dissent in Griffin [v. California, 380 U.S. 609 (1965)], But Griffin is now the law").

[251] Clark, Internal Operations of the United States Supreme Court, 43 J. Am. Jud. Soc'y 45 (1959).

[252] Felix Frankfurter on the Supreme Court 446 (Kurland ed. 1970).

[253] Douglas, note 95 *supra*, at 34.

TABLE 1

Precedent Situation	Best Choice (If Available)	Next Best	Least Credible
Stare decisis adherence	Original dissenter	Newcomer	Original author or majority member
Expansive application of the precedent	Original dissenter (if now a stare decisis adherent)	Newcomer	Original author or majority member
Restrictive application of the precedent	Original author or majority member	Newcomer	Original dissenter
Express overruling	Newcomer	Original author or majority member	Original dissenter

caused some discomfort to write. The example mentioned by Justice Douglas is only one of the many uses to which this principle of contrariety can be put.[254] In particular it can be applied to the basic attitudes toward precedent discussed in this paper. My nominees for most effective, second best, and least effective majority opinion writers are in table 1.

The choices above are no more than presumptive. In some circumstances a justice's special qualifications make him the Court's most persuasive author notwithstanding that my guidelines classify him "least credible." Certain justices, for example, draw opinion assignments because of their pre-Court accomplishments in a specialized field of law. For this or other reasons, including sheer writing skill, a particular justice may be invaluable in the spokesman's role[255]—even when he has serious reservations about the majority position and insists on expressing them openly.[256]

---

[254] Felix Frankfurter, a political liberal in his pre-Court days, made austerity the hallmark of his judicial career. Among the most self-denying of his opinions was his dissent in West Virginia Bd. of Educ. v. Barnette, 319 U.S. 624, 646–47 (1943).

[255] I note with approval the selection of Justice Powell, a past president of the American Bar Association, to speak for the Court in lawyer advertising cases despite his role as dissenter in the door-opening decision, Bates v. Arizona State Bar, 433 U.S. 350 (1977). Although I am not certain that Justice Powell accepts *Bates* in the full precedential sense, he has been willing to give wide scope to its First Amendment rationale. See Matter of R.M.J., 455 U.S. 191 (1982), and compare In re Primus, 436 U.S. 412 (1978), with Ohralik v. Ohio State Bar Ass'n, 436 U.S. 447 (1978). He would also be "best choice" under my guidelines if he now accepts *Bates* and is not merely acquiescing to it temporarily. (Illness kept Justice Powell from participating in the latest decision, Zauderer v. Office of Disciplinary Counsel, 105 S.Ct. 2265 [1985]). Note also the opinion assignment given to Justice Powell in a bar admission case, New Hampshire Supreme Court v. Piper, 105 S.Ct. 1272 (1985).

[256] See Justice Cardozo's dual opinions in Helvering v. Davis, 301 U.S. 619, 639 (1937); Justice Jackson's in Wheeling Steel Corp. v. Glander, 337 U.S. 562, 575 (1949); Justice

Although no justice holds the exclusive franchise to a field of decision making whatever his expertise or renown, it is an observable phenomenon that the authors of "landmark" opinions often develop a strong sense of proprietorship—an attitude that is reinforced by favoring them with opinion assignments in follow-up cases.[257] And when these justices see new majorities cabining or otherwise mistreating "their" decisions, they turn into especially waspish dissenters.[258] In this connection my guidelines do not recommend original authors as spokesmen for extended applications precisely because of the impression of willfullness in such opinions. (I find unpersuasive the counterargument that the author of the progenitor decision has a truer grasp of the Court's "original understanding" than any of the other justices.)[259]

The same concerns apply to opinions which reaffirm recent holdings in the face of fresh attacks. Thus I question the wisdom of

---

Brennan's in Abbate v. United States, 359 U.S. 187, 196 (1959); and Justice Blackmun's in Logan v. Zimmerman Brush Co., 455 U.S. 422, 438 (1982). The earliest instance of an expression of separate personal views in the course of an opinion for the Court is Lessee of Livingston v. Moore, 32 U.S. (7 Pet.) 469, 546 (1833) (per Johnson, J.). Similar but less eye-catching are cases in which the author of the majority opinion also joins a colleague's separate concurrence. E.g., Argersinger v. Hamlin, 407 U.S. 25 (1972) (Justice Douglas delivers the Court's opinion and subscribes to Justice Brennan's additional comments). Sometimes the "Court's opinion" is a patchwork consisting of portions of opinions written by different justices. See Arizona Governing Comm. v. Norris, 103 S.Ct. 3492 (1983) (Court's opinion is three parts Marshall and one part Powell, by reason of shifting five to four votes).

[257] Aside from catering to the personal wishes of the original author, a reason for staying with the same justice as the Court's spokesman is to avoid the inconsistency of language that often occurs when different justices deliver the opinions in a continuing line of cases. See Logan v. Zimmerman Brush Co., 455 U.S. 422, 443 n.* (1982) (Powell J., concurring).

[258] Note e.g., Justice Blackmun's active role in abortion matters and cases of commercial speech, both fields in which he wrote the cornerstone opinions. With respect to abortion, his opinions for the Court are Roe v. Wade, 410 U.S. 113 (1973); Doe v. Bolton, 410 U.S. 179 (1973); Planned Parenthood of Missouri v. Danforth, 428 U.S. 52 (1976); Colautti v. Franklin, 439 U.S. 379 (1979). He filed dissenting opinions in Beal v. Doe, 432 U.S. 438 (1977); Harris v. McRae, 448 U.S. 297 (1980); Planned Parenthood Ass'n of Kansas City v. Ashcroft, 103 S.Ct. 2517 (1983). With respect to commercial speech, Justice Blackmun's opinions for the Court are Bigelow v. Virginia, 421 U.S. 800 (1975); Virginia Bd. of Pharmacy v. Virginia Citizens Consumer Council, 425 U.S. 748 (1976); Bates v. Arizona State Bar, 433 U.S. 350 (1977). His later dissents are in Friedman v. Rogers, 440 U.S. 1 (1979), and Central Hudson Gas v. Public Serv. Comm'n, 447 U.S. 557 (1980).

[259] An example of this view is Bell, Race, Racism & American Law 635 (2d ed. 1980), commenting on Justice White's dissent in National Educ. Ass'n v. South Carolina, 434 U.S. 1026 (1976), summarily aff'g United States v. South Carolina, 445 F. Supp. 1094 (D.S.C. 1977), as a correct application of the principles of Washington v. Davis, 426 U.S. 229 (1976). Professor Bell describes Justice White "as the author of the Washington v. Davis opinion and thus entitled to more respect for his views than the Court's majority was willing to give him."

using Justice Powell, a charter member of the *Roe v. Wade* majority, to invoke the doctrine of stare decisis against *Roe* critics in 1983,[260] when another justice who joined the Court after *Roe* (Justice Stevens) was available for the job.[261]

In the category of outright overruling, I advise against handing the opinion assignment to an original dissenter. As Jerold Israel has shown,[262] a vindicated dissenter is given to gloating and less inclined to make use of "the traditional arts of overruling," which is to say, the diplomatic techniques available for correcting the Court's mistakes with a minimum of reproach.[263] According to my public relations precepts, the best qualified justice for an overruling assignment would seem to be a converted member of the original majority,[264] or, better still, the author of the discredited opinion ("Joy shall be in heaven over one sinner that repenteth, more than over ninety and nine just persons, which need no repentance").[265] The occasional act of contrition cleanses the judicial soul and is, as well, a powerful demonstration of intellectual openness. But there is a complication in using the recanter as the Court's voice, which is that the justice will have an autobiographical urge to explain his flip flop, and that is something that is done more comfortably through

---

[260] City of Akron v. Akron Center for Reproductive Health, Inc., 103 S.Ct. 2481 (1983).

[261] See Planned Parenthood of Missouri v. Danforth, 428 U.S. 52, 101 (1976) (Stevens, J., concurring in part and dissenting in part). *Cf.* the selection of newcomer Justice O'Connor as the Court's voice in Arizona v. Rumsey, 104 S.Ct. 2305 (1984), for adherence to a five to four decision predating her appointment to the Court: Bullington v. Missouri, 451 U.S. 430 (1981).

[262] Israel, Gideon v. Wainwright: The "Art" of Overruling, 1963 Supreme Court Review 211.

[263] Compare Gideon v. Wainwright, 372 U.S. 335 (1963), with Trammel v. United States, 445 U.S. 40 (1980). In *Gideon* a "new" justice (Harlan) wrote separately to say that the case being overruled was "entitled to a more respectful burial than has been accorded, at least on the part of those of us who were not on the Court when that case was decided." 372 U.S. at 349 (concurring opinion). In *Trammel* the overruling opinion was delivered by a newcomer (Chief Justice Burger), and it was left to the vindicated veteran, Justice Stewart, to suggest by separate concurrence that the Court was being too kind to the case it was overruling. See also Chandler v. Florida, 449 U.S. 560 (1981), in which Chief Justice Burger's majority opinion asserted that Estes v. Texas, 381 U.S. 532 (1965), had not totally banished television cameras from criminal trials, while *Estes* dissenters, Justices Stewart and White, maintained that *Estes* indeed imposed a per se ban and, for their part, they "would acknowledge our square departure from precedent." *Id.* at 586 (concurring opinion).

[264] As, *e.g.*, the choice of Justice Blackmun in Garcia v. San Antonio Metro. Transit Auth., 105 S.Ct. 1005 (1985), overruling National League of Cities v. Usery, 426 U.S. 833 (1976).

[265] Luke 15:7. For instances of such self-reversals, see note 267 *infra*.

the first-person medium of a separate concurring opinion.[266] Consequently, though the choice is close, I give the edge to a newcomer
as the spokesman for overruling.[267]

As for narrowing or distinguishing interpretations of precedent,
my objection to having the Court speak through an original dissenter is that such an assignment carries an implication of hostility
and of hidden agendas when what is wanted is the appearance of
objective analysis.[268] Of course, if key justices have developed mis-

---

[266] See West Virginia Bd. of Educ. v. Barnett, 319 U.S. 624, 643 (1943) (Black, J.,
concurring, joined by Douglas, J.) ("We are substantially in agreement with [the majority
opinion], but since we originally joined the Court in the [now overruled] Gobitis case, it is
appropriate that we make a brief statement of reasons for our change of view"). See also Reid
v. Covert, 354 U.S. 1, 65 (1957) (Harlan, J., concurring to explain his vote switch on
rehearing); Lewis v. Manufacturers Nat'l Bank, 364 U.S. 603, 610 (1961) (Harlan, J., concurring to recant views expressed as a Court of Appeals judge in Constance v. Harvey, 215
F.2d 571 [2d Cir. 1954]). What I find hard to understand is the unexplained vote switch. For
instance, Justice Stone joined Justice Roberts' unanimous opinion in Grovey v. Townsend,
295 U.S. 45 (1935), upholding the constitutionality of the Texas white primary. Some years
later, when Stone and Roberts were the only Grovey survivors on the Court, Grovey was
overruled by Smith v. Allwright, 321 U.S. 649 (1944). Justice Roberts, retaining his earlier
views, dissented. But Stone, now Chief Justice and the source of the opinion assignment,
joined Reed's majority opinion without adding a separate comment elaborating on (or drawing attention to) his change of heart. For a similar instance of unexplained vote switching, see
Dove v. United States, 423 U.S. 325 (1976) (Justice Brennan joins in eight to one per curiam
overruling of Durham v. United States, 401 U.S. 481 [1971], a six to three decision with
Justice Brennan then in the majority).

[267] Nevertheless there have been cases in which the overruling opinion was written without noticeable difficulty by the same justice who authored the overruled decision. See
Fairfield v. Gallantin Co., 100 U.S. 47 (1879) (per Strong, J.), overruling Town of Concord
v. Savings Bank, 92 U.S. 625 (1875); Hornbuckle v. Toombs, 85 U.S. 648 (1873) (per
Bradley, J.), overruling inter alia Dunphy v. Kleinsmith, 78 U.S. 610 (1870); Ry. Co. v.
McShane, 89 U.S. 444 (1874) (per Miller, J.), overruling Ry. Co. v. Prescott, 83 U.S. 603
(1872). And for a more contemporary illustration, see United States v. Scott, 437 U.S. 82
(1978) (per Rehnquist, J.), overruling United States v. Jenkins, 420 U.S. 358 (1975).

[268] Thus I question the selection of Justice White as majority writer in an aid-to-religion
case, Committee for Public Education v. Regan, 444 U.S. 646 (1980), requiring application
of the constitutional tests of Lemon v. Kurtzman, 403 U.S. 602 (1971), which Justice White
persistently rejects. See dissents cited in note 104 supra. The same objection applies to the
choice of Justice Powell in Middlesex Sewerage Auth. v. Nat'l Sea Clammers Ass'n, 453
U.S. 1 (1981), to apply the tests of Cort v. Ash, 422 U.S. 66 (1965), since Justice Powell was
and is a critic of the Cort approach to the implication of private remedies from federal
regulatory statutes. See his dissents in Cannon v. Univ. of Chicago, 441 U.S. 677, 730
(1979), and Merrill Lynch v. Curran, 456 U.S. 353, 395 (1982). I have a twofold objection to
the recent employment of Justice Marshall to deliver the Court's reversal of the death
sentence in Caldwell v. Mississippi, 105 S.Ct. 2633 (1985). First, Justice Marshall's abiding
belief in the unconstitutionality of capital punishment in any circumstances undermines his
value as administrator of the Court's precedents in such cases. Second, in order to reach the
Court's conclusion on the specific issue in Caldwell, concerning the propriety of prosecutorial
argument to the jury, it was necessary to distinguish a two-year-old decision, California v.
Ramos, 463 U.S. 992 (1983), in which Justice Marshall was a dissenter. It should be pointed

givings about the original decision, the choice of a former dissenter to deliver the Court's opinion can be seen as a calculated signal that the Court has begun to reverse direction.[269]

The justice who is a temporary acquiescer is always an unhappy choice as spokesman for the Court. True enough, when he agrees to a generous (albeit short-run) application of the precedent, he commands special respect. But if a temporary acquiescer is asked to be the Court's enforcer of recent holdings, a confusion of roles is bound to result. Consider the strange case of *Hudgens v. NLRB*.[270] The decision was meant to settle the Court's position on the question whether members of the public have First Amendment rights to mount demonstrations on the premises of privately owned shopping centers. Originally, in *Amalgamated Food Employees v. Logan Valley Plaza*,[271] the Court ruled five to four in favor of a constitutional right of access for labor pickets. Justice Stewart was part of the majority there. Later, in *Lloyd Corp. v. Tanner*,[272] the Court ruled five to four against political protestors, purporting to distinguish and narrow but not to overrule *Logan Valley*. Justice Stewart was with the dissenters in that case. Finally in *Hudgens* five justices took the view that the second case had overruled the first sub silentio and that the time had come to say so out loud, that is, to hold categorically that the First Amendment does not turn private business premises into a public forum for any cause.

Four of the five justice in *Hudgens* believed sincerely in the wisdom of that holding.[273] The fifth was Justice Stewart. His views on

---

out, however, that the Chief Justice was not responsible for the opinion assignment in *Caldwell*. That task fell to Justice Brennan (Marshall's alter ego on the subject of capital punishment) as senior member of the majority.

[269] See Foley v. Connelie, 435 U.S. 291 (1978), upholding the exclusion of aliens from jobs with the state police. The majority opinion was written by the Chief Justice, who only a year earlier dissented from a decision barring states from restricting aliens' eligibility for student scholarships. Nyquist v. Mauclet, 432 U.S. 1, 12 (1977). In a short concurrence in *Foley*, Justice Stewart wrote: "The dissenting opinions convincingly demonstrate that it is difficult if not impossible to reconcile the Court's judgment in this case with the full sweep of the reasoning and authority of some of our past decisions. It is only because I have become increasingly doubtful about the validity of those decisions (in at least some of which I concurred) that I join the opinion in this case." 435 U.S. at 300.

[270] 424 U.S. 507 (1976).

[271] 391 U.S. 308 (1968).

[272] 407 U.S. 551 (1972).

[273] Another, Justice White, accepted *Lloyd* at face value as compatible with *Logan Valley*, and classified the *Hudgens* facts as more closely aligned to *Lloyd*. 424 U.S. at 524–25 (concurring in result).

the constitutional merits had not changed since the first two cases but he too read *Lloyd Corp.* as the dispositive precedent. Now, if the main point of the *Hudgens* opinion was to give stare decisis reinforcement to *Lloyd Corp.*, Justice Stewart would have been an excellent author—assuming that for reasons of repose and certainty in the law he was prepared to abandon once and for all time his earlier opposition to *Lloyd*. But attend closely to Stewart's statement in *Hudgens*: "It matters not that some members of the Court may continue to believe that the *Logan Valley* case was rightly decided. Our institutional duty is to follow until changed the law as it now is, not as some members of Court might wish it to be."[274] Justice Stewart, of course, was among those who thought the overruled *Logan Valley* was "rightly decided," and nothing in his *Hudgens* opinion suggests that he did not "continue to believe" in the correctness of the first decision, although of the *Logan Valley* aficionados still on the Court Justice Stewart alone sacrifices himself to "our institutional duty." And yet notice the contingent manner in which he formulates the duty: it is "to follow *until changed* [my emphasis] the law as it now is." How might the law "as it now is" come to be changed? I doubt that Justice Stewart was thinking of constitutional amendment or of some sort of federally legislated right of access to shopping centers. Who will change the "law" of *Lloyd* and *Hudgens* if not the Court itself by a future act of judicial housecleaning? And if that is a welcome prospect to Justice Stewart, he is not a stare decisis capitulator but that rather different creature, a temporary acquiescer—a justice as subversive in his aspirations as any of the out-and-out dissenters in *Hudgens*. As such, he should be writing a reluctant concurrence and someone else should be speaking on behalf of the "the law as it now is."[275]

I realize that the proliferation of separate concurrences is disfavored in some quarters and even seen as an institutional pathology. But I cannot escape the conclusion that it ought to be *de rigueur*

---

[274] 424 U.S. at 518.

[275] I have the same criticism of the selection of Justice Stewart to write the Court's opinion in Crist v. Bretz, 437 U.S. 28 (1978), proceeding from a decision, Benton v. Maryland, 395 U.S. 784 (1969), in which Stewart was a dissenter. (Since the Chief Justice dissented in *Crist*, Justice Stewart's opinion assignment presumably came from the senior justice in the majority bloc, Justice Brennan.)

for all temporary acquiescers.[276] In addition, new justices, joining the Court in doctrinal midstream, have a special need for individual expression. If the newcomer joins with the majority in a decision based on previous holdings but is not the Court's assigned author, his vote is capable of several different interpretations. Is he implying that he would have joined the majority in the predecessor cases had he been on the Court? Or is he simply bowing to those decisions for reasons of stare decisis? Or is his acceptance that of a basically unfriendly temporary acquiescer? Certainly from the standpoint of the practicing bar—of lawyers who want to know where each justice stands on important propositions—it is desirable that recently appointed justices catch up to their senior colleagues by getting their own views on the record as soon as the opportunity occurs.

VII. CONCLUSION

There is no pat formula that routes dissenting justices to their proper role in future cases. The bracketing alternatives of stare decisis capitulation or stubborn dissent are fairly simple to understand—the former in terms of the need to settle the law once and for all, the latter by the urgings of abiding conviction. The more subtle choice is self-subordination "for the time being," a middle course whose pragmatic and institutional benefits are not always apparent. Yet on the whole I think it desirable that justices, having fully ventilated their disagreement with the Court's holding, ask themselves whether there are special reasons why they should persist in dissent. And "I still think I am right and my colleagues are wrong" is not, in my view, a fully sufficient basis for repetition of dissent. Self-subordination seems to me the better choice, pro-

---

[276] Justice Harlan's performance as temporary acquiescer shows that a separate opinion is the guarantor of clarity. That is why I not only question the choice of Justice Stewart as the Court's author in *Hudgens* but why I would not be satisfied had he merely signed another justice's opinion for the Court. For a recent instance of movement from dissent to cryptic concurrence, see United States v. Johns, 105 S.Ct. 1881 (1985), upholding seven to two a belated police search without warrant of an impounded automobile, on the authority and analogy of United States v. Ross, 456 U.S. 798 (1982). Justice White, a *Ross* dissenter, joined the majority opinion in *Johns*, while his fellow *Ross* dissenters, Justices Brennan and Marshall, took the occasion to renew their opposition to *Ross*. We must guess whether White's acceptance of *Ross* is temporary or permanent.

vided that two conditions are present: (1) that adherence to the earlier dissenting position would not adequately respond to the issues the Court has undertaken to decide, and (2) that the dissenter's conscience is not violated by the act of collegial acquiescence. As to the latter condition, it is well to bear in mind that not every intramural disagreement involves a matter of conscience or high principle, even when the point in dispute is one of constitutional law. In the final analysis, then, I admire the collegialism of Justice Harlan more than the soloism of Justice Black. By choosing temporary acquiescence a justice can, as Traynor says, avoid "the rata-plan" of renewed dissent while "abiding the time when he may win over the majority." But if this is the justice's chosen path, let him be sure to clarify by separate opinion the interim nature of his shifted position so that it will not be mistaken for permanent abandonment of original dissent.

MELVIN I. UROFSKY

THE BRANDEIS-FRANKFURTER

CONVERSATIONS

I. INTRODUCTION

Scholars and the general public have recently shown a renewed interest in the career of Louis D. Brandeis,[1] and especially his relationship with Felix Frankfurter.[2] In the past few years there have been not only major new biographies of both men[3] but also three separate studies of their partnership in legal and political affairs.[4] Although neither man during his life attempted to hide his

---

Melvin I. Urofsky is Professor of History, Virginia Commonwealth University; Philip E. Urofsky provided research assistance.

[1] Louis Dembitz Brandeis (LDB); born November 13, 1856, Louisville, Kentucky; died October 5, 1941, Washington, D.C.; educated in Louisville public schools and the Annen-Realschule in Dresden, Germany; LL.B., Harvard Law School, 1878; practiced law briefly in St. Louis, then in Boston until 1916; appointed by Woodrow Wilson as Associate Justice of the U.S. Supreme Court in 1916; retired in 1939.

[2] Felix Frankfurter (FF); born November 15, 1882, Vienna, Austria; died February 22, 1965, Washington, D.C.; educated in New York City schools; A.B., City College of New York, 1901; LL.B., Harvard Law School, 1905; in private practice in New York briefly, then served as assistant to Henry L. Stimson in U.S. Attorney's Office and in War Department; joined faculty of Harvard Law School in 1914; appointed by Franklin D. Roosevelt as Associate Justice of the Supreme Court in 1939; retired in 1962.

[3] Gal, Brandeis of Boston (1980); Urofsky, Louis D. Brandeis and the Progressive Tradition (1981); Paper, Brandeis (1983); Strum, Louis D. Brandeis, Justice for the People (1984). For Frankfurter, see Lash, From the Diaries of Felix Frankfurter (1975); Hirsch, The Enigma of Felix Frankfurter (1981); and Parrish, Felix Frankfurter and His Times: The Reform Years (1982).

[4] Dawson, Louis D. Brandeis, Felix Frankfurter, and the New Deal (1980); Murphy, The Brandeis/Frankfurter Connection (1982); and Baker, Brandeis and Frankfurter: A Dual Biography (1984).

friendship for the other, the depth of their collaboration after 1916, when Brandeis went on to the Supreme Court, was known to only a few close colleagues.

Brandeis once referred to Frankfurter as "half brother, half son,"[5] and the description is remarkably apt. In many areas, the younger Frankfurter looked up to Brandeis for fatherly advice. He accepted the professorship at the Harvard Law School, for example, despite the misgivings of most of his friends, on Brandeis's urging.[6] When Brandeis ascended the bench, it was Frankfurter who stepped in to take his place as counsel for the National Consumers' League in defending protective legislation.[7] During the New Deal, Frankfurter, who was close to Franklin Roosevelt, often operated as a surrogate for the jurist who, whatever his private dabblings in political affairs, could not himself act openly.[8]

But it was the brotherly aspect of their relationship that provided Brandeis something he sorely needed and missed after 1916, someone to whom he could talk freely, without fear that candid remarks would be repeated. This was especially true of his work on the Court, about which Brandeis spoke to no one, not even close friends and colleagues from reform and Zionist days, but which he discussed freely with Frankfurter, both orally and in an extensive correspondence.[9]

During the Court's summer recess, Brandeis and his family left the Washington heat for Chatham, on Cape Cod, to which Frankfurter came frequently, on occasion renting a nearby house. During these visits, the two men spoke of many things, and Frankfurter jotted down the gist of their conversations on loose pieces of paper and in blue-covered law school exam books. It is impossible to determine the full extent of the original notes since Frankfurter destroyed a number of papers relating to Brandeis after the latter's

---

[5] LDB to FF, September 24, 1925, in Urofsky and Levy (eds.), 5 Letters of Louis D. Brandeis 187 (5 vols. to date, 1971–) (hereafter cited as Brandeis Letters).

[6] Parrish, note 3 *supra*, at 57–61.

[7] *Id.* at 72.

[8] Murphy, note 4 *supra*, chs. 4, 5.

[9] Many of these letters are available in 4 and 5 Brandeis Letters, note 5 *supra*. A separate volume, including these as well as several hundred items from the recently opened Frankfurter Papers in the Library of Congress, is now in preparation.

death in 1941.[10] Those that are left are primarily for the years 1922–24 and are deposited in the Brandeis Papers in the Harvard Law School. Some are written in pencil, and the ravages of age as well as Frankfurter's nearly illegible handwriting make all of them difficult, and some words and phrases impossible, to read.[11]

But they do give us a remarkable portrait of the justices of the Supreme Court and their interaction during the early years of the Taft Court. Brandeis, along with Oliver Wendell Holmes and John H. Clarke, constituted a highly vocal minority in opposition to their conservative brethren. Many of their dissents later became accepted constitutional doctrine, and Brandeis was acutely aware of the changes that time could produce. He never saw himself as a prophet crying in the wilderness, but as a builder, laying a foundation on which others would later erect a proper modern jurisprudence.

Thus his opinions and dissents included enormous amounts of factual material, for he hoped to educate both bench and bar to the need to "guide by the light of reason."[12] He constantly urged Frankfurter to have his students write law-review articles to further the message and personally created the practice of citing law-review articles as authoritative sources in his footnotes. Alexander Bickel, utilizing drafts of dissents that Brandeis prepared but did not release, has shown the great effort the jurist made to educate his brethren to the realities of modern industrial life.[13] And as a number of his law clerks have recalled, after they had labored for weeks or months over an opinion, Brandeis would say: "Now I think the opinion is persuasive, but what can we do to make it more instructive?"[14]

---

[10] Information provided by the late Pearl von Allman, who was for many years curator of the Brandeis Collection at the University of Louisville, and who served as a research assistant to Alpheus T. Mason for his Brandeis: A Free Man's Life (1946).

[11] The original notes, contained in blue exam books and on loose leaf pages, are in The Louis Brandeis Papers in the Harvard Law School, along with a transcription, which can also be found in the Felix Frankfurter Papers in the Manuscript Division of the Library of Congress. Because of numerous errors in the original transcription, I have completely retranscribed the original Frankfurter notes, but some words remain indecipherable. Such words are indicated by [ ].

[12] LDB dissent in New State Ice Co. v. Liebman, 285 U.S. 262, 311 (1932).

[13] Bickel, The Unpublished Opinions of Mr. Justice Brandeis (1957).

[14] Freund, *Justice Brandeis: A Law Clerk's Remembrance*, 68 American Jewish History 7, 11 (1978).

Perhaps the most interesting part of these notes (of which scholars have long been aware but have seldom used) is Brandeis's
characterization of his brethren. Of especial interest is his appreciation of William Howard Taft, with whom he differed ideologically
and who had been a bitter political foe little more than a decade
earlier. Not surprising, of course, is his affection and esteem for
Oliver Wendell Holmes, whom Brandeis had known ever since his
early days as a young attorney in Boston.[15]

Finally, we get Brandeis on the law, in comments he could not
make in his writings but that reflect views he had articulated for
many years.[16] While there may be no surprises here, these notes
shed additional light on one of the great figures in modern American constitutional history and thought.

II. THE BRANDEIS-FRANKFURTER CONVERSATIONS

April 17, 1922. Taft[17] very nice—gentlemanly in dealing
with case involving Ballinger.[18] He talks long in Conference but
he's a cultivated man & only other except Holmes[19] you can talk to
about things other than law without need of diagrams & spelling it

---

[15] "Tuesday evening Holmes, Warren & I spent at Warren's room over a glass of ———
(mixture of Champagne & Beer) telling jokes & talking Summum bonum, i.e. Warren &
Holmes talked and I lay outstretched on a ship's chair." LDB to Alfred Brandeis, July 31,
1879, 1 Brandeis Letters, note 5 *supra*, at 45.

[16] Urofsky, A Mind of One Piece: Brandeis and American Reform, ch. 6 (1971).

[17] William Howard Taft (1857–1930) had realized his life's ambition when President
Harding named him Chief Justice of the United States in 1921; he served in that position
until shortly before his death. Taft had been a federal judge in Ohio, Solicitor General, then
Governor of the Philippines and Secretary of War before serving one term as President
(1909–1913).

[18] During Taft's administration, Progressives had accused his Secretary of the Interior,
Richard Achilles Ballinger (1858–1922), of plotting to give the nation's natural resources
away to private interests. LDB had served as counsel for Collier's Magazine, which broke the
story, and in the course of his investigation had shown that Taft had approved Ballinger's
action without having read the supporting materials, which Taft claimed to have done. The
full story is in Penick, Progressive Politics and Conservation: The Ballinger-Pinchot Affair
(1968). Taft, who had bitterly opposed LDB's appointment to the Court because of this
fight, had graciously made his peace with LDB during the war. See LDB to Alice Brandeis,
December 4, 1918, 4 Brandeis Letters, note 5 *supra*, at 370.

[19] Oliver Wendell Holmes, Jr. (1841–1935), had served for twenty years on the Supreme
Judicial Court of Massachusetts before Theodore Roosevelt named him to the Supreme
Court in 1902, where he sat for thirty years. LDB and known Holmes since the 1870s and
had attended his famous Lowell Lectures on the common law. For their collaboration on the
bench, see Konefsky, The Legacy of Holmes and Brandeis (1956).

out. Has no *Weltschmerz*.[20] He's the Taft we thought he was. He
has all the defects but also the advantages of the aristocratic order
that has done well by him. He accepts it, but doesn't sweat & labor
to maintain his position.

Holmes is as wonderful in character as in brain.

I suggested "Holmes more puritan than you" (L.D.B.)

L.D.B. (vehemently): "More so, much more so."

Re certiorari in turntable (Zinc Co. case),[21] "had no business to
grant it. Did so because Holmes wanted it, though he does not
know it & would be surprised to hear it.

June 25, 1922. Often wrong decisions due to haste and fatigue
of end of term. Saturday night at Chief's—preceding Monday—
have [   ] of cases (1) haste and (2) they are fatigued at end of term
and (3) at end of day.

June 26, 1972. Hughes'[22] statement that Court['s] hardest
work—(1) before [   ] Conference (2) two weeks before end of term.

L.D.B.: "Wouldn't you like to have job now that would enable
you to look forward to long vacation in two weeks."

C.E.H.: "Not at time you have to pay for it."

L.D.B. said White[23] told him Hughes at times so nervous bor-
dered on being crazy; took him home once at night, ministered an
electric treatment. After Conference Hughes spent an [*sic*] Sunday
in bed.

---

[20] "World-weariness."

[21] In United Zinc & Chemical Co. v. Britt, 258 U.S. 268 (1922), Holmes, speaking for a
six-man majority, held that a landowner had no duty to keep his property safe for children,
or even free from hidden dangers, if he had not directly or indirectly invited them onto
the land. The turntable case is the classic Railroad Co. v. Stout, 17 Wall. 657 (1873),
where the Court held that, when children had played on a turntable with knowledge of that
fact by the railroad's employees, there had been an implicit invitation, and the railroad was
liable for injuries sustained. Federal courts were then making general common law, a practice that Holmes disapproved in principle but exploited when an "interesting" question, such
as this one in torts, arose.

[22] Charles Evans Hughes (1862–1948), after a term as reform governor of New York, had
been appointed by Taft as Associate Justice of the Court in 1910 and resigned six years later
to run unsuccessfully as the Republican candidate for the Presidency. He served as Secretary
of State under Harding and Coolidge, and in 1930 President Hoover named him Chief
Justice, which he remained until his retirement in 1941.

[23] Edward Douglass White (1845–1921) of Louisiana had been appointed to the Supreme
Court by Grover Cleveland in 1894; in 1910 Taft elevated him to Chief Justice, in which
capacity he served until his death.

L.D.B.himself says in the beginning confinement of work—always have to be there and seven days a week etc.—"went hard with me." He—L.D.B.—accustomed to work when and how he willed—had freedom in work.[24]

June 18, 1922. Holmes—best intellectual machine. Thought so forty years ago. Yet he has two deep prejudices: Sherman Law, didn't and couldn't understand business fact involved in this machinery. Admits that he doesn't see social aspects of "big business" merely economic aspects. But believed it all is deep prejudice.

So also Doyle case[25]—recently overruled—here was chance to hit Missouri Court: worst Court (unless possibly Mississippi) that comes before us. Just shows no mind is immune from force of prejudice.

I asked whether influenced by counsel: e.g., Duplex,[26] Adair,[27] Coppage,[28] Truax[29] badly briefed and probably argued but [in] Truax (260) your (L.D.B.) dissent[30] had all counsel could give. L.D.B.: "Too late; by the time [of] my memo their backs were up and wouldn't change; we just show you we stick. Holmes would deny it but Ct doesn't heed dissents sufficiently. Holmes does—but not Court. Pitney[31] if he is fresh would consider. My experi-

---

[24] For LDB's apprehensions of how the Court would restrict him, see LDB to Amos Pinchot, June 27, 1916, 4 Brandeis Letters, note 5 *supra*, at 239.

[25] Doyle v. Continental Insurance Co., 94 U.S. 535 (1877), held that a state could not require, as a condition of doing business within the state, a foreign corporation to abstain from recourse to federal courts. However, the Court said there was nothing to stop a state from revoking the charter, for any reason it chose, and federal courts could not inquire into the reason. The holding was overruled in Terral v. Burke Constr. Co., 257 U.S. 529 (1922).

[26] In Duplex Printing Press Co. v. Deering, 254 U.S. 443 (1921), the Court, speaking through Pitney, held a secondary boycott could be enjoined under the antitrust laws, despite the Clayton Antitrust Act of 1914, which exempted unions from such attack. LDB, joined by Holmes and Clarke, entered a vigorous dissent at 479, urging the Court to leave policy decisions in the hands of the legislature.

[27] Adair v. United States, 208 U.S. 161 (1908), invalidated, under the due process clause of the Fifth Amendment, a federal law against "yellow dog" contracts, which required workers on interstate railroads, as a condition of employment, to promise not to join unions.

[28] Coppage v. Kansas, 236 U.S. 1 (1915), ruled unconstitutional a state prohibition of "yellow dog" contracts as violative of the Fourteenth Amendment's Due Process Clause.

[29] In Truax v. Corrigan, 257 U.S. 312 (1921), the Court nullified an Arizona statute forbidding state courts to grant injunctions against workers picketing during strikes.

[30] *Id.* at 354.

[31] Mahlon Pitney (1858–1924) of New Jersey had been appointed to the Court by Taft in 1912; he resigned in 1922.

ence on Ct. fortifies my views as to character. Taft, I believe, if he had to write whenever he concurred, might not reach results. Nor Holmes, of course. V.D.[32] wouldn't change, nor Clarke.[33] Day[34] couldn't be persuaded by anybody but himself. He does change his own views; he is a fighter, a regular game cock. Clarke practically never changes his views.

As to Coronado,[35] passed from week to week, once considered by Taft then brought in conclusions—(1) liable under Sherman Law (2) evidence to hold & (3) interstate commerce. I expressed views (1) liable at c[ommon]. l[aw]. and no evidence of conspiracy & (2) no interstate commerce. When Taft came to write changed his views & then carried Court with him.

I pounded on jurisdictional observance & glad to get Taft to say what he did in last P.[36]

June 30, 1922. L.D.B: There can't be too much apprehension about evil effects of old age. Marshall[37] and Story[38] outlived their usefulness not because of waning intellectual powers, but because

---

[32] Willis Van Devanter (1859–1941), after terms as Chief Justice of Wyoming, Assistant Attorney-General of the United States, and federal Circuit Court judge, had been named to the Supreme Court by Taft in 1910 and served until 1937. Although a conservative and often differing from LDB, the two men enjoyed cordial relations, and LDB respected "Van's" judicial ability. See L.D.B. to Willis VanDevanter, April 29, 1921, 5 Brandeis Letters, note 5 *supra*, at 171.

[33] John Hessin Clarke (1887–1945), a liberal Ohio lawyer and judge, had been appointed to the Court by President Wilson in 1916 only a few weeks after LDB's confirmation. He resigned in 1922 to work in the peace movement and for the League of Nations.

[34] William Rufus Day (1849–1923) of Ohio had been named to the Court by Theodore Roosevelt in 1903 and served until 1922.

[35] United Mine Workers v. Coronado Coal Co., 259 U.S. 344 (1922), voided damages assessed under the Sherman Act against a union during a violent strike since the Clayton Antitrust Act of 1914 had presumably exempted unions from such penalties. At first LDB did not believe the Court would vote this way and prepared a dissent should his brethren confirm the penalty. But Chief Justice White died, and Taft accepted LDB's reasoning. For the unpublished dissent and a history of the inner workings of the Court in this case, see Bickel, note 13 *supra*, ch. 5. See also FF, *The Coronado Case*, 31 New Republic 328 (August 16, 1922).

[36] At 259 U.S. 413 Taft had written: "The circumstances are such as to awaken regret that, in our view of the federal jurisdiction, we can not affirm the judgment. But it is of far higher importance that we should preserve inviolate the fundamental limitations in respect to the federal jurisdiction."

[37] John Marshall (1755–1835) served as Chief Justice from 1801 until his death; he fashioned the Supreme Court into a powerful instrument of government.

[38] Joseph Story (1779–1845) of Massachusetts was, after Marshall, the most influential justice of the early nineteenth century; he served on the Court from 1811 until his death.

of failure to grow. Holmes of course is a "sport"—can't reason from him at all. He works with as much intensity as I've ever known him to work. In forty years he has [had] spurts of rest but when he works he works with all the steam up there is and too often more. And again there is a great deal in him; in most men there isn't, there is no reservoir to draw on.

We ought to have provision for Presidents and members of our Ct. to sit, say, in [the] Senate, without vote. They could serve on Committees etc. I should think McKenna[39] & Day would love it. Like old war horses hearing the music again. Pension not enough—men want occupation.

It's the same problem as is met in all big businesses—old men are "retained" on boards, etc.

July 1922. Since I've been on Bench only one labor case well argued, Hughes' argument on first hearing of Coronado case.[40]

Day hot little gent—hot whenever Coppage[41] case mentioned and fierce about Truax v. C.[42]

F.F.: Why about latter?

L.D.B.: Because of facts in case—the poster "all who enter leave hope behind," etc.

July 1, 1922. At Bar chose jurors because of prejudice of judges but never realized until came on S. C. how much even these (?) men are diverted by passion & prejudice and how closed the mind can be. For instance Day & Clarke & Mc[Reynolds][43] are quite wild about prohibition.

After first argument of Truax case, Holmes, Clarke & I walked home together & Holmes said: "Well, at least in this case no one will vote for reversal." And I said: "We'll be lucky if we can sustain it five to four."

---

[39] Joseph McKenna (1843–1926) of California had been appointed to the Court by President McKinley in 1898 and served until 1925.

[40] Note 35 *supra.*

[41] Note 28 *supra.*

[42] Note 29 *supra.*

[43] James Clark McReynolds (1862–1946) had been named to the Court by Wilson in 1914 to get him out of the Cabinet, a political maneuver Wilson always regretted making. McReynolds was perhaps the most conservative member of the Court and disliked LDB not only because he was a liberal but also because he was a Jew. When LDB resigned from the Court in 1939, McReynold's name was conspicuously absent from the traditional letter sent by the remaining brethren. McReynolds resigned from the bench in 1941.

Holmes has no realization of what moves men—he is as innocent as a girl of sixteen is supposed to have been. And most of the time it doesn't matter in his position. Goes off sometimes in construing statutes because he doesn't understand or appreciate facts.

Holmes is more often quoted by lawyers but also leaves more loopholes for rehearing petitions than anyone else; he disregards some little fact or doesn't spell it out and it irritates him—as it irritates me with *myself* when it happens.

"Holmes ought to have more influence with the Ct—he is so guileless, so affable, so courteous, so gentle." I interrupted, "but he lives on so different and so elevated a plane compared with the others." "Yes," L.D.B., "it's a case of aristocracy against very ordinary bourgeoisie. Taft is the only other man with whom it is a pleasure to talk—you feel you talk with a cultivated man. He knows a lot, he *reads*, he has wide contacts. Taft's relations with Holmes are very loving, a fine banter, he is quick to catch his points and it's altogether fine."

Taft wants to get as good product as he can from Ct—uses materials he has. (In reply to my question as to L.D.B.'s writing int[erstate] com[merce] opinions) Taft wants Ct to guide Bar—indicate direction; doesn't sufficiently work over materials. Van D. does.

Dwells much on effect of close of term e.g. Coronado concurrences.[44] V.D. e.g., brings on his opinions. These they will take from Taft [but] wouldn't from us. If good enough for Taft good enough for us—they say, & a natural sentiment.

Concerned with how Ct can be made more favorably recognized by people. Admitted my comparison to days before C[ivil] War. Agreed evil effects of Truax v. Corrigan[45]—fierce passions—*you* ought to hear Day on that opinion—Ct ought to welcome criticism "approve the effort & vote against the measure" often.

July 9, 1922. L.D.B. thinks if no XIV [Amendment] there would have been extension of application of contract clause. Cites American Smelting Co. v. Colorado, 20—as sample.[46]

---

[44] Note 35 *supra.*

[45] Note 29 *supra.*

[46] American Smelting & Refining Co. v. Colorado, 204 U.S. 103 (1907), held that a foreign corporation, once admitted to do business in a state on an equal basis with domestic firms, could not later be subjected to a tax at twice the rate applied to local companies. Four members of the Court, including Holmes, dissented without opinion.

But agrees, generally, that XIV Amendment "much ado about nothing"—that absence would have brought home to States *their* responsibility more—both pass buck & don't consider sufficiently & also agrees that Charles Warren's numerical proof[47] of small % of state law nullifications by S.C. is an illusory test: Smythe case,[48] like Coppage[49] or Truax v. Corr[igan][50] may do mischief way beyond the arithmetic ratio to totality of decisions.

Thinks Schaefer case, 247 ? "dreadful".[51] Pitney's opinion as to presumed to have knowledge of "real" causes of war attributable to Pitney's Presbyterian doctrine of freedom of will. "These individuals having free choice of right & wrong, choose wrong." He—Pitney—personally is very kindly, tho in many ways naive & wholly without knowledge but still can't shake his Presbyterianism or doesn't realize he is in its grip.

L.D.B. says wage system is doomed—based on loyalty and there's no use talking. Workers won't have loyalty to absent stockholders with their "wrack-renting stewards." Answer is productive industry through building up markets & steadily supplying: Corporations all lack [   ]. Build up loyalty—as [   ] groundwork—go *without* rather than buy from nonCoop.

L.D.B. tremendously impressed with problem of "turning up" new physical instruments in factories etc. *a fortiori* political instruments better coop action (this in reply to absurd claims of people like Dr. Warbasse.)[52]

At bottom of most of L.D.B.'s philosophy—or rather opinions on affairs—is his sense of perfection together with his sense of

---

[47] Warren, *The Progressivism of the United States Supreme Court*, 13 Colum. L. Rev. 294 (1913).

[48] In Smyth v. Ames, 169 U.S. 466 (1898), the Court invalidated a Nebraska law setting intrastate freight rates because the law imposed rates so low as to be unreasonable and thus a deprivation of property without due process of law. The case launched courts into an extensive review of all administrative and legislative rate making for a generation.

[49] Note 28 *supra.*

[50] Note 29 *supra.*

[51] Schaefer v. United States, 251 U.S. 466 (1920), upheld the conviction of the publisher of a German-language periodical for pamphlets allegedly supporting the Central Powers. LDB, joined by Holmes, issued a powerful dissent at 482.

[52] James Peter Warbasse (1866–1957) was a surgeon who became interested in sociology and social problems; he gave up his practice and in 1916 became President of the Cooperative League of America, a position he held for twenty-five years. Warbasse traveled widely touting cooperatives as an answer to nearly all modern economic problems.

man's meager capacity—we are *not* great men—meager equipment
& difficulties of task.

Therefore don't undertake too vast or too big things. A sense of
humility about man.

July 20, 1922. Great difficulty of all group action of course is
when & what concessions to make. Can't always dissent—may
have dissented much just then or may think [   ] seems [   ] concur
in results to build on (such as the Trust opin 1922). Holmes in [   ]
Trust[53]—concur in result but ought not to sign such an opinion as
McKenna's. But law schools ought not to let Ct get by—country
ought to insist on quality. Infirmities of judgment are something
you got to put up with it, but not lack of quality—that men are
capable of. E.g., ought not to stand for McR's [   ]—he writes like
some of [   ] judges & is capable of effective writing.

Remedies inside of Ct are: (1) some one member of Ct should be
charged specially with going over opinions—to be appointed by
C.J. (2) opinions ought to lie over about 10 days—so a man can let
it rest on table and think about it—(except emergency agreed to by
all.)

Of course some wouldn't like it. Holmes would worry if not
returned at once as he does—apologies if not returned by messenger.

Two things furnish correction. (1) don't let Ct decide cases it has
no business [to] take jurisdiction. (2) Keep Ct up to best quality—in
its proper means. Frequent rehearings, I am as a rule vs. granting—
doesn't make for prestige of Ct.

Remedy is greater care in opinions—(1) holding over—(2) check
up by someone so charged. As to dissents—or different criticism—
don't want to vent feelings or raise rumpus. But if established
system would become tradition easy for newcomers.

September 2, 1922. Referring to Gooch v. Oregon[54] February 27,

---

[53] There are several words illegible in this sentence, making it impossible to determine to
which case FF is referring.

[54] Gooch v. Oregon Short Line R.R. Co., 258 U.S. 22 (1922), upheld a railroad requirement, approved by the Interstate Commerce Commission (I.C.C.), that claims for personal
injury had to be submitted in writing within thirty days after the accident, although Congress had set a ninety-day limit for claims of damages to goods. Holmes delivered the
opinion, from which Clarke, Taft, and McKenna dissented.

1922 (No ev.), "in such cases interpretation of S/L in indiv cases—I go with majority" (meaning not important enough to enter dissent.)

Also referring to my praise of Pitney in U.S. Fidelity v. Kentucky[55] & in N.Y. Workmen's Compensation[56]—"it was a job getting that by—getting a majority—a close shave!"

September 4, 1922. At freezer (came over to get [   ]) handed me envelope, "here's a memo of my views on present discontent" handling his 5 pp. dated Sept. 4. "What to do."[57]

November 30, 1922. "Van D. runs Court now," L.D.B. "Why." F.F.

B.: Well—he is like a jesuit general; he is always helpful to everybody, always ready for the C.J. He knows a deal of federal practice & federal specialities, particularly land laws and then he is "in" with all the Republican politicians.

Taft is great influence in filling vacancies (a propos Day & Pitney successors[58] & Pierce Butler's appointment).[59]

F. suggested his opinions are loose & mischievous in dicta & language even when *result* is right.

B.: "He can't help it—he can't write and think closely. But I am much disappointed in Sutherland.[60] He is a mediocre Taft, has all the latter's weaknesses."

B. spoke with concern about Holmes. He seems to have

---

[55] In United States Fidelity & Guar. Co. v. Kentucky, 231 U.S. 394 (1913), Pitney had ruled for a unanimous Court that persons engaged by a foreign corporation to check credit ratings are not themselves engaged in interstate commerce and are therefore subject to a state tax.

[56] In New York Cent. R.R. Co. v. White, 243 U.S. 188 (1917), a unanimous Court, speaking through Pitney, held the New York Workmen's Compensation statute constitutional.

[57] The memorandum, dealing with LDB's suggestions for a liberal labor agenda, is in 5 Brandeis Letters, note 5 *supra*, at 59, and also appeared as an unsigned article, *What to Do*, 32 New Republic 136 (October 4, 1922).

[58] Pierce Butler (see note 59 *infra*) succeeded Day, and Edward Sanford (see note 66 *infra*) took Pitney's place.

[59] Pierce Butler (1866–1939) of Minnesota was named to the Court by Harding in 1922 and took his seat at the beginning of 1923; he served until his death.

[60] George Sutherland (1862–1942), after two terms as Senator from Utah, was named by President Harding to the Court in 1922 and served until 1938. He once said of LDB: "My, how I detest that man's ideas. But he is one of the greatest technical lawyers I have ever known." Konefsky, note 19 *supra*, at 278n.

weakened his aim. "His aim is no longer sure tho his execution is brilliant." I mentioned Pittsburgh Party Wall case.[61]

B.: "Take that case. He actually voted & wrote the other way in that case." (Jackman v. Rosenbaum, dec. October 23, 1922). The great difficulty is his [ ] desire for speed. That always was a point of pride with him. Now it's a vice. He & McKenna run a race of diligence of finishing an opinion assigned to either. Holmes can't bear not to have case done the same day it's given to him.

The other day he asked C.J. about resigning, & Taft told him he more than carries his load. Which is true. He talked to me about it when we drove home & I told him the same. Speaking judicially I'm sure the public is the gainer by having him remain. No one conceivably likely to be appointed will give anywhere near his service. From the point of view of his reputation, I'm sure he will gain by staying on.

F.: Do you see much of him now?

B.: More than ever—for we ride down together in his carriage to [ ] Street where I get out and walk.

June 12, 1923. Saw L.D.B. at his old office, 160 Devonshire. Never looked better or happier. Almost his first words, "We've had some interesting times—but the atmosphere is very friendly. When we differ, we agree to differ, without any ill feeling. It's all very friendly."

He was happy over Sonneborn[62] decision (taxation on original packages at Rec[eip]t). "That's my opinion—Taft wrote it on basis

---

[61] Jackman v. Rosenbaum Co., 260 U.S. 22 (1922). Holmes, for a unanimous Court, held that a practice of ancient usage is unaffected by the Fourteenth Amendment and that, in having a wall torn down to be replaced by a required party wall, plaintiff was not entitled to incidental damages.

[62] Sonneborn Bros. v. Cureton, 262 U.S. 506 (1923). Ever since Brown v. Maryland, 12 Wheat. 419 (1827), the Court had provided imported goods constitutional immunity from state taxation so long as they remained in the original package. This rule at the time undoubtedly carried out the Framers' intent to prevent seaboard states enriching themselves on goods in transit, but by 1923 the doctrine had become confused and disruptive of state tax programs, and a series of cases (see note 63 *infra*) extended the doctrine to include goods imported not only from abroad but from another state as well. In this case the Court originally seemed bent on continuing the original package doctrine, and LDB prepared a dissent if the vote should go that way, in which he argued that the Court's attachment to a formal rule, and a wrong rule at that, disrupted commerce. The chief defender of the rule, Justice Day (see note 63 *infra*) retired, and LDB's argument won over a majority. Taft's opinion for the Court, striking down the century-old rule, incorporated LDB's major arguments. See Bickel, note 13 *supra*, ch. 6.

of memo in which I analyzed all cases. Earlier ones[63] I followed Pitney & Day, when I knew nothing and assumed they did. But upon study I found Court had gone off, largely through Day's strong, passionate talk & loose language. I don't know whether we could have gotten Sonneborn decision if Day had been on Court. He felt so fiercely about it.

As to valuation cases, we got by in Georgia case[64] holding that reconstruction is not the measure but merely a factor. It was with reference to that case that I wrote memorandum which eventually became dissent in S.W. Telephone case.[65] Also got by Court non-valuation of franchise etc. I think gradually Court will work out pretty satisfactorily on those cases. Trouble is they don't, most of them, understand the problem. Taft hasn't the slightest grasp of fiscal or utility aspects of these cases. P. Butler is about what people said he was. He is gunning after valuation of land grants in land grant roads. As to Sanford,[66] he is nice—but no spark of greatness; thoroughly bourgeois.

The most terrible thing Ct did was assumption of jurisdiction in West Virginia Natural Gas case.[67] Van D. by general phrases glides over total absence of jurisdictional bases in Record. I don't

---

[63] The Court had dealt with the original package rule in several recent cases, and in all of them LDB had joined in the unanimous decisions. The rule had been confirmed in Standard Oil Co. v. Graves, 249 U.S. 389 (1919); Askren v. Continental Oil Co., 252 U.S. 444 (1920); and Bowman v. Continental Oil Co., 256 U.S. 642 (1921), with Day delivering the first two opinions and Pitney the third. But in Wagner v. City of Covington, 251 U.S. 95 (1919), the Court, through Pitney, unanimously overlooked the rule because of the local nature of the allegedly interstate commerce.

[64] Georgia Ry. & Power Co. v. Railroad Comm'n of Ga., 262 U.S. 625 (1923). LDB delivered the opinion, with only McKenna dissenting, that valuation of property at replacement cost, less depreciation, was not the sole consideration but only one of several factors to be taken into account in setting rates for public utilities. This was a significant departure from the rule of Smyth v. Ames, note 48 supra.

[65] Missouri ex rel. Southwestern Bell Tel. Co. v. Public Serv. Comm'n of Mo., 262 U.S. 276 (1923). In this valuation case the Court, through McReynolds, held that public service companies were constitutionally entitled to a fair return on the current value (that is, replacement cost) of their property, not on the original cost. LDB, joined by Holmes, concurred in the result, that the company had not gotten a fair return under the Commission's scheme, but dissented as to the method. He proposed that the Court abandon the original cost/replacement cost argument and adopt as the appropriate standard "prudential return," that is, what a prudent investor would expect to receive on his capital. Id. at 289.

[66] Edward Terry Sanford (1865–1920) was named to the Court by Harding in 1922 and served from 1923 to 1920.

[67] Pennsylvania v. West Virginia, decided with Ohio v. West Virginia, 262 U.S. 553 (1923). West Virginia was planning to limit export of natural gas mined within its borders because of dwindling supply and a concern that local needs be met first. The Court, through VanDevanter, declared this was an unconstitutional interference with interstate commerce. Holmes, McReynolds, and LDB entered separate dissents. LDB argued that the Court

care much about natural gas—it will soon all be gone—but the decision is very important to hydroelectric. It means rich states can withdraw power from poor states—N[ew]. H[ampshire]. and N[orth]. C[arolina]. water power can be demanded by surrounding states through high power transmission lines."

I said that what bothers me most is that opinions of Ct all incoherent—they don't hang together from week to week.

L.D.B.: "They don't—the trouble is they don't know enough to keep them coherent."

June 28, 1923. "Nothing is decided without consideration, but hardly anything is decided with adequate consideration. On the personal side the present C.J. has admirable qualities, a great improvement on the late C.J.; he smoothes out difficulties instead of making them. It's astonishing he should have been such a horribly bad President, for he has considerable executive ability. The fact, probably, is that he cared about law all the time & nothing else. He has an excellent memory, makes quick decisions on questions of administration that arise & if a large output were the chief desideratum, he would be very good. He is a first-rate second-rate mind."

Few of them realize that questions of jurisdiction are really questions of power between States and Nations. Holmes and Taft for different reasons know little about it because they don't care. Taft because he likes to decide questions as a matter of expediency, where controversies arise; Holmes cares nothing about "expediency" but likes to decide cases where interesting questions are raised. Holmes is beginning to learn; intellectually he is beginning to appreciate our responsibility, tho not emotionally. I tell him, "the most important thing we do is *not* doing." "Van Dev. knows as much about jurisdiction as anyone—more than anyone. But when he wants to decide all his jurisdictional scruples go."

Referring to a writer in June 1923 Journal of Am Bar Assoc. who would suppress all dissenting opinions as "vanity of dissent,"[68] he

---

should not have heard the case because it was a premature suit; nothing had been done yet, the exporting companies in West Virginia were not parties to the suit, and therefore it was not justiciable as a case or controversy. *Id.* at 668.

[68] A letter from Frederick S. Tyler said that Supreme Court votes should not be made public, but only the result announced. Dissents, he claimed, weakened the force of the judgment and undermined the status of the Court. "Dissenting opinions merely afford play to the vanity of the dissenting justice." A.B.A. J. 398 (1923).

said "he isn't alone in that view. P. Butler rather regards dissents as vanity of dissenters & would like not to have them. He himself rarely dissents—partly because of newness, partly because of disbelief in them."

"The new men, Sanford, P. Butler—have contributed very little. I wrote original memo in S. W. Telephone Case,[69] in Ga. case[70]—wrote Ga. opinion according to Smyth v. Ames[71] then said "let's get away from it before it's too late—it makes for all kinds of difficulties, financial & legal." In Ga. case decided "franchise value" & also loss past years based on miscalculations. But they wouldn't, & then I hoped to get Ga. case out with Southwestern (May 21, 1923). But it was laid over for reconsideration & so was decided with full consideration, on June 11, & gained reinforcement through McKenna's dissent. Upshot is that reconstruction value is not measure but merely a factor and so needs to be considered, but in fact need not pay attention, as in Ga. case.

July 1, 1923. Spoke of my article in June Law Review (36 Har. L. Rev. 909) on Holmes.[72] "It's a very good paper—very good indeed. I am glad you wrote the introductory part, as to nature of constitutional adjudication. Two things need to be done, to spell out what you say, generally that ought to be done by someone who is not too close to Holmes and to me. First the special function of dissent in Const[itutional] cases. In ordinary cases there is a good deal to be said for not having dissents. You want certainty & definiteness & it doesn't matter terribly how you decide, so long as it is settled. But in these constitutional cases, since what is done is what you call statesmanship, nothing is ever settled—unless statesmanship is settled & at an end. That ought to be driven home—with your quote from Brewer[73] as a text & the quotation from

---

[69] Note 65 *supra*.

[70] Note 64 *supra*.

[71] Note 48 *supra*.

[72] F.F., *Twenty Years of Mr. Justice Holmes' Constitutional Opinions*, 36 Harv. L. Rev. 909 (1923).

[73] Justice David J. Brewer (1837–1910), in a Lincoln Day speech in 1898, said: "It is a mistake to suppose that the Supreme Court is either honored or helped by being spoken of as beyond criticism. On the contrary, the life and character of the justices should be the objects of constant watchfulness by all, and its judgments subject to the freest criticism. The time is past in the history of the world when any living man or body of men can be set on a pedestal

Mill[74] as a motto in another dealing with the general quasi-jurisdictional questions—not deciding unless you have to, etc. etc."

I spoke of coherence of Holmes' opinions—how all his writings hangs together—it's surprising. "It is and it isn't. For it's all been thought out—his work is a chemical composition and not a conglomerate. He has said many things in their ultimate terms and as new instances arise they just fit in."

Speaking of Ben Avon case (263 U.S.)[75] I argued against the result therein as unwarranted by prior state of law & on grounds of policy. "How came that to pass[?]" I asked.

"That came to pass, as so much is to be explained, on two grounds: 1st it wasn't adequately considered—they didn't understand what they pretended to do—'an independent inquiry into the facts in confiscation cases'—and secondly & largely on personal grounds—they didn't propose to follow my views. That isn't as much true now & of the present Chief—it was very considerably true under the old Chief [White]. I could have had my views prevail in cases of public importance if I had been willing to play politics. But I made up my mind I wouldn't—I would have had to sin against my light, and I would have hated myself. And I decided that the price was too large for the doubtful gain to the country's welfare. But you must constantly bear in mind the large part played by personal considerations & inadequacy of consideration.

To avoid latter, I wanted to have rule adopted that no case is to go down until eight days after opinion is circulated except by unanimous consent in special cases. Chief (Taft) was for it—Holmes was one of seniors against that—he would be miserable for eight days—he's worry all the time. He can't wait after he circulates his opinions, to have them back and "to shoot them off." So also McKenna—it's a race of diligence between them.

---

and decorated with a halo. True, many criticisms may be, like their authors, devoid of good taste, but better all sorts of criticism than no criticism at all. The moving waters are full of life and health; only in the still waters is stagnation and death." *Id.* at 932 n.59.

[74] "Improvement consists in bringing our opinions into nearer agreement with facts; and we shall not be likely to do this while we look at facts only through glasses colored by those very opinions." *Id.* at 914 n.16.

[75] Ohio Valley Water Co. v. Ben Avon Borough, 253 U.S. 287 (1920). McReynolds spoke for a six-man majority in holding that due process was violated if a state established an administrative rate system that did not permit the question of whether the rates set were confiscatory to be determined by courts, who could decide questions of fact as well as law. LDB dissented at 292, joined by Holmes and Clarke, and claimed the state procedures were fair, in that a limited, but appropriate, mode of judicial review was permitted.

But we have a better atmosphere for discussion—in valuation cases, last term, in S.W. Telephone case[76] there was much division & I suggested "I'll report on that if you want me to." So Taft asked me to report. I took months to prepare a memo, printed it & had it circulated, about 62 pp as a basis for discussion. I had a job holding in McReynolds who wrote his opinion in S.W. (My memo was evoked by Atlanta case.)[77] But through Chief and Van the thing was held up until my report was in. We then had a whole day set aside for discussion. And it was a thorough discussion. Some didn't grasp the facts & hadn't thoroughly mastered the memo but it was a new method in consideration of issues.

Van both in purpose & abilities can't be compared. He is too much superior to —P[ierce]. B[utler].

July 3, 1923. As to Arkansas Lynching case[78]—F. "How did it happen Frank case[79] was departed from?" L.D.B.: "Well—Pitney was gone, the late Chief was gone, Day was gone—the Court had changed."

Pitney had a great sense of justice affected by Presbyterianism but no imagination whatever. And then he was much influenced by his experience & he had had mighty little. He was connected with some small New Jersey institution, some company & frequently drew on that small experience. It was like White, who had been a bank director some 20 years ago & that experience constantly led him astray."

"The new men—P.B. & Sanford—are still very new. It takes three or four years to find oneself easily in the movements of the Court. Sanford's mind gives one blurs; it does not clearly register. Taft is the worst sinner in wanting to "settle things" by deciding them when we ought not to, as a matter of jurisdiction. He says, 'we will have to decide it sooner or later & better now.' I frequently

---

[76] Note 65 *supra.*

[77] Note 64 *supra.*

[78] Moore v. Dempsey, 261 U.S. 86 (1923). In an opinion delivered by Holmes, the Court held that a habeas corpus petition alleging that the original trial was held with a howling mob outside the door, that counsel, appointed on the day of the trial, had no time for preparation, and that the entire trial, resulting in death verdicts, took only forty-five minutes stated adequate grounds for relief as a deprivation of life without due process of law.

[79] Frank v. Magnum, 237 U.S. 309 (1915), deferred to local federal courts in determining if conditions in and around the trial warranted habeas corpus. Pitney had delivered the opinion in this case, from which Holmes and Hughes had dissented.

remind them of Dred Scott case[80]—Sutherland also had to be held in check. McR. cares more about jurisdictional restraints than any of them—Holmes is beginning to see it.

Of course there are all sorts of considerations that affect one in dissenting—there is a limit to the frequency with which you can do it, without exasperating men; then there may not be time, e.g. Holmes shoots them down so quickly & is disturbed if you hold him up; then you may have a very important case of your own as to which you do not want to antagonize on a less important case etc. etc.

McR. is a very extraordinary personality—what matters most to him are personal relations, the affections. He is a *Naturmensch*[81]— he has very tender affections & correspondingly hates. He treated Pitney like a dog—used to say the cruelest things to him. Pitney talked a good deal & he didn't like his voice & otherwise P got on McR's nerves & he treated him like a dog. But no one feels more P's sufferings[82] now—not as a matter of remorse but merely a sensitiveness to pain. He is a lonely person, has few real friends, is very dilatory in his work.

As to admiralty cases McR is beginning to see where he has led Court into by his talk of "uniformity." It's one of the striking instances of what you point out in your Holmes article—of turning specific questions of fact into "law". Of course, where uniformity is required, you want uniformity—but it's absurd by an *ipse dixit* to determine what does & what doesn't require uniformity, as they did in Jensen[83] and Knickerbocker[84] cases.

---

[80] Dred Scott v. Sandford, 19 How. 393 (1857), held slaves to be property and invalidated part of the 1820 Missouri Compromise. The case, which aroused enormous passions both North and South, resulted from Chief Justice Roger Taney's desire to "settle" the slavery question permanently.

[81] A "nature man," one who is not cultivated; see text at note 138 *infra*.

[82] In August 1922, Pitney had suffered a stroke that left him physically and mentally unable to continue his judicial responsibilities. He had resigned from the Court on December 31, 1922, and lived as an invalid in Washington until his death on December 9, 1924.

[83] Southern Pac. Co. v. Jensen, 244 U.S. 205 (1917). The Court, through McReynolds, held the New York Workmen's Compensation plan was inapplicable to harbor work, on the ground that federal maritime law governed. Holmes dissented at 218, Pitney at 223 in a lengthy opinion, while LDB and Clarke concurred with both dissenters.

[84] In Knickerbocker Ice Co. v. Stewart, 253 U.S. 149 (1920), McReynolds held that Congress had exclusive power of legislation in all maritime matters and that states could not impose their own workmen's compensation remedies in lieu of federal law. Holmes, together with LDB, Pitney, and Clarke, dissented at 166, claiming the Court had read the maritime

One of the warmest—in fact only near heated talks—I had with Chief was before beginning of 1922 Term, when he asked me about possible Democratic names for vacancies on Ct. He mentioned Manton[85] of New York. I told him I didn't believe in appointing men as Dem & Rep. Those are not the lines of cleavage on Ct & it's wrong to encourage such belief on part of people. Real line of difference is on progressive, so-called, views as to property. "I don't agree with you, at all," he said, "and we can't go around looking for men with certain creeds on property." "As a matter of fact, of course, they do" L.D.B. "He referred to what he had done as President, in appointing Dems to Ct. Don't you think I did a good thing?" To which L.D.B., "Times were different then." (Of course the real answer is—he didn't do a good thing and men he appointed *did* have certain views on property. White, Lamar[86] and Lurton.)[87]

July 14, 1923. Told him Wambaugh[88] for repeal of XIV. "Really?" with warm interest. "Why don't you tell Mrs. Kelley to go after that if she is in for amendment."[89] I told him that I did tell her so—that *that's* the real evil. There might be reason for protection of equality—of treatment of races, religion in country like ours—and equal protection clause—but that use made of that clause by Taft in Truax v. Corrigan[90] was fantastic. "Dreadful," he replied.

I asked him what he thought effect would have been if Minnesota

power too broadly and that the states did have room in which to act. The majority in this case still clung to the ruling in Jensen, even though Congress, by statute, had amended federal law to make state workmen's compensation laws applicable.

[85] Martin Thomas Manton (1880–1946) had been appointed to the U.S. District Court for Southern District of New York by Wilson in 1916 and then to the Second Circuit Court of Appeals in 1918. He served on that bench until 1939, when he was convicted of accepting loans and gifts from litigants appearing before him.

[86] Joseph Rucker Lamar (1857–1916), a Democrat from Georgia, had been appointed by Taft to the Court in 1910 and served until his death. It was to this seat that Wilson named LDB.

[87] Horace Harmon Lurton (1844–1914), a Democrat from Tennessee, sat on the Court from 1909 until his death.

[88] Eugene Wambaugh (1856–1940) had been at the Harvard Law School with LDB in the late 1870s; he later taught at the School from 1892 to 1925.

[89] Florence Kelley (1859–1932), a leading social reformer in the Progressive era, had worked with LDB in preparing his famous brief in Muller v. Oregon, 208 U.S. 412 (1908). At this time she was agitating for a constitutional amendment to permit the federal government to regulate child labor.

[90] Note 29 *supra*.

case[91] in 134 U.S. had gone the other way. "Nothing I think." To which I: "Don't you think it would have made legislatures more responsible & extended base of education of public." "That's precisely what would have happened. Legislatures would have realized that if they want proper improvements they must allow adequate return. Now they pass the buck to courts." To which I: "And to that extent fail in the process of public education & stir up conflict by blaming court." "Precisely."

A propos of not recognizing classes by Taft (referring to letter of Harcourt to Roseberry [sic] in 1894, in reply to latter's desire to avoid "cleavage of classes" and Harcourt's "you're too late" see Gardiner's Life of Harcourt, Vol. II).[92] L.D.B. says "& they think you are the one who makes class lines. That's the most awful part of it. If someone would take the cases & critically show them up once and for all, the showing would be dreadful."

F: "The labor cases, for instances."

L.D.B.: "They would make a terrible story. I don't suppose Sayre[93] is subtle enough to do it—it ought to be done in a leading law periodical so that the profession would see it."

"You know [Benjamin] Franklin's observation as to why so little progress is made—because we try to practice all the virtues at once. So articles like Powell's[94] have too much in them—that is scattered. If you deal with one or two ideas at a time there is a chance for lodgement of one's ideas & gradually it may sprout & blossom. The thing is to let no guilty man escape. Every fellow who writes ought to be kept up strictly in the law reviews."

---

[91] In Chicago, Milwaukee & St. Paul Ry. Co. v. Minnesota, 134 U.S. 418 (1890), the Court had ruled a state statute violated the due process and equal protection provisions of the Fourteenth Amendment because it did not provide for judicial review on administrative rate decisions. Pierce Butler had been the successful attorney for the railroad in this case.

[92] Gardiner, 2 The Life Of Sir William Harcourt 284 (1923). Sir William George Granville Venables Vernon-Harcourt (1827–1904) was a scholar who became one of the leaders of England's Liberal Party; Archibald Philip Primrose, the fifth Earl of Rosebery (1847–1929), was a rival to Harcourt within the party and in 1894 became Prime Minister.

[93] Francis Bowes Sayre (1885–1972), Woodrow Wilson's son-in-law, taught at the Harvard Law School; he would later be Assistant Secretary of State during the Second World War and then a member of the United Nations Trusteeship Council.

[94] Thomas Reed Powell (1880–1955), a fellow student of FF's, was then teaching at the Columbia Law School; the following year he would return to Harvard, where he taught until his retirement. Powell had written a number of articles on constitutional law and the Supreme Court, and it is impossible to tell to which particular ones LDB is referring.

July 19, 1923. Long talk on scope of due process as to freedom of speech and foreign language cases. Agreed.

1. d.p. should be restricted to procedural regularity, &

2. In favor of repeal, but

3. While it is, *must* -be applied to substantive laws & so as to things

> that are fundamental
>
> > Right to speech.
> >   ”   ” education.
> >   ”   ” choice of profession.
> >   ”   to locomotion.

are such fundamental rights not to be impaired or withdrawn except as judged by "clear and present danger" test.[95] Holmes says doesn't want to extend XIV. L.D.B. says it means—you are going to cut down freedom through striking down regulation of property but not give protection. Property, it is absurd as Holmes says, to deem fundamental in the sense that you can't curtail its use or its accumulation or power. There may be some aspects of property that are fundamental—but not regard as fundamental specific limitations upon it. Whereas right to your education & to utter speech is fundamental *except* clear and present danger.

Spoke of fear that Holmes will impair his own reputation by continuing—his own aim not sure. Changed in Jackman case[96] (260 U.S.), hadn't read local Ct's opinion to realize party wall regulation older than particular property & as old as property in Pennsylvania. When he had come around he brought Chief (Taft) around (who has open mind usually). H. is very powerful when he changes his mind, with others.

I asked L.D.B. how he accounts for Mahon (Kohler Act—260 U.S.) case.[97]

---

[95] Schenck v. United States, 249 U.S. 47 (1919), first established the test of "clear and present danger" for evaluating governmental restrictions on freedom of speech.

[96] Note 61 *supra*.

[97] Pennsylvania Coal Co. v. Mahon, 260 U.S. 393 (1922), invalidated Pennsylvania's Kohler Act, insofar as it applied to contracts made before its passage. The law prohibited coal mining within populated areas to avoid the dangers of buildings collapsing when mine tunnels gave way. Holmes delivered the opinion of the Court, ruling that property rights preexisting the statute remained inviolate. LDB, in a lone dissent (at 416), argued that the safety of the community took precedence over property rights, and that the state police power had been properly invoked.

"I account for it by what one would think Holmes is last man to yield to—class bias. He came back to views not of his manhood but childhood. I recalled when I saw that opinion that there is one of the indices of [ ] namely a denial of a heretofore conspicuous trait—a refined man becomes gross, a sensitive man does an act of injustice etc. Here is Holmes in a case where you would have thought he above all men could be insured against reaching the result he did."

[*Undated*]. L.D.B.: Heightened respect for property has been part of Holmes' growing old. The Mahon case[98] is a deep constitutional sentiment although they cut (caught) him when he was weak (after Holmes' prostate operation) & played him to go whole hog. But he said to me recently "I suppose miserliness is legitimate incident of age" a propos of accumulating & buying bonds. He is deeply worried about exhaustion of resources. I said to him, old sentiment N[ew]. E[ngland]. when there wasn't much. "Aren't you aware that men's apprehensions turn towards over-production & not under-production." Of course, he wasn't aware & intellectually he may try to rid himself of undue regard for property but emotionally he can't & it comes hard. (F.F.: I suppose nation's resources. See his Harvard Club speech. *Speeches* 103)[99]
All this a propos Ben Avon[100] & San Diego.[101]

August 6, 1923. L.D.B. talked about assigning cases—said Taft tries to distribute fairly, on whole. Many case C.J. takes for himself because important, others because points are interesting, though cases not important, others because some of justices don't like to take a case. Taft does about two men's work—with his added administrative tasks, extra work on certiorari etc. etc. Plans to give up his "outside activities" Yale Corporation etc. etc., for he has had

\

---

[98] Ibid.

[99] See *Reflections on the Past and Future*, a speech Holmes gave at the Alpha Delta Phi Club in Cambridge, Massachusetts, on September 27, 1912, in Howe (ed.), Occasional Speeches of Justice Oliver Wendell Holmes 163, 165 (1962).

[100] Note 75 *supra*.

[101] In San Diego Land & Town Co. v. Jasper, 189 U.S. 439 (1902), Holmes, speaking for a unanimous Court, held that town supervisors had some flexibility in determining the method of property evaluation they would use in settling water rates and were not locked into a single method.

signs of physical risks involved last term. But Taft is happy—life goes well with him.

Court is malleable almost on everything except trade unions. There its prejudices become active. Can never tell what court will do—what its mood will be when case reaches it.

Some assignments because of expertness—Van D. Land and Indian cases, now also go, in part, to Sutherland. I remarked "I.C.C. go to you." "Yes—but more ought to be, like Wisconsin Rate Cases,[102] 258 [U.S.], but first White and then Taft took it. Both asked me to talk with them about the cases. White's opinion was so bad I had it go over—then Taft took it, & though he knew practically nothing about it he felt he ought to write it. He was very nice in the suggestions he took from me."

"I could have had much influence with White—I did in beginning, but I made up my mind I couldn't pay the price it would have cost in want of directness & frankness. He required to be managed. Van D. was influential with White as he is with Taft—a very useful man. *Ein treuer Diener seines Herrn*.[103] He would make an ideal Cardinal. He has a mind that can adjust itself to two such different temperaments as Taft and White."

But things go happily in the Conference room with Taft—the judges go home less tired emotionally & less weary physically, than in White's days.

August 7, 1923. Spoke of Sonneborn case (260).[104] "I went with Day's opinion because I didn't know anything about subject—I thought there was some mystery about it. Then I began to study it & felt we must retrace our steps. Day was furious—he would change himself, but no one could change him.

Pitney was very different—real character. He welcomed correction and discussion. In an opinion he cited *Adair*,[105] *Coppage*[106] cases and I suggested they were like *Dred Scott*[107] and ought not to be cited. He eliminated reference!

---

[102] There was no case involving rate setting by Wisconsin or affecting a public utility that had "Wisconsin" in its name in 258 U.S. or in the entire October 1921 Term.

[103] "He is the true servant of his master."

[104] Note 62 *supra*.

[105] Note 27 *supra*.

[106] Note 28 *supra*.

[107] Note 80 *supra*.

Spoke of LaFollette[108]—his strong qualities of courage and persistence and real belief in people and serious intellectual limitations. (1) his assumption of "sin" in others & those in disagreement are wicked, as explanation of evil things. (2) his great belief in the curative powers of legislation & (3) his need for dramatic solutions. I never had any confidence in valuation proposal, thought it would be turned into an instrument against the people. But that was dramatic, whereas economics & elimination of waste are *not* dramatic.

Hoover[109] has lost talent for facts—misstated facts as to coal as L.D.B. corrected him from his own report. Has no confidence in popular education processes. Spoke of Hoover's talk that criticism should end at water's shore—criticism abroad hurts trade etc. L.D.B. said—"I felt just opposite—wrote those long dissents in Schaefer[110] & Pierce[111] cases to put on permanent record what we were not allowed to say."

Feels strongly Hyde Park free, unlicensed forum should be insisted upon in Commons, Boston—in *every* park.

August 8, 1923. "I have never been quite happy about my concurrence in Debs[112] and Schenk[113] cases. I had not then thought the

---

[108] Robert Marion LaFollette (1855–1925) was one of the towering figures of Progressive reform and a close personal friend and ally of LDB. LaFollette built a powerful political organization in Wisconsin that sent him first to Congress, then to the State House for three highly successful terms as Governor, and then to the U.S. Senate in 1905, where he served until his death. In 1924 he launched a third-party candidacy for the Presidency, charging that both the Democratic and the Republican nominees were too tied to conservative interests.

[109] Herbert Clark Hoover (1874–1964), after a successful career as a mining engineer, gained national attention first as director of Belgian relief and then as food administrator during World War I. He served as Secretary of Commerce from 1921 to 1929 and then one term as President. Until the early twenties, LDB thought highly of Hoover; see LDB to FF, February 11, 1920, 4 Brandeis Letters, note 5 *supra*, at 448.

[110] Note 51 *supra*.

[111] Pierce v. United States, 252 U.S. 239 (1920), was an Espionage Act case in which several antiwar pamphlets were judged false and seditious. Pitney wrote a brief opinion in which he casually observed that the pamphlets met the "clear and present danger" test. LDB, joined by Holmes, dissented and, in order to prove the innocuous nature of the pamphlet, reprinted it in full in his opinion. *Id.* at 253.

[112] In Debs v. United States, 249 U.S. 211 (1919), the Court, through Holmes, upheld the conviction of Socialist leader Eugene v. Debs under the 1917 Espionage Act, on grounds that he had obstructed the war effort by calling on men to resist the draft and not work in war plants. Debs's First Amendment defense was casually swept aside by reference to the "clear and present danger" test.

[113] Note 95 *supra*.

issues of freedom of speech out—I thought at the subject, not through it. Not until I came to write the Pierce [&] Schaefer cases did I understand it. I would have placed the Debs case on the war power—instead of taking Holmes' line about "clear and present danger." Put it frankly on war power—like Hamilton case[114] (251 U.S.)—and then the scope of espionage legislation would be confined to war. But in peace the protection against restrictions of freedom of speech would be unabated. You might as well recognize that during a war— F.F.: All bets are off.

L.D.B.: Yes, all bets are off. But we would have a clear line to go on. I didn't know enough in the early cases to put it on that ground. Of course you must also remember that when Holmes writes, he doesn't give a fellow a chance—he shoots so quickly.

But in Schaefer & Pierce cases I made up my mind I would put it all out, let the future know what we weren't allowed to say in the days of the war and following.

August 10, 1923. Re Hamilton Distillery case. At first went the other way 5 to 4, the Chief (White) was with me, Holmes against. Then White met Holmes on the street. H. told him he had doubts about his vote & he was ready to have it written the other way to see how it would go. White then came to see me & asked me to write it, because he thought I could get Holmes more easily.

Holmes balked on "Due Process"—the thing that prevailed with him in the Mahon case[115] later. I told him Mugler case[116] (123 U.S.) governed but he never has liked that case. Undoubtedly his impatience with prohibition explains this. I then wrote & gradually they all came with me—McR. & Pitney & others kicked—I said "let Pitney go over my opinion" & Pitney worked hard for a few days on it & we agreed. It was then that I began to know Pitney closely.

F.F. spoke of Holmes' pleasure in pointing out no special const. position of liquor & that "Fathers did not disapprove of it" in the First Child Labor case.[117]

---

[114] Hamilton v. Kentucky Distilleries & Warehouse Co., 251 U.S. 146 (1919), upheld the War-Time Prohibition Act under the war powers, even though the bill was passed after the Armistice. LDB, who delivered the Court's opinion, ruled that a war situation existed until either a peace treaty was signed or Congress declared an end to hostilities.

[115] Note 97 *supra.*

[116] Mugler v. Kansas, 123 U.S. 623 (1887), sustained a state prohibition law as within the police powers of the state.

[117] Hammer v. Dagenhart, 247 U.S. 251 (1918), invalidated the Federal Child Labor Law

L.D.B.: "That was a terrible decision—& of all people Day to have written who was so hot for Federal power in other cases."

Told him of Day & fears aroused by Adamson Law.[118] (Day spoke of it to Dr. Alice Hamilton[119] on Mackinac Island—) from that time on agin' social legislation. L.D.B.: "No, not social legislation. It did not affect his attitude on White Slave[120] & narcotic drugs[121] but only where property was involved."

F.F.: Yes, where property—the fear of power of labor & redistribution of economic power.

Agreed there is no answer except repeal of XIV Amend.

I spoke of that & necessity of putting an end to labor injunctions & difficulty of Truax v. Corrigan, 254,[122] towards accomplishing latter. L.D.B.: "Well—Court may reverse itself—I put it to them, to Taft that he has not hesitated to do so, once or twice when it mattered less than in valuation cases (Smyth v. Ames, 169 U.S.[123] to be repealed)—Genesee Chief,[124] Doyle, 94 U.S.,[125] vs. Burke Construction Co., 25(7 or 8)."[126]

What those fellows don't understand is that recognition of Federal powers does not men denial of State powers. I have not been

---

of 1916, with Justice Day espousing an especially narrow interpretation of the government's interstate commerce power. LDB, along with Clarke and McKenna, joined in Holmes's dissent at 277.

[118] The Adamson Act, establishing an eight-hour day for railroad workers and a federal mediation apparatus, was rushed through Congress at the end of August 1916 in order to avert a nationwide rail strike. The railroads challenged the law, but the Supreme Court upheld it, by a five-to-four vote, as a valid exercise of the interstate commerce power in Wilson v. New, 243 U.S. 332 (1917).

[119] Alice Hamilton (1869–1970) pioneered in the field of industrial medicine, which she taught at the Harvard Medical School from 1919 to 1935.

[120] Day had joined with the majority in Hoke v. United States, 227 U.S. 308 (1913), which sustained the 1910 Mann Act's prohibition against transporting women across state lines for immoral purposes. He also wrote the majority opinion in Caminetti v. United States, 242 U.S. 470 (1917), which held the law applicable to activities not constituting "commercialized vice."

[121] Day spoke for a bare five-to-four majority in United States v. Doremus, 249 U.S. 86 (1919), upholding the Harrison Act of 1914, which utilized the federal government's taxing power in an effort to control narcotics.

[122] Note 29 *supra*.

[123] Note 48 *supra*.

[124] The Genesee Chief, 12 How. 443 (1851), repudiated the tidal limitation on federal admiralty jurisdiction and extended it to include the Great Lakes.

[125] Note 25 *supra*.

[126] Terral v. Burke Constr. Co., 257 U.S. 529 (1922). With Taft speaking for the Court, it reversed the latter part of *Doyle* on the grounds that a state could not punish a corporation for exercising its constitutional rights.

against increase of federal powers, but curtailment [of] State's powers.

I spoke of Winfield case.[127] "That case laid me low," said L.D.B. (see his dissent).

August 11, 1923. Spoke on contingencies which govern opinions and dissents, as illustrated by National Bank Case in 257/146.[128] They were all wrong—made an assumption as to facts without knowing anything about it. I dissented but didn't get around to writing. Pitney could not go through throes of partuition periodically—his opinions came in an avalanche & then he was all worked up until they were disposed of & delivered. I said to him "I have some suggestions to submit as to that," & he said in the nicest way "Do it quick. Until you do I'll have no peace." Well, it would have spoiled his European trip, etc.—so I contented myself with registering a formal dissent.

F.F. spoke of mockery of Marshall's dictum "power to tax, is power to destroy."[129] Said "that was dreadful. Holmes always snorts at that. Marshall's dicta raised hell in all sorts of ways—taken terribly seriously." F.F. suggested that Marshall didn't (see Cohens v. Virginia).[130]

"June days are like March 3rd in Congress."

August 11, 1923. McKenna—only way of dealing with him is to appoint guardians for him. The Chief & Van D. are his guardians—McReynolds tries to handle him but does it badly. He knows

---

[127] New York Cent. R.R. Co. v. Winfield, 244 U.S. 147 (1917). In an opinion delivered by Justice VanDevanter, the Court ruled that compensation for injuries to an employee sustained on interstate carriers was governed exclusively by the Federal Employers Liability Act; Congress had covered the field and thus excluded the states. LDB, in his first dissent since joining the high court, disagreed and was joined by Clarke. *Id.* at 154.

[128] In Curtiss v. Connly, 257 U.S. 260 (1921), Holmes spoke for a unanimous Court in applying state and common-law statutes of limitations in a suit by receivers of a national bank against the former directors to recover for improper loans. LDB recused himself since his good friend and former law partner Edward McClennen was counsel for the receiver.

[129] McCullough v. Maryland, 4 Wheat. 316, 431 (1819).

[130] In Cohens v. Virginia, 6 Wheat. 264 (1821), Chief Justice Marshall, in very expansive language, upheld the constitutionality of §25 of the 1789 Judiciary Act, granting to federal courts review of decisions of the highest state court of law or equity that involved a federal law or treaty, even if a state was party to the suit. At 401 Marshall conceded that some of the dicta in Marbury v. Madison, 1 Cranch 137 (1803), were undoubtedly too broad and should not be taken literally.

he (McK) doesn't count, his suggestions are [not] taken, so every once in a while he sends up a balloon just to show that he is there. He breaks loose occasionally—he did in Atlanta case[131] (No. 260) but I was able to control myself and say nothing. Some of the others came to me & said "can't you do something to avoid his dissent, and make some changes." I said "I worked hard to make the opinion clear. It is clear now & I'd hate to change it & make it less clear, but if you can do anything, I'll be glad to consider it."

Every once in a while McK really does mischief—more often than appears. His opinions are often suppressed—they are held up & held up & gets mad & throws up the opinion and it's given to someone else.

September 1, 1923. Spoke of great part that "chance" plays in decisions & working of Ct. He instanced Britt v. Zinc Co. case[132] (25- U.S.). "Holmes saw a chance to decide one of his pet theories, & so certiorari was granted. I voted vs. cert. There was no earthly reason for granting it. I voted against the majority opinion, but I couldn't go Clarke's stuff, I was rushed with other work & so would have had to hold up Holmes if I was going to write a dissent & to hold him up from firing off is like sending an executioner after him. I had dissented recently in a number of cases, Holmes cared a good deal about this opinion, he had gone with me in my dissents so I let it go, without dissenting.

On the other hand, in another case where I disagreed with Holmes it happened to be recess time so that (1) I had time to think out the problem in my own mind, which takes me long time (2) I had time to go over to Holmes & talk things over with him at length and modify his views. Both were chance, that I had ample time to think the questions out (Holmes shoots so fast, often there is no time to think out) and time to talk things over with him.

Spoke of great want of historical data as to legislative history, even of very important legislation like Clayton Act[133]—had to dig it

---

[131] Note 64 *supra.*

[132] Note 21 *supra.*

[133] The Clayton Antitrust Act of 1914, 15 U.S.C.A. 12, was the crowning statute of Woodrow Wilson's New Freedom; and LDB had had a major role in shaping the Act. See Urofsky, Wilson, Brandeis and the Trust Issue, 1912–1914, 49 Mid-America 3 (1967).

out all first-hand so also Moreland case,[134] history of penal statutes. Spoke of great need of such historical studies.

July 2, 1924. L.D.B.: The Burns case (Burns Baking Co. v. Bryan, 264 U.S.)[135] was really 5 to 4, but Van Devanter "got busy," in his personal way, talking & laboring with members of Court, finally led Sutherland & Sanford to suppress their dissents. Holmes calls that private working with individuals, of which there is a great deal, "lobbying." Results are thus achieved not by legal reasoning, but by finesse & subtlety & in the old days, in the middle ages, Van Devanter would have been the best of Cardinals. He is indefatigable, on good terms with everybody, knows exactly what he wants & clouds over difficulties by fine phrases & deft language. He never fools himself, and his credit side is on the whole larger than his debit. But he is on the job all the time. One can achieve his results by working for them, but I made up my mind I wouldn't resort to finesse & subtlety & "lobbying." The drive against the Court has tended only to give us fewer & fewer 5 to 4— by making them 7 to 2 or 7 to 1.

After all there are reasons for withholding dissent, so that silence does not mean actual concurrence. (1) All depends on how frequent one's dissents have been when the question of dissenting comes, or (2) how important case, whether it's constitutionality or construction. So that I sometimes endorse an opinion with which I do not agree, "I acquiesce"; as Holmes puts [it] "I'll shut up."

July 3, 1924. L.D.B.: Pitney has real conscience & steady growth. But for him we would have had no Workmen's Compensa-

---

[134] In United States v. Moreland, 258 U.S. 433 (1922), McKenna ruled that the Fifth Amendment's requirement for a grand jury indictment in "capital or otherwise infamous crimes" included a charge for abandonment of family since conviction led to a term at hard labor. LDB entered a lengthy dissent at 441, joined by Holmes and Taft, on the changing meaning of "infamous crime" and believed that the original information would have been sufficient.

[135] Jay Burns Baking Co. v. Bryan, 264 U.S. 504 (1924), struck down a state statute that set minimum standard sizes for bread loaves as exceeding the state's police power. LDB, joined by Holmes, dissented at 517, arguing that there were legitimate reasons for the state's actions, that it was within the police power, and that the Court had no business questioning the judgment of the state legislature so long as it had the necessary power.

tion laws—he came around, upon study, though he had been the other way.[136]

In the Los Angeles case (26),[137] McReynolds first wrote an opinion that I couldn't stand for. I told the Chief that I have [no] love of union stations, was agin' them all, but McR's opinion had too many glaring errors to bother us in the future. Van D. worked with McR. & made changes and Chief asked me whether that will remove my sting. I had written a really stinging dissent. They didn't want the Court shown up that way, & corrections weren't adequate & finally the Chief took over the opinion & put out what is now the Ct's opinion (26) & I suppressed my dissent because after all it's merely a question of statutory construction & the worst things were removed by the Chief.

McR. is the Court's problem. Van D. takes him in hand often—he worries the Ct because of his offensiveness to counsel & in his opinions, & a sensitive temperament like Holmes is positively pained. Holmes now explains him as a "savage" with all the irrational impulses of a savage.[138] The Chief complained that McR. is everyday becoming more "meticulous" as to others though his own opinions are simply dreadful—he is lazy, stays away from Court when he doesn't feel like coming (more rearguments were ordered because McR was absent & didn't listen to arguments & called for a reargument). McR is hell on national powers in some ways—would have I.C.C. take over every grade crossing and again strongly against national powers, for instance, hates Federal Trade Com[mission].

Strongest argument is "it will hurt Court." In case involving admiralty rule (26- U.S.) Sanford privately asked me whether I didn't think it was unwise to show the rules promulgated by Court

---

[136] On March 6, 1917, the Court had handed down three decisions upholding the major types of state workmen's compensation plans. Pitney wrote the majority opinions in Hawkins v. Bleakley, 243 U.S. 210; and New York Cent. v. White, note 56 *supra*. The third case was Mountain Timber Co. v. Washington, 243 U.S. 219 (1917).

[137] In Railway Commission of California v. Southern Pacific Co., 320 U.S. 331 (1924), Chief Justice Taft, speaking for a unanimous Court, held that railroad companies could not abandon present junctions and stations to form a new union (central) station, either by voluntary agreement or even by order of a state commission, without the necessary certificate from the I.C.C. The decision nullified an order of the California Commission to have railroads build a new station in Los Angeles.

[138] Note 81 *supra*.

were obscure or tended to hardship. I said we are always criticizing legislatures' draftsmanship & legislative incompetence, we had better put out facts & let profession see that we are no better than the rest.

They—judges—are not conscious of any interest, though of course unconsciously operates—but they are defects of pettiness in character.

July 6, 1924. I have said that I was certain that Ct would decide NY statute prohibiting night work by women favorably as it did (Radice v. New York, 264 U.S.).[139] L.D.B. took me aside and said "you might have been certain but it was not at all certain. That was one of those 5 to 4 that was teetering back & forth for some time. The man who finally wrote—Sutherland was the fifth man & he had doubts & after a good deal of study (for whatever you may say of him he has character & conscience) came out for the act & then wrote his opinion. That swung the others around to silence. It was deemed inadvisable to express dissent and add another 5 to 4. The doubt as to the statute turned on unequal protection, which now looms up even more menacingly than due process, because the statute omitted some night work & only included some. The whole policy is to suppress dissents, that is the one positive result of Borah 7 to 2 business,[140] to suppress dissent so as not to make it 7 to 2. Holmes, for instance, is always in doubt whether to express his dissent, once he's "had his say" on a given subject & he's had his say on almost everything. You may look for fewer dissents. That's Van Devanter's particularly strong lobbying with the members individually, to have them suppress their dissents. He is perhaps closest with Butler, whom he treats as an elder brother, & while Butler is not easy to move, the prudential arguments of Van D. as to what is "good—or bad—for the Court" are weighty with him & with all of them.

---

[139] Radice v. New York, 264 U.S. 292 (1924), upheld a New York law prohibiting work by women in restaurants in large cities between 10:00 P.M. and 6:00 A.M.; Sutherland spoke for a unanimous Court.

[140] William Edgar Borah (1865–1940), a leading Progressive, served as U.S. Senator from Idaho from 1907 to 1940. In his frustration at the Court having nullified several reform measures, Borah had introduced a bill requiring at least seven judges to concur in an opinion holding an act of Congress unconstitutional. New York Times (February 6, 1923).

August 2, 1924. L.D.B: Next 25 years will compel us to think. European rehabilitation, my guess is, will make against us and not for us. They will be in condition to compete better than ever, & we shall have consequences of our expanded productive facilities. Oil and cotton our greatest exports—oil uses up our supply, fear reservoir not used & cotton more & more drawn from elsewhere. Copper now gotten more cheaply from So. America. Europe will buy elsewhere largely because she will sell more elsewhere. We'll be like England, great creditor nation, but our debtors won't be able to sell to us, unlike England's debtors.

Need is for new approach, quiet, unadvertised, solemn meetings like Const. conventions (see Farrand's book)[141] thinking out what *to do*, not what to put over. Say coal—have a dozen fellows get together for a month and think and think things out! So P[ublic]. U[tilities]. problems—law & economics & pol. scientists; but unofficial & unadvertised. Approach matter by dealing with *problems* and not *theses*.

In P.U. claims as to what investors will do, what will or won't frighten [them] off. Compare story of Granger laws and validation in Munn v. Illinois in 1877–78,[142] followed by vast investment of r.r. Built all anybody wanted, despite restrictive legislation from 1879–1884, not till 1885 freedom from state interference (Wabash case, 188 U.S.),[143] not till 1888 judicial protection (Minnesota, 134 U.S.),[144] not till 154 U.S. detailed items.[145] Truth is pressure of money & pressure of its manipulation (bankers) lead to investment & no causal connection between decisions & legislation & refusal to invest.

Examine in detail.

---

[141] Farrand, The Framing of the Constitution of the United States (1913).

[142] Munn v. Illinois, 94 U.S. 113 (1877), upheld the validity of state laws regulating rates for intrastate railroads and grain elevators, on the grounds that private property "affected with a public interest" could be controlled under the state's police power.

[143] Wabash, St. L. & P. Ry. Co. v. Illinois, 118 U.S. 557 (1886), held that state regulation of freight rates could not be enforced against interstate shipments since these were of a "national" rather than a "local" nature.

[144] Note 91 *supra*.

[145] Several cases at the October 1893 Term expanded the right of carriers to appeal administrative rate decisions to the courts. See Reagan v. Farmers' Loan & Trust Co., 154 U.S. 362 (1894); Pittsburgh, Cincinnati, Chicago & St. Louis Ry. Co. v. Backus, 154 U.S. 421 (1894); and I.C.C. v. Brimson, 154 U.S. 447 (1894).

August 3, 1924. L.D.B.: *A propos* limitation by carriers of liability beginning with New Jersey Navigation Co. v. Merchants, 6 How[146] to Lockwood case 17 Wall,[147] down to Hooker, 233 U.S.,[148] Esteve v. W.U., 254 U.S.,[149] L.D.B. said "we now have the situation in fully satisfactory shape. We *made it a rule of law* and people know *where* they are & it is pretty rational."

That led to Clarke, J. "He always 'dilated with a wrong emotion,' as Rufus Choate[150] said, on the subject, sustaining power of carrier to limit amount of his liability." And F.F. added: "or Employers Liability cases." "Yes, and Employers Liability cases.[151] Those cases never wearied of calling forth his long and weary dissent." I said to him about Employers Liability, "Don't you see that the worse the law is the more it will stimulate the unions to demand workmen's compensation laws, for the union railroad men are to blame, for having resisted it." "No—he would shake his head and go on writing dissents." F.: "One more subject—a loose inter-

---

[146] New Jersey Steam Navigation Co. v. Merchants' Bank of Boston, 47 U.S. (6 How.) 344 (1848), ruled that a common carrier could not restrict its common-law liability, even if a contract with a special agent provided that the latter would assume all risk.

[147] In Railroad Co. v. Lockwood, 89 U.S. (17 Wall.) 357 (1873), the Court held that common carriers cannot contract out of their normal responsibilities for care, even for free passengers; such duties were essential to public security, and failure to fulfill them would be negligence.

[148] Boston & Maine R.R. v. Hooker, 233 U.S. 97 (1914). Congress, through the I.C.C., provided for railroads to compensate passengers for lost or damaged baggage. Railroads cannot unilaterally change the schedule controlling this liability without the permission of the I.C.C. The statute did not alter the carrier's common-law liability in substance, only in degree.

[149] Western Union Tel. Co. v. Esteve Bros. & Co., 256 U.S. 566 (1921). LDB delivered the opinion of the Court ruling that, when the telegraph company provided two types of service and one of them carried greater liability for error in return for an increased fee, a customer could not sue for full damages resulting from an error if the lesser service had been used. Pitney and Clarke dissented without opinion.

[150] Rufus Choate (1799–1859) had been a Senator from Massachusetts and one of the founders of the Whig Party.

[151] The Court had consistently upheld state statutes changing the old common-law limitations on employer liability for injuries to workers, beginning in 1888 with Missouri Pac. Ry. Co. v. Mackey, 127 U.S. 205; and Minnesota & St. Louis Ry. Co. v. Herrick, 127 U.S. 210. It had struck down the first federal statute on this subject governing common carriers in First Employers' Liability Case, 207 U.S. 463 (1908), although a majority of the justices felt that Congress had the power to do so if it drew up a more careful law. This Congress did in the Federal Employers' Liability Act of 1908, which received unanimous approval by the Court in Mondou v. New York, New Haven & Hartford R.R. Co., 233 U.S. 1 (1912). However, the Court frequently granted review to cases arising under this law and often reversed verdicts for employees. These verdicts often turned on essentially factual issues, *i.e.*, had there been negligence, was the train in interstate commerce at the moment of injury, etc., that should not have concerned an appellate court. LDB thought the futility of this litigation would lead to the enactment of workmen's compensation statutes.

pretation of municipal franchises." L.D.B.: "Yes, though on that subject he became less intense."

Speaking of Fuller,[152] "it is said of him that he said 'opinions ought not to disclose the process of the decisions.' The fact is that his opinions are rarely quoted except on procedural matters & then he made some mischief as in questions of patent review (see 1923 Term, 263 [U.S.]).[153] He did shed dignity over the Court. He had gentleness & gentlemanliness & Holmes will never allow any ill word spoken about Fuller.

"As a matter of fact the present Chief, with all his good nature & kindliness & the quality that makes everybody like him, looks like many a benevolent, good-natured distillery drummer I used to see in the days when I was counsel for some distilleries. His face has nothing in it—it's so vapid. Unlike the late Chief[154]—who had the grand manner and was of the 18th Century.

"As a matter of fact, McReynolds is one of the most interesting men on the present Court. He would have given Balzac great joy. I watch his face closely & at times, with his good features, he has a look of manly beauty, of intellectual beauty & at other times he looks like a moron and an infantile moron. I've seen him struggle painfully to think & to express himself & just can't do it coherently. There is the greatest play about his countenance, like the sky on a variable day. It's more than mere temperament, moodiness, how-ever—of course, Holmes says "he isn't civilized—he is a primitive man." His health may have something to do with it, but he is certainly an interesting study. His [ ] boorishness gives Holmes pain, much pain—who sits next to him and has to hear him blurt out."

"As to White, I remarked that his earlier opinions, both in Louisiana[155] and e.g. his dissent in the Income Tax case (157/157)[156]

---

[152] Melvin Weston Fuller (1833–1910) of Illinois was appointed Chief Justice by President Cleveland in 1888 and served until his death.

[153] There are only three cases in 263 U.S. involving patent law, and in none of them does the Court either quote Fuller or refer to a decision he wrote. The same is true for the other two volumes of cases decided during the October 1922 Term.

[154] Edward Douglass White.

[155] In Louisiana Navigation Co. v. Oyster Comm'n of La. 226 U.S. 99 (1912), White had dismissed a suit to review a remand by the state's highest court to a lower court, on grounds that such an action did not constitute a final judgment and therefore was not ripe for review by the Supreme Court.

[156] Pollock v. Farmer's Loan & Trust Co., 157 U.S. 429 (1895), invalidated the income-tax provision of the Wilson-Gorman Tariff of 1894. White dissented on the grounds that the

are wanting in his later turgidity & involutions. "Holmes says, and some of the others, that he, White, lapsed into Jesuitism, an atavistic movement into his early training."

August 4, 1924. L.D.B.: A propos power to impose conditions to relinquish "constitutional rights" as a basis of new grounds of power by a state which state has power to withhold, in connection with discussion as to "doing something" on valuation cases to avoid morass of *Smyth v. Ames*[157] and reach "prudential investment" basis. (Brandeis dissent in Telephone cases, 261 U.S.),[158] talked of Pullman v. Adams Express Co. doctrine (216 U.S.)[159] & Holmes' rephrasing of it in W.U. v. Foster (247 U.S. 105)[160] as to prohibition of imposing "unconstitutional conditions." F.F. spoke of Holmes' occasional indulgence of a large phrase, "general principles which do not decide concrete cases," which begets heaps of mischief, as in Mahon case (260 U.S.)[161] L.D.B.: "Truth of matter is he takes joy in the trick of working out what he calls 'a form of words' in which to express desired result. He occasionally says, 'I think I can find a form of words' to which I reply, 'of course you can, you can find a form of words for anything.' "

F.F.: "He goes along carefully, moderately, step by step and every once in a while he indulges himself at large; he is on a spree."

L.D.B.: "That's exactly what it is. It's perfectly amazing that a man who has had no practical experience to speak of, and no experi-

---

means by which the statute had been attacked, a suit by a stockholder against the company, was clearly a collusive suit and designed to bypass the express Congressional prohibition of 1867 banning suits for the purpose of restraining the collection of a tax.

[157] Note 48 *supra.*

[158] Note 65 *supra.*

[159] The case is Pullman Co. v. Kansas, 216 U.S. 56 (1910), which held that the sleeping-car company could not be restrained from doing local business in a state by its refusal to pay a charter fee since such a tax impinged on interstate commerce. The issue was whether a state, having power to admit or exclude a corporation, could condition such a decision on conditions that, standing alone, would violate the commerce clause or other constitutional limitation. In this case, Holmes dissented from the doctrine at 75, arguing that the state had the right to levy such a tax since the property was involved in local commerce.

[160] In Western Union Tel. Co. v. Foster, 247 U.S. 105 (1918), Holmes spoke for a unanimous Court in ruling that information on stock exchange transactions, while in transit over the telegraph, was in interstate commerce and not subject to state regulation. In his opinion, Holmes endorsed the "unconstitutional conditions" doctrine that he had rejected in Pullman, and in the broadest terms. LDB, according to Paul Freund, had very little use for the "unconstitutional conditions" doctrine; letter to author, October 12, 1984.

[161] Note 97 supra.

ence at statesmanship, should be so frequently right as to matters that have significance only in their application. I have told him so—how amazing it is. And once told him that if he really wants to "improve his mind" (as he always speaks of it), the way to do it is not to read more philosophic books, he has improved his mind that way as far as it can go, but to get some sense of the world of fact. And he asked me to map out some readings, he became much interested & I told him that I'd see—get some books, that books could carry him only so far & that then he should get some exhibits from life. I suggested the textile industry & told him in vacation time he's near Lawrence & Lowell & he should go there & look about. He became much interested although he said he was "too old." I told him he was too old to acquire knowledge in many fields of fact but not too old to realize through one field what the world of fact was and to be more conscious & understanding of it. With his mind as an instrument, there wasn't anything he couldn't acquire. And so he undertook to do the textiles, but very unfortunately it was the time Mrs. Holmes was very sick & he had her on his mind & studying became a duty instead of, as I hoped, a new interest & possibly, therefore, a relaxation. And so he reported to me, very apologetically, in the Fall his inability to pursue the study.[162]

But he highly approved the inquiry into & reference to facts as the basis of my opinions, tho he does not wholly reconcile himself to my footnotes.[163] He doesn't realize that others haven't his precipitate of knowledge, they don't know as he knows, and secondly he doesn't sufficiently consider the need of others to understand or sufficiently regard the difficulties or arguments of others. So that he

---

[162] Actually, Holmes detested facts, and he seems to have acquiesced in LDB's suggestion so as to avoid a lengthy lecture by LDB on the subject. As he had written to a friend when LDB urged a study of facts: "[T]alking with Brandeis yesterday he drove a harpoon into my midriff by saying that it would be for the good of my soul to devote my next leisure to the study of some domain of fact—suggesting the textile industry, which, after reading many reports &c, I could make living to myself by a visit to Lawrence. . . . Well, I hate facts." Although Holmes took several volumes with him, he did not read them, and the following summer he gratefully recorded that, "in consideration of my age and moral infirmities, [Brandeis] absolved me from facts for the vacation and allowed me my customary sport with ideas." Holmes to Harold Laski, June 16, 1919, and June 11, 1920, in Howe (ed.), 1 Holmes-Laski Letters 212, 268 (1953).

[163] Holmes often received complaints from mutual friends about LDB's insistence on extensive footnoting of opinions. "If you could hint to Brandeis," Laski wrote him, "that judicial opinions aren't to be written in the form of a brief it would be a great relief to the world. [Roscoe] Pound spoke rather strongly as to the advocate in B. being over-prominent in his decisions." Laski to Holmes, January 13, 1918, id. at 127; see also 556, 675.

has a surprisingly large [number of] petitions for rehearing in his cases, because he does not seem to have considered arguments of counsel that are very weighty with them and often he hasn't. Philosophically he would admit difference between truth and consent of others to truth, but he does not regard difference in practice.

June 15–16, 1926. Stone:[164] "I think it's wrong, *but*. I think it's right, *but*,"

Doesn't know & doesn't take trouble to find out. Van D. (says) if he would only take time enough to think.

"Hasn't written one really good opinion" Van D. thinks. I agree—least valuable member at present.

Van D. keeps close track of Chief & of some others—Mc. (who has to be tactfully treated), Sanford, Sutherland. Intimidates some, influence that [comes] from experience, he has influence so he gets more cases about standing of Court—criticizes as to dangers in future.

Many 5 to 4 even where no dissent *at all*.

Butler has grown—one of the most powerful on Bench.

Sanford ought never to have been above D.J.—a dull bourgeois mind—terribly tiresome.

Taft has open mind, poor judgment, likes to write many opinions but is most generous to his colleagues, praises where [ ] seemingly praise is deserved though often wrongly. Has his hands full with legislative matters.

June 17, 1926. Van D.—conflict of 2 deep impulses. Appetite for power & ambition that Court be right. If first is satisfied and not involved, second is strong way (a propos *Bondurant* case).[165] That's great thing about V. Once having established power he will try to confine his own errors.

---

[164] Harlan Fiske Stone (1872–1946), after serving as Dean of the Columbia Law School and Attorney-General of the United States, was appointed by President Coolidge to the Supreme Court to replace Joseph McKenna in 1925. In 1941, President Franklin D. Roosevelt elevated Stone to the center chair, where he served until his death.

[165] *Dahnke-Walker Milling Co. v. Bondurant,* 257 U.S. 282 (1921), involved a Kentucky farmer and a Tennessee feed mill, with the former breaching a contract on grounds that a Kentucky statute involving foreign corporations had not been complied with. LDB dissented at 293, claiming that the Court should never have accepted the case since, under the 1916 revision of its jurisdiction, it now had discretion in which cases to review. Moreover, the state statute at question had never actually been invoked but merely used as a pretext for the breach.

Stone it's a refrain "had I been on Court I would, or wouldn't have done" *e.g.* Ben Avon[166] (let's watch what he'll do).

If he'd only think.

Court makes these men better men.

February 25, 1935. Gold clause[167]

L.D.B. Why no questions (he had asked none on argument).

(1) Q = answer in sensitized state of public mind.

(2) Knew what my legal conclusions were, at the outset, & so completely out of sympathy on matters of policy with what Gov't did that I thought it best to say nothing.

I was very glad that I was not asked to write opinion as I well might have been.

Economics doubtful at best. Morals were plain & most important. I don't know whether we shall recover.

But I did have a great deal to do with "hot oil" case.[168] Chief[169] came to me and said that in view of Johnson's criticism earlier in year[170] he wondered whether I would not like to write opinion. I told him I would not object to writing it but I have no desire to do so. As a matter of fact I felt he was anxious to write it himself. But I had a good deal to do with shaping opinion & setting my brethren on either side to ask some of their questions.

---

[166] Note 75 *supra*.

[167] In 1933, as part of its inflationary policy to fight the Depression, the Roosevelt administration went off the gold standard and nullified clauses in both public and private contracts requiring payment in gold. In Norman v. Baltimore & Ohio R.R. Co., 294 U.S. 240 (1935), the Court sustained the government's power to cancel the gold clause in private contracts under the federal monetary power. In Perry v. United States, 294 U.S. 330 (1935), however, the Court said that Congress did not have the power to repudiate its own promises but that, since the defendant had been unable to show any damages, there was no effective remedy for him. The repudiation of the gold clause horrified many conservatives; Justice McReynolds, who dissented in these cases, complained that, "as for the Constitution, it does not seem too much to say that it is gone. Shame and humiliation are upon us now." Leuchtenburg, Franklin D. Roosevelt and the New Deal 144 (1963).

[168] Panama Ref. Co. v. Ryan, 293 U.S. 388 (1935). In an eight to one decision, with Cardozo dissenting strongly, the Court struck down the National Industrial Recovery Act's provision forbidding the interstate transportation of oil produced in excess of state-allotted quotas, primarily because of the sloppy administrative procedures. The decision, which criticized the government for not informing the public of administrative rules, led to the establishment of the Federal Register.

[169] Charles Evans Hughes was then Chief Justice.

[170] Hugh S. Johnson (1882–1942), after rising to rank of general in the Army, had gone into business and public service and in 1933 and 1934 headed the National Recovery Admin-

[*Undated*]. Butler watching valuation for r.r. though he pretends it's a gas co. of which he was counsel. But he is alert to protect accused. (See Butler in *Olmstead*,[171] *Sorrell*,[172] *Snyder*)[173]

[*Undated*]. Sutherland Far-Western Bourgoisie. More cultured than Butler but mechanical & his law is collected but not digested. But fine character.

Butler eye on ball. Great will & shows much self-mastery to control. Hates to be corrected—hangs on a word but hates dissents from him so will yield.

The work of a judge should never be done in a hurry.

February 5, 1939. [   ] resignation:
   age and health
   judgment as good as ever
   never have done anything can't do thoroughly—don't know
how
   quantitatively not able to do as much
   opinion writing demands an intensity & I find it gets to be hard.

   Several times during last few years. At end of 1936 T[erm]. put it to the C.J., & he thought there was no justification. Again at end of

---

istration (NRA). The episode involved a claim by Johnson that, in establishing the NRA's policies, he had been in frequent contact with LDB for advice. For details, see Murphy, note 4 *supra*, at 145–49.

[171] In Olmstead v. United States, 277 U.S. 438 (1928), a sharply divided Court, speaking through Chief Justice Taft, held that government wiretapping did not violate the Fourth Amendment's ban on search and seizure without a warrant. Butler, in a carefully reasoned dissent at 485, condemned Taft's argument for ignoring the common-sense historical meaning of the Fourth Amendment. Holmes also dissented, terming wiretapping a "dirty business" and declaring bluntly that it was "less evil that some criminals should escape than that the government should plan an ignoble role." *Id.* at 469, 470. LDB, in one of his most eloquent and powerful dissents, declared that, "if the Government becomes a lawbreaker, it breeds contempt for the law. . . . To declare that the Government may commit crimes in order to secure the conviction of a private criminal would bring terrible retribution. Against that pernicious doctrine the Court should resolutely set its face." And in one of his most quoted statements, he said: "[T]he right to be let alone [is] the most comprehensive of rights and the right most valued by civilized men." *Id.* at 471, 485, 476.

[172] Sorrells v. United States, 287 U.S. 435 (1932). Butler joined in an eight-to-one decision (with only McReynolds dissenting) striking down a conviction under the Prohibition Act because of entrapment.

[173] In Snyder v. United States, 291 U.S. 97 (1934), Cardozo spoke for a bare majority of the Court in holding that due process was not violated if a defendant was not permitted to accompany the court to visit the scene of the crime. Owen Roberts wrote a lengthy dissent at 123, in which he was joined by LDB, Butler, and Sutherland.

1937 I talked to Chief about retiring & he gave cogent reasons for not retiring & I yielded. I talked to him again yesterday, inviting his views but reserving my own judgment. He again offered counter considerations, but I have decided to retire, & promptly. Though I would sit tomorrow, unless weather forbids, & this will not give notice of intent & go on sitting, but to send letter to Pres[iden]t the day I retire & give no reasons, but just briefly say I retire this day, unless you think that an unwise procedure.

Retired 13.[174]

---

[174] LDB wrote to President Roosevelt on February 13, 1939: "Dear Mr. President: Pursuant to the Act of March, 1937, I retire this day from regular active service on the bench. Cordially, Louis D. Brandeis." 5 Brandeis Letters, note 5 *supra*, at 610.

ANDRZEJ RAPACZYNSKI

FROM SOVEREIGNTY TO PROCESS: THE JURISPRUDENCE OF FEDERALISM AFTER GARCIA

I. Introduction

On February 19, 1985, the Supreme Court, in *Garcia v. San Antonio Metropolitan Transit Authority*,[1] overruled its 1976 decision in *National League of Cities v. Usery*.[2] Although the continued vitality of *National League of Cities* had been in question in recent years,[3] the Court's abrupt repudiation of the very principle announced in that case[4] is an event of considerable significance, beyond showing, one more time, that the rule of *stare decisis* has a limited application in the Court's modern constitutional adjudication.[5] *Garcia*'s impor-

Andrzej Rapaczynski is Assistant Professor of Law, Columbia University.

AUTHOR'S NOTE: I wish to express my gratitude to my colleagues, Professors Henry Monaghan, Peter Strauss, Alan Farnsworth, and Alfred Hill for their comments on an earlier draft of this paper. I owe a special debt to Professor Bruce Ackerman for encouraging me to write this article and for his insightful comments at all stages of the writing process.

[1] 105 S.Ct 1005 (1985).

[2] 426 U.S. 833 (1976).

[3] None of the Supreme Court decisions in the post-1976 period in which the question of state immunity from federal interference was raised was favorable to the state interest. Hodel v. Virginia Surface Mining and Reclamation Association, 452 U.S. 264 (1981); Hodel v. Indiana, 452 U.S. 314 (1981); United Transportation Union v. Long Island R. Co., 455 U.S. 742 (1982); FERC v. Mississippi, 456 U.S. 742 (1982); EEOC v. Wyoming, 460 U.S. 226 (1983).

[4] At one or another point between 1976 and 1985 all nine Justices declared their overt adherence to the *National League of Cities* decision. See the cases cited in the preceding note.

[5] *National League of Cities* itself had overruled Maryland v. Wirtz, 392 U.S. 183 (1968).

tance lies, above all, in revealing the absence of anything approaching a well elaborated theory of federalism that would provide a solid intellectual framework for an articulation of the Justices' divergent views on state-national relations. Three dissenting members of the *Garcia* Court state in no uncertain terms that they are prepared to reverse the course again in the near future.[6] It is very important, therefore, for the scholarly community and the profession to conduct a thorough inquiry into the theoretical foundations of federalism before the Court embarks on further adventures.

The position of federalism in our constitutional law is peculiar. On the one hand, next to separation of powers and individual rights, federalism is clearly one of the three main branches of our constitutional structure. On the other hand, judicial enforcement of any limits on national power that the concept of federalism might entail has a rather unfortunate history and, at least insofar as the limitations on national commerce power are concerned, seems to have been abandoned in the *Garcia* case in favor of what Professor Wechsler has called "the political safeguards of federalism."[7]

More than in any other area of constitutional adjudication, the Court's attempts to impose federalism-related limitations on the national government have been, throughout history, frustrated by the political process, resulting three times in constitutional amendments. The Court's decision in the *Dred Scott* case[8] that slavery was a municipal institution outside federal control, was "overruled" by the Civil War Amendments. The decision in *Pollock v. Farmers' Loan and Trust Co.*[9] that "the boundary between the Nation and the States . . . would have disappeared"[10] if the national taxing power had been extended to taxing income from real estate, led to the enactment of the Sixteenth Amendment. The Court's attempts to

---

[6] Garcia v. San Antonio MTA, 105 S.Ct. at 1033 (Justice Rehnquist dissenting) and 105 S.Ct. at 1038 (Justice O'Connor, with whom Justice Powell and Justice Rehnquist join, dissenting).

[7] Wechsler, The Political Safeguards of Federalism: The Role of the States in the Composition and Selection of the National Government, 54 Colum. L. Rev. 543 (1954). Garcia v. San Antonio MTA, 105 S.Ct. 1018 ("the principal means chosen by the Framers to ensure the role of the States in the federal system lies in the structure of the Federal Government itself").

[8] 19 How. 393 (1857).

[9] 157 U.S. 429 (1895).

[10] 157 U.S. at 583.

give meaning to the Tenth Amendment by limiting national regulation of private activities under the Commerce Clause[11] were instrumental in precipitating the "constitutional crisis" of 1937 and led to
a wholesale judicial retreat.[12] As recently as 1970, the Court's decision in *Oregon v. Mitchell*,[13] holding that Congress lacked the power
to enfranchise eighteen-year-olds in state elections, resulted in passing the Twenty-Sixth Amendment, which it took the country only
three months to ratify.

It is important to inquire into the reasons for this rather dismal
record of judicial intervention.[14] The most common explanation,
seemingly adopted by the *Garcia* Court, is that federalism is essentially a political arrangement and that the policing of it is, for one
reason or another, unsuited to the *modus operandi* of the judicial
department.[15] The extreme version of this argument is exemplified
by Professor Choper's claim that the Court is most needed and
most effective in protecting individual rights against governmental
encroachments and that its reservoir of legitimacy is only dissipated
if the Court intervenes in the distribution of institutional competences among governmental entities.[16] Whatever merit this view
may have, it is clearly not shared by the Court, which has not shied
away from highly charged, controversial issues of institutional
competence in the area of separation of powers, most recently in
Immigration and Naturalization Service v. Chadha.[17] Instead, the
Court's reasoning in *Garcia* singles out the federalism-related limita-

---

[11] Art. I, Section 8, of the Constitution. See cases listed in notes 38, 43 *infra*.

[12] See cases listed in note 45 *infra*.

[13] 400 U.S. 112 (1970).

[14] According to Professor Choper, "there is virtually no states' rights decision of any note
that retains current meaningful force." Choper, Judicial Review and the National Political
Process 170 (1980). The exception made by Choper in 1980 for the *National League of Cities*
case, *ibid.*, is no longer necessary.

[15] While stressing the "political safeguards of federalism," the Court's opinion in the *Garcia*
case stops short of declaring outright that federalism-related limits on the national commerce
power present a nonjustifiable political question (". . . we need to go no further than to state
that we perceive nothing in the overtime and minimum-wage requirements of the FLSA, as
applied to SAMTA, that is destructive of state sovereignty or violative of any constitutional
provision." 105 S.Ct at 1020). Indeed, I shall argue later in this article that *Garcia* should be
understood as calling for a new jurisprudence of federalism.

[16] Choper, note 14 *supra*. For a critique of Choper's views on federalism, see Nagel,
Federalism as a Fundamental Value: National League of Cities in Perspective, 1981 Supreme
Court Review 81.

[17] 462 U.S. 919 (1983).

tions on the national power as peculiarly unsuitable for judicial resolution. We are not really told, however, what distinguishes federalism from the separation of powers in this respect: it is certainly not the absence of the "political safeguards" of the latter, for the Constitution abounds in provisions guaranteeing that at least the Congress and the President have ample means to protect themselves in the political arena. More likely, the reason for singling out federalism is to be found in the absence from the Constitution of any affirmative state-rights limitations on the scope of national powers, beyond those that specify the role of the states in functioning of the *federal* institutions.

But is unlikely that this reason could be genuinely decisive. To begin with, many, if not most, hard cases in the area of separation of powers do not deal with any straightforward violation of affirmative constitutional limitations.[18] From the very beginning, the Court's most important decisions have often proceeded from what came to be called the "structure" of the Constitution.[19] It is not unreasonable to state that all constitutional interpretation, even when a specific affirmative provision is at issue, requires a background understanding of the general institutional framework of governmental bodies and an appreciation of the context within which they operate. In this connection, the centrality of the concept of federalism within the structure established by the Constitution does not admit of serious question. In setting up the national government, the Framers worked against the background of already existing state institutions, and, unlike in the case of the federal authorities established by the Constitution, they were not conferring any new powers on the states. While they undoubtedly

---

[18] The one-House veto, for example, is nowhere explicitly prohibited in the Constitution, and such a prohibition cannot be inferred from the bicameralism and Presidential veto provisions without assuming the doctrine of nondelegation which is nowhere to be found in the Constitution. INS v. Chadha, *ibid.* See also Schechter Poultry Corp. v. United States, 295 U.S. 495 (1935). The Presidential removal power, at issue in Myers v. United States, 272 U.S. 52 (1926), Humphrey's Executor v. United States, 259 U.S. 602 (1935), and Wiener v. United States, 357 U.S. 349 (1958), is not subject to any explicit Constitutional provision. The Congressional power over Presidential papers, Nixon v. Administrator of General Services (Nixon II), 433 U.S. 425 (1977), as well as the matter of executive privilege, United States v. Nixon (Nixon I), 418 U.S. 638 (1974), are equally unmentioned. Indeed, judicial review, Marbury v. Madison, 1 Cranch 137 (1803), is not governed by any explicit provision.

[19] See Black, Structure and Relationship in Constitutional Law (1969). For an example of a structural approach to the separation of powers questions and the relation between this approach and the textual analysis of the Constitution, see Strauss, The Place of Agencies in Government: Separation of Powers and the Fourth Branch, 84 Colum. L. Rev. 573 (1984).

chose broad language in describing the competence of the national government, their assumption of the continued existence and vitality of state governments is visible throughout the Constitution. Thus, the absence of affirmative limitations on the national power, especially in the light of the enumeration technique in Article I, Section 8, cannot be viewed as preclusive of a judicial enforcement of the principles related to the federal structure of our government.

The most plausible explanation of the repeated frustration of judicial intervention in the area of state-national relations is the failure of judges and scholars to produce a viable theory of federalism that would help to develop workable principles for the judicial resolution of federalism-related disputes. To begin with, rather than focusing on a functional analysis of the role of the states in the federal system—an analysis that would parallel the Court's jurisprudence in the area of separation of powers—the basic intellectual inquiry has been concentrated on the concept of state sovereignty and its implications for the limitation of national authority. Furthermore, it was in the light of the idea of state sovereignty that the constitutional doctrine of the enumeration of federal powers was interpreted, which led to the conclusion that the enumeration implied some reserved area of exclusive state control. Despite the fact that this view of the intergovernmental division of competences had always created some tensions,[20] as long as the actual exercise of the federal commerce power was relatively restricted, the inadequacy of the concept of sovereignty for analyzing the role of the states in the federal system was not immediately apparent. Nevertheless, even after the massive shift toward national regulation of economic and social life has revealed that the enumeration doctrine provided no viable standards for the protection of the states, the constitutional defense of state rights has continued to rely on the concept of state sovereignty. No serious attempt has been made to go beyond the few standard shibboleths associated with this way of thinking. It is also possible that a political disinclination toward the state-rights doctrine, stemming from the Civil War divisions and the intellectual ascendancy of the New Deal, further contributed to the neglect of a theory of federalism. But the past failures should not be taken to preclude the possibility of future success. Indeed, even if the protection of the federal structure of the United States is to rest ultimately with the political process, and not the courts, the actors

---

[20] See Frankfurter, Commerce Clause under Marshall, Taney, and Waite (1937).

in that process, no less than judges, must have some idea of the basic purposes of federalism and the reasons behind their constitutional protection. A new theory of federalism is thus necessary to allow us a more comprehensive understanding of the American institutions. In the following pages I shall attempt to clear the ground for such a theory of federalism and point in the directions in which I think it should develop.

II. FEDERALISM AND THE DOCTRINE OF STATE SOVEREIGNTY: A CRITIQUE

The rhetoric of state sovereignty is responsible for much of the intellectual poverty of our federalism-related jurisprudence. No assignment of meanings to the words of a language is sacred, and words can be made to serve different purposes. It is thus possible, of course, to preserve the use of the word "sovereignty" in speaking of American federalism by making it stand for the precise assortment of characteristics possessed by the states in our constitutional system. But the price for doing so is quite high, for the word carries with it an array of traditional meanings, and I will try to show that none of these meanings make much sense when used in the American context. Thus, while the use of the word "sovereign" with respect to the states may have carried a welcome implication of some dignity attributable to state governmental institutions (and I doubt that much more by way of a clear meaning could be assigned to its use in the conventional legal discourse of federalism outside the area of state sovereign immunity[21]), the confusion resulting from this usage far outweighs any of its advantages and the word should be abandoned.

Even in political philosophy, where the term originated, "sovereignty" does not have any clear, undisputed meaning. In most of its classical formulations, however, it was used to identify the peculiar kind of authority that only a state could possess. The concept, as originally introduced by Bodin,[22] was designed to strengthen the hand of the French king in his struggle against the nobility and to

---

[21] The state's sovereign immunity is, by and large, irrelevant to the problems of federalism since the states are not immune to suits by the United States or by other states. Monaco v. Mississippi, 292 U.S. 313 (1934).

[22] Bodin, The Six Books of a Commonweale (McRae ed.) (1962).

assert the necessity, as well as the legitimacy, of a single source of authority in the political realm. Bodin himself did not deny that the sovereign was constrained by the higher principles of natural law and the divine commandments, and he understood the concept of sovereignty as pertaining to the King's ultimate and exclusive authority to lay down the principles of positive law. Nevertheless, within a legal or institutional context, the concept was designed to deny the legitimacy of any opposition to royal authority. It is this feature of the concept of sovereignty that made it attractive to legal positivists for whom it provided a seemingly sound basis for explaining the binding force of legal norms. From Hobbes to Austin,[23] the idea of sovereignty came to stand for an ultimate source of authority, capable of enacting laws binding on everyone else, but not itself bound by any laws and capable of changing them at will.

The precise status of the theory of sovereignty has never been entirely clear. It could be understood as a descriptive theory claiming that in every actual political society there exists de facto an ultimate source of authority, legal or political, and that the task of a political scientist is to identify it. But it could also be understood as a normative theory claiming that in each political society there ought to be such an authority, for otherwise instability or illegitimacy would ensue. And finally, the theory could be understood as axiomatic, simply spelling out a condition that must necessarily be satisfied for a society to be recognized as "political" or as forming a "state." But what constitutes the common core of the theory is the claim that only a state could be sovereign, so that the term is not applicable to individuals or institutions of another kind. To be sure, sovereignty implies such things as "autonomy," "dignity," "freedom," "power," "authority," and so on. But if the term does not simply duplicate one or more of these things, it means something more than that, and this "something more" only a state can possess.

There are essentially three components defining the *differentia specifica* of sovereignty: (1) A sovereign must be sovereign (have authority) over someone and something (that is, there must be subjects and a domain over which the sovereign rules); (2) the authority of a sovereign over the subjects within the sovereign's domain must be of a political nature (that is, at a minimum, the types

---

[23] Hobbes, Leviathan (Macpherson ed.) (1968); Austin, The Province of Jurisprudence Determined (Hart ed.), esp. at 193ff. (1954).

of commands issued by the sovereign must be capable of acquiring a *legal* status and be backed by an appropriate enforcement mechanism);[24] and (3) the authority of a sovereign must be final (that is, the sovereign cannot in turn be dependent on another person or institution, and there is no further recourse for subjects who are not prepared to obey the sovereign's commands).

It follows immediately from these postulates that it is impossible to be a sovereign and a subject at the same time, at least with respect to the same command. For if the subject must obey the sovereign, while the sovereign is always free to change his mind, then it cannot be said, in a literal sense, that one is both the subject and the sovereign or that one is a sovereign over oneself.[25]

The power of the theory of sovereignty is considerable. If one accepts it, the mere location of the sovereign in a given community allows one to deduce some very important attributes of the person or institution in question. Thus, for example, if the English courts are persuaded that Parliament is the British sovereign, then it immediately follows that, like the most absolute of monarchs, it "can do no wrong," that is, it must be treated as a source of all legal norms and never a subject of any of them.[26] If it does not permit suits against itself, no one can challenge its decrees. If it tramples on even the most cherished British traditions, it may perhaps cause a revolution, but nothing short of that will release the courts from their duty to enforce its commands.

Simply to state the proposition that the American states are sovereign in this sense is to refute it. The problem is not so much that the states have written constitutions that limit the powers of their

---

[24] The requirement that the sovereign's commands must be able to acquire a legal status may appear circular if the concept of sovereignty is then used to explain the binding force of legal commands. But there is more to law than merely its binding force, such as, for example, the general character of its commands or a standard mode of enforcement.

[25] This poses some problems for the idea of popular sovereignty. They can perhaps be overcome by distinguishing the people as a collective body from private individuals and such must be the sense of Rousseau's distinction between the general will (*volonté générale*) and the wills of particular individuals, even when the particular wills perfectly coincide (the will of all or *volonté des tous*). Similarly, the Kantian idea of autonomous sovereign individuality presupposes a distinction between the agent as a purely rational will and as an empirical consciousness driven by inclinations. Even so, Austin believed that all such uses of the term "sovereignty" were at best metaphorical. Austin, The Province of Jurisprudence Determined 255 (1954).

[26] In practice a legal fiction is maintained that it is the "King in Parliament" that is the British sovereign, but nothing hinges on this here. *Cf.* Austin, note 23 *supra*, at 230–33.

governments, for one may perhaps look to the bodies that can change these constitutions as the true sovereigns and view the state governments as their delegates or representatives. The problem rather is that the federal Constitution imposes a variety of limits on the states that are clearly incompatible with the absolute authority entailed by state sovereignty in this strong sense.[27]

The reason why this obvious fact does not by itself preclude viewing the American states as sovereign in some weaker sense is that, even for the most ardent positivist, the concept of a sovereign cannot refer exclusively to a divinelike entity that has an absolute power over everyone and everything everywhere. The least problematic case of sovereignty is that of an independent state viewed from outside, in the domain of foreign relations, where the domestic division of authority is largely ignored and the person representing the state is viewed as empowered to speak without any limitation for the country as a whole. Clearly, even in this case, to say that a state is sovereign is an abbreviated way of saying that its sovereignty is limited to some domain. This domain is defined geographically by the territory of the country, and the state's authority is restricted to power over the state's own citizens or those citizens of other countries who are within its territory.[28] Whether we view these limitations of sovereignty as a matter of power alone, or of some voluntary agreement on the part of the sovereign, or of some higher law (the law of nations or of nature) does not seem to

---

[27] The Supremacy Clause, Art. VI, Section 2, not only assures the supremacy of federal over state laws but also forces state judges to apply federal law in appropriate cases. Art. IV, Section 1 obliges state courts to give full faith and credit to public records and judicial proceedings in other states as a matter of duty and not of comity. Art. IV, Section 2 limits the power of the states to give preference to their own residents and thus takes away much of their power to determine their citizenship. Art. IV, Section 3 limits the power of the states to control their geographical boundaries. Art. IV, Section 4 limits the states' right to choose their own form of government by obligating the United States to assure that each state government is "republican." Art. I, Section 10 prohibits the states to conduct foreign policy (including entering into compacts or agreements with other states and engaging in war), to conduct an independent monetary policy, impose export duties, impair obligations of contract, grant titles of nobility, pass bills of attainder or ex post facto laws. Judicial decisions subordinated state courts to federal review. Martin v. Hunter's Lessee, 1 Wheat. 304 (1816); Cohens v. Virginia, 6 Wheat. 264 (1821). Art. 3, Section 2 has been interpreted to imply no sovereign immunity for the states in suits by other states or the United States. Monaco v. Mississippi, 292 U.S. 313 (1934).

[28] There is also in some cases more questionable jurisdiction over foreigners abroad or on the high seas, see Leech, Oliver, & Sweeny, Cases and Materials on the International Legal System, Part I (1973), but these complications need not detain us.

destroy the usefulness of the concept in international relations.[29]
One way or another, the existence of many states implies a division
of sovereignty (or at least of sovereigns), while at the same time the
dominion of each state within its boundaries may still be seen as in
principle absolute.

The use of the concept of sovereignty in analyzing the relation
between the states and the federal government most likely derives
from an analogy to this least problematic case of international relations. If sovereignty may be parceled out among various nations,
the argument seems to run, why couldn't it be parceled out somewhat differently in the case of the United States. At this point, a
story is usually told that runs something like this: After the separation of the colonies from Great Britain, the American states became
independent and sovereign within their boundaries. The Articles of
Confederation were essentially akin to an international compact
since their efficacy depended on the voluntary cooperation of the
states. The Constitution of 1789 changed this situation in important respects because it allowed the federal government to operate
directly on the people in the states and imposed binding restrictions
on state power. Still—the story continues—the powers of the federal government are not general but limited to those enumerated in
the Constitution. Since that leaves a residuum of powers not delegated, the states, which have existed continuously throughout this
period, have remained sovereign, although their sovereignty has
become limited to the residuum of the powers not delegated to the
United States. Thus, it might be argued, even if the sovereignty
was parceled out between the states and the federal government in a
way that is different from its division among the many nation
states, the remaining areas of state and federal competence are
nevertheless partially exclusive, and this exclusiveness allows for an
absolute (sovereign) authority of each government in its own
sphere.

Put in this way, the idea of state sovereignty is not self-refuting.
To be sure, a positivist purist would immediately point out that
any limitation of a sovereign nation's power in international relations is due exclusively to the sovereign's own voluntary agreement—the idea of international *law* being, for such a positivist,

---

[29] The case becomes more problematic if some international body has the authority to
enforce the norms of international law.

incompatible with national sovereignty—while the limitations of the American states' power comes from the federal Constitution over which the states have only a very limited authority. But we need not be detained by this objection, for so long as some domain of exclusive state power can be meaningfully identified, even if a state is not itself free to change it, the idea of state sovereignty does not lose all its utility. The real problem is that even a moderately searching scrutiny of the powers of the federal government shows that the alleged existence of a residual category of exclusive state powers over any private, nongovernmental activity is in fact illusory. This does not mean, of course, that the idea of federalism, with its notion of independent state governments, is also illusory. It may very well be, for example, that state governments are not merely local branches of the United States government anymore than the League of Women Voters is such a branch and that state governments enjoy a panoply of immunities by virtue of the principles of federalism. But the idea of sovereignty implies at a minimum that the sovereign must be the ultimate source of legal authority over someone other than himself, so that not every immunity which allows for some person or institution to have his or its own sphere of autonomy amounts to carving out a new sovereign domain.[30] It is not surprising, therefore, that the history of the American idea of state sovereignty turns out, on closer inspection, to be the story of a succession of vain attempts to define some substantive domain over which exclusive and ultimate state authority could be confidently asserted.

A simple comparison with nation states reveals that the American states lack a domain defined in precisely those terms that make the notion of national sovereignty relatively unproblematic. The domain in which national governments are sovereign can be easily delimited by their geographical boundaries. The case of the American states is different because, although state jurisdictions are geographically determined, their sovereignty over their territory is vitiated by the geographically coextensive reach of the federal gov-

---

[30] It is only if the concept of autonomy (self-determination) is thoroughly confused with the concept of sovereignty (control over others) that one can still maintain that the American states are "sovereign." While it is, of course, impossible to forbid anyone to use the word in this way, doing this will also entail calling individuals, private associations, and single branches of the federal government "sovereign," for they also have their own spheres of autonomy within our constitutional order.

ernment. Neither can the sovereign domain of the American states be defined in terms of their authority over their people, for it is the same people who are also subject to the jurisdiction of the federal government. Faced with this, the attempts to carve out a sphere of exclusive state authority have traditionally proceeded to define it in terms of some substantive fields of regulation, such as production versus commerce, social versus economic regulation, local versus interstate commerce, and so forth.[31] It is, of course, not *a priori* impossible to make such distinctions. By a peculiar hypertrophy of logic over reality, one may separate commerce from production, for example, by a set of rigid definitions and enforce such distinctions regardless of practical consequences. It is scarcely worth considering such an alternative, however, for it would be a prime example of putting the cart before horse: instead of thinking of state sovereignty as a way of ensuring the viability of federalism, this approach can only explode the concept of federalism to save the fiction of state sovereignty.

A defensible use of the concept of state sovereignty presupposes that the domain over which a state exercises supreme authority corresponds to some reality, that is, that the areas cordoned off from federal interference have some practical separateness from the point of view of the purposes of good government. The reason why the idea of sovereignty retains some significance in the area of international relations does not lie in pure philosophy but precisely in the fact that most actual states constitute relatively viable social, economic, and cultural units. People united by a long-standing tradition, speaking a distinctive common language, living within boundaries that roughly correspond to the relevant economic market, can be grouped into a political unit that exercises ultimate authority over all the matters that concern them. When these independently unifying factors are missing, such as in the case of some states created by artificial colonial lines, or in the case of artificially small states,[32] or in the case of countries tied to their neighbors by increasing economic, social, and cultural interdependence, even the traditional concept of geographically defined sovereignty becomes an increasingly artificial construct, reversing the natural order of

---

[31] See notes 38–44 *infra* and accompanying text.

[32] The free city of Danzig in the period 1920–39 comes to mind here.

dependence between the needs to be served by political authority
and purely political organization. In such situations, politics begins
to exert an entirely autonomous influence over social and economic
life to the detriment of unhampered development. In some (rather
fortunate) cases, the political organization collapses under the
weight of its own irrelevance and new, more viable units are
formed. In other cases, politics comes out victorious over reality,
but only at the cost of repression and the ultimate stifling of the
vitality of those who have the misfortune to be the subjects of the
artificial sovereign. In only rare cases can a viable socio-economico-
cultural unit be created by purely political means.[33] In the area of
international relations, where the concept of sovereignty constitutes one of the few barriers against anarchy and constant interference of some states in the "internal affairs" of other countries, the
emergence of an artificial and unviable sovereign may nevertheless
dictate a restraint on the behavior of other members of the international community. In the case of state-federal relations, however,
no such justification exists. The original impetus behind the enactment of the United States Constitution was precisely to avoid the
loss of welfare inherent in the recognition of state sovereignty.[34]
The Commerce Clause in particular reflected a widespread recognition of the economic interdependence of the states. The fact that
even under the Articles of Confederation, the United States represented a unit insofar as foreign relations were concerned means that
state sovereignty had never been taken very seriously in this area.[35]
The Constitution of 1789 made this even more clear by entirely
excluding the states from participation in foreign affairs and by
omitting any reference to state sovereignty.[36] The very recognition

---

[33] This, I presume, would be the happy outcome for some postcolonial entities now in
existence.

[34] See Wood, The Creation of the American Republic, 1776–1887, 463–67 (New York,
1972).

[35] Rakove, The Beginnings of National Politics: An Interpretive History of the Continental Congress, 173 note (1982). See also United States v. Curtiss-Wright Co., 299 U.S. 304,
315-19 (1936), although the historical accuracy of Justice Sutherland's claims may be questioned.

[36] Article II of the Articles of Confederation stated: "Each State retains its sovereignty,
freedom and independence, and every power, jurisdiction and right, which is not by this
confederation expressly delegated to the United States, in Congress assembled." By contrast,
even the Tenth Amendment speaks only of "powers" not delegated to the United States as
remaining in the States (if not prohibited to them by the Constitution.)

of the existence of the American nation and the creation of the United States as the expression of its political will mean that the Framers recognized the degree of real interdependence among the states that made thinking of them in terms of sovereignty largely inappropriate. States may have rights, powers, and immunities within the federal compact, but they cannot be conceived as staying outside of it.

The shape ultimately taken by the structure of governmental authority under the United States Constitution was one of compromise between the social, economic, and international realities and some more purely political desiderata. The power represented by the states had to be reckoned with and indeed was welcome insofar as it could be harnessed into the complex structure of divided authority that was to be the main protection against what the Framers called "tyranny"—a rather amorphous term referring to most forms of governmental oppression. But at the same time the Framers wanted to ensure that the federal government would be unquestionably independent and superior in all matters of national importance. Only "local" matters were to be left in the hands of the states.

Had the compromise of 1787 clearly left it to the federal government to determine what issues were or were not "local" (by, for example, making such determinations largely political),[37] the question of state sovereignty would have become meaningless then and there. But the Constitution appears to go further and attempts to define negatively the scope of state power by the enumeration of the powers of the national government. This could be, and often was, interpreted as an effort to give an ahistorical definition of what is "local." The enumeration technique of Article I, Section 8, thus appears to constitutionalize the issue of state sovereignty by proposing a rigid, *a priori* distinction between the separate domains of the two governments, instead of a more practical, ad hoc determination of their appropriate law-making functions.

---

[37] Proposals of this kind were, indeed, before the Convention. The Virginia plan proposed that "the National Legislature ought to be empowered . . . to legislate in all cases, to which the separate States are incompetent or in which the harmony of the United States may be interrupted by exercise of individual legislation." The Convention voted on two occasions for similar general formulations. See Farrand, I Records of the Federal Convention of 1787 47, 53 (1911); II *id.* at 21. The present scheme of enumeration emerged in the Committee of Detail. See Gunther, Cases and Materials on Constitutional Law 83 (11th ed. 1985).

If the matter of determining whether the Constitutional enumeration of the powers of the federal government implied a substantively defined domain of state sovereignty had arisen here for the
first time, an extensive discussion of all relevant considerations
would have been necessary. But the matter seems so definitively
settled by historical experience and the Supreme Court's decisions
that to rehearse once more the vicissitudes of the Commerce Clause
disputes would be an improvident expenditure of energy. In case
after case, the distinctions drawn by the courts that were supposed
to insure state supremacy over some substantive fields of regulation
have proved to be unworkable. In part, these efforts were designed
to map what the Court perceived as the political desiderata of
federalism onto the contours of economic life and to translate the
concept of dual sovereignty into the language of economics by
separating commerce from production.[38] Whatever validity a distinction between production and external commerce may have in
the case of international relations, one look at the supermarkets in
New York and California is enough to convince one of its inappropriateness in the context of the United States economy. Within the
American federal system, state boundaries have long lost most of
their economic significance,[39] and as early as the distinction between commerce and production appeared, the Court was forced to
modify it by the introduction of the concept of the "current" or
"flow" of commerce[40] and to draw another, economically irrelevant, distinction between "direct" and "indirect" effects of the regulated activity on interstate commerce.[41] Similarly unsuccessful
were the Court's efforts to correlate the concept of dual sovereignty
with a distinction between the regulation of economic and social
activities. It was rightly observed that, in the absence of other
limitations, the power to regulate commerce could obviously be

---

[38] United States v. E. C. Knight Co. (The Sugar Trust Case), 156 U.S. 1 (1895); Schechter Poultry Corp. v. United States, 295 U.S. 495 (1935); Carter v. Carter Coal, 298 U.S. 238
(1936). For a discussion of the heterogeneity of the political categories of federalism with
respect to economic reality, see Frankfurter, note 20 *supra*, at 21 (1937).

[39] See H. P. Hood & Sons v. DuMond, 336 U.S. 525, 537–38 (1949).

[40] Swift & Co. v. United States, 196 U.S. 375 (1905); Stafford v. Wallace, 258 U.S. 495,
514–16 (1922).

[41] Addyston Pipe & Steel Co. v. United States, 175 U.S. 211 (1899); Northern Securities
Co. v. United States, 193 U.S. 197 (1904). These two decisions prevented a total emascula-
tion of the antitrust laws by the Sugar Trust Case.

used to reach most activities related to morals and social, rather than purely economic, concerns. Given the centrality of the states' police powers to their function as independent governments, the Court, after a period of relative toleration of federal social legislation,[42] attempted to reserve for the states the exclusive authority to regulate general welfare by restricting federal regulation to the "improvement" or "facilitation" of commerce (so that Congress could prohibit commerce only in the case of intrinsically "harmful" objects),[43] and interpreting the Article I, Section 8 delegation as specifying not the permissible areas, but the permissible purposes, of federal regulation.[44]

All these efforts, designed to preserve some exclusive domains of state authority, have by and large collapsed with the New Deal changes.[45] The cases since then have oscillated between the language requiring a "substantial effect" of the regulated activity on interstate commerce as a condition of the federal power to regulate it[46] and a virtual repudiation of any judicial authority to place limits on the Congressional power to determine the meaning of "local" activities.[47] No decision, however, has in principle exempted any substantive field from federal regulation. Also, even if some new constitutional jurisprudence were to call for some limits on the federal power over the private sector, an articulation of such limits would require an essentially pragmatic analysis of the national and local effects of the regulated activities and a search for solutions that

---

[42] See Champion v. Ames (The Lottery Case), 188 U.S. 321 (1903); Hipolite Egg Co. v. United States, 220 U.S. 45 (1911) (upholding the Pure Food and Drug Act of 1906); Hoke v. United States, 227 U.S. 308 (1913) (upholding the Mann Act).

[43] Hammer v. Dagenhart (The Child Labor Case), 247 U.S. 251 (1918).

[44] See Bailey v. Drexel Furniture Corp. (The Child Labor Tax Case), 259 U.S. 20 (1922); United States v. Butler, 297 U.S. 1 (1936).

[45] See National Labor Relations Board v. Jones & Laughlin Steel Corp., 301 U.S. 1 (1937) (upholding extensive federal regulation of labor relations and abandoning the "stream of commerce" analysis); United States v. Darby, 312 U.S. 100 (1941) (overruling Hammer v. Dagenhart); Wickard v. Filburn, 317 U.S. 111 (1942) (upholding federal regulation of agriculture); Perez v. United States, 402 U.S. 146 (1971) (upholding federal criminal prohibition of "extortionate credit transactions" in the context of a "local" loan-sharking); Heart of Atlanta Motel v. United States, 379 U.S. 241 (1964) (upholding Title II of the Civil Rights Act of 1964); Daniel v. Paul, 395 U.S. 298 (1969) (extending the *Heart of Atlanta Motel* rationale to all arguably purely local acts of discrimination).

[46] National Labor Relations Board v. Jones & Laughlin Steel Corp., 301 U.S. 1 (1937).

[47] Garcia v. San Antonio Metropolitan Transit Authority, 105 S.Ct. 1005 (1985).

are the most adequate for the national welfare. The concerns of federalism would not, of course, be irrelevant for this analysis, but they would have to be viewed in terms of the values and functions to be served by the states within the federal system and the *a priori* concept of state sovereignty would have no role to play in such an inquiry.

As a matter of fact, the usefulness of the idea of sovereignty in discussing the governmental system of the United States at any level, be it state or federal, is also quite limited. To be sure, in terms of the relations between the United States and foreign countries, the Framers thought of the national (but not state) government, insofar as it represented the American people, as fully equal to other powers and entitled to the same respect as any "sovereign" nation. But in terms of domestic relations, the structure of government established by the Framers, with its written Constitution, tripartite division of powers on the national level, decentralization of authority involved in the federal system, and constraints imposed on the governments at all levels in favor of individuals and private institutions, makes the positivistic concept of sovereignty of questionable value both as an analytical tool and as a norm defining a desirable feature of political organization. The very legitimation of political authority in the United States seems to rest on a theory that views unfavorably the location of sovereignty in any well-defined institution, preferring instead a dispersion of power and authority as a mode of increasing political accountability. Even with respect to the national government, therefore, it would be impossible to point to a single body that "could do no wrong" as a matter of principle and spread the protective mantle of sovereignty to insulate itself in an *a priori* fashion from some superior form of control.

If the Framers thought of anyone as "sovereign" in the United States, they thought this of the people in whose name they purported to write the Constitution. The idea of popular sovereignty had, of course, enjoyed widespread acceptance in the progressive thought of the eighteenth century, and I am not prepared to discount the usefulness of such a conceptualization. What is characteristic, however, of the Framers' idea of the people, as it is spelled out in the Constitution, is its complexity, if not amorphousness: the Constitution neither defines the term in any unitary fashion nor considers its meaning self-evident.[48] Rather, the Constitution admits of a whole set of voices with which the people may speak, and each of these voices is identified with one or another institutional arrangement. It may be a set of conventions or a mixture of the federal and state legislatures (in the case of constitutional amendments), or the Congress and the President acting together (in the case of ordinary laws), or the Supreme Court (in the case of constitutional interpretation), but at no point, short of some violent revolutionary changes that would sweep away the present constitutional order, does the Constitution envisage the people speaking directly or with a voice that would trump all other voices by a simple fiat.[49]

The complexity of the concept of the people, as spelled out in the Constitution, makes the idea of popular sovereignty very difficult to work with and, in any case, useless for a defense of the *a priori* notion of state sovereignty. For the voices with which the "people speak" are always delegated. Even if some of them are institutionalized in the organs of the states, the whole difficulty lies in identifying precisely those occasions on which the states exercise the sovereign capacity that is delegated *to them*. It is, in fact, enough to put it in this way to see that the word "sovereign" does not add anything to what we must already know in order to apply it. In the context of the positivist theory of sovereignty, a mere identification of some person as the sovereign would allow one to learn something one would not have necessarily known without it, such as that the authority of that person is final not only in this particular instance but also in all other instances of his actions on his subjects. But if the sovereign authority is simply delegated, then we must know the extent of the delegation. If we know this, however, we learn nothing more by saying that the representative speaks for the sovereign. When speaking of the states, therefore, the task is to articulate some independent grounds for saying that some of their decisions are immune from federal interference, and not to call the states "sover-

---

[48] I have derived much enlightenment on the meaning of the term "the people" in the Constitution from my colleague, Bruce Ackerman. See his Storrs Lectures, Discovering the Constitution, 93 Yale L.J. 1013 (1984).

[49] Even in its capacity to amend the Constitution, the people are limited by the nonamendability of the states' suffrage in the Senate. That the process of legislation is limited by the requirement of constitutionality is obvious. The same is in principle true of the Supreme Court's decisions, even if only an amendment can in practice overrule them.

eign" in order to deduce anything from that. At the very least, then, the idea of state sovereignty is of no help in elaborating a theory of federalism.[50]

III. PROCESS JURISPRUDENCE: AN ALTERNATIVE APPROACH

A. GARCIA AND NATIONAL LEAGUE OF CITIES

The rejection of the label of "sovereignty" as inapplicable in any meaningful sense to the American states does not mean that the American federal system does not differ very significantly from other well known systems of government, centralized or decentralized. Neither does it mean that the problems of federalism lack a constitutional dimension, so that judicial review of federalism-related limitations on the authority of the Congress or the Executive is necessarily inappropriate. My only point so far is that the idea of state sovereignty is not useful in elaborating a respectable theory of federalism and, a fortiori, in devising the adequate standards of judicial enforcement.

Seen in this light, the Supreme Court's decision in *Garcia v. San Antonio MTA*, coming down rather hard on the notion of state sovereignty, should be viewed as the last logical step in a long evolution of the sovereignty-based jurisprudence of federalism. The bitter historical experience of the Supreme Court in trying to apply the sovereignty-based limitations on national legislative powers, leading to the constitutional crisis of 1937, had long ago convinced the Court and most commentators that the Article I enumeration of national powers provided no helpful ground for judicial

---

[50] Very similar conclusions would follow if one were to look to the more recent discussions of sovereignty by such political scientists as Leon Duguit (Souveraineté et Liberté (1922)), Hugo Krabbe (The Modern Idea of the State (1922)), and Harold J. Laski (Studies in the Problem of Sovereignty (1917), Authority in the Modern State (1919)). The upshot of these discussions is that the traditional concept of sovereignty simply obfuscates the fact that actual authority in the modern states resides in an often shifting configuration of political, economic, and social groups, with the state being only one of the contenders. In view of these theories, which also blur the distinction between various kinds of de facto authority possessed by extragovernmental interests and the control over legal forms possessed by governmental institutions, to say that the American states are sovereign would be patently false. At most, one could say that the states should be counted among the various groups that constitute the pluralistic sovereign that is the United States, but the same could be said of the Congress, the President, or even the Democratic Party. And to say this would, again, mean no more than that the states in fact exercise some influence over the political and legal decisions in the United States but would not make it any easier to determine what this influence is or should be.

intervention in the national political process, so that the courts were left with only an ultraminimal role in this area, if any. Quite significantly, however, the rhetoric of the Court's decisions did not fully reflect what appeared to be the practice of Commerce Clause adjudication: despite the fact that since 1937 no private activity has ever been found in principle beyond the reach of the Commerce Clause legislation, the "substantial effect" standard,[51] tied as it was to the idea that the regulation of purely local activities was reserved exclusively to the states (and thus potentially to the notion of the states' sovereign domains), was upheld in theory and a certain amount of unease, occasionally rising to the level of a dissent, could be detected in the pronouncements of various justices with respect to the absence of any genuine judicial check on real or hypothetical encroachments on state prerogatives by the federal government.[52] Although the *Garcia* decision does not in its terms overrule the "substantial effect" standard and although its own language is not entirely free from the rhetoric of state sovereignty,[53] its main thrust is to reject the usefulness of the sovereignty-based analysis and to replace it with a focus on the nature of the political process responsible for making the federalism-related decisions. Consequently, *Garcia* stresses the fact that the Constitution "divested" the states of "their original powers" and that it is futile to try to "identify principled constitutional limitations on the scope of Congress' Commerce Clause powers over the States merely by relying on *a priori* definitions of state sovereignty."[54] Instead, the decision proposes to

---

[51] Congress has the power to exercise control over activities that have "close and substantial relation to interstate commerce." NLRB v. Jones & McLaughlin Steel Corp., 301 U.S. 1, 37 (1937); see also Wickard v. Filburn, 317 U.S. 111, 125 (1942); Heart of Atlanta Motel v. United States, 379 U.S. 241, 258 (1964).

[52] A good example of such unease may be found in Justice Black's dissent in Daniel v. Paul, 395 U.S. 298, 315 (1969). Another, and quite interesting, expression of the same unease may be found in Justice Jackson's opinion in United States v. Five Gambling Devices, 346 U.S. 441 (1953). *Cf.* Justice Rehnquist's concurrence in Hodel v. Virginia Surface Mining & Recl. Ass'n., 452 U.S. 264, 307 (1981), where he states that the idea that Congress's power to reach private activities is limited is "one of the greatest 'fictions' of our federal system."

[53] Justice Blackmun's opinion affirms that while "the sovereignty of the States is limited by the Constitution," 105 S.Ct. at 1017, "[t]he States unquestionably 'retain a significant measure of sovereign authority' . . . to the extent that the Constitution has not divested them of their original powers and transferred those powers to the Federal Government." *Id.* Similar statements appear throughout the opinion, and its ultimate holding is that the contested provisions of the FLSA are not "destructive of state sovereignty." 105 S.Ct. at 1020.

[54] 105 S.Ct. at 1016.

rely primarily on the political safeguards of federalism[55] and to ground any future judicial intervention not in a defense of state sovereignty but in the idea of compensating for possible failings in the national political process.[56]

The only exception to the steady move away from the sovereignty-based jurisprudence of federalism since 1937 seems to have been the 1976 *National League of Cities* decision, overruled in *Garcia*. Justice Rehnquist's opinion for the Court in *National League of Cities* drew very heavily on the "fact" that the immunities enjoyed by the states derived from their "sovereignty"[57] and the main holding of the case was anchored in his observation that "[o]ne undoubted attribute of state sovereignty is the States' power to determine the wages which shall be paid to those whom they employ to carry out their governmental functions."[58] The subsequent reformulation of the holding of *National League of Cities*, given in Justice Marshall's opinion for the Court in *Hodel v. Virginia Surface Min. & Recl. Ass'n*,[59] made the concept of state sovereignty into the focal point of its three-pronged test[60] and it was this focus that shaped the *Garcia* response.

It is an important question, however, whether *National League of Cities* really needed to rely on the idea of state sovereignty to justify its holding and, if it did not, whether the *Garcia* response was not, at least in part, inapposite.

The first point to note in this context is that the principle announced in *National League of Cities*, namely, that the states should be immune from federal interference in structuring their own governmental operations, was significantly different from the previous

---

[55] See note 7 *supra*.

[56] Garcia v. San Antonio MTA, 105 S.Ct. at 1019–20: "[A]ny substantive restraint on the exercise of Commerce Clause powers must find its justification in the procedural nature of [the] basic limitation [the Constitution imposes to protect the states], and it must be tailored to compensate for possible failings in the national political process rather than to dictate a 'sacred province of state autonomy.' "

[57] 426 U.S. at 833, 843 n.14.

[58] 426 U.S. at 845.

[59] 452 U.S. 264, 287–88 (1981).

[60] "[A] claim that congressional commerce clause legislation is invalid under the reasoning of National League of Cities must satisfy each of three requirements. First, there must be a showing that the challenged statute regulates the 'States as States.' Second, the federal regulation must address matters that are indisputably 'attribute[s]' of state sovereignty.' And third, it must be apparent that the States' compliance with the federal law would directly impair their ability 'to structure integral operations in areas of traditional function.' " *Ibid.*

attempts to protect state rights that had concentrated on assuring the states' supremacy in regulating substantive, private activities supposedly outside the enumerated powers of the national government. The significance of this difference lay precisely in the fact that the immunity granted to the states by the *National League of Cities*, like most other limitations imposed on the authority of the national (or, for that matter, state) government—by the Bill of Rights, for example—did not have to derive from the displacement of the federal power by another sovereign but could rather be conceptualized as yet another check on the concentration of power in general, for the sake of protecting certain forms of life or preventing arbitrary and tyrannical imposition by some interests upon others. To say that the federal government cannot unduly interfere with the states' ability to structure their governmental operations or that it cannot destroy their "separate and independent existence"[61] need, in and of itself, no more rely on the concept of state sovereignty than the prohibition of state interference with the membership of a private association[62] must recognize that association's "sovereignty" or the protection of the Episcopalians' right to associate and exercise their religion must imply the "sovereignty" of the Episcopal Church. What seems rather to be true in all of these cases is that the very principle of sovereignty, wherever located, is circumscribed by the Constitution, in favor of the idea of limited government.

It is the case, of course, that the holding of *National League of Cities* attempted to protect governmental, and not private, institutions. This fact is not without significance, but the decision did not protect the states as governmental institutions in the sense—crucial for the preservation of state sovereignty—of assuring their ability to impose the ultimate rules of conduct in any given area of extragovernmental activities. In interpreting the Tenth Amendment, the *National League of Cities* Court did not rely on any "residue" of nondelegated state powers; the opinion straightforwardly admitted that the regulation of wages at issue in the case was "undoubtedly within the scope of the Commerce Clause."[63] The exception carved

---

[61] National League of Cities v. Usery, 426 U.S. at 845 (citing Coyle v. Smith, 221 U.S. 559, 580 (1911)).

[62] *Cf.* NAACP v. Alabama, 357 U.S. 449 (1958).

[63] 426 U.S. at 841.

out from the federal powers pertained exclusively to the immunity
of internal state governmental processes, and nothing in the opinion
even remotely implied that the federal government could not reach
any private activity. Whatever sovereign power (in the sense of an
ultimate power to control the activities of third parties) was therefore seen as vested in any governmental body in the United States
was squarely seen as vested in the national authorities, all the
rhetoric of "state sovereignty" notwithstanding.

This aspect of *National League of Cities* was not sufficiently ap-
preciated in the subsequent decisions of the Court. For example,
Justice Blackmun, in his opinion for the majority in *FERC v. Mississippi*,[64] intimates that the existence of the federal power to preempt
state utilities regulation justified, or at least mitigated the constitutional problems with, federal interference with state regulatory
processes in the area.[65] If this argument were to be taken seriously,
then it either rendered *National League of Cities* meaningless long
before its ultimate overruling (for, given universal preemptibility, it
left no state governmental function immune from federal interference) or conditioned its continued vitality on the existence of some
areas of regulation reserved exclusively to the states. But if the
latter interpretation were to be chosen, the novelty of *National
League of Cities* had to disappear since it no longer could be viewed
as protecting merely the structural integrity of state governments
and required the continuation of the old sovereignty-based analysis. Thus interpreted, *National League of Cities* would have indeed
deserved to be overruled.

In fact, however, putting aside the unfortunate references to
state sovereignty in *National League of Cities* and its progeny, there is
a certain jurisprudential affinity between the approaches taken in
Garcia and in the 1976 decision. While the practical chances of any

---

[64] 456 U.S. 742, 761–66 (1982).

[65] Strictly speaking, Justice Blackmun stopped short of finding that the possibility of
preemption justified direct federal control of state instrumentalities since he also found that
the state was free to withdraw from the field of utilities regulation altogether if it did not wish
to submit to the federal commands. Nevertheless, Justice Blackmun himself saw that the
possibility of state withdrawal was no more than theoretical, especially in view of the
Congressional failure to provide for any alternative regulatory mechanism. 456 U.S. at 766.
For all practical purposes, therefore, the argument amounted to legitimizing federal control
over the state regulatory processes in all preemptible fields. It must be noted, however, that
the question of when a federal action on the states amounts to coercion was one of the
fundamental issues not sufficiently addressed by the *National League of Cities* and its progeny.

future invalidation of national legislation on the grounds of conflict
with the requirements of federalism appear to be small for the time
being, in theory at least *Garcia* leaves the door open for a certain
amount of judicial supervision of the national political process. The
safeguards of federalism, according to the *Garcia* majority, lie
primarily "in the structure of the Federal Government itself,"[66]
which guarantees to the states a certain amount of influence on the
national level. Clearly, should the constitutionally required composition of the federal government be directly infringed on (for example by decoupling the choice of the Senators from the state
electoral base), the Court would be obliged to intervene. But *Garcia*
goes significantly further, for it does not preclude the possibility
that even a properly composed national authority may insufficiently protect the interests of the states. All that *Garcia*, on its face,
requires is that a justification of any federalism-related limitation on
the national government be one of "process" (rather than relying on
the alleged existence of some " 'sacred province of state autonomy' ") and that the process failure, required for judicial intervention, be on the national level.[67] But while the justification of the
"restraint on the exercise of Commerce Clause powers" must be one
of "process," the restraint itself may be "substantive,"[68] that is,
need not be limited to assuring the proper amount of state influence
on the federal level but may instead address itself directly to the
problem of national overreaching.

Viewed from this perspective, the gist of *Garcia*'s holding lies not
in ruling out as nonjusticiable all matters of federalism-related limitations on national power, but rather in formulating an approach to
the elaboration of the judicial standards of review. This approach
has much in common with the "process jurisprudence" originating
in the famous footnote four of the *Carolene Products* decision[69] and
subsequently elaborated in the scholarly literature.[70] The assumption of this approach is that the Constitution largely confines the
outcomes of governmental action to the political process and that

---

[66] 105 S.Ct. at 1018.

[67] 105 S.Ct. at 1019–20 (citing EEOC v. Wyoming, 460 U.S. 226, 236 (1983)).

[68] *Ibid.* (emphasis added).

[69] United States v. Carolene Products Co., 304 U.S. 144, 152-53 n.4 (1938).

[70] See, above all, Ely, Democracy and Distrust (1980), and Lusky, By What Right?
(1975).

judicial review should, with a few exceptions related to very concrete substantive provisions in the Constitution, be directed toward
preserving the integrity of the political process, keeping open the
channels of political change, and so on. In elaborating this theory of
judicial review, however, process jurisprudence does not limit the
scope of judicial intervention to explicitly procedural remedies or to
the enforcement of specifically procedural principles. It aims rather
at an elaboration of judicial standards, the justification of which
does not rely on the desirability of specific substantive results but
rests instead on the identification of some defects in the political
process that prevent it from operating in accordance with the function assigned to it in the Constitution. Thus, for example, in reviewing governmental actions that may inhibit free speech or discriminate against certain minorities, a court sympathetic to the
tenets of process jurisprudence will feel free to elaborate the standards of review that will directly address the substantive issues of
free speech or minority rights, but it will justify them not so much
in terms of the autonomous values of speech or equality as in terms
of their role in the properly functioning democratic process and will
attempt to identify some distortions in that process that account for
its presumably abnormal results. Seen in this light, the protection
of free speech will be related, say, to the idea of informed consent
as a basis of democratic legitimation, while discriminatory legislation will be viewed, say, as an outcome of restricted access by
discrete and insular minorities to the trade-offs and compromises
that are supposed to prevent systematic exploitation of minority
interests in a well-functioning democratic society.[71]

In the context of federalism, the process jurisprudence endorsed
by *Garcia*, if I interpret it correctly, does not imply, therefore, an
unconditional rejection of even the specific principle of the protection of the integrity of state governmental operations put forth by
the *National League of Cities* so long as this principle is not rooted in

---

[71] By giving these examples, I do not mean to suggest that they represent the correct
applications of the principles of process jurisprudence. For a critique of the reasoning underlying the protection of minority rights indicated in the text, see Ackerman, Beyond Carolene
Products, 98 Harv. L. Rev. 713 (1985). I also recognize that it may be impossible to specify
the characteristics of a well-functioning political process without anchoring them in a theory
of substantive values that the process is supposed to realize. See Brest, The Substance of
Process, 42 Ohio St. L.J. 131, 134–37 (1981); Tribe, The Puzzling Persistence of Process-
Based Constitutional Theories, 89 Yale L.J. 1063, 1072–77 (1980). This last issue will be
considered further in section B *infra*.

the assumption of state sovereignty. Should it turn out, for example, on the basis of a well-grounded analysis of the significance of local politics for the proper functioning of the national political process, that certain systemic characteristics of the national government make it prone to fail to recognize the interdependence between its own health and the robustness of political life in the states, the Court might view with suspicion federal interference with the integrity of some vital governmental operations of the states, in much the same way as it applied its "strict scrutiny" analysis to governmental actions involving race-based classifications.[72]

Moreover, if one can abstract from the rhetoric of sovereignty in *National League of Cities* and some of its progeny, the ideas of process jurisprudence are not entirely absent from their analyses and could profitably be further developed. Thus, for example, much of Justice Rehnquist's opinion in *National League of Cities* is not directed to the problem of state sovereignty but rests on an analysis of the impact of the 1974 FLSA Amendments (requiring that minimum wages be paid to state employees) on the states' ability to structure their internal operations and the relation between the need to preserve this ability and the role assigned to the states within the federal system. Posing the issue in this way implies that the principles of *National League of Cities* derive from the structure of government set up under the Constitution, rather than from some preexisting immunity of the states, due to their status as sovereigns that the Constitution could not or did not abrogate. This is even more clear in the elaboration of the principles of *National League of Cities* given by Justice O'Connor in her dissent in *FERC v. Mississippi*.[73] After making a questionable statement that "each State is sovereign within its own domain, governing its citizens and providing for their general welfare,"[74] Justice O'Connor proceeded to analyze the statute at issue in terms of its impact on the states' ability to func-

---

[72] See Korematsu v. United States, 323 U.S. 214 (1944).

[73] 456 U.S. 742, 775 (1982). Justice O'Connor's dissent in *FERC* was joined by Justice Rehnquist and Chief Justice Berger, both of whom were in the majority in *National League of Cities*. Additionally, Justice Powell, another member of the *National League of Cities* majority, expressed his agreement with the "wisdom" of "Justice O'Connor's evocation of the principles of federalism." FERC v. Mississippi, 456 U.S. at 775 (Justice Powell, concurring and dissenting).

[74] *Id.* at 777.

tion within the federal system and pointed to the values to be
served by state autonomy under our constitutional scheme. Among
these values and functions, Justice O'Connor listed the enhancement of the political accountability of officials, the function of the
states as "laboratories for the development of new social, economic,
and political ideas,"[75] the enhancement of "the opportunity of all
citizens to participate in representative government,"[76] and the provision of "a salutary check on governmental power."[77]

No special attempt was made in most of these statements to
relate the protection of the integrity of state governmental operations to any specific analysis of the failure of the political process on
the national level, as eventually required by *Garcia*, since the protection of state interests was presumed by Justice O'Connor to be
constitutionally required by the principles of federalism, independently of the specific guarantees of local representation on the national level. But it might not be very difficult to relate the concerns
of the *National League of Cities*'s proponents to the problems inherent
in the national government as it has developed in the post–Civil
War period, and particularly in the last fifty years and to point out
the effect of those changes on the political protection of the interests
of the states as envisaged by the Framers.[78] What is more important, however, than the question of where the protection of the
states is textually anchored in the Constitution (in the provisions
specifying the composition of the federal government or in the
Tenth Amendment) is the elaboration of a constitutional theory of
federalism in terms of the functions assigned to the political processes envisaged by the Constitution and the relation between those
functions and the actual operation of governmental institutions. In
this respect, both *Garcia* (insofar as it leaves room for a judicial
review of the federalism-related implications of national action) and
National League of Cities (insofar as it may have grounded its holding
in a functional analysis of the role of the states within the federal
system) are on the right track. They both recognize the special role

---

[75] *Id.* at 788.

[76] *Id.* at 789.

[77] *Id.* at 790.

[78] An argument of this kind is indicated in Part B of Justice Powell's dissenting opinion in
Garcia. 105 S.Ct. 1025–27; see particularly footnote 9. Among scholarly contributions, of
particular importance in this context is Kaden, Politics, Money, and State Sovereignty: The
Judicial Role, 79 Colum. L. Rev. 847 (1979).

of the analysis of institutional arrangements and processes set up by the Constitution for the judicial evaluation of the substantive outcomes that these arrangements and processes engender. But both these cases fail to move beyond the programatic stages in the formulation of the analysis they require and proceed to a conclusory resolution of complex problems of federalism: *National League Cities* by laying down a blanket prohibition on the interference with the vaguely defined "traditional governmental functions" of the states,[79] *Garcia* by simply relegating the protection of unspecified state interests to an insufficiently analyzed national political process.

B. THE NATURE OF PROCESS JURISPRUDENCE AND ITS MISCONCEPTIONS

1. *Substantive values and process jurisprudence.* To develop a theory of federalism along the lines of process jurisprudence, we must have a fairly good idea of the nature of the political processes envisaged by the Constitution and the functions that the document assigns to them. On this point the opinions in both *Garcia* and *National League of Cities* are most deficient. *National League of Cities*, in laying down its principle of the protection of state governmental processes, simply stated that the protection extended to governmental functions and activities that were termed "traditional,"[80] "integral,"[81] "typical,"[82] "important," "essential" or "required,"[83] without explaining how and why these terms related to the basic values of federalism. *Garcia*, on the other hand, seized on the lack of clarity in these criteria and declared that the values of federalism are "more properly protected by procedural safeguards inherent in the federal system."[84] The opinion of the Court lists a series of constitutional provisions assuring to the states a role in the operation of the national government,[85] but it never attempts to specify

---

[79] 426 U.S. at 851, 852, 855.

[80] *Ibid.*

[81] *Id.* at 851, 852, 854 n.18, 855.

[82] *Id.* at 851.

[83] *Id.* at 845, 846, 847, 850, 851.

[84] 105 S.Ct. at 1018.

[85] *Ibid.*

what the protected values are or how they are related to the procedural safeguards referred to by the Court.

The other sources inspired by the ideas of process jurisprudence
are not of much help either. To begin with, the issue of federalism
is simply absent from the list of problems that the *Carolene Products*
footnote[86] identified as potentially enhancing the level of judicial
scrutiny, and the issue rarely appears in the further elaborations of
its doctrine.[87] But more importantly than that, even though the
idea that constitutional adjudication is primarily concerned with
protecting the integrity of the political process, rather than some
substantive outcomes or entitlements, has been much in vogue for a
while, the legal profession has been rather slow in developing a
sophisticated theory of political processes or in applying the results
available from political science to the problems of constitutional
interpretation. The basic problem with the concept of process, as
understood by the exponents of process jurisprudence, is its narrow
focus on representative political institutions and their function of
expressing the will of the majority.

The crudest version of the process theory would look something
like this: The Constitution is a democratic document, which means
that the decisions of the majority of the representatives freely
elected by the majority of the people should not be upset, and
judicial intervention—which always raises a prima facie presumption of countermajoritarianism—should be limited to cases in
which something in the process suggests that the decision deviates
from the majority's will.

While this version of the theory may look too simplistic, the
more sophisticated versions seem to proceed from it as a starting
point in order to add a few refinements. This is done by Ely, for

---

[86] Note 69 *supra.*

[87] Some efforts at applying the footnote's ideas to the review of state legislation that might
conflict with the "dormant" federal Commerce Clause powers were made by Justice Stone in
South Carolina State Highway Dept. v. Barnwell Bros., Inc., 303 U.S. 177, 184 n.2 (1938),
and Southern Pacific Co. v. Arizona, 325 U.S. 761, 767 n.2 (1945), where he explained that
the usual deference to state legislative judgments is suspended in cases when such legislation
may discriminate against out-of-state interests because of the absence of the representation
(even in the virtual sense) of those interests in the state legislature. The idea of "virtual
representation" is further picked up by Ely in his Democracy and Distrust, note 70 *supra*, at
82–87. While no explicitly process-oriented work approaches the subject of federalism-
related limitations on the national authorities, of great value in this context is Kaden, note 78
supra.

example,[88] by concentrating on two aspects of the majoritarian rule: (1) assuring that the selecting process is truly responsive to the interests of those who are represented and (2) protecting minority interests from systematic exploitation by the majority due to the majority's "simple hostility or a prejudiced refusal to recognize commonalities of interest."[89] The first of these considerations yields such normative postulates as guaranteeing the right to vote, assuring the proper dissemination of information, and facilitating the expression and advocacy of citizens' interests. The second type of consideration (as well as those aspects of the first that guard against the evils of ignorance) introduces a certain modification into the premise of unqualified majoritarianism. Majority rule is not perhaps a good per se but rather a system in which every interest has a chance to succeed some of the time in the political world of the trade-offs and compromises that are necessary to form a majority in a universe of diverse interests. The ultimate justification of majority rule is thus its basic fairness, but this would be undermined if some groups were to be systematically excluded from the political give-and-take because other people are either uninformed or motivated by irrational hostility, and this gives rise to the jurisprudence of "suspect classifications."[90]

Something along the lines of this version of the process theory must have been at the bottom of the famous state reapportionment cases,[91] which laid down the blanket rule of "one man, one vote" as the logical conclusion of the majoritarian democratic theory. What is rather amazing about it, however, is that the theory, without more (indeed, much more), is incapable of giving any account of most of the processes and structures set up by the federal Constitution, be they related to the separation of powers or (in particular) to the representative imbalance characteristic of the federal system.[92] Ely himself does not believe that the "one man, one vote" conclusion is ineluctable and explains it with reference to administrative

---

[88] Ely, note 70 *supra.*

[89] *Id.* at 103.

[90] See Korematsu v. United States, 323 U.S. 214 (1944).

[91] Baker v. Carr, 369 U.S. 186 (1962); Reynolds v. Sims, 377 U.S. 533 (1964); Lucas v. Forty-Fourth General Assembly, 377 U.S. 713 (1964); WMCA Inc. v. Lomenzo, 377 U.S. 633 (1964).

[92] See Bishin, Judicial Review in Democratic Theory, 50 S. Cal. L. Rev. 1099 (1977).

concerns,[93] but neither does his book contain any explanation of the peculiarly procedural provisions unrelated to, or deviating from, the principle of majority rule that occupy the bulk of the Constitution.[94] To be sure, Ely does say that deviations from the "one man, one vote" principle are not inherently irrational,[95] but what passes in silence is that the rationality of such deviations cannot, in most instances, be judged with reference to some exclusively procedural principles.[96] Even a genuine legitimation of majority rule calls for some further substantive justification, such as the Rousseauean theory of popular sovereignty or the Madisonian (and Ely's) theory of fairness resulting from pragmatic accommodations. But in a system as complex as that of the American government, the dominance of any one principle of legitimation (such as the democratic concept of popular sovereignty or fairness in the distribution of governmental favors) is very unlikely to provide a good explanation of the whole structure of governmental institutions. Even a cursory reading of the Constitution and the work of those who wrote it or participated in the ratification debates will immediately show the crucial role of such values as individual autonomy, citizen participation, the sanctity of property, secularism, economic growth, the fostering of civic virtues, and so on. And it is even more doubtful that this plurality of substantive values underlying the constitutional order could find its expression in a single dominant procedural feature, such as majority rule. As a matter of fact, the

---

[93] Ely, note 70 *supra*, at 116–25.

[94] The only facet of the separation of powers that receives a plausible justification in Ely's book (and indeed is its basic leitmotif) is, ironically, the one not explicitly mentioned in the text of the Constitution: judicial review.

[95] Ely, note 70 *supra*, at 121.

[96] Ely, *ibid.*, mentions in this context that the Equal Protection Clause often allows for unequal treatment if it is "rationally explainable." But this remark, while relevant to the Court's ostensible grounding of the reapportionment cases in the Equal Protection Clause, is inapposite in the context of the underlying Republican Form of Government Clause that he admits is also relevant here. The mere rationality of some decision is a far cry from its legitimacy: a lot of perfectly abhorrent laws might be rational and still unacceptable. What legitimizes most laws challenged under equal protection, on Ely's own terms, is that they have been passed by a democratically legitimate legislature, with rationality being an only minimal additional component. But in the case of a decision that disenfranchises (or dilutes the votes of) a part of the population or, even more clearly, that results from such a disenfranchisement (or dilution), the usual democratic legitimation is precisely absent and some other form of legitimation is necessary. It seems to me very doubtful that an ultimately satisfying form of legitimation (even in the same degree as a simple reference to majority rule may be satisfying) of such decisions could be purely procedural.

Constitution reveals many clearly antimajoritarian features that are probably incomprehensible without a reference to some of the substantive values just mentioned.

2. *Process jurisprudence and individual rights.* Where does this leave us with respect to the utility of process jurisprudence for the formulation of the effective standards of judicial review, particularly in the area of federalism? Doesn't the account given here, by requiring an explanation of the procedural features of political institutions in terms of the substantive values underlying the political process, negate the whole enterprise of process jurisprudence and lead us back to evaluating the outcomes of the political process in terms of some substantive "fundamental values" that the whole approach was designed to avoid?

The answer is that the idea of process jurisprudence need not be abandoned simply because the theory must admit of the existence of some substantive values, but rather that the purpose and the methods of process jurisprudence must be further clarified and its ambitions somewhat scaled down. The primary aim of a process theory, which may have been widely misconceived, is not to eliminate the idea of substantive values from constitutional interpretation or to reduce them to purely procedural terms but to understand the specific role played by institutions in the realm of social and political life. And in this context, to say that an institution has a particular function that must be accounted for in terms of some substantive values the institution is supposed to serve does not mean that the peculiar process-related characteristics of the institution do not acquire independent significance or that one may ignore its internally generated interests and purposes. What I take to be the most promising aspect of *Garcia*'s endorsement of the process-analysis approach to the problem of federalism is not, therefore, its arguable reduction of the meaning of federalism to a few purely procedural arrangements through which the states have some voice in national politics, but rather its implicit call for a complex account of the nature of the federalist institutions. Even to begin to vindicate *Garcia*'s promise in this respect, one must, above all, have the rudiments of a general theory of political processes that would allow us to understand why the Constitution concentrates as heavily as it does on the protection of the integrity of processes and institutions rather than directly on the substantive values these processes and institutions are supposed to serve. Armed with such a general theory, one may then apply it to explain the functioning of a particular institutional arrangement, such as federalism, and its possible pathological distortions. The process-oriented analysis of federalism would thus not deny that the federalist institutions do indeed serve further substantive purposes, such as the preservation of individual freedom or citizen participation in government, but it would also not stop at a mere identification of such purposes. Instead, it would proceed to show how respect for the integrity of the federalist political process might more effectively promote the very substantive values federalism is supposed to serve than any attempt to enforce those values directly. It would also identify those features of the federalist institutions that might be susceptible to pathological developments.

We must begin, then, by outlining the general considerations that explain the importance of focusing on the inner dynamic of political processes. The reason why, without deeper reflection, it is easy to miss the point of a theory of political institutions that entails the idea that political structures and processes have their own, self-generated claims to autonomy is that most of us simply assume that government should serve the people. On this assumption and the one that the "people" is not a mystical, abstract entity but rather the sum of the individuals concerned, it can easily be shown that the well-being of individuals is the ultimate justification of *any* governmental arrangement or institution. It is only a step from this, in turn, to an approach that neglects the analysis of the structures of political life and concentrates on assuring that the individuals are protected against governmental abuse through a system of rights. Nevertheless, without ever questioning the self-evident proposition that governments are ultimately supposed to serve the people, it is not the case that all constitutional principles concerning institutional arrangements can be translated directly into the language of individual rights. Everyone, or at least every lawyer, seems to understand this when, say, a question concerning separation of powers is raised. Clearly, separation of powers was designed to prevent the oppression of individuals. Nevertheless, there exists no individual right, inhering in United States citizens as such, to have a government composed of the three branches listed in the Constitution. Indeed, separation of powers seems to have been conceived as an institutional arrangement precisely because it was thought unrealistic to expect that any system of individual rights would be sufficient to guarantee that the government would respect those rights and that what the framers called "tyranny" would not ensue. The creation of some stronger interest than an individual one was deemed necessary for this, and supraindividual (institutional) bodies were created to watch over each other to forestall the rise of an oppressive government. The Framers seem in fact to have had such confidence in this institutional approach that they at first neglected to provide the alternative guarantees of individual rights, and many argued that the Bill of Rights was unnecessary. But even the enactment of the Bill of Rights did not change the fact that the two approaches—the institutional one and the one promoting individual rights—are profoundly distinct and that the foundation of the institutional approach derives from an acknowledgment of the autonomy of supraindividual bodies within any well-conceived constitutional theory. It is tempting, indeed, under the guise of avoiding mystification or through simple ignorance, to view political and institutional phenomena through the prism of individual relations. Quite sophisticated politicians are not unknown to have argued that budget deficits are bad because a family that goes too deeply into debt is bound to face disastrous consequences.[97] Nevertheless, such a reductionist approach misses one of the fundamental verities of the political theory underlying much of our constitutional law.

In explaining why an institutional or group-oriented approach is a necessary complement to the individual-rights-oriented approach to protecting individuals, we do not have to rely exclusively on the insights of the Framers, valuable as they are, because there are also some very important data of more recent vintage that throw new light on many of the old problems. I have particularly in mind the achievements of the so-called theory of public goods, developed by modern economics and social science,[98] which allows us to explain some peculiar features of institutional arrangements.

A "public good" is something that many people consider desir-

[97] President Roosevelt is reported to have made this argument in this first presidential campaign.

[98] The following discussion is heavily influenced by Olson's The Logic of Collective Action (1965). Olson's theory, which has potentially enormous implications with respect to many legal issues, has been rarely used by lawyers outside the law and economics area. For a summary of more recent research on the subject, see Hardin, Collective Action (1982).

able and would be willing to pay for[99] but which has the following
two characteristics: First, the good is of such a nature that once it is
available it is not possible to discriminate between those who actually paid for it and those who did not by making the good available
only to the former and not the latter. Thus, clean environment and
living in a democratic society are examples of public goods, because
once the environment has been cleaned up it benefits both those
who paid for the clean-up and those who did not, and once a
democratic government is installed it is not possible to take away
most of its benefits from those who did not vote. Second, because a
large number of contributors, each of whose contributions is relatively small, is necessary for the achievement of the good, no individual contribution "matters" by itself, that is, no individual's contribution can be said to be decisive with respect to whether or not
the good will in fact be made available. Thus, for example, since
almost no election is decided by one vote, it is extremely unlikely
that any individual's voting or not voting will significantly affect
the outcome of a large election.

The problem posed by the existence of public goods is that each
self-maximizing individual has an incentive to "free ride" on the
contributions of others in the achievement of any goods of this
kind. Imagine, for example, that a contribution of no more than one
dollar from each consumer of automobiles would be more than
enough to organize a lobby that would successfully persuade the
legislature to pass antiprotectionist laws that would lower the price
of automobiles and benefit each consumer at least $100. Never-
theless, each self-interested consumer is tempted by the following
reasoning: "If a sufficiently large number of other consumers contribute $1.00 each, the legislation will pass and I will gain $100
even if I don't contribute anything. If, on the other hand, a
sufficiently large number of other consumers do not make their
contributions, then even if I contribute $99.99 (the largest amount
that it could still make sense for me to contribute), the legislation
will not pass anyway and I will have simply lost my money. One

---

[99] By "willingness to pay" I understand the willingness to contribute not only a monetary
payment but also any expenditure of time or energy that an individual may be ready to make
to obtain the good in question. Thus, the time and effort required to go to the polls, for
example, is something that an individual must "pay" for the exercise of his or her voting
rights.

way or the other, therefore, I am better off by not contributing at all." As a consequence of such perfectly rational behavior it is clear that in a society composed of self-maximizing individuals, the provision of public goods will be inherently suboptimal: some, if not most, such goods will not be made available, even though each individual will be made worse off as a result.[100]

It should be quite obvious—though the consequences of this fact are rather complex—that most benefits derived from a democratic government, and in particular freedom from governmental oppression, are public goods. It is, of course, possible for a government to discriminate among its subjects by conferring some benefits—including political or civil rights—on some people and not others, but at least insofar as the groups targeted for oppression are concerned, the availability of civic and political rights to some individuals is inextricably linked with their availability to others. Indeed, it is a well-known strategy of many oppressive governments to maintain their power over everyone by a policy of pitting their opponents against each other. And insofar as our views of freedom may link it to a certain amount of basic equality of rights among the citizens—surely a view congenial to the American constitutional tradition—the possibility that some, but not all, can be free may even be theoretically unsound.

At a minimum, then, success in protecting individual rights against a tyrannical government is a public good and its achievement may be seriously frustrated by the free-rider phenomenon. For while republican rhetoric often claims that to die in the struggle for freedom is an honor and a privilege, only a very few subjects of tyrannical governments seem to covet this distinction. Despite the claims made by such governments that the lack of resistance is a sign of popular support, the more plausible explanation is that individual acts of heroism, in the absence of some assurance that one's fellow citizens are going to join the resistance in sufficient

---

[100] Note that the realization on the part of the free riders that this is indeed so is not sufficient to change anything. Thus, the common objection to free riding—"If everyone were to behave in this way (say, refuse to contribute $1.00 to consumer legislation), we would all be worse off"—is based on a fallacy since the free rider grants the truth of this statement but adds that, since his contribution is insignificant and since whether or not others contribute does not depend in any way on whether or not he contributes, it by no means follows from the objection just raised that he should contribute. It is important to understand that the free rider's answer is not a gimmick but rather expresses a real conflict between private and collective interests.

numbers to offer at least a chance of success, are perceived as wasted efforts. Those who are willing to pay the greatest price for regaining their freedom turn in such situations to *organizing* their fellow citizens rather than to overt acts of disobedience.

A theory of organization as the most effective weapon in defeating the free-rider phenomenon is thus, not surprisingly, one of the most important aspects of the public-goods theory. In general, the free-rider phenomenon can be overcome, in the absence of significant moral or other altruistic motivations, only by a modification of the incentives of some or all the potential beneficiaries. Outright compulsion—in the form of a threat of violence or other retaliation for noncontribution—is one form in which such incentives are modified.[101] Peer pressure, in cases in which the fact of noncontribution is known and exposes the noncontributor to disapproval of those with whose opinions he must reckon, is another. Tying one's contribution to those of others, as when, for example, a donor to some cause promises to match the contributions of other donors, is also a way of diminishing the incentive to free ride. Finally, a creation of some additional benefit, other than the public good, that a contributor may derive from his contribution (such as the availability of a special insurance offered only to dues-paying union members)[102] is sometimes an effective way of overcoming the free-rider phenomenon. But if the group of potential beneficiaries is large and diffuse enough for peer pressure not to have great significance, the employment of all these incentive modifications can be effective only when the group is organized.

To begin with, an organization with some financial means at its disposal is able to hire a group of persons who, being paid, have a special incentive to devote much more time and energy to the cause of achieving the public good in question than would be rational for any individual with only limited stakes (such as the consumer of automobiles who can gain at most $100 from antiprotectionist legislation). Second, once an organization with established links to the group members exists, the cost of identifying all potential contributors and of disseminating information among them is greatly reduced and this is often the single most important cost involved in

---

[101] Thus, the state, by providing criminal penalties, modifies the incentive not to pay taxes; a labor union, by threatening violence, modifies the incentives of strike breakers.

[102] See Olson, note 98 *supra*, at 72–73.

bringing a collective effort to fruition. Third, the existence of special benefits to modify the incentives of individual contributors is very often already implied in an existing organization, as when the approval of church authorities is an important factor in the motivation of individual members, and the devising of new special benefits of this kind is greatly facilitated. Finally, while the threat of violence with respect to noncontributors may be prohibited by law, a whole host of sanctions may be available to an organization the members of which derive some independent benefits from their membership.

While the existence of an organization is the single most important factor in enhancing the effective achievement of a public good, it is at the same time the most difficult to bring about. Not only are the initial costs of organizing the highest, but also the incentives of any member of an unorganized group to incur them are the lowest. Once an organization is in place, on the other hand, it tends to develop a set of incentives, both for the leadership and the rank-and-file members, to perpetuate and expand the existing structure, so that the efficacy of collective action is radically improved. And it is this set of factors that explains why an institutional approach to protecting the well-being of individuals is a necessary complement to an individual-rights approach.[103] For, if most benefits of democracy are public goods, and if organization is necessary for their effective defense, it is logical, in structuring a constitutional order, to make sure that in addition to any protection of individual rights, an institutionalized framework is always available for the protection of the collective interest of the individuals who might find themselves threatened with exclusion and exploitation. In fact, the solutions adopted by the Framers are best analyzed in light of this consideration.

But while the process-oriented approach to constitutional law confers an independent status on institutional arrangements and does not permit a direct translation of the talk about institutions into a language of individual rights, it is also incorrect to say, as

---

[103] It is to be noted, however, that even the individual-rights approach, insofar as it does not simply confer entitlements on individuals but rests on a creation of a judicial machinery of enforcement, contains an important element of institutional support. It was, however, the inherent weakness of judicial institutions, when not backed up by more complex political arrangements, that made the Framers look beyond them.

some commentators have argued[104] and as the *Garcia* Court sometimes implies with respect to federalism, that the Framers' choice of
a primarily institutional approach to the protection of constitutionally significant values and interests renders those values and interests inherently "political" and, in the absence of specific constitutional provisions in favor of individuals, unsuitable for judicial
enforcement. In fact, an argument of this kind would constitutionally degrade those very objectives and purposes which, while peculiarly incapable of conceptualization in terms of judicially enforceable individual rights, may lie close to the core of constitutional
government. For the very essence of the process-oriented approach
is that certain fundamental values cannot be sufficiently protected
by a conferral of entitlements on individuals, either because their
enforcement would be inefficient or because the courts would lack
any manageable standards of adjudication. But precisely because
the values at stake are fundamental, if some institutional arrangements can be devised to protect them indirectly, such arrangements
may themselves become a part of the constitutional structure and
their protection (insofar as it does not raise the difficulties related to
the enforcement of a corresponding individual right) might be
vested in the judicial department rather than left to the vagaries of
momentary political expediency.[105] Thus, while the courts would,
for the most part, respect the outcomes of the political process, they
would also police it by making sure that the process does not distort

---

[104] See note 16 *supra* and accompanying text.

[105] According to two prominent scholars, such was indeed the reason why *National League
of Cities* protected the integrity of state governmental institutions. Tribe, Unraveling National League of Cities: The New Federalism and Affirmative Rights to Essential Government Services, 90 Harv. L. Rev. 1065-1104 (1977); Michelman, States' Rights and States'
Roles: Permutations of 'Sovereignty' in National League of Cities v. Usery, 86 Yale L.J.
1165-1195 (1977). It was the claim of Tribe and Michelman that the immunity granted to
state governments in *National League of Cities* should be understood not as deriving from
the federalist concerns of the Tenth Amendment but as a roundabout way of protecting an
individual right to governmental services provided by the states and threatened by federal
action in the absence of a separate national commitment to the provision of such services by
officials accountable to local constituencies. For an argument that an individual right to
essential services might be implied by the Constitution, see also Michelman, Foreword: On
Protecting the Poor Through the Fourteenth Amendment, 83 Harv. L. Rev. 7 (1969). But
both Tribe, *supra* at 1092, and Michelman, States' Rights, at 1178, 1183, admit that any
judicial effort to enforce the right to essential services would encounter great difficulties.
Thus, even if one were to accept their claim that one of the main functions of federalism is to
assure the provision of services to individuals, it would be more appropriate to view Tribe's
and Michelman's defense as a second-order theory of federalism, rather than an argument for
the existence of an individual right to essential services.

the functions assigned to it by the Constitution. And it is very much in this light that, in the wake of the *Garcia* decision, we should look at the function of the states within the federal system.

IV. The Function of the States within the Federal System

Having developed the general idea of process jurisprudence endorsed in the *Garcia* case, I shall now move to a more concrete discussion of the functions assigned to the states in our constitutional system. My purpose is not to come up with some entirely new rationale behind the federal structure of American government, but rather to examine its oft-mentioned justifications in the light of the process-oriented approach and to clarify the way in which federalist institutions were designed to serve the fundamental values envisaged in the Constitution. What will, I hope, emerge from my discussion is that the intellectual agenda endorsed in the *Garcia* case, when properly carried out, is by no means inimical to the protection of the integrity of state political processes recognized in *National League of Cities*, despite the seemingly contradictory holdings in these two cases. In examining the most important functions of the states within the federal system, we should keep in mind the two prongs of inquiry necessary to bring out the full implications of *Garcia*: the identification and analysis of the political processes by which federalism protects important constitutional values and the identification of potential failures or shortcomings in the national political process which may endanger the vital role of the states in the constitutional scheme.

A. TYRANNY PREVENTION

1. *Governmental pathologies and the role of the states.* Perhaps the most frequently mentioned function of the federal system is the one it shares to a large extent with the separation of powers, namely, the protection of the citizen against governmental oppression—the "tyranny" that the Framers were so concerned about.

The fear expressed rather generally at the time of the adoption of the Constitution was that the central government, ruling over a large territory and population, would be far removed from the people and would rely on a caste of bureaucrats and politicians, wielding an enormous governmental machine that could be turned against the interests of individuals and used to build a Romanlike empire.[106] The odds of such a turn of events did not appear inconsiderable in light of historical experience. The history of Rome was, after all, not a bad analogy. Like the American colonies, Rome was essentially a small country when the republican system was installed. Like America, the republican Rome was a rapidly expanding country, with respect to both territory and population. The new wealth, the need for an enormous military and administrative machine, the disintegration of traditional communities and of the old class structure, the rapid growth of external cultural influences—all these factors, which were ultimately responsible for the decay of the Roman Republic and the birth of the Empire, also seemed a fair prospect for the United States. More recent, and equally unhappy, experience was also available—since in all European countries (except for England) in which governmental centralization had been successfully accomplished, its concomitant was the development of absolutist royal authority. Finally, shortly after the adoption of the Constitution, the experience of the French Revolution, with its bloody transition to the Napoleonic system, provided quick confirmation of the possible dangers of centralized authority.

As I have explained,[107] the Framers did not believe that a bill of rights was a sufficient guarantee against the danger of "tyranny," and they insisted in the first place on institutional rather than individual-rights-oriented solutions. Some of these institutional arrangements were quite specific, such as the provision for civilian control of the military,[108] but most had a more general purpose of fragmenting governmental authority and of creating special interest groups. In this category, next to the separation of powers, federalism plays the most important role.

---

[106] Bailyn et al., The Great Republic 335-36 (1977); Storing, What the Anti-Federalists Were For 15-23 (1981). For the hold of antiquity on the Revolutionary generation, see Wood, note 34 *supra*, at 48-53.

[107] See text preceeding note 97 *supra*.

[108] Art. I, Section 8, prohibits appropriation of money to raise and support armies for a longer term than two years; Art. II, Section 2, makes the President Commander-in-Chief of the armed forces; Art. I, Section 6 prohibits persons holding office under the United States to be members of either House of the Congress or (*per* Art. II, Section 1) presidential electors.

There are three somewhat different scenarios of governmental oppression that the Framers seem to have had in mind when they spoke of the danger of "tyranny." First, they were clearly concerned that a small minority might be oppressed by a sufficiently homogeneous majority. Second, they were concerned with the danger that a few powerful minority interests might gain ascendancy over the political process and exploit the rest of society. And third, they were afraid that a powerful central government may itself develop its own separate interest and oppress the citizenry.

With respect to the first two scenarios, Madison, the most profound and influential thinker among the Framers, believed that the very size of the population subject to the national government made it less likely that oppression would result.[109] Madison's point was rather straightforward: if you increase the number of people involved, there will be a greater variety of interests and, consequently, a lesser chance of one faction acquiring a monopoly on political power or of a sufficiently large number of interests entering into a viable and stable coalition. At first sight, Madison's reasoning is not without problems, especially in the light of some modern developments. There is a rather old argument that in a large state a great number of people are removed from direct participation in politics and that the absence of active citizenship makes great masses of people susceptible to political demagoguery.[110] Whatever the historical truth of this observation, it seems to acquire additional support in the light of the more recent phenomenon of "mass society." If it is indeed true that technological progress is a great leveler and that it eliminates a great number of traditional, regional, and professional differences among people, then the resulting uniformity, unknown in the smaller societies of old, may contradict Madison's optimistic reliance on the diversity of factions in a large state. Nevertheless, the public goods theory comes to shore up the Madisonian point to some extent. In a large society, regardless of the uniformity of interests, there is a lesser chance that any one interest large enough to aspire to the monopoly of power can achieve an effective level of organization. Since the more numerous the interest group the more difficult and costly it is

---

[109] The Federalist Papers, No. 10.

[110] The argument goes as far back as Plato's Republic, 564c–566d. For a modern version, see Sartori, Democratic Theory (1962).

to organize, small interests have a natural advantage over large ones and the "mass society" phenomenon is to some degree counteracted by the very size of the masses involved. Thus, despite the perhaps greater uniformity of modern societies, numerically small interest groups that possess a high degree of cohesion or whose members are easily identified are not particularly threatened by majoritarian oppression.[111]

If this were the whole story, one could say perhaps—along with many liberal thinkers—that the primary means of preventing the oppression of some interests by others consists not so much in devising an elaborate structure of government as in making sure that extragovernmental, social organisms are allowed to grow undisturbed and watch over each other. By simply assuring that the access to the machine of government remains open to those who want to influence its policies, one will then also assure that those policies will reflect a wide range of interests and that no significant majority will be systematically excluded from the benefits the government provides. By adopting the principle of majority rule, therefore, one would in fact endorse the reality of genuine pluralism.

But unfortunately, this is not the whole story, and the most important complications arise because of the disparity between the short- and long-term dynamics of social growth and because of the role that the government itself can play in this development. While the public-goods theory tells us that, all things being equal, small interests are easier to organize than larger ones, it also tells us that existing organizations have a definite advantage over still unorganized interests and that even originally weak organizations have a tendency to grow and become stronger if they can devise mechanisms, such as a hierarchical structure, individualized incentives,

---

[111] As Professor Ackerman has pointed out, note 71 *supra*, this indicates a serious flaw in the argument, based on the *Carolene Products* footnote, that racial minorities deserve special legal protection because they are "insular and discrete." While I do not, of course, wish to imply that these minorities do not deserve special protection, their discreteness and insularity, given that it helps to assure their political representation, tends to argue against, rather than for, such special solicitude. This might also be the reason why judicial protection of individual rights is relatively effective in preventing the oppression of discrete minorities. Given the difficulty of forming stable and cohesive majorities in a large society, oppression of small, better organized groups is likely to be exceptional and sporadic. The courts, which may have difficulties in resisting systematic majority policy, can, without undermining the perception of their legitimate role, correct such sporadic excesses.

and so on, to counteract the free-rider phenomenon. This, in turn, means that the social structure of a large state tends, in the long run, to ossify into a relatively small number of powerful interests that come to dominate the political scene.[112] This phenomenon is quite disturbing in itself since it undermines our confidence in the ultimate representativeness of a government, which is in fact beholden to a few powerful interests. The phenomenom also decreases the likelihood of needed reforms that may be in the general interest of the community at large but not of those groups that are most powerfully entrenched in the status quo. Even more disturbing is the prospect that a small number of powerful interests may derive their strength not so much from having their wishes disproportionately reflected in governmental policies as from using the machine of government, specifically designed to defeat the free-rider phenomenon through its power to coerce, to reinforce their own internal cohesion or to prevent the competing interests from effective organization.

But while the threat of the government's being used by a few powerful interests (or perhaps even one) to oppress the rest of society was very much in the minds of the Framers, of even more importance in our own time is the third scenario of governmental oppression they envisioned, that of the government itself becoming the most powerful special interest, which can devour those whom it is supposed to serve.[113] At any time, a government is more than a merely passive vessel through which flows the diversity of private interests. Like any large organization, it has many members who have a special interest in their own position within the organization as well as in the power of the organization itself. And while any organization tends to develop its own institutional interests and cohesion independent from the interest of the individuals it is supposed to represent, the more amorphous the organization's constituency the more likely is this tendency to grow. The government machine, being very hierarchically structured, possessing an enormous ability to strengthen its own cohesion, having the most amor-

---

[112] For the tendencies of social structures to ossify, see Olson, The Rise and Decline of Nations: Economics and Growth, Stagflation and Social Rigidities (1982).

[113] For a view that this third scenario was also the most prominent in the thought of Madison, see Carey, Separation of Powers and the Madisonian Model: A Reply to Critics, 72 Am. Pol. Sci. Rev. 151 (1978).

phous constituency of all (citizens in general), and having a virtual monopoly on coercion, is more than likely, in the absence of other centrifugal forces, to be a potential threat in any society. The threat intensifies, however, when the traditional liberal policy of restricting the government to a few limited tasks is no longer feasible and the expansion of the "activist state" is necessary to accomplish a whole gamut of tasks that can no longer be entrusted to an unregulated private sector. Not only does the government then become a primary dispenser of some of the most valuable resources[114] but also the variety of competing private interests, on which the liberal model so heavily depended for the prevention of governmental oppression, becomes increasingly dependent on government policies for their survival and subject to often minute governmental regulation.[115] One needs no reminder of the horrors of totalitarianism to realize the dangers that this process entails if the wheels of the modern governmental machine were to turn against the individual members of the community.

How is federalism related to the Framers' objective of preventing the three-headed specter of tyranny? Many American liberals tend to look with skepticism on the states as the protectors of individual freedom and they point to a whole host of situations in which the states, much more than the federal government, have engaged in practices violative of individual rights. Quite apart from the special problem of racial discrimination, which is historically tied to the regional character of slavery in the United States, there are in fact good reasons to believe that the states represent a more direct threat than the national authorities to the rights of small minorities and that the states have only a secondary role to play in protecting such minorities—so long as these minorities are not geographically defined. The explanation for this lies in the fact that local constituencies are much more homogenous and cohesive than the national one, both because their members share more common interests and values and because, the constituencies being less numerous, stable majoritarian interests are more likely to exist within

---

[114] For the role of the government-dispensed largesse and the concomitant transformation of the type of resources on which the livelihood of individuals depends in contemporary America, see Reich, The New Property, 73 Yale L.J. 733 (1964).

[115] For the role of the state in running the corporate America, see Berle, Property, Production and Revolution, 65 Colum. L. Rev. 1 (1965).

them and to be easier to organize. Consequently, at least insofar as the first of the Framers' scenarios of governmental oppression is concerned, state governments are more likely than the national one to be captured by powerful majoritarian interests and to oppress small minorities with little power to resist. In this light, the Civil War Amendments, with their emphasis on the federal protection of individual rights, acquire a justification independent of the particular circumstances of their adoption. For the federal government, being less likely to be dominated by one majoritarian interest, seems better suited than any political forces within the average state to guarantee the basic equality of treatment to state citizens (most commonly by the enforcement of the federal Bill of Rights).[116]

But if the liberal mistrust of the states' power is partially justified in this way, the more comprehensive neglect on the part of liberals of the importance of the states for the prevention of governmental oppression is somewhat myopic. To begin with, while the states are more easily captured by relatively undifferentiated majoritarian interests intent on suppressing small minorities, the federal government may be a more likely subject of capture by a set of special minoritarian interests, precisely because the majority interest of the national constituency is so large, diffuse, and enormously difficult to organize. The problem that this raises is not only that those particular interests that are shared by the majority (such as the interest of the consumers, for example) may be systematically underrepresented on the federal level, for there may be few such interests in a country as diverse as the United States. A more disturbing prospect is that the ossification of the social structure may result in a virtual exclusion of quite a large number of diverse interests that suffer under all kinds of organizational disadvantages but which together constitute a majority the federal government is supposed to serve. And here the existence and vitality of local governments may provide an important counterbalance to the constellation of forces on the national level.

It is quite easy to see how a system weighted in favor of local interests (either through the importance of state institutions or through a regional representation on the national level) will provide

---

[116] It is significant in this context that the federal action under the Fourteenth Amendment was not subject to the limitations imposed in the *National League of Cities* on the exercise of the Commerce Clause powers. City of Rome v. United States, 446 U.S. 156, 179 (1980).

an institutional support to geographically defined groups that may
be subject to exclusion or exploitation by the more powerful regions. But it is no less important to see that the existence of a strong
system of local government may also modify those divisions between the potential ins and outs that are essentially social in nature
(such as between the traditional and new industries, organized and
unorganized labor, producers and consumers, and so on) rather
than primarily geographically determined. As I have noted, the
very scale on which an organization must succeed before it gains
meaningful access to the political process and can use the machine
of the government to improve its position vis à vis other groups is
very often decisive with respect to whether an effective collective
action takes place. It is thus quite likely that an effort to exclude
certain groups may be more successful on the federal than on the
state level and that maintaining the domination of an already existing power elite is much more difficult on the local level. Insofar,
then, as a large proportion of governmental benefits is dispensed on
an independent local level or as the constellation of forces on the
local level determines the influence on the national level, the danger
of minoritarian oppression is significantly diminished.

A simple example[117] may bring this out. Suppose that an existing
union movement, which is very well entrenched on the federal
level, is committed to supporting traditional industries, where its
leadership has the greatest power base, and systematically neglects
the interests of a newer type of employee, mostly white collar and
working in the service sector. In a situation of this kind, the likelihood of successful organization of the white-collar workers is rather
small, even on the local level, if the only reward to be expected is a
certain measure of influence over one or two federal politicians. If,
however, independently of any influence on the federal level, a
local white-collar organization can expect to influence in a significant manner a great number of state legislators, then the possibility
of effective collective action increases because the resulting state
legislation will immediately deliver tangible benefits to the new
union as well as strengthen its organizational status (by, for example, outlawing some employer practices or allowing closed-shop

---

[117] In elaborating this example, I want to make a general point. I will consequently ignore
the complexities that would be introduced if one were to consider the impact of actually
existing federal labor legislation.

contracts). Given this incentive modification, it is much more likely that the new union will be successful in an increasing number of states and ultimately will make itself felt on the national level.

There are at least three important lessons that may be drawn from this example. First, the existence of effective local authorities is an independent factor in allowing certain vital interests to organize. Second, the health of the national government crucially depends on the preservation of those local authorities, for otherwise the national government is much more seriously threatened with ossifying into a mouthpiece of a few powerful special interests. And third, if federal legislators are primarily tied to the constituencies that elect them (that is, in practice, to the already—often nationally—organized interest groups in their districts), then they do not have any special incentive to strengthen the state governmental machinery which may be the most important factor in readjusting the local configuration of forces that in turn influences the actions of the national representatives. In fact, the already established national interests, threatened by their new competitors on the local level, may look to their still unbroken power on the national level to remove their competition by a federal preemption mechanism or by causing the national authorities to interfere with the state governmental operations and prevent the victory of their opponents on the local level.[118]

But the most influential protection that the states offer against tyranny is the protection against the special interest of the government itself. For the fact that the federal government may be less likely than the states, in what we may call "normal times," to oppress small minorities whose mode of life offends a homogeneous majority does not mean that it is never likely to oppress them as well as to deprive the citizenry as a whole of their legitimate voice in running the national affairs. Should the federal government ever be captured by an authoritarian movement or assert itself as a special cohesive interest, the resulting oppression would almost certainly be much more severe and durable than that of which any state would be capable. In such a situation, both private individuals and private-interest groups prepared to defend their rights would face very grave organizational obstacles and could not provide any-

---

[118] See Elliott, Ackerman, & Millian, Toward a Theory of Statutory Evolution: The Federalization of Environmental Law, 1 J. L. Econ. Org. 313 (1985).

thing even approaching in effectiveness the resistance that may be offered by a governmental institution, endowed with the power of coercing those who may lack a sufficient individual motivation to contribute (if even only financially) to the common good. It is precisely because the states are governmental bodies that break the national authorities' monopoly on coercion that they constitute the most fundamental bastion against a successful conversion of the federal government into a vehicle of the worst kind of oppression.[119]

Viewed from this perspective, freedom from federal interference enjoyed by state governmental machinery, and especially by those of its organs that potentially provide the easiest means by which the citizenry can organize itself against a tyrannical movement on the national level, turns out to be a value quite independent from any limitation of the federal power to regulate any substantive field of private activity. While traditional liberal doctrine relied quite heavily on the exclusion of government from most private activities and hoped to guard us in this way from tyrannical overreaching, the realization of the pervasiveness of market failures in a complex, advanced society has made the doctrine of *laissez-faire* of less use under modern conditions. Similarly, the increasing interdependence of social and economic problems on the national scale makes

---

[119] Despite all the differences between the American and German federal systems, an interesting lesson supporting our conclusions may perhaps be drawn from the experiences of Germany around the time of the Nazi takeover. In post-Bismarckian Germany, the state of Prussia constituted two-thirds of Germany's territory and three-fifths of its population, and it had its own police force of close to 90,000 men. In 1932, when the Nazi threat was very clear and the German Right embarked on its fateful policy to tame Hitler—the policy that was ultimately to lead to the Nazi seizure of power—the Prussian government was controlled by the Social Democrats intent on entrenching their own power and keeping the Nazis from taking over. Faced with this, the Right, which controlled the central, Reich, government, placed Prussia under martial law, removed the state government, and appointed a special Reich Commissioner to rule by decree. The Prussian government appealed the constitutionality of this move and, after a celebrated trial, the Staatsgerichtshof, despite an apparently Solomonic ruling, failed to preserve the Prussian autonomy. As a consequence, the confidence in Weimar institutions was drastically undermined, the Social Democrats lost the real control of Prussia, and a few months later the Prussian police, under the control of Hermann Goering, was instrumental in the Nazi intimidation of political opposition and enabled Hitler to establish himself as a dictator in Germany. One of his first acts was to destroy the remaining state governments. For the account of the trail, see Bendersky, Carl Schmitt—Theorist for the Reich, 175ff. (1983); for the whole episode, see Grund, "Preussenschlag" und Staatsgerichtshof im Jahre 1932 (1976); for its effect on the Weimar Republic, see Bullock, Hitler: A Study in Tyranny, 214–15 (1964); for the lessons drawn by Germany after World War II, see Fromme, Von der Weimarer Verfassung zum Bonner Grundgesetz, Tuebinger Studien zur Geschichte und Politik, 142–43 (1960).

it unrealistic to expect that the federal government can be kept away from regulating the ever increasing details of what had previously been thought to be essentially local activities. In this situation, when it is no longer an option simply to resist most forms of federal involvement in the private sector, the federalist idea of the separation of the national and local governmental institutions acquires more, and not less, significance for the prevention of governmental oppression.[120] For the independence of the very process of state government, without seriously hampering the national authorities in regulating most private activities, assures the existence of an organizational framework, more efficient than any private institution could provide, that may always be used as an effective tool for bringing together otherwise defenseless individuals with some stakes in resisting the overreaching of the national government. The value of this organizational apparatus thus lies not so much in any of its concrete regulatory activities that the national government could not do as well (or better), as in the very fact that it eliminates the national monopoly on the power to coerce. Moreover, it is this feature of the federal system that distinguishes it most clearly from other forms of decentralization. An intelligently structured unitary national government can probably accommodate the need for local experimentation by giving its local branches a degree of discretion in applying national policies. Such a government may also perhaps draw on local talent or involve many local interests in the formulation of the national policy. But only in a system in which some forms of governmental authority exist independently from one another, and not as emanations from a single source of legitimate power, is the monopoly on coercion truly broken. It seems not unreasonable therefore to see this break as the essence of the American federal system and to acknowledge its

---

[120] The vertical separation characteristic of the federalist system may become even more important under modern conditions, given the evolution of the separation of powers on the national level. For the complexity of the national government's task in contemporary America necessitates a far greater degree of cooperation between the three branches of the national government and often requires that the day-to-day task of regulation be conferred on a whole host of agencies that combine legislative, administrative, and judicial functions. Without denying the continued importance of maintaining the constitutional lines of division between the three branches as well as those between the federal government and the states, the tendency of all governmental institutions to interlock requires an increasingly fine tuning of the constitutional theory to preserve the balance required to avoid governmental oppression. In this situation, the continued neglect of the federalist ideas among constitutional lawyers may be more dangerous today than ever before.

constitutional status, not subject to the vagaries ordinary political arrangements.

2. *The failures of national representation.* The idea that the independence of state political processes is an essential feature of American federalism was, of course, at the heart of *National League of Cities,* although it was largely obfuscated by being draped in the mantle of state sovereignty. And, despite the explicit overruling of *National League of Cities* by *Garcia,* the recognition of the states' role in preventing governmental oppression can not only withstand, but is in fact strengthened, by the process-oriented analysis endorsed in *Garcia.* The extent, however, to which a judicial enforcement of federalist concerns can be incorporated into the *Garcia* rationale depends on how the Court will interpret *Garcia's* focus on failures of the political processes at the national level as the exclusive justification of any future judicial intervention.[121]

What is exactly meant by a "process failure" that *Garcia* makes into a condition of judicial intervention? The easiest answer would be to say that the national political process functions flawlessly, from the constitutional point of view, when the states' formal role in choosing the national representatives (their role in the Senate, in drawing the boundaries of Congressional districts, or in choosing Presidential electors) is not impaired, and that only such an impairment would give grounds for judicial intervention. But this answer—which would simply amount to a repudiation of judicial responsibility in the area of federalism—would represent a very poor application of process jurisprudence, unless one were also to show that there could be no other features of the national political process that could seriously endanger the constitutional function of the states within the federal system. In fact, however, it is rather easy to show that there are very serious incentives built into the very system of national representation that would make the exclusive reliance on the mere composition of the national government for the protection of the states' tyranny-prevention functions quite misplaced. A brief analysis will bring this to light.

The tyranny-prevention functions of state governments that we have identified are, roughly, three (in increasing order of import-

---

[121] "Any substantive restraint on the exercise of Commerce Clause powers . . . must be tailored to compensate for possible failings in the national political process." 105 S.Ct. at 1019–20.

ance): the protection of geographically defined minorities; the facilitation of the expression of those interests that face organizational disadvantages if they have to succeed on a very large scale; and the provision of an organizational framework for resisting a wholesale attack on individual freedoms by the federal government. The question then is whether the role assigned to the states in the composition of the national government is by itself sufficient to prevent those forms of federal interference with state governmental processes that may impede the states in performing the three functions identified.

The least problematic aspect of concentrating on the composition of the federal government is the reliance on the local representation on the federal level for the protection of geographically defined interests. Even if state governments were not available to give expression to such interests, the American system of representation, unlike proportional representation or the British party system, makes the link between a representative and his district into the strongest determinant of his voting behavior.[122] But already with respect to the facilitation of the expression of those interests that are not local in nature, but which may face organizational obstacles if they must succeed over wide geographical areas, the simple fact of local districting will likely not suffice for those interests to make themselves heard. For, as I have argued earlier,[123] large and well-established interests have a definite advantage on the national level, and it is primarily the possibility of using state governmental machinery as a counterweight to the federal government that gives the less well-organized interests their fighting chance. It is therefore not only insufficient for newer interests to count on their capture of a few national representatives to realize their goals but also there are good reasons to believe that the very challenge by newer interests on the local level provides an incentive for the older interests to use their influence on the federal level in order to weaken state governments and thus to disarm their opponents.

This does not mean, of course, that the state governmental ma-

---

[122] For studies of the determinants of congressional voting see Mayhew, Congress: The Electoral Connection (1974); Clansen, How Congressmen Decide: A Policy Focus (1973); Kingdon, Congressmen's Voting Decisions (1973); Miller & Stokes, Constituency Influence in Congress, 57 Am. Pol. Sci. Rev. 45 (1963).

[123] See text *supra* at note 112. See in particular the example given in text following note 117 *supra*.

chinery, with its capacity to propel aspiring politicians to power or its ability to influence the shape of congressional districts, does not have a considerable impact on the behavior of national politicians. Nevertheless, ever since the adoption of the Seventeenth Amendment (providing for direct election of Senators), and in particular during the last thirty years, there has been a marked decrease in the dependence of the national representatives on the processes of local governments and an increase in their reliance on both national and local private interests.[124] There is also, perhaps not accidentally, a radical increase in the federal government's tendency to regulate the states themselves, either through a system of commands or conditional spending, which makes the very operations of state governments increasingly dependent on federal decisions.[125] Faced with this situation, it would be quite fatuous to rely on the mere composition of the federal government as a sufficient defense against a minoritarian ossification on the national level.

Many of the same reasons counsel against the hope that the mere composition of the federal government would protect the states in their role of providing an organizational framework for resisting a potential tyranny by the federal government itself. To be sure, the primary constituencies of the national representatives, along with most of the citizenry, probably have an interest in preventing authoritarian oppression, and, in extraordinary circumstances of a direct authoritarian assault on the constitutional system, those national representatives who might be inclined to resist would also try to lean on state governments for support. But it is also the case that in normal times, in which most of the pressure to erode the independence of the states is exerted, the primary constituencies of the national representatives may, as we have seen, be precisely those that advocate an extension of the federal power to the disadvantage of the states. As one scholar observed, "[N]o one expects Congress to obliterate the states in one fell swoop. If there is any danger, it

---

[124] See Kaden, note 78 *supra*, at 857–68. Among the factors listed by Kaden as influencing this change are: the role of mass media, the decreasing role of the states in shaping electoral districts, the increasing importance of incumbency, the decreasing role of the party machine, the changes in campaign financing, and the increasing role of the federal government.

[125] For a review of this process as well as the empirical studies of it, see ACIR, Regulatory Federalism: Policy, Process, Impact and Reform (1984). The ruling of *National League of Cities*, when still in effect, had only a limited impact of this tendency. *Id.* at 38ff.

lies in the tyranny of small decisions."[126] which may over time remove the states as a force to reckon with in the national politics and prepare the ground for a tyrannical assault. It is thus clear that the national government, even when it operates "normally" and the states' role in its composition is not impaired, is capable of endangering the values underlying the federalist system. But if in all this the national government operates "normally," in what sense can a judicial defense of state interests still be viewed as correcting for a "failure" of the national process, rather than as imposing an external constraint on this process (a constraint rooted, for example, in the Tenth Amendment)?

I have said[127] that it does not strike me as extremely important whether the constitutional protection of federalism is textually rooted in the Tenth Amendment or in the main body of the Constitution. What is more important is that it be anchored in a comprehensive theory of the governmental processes set up by the Constitution and that it provide intelligible standards of adjudication. But with this caveat, it is by no means inappropriate to speak of a "failure" of the national government when its operation undermines the constitutional role of the states. The primary reason for saying this is that, in undermining the states, the federal government at the same time undercuts those very features of the national political process as a whole (both on the state and national level) on which its *own* health crucially depends. To repeat, the main thrust of the states' tyranny-prevention function is to guard against the minoritarian ossification of the national government and the possibility of its tyrannical degeneration. On both these counts, the very representativeness of the federal government and its own robustness depends on whether the states are afforded adequate protection.

To be sure, the "process failure" that I have identified is not a result of any simple "mistake" on the part of the Framers. It rather reflects an inherent tension in our constitutional system between the desire to assure the independence of the federal government from the states and at the same time to preserve the states as vital protectors against national overreaching. It was inadvisable to strengthen the link between the federal representatives and the

---

[126] Tribe, American Constitutional Law 302 (1978).

[127] See the text following note 78 *supra*.

state governments, for this would impair the necessary power of the national authorities, but it was also impossible to rely on the composition of the national government as an exclusive remedy against a federal assault on the states. Still, even if the composition of the national government is inherently biased against important interests of the states, it would be in the name of keeping the federal political process open and healthy that the judiciary would oversee its policies toward the states.

Finally, it should be noted that the more sophisticated concept of process failure under examination is in full accord with the general trend of American process jurisprudence. A comparison that comes to mind would be a judicial decision to scrutinize closely an outcome of the political process that impairs the channels of communication necessary for its own future health or discriminates against minorities that face organizational obstacles in getting a fair share of governmental benefits. In both these cases, as in the case of a federal action endangering the states, it would be impossible to say that, as long as the formal requirements of representation are satisfied, the courts should stay out of the conflict because the process did not fail. For in all such cases, the responsible governmental authorities—designed to fulfill a great variety of tasks and not geared to any one of them exclusively—may occasionally fail with respect to an aspect of their constitutional mission. It is to be hoped therefore that *Garcia*'s focus on the political process at the federal level will not be misunderstood and undermine its promise of a new jurisprudence of federalism.[128]

B. PROVIDING A SPACE FOR PARTICIPATORY POLITICS

The value of citizen participation in governmental operations has often been stressed in legal literature and its enhancement has often

---

[128] *Garcia* itself clearly accepts the possibility that the process failure required for judicial intervention may be of the kind we have identified, for its statement that "[a]ny substantive restraint on the exercise of Commerce Clause powers . . . must be tailored to compensate for possible failings in the national political process" is made in response to (and acknowledgment of) the argument that the "changes in the structure of the Federal Government . . . since 1789, not the least of which . . . the adoption of the Seventeenth Amendment . . . may work to alter the influence of the States in the federal political process." 105 S.Ct. at 1019–20. If the only cognizable process failure were to consist in depriving the states of their formal representation required by the Constitution, it would be, of course, impossible to argue that the adoption of the Seventeenth Amendment (which is an integral part of the Constitution) could lead to any process failure in this restrictive sense.

been viewed as one of the most important purposes of federalism.[129] But the objectives of citizen participation are usually seen as clustered around such things as the facilitation of the flow of information between the citizens and the government, improving the efficiency of governmental decisions, and the enhancement of the accountability of public officials or of the public acceptance of governmental decisions.[130] Viewed in this way, citizen participation appears, above all, as a means of strengthening the representativeness of governmental institutions and enhancing the perception of its legitimacy.[131] This view has much to recommend it and fits quite well with the general inclination of the proponents of process jurisprudence to focus on the role of undistorted representation for the expression of the will of the majority; nonetheless, the view ignores the independent significance of citizen participation that may have been one of the controlling considerations in the Framers' thinking about federalism. In this context, citizen participation is understood as a separate process of direct self-government, quite distinct from the very idea of representative democracy.

1. *Representation-enhancing participation.* Even in arguing that citizen participation strengthens and legitimizes the representativeness of governmental institutions—that is, in viewing participation primarily as a means rather than the end of political life—the legal literature remains most often at a common-sense, largely anecdotal level of analysis that tends to ignore much of other disciplines' (above all, political science's) learning on the subject and is likely to miss some of the less obvious problems with its arguments.[132] The

---

[129] See, *e.g.*, FERC v. Mississippi, 456 U.S. 742, 789 (1982) (opinion of O'Connor, J.). For the most extensive treatment in legal literature, see Advisory Commission on Intergovernmental Relations, Citizen Participation in the American Federal System (1979) (hereafter cited as ACIR, Citizen Participation).

[130] See, *e.g.*, ACIR, Citizen Participation, at 2, 62–64.

[131] It is in this way that the concept of participation functions in Ely's version of the process theory. Ely defines the goals of participation as those of the "broadened access to the processes and bounty of representative government." Ely, note 70 *supra*, at 74. See also *id.* at 75, footnote. An exception to such an instrumental view of participation in legal literature may be found in Frug, The City as a Legal Concept, 93 Harv. L. Rev. 1057 (1980).

[132] The level of sophistication of the legal literature on the subject is not, however, uniformly low. Thus, for example, the ACIR study on Citizen Participation, while making little use of the more theoretical sources, contains a wealth of interesting data and insightful analyses. But no effort is made in the ACIR study to relate this to the constitutional dimension of federalism. The constitutional problems of federalism are to some extent addressed in another ACIR study, Regulatory Federalism: Policy, Process, Impact and Reform (1984), but with little attention to the issue of participation.

operative assumption in most of these discussions is, again, that
the government should serve the interests of the people and that the
"closer" it remains to the people, the better it is likely to succeed.
Citizen participation being the method of involving the people directly in the affairs of the government, it must be a good idea.

Undoubtedly, there is much truth in these observations but also
much that is problematic. Even if we do not question the assumption that the interest of the "people" is ultimately identical to the
interest of individuals,[133] it is by no means clear that individuals
themselves are best able to articulate the types of considerations
that will most affect their interests or identify the decisions that will
maximize them.[134] In fact, one of the basic tenets of the classical
theory of representation is that it is both wasteful and dangerous for
the masses to busy themselves with the complex matters of policy
making that may be better handled by professional politicians who
choose this as their full-time occupation.[135] Naturally, a certain
element of outside control on the political process is necessary for
preventing its authoritarian degeneration, but what the required
level of such control is and who will best exercise it are matters of
considerable complexity. While there is not much controversy
among political scientists that the electoral process plays an important role in this respect,[136] even on this score there is much evidence
that the extent of popular participation in elections is not necessarily a sign of the government's political health or legitimacy.[137]
There are also persuasive arguments that too much electoral control
may in some situations unproductively divert the efforts of the
legislators[138] or make them systematically ignore those issues that

---

[133] For the problematic nature of the concept of the "people," see, *e.g.*, Schumpeter,
Capitalism, Socialism, and Democracy 250ff. (1947).

[134] *Ibid.*

[135] See Mill, Essays on Politics and Culture, 17 (Himmelfarb ed.) (1963); see also Sartori,
Democratic Theory (1962) (although Sartori may misrepresent the "classical" theory, his
own view is very much in point). *Cf.* Lippmann, Public Opinion 251ff. (1965 ed.); Schumpeter, note 128 *supra*, at 295; Berelson, Lazarsfeld & McPhee, Voting: A Study of Opinion
Formation in a Presidential Campaign 314–15 (1954).

[136] See Dahl, A Preface to Democratic Theory, *passim*, but esp. at 125ff. (1956).

[137] Lipset, Political Man: The Social Bases of Politics, 216–19. Chapter VI, at 179–219,
contains a wealth of data on this issue. These data are not entirely unambiguous and do not
mean, of course, that disenfranchisement, as opposed to actual nonparticipation, does not
lead to the neglect of the interests that cannot make themselves felt at the polls.

[138] For evidence that Congressmen spend a staggering portion of their time on reelection
concerns, see Mayhew, Congress. The Electoral Connection (1974), passim.

do not provide an immediate payoff at the polls—even though they may have an ultimately greater impact on the electorate's welfare.[139] Moreover, many electoral systems that seemingly provide a more adequate and more direct representation to a greater variety of interests in fact lead to less governmental stability, decreased efficiency, and shakier long-term legitimacy.[140] Finally, it is not difficult to conceive of situations in which a competent bureaucrat, operating in a clear hierarchical structure in which he expects to make his career, may do a much better job at serving the public than a politician directly responsible to the electorate.[141]

If even with respect to the electoral process, the degree of citizen participation is subject to much controversy, there are still more serious doubts as to other forms of citizen involvement. The basic problem with many forms of direct citizen involvement is that while we may accept the individuals' welfare as the ultimate object of good government, the identification of the "people" with the sum of the individuals composing it is too simplistic. In the same way as I have argued that only the proper appreciation of the special role of political and governmental institutions can allow us to understand the design of our constitutional system,[142] it can also be argued that the extragovernmental social fabric crucially depends on a variety of structures or processes that may have a more or less concrete institutional existence but which all have their own interests and claims that must be taken into account. Unions, corporations, churches, families, educational institutions, consumer organizations, and others simply cannot be reduced to the individuals who compose them for the very reason they are often formed is because the interests they represent and the functions they fulfill cannot be adequately pursued by uncoordinated individuals.[143] One of the most influential trends in political science has been to think of

---

[139] Ibid. See also *infra* note 175 and accompanying text.

[140] Lipset, note 137 *supra*, at 45–46, 179ff.

[141] Lawyers often make arguments of this kind against the elective judiciary. But the problem is equally apparent in other areas and does not depend only on the need for expertise. See also text at note 175 *infra*.

[142] See Part III.B.2 *supra*.

[143] We have considered the reasons why institutions are necessary for the achievement of public goods. See text at notes 101–3 *supra*. A classic work explaining the particular significance of the institutions mentioned in the text is Tocqueville's Old Regime and the French Revolution (1955).

society as a collection of groups, rather than of individuals, vying
for political influence, and it is the pressure of those groups that is
often seen as the most effective form of outside control of governmental abuse.[144] But if this view is seriously considered, the problem of assuring the representativeness of political institutions is by
no means solved by uncritically striving for increased citizen participation. For while some forms of outside influence and control
(and hence participation) must be assured for the government to be
legitimately representative, it is clear that the direct involvement of
individual citizens is not always, or even most often, the best way
of achieving this. It would be at least not surprising if many of the
basic institutional concerns, on which the individuals' welfare ultimately depends, were to be in fact neglected or diluted within the
framework of directly participatory politics.

2. *Participation as an independent value.* All the foregoing complexities concerning the relation between participation and representation are no more than that—complexities that must be taken into
consideration, but that do not in a wholesale fashion invalidate the
idea that citizen participation has an important role to play in the
process of representative democratic politics and that the governmental decentralization characteristic of the American federal system may be one of the principal constitutional means of assuring
the desired level of citizen involvement. But in order to transform
this idea into a full-fledged argument, the legal profession would
have to conduct a much more detailed inquiry into the way in
which the political institutions set up by the Constitution are supposed to accommodate the participatory elements of the political
process and to establish how the Constitution resolves the tension
between the disruptive and the constructive aspects of participation
in a representative democratic system.

While the task just mentioned is beyond the ambitions of this
paper, citizen participation may also be viewed quite independently from the mechanics of representation. This view is directly
related to the ideas of federalism.

The model of representative politics rests on the idea that the
main task of political institutions consists in providing a method of
selecting a social policy that reflects in a fair and acceptable manner

---

[144] See, *e.g.*, Truman, The Governmental Process (1951); Dahl, Dilemmas of Pluralist
Democracy (1982).

the preferences and interests of those groups or individuals who are members of a given political society.[145] What is distinctive in this model is its essentially atomistic conception of society in which the basic interests of social actors do not derive from their being members of the political community and in which the government serves an essentially instrumental function of aggregating the actors' primary preferences into social policies.

Against this representative model, the model of participatory government, which goes as far back as Aristotle, views political activity not as instrumental toward achieving a proportionate share in the distribution of available resources, to be used in a variety of private pursuits, but rather as a good in itself, something essentially implicated in the very concept of human freedom. This way of thinking, which stresses the role of the community in the very shaping of the "interests" of its members and in infusing their lives with a sense of purpose, was by no means absent from the thought of the Founding Fathers. To be sure, the Framers were very strongly influenced by the liberal theories of Locke and de Montesquieu, which placed a high value on the individualistic ideal of liberty understood as freedom from politics that would allow men to focus on the private pursuit of happiness and salvation. This, and the Founders' realization of the difficulty of devising meaningful and workable participatory institutions in a modern society, operating on a very large, national scale, are clearly responsible for their choice of the representative model as, by and large, the most appropriate form of government on the federal level. As we have seen, they also thought of the representative federal model as a way of checking the potentially illiberal tendencies of the more homogeneous political life on the local level (an area in which the federal government has been particularly active since the adoption of the Civil War Amendments)[146] and as a check on the danger of balkani-

---

[145] For a comprehensive argument that the very concept of representation, so understood, may be quite problematic on its own terms and that every widely used method of aggregating individual preferences into social choices underdetermines the ultimate outcome and lends itself to extensive manipulation, see the seminal work of Arrow, Social Choice and Individual Values (1951). Arrow's work in turn gave rise to a very extensive literature that has unfortunately had only a minimal impact on the legal profession. For a review of some of that literature, see Barry & Hardin, Rational Man and Irrational Society? (1982), Part II.

[146] For a discussion of the differential impact of the state and federal authorities with respect to the protection of individual rights, see text following note 115 *supra*.

zation inherent in local autonomy. But it does not take very much effort or perspicacity to notice that the Founding Fathers did not look forward to a society reduced to atomistic pursuits of individual well-being, nor did they, like many liberals, see the extragovernmental sphere of "civil society" (such as private associations, churches, and interest groups) as the exclusive locus where the social aspirations of individuals are realized. On the contrary, their ever present concern with what they called public, civic, or "republican" virtue testifies clearly to their belief that the "good life," as Aristotle would have termed it, involves a commitment to a political community and participation in a process by which individuals shape in common the mode of life they are going to share. Not only is it not unlikely that the Framers were familiar with the extremely influential work of Rousseau and not only did they aspire to recreate some of the features and glory of the ancient republics (which had relied much more on participation than representation) but also the most indigenous American political tradition, especially but not exclusively in the North, was inextricably linked to the idea of direct popular control over the matters involving the life of each locality.[147] It should then be by no means surprising if, given the limited possibility of direct participation on the national level, the Framers envisaged the states, and particularly their subdivisions, as the most fertile ground for the development of the alternative political processes, responsive to the need for participatory forms of political life.[148]

The tie between the idea of federalism and that of preserving the public space of participatory politics cannot, however, rely exclusively on the Framers' assumptions, but must also correspond to the realities of contemporary American politics. Even a cursory look at the modern political scene is enough to convince one that state governments are very different from the Greek *agora* or the *forum* of the early republican Rome and that representation is a standard feature of each state's political life. There have even been some arguments that it is the states, rather than the federal government, that have most interfered with those local bodies, such as

---

[147] See Frug, note 131 *supra*, at 1095ff., and the sources cited therein.

[148] The most radical expression of the Framers' endorsement of local participatory politics may be found in Jefferson's famous proposal for the "ward system." See his letter to Samuel Kercheval of July 13, 1816.

municipal governments, in which participatory politics could still be realistically envisaged in the modern world.[149] Nevertheless, these observations do not necessarily undermine the link between federalism and participatory ideals.

First of all, if there is some genuine room for noninstrumental participation in American political life, it can realistically exist only on the local level. There have been some efforts to devise new means, using modern communications technology, of reviving participatory politics on a large scale,[150] but the dominant view is that the optimum size of a political body that can afford significant citizen participation is nowhere near the size of the modern nation state or even of its main provincial subdivisions.[151] Whatever else may be obscure, it also seems clear that within our political structure, practically all the local political bodies that may be suitable for the development of participatory politics function under the umbrellas of state governments. Even if these bodies are often hampered by state governments run on a representative model, the remedy for this cannot come at the federal constitutional level (though at the state level, constitutional as well as political solutions may be sought). Thus, if the protection of the participatory political processes does indeed rise to the federal constitutional level, it must take the form of limiting federal interference with the governmental operations run under the auspices of the states, although it might be focused on checking particularly those forms of federal action that interfere with the institutions run on the participatory model.[152]

Secondly, the existence of participatory politics on the state level and on the level of state subdivisions is by no means a fiction. From

[149] Frug, note 131 *supra*, at 1059.

[150] See Barber, Strong Democracy: Participatory Politics for a New Age (1984), esp. at 261 *et seq.* and the sources cited therein.

[151] See Dahl, The City in the Future of Democracy, 61 Am. Pol. Sci. Rev. 953 (1967).

[152] It might be noted in this context that however faulty was the identification of the governmental processes protected by the rule of the *National League of Cities*, the immunity established in that case was extended not only to the highest organs of state governments but also to their local emanations, such as townships and municipalities. 426 U.S. at 855 n.20. Had the Court decided this issue primarily on the ground of state "sovereignty," it would have been likely to track more closely the Eleventh Amendment jurisprudence, which refused to extend sovereign immunity to the local units on the county and municipal level. See Mt. Healthy City School Dist. v. Doyle, 429 U.S. 274, 277–79 (1977); Lincoln County v. Luning, 133 U.S. 529 (1980).

a comprehensive study, based on a number of empirical surveys, by the Advisory Commission on Intergovernmental Relations,[153] there emerges a picture of interlocking participatory institutions at all levels of government, with a particular success on the local level. To begin with, the study shows, the most traditional American mechanism of participatory democracy—the town meeting—is very much alive in a large section of the country, extending significantly beyond New England.[154] The levels of attendance at these meetings are quite high, especially where they have a significant role in the budgetary process and school matters. Further, throughout the country, there is significant citizen involvement in the local planning process, school boards, the budget process, and other governmental functions. Among the techniques used to foster participation are a set of hearing mechanisms, volunteer programs, conferences, opinion-polling mechanisms, open meeting and records laws, drop-in centers, hot lines, as so on.[155] Finally, a special role of the most powerful tool of direct government on a larger scale—the referendum—must be mentioned. The referendum exists in some form in forty-two states, of which thirty-eight allow referenda on the local level. Most of these states leave room for citizen-initiated referenda, and in seventeen states the state constitution may be amended through this process (other states requiring citizen-approved conventions). In thirty-nine states statutory laws are, or may be, subject to popular ratification.[156] In a large measure, these referenda were designed (mostly during the Progressive era) to permit direct citizen involvement in the governing process, and, in addition to allowing the bypassing of the representative system, offer an important incentive for the citizens to keep abreast of the substantive issues in the political life of their communities. While the federal government is by no means always hostile to some forms of citizen participation, its own attempts at creating more room for it are, by and large, much less successful than the practices of the states and largely rely on the opportunities provided by state institutions.[157]

---

[153] ACIR, Citizen Participation, passim, but see esp. chs. 3, 5.

[154] Id. at 238–39. Town meetings are used in portions of twenty states, principally in New England, mid-Atlantic and midwestern states.

[155] Id., esp. at 65.

[156] Id. at 247–49.

[157] Id. at 3–6 and ch. 4.

If one of the primary functions, within the federalist framework, of state-run institutions is to provide the public space for participatory politics, then from this point of view federalism does not conceive the division between the state and national governments as a way of parceling out "sovereignty"—the control over substantive fields of regulation—but rather as a way of preserving alternative modes of decision making. Naturally, the vitality of the participatory state institutions depends in part on the types of substantive decisions that are left for the states. Should the federal government preempt them from most fields that touch directly on the life of local communities, the states would become but empty shells within which no meaningful political activity could take place. But whatever the effect of preemption, the principles of federalism provide an important and independent reason for protecting the autonomy of the political processes of local governments, and this not just in the name of democratic control (for the federal government is also subject to such control), but also in the name of protecting a different form of political space that the national government is very unlikely to provide.

Viewed from this perspective, federalism is not entirely of one piece with liberal individualism and its ideology of privacy and individual rights.[158] To be sure, the fear of national power, unchecked by local authority, was inextricably linked in the Framers' mind with the fear of what they called "tyranny"; federalism, like separation of powers, was one of the whole panoply of institutional devices to protect individual rights.[159] Yet it is not correct to view federalism as nothing more than yet another expression of the American commitment to pluralism. On the contrary, federalism seems to be at least partially inspired by an ideal of a tightly knit community of persons who share each other's values and concerns and for whom politics does not resolve to a periodical exercise of voting rights but rather stands for the most general expression of their common aspirations. For this reason, it should come as no surprise that throughout the course of postrevolutionary American history the banner of "state rights" was more often than not raised in opposition to the individualistic ideology of traditional liberal-

---

[158] For a discussion of the conflict between liberalism and the idea of participatory democracy within our political system, see Frug, note 131 *supra*.

[159] See *supra*, section IV A.

ism. It was populism, rather than liberalism, as well as the defense of a peculiar, provincial mode of life that found the ideology of federalism useful and congenial.[160] This fact is more than a coincidence, for a protest against the centralization of political authority, far from being a liberal monopoly, has been a standard feature of most conservative as well as romantic or populist ideologies opposed to the impersonal character of modern states.[161] The Constitution is not an exclusively liberal product, however; its greatness and durability may in fact lie in finding a way to accommodate a variety of values and political visions that have exploded many other societies.

3. *Judicial enforcement.* As in the case of the states' tyranny-prevention function, *Garcia*'s focus on the national political process makes the future of any judicial protection of the states' role as providers of a space for participatory politics depend on whether it can be conceptualized as a correction of some process failure on the federal level. There is, again, no doubt that the structure of the national government manifests an unavoidable and intentional bias that makes it unlikely to do justice to the constitutional importance of participatory politics. The federal government was clearly designed to channel the pluralist interest politics through a system of representation, and its ability to accommodate the need for citizen participation is quite limited. Insofar as participatory local institutions also have a representation-enhancing function and aid in legitimizing governmental institutions in general, there is, of course, some pressure on the national government to maintain them. Also, as I have shown,[162] the different mechanics of representation on the state and national levels result in the two governments having different constituencies whose interests are, from time to time, likely to clash. Consequently, the more established interest groups, which are usually more influential on the national level, may very well view favorably a federal policy of fostering direct participatory institutions on the state level since that may

---

[160] As opposed to the more explicitly political uses of federalism, the judicial enforcement of state rights, in such cases as those cited in notes 43 and 44, was often viewed as motivated by *laissez-faire* liberalism. See Corwin, The Commerce Power versus States' Rights (1936).

[161] For a discussion of the dangers that the ideal of a tightly knit community may represent for individual rights and the role of the federal government in protecting them, see text at note 116 *supra*.

[162] See text following note 116 *supra* and text at notes 122–26 *supra*.

generally diminish the effectiveness with which any special interest groups may use the state apparatus for their own purposes and thus decrease the competition for the groups well entrenched on the federal level.[163] But, on the whole, it would be too much to expect that such factors would be enough to make the federal government properly attuned to the needs of local participation. The requirements of long-term legitimacy are more than likely to be sacrificed for the perceived efficiency of short-term measures inimical to local autonomy. It is equally likely that an intermittent special-interest pressure would result in federal solicitude for participatory citizen involvement in the least appropriate aspects of local politics.[164] Consequently, the protection of the participatory processes of local government must come in part at least from judicial supervision over the outcomes of national politics.

It may be possible to characterize the inability of the national political process to protect fully the participatory function of local government as a "failure" of this process. It is much harder, however, to claim that the aim of scrutinizing the outcomes of the national process in this area is to protect the health of the federal government itself. Insofar as citizen participation can be said to have a representation-enhancing role, an argument of this kind could be quite persuasive. But insofar as citizen participation is an independent constitutional value, it would be somewhat disingenuous to try to argue for it in the same way. An alternative justification would thus probably be more appropriate.

I have said that the federalist concern with state participatory institutions is not of one piece with the liberal ideology underlying other parts of the Constitution. There is, however, one point that the two views share—the idea of limiting the sovereignty of the national government in favor of the associational rights of individ-

---

[163] This will be so because participation, understood as a form of direct self-government, relies on an unimpeded access of individuals to the political process and thus dilutes the advantage that any organized groups enjoy in a representative system. Thus, to go back to my previous example, if the organizers of a new white-collar union hope to strengthen themselves by capturing a state agency dealing with labor issues, the employers and the old union can, by transforming the agency into a wide-open participatory institution (for example, through pressing the federal government to "open up the machine-dominated state bodies") significantly lessen the agency's value to the new union. What this shows, incidentally, is that the states' participation-enhancing function may sometimes be in conflict with their tyranny-prevention function.

[164] See the immediately preceding note.

uals. While it has been a rather common tendency in our legal system to think of institutions on the model of individuals and to neglect the peculiar character of collective entities, there is nevertheless a significant body of constitutional law derivatively protecting private associations from governmental interference that could destroy those institutions. Liberals consider this jurisprudence to be particularly important not only for aiding resistance to governmental oppression but also for leaving sufficient room for individuals to develop the forms of life they consider meaningful. Perhaps because liberals have traditionally viewed governmental bodies as playing no more than an instrumental role and because they usually associated them with a threat to—rather than a forum for—the realization of individual aspirations, no corresponding body of constitutional law has ever developed for the protection of the associational values that may inhere in public, governmental institutions, especially when they are not protected by the usual mantle of state sovereignty. Thus, if the shibboleth of state sovereignty is finally discarded, as it should be, there is a distinct need to revitalize those aspects of the Bill of Rights that may be used to protect the autonomy of state political processes. Whether such need may be best accommodated through a reading of the First or the Tenth (or even the Ninth) Amendment is not of particular importance. But an additional benefit of doing this may be a development of a body of law geared to the peculiar claims to process integrity that institutions in general could raise within our constitutional system, rather than dealing with all limitations of national sovereignty through the prism of individual rights.

If what I have said so far is accepted, then certain features of the *National League of Cities* decision acquire a very special significance not sufficiently brought out in that case. The rule formulated there singles out the very integrity of the political processes of local governments as a value quite independent of any outcomes that these processes generate, and the rationale of that rule need no longer depend entirely on the type of protection of which only governmental institutions could avail themselves in the past. Instead, it brings the federalist ideas within the general orbit of a theory of limited representative government and points to the special role of associational values in the political structure of American democracy. In this context, one of the basic purposes of federalism is to assure that, insofar as politics is per se an indispensable communal component of the good life, the nationalization of political decision making does not deprive the communities and individuals of an essential sphere of their self-realization. Freedom to participate in government, rather than freedom from government, is the issue at stake. The meaning of some activity's being "local" does not lie in its being "reserved for the states" or apt to be more efficiently handled by a local authority but in the fact that, unlike most national issues, it is being handled by a participatory institution.

C. LABORATORIES OF EXPERIMENT

Courts as well as commentators are very fond of repeating Justice Brandeis's dictum that "[i]t is one of the happy incidents of the federal system that a single courageous state may, if its citizens choose, serve as a laboratory; and try novel social and economic experiments without risk to the rest of the country."[165] While the context of Justice Brandeis's remark had nothing to do with protecting the states from Congressional interference[166] and while his point concerned only an "incident" of the federal system, the claim that the states constitute "national laboratories of experiment" came to be viewed by many as a cornerstone of the federalist thinking and has quickly become one of the least examined verities of constitutional theory. Only recently has there been some scholarly effort to assess the accuracy of this claim,[167] and the most that can be said is that the jury is still out.

The importance attached by many to the states' function as laboratories of experiment is at least in part exaggerated and, in any case, of little significance for constitutional adjudication. This is true for three reasons. First, whether a strong protection of the states' autonomy would actually contribute to the efficiency of the American government is a very complex question that does not admit of an easy answer. In fact, there are many arguments to the contrary. Second, insofar as there is something to the laboratory-of-experiment argument, a unitary government could avail itself of

---

[165] New State Ice Co. v. Liebman, 285 U.S. 262, 311 (1932) (Brandeis, J., dissenting).

[166] At stake in *Liebman* was a due process claim by an individual against the state of Oklahoma.

[167] A list of the most important works on the subject may be found in Mashaw & Rose-Ackerman, Federalism and Regulation, in The Reagan Regulatory Strategy: An Assessment 111–52 (Eads & Fix eds.) (1984).

the same advantages by a partial delegation of authority to its local branches, so that there may be nothing in the laboratory rationale that is peculiarly related to the federal structure of American government. Finally, even if it turns out that decentralization does contribute to governmental efficiency, the analysis necessary to determine which aspects of local governance should be protected from central interference is of a very complex and largely pragmatic nature and thus unsuitable either for elevation to the constitutional level or for judicial assessment. In sum, then, in developing their federalist jurisprudence, the courts should concentrate on the other, more fundamental state functions within the federal framework: the protection against tyranny and the provision of a space for participatory politics.

We should begin with the observation that if the laboratory-of-experiment argument were fully accepted, it would be hard to limit its conclusions to the protection of the internal mode of state governmental operations, as proposed by *National League of Cities*, and not to apply them to the states' control over the private sector. After all, to take the facts of *National League of Cities* as an example, the imposition of minimum-wage requirements for private hospitals reduces the possibility of state experimentation (to say nothing of private experimentation) in this area no less than in the case of public hospitals. Indeed, the very possibility of federal preemption of the regulation of any field of private activity decreases the possibility of state-introduced innovation. Thus, unless we are seriously prepared to consider reversing the long tradition of the Commerce Clause jurisprudence and go back to the idea of preserving some areas of exclusive state regulation, the laboratory-of-experiment argument proves too much.[168]

---

[168] It is, of course, possible to say that direct regulation of state governmental processes not only affects the possibility of experimentation in one area but also depletes state resources that could be used to experiment elsewhere. See Justice O'Connor's argument in her dissent in FERC v. Mississippi, 456 U.S. 742, 786–87 (1982). But quite apart from the fact that, to the extent that any inefficient regulation is bound to decrease the tax base of the state, the same also seems to be true in the case of federal regulation of private activities, it is also true that, so long as the federal government is prepared to back its commands with some monetary incentives, the states are free to move their previously committed financial resources elsewhere and the federal government may acquire less control over local behavior by trying to use the state administrative machinery for its own programs than in the case of an outright preemption. See Rose-Ackerman, Cooperative Federalism and Co-optation, 92 Yale L.J. 1344, 1347 (1983).

On closer scrutiny, however, the laboratory-of-experiment argument may turn out to prove not too much but too little. It is, of course, quite intuitive and largely true that a locally made decision, in the absence of countervailing factors, has a good chance of being better adapted to local conditions. Similarly, when there are many independent centers of decision and no countervailing factors, chances are that this very fact may increase the probability of an innovative solution being adopted somewhere that may then be taken over by others. But the caveats about there being no countervailing factors present are important. Both theoretical and empirical studies show that Justice Brandeis's offhand confidence that the states may engage in interesting experiments "without risk to rest of the country"[169] may be quite unfounded. There are, in fact, a number of different considerations that have only rarely been taken into account in assessing the laboratory-of-experiment argument but without which its validity cannot be ascertained. The following list is probably incomplete, but it may suffice to force a reconsideration:

a). If, as has been argued, the states are political units that may have their justification in history but do not necessarily correspond to the economic and social realities of contemporary America,[170] then the forces that determine the direction of local policies may be much less than ideally suited to foster the most efficient governmental solutions. A central government possessed of a power to reshuffle the boundaries and powers of its territorial subdivisions could perhaps produce much better (more efficient) local administration.

b). State regulation is often likely to have spillover effects on other states and produce inefficient solutions by ignoring the costs borne by outsiders. Again, a central government may tailor its delegations of regulatory powers to jurisdictions designed to minimize such externalities.[171]

c). States will often compete with one another for various resources, such as capital, which can move relatively easily to those

---

[169] Note 165 *supra*.

[170] See note 39 *supra*.

[171] Rose-Ackerman, Does Federalism Matter? Political Choice in a Federal Republic, 89 J. of Pol. Econ. 152–65 (1981). The spillover effects Rose-Ackerman talks about arise when one state adopts a policy that imposes costs on other states or creates differential costs of doing business in different states and causes a migration of capital from one state to another.

jurisdictions that offer them the most favorable conditions. As a by-product of this rivalry, however, states may have to forgo many redistributive and social programs that make the cost of doing business higher.[172] These programs, in addition to being otherwise socially desirable, may also in the long run raise productivity and contribute to better business efficiency, but no state may be able to afford them in the short run and all will be reduced to the lowest common denominator.[173] A central government capable of devising national solutions can afford to be much more innovative in such situations.

d). The costs involved in certain types of innovative regulatory activity (such as the costs of collecting and transmitting information or administering a program) may be too high for a local government to bear, but economies of scale on the national level may make regulations more cost effective.[174] Of particular importance here is the comparative quality of state and federal officials, bureaucrats, and administrators. The increased cost of competence, which may be too high for a state agency, may result in much more innovative solutions on the federal level. The lower quality of local bureaucrats may also contribute to their greater corruptibility.

e). Related to the previous point is the question of incentives that local elective politicians may have, as compared to a professional looking to improve his career prospects in a national bureaucratic hierarchy.[175] While many are prepared to manifest a knee-jerk preference for a politician subject to electoral control over a "faceless bureaucrat," the former's incentives to innovate are significantly reduced by his desire for reelection. First, unlike a competitive economic market, the federal system does not allow a local official to "sell" his product (i.e., to gain additional votes) outside his jurisdiction, and this limits his incentive to innovate. Second, the fact that beneficiaries of governmental innovation do not, as a rule,

---

[172] Mashaw & Rose-Ackerman, note 167 *supra*, at 117–18.

[173] Problems with local child-labor laws under the regime of Hammer v. Dagenhart, 247 U.S. 251 (1918), and the resulting clamor for a constitutional amendment, are a good historical example of these drawbacks of local control.

[174] Mashaw & Rose-Ackerman, note 163 *supra*, at 118.

[175] For a more complete discussion of this subject see Rose-Ackerman, Risk Taking and Reelection: Does Federalisms Promote Innovation? 9 J. Legal Stud. 593–616 (1980). The reader may have by now observed how much the author owes to the work of Professor Susan Rose-Ackerman.

move from one jurisdiction to another, so as to find the one in which the government's willingness to take risks matches their own preferences, the politician's "portfolio" of governmental projects will tend to cater to the risk preferences of those around the population median (rather than gravitating toward more risky innovations). Third, the possibility of free riding on the innovative solutions of other jurisdictions further reduces a politician's incentive to take new and more risky paths. Compared to that, a career bureaucrat, looking to the approval of his superiors and the effects of his work in a well-designed national hierarchy of administrators may (though, of course, only may) have a system of incentives more favorable to innovation.

f). Finally, the advantages of uniformity may often outweigh the benefits of local innovation, even if some local solutions may have more intrinsic merit.[176] Thus, for example, all states, except for Louisiana, have recognized the advantages of adopting the Uniform Commercial Code. But similar advantages to commerce could perhaps accrue from a uniformity in at least parts of tort or insurance law. Again, a central government, not subject to local political or constitutional constraints, could probably be much more efficient in this respect.

The considerations just listed do not, of course, mean that the function of the states as the laboratories of experiment is entirely illusory.[177] They do mean, however, that the question of how to structure the division of competences among different levels of government to achieve the most desirable degree of innovation and efficiency is a very complex one and that the answer to it hinges on a variety of empirical and constantly shifting factors. It is thus quite likely that some forms of unitary government, with a flexible system of delegation that would not be limited by constitutional provisions concerning the structure of local authorities, could accommodate much better the demands of governmental efficiency than our own federal system. It is, of course, possible that the question of

---

[176] See Mashaw & Rose-Ackerman, note 163 *supra*, 118–20.

[177] Nor does the list given here pretend to be complete. On a more general level, for example, it has been argued by one commentator that federalism simply delayed national regulation of business in the United States and helped perpetuate racist acts but had no long-run impact on the character of national legislation. Riker, Federalism in 5 Handbook of Political Science 154–56 (1975).

governmental efficiency may have its constitutional dimensions. The basic structure of government, which determines the nature of the political pressures to which a government is primarily responsive, is also decisive as to whether the operations of that government will produce efficient results. But what seems doubtful is that governmental efficiency is among the primary functions of our constitutional division of authority between the states and the federal government. Quite to the contrary, if my analyses of the role to be played by the states in protecting the citizens from the dangers of governmental oppression and in providing a public space for participatory politics are correct, then the protection of these constitutional functions of the states requires that a certain price be paid for them in terms of a degree of governmental inefficiency. To the extent that the federal structure of government also allows for state experimentation that may prove beneficial, this fact is, as Justice Brandeis said, "one of the happy incidents of the federal system" rather than its basic justification.

There is, moreover, a significant price to be paid for misjudging the role of governmental efficiency in the process of federalism-related constitutional adjudication. As in every complex area of constitutional adjudication, the text of the Constitution does not by itself unambiguously control the outcome of judicial decisions—an interpretation of the text is always necessary to resolve the questions presented. But if the laboratory-of-experiment argument becomes a basic tool for interpreting the federalism-related provisions of the text, the resulting harm will not be limited to the neglect of the more important functions of the states within the federal system. First, it is unlikely that the courts could really collect all the relevant information and make the cost-benefit analysis necessary for striking a proper balance between the advantages of decentralization and the need for intergovernmental coordination. They will therefore more likely resort to abstract legal rules that would ignore the complex empirical factors involved and ultimately harm more than help the very cause of governmental efficiency. Second, while the political process may be far from flawless in responding to the demands of efficiency, the legitimacy of judicial intervention is usually at its lowest when the courts occupy themselves with primarily economic concerns. In fact, the very perception that the Supreme Court was involved in such policy choices was a signifi-

cant factor in the resistance to much of its federalism-related jurisprudence.[178] Third, even if the courts were able to do justice to the
complexities of the cost-benefit analysis of decentralization, it is
doubtful that considerations of this kind should be allowed to rise
to the constitutional level, for the shifting nature of most of the
factors involved makes the decisions at hand more a matter of ad
hoc managerial accommodation than one of a principled resolution
that could endure over time. To be sure, even in the process of
constitutional adjudication, the courts cannot be entirely blind to
the question of the efficiency of the policies they scrutinize. But as
in other areas of constitutional adjudication, the courts should
largely defer to legislative assessments of such matters and focus on
other, more properly judicial concerns.

V. FUTURE DOCTRINAL DEVELOPMENTS

The outcome of my discussion is that the process-oriented
analysis of the constitutional functions of federalism, endorsed but
not really carried out in the *Garcia* decision, leads to a more
affirmative procedural role of the states within the federal system
than suggested on the face of Justice Blackmun's opinion. Also, two
important functions of the states—tyranny prevention and the provision of a space for participatory politics—are likely to be en-
dangered by the national government and warrant a close judicial
scrutiny of federal interference with state and local governmental
operations. To some extent, then, my analysis confirms the accuracy of the insights implicit in *National League of Cities* by showing
that its insistence on the protection of the political process of local
governments, rather than on a guarantee of some exclusive state
controls over the private sector, responded to the most fundamental
desiderata of federalism, while also showing that some of these
insights need not be viewed as incompatible with the *Garcia* approach.

Nevertheless, developing a constitutional theory of federalism
does not automatically translate into a clear judicial doctrine specifying a set of genuinely manageable standards of review. In fact, it
is the problematic character of such standards that occupies the
bulk of the Court's opinion in *Garcia* and the unmanageability

---

[178] See, for example, Corwin, The Commerce Power versus States' Rights (1936).

of the "traditional governmental functions" test laid down by
National League of Cities seems to have been one of the main reasons
for its overruling.[179] What needs to be seen is whether the theory of
federalism I have articulated can provide more reliable guidance for
judicial application.

A full-fledged elaboration of the doctrinal implications of the
process-oriented approach to federalism would probably be premature at this point. Given the collapse of *National League of Cities*, my
aim has been to show that the process jurisprudence endorsed in
Garcia does not signify an utter abandonment of a judicial role in
this area. Nevertheless, a few preliminary observations on doctrinal
matters may be in order.

To begin with, the delimitation of the protected processes of
state governments with reference to traditional state functions—the
road chosen by *National League of Cities*—is indeed deeply unsatis-
factory. It is, of course, not a priori precluded that the traditional
functions of state governments are also the very ones that are the
most important from the point of view of the federalist concerns,
although it is not clear why this should be so. On closer inspection,
the traditional functions are much more likely to be a product of the
historical role of the states in regulating the private sector and they
are much more likely to have been shaped by outdated notions
of state sovereignty and more modern ideas of governmental efficiency than by the more properly constitutional concerns with tyranny prevention and political participation.

At the same time, *Garcia*'s merciless critique of the criterion of
tradition seems to evince a desire for watertight, mechanical tests of
protected governmental functions that simply cannot be had in an
area as complex as that of federalism. Constitutional adjudication is
not, after all, a field in which simple standards predominate, and
there can be no substitute for a painful case-by-case refinement and
elaboration. Still, there are a number of ways in which the concerns
of federalism may be intelligibly used as a guide for judicial review.

First, there are some state governmental functions so directly
related to the federalist concern with preventing tyranny that they
present rather easy cases for judicial intervention (though perhaps

---

[179] The criterion of "tradition" had been criticized by scholars prior to the *Garcia* case. See
Tribe, note 105 *supra*, at 1072–74; Kaden, note 78 *supra*, at 887; Alfange, Congressional
Regulation of the "States qua States": From National League of Cities to EEOC v. Wyo-
ming, 1983 Supreme Court Review 215, 233ff.

they are also, at this moment, the least likely to meet with serious interference). Under any approach, for example, federal interference with the agenda of the highest state legislative and executive organs is likely to undermine the overall autonomy of the political processes in the states and eliminate their constitutional role within the federal system. Similarly, an interference with the state electoral processes, insofar as it is not clearly related to the protection of individual rights but threatens to gerrymander the local districts in order to change the configuration of political forces in favor of the nationally powerful interests, would be clearly beyond the pale. A gradual subordination of state police forces to a federal command structure would cripple the states' ability to enforce their basic choices and resist tyrannical pressures from above. A radical limitation of the states' ability to tax would make their fiscal solvency a matter of federal grace and ultimately make a mockery of the federalist concerns.

It may be a little harder to come up with equally clearly unconstitutional instances of federal interference with the states' function of enhancing participation, especially since, as I have noted,[180] it is mostly not the state governments themselves but rather their local emanations that provide the primary locus of direct citizen involvement in the political life in America. Even here, though, there may be clear enough cases. For example, given the special participatory mode in which school boards operate in most states, a federal education law that would attempt to transform those boards into an extension of the federal bureaucratic machinery would strike at the very core of participatory politics in the United States.[181]

Furthermore, it would be a mistake to think that cordoning off some areas of state governments from federal interference is the only possible method of implementing the principles of federalism. After all, if it is not the protection of state sovereignty that is at stake here but rather the basic functions of the states within the federal system, it is quite likely that the nature of the central intervention itself should be more determinative of its constitutionality than the local activity interfered with. Thus, for example, many federal laws that depend on state governmental machinery for their

---

[180] See text at notes 149–52 *supra*.

[181] Even in the area of the enforcement of individual rights, where the courts have been quite willing to interfere with local control over schools to promote racial integration, they have stopped short of a radical transformation of the very structure of local school districting. Milliken v. Bradley, 418 U.S. 717 (1974).

implementation attempt, though usually with only very modest success, to assure that the states open the administrative process to citizen involvement.[182] Insofar as such programs attempt to open up state politics to citizen participation, without undermining those aspects of local representative systems that may be important to preventing tyranny, they may be subject to a looser form of control than laws that have the opposite effect. Similarly, federal laws that provide reimbursements for costs imposed on local governments may be more acceptable than those that constitute a serious drain on state fiscal resources.[183]

Finally, although *National League of Cities* concentrated exclusively on federal interference through a system of direct commands to local governments, federalist concerns also have some implications with respect to national action under the spending power. The common issue that is bound to arise in both contexts, but which was left unanalyzed by *National League of Cities* and its progeny, is the question of when the states are unconstitutionally induced by the national government into something that may impair their ability to fulfill their consitutional functions. In the context of the Commerce Clause, the question arose in *FERC v. Mississippi* as a result of Justice Blackmun's intimation that if the federal government had the power to preempt the states from the field of utility regulation, it could also condition its permission for the states to engage in the regulation of utilities on their acceptance of federally mandated standards and procedures.[184] The ostensible explanation was that since the states were free to withdraw from the field altogether, they were not coerced by the federal requirements. Justice O'Connor's dissent in *FERC* disputed this approach but gave no real criteria for distinguishing incentives from coercion. It is this issue that becomes central when *National League of Cities'* concern with the federal coercion of the states is carried over to spending power legislation,[185] which constitutes the national government's main tool of securing state compliance with its demands.[186] The reason why federalist concerns are usually ignored

---

[182] For examples of such legislation, see ACIR, Citizen Participation, ch. 4.

[183] The Garcia Court mentioned this aspect of the federal legislation at issue there but discounted its relevance in a footnote. 105 S.Ct. at 1020 and *id.* n.21.

[184] See note 65 *supra* and accompanying text.

[185] The issue was specifically left open in *National League of Cities*, 426 U.S. 833, 852 n.17.

[186] See ACIR, Regulatory Federalism, passim, but see esp. the table at 19–21; Kaden, note 78 *supra*, at 871ff.

in the judicial review of spending power legislation is primarily related to the claim that the states are free to refuse to participate in the federal spending programs and thus are not really coerced into anything.[187] Nevertheless, while emphasis on the consent given by the states to the various conditions in federal grants (often quite unrelated to the purposes of the grant itself)[188] may comport quite well with the idea of state sovereignty, the states' consent is often likely to be free in a rather Pickwickian sense.[189] Even apart from coercion, the emphasis on consent may sometimes raise serious questions under the process analysis developed here. Even if the states should "consent" to measures that weaken their organizational capacity to resist tyrannical pressures from the national government or their ability to protect local participatory institutions, it is not clear that the Constitution allows the federal government to undermine its own democratic character by proposing such measures.

Clearly, the prospect of increased judicial control over the federal spending power raises problems of its own, and they are beyond the scope of this article. To recognize, however, the need for judicial concern, based in a well-thought-out theory of constitutional interpretation, does not necessitate an overly active judicial posture. Particularly in those areas in which the determinations required to assess the validity of federal enactments cannot, for some reason, be confidently made by the judiciary, it is always open for the courts to assume a more deferential posture to legislative assessments but to try to assure at the same time that the legislators themselves pay more attention to the factors that judges view as constitutionally important. This has been done in fact by the Court in some areas of Commerce Clause adjudication where judicial deference to a Congressional determination that a given activity concerned interstate commerce was conditioned on the Congress's explicit statement to this effect or a requirement of a series of specific findings.[190] This kind of technique, particularly suited to *Garcia's*

---

[187] This doctrine was spelled out in Steward Machine Co. v. Davis, 301 U.S. 548 (1937). Somewhat paradoxically, the Court elaborated its doctrine concerning the states' unconditional freedom at about the same time as it started to doubt to old *Lochner* wisdom that regulating hours of work was an abridgement of the workers' freedom of contract.

[188] See note 186 *supra*.

[189] ACIR, Regulatory Federalism, at 39ff.; Kaden, note 78 *supra*, at 871ff.

[190] See United States v. Five Gambling Devices, 346 U.S. 441 (1953) (registration and

confidence in political accountability, deserves more sustained consideration.

VI. CONCLUSION

The historical reasons why our federalist jurisprudence has been for so long so barren of new thoughts are not very difficult to fathom. While the Framers had been very much aware that they were creating a new type of government, it was the sterile idea of state sovereignty, basically more appropriate to the old Confederation than the new Union, that came to dominate the thinking about the states. The Civil War, further shifting the balance of the federal system, and the New Deal, which relied so heavily on building up a national bureaucracy, made the old theories even more inadequate. At the same time, however, the best legal minds had little incentive to shore up the jurisprudence of federalism. "Progress" seemed to lie with centralization and chipping away at state rights; the defense of the states seemed to have too many reactionary and racist overtones.

It is time, however, to think again about federalism. Practically all the barriers that federalism once posed for the efficient national regulation of private activities have by now been swept away. One of the positive effects of *Garcia* was to put to rest the old ideas of state sovereignty. In the long run, however, unless we reassess the meaning of our dual system of government, we may not have any more federalism as we know it. This is not to say, of course, that the states will cease to exist altogether, but only that if the message of *Garcia* is misunderstood, the separateness of the state and national bureaucracies may be gradually undermined by ever more complex forms of national control over the local agencies of government. The era of weak national governments is clearly behind us. But for this very reason we should think twice before leaving behind us the era of strong local government as well. It is to be hoped that *Garcia* will come to be seen not as the last word on the subject of federalism but as the new and clean slate on which to inscribe the future jurisprudence of state-national relations.

---

reporting provisions of a law prohibiting interstate shipment of gambling devices not applicable to local owners of such devices in the absence of specific congressional findings); United States v. Bass, 404 U.S. 336 (1971) (narrow reading of a federal criminal statute). *Cf.* Rewis v. United States, 401 U.S. 808 (1971) (narrow reading of the Travel Act).